Beginning Java 8 Fundamentals

Language Syntax, Arrays, Data Types, Objects, and Regular Expressions

Kishori Sharan

Apress

Beginning Java 8 Fundamentals: Language Syntax, Arrays, Data Types, Objects, and Regular Expressions

ISBN-13 (pbk): 978-1-4302-6652-5

ISBN-13 (electronic): 978-1-4302-6653-2

Publisher: Heinz Weinheimer
Lead Editor: Steve Anglin
Development Editor: Matthew Moodie
Technical Reviewer: John Zukowski
Editorial Board: Steve Anglin, Mark Beckner, Ewan Buckingham, Gary Cornell, Louise Corrigan, James T. DeWolf, Jonathan Gennick, Jonathan Hassell, Robert Hutchinson, Michelle Lowman, James Markham, Matthew Moodie, Jeff Olson, Jeffrey Pepper, Douglas Pundick, Ben Renow-Clarke, Dominic Shakeshaft, Gwenan Spearing, Matt Wade, Steve Weiss
Coordinating Editors: Anamika Panchoo, Kevin Shea
Copy Editor: Mary Behr
Compositor: SPi Global
Indexer: SPi Global
Artist: SPi Global
Cover Designer: Anna Ishchenko

Distributed to the book trade worldwide by Springer Science+Business Media New York, 233 Spring Street, 6th Floor, New York, NY 10013. Phone 1-800-SPRINGER, fax (201) 348-4505, e-mail orders-ny@springer-sbm.com, or visit www.springeronline.com. Apress Media, LLC is a California LLC and the sole member (owner) is Springer Science + Business Media Finance Inc (SSBM Finance Inc). SSBM Finance Inc is a Delaware corporation.

For information on translations, please e-mail rights@apress.com, or visit www.apress.com.

Apress and friends of ED books may be purchased in bulk for academic, corporate, or promotional use. eBook versions and licenses are also available for most titles. For more information, reference our Special Bulk Sales–eBook Licensing web page at www.apress.com/bulk-sales.

Any source code or other supplementary material referenced by the author in this text is available to readers at www.apress.com. For detailed information about how to locate your book's source code, go to www.apress.com/source-code/.

To

My parents, Ram Vinod Singh and Pratibha Devi

Contents at a Glance

Contents

Foreword

Java is a very versatile programming language. It began over 20 years ago in the depths of Sun Microsystems, which has since been taken over by Oracle. The original version of Java—including the compiler, runtime, source code, and documentation—could fit onto a single 720KB floppy disk. Nowadays, the closest thing to a floppy disk one can find is one of those micro SD cards you plug into your phone, and you'll be lucky if the whole of the Java world could fit on it. Instead of just the single desktop version of the Java platform, today you'll find separate versions for micro devices and the enterprise, and even multiple desktop profiles. You'll find specialized libraries for security, databases, 3D graphics, TV, messaging, expressions, e-mail, and so many other things.

This large library set is what makes the Java platform so great. You don't need to keep reinventing the wheel. More than likely, somebody else has already done it for you. Most of the custom code done these days is for the business logic behind a project, not the management of data structures nor the marshaling and unmarshalling of data sent across the wire. This large library set is also what makes learning the Java platform so hard. There is just so much out there! You must focus on a small part of it to get started before you can tackle Java as a whole.

This book takes a focused approach to learning the fundamentals of the Java platform. Author Kishori Sharan has weeded through all there is to the core Java development environment and focuses on those parts you need to know to get yourself started with object-oriented development using the Java programming language. There is certainly much more out there than can fit in one introductory text. Until you're comfortable with the basics, just don't worry about the rest. You'll learn about them soon enough, when you need to. For now, read on, and you'll be glad you picked up this text.

—John Zukowski
Java Author and Senior Software Engineer, TripAdvisor.com
@JavaJohnZ

About the Author

Kishori Sharan is a senior software consultant at Doozer, Inc. He holds a Master of Science in Computer Information Systems from Troy State University in Montgomery, Alabama. He is a Sun Certified Java programmer and Sybase Certified PowerBuilder Developer Professional. He specializes in developing enterprise application using Java SE, Java EE, PowerBuilder, and Oracle database. He has been working in the software industry for over 16 years. He has helped several clients to migrate legacy applications to the Web. He loves writing technical books in his free time. He maintains his web site at www.jdojo.com where he posts blogs on Java and JavaFX.

About the Technical Reviewer

John Zukowski is currently a software engineer with TripAdvisor, the world's largest travel site (www.tripadvisor.com). He has been playing with Java technologies for 20 years now and is the author of 10 Java-related books. His books cover Java 6, Java Swing, Java Collections, and JBuilder from Apress, Java AWT from O'Reilly, and introductory Java from Sybex. He lives outside Boston, Massachusetts and has a Master's degree in software engineering from The Johns Hopkins University. You can follow him on Twitter at http://twitter.com/javajohnz.

Acknowledgments

My heartfelt thanks are due to my father-in-law, Mr. Jim Baker, for displaying extraordinary patience in reading the initial draft of the book. I am very grateful to him for spending so much of his valuable time teaching me quite a bit of English grammar that helped me produce better material.

I would like to thank my friend Richard Castillo for his hard work in reading my initial draft of the book and weeding out several mistakes. Richard was instrumental in running all examples and pointing out errors.

My wife, Ellen, has always been patient when I spent long hours at my computer desk working on this book. She would happily bring me snacks, fruit, and a glass of water every 30 minutes or so to sustain me during that period. I want to thank her for all her support in writing this book. She also deserves my sincere thanks for letting me sometimes seclude myself on weekends so I could focus on this book.

I would like to thank my family members and friends for their encouragement and support for writing this book: my elder brothers, Janki Sharan and Dr. Sita Sharan; my sister and brother-in-law, Ratna and Abhay; my nephews Babalu, Dabalu, Gaurav, Saurav, and Chitranjan; my friends Shivashankar Ravindranath, Kannan Somasekar, Mahbub Choudhury, Biju Nair, Srinivas Kakkera, Anil Kumar Singh, Chris Coley, Willie Baptiste, Rahul Jain, Larry Brewster, Greg Langham, Ram Atmakuri, LaTondra Okeke, Rahul Nagpal, Ravi Datla, Prakash Chandra, and many more friends not mentioned here.

My sincere thanks are due to the wonderful team at Apress for their support during the publication of this book. Thanks to Anamika Panchoo, the Senior Coordinating Editor, for providing excellent support and for being exceptionally patient with me when I asked her so many questions in the beginning. Thanks to Matthew Moodie and John Zukovski for their technical insights and feedback during the editing process. Last but not least, my sincere thanks to Steve Anglin, the Lead Editor at Apress, for taking the initiative for the publication of this book.

Introduction

How This Book Came About

My first encounter with the Java programming language was during a one-week Java training session in 1997. I did not get a chance to use Java in a project until 1999. I read two Java books and took a Java 2 Programmer certification examination. I did very well on the test, scoring 95 percent. The three questions that I missed on the test made me realize that the books that I had read did not adequately cover details of all the topics necessary about Java. I made up my mind to write a book on the Java programming language. So, I formulated a plan to cover most of the topics that a Java developer needs to use the Java programming language effectively in a project, as well as to get a certification. I initially planned to cover all essential topics in Java in 700 to 800 pages.

As I progressed, I realized that a book covering most of the Java topics in detail could not be written in 700 to 800 hundred pages. One chapter alone that covered data types, operators, and statements spanned 90 pages. I was then faced with the question, "Should I shorten the content of the book or include all the details that I think a Java developer needs?" I opted for including all the details in the book, rather than shortening its content to keep the number of pages low. It has never been my intent to make lots of money from this book. I was never in a hurry to finish this book because that rush could have compromised the quality and the coverage of its contents. In short, I wrote this book to help the Java community understand and use the Java programming language effectively, without having to read many books on the same subject. I wrote this book with the plan that it would be a comprehensive one-stop reference for everyone who wants to learn and grasp the intricacies of the Java programming language.

One of my high school teachers used to tell us that if one wanted to understand a building, one must first understand the bricks, steel, and mortar that make up the building. The same logic applies to most of the things that we want to understand in our lives. It certainly applies to an understanding of the Java programming language. If you want to master the Java programming language, you must start by understanding its basic building blocks. I have used this approach throughout this book, endeavoring to build each topic by describing the basics first. In the book, you will rarely find a topic described without first learning its background. Wherever possible, I have tried to correlate the programming practices with activities in our daily life. Most of the books about the Java programming language available in the market either do not include any pictures at all or have only a few. I believe in the adage, "A picture is worth a thousand words." To a reader, a picture makes a topic easier to understand and remember. I have included plenty of illustrations in the book to aid readers in understanding and visualizing the contents. Developers who have little or no programming experience have difficulty in putting things together to make it a complete program. Keeping them in mind, the book contains over 240 complete Java programs that are ready to be compiled and run.

I spent countless hours doing research for writing this book. My main source of research was the Java Language Specification, white papers and articles on Java topics, and Java Specification Requests (JSRs). I also spent quite a bit of time reading the Java source code to learn more about some of the Java topics. Sometimes, it took a few months researching a topic before I could write the first sentence on the topic. Finally, it was always fun to play with Java programs, sometimes for hours, to add them to the book.

Structure of the Book

This book contains 18 chapters and three appendixes. The chapters contain fundamental topics of Java such as syntax, data types, operators, classes, objects, etc. The chapters are arranged in an order that aids learning the Java programming language faster. The first chapter, "Programming Concepts," explains basic concepts related to programming in general, without going into too much technical details; it introduces Java and its features. The second chapter, "Writing Java Programs," introduces the first program using Java; this chapter is especially written for those learning Java for the first time. Subsequent chapters introduce Java topics in an increasing order of complexity. The new features of Java 8 are included wherever they fit in the chapter. The new Date-Time API, which is one of the biggest addition in Java 8, has been discussed in great detail in over 80 pages in Chapter 12.

After finishing this book, to take your Java knowledge to the next level, two companion books are available by the author: *Beginning Java 8 Language Features* (ISBN 978-1-4302-6658-7) and *Beginning Java 8 APIs, Extensions, and Libraries* (ISBN 978-1-4302-6661-7).

Audience

This book is designed to be useful for anyone who wants to learn the Java programming language. If you are a beginner, with little or no programming background, you need to read from the first chapter to the last, in order. The book contains topics of various degrees of complexity. As a beginner, if you find yourself overwhelmed while reading a section in a chapter, you can skip to the next section or the next chapter, and revisit it later when you gain more experience.

If you are a Java developer with an intermediate or advanced level of experience, you can jump to a chapter or to a section in a chapter directly. If a section uses an unfamiliar topic, you need to visit that topic before continuing the current one.

If you are reading this book to get a certification in the Java programming language, you need to read almost all of the chapters, paying attention to all the detailed descriptions and rules. Most of the certification programs test your fundamental knowledge of the language, not the advanced knowledge. You need to read only those topics that are part of your certification test. Compiling and running over 240 complete Java programs will help you prepare for your certification.

If you are a student who is attending a class in the Java programming language, you need to read the first six chapters of this book thoroughly. These chapters cover the basics of the Java programming languages in detail. You cannot do well in a Java class unless you first master the basics. After covering the basics, you need to read only those chapters that are covered in your class syllabus. I am sure, you, as a Java student, do not need to read the entire book page-by-page.

How to Use This Book

This book is the beginning, not the end, for you to gain the knowledge of the Java programming language. If you are reading this book, it means you are heading in the right direction to learn the Java programming language that will enable you to excel in your academic and professional career. However, there is always a higher goal for you to achieve and you must constantly work harder to achieve it. The following quotations from some great thinkers may help you understand the importance of working hard and constantly looking for knowledge with both your eyes and mind open.

> *The learning and knowledge that we have, is, at the most, but little compared with that of which we are ignorant.*

—Plato

> *True knowledge exists in knowing that you know nothing. And in knowing that you know nothing, that makes you the smartest of all.*

—Socrates

Readers are advised to use the API documentation for the Java programming language, as much as possible, while using this book. The Java API documentation is the place where you will find a complete list of documentation for everything available in the Java class library. You can download (or view) the Java API documentation from the official web site of Oracle Corporation at `www.oracle.com`. While you read this book, you need to practice writing Java programs yourself. You can also practice by tweaking the programs provided in the book. It does not help much in your learning process if you just read this book and do not practice by writing your own programs. Remember that "practice makes perfect," which is also true in learning how to program in Java.

Source Code and Errata

Source code and errata for this book may be downloaded from `www.apress.com/source-code`.

Questions and Comments

Please direct all your questions and comments for the author to `ksharan@jdojo.com`.

CHAPTER 1

■ ■ ■

Programming Concepts

In this chapter, you will learn

- The general concept of programming
- Different components of programming
- Major programming paradigms
- The object-oriented paradigm and how it is used in Java

What Is Programming?

The term "programming" is used in many contexts. We will discuss its meaning in the context of human-to-computer interaction. In the simplest terms, programming is the way of writing a sequence of instructions to tell a computer to perform a specific task. The sequence of instructions for a computer is known as a program. A set of well-defined notations is used to write a program. The set of notations used to write a program is called a programming language. The person who writes a program is called a programmer. A programmer uses a programming language to write a program.

How does a person tell a computer to perform a task? Can a person tell a computer to perform any task or does a computer have a predefined set of tasks that it can perform? Before we look at human-to-computer communication, let's look at human-to-human communication. How does a human communicate with another human? You would say that human-to-human communication is accomplished using a spoken language, for example, English, German, Hindi, etc. However, spoken language is not the only means of communication between humans. We also communicate using written languages or using gestures without uttering any words. Some people can even communicate sitting miles away from each other without using any words or gestures; they can communicate at thought level.

To have a successful communication, it is not enough just to use a medium of communication like a spoken or written language. The main requirement for a successful communication between two parties is the ability of both parties to understand what is communicated from the other party. For example, suppose there are two people. One person knows how to speak English and the other one knows how to speak German. Can they communicate with each other? The answer is no, because they cannot understand each other's language. What happens if we add an English-German translator between them? We would agree that they would be able to communicate with the help of a translator even though they do not understand each other directly.

Computers understand instructions only in binary format, which is a sequence of 0s and 1s. The sequence of 0s and 1s, which all computers understand, is called machine language or machine code. A computer has a fixed set of basic instructions that it understands. Each computer has its own set of instructions. For example, 0010 may be an instruction to add two numbers on one computer and 0101 is an instruction to add two numbers on another computer. Therefore, programs written in machine language are machine-dependent. Sometimes machine code is referred to as native code as it is native to the machine for which it is written. Programs written in machine language are very difficult, if not impossible, to write, read, understand, and modify. Suppose you want to write a program that adds two numbers, 15 and 12. The program to add two numbers in machine language will look similar to the one shown below. You do not need to understand the sample code written in this section. It is only for the purpose of discussion and illustration.

```
0010010010   10010100000100110
0001000100   01010010001001010
```

The above instructions are to add two numbers. How difficult will it be to write a program in machine language to perform a complex task? Based on the above code, you may now realize that it is very difficult to write, read, and understand a program written in a machine language. But aren't computers supposed to make our jobs easier, not more difficult? We needed to represent the instructions for computers in some notations that were easier to write, read, and understand, so computer scientists came up with another language called an assembly language. An assembly language provides different notations to write instructions. It is little easier to write, read, and understand than its predecessor, machine language. An assembly language uses mnemonics to represent instructions as opposed to the binary (0s and 1s) used in machine language. A program written in an assembly language to add two numbers looks similar to the following:

```
li $t1, 15
add $t0, $t1, 12
```

If you compare the two programs written in the two different languages to perform the same task, you can see that assembly language is easier to write, read, and understand than machine code. There is one-to-one correspondence between an instruction in machine language and assembly language for a given computer architecture. Recall that a computer understands instructions only in machine language. The instructions that are written in an assembly language must be translated into machine language before the computer can execute them. A program that translates the instructions written in an assembly language into machine language is called an assembler. Figure 1-1 shows the relationship between assembly code, an assembler, and machine code.

Figure 1-1. *The relationship between assembly code, assembler, and machine code*

Machine language and assembly language are also known as low-level languages. They are called low-level languages because a programmer must understand the low-level details of the computer to write a program using those languages. For example, if you were writing programs in machine and assembly languages, you would need to know what memory location you are writing to or reading from, which register to use to store a specific value, etc. Soon programmers realized a need for a higher-level programming language that could hide the low-level details of computers from them. The need gave rise to the development of high-level programming languages like COBOL, Pascal, FORTRAN, C, C++, Java, C#, etc. The high-level programming languages use English-like words, mathematical notation, and punctuation to write programs. A program written in a high-level programming language is also called source code. They are closer to the written languages that humans are familiar with. The instructions to add two numbers can be written in a high-level programming language, for example. Java looks similar to the following:

```
int x = 15 + 27;
```

You may notice that the programs written in a high-level language are easier and more intuitive to write, read, understand, and modify than the programs written in machine and assembly languages. You might have realized that computers do not understand programs written in high-level languages, as they understand only sequences of 0s and 1s. So there's a need for a way to translate a program written in a high-level language to machine language. The translation is accomplished by a compiler, an interpreter, or a combination of both. A compiler is a program that translates programs written in a high-level programming language into machine language. Compiling a program is an overloaded phrase. Typically, it means translating a program written in a high-level language into machine language. Sometimes it is used to mean translating a program written in a high-level programming language into a lower-level programming language, which is not necessarily the machine language. The code that is generated by a compiler is called compiled code. The compiled program is executed by the computer.

Another way to execute a program written in high-level programming language is to use an interpreter. An interpreter does not translate the whole program into machine language at once. Rather, it reads one instruction written in a high-level programming language at a time, translates it into machine language, and executes it. You can view an interpreter as a simulator. Sometimes a combination of a compiler and an interpreter may be used to compile and run a program written in a high-level language. For example, a program written in Java is compiled into an intermediate language called bytecode. An interpreter, specifically called a Java Virtual Machine (JVM) for the Java platform, is used to interpret the bytecode and execute it. An interpreted program runs slower than a compiled program. Most of the JVMs today use just-in-time compilers (JIT), which compile the entire Java program into machine language as needed. Sometimes another kind of compiler, which is called an ahead-of-time (AOT) compiler, is used to compile a program in an intermediate language (e.g. Java bytecode) to machine language. Figure 1-2 shows the relationship between the source code, a compiler, and the machine code.

Figure 1-2. *The relationship between source code, a compiler, and machine code*

Components of a Programming Language

A programming language is a system of notations that are used to write instructions for computers. It can be described using three components:

- Syntax

- Semantics

- Pragmatics

The syntax part deals with forming valid programming constructs using available notations. The semantics part deals with the meaning of the programming constructs. The pragmatics part deals with the use of the programming language in practice.

Like a written language (e.g. English), a programming language has a vocabulary and grammar. The vocabulary of a programming language consists of a set of words, symbols, and punctuation marks. The grammar of a programming language defines rules on how to use the vocabulary of the language to form valid programming constructs. You can think of a valid programming construct in a programming language like a sentence in a written language. A sentence in a written language is formed using the vocabulary and grammar of the language. Similarly, a programming construct is formed using the vocabulary and the grammar of the programming language. The vocabulary and the rules to use that vocabulary to form valid programming constructs are known as the syntax of the programming language.

In a written language, you may form a grammatically correct sentence, which may not have any valid meaning. For example, "The stone is laughing," is a grammatically correct sentence. However, it does not make any sense. In a written language, this kind of ambiguity is allowed. A programming language is meant to communicate instructions to computers, which have no room for any ambiguity. We cannot communicate with computers using ambiguous instructions. There is another component of a programming language, which is called semantics. The semantics of a programming language explain the meaning of the syntactically valid programming constructs. The semantics of a programming language answer the question, "What does this program do when it is run on a computer?" Note that a syntactically valid programming construct may not also be semantically valid. A program must be syntactically and semantically correct before it can be executed by a computer.

The pragmatics of a programming language describe its uses and its effects on the users. A program written in a programming language may be syntactically and semantically correct. However, it may not be easily understood by other programmers. This aspect is related to the pragmatics of the programming language. The pragmatics are concerned with the practical aspect of a programming language. It answers questions about a programming language like its ease of implementation, suitability for a particular application, efficiency, portability, support for programming methodologies, etc.

Programming Paradigms

The online Merriam-Webster's Learner's dictionary defines the word "paradigm" as follows:

> *"A paradigm is a theory or a group of ideas about how something should be done, made, or thought about."*

In the beginning, it is a little hard to understand the word "paradigm" in a programming context. Programming is about providing a solution to a real-world problem using computational models supported by the programming language. The solution is called a program. Before we provide a solution to a problem in the form of a program, we always have a mental view of the problem and its solution. Before I discuss how to solve a real-world problem using a computational model, let's take an example of a real-world social problem, one that has nothing to do with computers.

Suppose there is a place on Earth that has a shortage of food. People in that place do not have enough food to eat. The problem is "shortage of food." Let's ask three people to provide a solution to this problem. The three people are a politician, a philanthropist, and a monk. A politician will have a political view about the problem and its solution. He may think about it as an opportunity to serve his countrymen by enacting some laws to provide food to the hungry people. A philanthropist will offer some money/food to help those hungry people because he feels compassion for all humans and so for those hungry people. A monk will try to solve this problem using his spiritual views. He may preach to them to work and make livings for themselves; he may appeal to rich people to donate food to the hungry; or he may teach them yoga to conquer their hunger! Did you see how three people have different views about the same reality, which is "shortage of food"? The ways they look at the reality are their paradigms. You can think of a paradigm as a mindset with which a reality is viewed in a particular context. It is usual to have multiple paradigms, which let one view the same reality differently. For example, a person who is a philanthropist and politician will have his ability to view the "shortage of food" problem and its solution differently, once with his political mindset and once with his philanthropist mindset. Three people were given the same problem. All of them provided a solution to the problem. However, their perceptions about the problem and its solution were not the same. We can define the term paradigm as a set of concepts and ideas that constitutes a way of viewing a reality.

Why do we need to bother about a paradigm anyway? Does it matter if a person used his political, philanthropical, or spiritual paradigm to arrive at the solution? Eventually we get a solution to our problem. Don't we?

It is not enough just to have a solution to a problem. The solution must be practical and effective. Since the solution to a problem is always related to the way the problem and the solution are thought about, the paradigm becomes paramount. You can see that the solution provided by the monk may kill the hungry people before they can get any help. The philanthropist's solution may be a good short-term solution. The politician's solution seems to be a long term solution and the best one. It is always important to use the right paradigm to solve a problem to arrive at a practical and the most effective solution. Note that one paradigm cannot be the right paradigm to solve every kind of problem. For example, if a person is seeking eternal happiness, he needs to consult a monk and not a politician or a philanthropist.

Here is a definition of the term "programming paradigm" by Robert W. Floyd, who was a prominent computer scientist. He gave this definition in his 1978 ACM Turing Award lecture titled "The Paradigms of Programming."

"A programming paradigm is a way of conceptualizing what it means to perform computation, and how tasks that are to be carried out on a computer should be structured and organized."

You can observe that the word "paradigm" in a programming context has a similar meaning to that used in the context of daily life. Programming is used to solve a real-world problem using computational models provided by a computer. The programming paradigm is the way you think and conceptualize about the real-world problem and its solution in the underlying computational models. The programming paradigm comes into the picture well before you start writing a program using a programming language. It is in the analysis phase when you use a particular paradigm to analyze a problem and its solution in a particular way. A programming language provides a means to implement a particular programming paradigm suitably. A programming language may provide features that make it suitable for programming using one programming paradigm and not the other.

A program has two components, data and algorithm. Data is used to represent pieces of information. An algorithm is a set of steps that operates on data to arrive at a solution to a problem. Different programming paradigms involve viewing the solution to a problem by combining data and algorithms in different ways. Many paradigms are used in programming. The following are some commonly used programming paradigms:

- Imperative paradigm
- Procedural paradigm
- Declarative paradigm
- Functional paradigm
- Logic paradigm
- Object-oriented paradigm

Imperative Paradigm

The imperative paradigm is also known as an algorithmic paradigm. In the imperative paradigm, a program consists of data and an algorithm (sequence of commands) that manipulates the data. The data at a particular point in time defines the state of the program. The state of the program changes as the commands are executed in a specific sequence. The data is stored in memory. Imperative programming languages provide variables to refer to the memory locations, an assignment operation to change the value of a variable, and other constructs to control the flow of a program. In imperative programming, you need to specify the steps to solve a problem. Suppose you have an integer, say 15, and you want to add 10 to it. Your approach would be to add 1 to 15 ten times and you get the result, 25. You can write a program using an imperative language to add 10 to 15 as follows. Note that you do not need to understand the syntax of the following code; just try to get the feeling of it.

```
int num = 15;     // num holds 15 at this point
int counter = 0; // counter holds 0 at this point

while(counter < 10) {
        num = num + 1;          // Modifying data in num
        counter = counter + 1; // Modifying data in counter
}
// num holds 25 at this point
```

The first two lines are variable declarations that represent the data part of the program. The while loop represents the algorithm part of the program that operates on the data. The code inside the while loop is executed 10 times. The loop increments the data stored in the num variable by 1 in its each iteration. When the loop ends, it has incremented the value of num by 10. Note that data in imperative programming is transient and the algorithm is permanent. FORTRAN, COBOL, and C are a few examples of programming languages that support the imperative paradigm.

Procedural Paradigm

The procedural paradigm is similar to the imperative paradigm with one difference: it combines multiple commands in a unit called a procedure. A procedure is executed as a unit. Executing the commands contained in a procedure is known as calling or invoking the procedure. A program in a procedural language consists of data and a sequence of procedure calls that manipulate the data. The following piece of code is typical code for a procedure named addTen:

```
void addTen(int num) {
        int counter = 0;
        while(counter < 10) {
                num = num + 1;          // Modifying data in num
                counter = counter + 1;  // Modifying data in counter
        }
        // num has been incremented by 10
}
```

The addTen procedure uses a placeholder (also known as parameter) num, which is supplied at the time of its execution. The code ignores the actual value of num. It simply adds 10 to the current value of num. Let's use the following piece of code to add 10 to 15. Note that the code for addTen procedure and the following code are not written using any specific programming language. They are provided here only for the purpose of illustration.

```
int x = 15; // x holds 15 at this point
addTen(x);  // Call addTen procedure that will increment x by 10
// x holds 25 at this point
```

You may observe that the code in imperative paradigm and procedural paradigm are similar in structure. Using procedures results in modular code and increases reusability of algorithms. Some people ignore this difference and treat the two paradigms, imperative and procedural, as the same. Note that even if they are different, a procedural paradigm always involves the imperative paradigm. In the procedural paradigm, the unit of programming is not a sequence of commands. Rather, you abstract a sequence of commands into a procedure and your program consists of a sequence of procedures instead. A procedure has side effects. It modifies the data part of the program as it executes its logic. C, C++, Java, and COBOL are a few examples of programming languages that support the procedural paradigm.

Declarative Paradigm

In the declarative paradigm, a program consists of the description of a problem and the computer finds the solution. The program does not specify how to arrive at the solution to the problem. It is the computer's job to arrive at a solution when a problem is described to it. Contrast the declarative paradigm with the imperative paradigm. In the imperative paradigm, we are concerned about the "how" part of the problem. In the declarative paradigm, we are concerned about the "what" part of the problem. We are concerned about what the problem is, rather than how to solve it. The functional paradigm and the logic paradigm, which are described next, are subtypes of the declarative paradigm.

Writing a database query using a structured query language (SQL) falls under programming based on the declarative paradigm where you specify what data you want and the database engine figures out how to retrieve the data for you. Unlike the imperative paradigm, the data is permanent and the algorithm is transient in the declarative paradigm. In the imperative paradigm, the data is modified as the algorithm is executed. In the declarative paradigm, data is supplied to the algorithm as input and the input data remains unchanged as the algorithm is executed. The algorithm produces new data rather than modifying the input data. In other words, in the declarative paradigm, execution of an algorithm does not produce side effects.

Functional Paradigm

The functional paradigm is based on the concept of mathematical functions. You can think of a function as an algorithm that computes a value from some given inputs. Unlike a procedure in procedural programming, a function does not have a side effect. In functional programming, values are immutable. A new value is derived by applying a function to the input value. The input value does not change. Functional programming languages do not use variables and assignments, which are used for modifying data. In imperative programming, a repeated task is performed using a loop construct, for example, a while loop. In functional programming, a repeated task is performed using recursion, which is a way in which a function is defined in terms of itself. In other words, it does some work, then calls itself.

A function always produces the same output when it is applied on the same input. A function, say add, that can be applied to an integer x to add an integer n to it may be defined as follows:

```
int add(x, n) {
        if (n == 0) {
                return x;
        }
        else {
                return 1 + add(x, n-1); // Apply add function recursively
        }
}
```

Note that the add function does not use any variable and does not modify any data. It uses recursion. You can call the add function to add 10 to 15 as follows:

```
add(15, 10); // Results in 25
```

Haskell, Erlang, and Scala are a few examples of programming languages that support the functional paradigm.

■ **Tip**   Java 8 added a new language construct called a lambda expression, which can be used to perform functional programming in Java.

Logic Paradigm

Unlike the imperative paradigm, the logic paradigm focuses on the "what" part of the problem rather than how to solve it. All you need to specify is what needs to be solved. The program will figure out the algorithm to solve it. The algorithm is of less importance to the programmer. The primary task of the programmer is to describe the problem as closely as possible. In the logic paradigm, a program consists of a set of axioms and a goal statement. The set of axioms is the collection of facts and inference rules that make up a theory. The goal statement is a theorem. The program uses deductions to prove the theorem within the theory. Logic programming uses a mathematical concept called a relation from set theory. A relation in set theory is defined as a subset of the Cartesian product of two or more sets. Suppose there are two sets, Persons and Nationality, which are defined as follows:

```
Person = {John, Li, Ravi}
Nationality = {American, Chinese, Indian}
```

The Cartesian product of the two sets, denoted as Person x Nationality, would be another set, as shown:

```
Person x Nationality = {{John, American}, {John, Chinese},
                        {John, Indian}, {Li, American}, {Li, Chinese},
                        {Li, Indian}, {Ravi, American}, {Ravi, Chinese},
                        {Ravi, Indian}}
```

Every subset of Person x Nationality is another set that defines a mathematical relation. Each element of a relation is called a tuple. Let PersonNationality be a relation defined as follows:

```
PersonNationality = {{John, American}, {Li, Chinese}, {Ravi, Indian}}
```

In logic programming, you can use the PersonNationality relation as the collection of facts that are known to be true. You can state the goal statement (or the problem) like

```
PersonNationality(?, Chinese)
```

which means "give me all names of people who are Chinese." The program will search through the PersonNationality relation and extract the matching tuples, which will be the answer (or the solution) to your problem. In this case, the answer will be Li.

Prolog is an example of a programming language that supports the logic paradigm.

Object-Oriented Paradigm

In the object-oriented (OO) paradigm, a program consists of interacting objects. An object encapsulates data and algorithms. Data defines the state of an object. Algorithms define the behavior of an object. An object communicates with other objects by sending messages to them. When an object receives a message, it responds by executing one of its algorithms, which may modify its state. Contrast the object-oriented paradigm with the imperative and functional paradigms. In the imperative and functional paradigms, data and algorithms are separated, whereas in the object-oriented paradigm, data and algorithms are not separate; they are combined in one entity, which is called an object.

Classes are the basic units of programming in the object-oriented paradigm. Similar objects are grouped into one definition called a class. A class' definition is used to create an object. An object is also known as an instance of the class. A class consists of instance variables and methods. The values of instance variables of an object define the state of the object. Different objects of a class maintain their states separately. That is, each object of a class has its own copy of the instance variables. The state of an object is kept private to that object. That is, the state of an object cannot be accessed or modified directly from outside the object. Methods in a class define the behavior of its objects. A method is like a procedure (or subroutine) in the procedural paradigm. Methods can access/modify the state of the object. A message is sent to an object by invoking one of its methods.

Suppose you want to represent real-world people in your program. You will create a `Person` class and its instances will represent people in your program. The `Person` class can be defined as shown in Listing 1-1. This example uses the syntax of the Java programming language. You do not need to understand the syntax used in the programs that you are writing at this point; I will discuss the syntax to define classes and create objects in subsequent chapters.

Listing 1-1. The Definition of a Person Class Whose Instances Represent Real-World Persons in a Program

```
package com.jdojo.concepts;

public class Person {
        private String name;
        private String gender;

        public Person(String initialName, String initialGender) {
                name = initialName;
                gender = initialGender;
        }

        public String getName() {
                return name;
        }

        public void setName(String newName) {
                name = newName;
        }

        public String getGender() {
                return gender;
        }
}
```

The Person class includes three things:

- Two instance variables: name and gender.

- One constructor: Person(String initialName, String initialGender)

- Three methods: getName(), setName(String newName), and getGender()

Instance variables store internal data for an object. The value of each instance variable represents the value of a corresponding property of the object. Each instance of the `Person` class will have a copy of name and gender data. The values of all properties of an object at a point in time (stored in instance variables) collectively define the state of the object at that time. In the real world, a person possesses many properties, for example, name, gender, height, weight, hair color, addresses, phone numbers, etc. However, when you model the real-world person using a class, you include only those properties of the person that are relevant to the system being modeled. For this current demonstration, let's model only two properties, name and gender, of a real-world person as two instance variables in the Person class.

A class contains the definition (or blueprint) of objects. There needs to be a way to construct (to create or to instantiate) objects of a class. An object also needs to have the initial values for its properties that will determine its initial state at the time of its creation. A constructor of a class is used to create an object of that class. A class can have many constructors to facilitate the creation of its objects with different initial states. The Person class provides one constructor, which lets you create its object by specifying the initial values for name and gender. The following snippet of code creates two objects of the Person class:

```
Person john = new Person("John Jacobs", "Male");
Person donna = new Person("Donna Duncan", "Female");
```

The first object is called john with John Jacobs and Male as the initial values for its name and gender properties, respectively. The second object is called donna with Donna Duncan and Female as the initial values for its name and gender properties, respectively.

Methods of a class represent behaviors of its objects. For example, in the real world, a person has a name and his ability to respond when he is asked for his name is one of his behaviors. Objects of the Person class have abilities to respond to three different messages: getName, setName, and getGender. The ability of an object to respond to a message is implemented using methods. You can send a message, say getName, to a Person object and it will respond by returning its name. It is the same as asking "What is your name?" and having the person respond by telling you his name.

```
String johnName = john.getName();   // Send getName message to john
String donnaName = donna.getName(); // Send getName message to donna
```

The setName message to the Person object asks him to change his current name to a new name. The following snippet of code changes the name of the donna object from Donna Duncan to Donna Jacobs:

```
donna.setName("Donna Jacobs");
```

If you send the getName message to donna object at this point, it will return Donna Jacobs and not Donna Duncan.

You may notice that your Person objects do not have the ability to respond to a message such as - setGender. The gender of Person object is set when the object is created and it cannot be changed afterwards. However, you can query the gender of a Person object by sending getGender message to it. What messages an object may (or may not) respond to is decided at design-time based on the need of the system being modeled. In the case of the Person objects, we decided that they would not have the ability to respond to the setGender message by not including a setGender(String newGender) method in the Person class.

Figure 1-3 shows the state and interface of the Person object called john.

Figure 1-3. *The state and the interface for a Person object*

The object-oriented paradigm is a very powerful paradigm for modeling real-world phenomena in a computational model. We are used to working with objects all around us in our daily life. The object-oriented paradigm is natural and intuitive as it lets you think in terms of objects. However, it does not give you the ability to think in terms of objects correctly. Sometimes the solution to a problem does not fall into the domain of an object-oriented paradigm. In such cases, you need to use the paradigm that suits the problem domain the most. The object-oriented paradigm has a learning curve. It is much more than just creating and using objects in your program. Abstraction, encapsulation, polymorphism, and inheritance are some of the important features of the object-oriented paradigm. You must understand and be able to use these features to take full advantage of the object-oriented paradigm. I will discuss these features of the object-oriented paradigm in the sections to follow. In subsequent chapters, I will discuss these features and how to implement them in a program in detail.

To name a few, C++, Java and C# (pronounced as C sharp) are programming languages that support the object-oriented paradigm. Note that a programming language itself is not object-oriented. It is the paradigm that is object-oriented. A programming language may or may not have features to support the object-oriented paradigm.

What Is Java?

Java is a general purpose programming language. It has features to support programming based on the object-oriented, procedural, and functional paradigms. You often read a phrase like "Java is an object-oriented programming language." What is meant is that the Java language has features that support the object-oriented paradigm. A programming language is not object-oriented. It is the paradigm that is object-oriented, and a programming language may have features that make it easy to implement the object-oriented paradigm. Sometimes programmers have misconceptions that all programs written in Java are always object-oriented. Java also has features that support the procedural and functional paradigms. You can write a program in Java that is a 100% procedural program without an iota of object-orientedness in it.

The initial version of the Java platform was released by Sun Microsystems (part of Oracle Corporation since January 2010) in 1995. Development of the Java programming language was started in 1991. Initially, the language was called Oak and it was meant to be used in set-top boxes for televisions.

Soon after its release, Java became a very popular programming language. One of the most important features for its popularity was its "write once, run anywhere" (WORA) feature. This feature lets you write a Java program once and run it on any platform. For example, you can write and compile a Java program on UNIX and run it on Microsoft Windows, Macintosh, or UNIX machine without any modifications to the source code. WORA is achieved by compiling a Java program into an intermediate language called bytecode. The format of bytecode is platform-independent. A virtual machine, called the Java Virtual Machine (JVM), is used to run the bytecode on each platform. Note that JVM is a program implemented in software. It is not a physical machine and this is the reason it is called a "virtual" machine. The job of a JVM is to transform the bytecode into executable code according to the platform it is running on. This feature makes Java programs platform-independent. That is, the same Java program can be run on multiple platforms without any modifications.

The following are a few characteristics behind Java's popularity and acceptance in the software industry:

- Simplicity
- Wide variety of usage environments
- Robustness

Simplicity may be a subjective word in this context. C++ was the popular and powerful programming language widely used in the software industry at the time Java was released. If you were a C++ programmer, Java would provide simplicity for you in its learning and use over the C++ experience you had. Java retained most of the syntax of C/C++, which was helpful for C/C++ programmers trying to learn this new language. Even better, it excluded some of the most confusing and hard-to-use-correctly features (though powerful) of C++. For example, Java does not have pointers and multiple inheritance, which are present in C++.

If you are learning Java as your first programming language, whether it is a simple language to learn may not be true for you. This is the reason why I said that the simplicity of Java or any programming language is very subjective. The Java language and its libraries (a set of packages containing Java classes) have been growing ever since its first release. You will need to put in some serious effort in order to become a serious Java developer.

Java can be used to develop programs that can be used in different environments. You can write programs in Java that can be used in a client-server environment. The most popular use of Java programs in its early days was to develop applets. An applet is a Java program that is embedded in a web page, which uses the HyperText Markup Language (HTML), and is displayed in a web browser such as Microsoft Internet Explorer, Google Chrome, etc. An applet's code is stored on a web server, downloaded to the client machine when the HTML page containing the reference to the applet is loaded by the browser, and run on the client machine. Java includes features that make it easy to develop distributed applications. A distributed application consists of programs running on different machines connected through a network. Java has features that make it easy to develop concurrent applications. A concurrent application has multiple interacting threads of execution running in parallel. I will discuss these features of the Java platform in detail in subsequent chapters in this book.

Robustness of a program refers to its ability to handle unexpected situations reasonably. The unexpected situation in a program is also known as an error. Java provides robustness by providing many features for error checking at different points during a program's lifetime. The following are three different types of errors that may occur in a Java program:

- Compile-time error

- Runtime error

- Logic error

Compile-time errors are also known as syntax errors. They are caused by incorrect use of the Java language syntax. Compile-time errors are detected by the Java compiler. A program with a compile-time error does not compile into bytecode until the errors are corrected. Missing a semicolon at the end of a statement, assigning a decimal value such as 10.23 to a variable of integer type, etc. are examples of compile-time errors.

Runtime errors occur when a Java program is run. This kind of error is not detected by the compiler because a compiler does not have all of the runtime information available to it. Java is a strongly typed languages and it has a robust type checking at compile-time as well as runtime. Java provides a neat exception handling mechanism to handle runtime errors. When a runtime error occurs in a Java program, the JVM throws an exception, which the program may catch and deal with. For example, dividing an integer by zero (e.g. 17/0) generates a runtime error. Java avoids critical runtime errors, such as memory overrun and memory leaks, by providing a built-in mechanism for automatic memory allocation and deallocation. The feature of automatic memory deallocation is known as garbage collection.

Logic errors are the most critical errors in a program, and they are hard to find. They are introduced by the programmer by implementing the functional requirement incorrectly. This kind of error cannot be detected by a Java compiler or Java runtime. They are detected by application testers or users when they compare the actual behavior of a program with its expected behavior. Sometimes a few logic errors can sneak into the production environment and they go unnoticed even after the application is decommissioned.

An error in a program is known as a bug. The process of finding and fixing bugs in a program is known as debugging. All modern integrated development environments (IDEs) such as NetBeans, Eclipse, JDeveloper, JBuilder, etc, provide programmers with a tool called a debugger, which lets them run the program step-by-step and inspect the program's state at every step to detect the bug. Debugging is a reality of programmer's daily activities. If you want to be a good programmer, you must learn and be good at using the debuggers that come with the development tools that you use to develop your Java programs.

The Object-Oriented Paradigm and Java

The object-oriented paradigm supports four major principles: abstraction, encapsulation, inheritance, and polymorphism. They are also known as four pillars of the object-oriented paradigm. Abstraction is the process of exposing the essential details of an entity, while ignoring the irrelevant details, to reduce the complexity for the users. Encapsulation is the process of bundling data and operations on the data together in an entity. Inheritance is used to derive a new type from an existing type, thereby establishing a parent-child relationship. Polymorphism lets an entity take on different meanings in different contexts. The four principles are discussed in detail in the sections to follow.

Abstraction

A program provides solutions to a real-world problem. The size of the program may range from a few lines to a few million lines. It may be written as a monolithic structure running from the first line to the millionth line in one place. A monolithic program becomes harder to write, understand, and maintain if its size is over 25 to 50 lines. For easier maintenance, a big monolithic program must be decomposed into smaller subprograms. The subprograms are then assembled together to solve the original problem. Care must be taken when a program is being decomposed. All subprograms must be simple and small enough to be understood by themselves, and when assembled together, they must solve the original problem.

Let's consider the following requirement for a device:

> *Design and develop a device that will let its user type text using all English letters, digits, and symbols.*

One way to design such a device is to provide a keyboard that has keys for all possible combinations of all letters, digits, and symbols. This solution is not reasonable as the size of the device will be huge. You may realize that we are talking about designing a keyboard. Look at your keyboard and see how it has been designed. It has broken down the problem of typing text into typing a letter, a digit, or a symbol one at a time, which represents the smaller part of the original problem. If you can type all letters, all digits, and all symbols one at a time, you can type text of any length.

Another decomposition of the original problem may include two keys: one to type a horizontal line and another to type a vertical line, which a user can use to type in E, T, I, F, H, and L because these letters consist of only horizontal and vertical lines. With this solution, a user can type six letters using the combination of just two keys. However, with your experience using keyboards, you may realize that decomposing the keys so that a key can be used to type in only part of a letter is not a reasonable solution, although it is a solution.

Why is providing two keys to type six letters not a reasonable solution? Aren't we saving space and number of keys on the keyboard? The use of the phrase "reasonable" is relative in this context. From a purist point of view, it may be a reasonable solution. My reasoning behind calling it "not reasonable" is that it is not easily understood by users. It exposes more details to the users than needed. A user would have to remember that the horizontal line is placed at the top for T and at bottom for L. When a user gets a separate key for each letter, he does not have to deal with these details. It is important that the subprograms that provide solutions to parts of the original problem must be simplified to have the same level of detail to work together seamlessly. At the same time, a subprogram should not expose details that are not necessary for someone to know in order to use it.

Finally, all keys are mounted on a keyboard and they can be replaced separately. If a key is broken, it can be replaced without worrying about other keys. Similarly, when a program is decomposed into subprograms, a modification in a subprogram should not affect other subprograms. Subprograms can also be further decomposed by focusing on a different level of detail and ignoring other details. A good decomposition of a program aims at providing the following characteristics:

- Simplicity

- Isolation

- Maintainability

Each subprogram should be simple enough to be understood by itself. Simplicity is achieved by focusing on the relevant pieces of information and ignoring the irrelevant ones. What pieces of information are relevant and what are irrelevant depends on the context.

Each subprogram should be isolated from other subprograms so that any changes in a subprogram should have localized effects. A change in one subprogram should not affect any other subprograms. A subprogram defines an interface to interact with other subprograms. The inner details about the subprogram are hidden from the outside world. As long as the interface for a subprogram remains unchanged, the changes in its inner details should not affect the other subprograms that interact with it.

Each subprogram should be small enough to be written, understood, and maintained easily.

All of the above characteristics are achieved during decomposition of a problem (or program that solves a problem) using a process called abstraction. What is abstraction? Abstraction is a way to perform decomposition of a problem by focusing on relevant details and ignoring the irrelevant details about it in a particular context. Note that no details about a problem are irrelevant. In other words, every detail about a problem is relevant. However, some details may be relevant in one context and some in another. It is important to note that it is the "context" that decides what details are relevant and what are irrelevant. For example, consider the problem of designing and developing a keyboard. For a user's perspective, a keyboard consists of keys that can be pressed and released to type text. Number, type, size, and position of keys are the only details that are relevant to the users of a keyboard. However, keys are not the only details about a keyboard. A keyboard has an electronic circuit and it is connected to a computer. A lot of things occur inside the keyboard and the computer when a user presses a key. The internal workings of a keyboard are relevant for keyboard designers and manufactures. However, they are irrelevant to the users of a keyboard. You can say that different users have different views of the same thing in different contexts. What details about the thing are relevant and what are irrelevant depends on the user and the context.

Abstraction is about considering details that are necessary to view the problem in the way that is appropriate in a particular context and ignoring (hiding or suppressing or forgetting) the details that are unnecessary. Terms like "hiding" and "suppressing" in the context of abstraction may be misleading. These terms may mean hiding some details of a problem. Abstraction is concerned with which details of a thing should be considered and which should not for a particular purpose. It does imply hiding of the details. How things are hidden is another concept called information hiding, which is discussed in the following section.

The term "abstraction" is used to mean one of the two things: a process or an entity. As a process, it is a technique to extract relevant details about a problem and ignore the irrelevant details. As an entity, it is a particular view of a problem that considers some relevant details and ignores the irrelevant details.

Abstraction for Hiding Complexities

Let's discuss the application of abstraction in real-world programming. Suppose you want to write a program that will compute the sum of all integers between two integers. Suppose you want to compute the sum of all integers between 10 and 20. You can write the program as follows. Do not worry if you do not understand the syntax used in programs in this section; just try to grasp the big picture of how abstraction is used to decompose a program.

```
int sum = 0;
int counter = 10;
while(counter <= 20) {
        sum = sum + counter;
        counter = counter + 1;
}
System.out.println(sum);
```

This snippet of code will add 10 + 11 + 12 + ... + 20 and print 165.

Suppose you want to compute sum of all integers between 40 and 60. Here is the program to achieve just that:

```
int sum = 0;
int counter = 40;
while(counter <= 60) {
        sum = sum + counter;
        counter = counter + 1;
}
System.out.println(sum);
```

This snippet of code will perform the sum of all integers between 40 and 60, and it will print 1050. Note the similarities and differences between the two snippets of code. The logic is the same in both. However, the lower limit and the upper limit of the range are different. If you can ignore the differences that exist between the two snippets of code, you will be able to avoid the duplicating of logic in two places.

Let's consider the following snippet of code:

```
int sum = 0;
int counter = lowerLimit;
while(counter <= upperLimit) {
        sum = sum + counter;
        counter = counter + 1;
}
System.out.println(sum);
```

This time, you did not use any actual values for the lower and upper limits of any range. Rather, you used lowerLimit and upperLimit placeholders that are not known at the time the code is written. By using lowerLimit and upperLimit placeholders in your code, you are hiding the identity of the lower and upper limits of the range. In other words, you are ignoring their actual values when writing the above piece of code. You have applied the process of abstraction in the above code by ignoring the actual values of the lower and upper limits of the range.

When the above piece of code is executed, the actual values must be substituted for lowerLimit and upperLimit placeholders. This is achieved in a programming language by packaging the above snippet of code inside a module (subroutine or subprogram) called a procedure. The placeholders are defined as formal parameters of that procedure. Listing 1-2 has the code for such a procedure.

Listing 1-2. A Procedure Named getRangeSum to Compute the Sum of All Integers Between Two Integers

```
int getRangeSum(int lowerLimit, int upperLimit) {
        int sum = 0;
        int counter = lowerLimit;
        while(counter <= upperLimit) {
                sum = sum + counter;
                counter = counter + 1;
        }
        return sum;
}
```

A procedure has a name, which is getRangeSum in this case. A procedure has a return type, which is specified just before its name. The return type indicates the type of value that it will return to its caller. The return type is int in this case, which indicates that the result of the computation will be an integer. A procedure has formal parameters (possibly zero), which are specified within parentheses following its name. A formal parameter consists of data type and a name. In this case, the formal parameters are named as lowerLimit and upperLimit, and both are of the data type int. It has a body, which is placed within braces. The body of the procedure contains the logic.

When you want to execute the code for a procedure, you must pass the actual values for its formal parameters. You can compute and print the sum of all integers between 10 and 20 as follows:

```
int s1 = getRangeSum(10, 20);
System.out.println(s1);
```

This snippet of code will print 165.

To compute the sum all integers between 40 and 60, you can execute the following snippet of code:

```
int s2 = getRangeSum(40, 60);
System.out.println(s2);
```

This snippet of code will print 1050, which is exactly the same result you had achieved before.

The abstraction method that you used in defining the getRangeSum procedure is called abstraction by parameterization. The formal parameters in a procedure are used to hide the identity of the actual data on which the procedure's body operates. The two parameters in the getRangeSum procedure hide the identity of the upper and lower limits of the range of integers. Now you have seen the first concrete example of abstraction. Abstraction is a vast topic. I will cover some more basics about abstraction in this section.

Suppose a programmer writes the code for the getRangeSum procedure as shown in Listing 1-2 and another programmer wants to use it. The first programmer is the designer and writer of the procedure; the second one is the user of the procedure. What pieces of information does the user of the getRangeSum procedure need to know in order to use it?

Before you answer this question, let's consider a real-world example of designing and using a DVD player (Digital Versatile Disc player). A DVD player is designed and developed by electronic engineers. How do you use a DVD player? Before you use a DVD player, you do not open it to study all the details about its parts that are based on electronics engineering theories. When you buy it, it comes with a manual on how to use it. A DVD player is wrapped in a box. The box hides the details of the player inside. At the same time, the box exposes some of the details about the player in the form of an interface to the outside world. The interface for a DVD player consists of the following items:

- Input and output connection ports to connect to a power outlet, a TV set, etc.

- A panel to insert a DVD

- A set of buttons to perform operations such as eject, play, pause, fast forward, etc.

The manual that comes with the DVD player describes the usage of the player's interface meant for its users. A DVD user need not worry about the details of how it works internally. The manual also describes some conditions to operate it. For example, you must plug the power cord to a power outlet and switch on the power before you can use it.

A program is designed, developed, and used in the same way as a DVD player. The user of the program, shown in Listing 1-1, need not worry about the internal logic that is used to implement the program. A user of the program needs to know only its usage, which includes the interface to use it, and conditions that must be met before and after using it. In other words, you need to provide a manual for the getRangeSum procedure that will describe its usage. The user of the getRangeSum procedure will need to read its manual to use it. The "manual" for a program is known as its specification. Sometimes it is also known as documentation or comments. It provides another method of abstraction, which is called abstraction by specification. It describes (or exposes or focuses) the "what" part of the program and hides (or ignores or suppresses) the "how" part of the program from its users.

Listing 1-3 shows the same getRangeSum procedure code with its specification.

Listing 1-3. The getRangeSum Procedure with its Specification for Javadoc Tool

```
/**
 * Computes and returns the sum of all integers between two
 * integers specified by lowerLimit and upperLimit parameters.
 *
 * The lowerLimit parameter must be less than or equal to the
 * upperLimit parameter. If the sum of all integers between the
 * lowerLimit and the upperLimit exceeds the range of the int data
 * type then result is not defined.
 *
```

```
 * @param lowerLimit The lower limit of the integer range
 * @param upperLimit The upper limit of the integer range
 * @return The sum of all integers between lowerLimit (inclusive)
 *         and upperLimit (inclusive)
 */
public static int getRangeSum(int lowerLimit, int upperLimit) {
        int sum = 0;
        int counter = lowerLimit;
        while(counter <= upperLimit) {
                sum = sum + counter;
                counter = counter + 1;
        }
        return sum;
}
```

It uses Javadoc standards to write a specification for a Java program that can be processed by the Javadoc tool to generate HTML pages. In Java, the specification for a program element is placed between /** and */ immediately before the element. The specification is meant for the users of the getRangeSum procedure. The Javadoc tool will generate the specification for the getRangeSum procedure, as shown in Figure 1-4.

getRangeSum

```
public static int getRangeSum(int lowerLimit,
                              int upperLimit)
```

Computes and returns the sum of all integers between two integers specified by lowerLimit and upperLimit parameters. The lowerLimit parameter must be less than or equal to the upperLimit parameter. If the sum of all integers between the lowerLimit and the upperLimit exceeds the range of the int data type then result is not defined.

Parameters:

lowerLimit - The lower limit of the integer range

upperLimit - The upper limit of the integer range

Returns:

The sum of all integers between lowerLimit (inclusive) and upperLimit (inclusive)

Figure 1-4. *The specification for the getRangeSum procedure*

The above specification provides the description (the "what" part) of the getRangeSum procedure. It also specifies two conditions, known as pre-conditions, that must be true when the procedure is called. The first pre-condition is that the lower limit must be less than or equal to the upper limit. The second pre-condition is that the value for lower and upper limits must be small enough so that the sum of all integers between them fits in the size of the int data type. It specifies another condition that is called post-condition, which is specified in the "Returns" clause. The post-condition holds as long as pre-conditions hold. The pre-conditions and post-conditions are like a contract (or an agreement) between the program and its user. It states that as long as the user of the program makes sure that the pre-condition holds true, the program guarantees that the post-condition will hold true. Note that the specification never tells the user about how the program fulfils (implementation details) the post-condition. It only tells "what" it is going to do rather than "how" it is going to do it. The user of the getRangeSum program, who has the specification, need not look at the body of the getRangeSum procedure to figure out the logic that it uses. In other words, you have hidden the details of implementation of getRangeSum procedure from its users by providing the above specification to them. That is, users of the getRangeSum procedure can ignore its implementation details for the purpose of using it. This is another concrete example of abstraction. The method of hiding implementation details of a subprogram (the "how" part) and exposing its usage (the "what" part) by using specification is called abstraction by specification.

Abstraction by parameterization and abstraction by specification let the users of a program view the program as a black box, where they are concerned only about the effects that program produces rather than how the program produces those effects. Figure 1-5 depicts the user's view of the getRangeSum procedure. Note that a user does not see (need not see) the body of the procedure that has the details. The details are relevant only for the writer of the program, not its users.

Figure 1-5. *User's view of the getRangeSum procedure as a black box using abstraction*

What advantages did you achieve by applying the abstraction to define the getRangeSum procedure? One of the most important advantages is isolation. It is isolated from other programs. If you modify the logic inside its body, other programs, including the ones that are using it, need not be modified at all. To print the sum of integers between 10 and 20, you use the following program:

```
int s1 = getRangeSum(10, 20);
System.out.println(s1);
```

The body of the procedure uses a while loop, which is executed as many times as the number of integers between lower and upper limits. The while loop inside the getRangeSum procedure executes n times where n is equal to (upperLimit - lowerLimit + 1). The number of instructions that needs to be executed depends on the input values. There is a better way to compute the sum of all integers between two integers, lowerLimit and upperLimit, using the following formula:

```
n = upperLimit - lowerLimit + 1;
sum = n * (2 * lowerLimit + (n-1))/2;
```

If you use the above formula, the number of instructions that are executed to compute the sum of all integers between two integers is always the same. You can rewrite the body of the getRangeSum procedure as shown in Listing 1-4. The specification of getRangeSum procedure is not shown here.

Listing 1-4. Another Version of the getRangeSum Procedure with the Logic Changed Inside its Body

```
public int getRangeSum(int lowerLimit, int upperLimit) {
        int n = upperLimit - lowerLimit + 1;
        int sum = n * (2 * lowerLimit + (n-1))/2;
        return sum;
}
```

Note that the body (implementation or the "how" part) of the getRangeSum procedure has changed between Listing 1-2 and Listing 1-3. However, the users of the getRangeSum procedure are not affected by this change at all because the details of the implementation of this procedure were kept hidden from its users by using abstraction. If you want to compute the sum of all integers between 10 and 20 using the version of the getRangeSum procedure as shown in Listing 1-3, your old code (shown below) is still valid.

```
int s1 = getRangeSum(10, 20);
System.out.println(s1);
```

You have just seen one of the greatest benefits of abstraction, in which the implementation details of a program (in this case, a procedure) can be changed without warranting any changes in the code that uses the program. This benefit also gives you a chance to rewrite your program logic to improve performance in the future without affecting other parts of the application.

I will consider two types of abstraction in this section:

- Procedural abstraction
- Data abstraction

Procedural Abstraction

Procedural abstraction lets you define a procedure, for example, getRangeSum, that you can use as an action or a task. So far, in this section, I have been discussing procedural abstraction. Abstraction by parameterization and abstraction by specification are two methods to achieve procedural abstraction as well as data abstraction.

Object-oriented programming is based on data abstraction. However, I need to discuss data type briefly before I discuss data abstraction. A data type (or simply a type) is defined in terms of three components:

- A set of values (or data objects)
- A set of operations that can be applied to all values in the set
- A data representation, which determines how the values are stored

Programming languages provide some predefined data types, which are known as built-in data types. They also let programmers define their own data types, which are known as user-defined data types. A data type that consists of an atomic and indivisible value, and that is defined without the help of any other data types, is known as a primitive data type. For example, Java has built-in primitive data types such as int, float, boolean, char, etc. Three components that define the int primitive data type in Java are as follows:

- An int data type consists of a set of all integers between -2147483648 and 2147483647.

- Operations such as addition, subtraction, multiplication, division, comparison, and many more are defined for the int data type.

- A value of int data type is represented in 32-bit memory in 2's compliment form.

All three components of the int data type are predefined by Java language. You cannot extend or redefine the definition of the int data type as a programmer. You can give a name to a value of the int data type as

```
int n1;
```

The above statement states that n1 is a name (technically called an identifier) that can be associated with one value from the set of values that defines values for int data type. For example, you can associate integer 26 to the name n1 using an assignment statement as

```
n1 = 26;
```

At this stage, you may be asking, "Where is the value 26, which is associated with the name n1, stored in memory?" You know from the definition of int data type that n1 will take 32-bit memory. However, you do not know, cannot know, and do not need to know where in the memory that 32-bit is allocated for n1. Do you see an example of abstraction here? If you see an example of abstraction in this case, you are right. This is an example of abstraction, which is built into the Java language. In this instance, the pieces of information about the data representation of the data value for int data type are hidden from the users (programmers) of the data type. In other words, a programmer ignores the memory location of n1 and focuses on its value and the operations that can be performed on it. A programmer does not care if the memory for n1 is allocated in a register, RAM, or the hard disk.

Data Abstraction

Object-oriented programming languages such as Java let you create new data types using an abstraction mechanism called data abstraction. The new data types are known as abstract data types (ADT). The data objects in ADT may consist of a combination of primitive data types and other ADTs. An ADT defines a set of operations that can be applied to all its data objects. The data representation is always hidden in ADT. For users of an ADT, it consists of operations only. Its data elements may only be accessed and manipulated using its operations. The advantage of using data abstraction is that its data representation can be changed without affecting any code that uses the ADT.

■ **Tip**   Data abstraction lets programmers create a new data type called an abstract data type, where the storage representation of the data objects is hidden from the users of the data type. In other words, ADT is defined solely in terms of operations that can be applied to the data objects of its type without knowing the internal representation of the data. The reason this kind of data type is called abstract is that users of ADT never see the representation of the data values. Users view the data objects of an ADT in an abstract way by applying operations on them without knowing the details about representation of the data objects. Note that an ADT does not mean absence of data representation. Data representation is always present in an ADT. It only means hiding of the data representation from its users.

Java language has constructs, for example, class, interface, and enum, that let you define new ADTs. When you use a class to define a new ADT, you need to be careful to hide the data representation, so your new data type is really abstract. If the data representation in a Java class is not hidden, that class creates a new data type, but not an ADT. A class in Java gives you features that you can use to expose the data representation or hide it. In Java, the set of values of a class data type are called objects. Operations on the objects are called methods. Instance variables (also known as fields) of objects are the data representation for the class type.

A class in Java also lets you provide an implementation of operations that operates on the data representation. An interface in Java lets you create a pure ADT. An interface lets you provide only the specification for operations that can be applied to the data objects of its type. No implementation for operations or data representation can be mentioned in an interface. Listing 1-1 shows the definition of the Person class using Java language syntax. By defining a class named Person, you have created a new ADT. Its internal data representation for name and gender uses String data type (String is built-in ADT provided by Java class library). Note that the definition of the Person class uses the private keyword in the name and gender declarations to hide it from the outside world. Users of the Person class cannot access the name and gender data elements. It provides four operations: a constructor and three methods (getName, setName, and getGender).

A constructor operation is used to initialize a newly constructed data object of Person type. The getName and setName operations are used to access and modify the name data element, respectively. The getGender operation is used to access the value of the gender data element.

Users of the Person class must use only these four operations to work with data objects of Person type. Users of the Person type are oblivious to the type of data storage being used to store name and gender data elements. I am using three terms, "type," "class," and "interface," interchangeably because they mean the same thing in the context of a data type. It gives the developer of the Person type freedom to change the data representation for the name and gender data elements without affecting any users of Person type. Suppose one of the users of Person type has the following snippet of code:

```
Person john = new Person("John Jacobs", "Male");
String intialName = john.getName();
john.setName("Wally Jacobs");
String changedName = john.getName();
```

Note that this snippet of code has been written only in terms of the operations provided by the Person type. It does not (and could not) refer to the name and gender instance variables directly. Let's see how to change the data representation of the Person type without affecting the above snippet of code. Listing 1-5 shows the code for a newer version for the Person class.

Listing 1-5. Another Version of the Person Class That Uses a String Array of Two Elements to Store Name and Gender Values as Opposed to Two String Variables

```
package com.jdojo.concepts;

public class Person {
        private String[] data = new String[2];

        public Person(String initialName, String initialGender) {
                data[0] = initialName;
                data[1] = initialGender;
        }

        public String getName() {
                return data[0];
        }

        public void setName(String newName) {
                data[0] = newName;
        }

        public String getGender() {
                return data[1];
        }
}
```

Compare the code in Listing 1-1 and Listing 1-5. This time you have replaced the two instance variables (name and gender), which were the data representation for the Person type in Listing 1-1, with a String array of two elements. Since operations (or methods) in a class operate on the data representation, you had to change the implementations for all four operations in the Person type. The client code in Listing 1-5 was written in terms of the specifications of the four operations and not their implementation. Since you have not changed the specification of any of the operations, you do not need to change the snippet of code that uses the Person class; it is still valid with the newer definition of the Person type as shown in Listing 1-5. Some methods in the Person class use the abstraction by parameterization and all of them use the abstraction by specification. I have not shown the specification for the methods here, which would be Javadoc comments.

You have seen two major benefits of data abstraction in this section.

- It lets you extend the programming language by letting you define new data types. The new data types you create depend on the application domain. For example, for a banking system, Person, Currency, and Account may be good choices for new data types whereas for an auto insurance application, Person, Vehicle, and Claim may be good choices. The operations included in a new data type depend on the need of the application.

- The data type created using data abstraction may change the representation of the data without affecting the client code using the data type.

Encapsulation and Information Hiding

The term encapsulation is used to mean two different things: a process or an entity. As a process, it is an act of bundling one or more items into a container. The container could be physical or logical. As an entity, it is a container that holds one or more items.

Programming languages support encapsulations in many ways. A procedure is an encapsulation of steps to perform a task; an array is an encapsulation of several elements of the same type, etc. In object-oriented programming, encapsulation is bundling of data and operations on the data into an entity called a class.

Java supports encapsulation in various ways.

- It lets you bundle data and methods that operate on the data in an entity called a class.

- It lets you bundle one or more logically related classes in an entity called a package. A package in Java is a logical collection of one or more related classes. A package creates a new naming scope in which all classes must have unique names. Two classes may have the same name in Java as long as they are bundled (or encapsulated) in two different packages.

- It lets you bundle one or more related classes in an entity called a compilation unit. All classes in a compilation unit can be compiled separately from other compilation units.

While discussing the concepts of object-oriented programming, the two terms, encapsulation and information hiding, are often used interchangeably. However, they are different concepts in object-oriented programming, and they should not be used interchangeably as such. Encapsulation is simply the bundling of items together into one entity. Information hiding is the process of hiding implementation details that are likely to change. Encapsulation is not concerned with whether the items that are bundled in an entity are hidden from other modules in the application or not. What should be hidden (or ignored) and what should not be hidden is the concern of abstraction. Abstraction is only concerned about which item should be hidden. Abstraction is not concerned about how the item should be hidden. Information hiding is concerned with how an item is hidden. Encapsulation, abstraction, and information hiding are three separate concepts. They are very closely related, though. One concept facilitates the workings of the others. It is important to understand the subtle differences in roles they play in object-oriented programming.

It is possible to use encapsulation with or without hiding any information. For example, the Person class in Listing 1-1 shows an example of encapsulation and information hiding. The data elements (name and gender) and methods (getName(), setName(), and getGender()) are bundled together in a class called Person. This is encapsulation. In other words, the Person class is an encapsulation of the data elements name and gender, plus the methods getName(), setName(), and getGender(). The same Person class uses information hiding by hiding the data elements from the outside world. Note that name and gender data elements use the Java keyword private, which essentially hides them from the outside world. Listing 1-6 shows the code for a Person2 class.

Listing 1-6. The Definition of the Person2 Class in Which Data Elements Are Not Hidden by Declaring Them Public

```
package com.jdojo.concepts;

public class Person2 {
        public String name;    // Not hidden from its users
        public String gender; // Not hidden from its users

        public Person2(String initialName, String initialGender) {
                name = initialName;
                gender = initialGender;
        }

        public String getName() {
                return name;
        }

        public void setName(String newName) {
                name = newName;
        }

        public String getGender() {
                return gender;
        }
}
```

The code in Listing 1-1 and Listing 1-6 is essentially the same except for two small differences. The Person2 class uses the keyword public to declare the name and the gender data elements. The Person2 class uses encapsulation the same way the Person class uses. However, data elements name and gender are not hidden. That is, the Person2 class does not use data hiding (Data hiding is an example of information hiding). If you look at the constructor and methods of Person and Person2 classes, their bodies use information hiding because the logic written inside their bodies is hidden from their users.

■ **Tip** Encapsulation and information hiding are two distinct concepts of object-oriented programming. The existence of one does not imply the existence of the other.

Inheritance

Inheritance is another important concept in object-oriented programming. It lets you use abstraction in a new way. You have seen how a class represents an abstraction in previous sections. The Person class shown in Listing 1-1 represents an abstraction for a real-world person. The inheritance mechanism lets you define a new abstraction by extending an existing abstraction. The existing abstraction is called a supertype, a superclass, a parent class, or a base class. The new abstraction is called a subtype, a subclass, a child class, or a derived class. It is said that a subtype is derived (or inherited) from a supertype; a supertype is a generalization of a subtype; and a subtype is a specialization of a supertype. The inheritance can be used to define new abstractions at more than one level. A subtype can be used as a supertype to define another subtype and so on. Inheritance gives rise to a family of types arranged in a hierarchical form.

Inheritance allows you to use varying degrees of abstraction at different levels of hierarchy. In Figure 1-6, the Person class is at the top (highest level) of the inheritance hierarchy. Employee and Customer classes are at the second level of inheritance hierarchy. As you move up the inheritance level, you focus on more important pieces information. In other words, at a higher level of inheritance, you are concerned about the bigger picture; and at lower levels of inheritance, you are concerned about more and more details. There is another way to look at inheritance hierarchy from abstraction point of view. At the Person level in 5, you focus on the common characteristics of Employee and Customer, and you ignore the difference between them. At Employee level, you focus on common characteristics of Clerk, Programmer, and Cashier, and you ignore the differences between them.

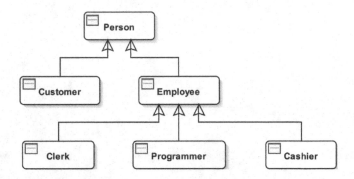

Figure 1-6. *Inheritance hierarchy for the Person class*

In inheritance hierarchy, a supertype and its subtype represent an "is-a" relationship. That is, an Employee is a Person; a Programmer is an Employee, etc. Since the lower level of inheritance means more pieces of information, a subtype always includes what its supertype has and maybe some more. This characteristic of inheritance leads to another feature in object-oriented programming, which is known as the principle of substitutivity. It means that a supertype can always be substituted with its subtype. For example, you have considered only name and gender information for a person in your Person abstraction. If you inherit Employee from Person, Employee includes name and gender information, which it inherits from Person. Employee may include some more pieces of information such as employee id, hire date, salary, etc. If a Person is expected in a context, it implies that only name and gender information are relevant in that context. You can always replace a Person in this context with an Employee, a Customer, a Clerk, or a Programmer because being a subtype (direct or indirect) of the Person these abstractions guarantee that they have the ability to deal with at least name and gender information.

At programming level, inheritance provides a code reuse mechanism. The code written in supertype may be reused by its subtype. A subtype may extend the functionality of its supertype by adding more functionality or by redefining existing functionalities of its supertype.

■ **Tip**   Inheritance is also used as a technique to implement polymorphism, which is discussed in the next section. Inheritance lets you write polymorphic code. The code is written in terms of the supertype and the same code works for subtypes.

Inheritance is a vast topic. This book devotes a complete chapter to inheritance. I will discuss how Java allows us to use inheritance mechanisms in Chapter 9.

Polymorphism

The word "polymorphism" has its root in two Greek words: "poly" (means many) and "morphos" (means form). In programming, polymorphism is the ability of an entity (e.g. variable, class, method, object, code, parameter, etc.) to take on different meanings in different contexts. The entity that takes on different meanings is known as a polymorphic entity. Various types of polymorphism exist. Each type of polymorphism has a name that usually indicates how that type of polymorphism is achieved in practice. The proper use of polymorphism results in generic and reusable code. The purpose of polymorphism is writing reusable and maintainable code by writing code in terms of a generic type that works for many types (or ideally all types).

Polymorphism can be categorized in the following two categories:

- Ad hoc polymorphism

- Universal polymorphism

If the types for which a piece of code works are finite and all those types must be known when the code is written, it is known as ad hoc polymorphism. Ad hoc polymorphism is also known as apparent polymorphism because it is not a polymorphism in a true sense. Some computer science purists do not consider ad hoc polymorphism as polymorphism at all. Ad hoc polymorphism is divided into two types: overloading polymorphism and coercion polymorphism.

If a piece of code is written in such a way that it works for infinite number of types (will also work for new types not known at the time the code is written), it is called universal polymorphism. In universal polymorphism, the same code works on many types, whereas in ad hoc polymorphism, different implementations of code are provided for different types giving an apparent impression of polymorphism. Universal polymorphism is divided into two types: inclusion polymorphism and parametric polymorphism.

Overloading Polymorphism

Overloading is an ad hoc polymorphism. Overloading results when a method (called a method in Java and a function in other languages) or an operator has at least two definitions that work on different types. In such cases, the same method or operator name is used for their different definitions. That is, the same name exhibits many behaviors and hence the polymorphism. Such methods and operators are called overloaded methods and overloaded operators. Java lets you define overloaded methods. Java has some overloaded operators. Java does not let you overload an operator for an ADT. That is, you cannot provide a new definition for an operator in Java.

Listing 1-7 shows code for a class named `MathUtil`.

Listing 1-7. An Example of an Overloaded Method in Java

```java
package com.jdojo.concepts;

public class MathUtil {
    public static int max(int n1, int n2) {
        /* Code to determine the maximum of two integers goes here */
    }

    public static double max(double n1, double n2) {
        /* Code to determine the maximum of two floating-point numbers goes here */
    }

    public static int max(int[] num) {
        /* Code to determine the maximum of an array of int goes here */
    }
}
```

The max() method of the MathUtil class is overloaded. It has three definitions and each of its definitions performs the same task of computing maximum, but on different types. The first definition computes a maximum of two numbers of int data type, the second one computes a maximum of two floating-point numbers of double data type, and the third one computes a maximum of an array of numbers of int data type. The following snippet of code makes use of all three definitions of the overloaded max() method:

```
int max1 = MathUtil.max(10, 23);              // Uses max(int, int)
double max2 = MathUtil.max(10.34, 2.89);      // Uses max(double, double)
int max3 = MathUtil.max(new int[]{1, 89, 8, 3}); // Uses max(int[])
```

Note that method overloading gives you only sharing of the method name. It does not result in the sharing of definitions. In Listing 1-7, the method name max is shared by all three methods, but they all have their own definition of computing maximum of different types. In method overloading, the definitions of methods do not have to be related at all. They may perform entirely different things and share the same name.

The following code snippet shows an example of operator overloading in Java. The operator is +. In the following three statements, it performs three different things:

```
int n1 = 10 + 20;          // Adds two integers
double n2 = 10.20 + 2.18;   // Adds two floating-point numbers
String str = "Hi " + "there"; // Concatenates two strings
```

In the first statement, the + operator performs addition on two integers, 10 and 20, and returns 30. In the second statement, it performs addition on two floating-point numbers, 10.20 and 2.18, and returns 12.38. In the third statement, it performs concatenation of two strings and returns "Hi there".

In overloading, the types of the actual method's parameters (types of operands in case of operators) are used to determine which definition of the code to use. Method overloading provides only the reuse of the method name. You can remove method overloading by simply supplying a unique name to all versions of an overloaded method. For example, you could rename the three versions of the max() method as max2Int(), max2Double(), and maxNInt(). Note that all versions of an overloaded method or operator do not have to perform related or similar tasks. In Java, the only requirement to overload a method name is that all versions of the method must differ in number and/or type of their formal parameters.

Coercion Polymorphism

Coercion is an ad hoc polymorphism. Coercion occurs when a type is implicitly converted (coerced) to another type automatically even if it was not intended explicitly. Consider the following statements in Java:

```
int num = 707;
double d1 = (double)num; // Explicit conversion of int to double
double d2 = num;         // Implicit conversion of int to double (coercion)
```

The variable num has been declared to be of int data type, and it has been assigned a value of 707. The second statement uses cast, (double), to convert the int value stored in num to double, and assigns the converted value to d1. This is the case of explicit conversion from int to double. In this case, the programmer makes his intention explicit by using the cast. The third statement has exactly the same effect as the second one. However, it relies on implicit conversion (called widening conversion in Java) provided by Java language that converts an int to double automatically when needed. The third statement is an example of coercion. A programming language (including Java) provides different coercions in different contexts: assignment (shown above), method parameters, etc.

Consider the following snippet of code that shows a definition of a square() method, which accepts a parameter of double data type:

```
double square(double num) {
        return num * num;
}
```

The square() method can be called with actual parameter of double data type as

```
double d1 = 20.23;
double result = square(d1);
```

The same square() method may also be called with actual parameter of int data type as

```
int k = 20;
double result = square(k);
```

You have just seen that the square() method works on double data type as well as int data type although you have defined it only once in terms of a formal parameter of double data type. This is exactly what polymorphism means. In this case, the square() method is called a polymorphic method with respect to double and int data type. Thus the square() method is exhibiting polymorphic behavior even though the programmer who wrote the code did not intend it. The square() method is polymorphic because of the implicit type conversion (coercion from int to double) provided by Java language. Here is a more formal definition of a polymorphic method:

Suppose m is a method that declares a formal parameter of type T. If S is a type that can be implicitly converted to T, the method m is said to be polymorphic with respect to S and T.

Inclusion Polymorphism

Inclusion is a universal polymorphism. It is also known as subtype (or subclass) polymorphism because it is achieved using subtyping or subclassing. This is the most common type of polymorphism supported by object-oriented programming languages. Java supports it. Inclusion polymorphism occurs when a piece of code that is written using a type works for all its subtypes. This type of polymorphism is possible based on the subtyping rule that a value that belongs to a subtype also belongs to the supertype. Suppose T is a type and S1, S2, S3... are subtypes of T. A value that belongs to S1, S2, S3... also belongs to T. This subtyping rule makes us write code as follows:

```
T t;
S1 s1;
S2 s2;
...
t = s1; // A value of type s1 can be assigned to variable of type T
t = s2; // A value of type s2 can be assigned to variable of type T
```

Java supports inclusion polymorphism using inheritance, which is a subclassing mechanism. You can define a method in Java using a formal parameter of a type, for example, Person, and that method can be called on all its subtypes, for example, Employee, Student, Customer, etc. Suppose you have a method processDetails() as follows:

```
void processDetails(Person p) {
        /* Write code using the formal parameter p, which is of type Person. The same code will
           work if an object of any of the subclass of Person is passed to this method.
        */
}
```

The processDetails() method declares a formal parameter of Person type. You can define any number of classes that are subclasses of the Person class. The processDetails() method will work for all subclasses of the Person class. Assume that Employee and Customer are subclasses of the Person class. You can write code like

```
Person p1 = create a Person object;
Employee e1 = create an Employee object;
Customer c1 = create a Customer object;
processDetails(p1); // Use Person type
processDetails(e1); // Use Employee type, which is a subclass of Person
processDetails(c1); // Use Customer type, which is a subclass of Person
```

The effect of the subtyping rule is that the supertype includes (hence the name inclusion) all values that belong to its subtypes. A piece of code is called universally polymorphic only if it works on an infinite number of types. In the case of inclusion polymorphism, the number of types for which the code works is constrained but infinite. The constraint is that all types must be the subtype of the type in whose term the code is written. If there is no restriction on how many subtypes a type can have, the number of subtypes is infinite (at least in theory). Note that inclusion polymorphism not only lets you write reusable code, it also lets you write extensible and flexible code. The processDetails() method works on all subclasses of the Person class. It will keep working for all subclasses of the Person class, which will be defined in future, without any modifications. Java uses other mechanisms, like method overriding and dynamic dispatch (also called late binding), along with subclassing rules to make the inclusion polymorphism more effective and useful.

Parametric Polymorphism

Parametric is a universal polymorphism. It is also called "true" polymorphism because it lets you write true generic code that works for any types (related or unrelated). Sometimes it is also referred to as generics. In parametric polymorphism, a piece of code is written in such a way that it works on any type. Contrast parametric polymorphism with inclusion polymorphism. In inclusion polymorphism, code is written for one type and it works for all of its subtypes. It means all types for which the code works in inclusion polymorphism are related by a supertype-subtype relationship. However, in parametric polymorphism, the same code works for all types, which are not necessarily related. Parametric polymorphism is achieved by using a type variable when writing the code, rather than using any specific type. The type variable assumes a type for which the code needs to be executed. Java supports parametric polymorphism since Java 5 through generics. Java supports polymorphic entity (e.g. parameterized classes) as well as polymorphic method (parameterized methods) that use parametric polymorphism.

All collection classes as of Java 5 have been retrofitted to use generics (parametric polymorphism is achieved in Java using generics). You can write code using generics as shown below. This code uses a List object as a list of String type and a List object as a list of Integer type. Using generics, you can treat a List object as a list of any type in Java. Note the use of <XXX> (angle brackets) in code to specify the type for which you want to instantiate the List object.

```
// Use List for String type
List<String> sList = new ArrayList<String>();
sList.add("string 1");
sList.add("string 2");
String s2 = sList.get(1);

// Use List for Integer type
List<Integer> iList = new ArrayList<Integer>();
iList.add(10);
iList.add(20);
int i2 = iList.get(1);
```

Summary

Writing the set of instructions for a computer to accomplish a task is known as programming. The set of instructions is known as a program. Different types of programming languages exist. They differ in their closeness to the instructions that the hardware can understand or the paradigm. A machine language lets you write programs using 0s and 1s, and it is the lowest level programming language. A program written in machine language is known as machine code. An assembly language lets you write programs using mnemonics. A program written using an assembly language is known as assembly code. Later, higher-level programming languages were developed, using an English-like language.

Several types of programming paradigms are in practice. A programming paradigm is a thinking cap for viewing and analyzing real-world problems in a particular way. Imperative, procedural, functional, and object-oriented are some widely used paradigms in software development. Java is a programming language that supports procedural, functional, and object-oriented programming paradigms.

Abstraction, encapsulation, inheritance, and polymorphism are the four pillars of object-oriented paradigms. Abstraction is the process of hiding details of a program that are irrelevant to the users. Encapsulation is the process of bundling multiple items into one entity. Inheritance is the process of arranging classes in a hierarchical manner to build supertype/subtype relationships. Inheritance promotes reusability of code by allowing programmers to write the code in terms of a supertype that also works for all of the subtypes. Polymorphism is the way of writing a piece of code once that can operate on multiple types. Method overloading, method overriding, subtyping, and generics are some of the ways to implement polymorphism.

■ ■ ■

Writing Java Programs

In this chapter, you will learn

- How to write, compile, and run Java programs using command prompts and the NetBeans integrated development environment (IDE)
- How to set the CLASSPATH for running Java programs
- Briefly about the Java Virtual Machine (JVM) and the Java Platform

What is a Java Program?

A Java program, which is written using the Java programming language, is a set of instructions to be executed by a computer to perform a task. In this chapter, you will write a simple Java program that prints a message on the console, for example, a command prompt on Windows. This chapter explains only the basics involved in writing a Java program. A detailed explanation of all aspects of a Java program will be covered in subsequent chapters.

Writing a Java program involves three steps:

- Writing the source code
- Compiling the source code
- Running the compiled code

You can write Java programs using a text editor of your choice, such as Notepad on Windows, vi editor on UNIX, etc. The source code is compiled into object code, also known as bytecode, using a Java compiler. The compiled code (object code or bytecode) is run by a JVM. You can also use an IDE such as NetBeans to write Java programs. This chapter shows how to write Java programs using both a text editor and the NetBeans IDE.

System Requirements

You need to have the following software installed on your computer:

- Java Development Kit 8
- NetBeans IDE 7.4 or later

It is not necessary to have NetBeans to use the programs in this book. However, the NetBeans IDE makes working with Java programs easy. You can use any other IDE, for example, Eclipse, JDeveloper, IntelliJ IDEA, etc. The source code for this book contains a NetBeans project. If you use an IDE other than NetBeans, you will have to copy the contents of the src directory, from the source code bundle for this book, to the source code directory created for the project by your IDE.

■ **Note**   Java SE 8 is not supported on Windows XP.

Writing the Source Code

This section will cover the details of writing the source code. I will demonstrate this by using Notepad on Windows. You can use a text editor of your choice that is available on your system.

■ **Note**   I will cover using the NetBeans IDE in the following section. I want to cover using a text editor because the process reveals a lot about Java programs that you need to know.

When you finish writing the source code, you must save the file with the extension .java. You are going to name your source code file Welcome.java. Note that any extension to the file other than .java is not acceptable. For example, the names Welcome.txt and Welcome.doc are not valid source code file names.

Whenever you use a language to write something (in your case, Java source code), you need to follow the grammar of that language, and use a specific syntax depending on the thing you are writing. Let's take an example of writing a letter to your friend. The letter will have several parts: a heading, a greeting, a body, closing statement, and your signature. The parts of the letter should be placed in order. In a letter, it is not just important to put all five parts together; rather, they should also be placed in a specific order. For example, the closing needs to follow the body, etc. Some parts in a letter may be optional and others mandatory. For example, it is fine to exclude the return address in a letter to your friend, whereas it is mandatory in a business letter.

In the beginning, you can think of writing a Java program as similar to writing a letter. Let's start writing the Java source code. Java source code consists of three parts

- Zero or one package declaration

- Zero, one, or more import declarations

- Zero, one, or more type declarations: class, interface, or enum declarations

All three parts are optional. The three parts, if present, must be specified in the above-mentioned order. Figure 2-1 shows the three parts of a Java programs.

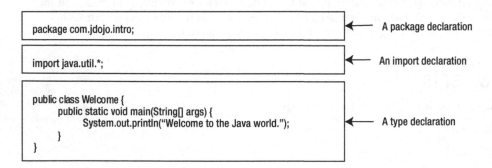

Figure 2-1. *Parts of a Java program*

Package Declaration

The general syntax for a package declaration is

```
package <your-package-name>;
```

A package declaration starts with the keyword package followed with a user-supplied package name. One or more whitespaces (spaces, tabs, new lines, carriage returns, tabs, and form-feeds) separate the keyword package and the package name. A semicolon (;) ends the package declaration. For example, the following is the package declaration for a package named com.jdojo.intro:

```
package com.jdojo.intro;
```

Figure 2-2 shows the parts of a package declaration.

Figure 2-2. *Parts of a package declaration in a Java program*

The programmer supplies the package name. A package name may consist of one or more parts. In this example, two parts are separated by a dot (.). This package name consists of three parts: com, jdojo, and intro. There is no limit on the number of parts in a package name. However, if a package declaration appears in Java source code, it must contain a package name, which must have at least one part. You can have maximum of one package declaration in a Java source file (to be more specific, in a compilation unit). The following are some examples of valid package declarations:

```
package intro;
package com.jdojo.intro.common;
package com.ksharan;
package com.jdojo.intro;
```

Why do we use a package declaration? A package is a logical repository for Java types (class, interface, and enum). In other words, it provides a logical grouping for related Java types. A package can be stored in a host-specific file system, a database, or a network location. In a file system, each part of a package name denotes a directory on the host system. For example, the package name com.jdojo.intro indicates the existence of a directory named com, which contains a subdirectory jdojo, which contains a subdirectory intro. The directory intro will contain the compiled Java code. If you are working on Windows, you can think of a directory structure com\jdojo\intro\<<Class File Name>> whereas on UNIX-like operating systems (for example, Linux, Solaris, and Mac OS X), it will look like com/jdojo/intro/<<Class File Name>>. A dot, which is used to separate parts in the package name, is treated as a file-separator character on the host system. A back slash (\) is the file-separator character on Windows, and a forward slash (/) on UNIX-like operating system.

The package name specifies only the partial directory structure in which the compiled Java program (class files) must exist. It does not specify the full path of the class files. In this example, the package declaration com.jdojo.intro does not specify where the com directory will be placed. It may be placed under C:\ directory or C:\myprograms directory or under any other directory in the file system.

Knowing just the package name is not enough to locate a class file, because it specifies only a partial path to the class file. The leading part of the class file path on the file system is obtained from an environment variable called CLASSPATH. I will discuss CLASSPATH in detail shortly.

The package declaration is optional. What repository does your Java program belong to if you omit the package declaration? A Java program (strictly speaking, a Java type), which does not have a package declaration, is said to be part of an unnamed package (also called default package). I will discuss unnamed package in more detail in the sections to follow.

Java source code is case sensitive. The keyword package has to be written as is—in all lowercase. The word Package or packAge cannot replace the keyword package. The package name is also case sensitive. On some operating systems, the names of files and directories are case sensitive. On those systems, the package names will be case sensitive, as you have seen: the package name is treated as a directory name on the host system. The package names com.jdojo.intro and Com.jdojo.intro may not be the same depending on the host system that you are working on. It is recommended to use package names in all lowercase.

The package declaration is a simple and important part of Java source code. It is recommended that you always use a package declaration in your source code. Typically, a package name starts with a reverse domain name of the company, such as com.yahoo for Yahoo, com.google for Google etc. Using the reverse domain name of the company as the leading part of the package name guarantees that a package name will not conflict with package names used by other companies, provided they follow the same guidelines. If you do not own a domain name, make up one that is likely to be unique. This is just a guideline. There is nothing in practice that guarantees a unique package name for all Java programs written in the world.

Import Declarations

Import declarations in Java source code are optional. You may develop a Java application without using even a single import declaration. Why is an import declaration needed at all? Using import declarations in your code makes your life easier. It saves you some typing and makes your code cleaner and easier to read. In an import declaration, you tell the Java compiler that you may use one or more classes from a particular package. Whenever a type (a class, an interface, or an enum) is used in Java source code, it must be referred to by its fully qualified name. Using an import declaration for a type lets you refer to a type using its simple name. I will discuss simple and fully qualified names of a type shortly.

Unlike a package declaration, there is no restriction on the number of import declarations in the source code. The following are two import declarations:

```
import com.jdojo.intro.Account;
import com.jdojo.util.*;
```

I will discuss import declarations in detail in the chapter on classes and objects. In this section, I will discuss only the meaning of all parts of an import declaration. An import declaration starts with the keyword import. The second part in an import declaration consists of two parts:

- A package name from which you want to use the classes in the current source code

- A class name or an asterisk (*) to indicate that you may use one or more of the classes stored in the package.

Finally, an import declaration ends with a semicolon. The above two import declarations state the following:

- We may use a class named Account by its simple name from com.jdojo.intro package.

- We may use any classes, interfaces, and enums by their simple names from the com.jdojo.util package.

If you want to use a class named `Person` from `com.jdojo.common` package in the source code, you need to include one of the following two import declarations in your source code:

```
import com.jdojo.common.Person;
```

or

```
import com.jdojo.common.*;
```

The following import declarations do not include classes in the package `com` or `com.jdojo`:

```
import com.jdojo.intro.Account;
import com.jdojo.intro.*;
```

You might think that an import declaration like

```
import com.*.*;
```

would let you use the simple names of all classes whose first part of package declaration is com. Java does not support this type of wildcard use in an import declaration. You are allowed only to name one class in a package (`com.jdojo.intro.Account`) or all classes in a package (`com.jdojo.intro.*`); any other syntax to import classes is invalid.

The third part in a Java source code contains type declarations, which may contain zero or more declarations for class, interface, and/or enum. According to the Java Language Specification, type declaration is also optional. However, if you omit this part, your Java program does not do anything. To make your Java program meaningful, you must include at least one class, interface, or enum declaration in your Java source code. I will defer the discussion of interface and enum until later chapters in this book. Let's discuss how to declare a class in a Java source code.

Class Declaration

In the simplest form, a class declaration looks like

```
class Welcome {
        // Code for the class body goes here
};
```

Figure 2-3 shows parts of the above class declaration.

Figure 2-3. *Parts of a class declaration in a Java source code*

A class is declared by using the keyword class, which is followed by the name of the class. In this example, the name of the class is Welcome.

The body of the class is placed between an opening brace and a closing brace. The body may be empty. However, you must include the two braces to mark the beginning and the end of the body. Optionally, a class declaration may end with a semicolon. This book will not use the optional semicolon to end a class declaration. Before continuing the discussion of a class declaration, let's discuss the following line from the body of the class in our example:

```
// Code for the class body goes here
```

This line is called a comment. Comments are non-executable code. The Java compiler ignores them. They are included in a program to document the program's functionality and logic. There are three types of comments in a Java program:

- Single-line comment

- Multi-line comment

- Documentation comment or Javadoc comment

The first type of comment is called a single-line comment. It starts with two forward slashes (//) followed by text. For example,

```
// This is a single-line comment
package com.jdojo.intro; // This is also a single-line comment
```

This type of comment may start at any position in a line. The part of the line starting from two forward slashes to the end of the line is considered the comment. As shown above, you can also mix Java source code, for example, a package declaration and a comment in one line. Note that this type of comment cannot be inserted in the middle of the Java code. The following package declaration is incorrect as the package name and the semicolon are also considered as part of the comment:

```
package // An incorrect single-line comment com.jdojo.intro;
```

The following line is a single-line comment. It has a valid package declaration as the comment's text. It will be treated as a comment, not as a package declaration.

```
// package com.jdojo.intro;
```

The second type of comment is called a multi-line comment. A multi-line comment may span multiple lines. It starts with a forward slash immediately followed by an asterisk (/*) and ends with an asterisk immediately followed by a forward slash (*/). An example of a multi-line comment in a Java source code is as follows:

```
/*
    This is a multi-line comment.
    It can span more than one line.
*/
```

The above comment can also be written using two single-line comments, as follows:

```
// This is a multi-line comment.
// It can span more than one line
```

The style of comment that you use in the source code is your personal choice. A multi-line comment may be inserted in the middle of Java code as shown below. The compiler ignores all text starting from /* to */.

```
package /* A correct comment */ com.jdojo.intro;
```

The third type of comment is called documentation (or Javadoc) comment, which is also a multi-line comment. It is used to generate documentation for Java programs. This kind of comment begins with a forward slash that is immediately followed by two asterisks (/**) and ends with an asterisk that is immediately followed by a forward slash (*/). The following is a simple example of a documentation comment:

```
/**
This is a documentation comment. javadoc generates documentation from such comments.
*/
```

■ **Note** Writing documentation comment is a big topic. It is covered in Appendix B in detail.

The simplest class declaration in a Java program may look like

```
class Welcome { }
```

This time, I have placed the whole class declaration in one line. You can place the keyword `class`, the name of the class `Welcome`, and the two braces in any position you want, except that you must include at least one whitespace (space, newline, tab, etc.) between the keyword `class` and class name `Welcome`. Java allows you to write source code in a freeform text format. All of the following three class declarations are the same:

- Class Declaration #1

    ```
    class
    Welcome { }
    ```

- Class Declaration #2

```
class
        Welcome {
}
```

- Class Declaration #3

```
class Welcome {
}
```

This book uses the following class declaration format: the opening brace is placed on the same line following the class name, and the closing brace is placed on a separate line and it is aligned with the first character of the first line of the class declaration, like so:

```
class Welcome {
}
```

The body of a class consists of four parts. All parts are optional, may appear in any order, and can be split into multiple sections, not all together.

- Field Declarations

- Initializers: Static initializers and instance initializers

- Constructors

- Method Declarations

Java language does not impose any order in which the four parts of the body of a class may appear. I will start with method declarations and confine the discussion only to simple method declarations in this chapter. I will discuss advanced aspects of method declarations and other parts of class body declarations in the chapter on classes and objects.

Let's discuss how to declare a method for a class. You might guess that the method declaration would begin with a keyword method, as package and class declarations began with the keywords package and class, respectively. However, a method declaration does not begin with a keyword method. In fact, method is not a keyword in Java language. You begin a class declaration with the keyword class indicating that you are going to declare a class. However, in case of a method declaration, the first thing you specify is the type of value that a method will return to its caller. If a method does not return anything to its caller, you must mention that fact in the beginning of the method declaration, so you use the keyword void to indicate that a method does not return anything. The name of the method follows the return type of the method, and left and right parentheses follow the method name. Like a class, a method has a body part, which is enclosed in braces. The simplest method declaration in Java looks like the following:

```
<<MethodReturnType>> <<MethodName>> (<<arguments>>) {
        // Body of the method goes here
}
```

The following is an example of a method declaration:

```
void main() {
        // Empty body of the main method
}
```

This method declaration contains four things:

- The method does not return anything as indicated by the keyword void.

- The name of the method is main.

- The method requires no arguments.

- The method does not do anything as its body is empty.

The return value of a method is something that the method returns to its caller. The caller of the method may also want to pass some values to the method. If a method requires its caller to pass some values to it, this fact must be indicated in method's declaration. The fact that you want to pass some value to a method is specified within the parentheses that follow the method name. You need to specify two things about the values you want to pass to the method:

- The type of the value you want to pass. Suppose you want to pass an integer (say 10) to the method. You need to indicate this by using a keyword int, which is used to indicate an integer value like 10.

- The identifier, which will hold the value you pass to the method. Identifier is a user-defined name. It is called a parameter name.

If you want the main method to accept one integer value from its caller, its declaration will change to the following one:

```java
void main(int num) {

}
```

Note that num is the identifier, which will hold the value passed to this method. Instead of num, you may choose to use another identifier, for example, num1, num2, num3, etc. The above declaration of the main method is read as

The method main accepts one parameter of the type int and it does not return any value to its caller.

If you want to pass two integers to the main method, its declaration will change to the following:

```java
void main(int num1, int num2) {

}
```

It is clear from the above declaration that you need to separate the parameters passed to a method by a comma (,). What will you do if you want to pass 50 integers to this method? You will end up with a method declaration like

```java
void main(int num1, int num2, ..., int num50) {

}
```

I have shown only three parameter declarations. However, when you write a Java program, you will have to type all 50 parameter declarations. Let's look for some alternate ways to passing 50 parameters to this method. There is one similarity among all 50 parameters that they are all of the same type—integer. No values will contain fraction like 20.11 or 45.09. This similarity among all parameters allows you to use a magical creature in the Java language called an array. What is required to use array to pass 50 integer parameters to this method? When you write

```java
int num
```

it means that num is an identifier of the type int and it can hold one integer value. If you place two magic brackets ([ ]) after int, as in

```
int[] num
```

it means that num is an array of int and it can hold as many integer values as you want. There is a limit to the number of integers that num can hold. However, that limit is very high and I will discuss that limit when I discuss arrays in detail. The values stored in num can be accessed using subscripts: num[0], num[1], num[2], etc. Note that in declaring an array of the type int, you have not mentioned the fact that you want num to represent 50 integers. Your modified declaration for main method, which can accept 50 integers, would be as follows:

```
void main(int[] num) {

}
```

How will you declare the main method, which will let you pass names of 50 persons? Since int can only be used for passing integers, you must look for some other type that represents a text in Java language because the name of a person will be text, not an integer. There is a type String (note the uppercase S in String) that represents a text in Java language. Therefore, to pass 50 names to the method main, you can change its declaration as follows:

```
void main(String[] name) {

}
```

In this declaration, you need not necessarily change the parameter name from num to name. You changed it just to make the meaning of the parameter clear and intuitive. Now let's add some Java code in the body of the main method, which will print a message on the console.

```
System.out.println("The message you want to print");
```

This is not the appropriate place to discuss what System, out, and println are all about. For now, just type in System (note uppercase S in System), a dot, out, a dot, println followed by two parentheses that contain the message you want to print within double quotes. You want to print a message "Welcome to the Java world" and your main method declaration will be as follows:

```
void main(String[] name) {
        System.out.println("Welcome to the Java world");
}
```

This is a valid method declaration that will print a message on the console. Your next step is to compile the source code, which contains the Welcome class declaration, and run the compiled code. However, when you run a class, the JVM looks for a method main in that class and the declaration of the method main must be as follows, though name could be any identifier.

```
public static void main(String[] name) {

}
```

Apart from two keywords, public and static, you should be able to understand the above method declaration, which states: "main is a method, which accepts an array of String as a parameter and returns nothing."

For now, you can think of `public` and `static` just as two keywords, which must be present to declare the `main` method. Note that the JVM also requires that the name of the method must be `main`. This is the reason that I chose `main` as the name of the method from the very beginning. It is just a rule imposed by the JVM to run a class that the class must have a method named `main` whose declaration must look similar to as shown above. The final version of the source code is shown in Listing 2-1. Save the source code in a file named `Welcome.java`.

Listing 2-1. Source Code for the Welcome Class

```java
// Welcome.java
package com.jdojo.intro;

class Welcome {
        public static void main(String[] args) {
                System.out.println("Welcome to the Java world.");
        }
}
```

The Java compiler imposes restrictions on the file name of the source code. In this example, the name of the file in which the source code for `Welcome` class is saved need not be `Welcome.java`. You could use another file name, for example, `MyWelcome.java`, `JWelcome.java`, etc. If you declare a class as public, the source code for that class must be saved in a file that has exactly the same name as the name of the class, plus the `.java` extension. You declare a class public by using the `public` keyword before the `class` keyword in its declaration. The following snippet of code declares the `Welcome` class public. For this purpose, it does not matter whether you declare the `Welcome` class public.

```java
// Welcome class is public now
public class Welcome {

}
```

Every class in Java has two names

- A simple name
- A fully qualified name.

The simple name of a class is the name that appears after the `class` keyword in the class declaration. In this example, `Welcome` is the simple name of the class. The fully qualified name of a class is its package name followed by a dot and its simple name. Thus, in this example, `com.jdojo.intro.Welcome` is the fully qualified name of the class.

The next question that might arise in your mind is "What is the fully qualified name of a class that does not have a package declaration?" The answer is simple. In such a case, the simple name and the fully qualified name of the class are the same. If you remove the package declaration from the source code, `Welcome` will be both names for your class.

You might notice that the name of the class (`Welcome`) and the name of the file you saved the source code in (`Welcome.java`) match (excluding the file extension `.java`). This did not happen by chance. I did select the file name `Welcome.java` on purpose. Is it required to name the source code file the same as the name of the class? Yes, but not always. This raises another question. What should be the name of the source code file if you declare two classes in the same source code? Suppose you declare two classes, `Welcome` and `Bye`, in your source code. What name should you give to the source file: `Welcome.java`, `Bye.java`, or something else? In some cases, Java forces you to keep the name of a class and the file name the same. In your example, you do not need to stick to any source code file-naming rules. It is correct even if you name your source file as `Bye.java` or `Test.java`. However, let's continue with this example, assuming that the source code has been saved in the file `Welcome.java`.

Compiling the Source Code

Compiling is the process of translating the source code into a special binary format called *bytecode*. This is accomplished using a program (usually called a compiler) javac, which comes with JDK from Oracle Corporation. The process of compiling Java source code is shown in Figure 2-4.

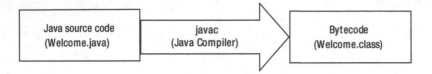

Figure 2-4. *The process of compiling a Java source code into bytecode*

You supply the source code (in your case, Welcome.java) as input to the Java compiler and it generates a new file (or a set of files) with extension .class. The file with extension .class is called a class file. A class file is in a special format called bytecode. Bytecode is a machine language for Java virtual machine (JVM). I will discuss the JVM and bytecode later in this chapter.

Now, I will walk through the steps that are needed to compile the source code on Windows. For other platforms, for example, UNIX and Mac OS X, you will need to use the file path syntax specific to those platforms.

It is assumed that you have installed JDK from Oracle Corporation on your machine. It is further assumed that you have stored your source code in a directory such as

`C:\javaprograms\com\jdojo\intro\Welcome.java`

Open a command prompt and change the directory, so intro should be your current working directory. The prompt should look as follows:

`C:\javaprograms\com\jdojo\intro>`

To compile the Welcome.java, execute the following command:

`C:\javaprograms\com\jdojo\intro>javac Welcome.java`

If you do not get any error message, it means your source code was compiled successfully and it generated a new file named Welcome.class in intro directory. However, if you get any error, there could be one of the three reasons:

- You have not saved the Welcome.java file in the directory C:\javaprograms\com\jdojo\intro.

- You may not have installed the JDK on your machine.

- If you have already installed the JDK, you have not added the JAVA_HOME\bin directory to the PATH environment variable, where JAVA_HOME refers to the directory where you installed the JDK on your machine. If you installed JDK 8 in the directory C:\java8, you need to add C:\java8\bin to the PATH environment variable on your machine.

If the above discussion about setting PATH environment variable did not help, you can use the following command. This command assumes that you have installed JDK in the directory C:\java8.

`C:\javaprograms\com\jdojo\intro>C:\java8\bin\javac Welcome.java`

If you do not want to change the current working directory to C:\javaprograms\com\jdojo\intro, you can compile your source code using the full path for Welcome.java file as follows:

```
C:\>C:\java8\bin\javac C:\javaprograms\com\jdojo\intro\Welcome.java
```

It does not matter how you specify the path for the javac command and the Welcome.java file. If the command prompt can find it, your Java source code will be compiled successfully. Below is another way to compile the Welcome.java file. This time, I assume that the javac.exe command file is in PATH and the current directory is C:\javaprograms.

```
C:\javaprograms>javac com\jdojo\intro\Welcome.java
```

At this point, it is assumed that you have compiled the source code in Welcome.java successfully, which has generated a new file named Welcome.class in the C:\javaprograms\com\jdojo\intro directory.

You are now ready to run your first Java program. Before you run this program, let's discuss one important point about the file name that is generated by the compiler. The name of the bytecode file (the .class file) is Welcome.class. Why did the compiler choose to name the class file Welcome.class? You have used the word "Welcome" at three places when you wrote the source code and compiled it.

- First, you declared a class named Welcome.

- Second, you saved the source code in a file named Welcome.java.

- And third, you passed Welcome.java file name to the compiler as an input.

Which one of your three steps prompted the compiler to name the generated bytecode file as Welcome.class? As a first guess, it appears to be the third step, which is passing Welcome.java as an input file name to the Java compiler. However, the guess is wrong. It is the first step, which is declaring a class named Welcome in the source code Welcome.java, which prompted the compiler to name the output bytecode file Welcome.class. You can declare as many classes as you want in one Java source code. Suppose you declare two classes, Welcome and Bye, in the Welcome.java file. What file name will the compiler choose to name the output class file? The compiler scans the whole source code file. It creates one class file for each class declared in the source code. If the Welcome.java file had three classes, Welcome, Thanks and Bye, the compiler would have generated three class files, Welcome.class, Thanks.class, and Bye.class.

Running the Compiled Code

A Java program is run by a JVM. A JVM is invoked using a program called java, which is the java.exe file installed on your machine along with the JDK. The java program accepts the fully qualified name of the Java class you want to run. Recall that a class has two names: a simple name and a fully qualified name. The fully qualified name must be used to run the class. You are going to run Welcome class whose fully qualified name is com.jdojo.intro.Welcome. Use the following command at the command prompt to run the class:

```
C:\javaprograms>java com.jdojo.intro.Welcome
```

What happens when you use the above command? First, the JVM tries to locate the bytecode (here, Welcome.class file) for the com.jdojo.intro.Welcome class on your machine. JVM replaces every dot in the fully qualified name of the class with the file-separator character on the host system. A backslash is the file-separator character on Windows and a forward slash on UNIX-like operating systems. This step converts the com.jdojo.intro.Welcome class name that was passed to the JVM to com\jdojo\intro\Welcome. Note that on a UNIX-like operating system, the same class name will be converted to com/jdojo/intro/Welcome.

■ **Tip** The JVM also allows you to use a forward slash in place of a dot in the fully qualified name of the class to run. For example, you can also use the following command to run the `Welcome` class:

```
C:\javaprograms>java com/jdojo/intro/Welcome
```

When you use forward slashes in place of dots in the fully qualified name of the class to run, you must use only forward slashes, irrespective of the operating system. For example, you cannot use backslashes on Windows and forward slashes on UNIX.

The second step the JVM takes is to append the word ".class" to the class name thus converted. The resulting string out of the fully qualified name of the class becomes

```
com\jdojo\intro\Welcome.class
```

Now the JVM looks for the `Welcome.class` file, which must be under the `intro` directory, which in turn must be under the `jdojo` directory, which in turn must be under the `com` directory. The JVM is not only looking for a `Welcome.class` file. Rather, it is looking for a `Welcome.class` file in a directory structure like `com\jdojo\intro`. You may realize that there could be many directory paths on your machine, which can lead the JVM to a `com\jdojo\intro\Welcome.class` file. Suppose you have three `Welcome.class` files on your machine as follows:

```
C:\jp1\com\jdojo\intro\Welcome.class
C:\jp2\com\jdojo\intro\Welcome.class
C:\javaprograms\com\jdojo\intro\Welcome.class
```

How does the JVM know which one of the three `Welcome.class` files it has to run? Here comes the concept of a mysterious (sometimes confusing and frustrating) creature called the `CLASSPATH` environment variable. The JVM uses the `CLASSPATH` environment variable to locate a class file on your machine. Many questions about `CLASSPATH` may have arisen in your mind. Who defines the `CLASSPATH`? Where is it stored? How is it used? I will discuss all these questions and their answers one by one.

The user of the machine sets the `CLASSPATH`. It can be set permanently, temporarily, or at runtime. If it is set permanently, the JVM will use it whenever it needs to locate a class file. It can be set temporarily for the duration of a command prompt session. It can be set at runtime by using `-cp` or `-classpath` option at the command line.

On Windows, the value of the `CLASSPATH` environment variable is a semicolon separated list of directories, ZIP files, and JAR files. A typical setting for the `CLASSPATH` looks as follows:

```
SET CLASSPATH=C:\;C:\jbook;C:\javaprograms
```

On Windows, you can set the `CLASSPATH` environment variable using Settings ➤ Control Panel ➤ System ➤ Advanced Tab ➤ Environment Variables button. It displays the Environment Variables dialog box shown in Figure 2-5. Under the System Variables group box, you should select `CLASSPATH` under the Variable column. If you do not find `CLASSPATH` variable, it means that it has not been set previously. If the `CLASSPATH` variable has not been set previously, click the New button. Otherwise, click the Edit button. Clicking the New or Edit button will display a dialog box as shown in Figure 2-6 in which you can add/modify the value for the `CLASSPATH`.

Figure 2-5. *Environment Variables dialog box for setting CLASSPATH on Windows*

Figure 2-6. *New/Edit System variable dialog box for setting CLASSPATH on Windows*

■ **Tip** The value for CLASSPATH is a list of directories, JAR files, and ZIP files that are separated by a path-separator. The path-separator is operating system dependent. On a Windows operating system, the separator is a semicolon. On a UNIX-like operating systems, for example, Linux, Solaris, and Mac OS X, the separator is a colon (:). On Windows operating system, a CLASSPATH entry looks like `C:\;C:\jbook;C:\jp;c:\myapps.jar`. On UNIX-like operating systems, it looks like `/usr/jp/classes:/usr/myapps.jar`.

You can also set CLASSPATH by typing the following command on command prompt. However, such CLASSPATH setting is valid only for the current command prompt session.

```
C:\>SET CLASSPATH=C:\;C:\jbook;C:\javaprograms
```

After you have set the CLASSPATH, you can use the following command to run the Welcome class:

```
C:\>java com.jdojo.intro.Welcome
```

As I have already discussed, the JVM will convert the class name to a class file, `com\jdojo\intro\Welcome.class`. The JVM reads the CLASSPATH value, which it will use to locate the class file. It reads the first entry from the CLASSPATH value, which is `C:\`, and concatenates the converted class name string to it. The JVM may use an extra backslash if needed to create a valid file name. In your case, the resulting string will be

```
C:\com\jdojo\intro\Welcome.class
```

The JVM checks if a file with the above path exists on the machine. In this case, this check will fail, because you do not have a `C:\com\jdojo\intro\Welcome.class` file on your machine. If the JVM fails to locate a class file using an entry in the CLASSPATH, it repeats the class file search using next entry from the CLASSPATH. This process continues until the JVM locates the class file or it has exhausted all entries in the CLASSPATH. In your case, the JVM will find the class file in the third attempt. It will find the `C:\javaprograms\com\jdojo\intro\Welcome.class` file. This is not the end of the story. Since you passed the class name `com.jdojo.intro.Welcome` to the JVM, the JVM makes sure that the `C:\javaprograms\com\jdojo\intro\Welcome.class` was generated by a Java compiler for a class named Welcome, whose package declaration was `com.jdojo.intro`. In your case, this criterion is fulfilled.

What does the JVM do next? Now, it looks for a method declaration in the Welcome class whose declaration must look as follows:

```
public static void main (String[] args)
```

If the JVM does not find the main method declaration, or the main method is not declared static final, it prints an error message and aborts the execution. This is the reason why you declared the main method in your Welcome class. In your case, the JVM will find the correct declaration for the method main. It executes the body of the main method, which prints the following message on the console:

```
Welcome to the Java world.
```

There is another way of setting the CLASSPATH. You can set the CLASSPATH when you run your Java class. You can use –cp or –classpath option with the java command to set the CLASSPATH while running the class. For example, you can run the Welcome class as follows. Note that the command is entered on the command line in one line, like.

```
C:\>java -cp C:\;C:\jbook;C:\javaprograms com.jdojo.intro.Welcome
```

or

```
C:\>java -classpath C:\;C:\jbook;C:\javaprograms com.jdojo.intro.Welcome
```

Can you run your Welcome class example without worrying about the CLASSPATH setting? The answer is yes and no. Sometimes, CLASSPATH setting becomes a bit tricky. If you don't set any value for CLASSPATH as in

```
SET CLASSPATH=
```

the JVM uses the current working directory as the one and the only entry for the CLASSPATH. The current working directory is specified by a dot. Therefore, the following two CLASSPATH settings are the same for the JVM:

```
SET CLASSPATH=
```

and

```
SET CLASSPATH=.
```

If you set some value for the CLASSPATH, you have to add a dot separately to indicate that you also want to include the current working directory in the CLASSPATH. Note that you lose the default CLASSPATH setting (which is the current working directory) when you set it explicitly. Suppose you have set the CLASSPATH using the following command:

```
SET CLASSPATH=
```

Now, you want to run your Welcome class. The only thing you have to do is that you must change your working directory to C:\javaprograms, so C:\javaprograms becomes your current working directory. Using this directory as the default entry for CLASSPATH, the JVM will find your class correctly. The command prompt should look as follows:

```
C:\javaprograms>java com.jdojo.intro.Welcome
```

Finally, there are some words of caution for you when you work with the CLASSPATH and the package of a class to locate the class file. The JVM uses CLASSPATH and fully qualified name of the class to locate the actual class file on the machine. However, you cannot take some part from one and add it to another, even though the resulting path is the same. Always keep in mind that it is not enough for the JVM just to locate the class file. It also verifies the bytecode in a class file to make sure that it contains the class definition with proper package name. The following commands are not the same. Note the use of the space in each of the commands to separate the CLASSPATH value and the fully qualified name of the class.

```
C:\>java -cp C:\ javaprograms.com.jdojo.intro.Welcome
C:\>java -cp C:\javaprograms com.jdojo.intro.Welcome
C:\>java -cp C:\javaprograms\com jdojo.intro.Welcome
C:\>java -cp C:\javaprograms\com\jdojo intro.Welcome
C:\>java -cp C:\javaprograms\com\jdojo\intro Welcome
```

In the above examples, all the commands will look for the same class file C:\javaprograms\com\jdojo\intro\Welcome.class. However, only the second command will run successfully, because the package declaration for the Welcome class is com.jdojo.intro.

The path of the class file is determined by the JVM on Windows as shown in Figure 2-7. On other platforms, the JVM uses the file-separator character specific to the platforms.

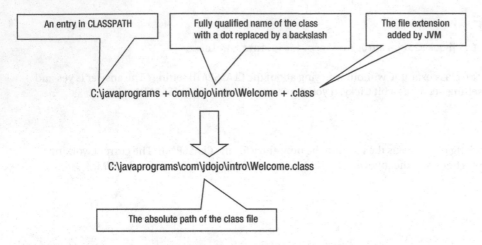

Figure 2-7. *The process of finding a class file when the class is run*

Using NetBeans IDE

You can use the NetBeans IDE to write, compile, and run Java programs. In this section, you will walk through the steps of working with NetBeans. First, you will learn how to create a new Java project, write a simple Java program, compile, and run it. At the end, you will learn how to open the NetBeans project for this book and use the source code for this book.

It is assumed that you have installed NetBeans 7.4 or later. You can download it from www.netbeans.org. The NetBeans IDE comes in different bundles: Java SE, Java EE, C/C++, HTML5 & PHP, and "All." For running all examples in this book, you need Java SE or "All" bundle.

■ **Note**   At the time of this writing, NetBeans IDE 8.0 is in its beta release. By the time you read this chapter, the final release version 8.0 should be available. In this section, I will use the NetBeans 8.0 beta version.

Creating a Java Project

When you start the NetBeans IDE, the startup page is displayed as shown in Figure 2-8. The startup page contains useful links for developers, such as links for tutorials for Java, JavaFX, C++, etc. If you don't want the startup page to display every time you start the IDE, you need to uncheck the "Show on Startup" checkbox in the upper-right corner of the startup page. You can close the startup page by clicking the X icon displayed in the Start Page tab.

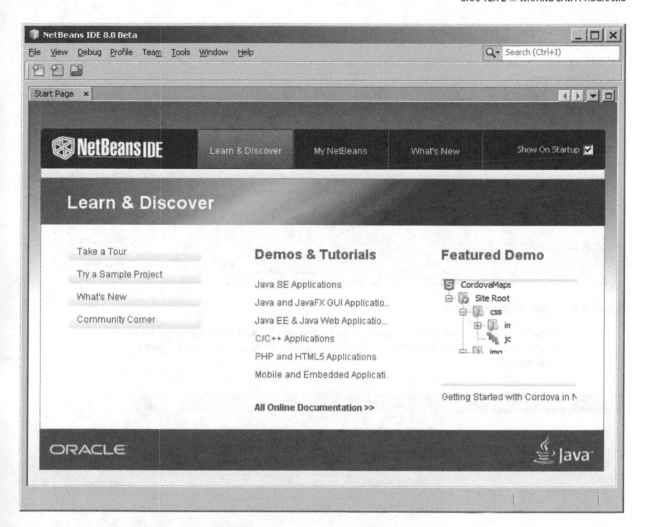

Figure 2-8. *The NetBeans IDE with the startup page*

To create a new Java project, follow these steps.

1. Select the menu item New Project under the File menu. A New Project dialog is displayed, as shown in Figure 2-9.

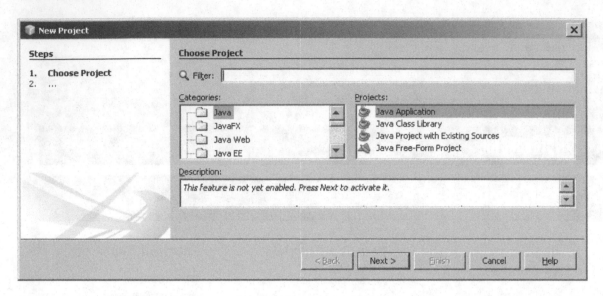

Figure 2-9. *A New Project dialog*

2. In the New Project dialog, select "Java" in the Categories list and "Java Application" in the
    Projects list. Click the Next button. A New Java Application dialog, shown in Figure 2-10,
    is displayed.

Figure 2-10. *A New Java Application dialog*

3. In the New Java Application dialog, enter TestApp as the project name. Enter or browse for a location where you want to save the project files. Make sure the checkbox "Create Main Class" is selected and a class name com.jdojo.intro.Welcome is entered next to the checkbox. Click the Finish button when you are done. The new TestApp project with a Welcome class will be opened in the IDE, as shown in Figure 2-11. You might see some more comments for the Welcome class, which are added by NetBeans when it creates a new class; I removed most of the comments before taking the screenshot.

Figure 2-11. *The NetBeans IDE with TestApp Java Project*

Replace the TODO comments in the main() method of the Welcome class with the following statement. The IDE should look similar to the one shown in Figure 2-12.

```
System.out.println("Welcome to the Java world.");
```

Figure 2-12. *The Welcome class after adding a statement in the main() method*

NetBeans lets you run a project or a single Java class.

- To run a project, you need to set a main class, which is the fully qualified name of a class with a main() method, as you had for the Welcome class. In this case, enter com.jdojo.intro.Welcome as the main class for the TestApp project. If you run the project, the com.jdojo.intro.Welcome class will be run. To run a project, select the Run Project menu item from the Run menu or press F6 when the project is active in the IDE. You can change the main class for a project using project properties. I will discuss how to change project properties shortly.

- To run a file, select a file and select the Run File menu item from the Run menu. Alternatively, you can select a Java class in the IDE and press Shift + F6 to run it.

To run the Welcome class, press F6. The class will be compiled and run. The output will be displayed in the output pane, as shown in Figure 2-13.

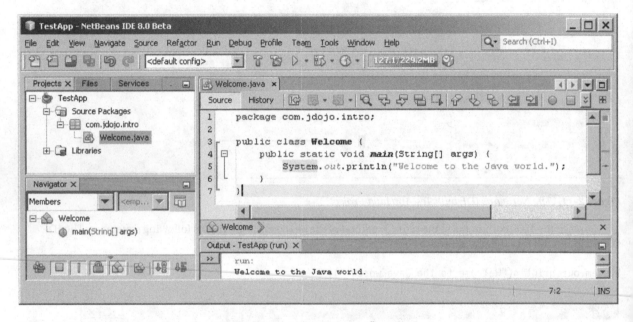

Figure 2-13. *The Welcome class after adding a statement in the main() method*

Adding Classes to the Project

To add a new class, follow these steps.

1. Select a Java project or a package in the IDE and right-click to access the menu options. Figure 2-14 shows the menu options when the package com.jdojo.intro is selected.

Figure 2-14. *Accessing new option to add a new class*

2. Select the New ➤ New Class menu item from the right-clicked menu list. Selecting the New Class menu option displays a New Java Class dialog, as shown in Figure 2-15.

New Java Class	
Steps	**Name and Location**
1. Choose File Type 2. **Name and Location**	Class Name: Bye Project: TestApp Location: Source Packages Package: com.jdojo.intro Created File: C:\testproject\TestApp\src\com\jdojo\intro\Bye.ja

< Back   Next >   Finish   Cancel   Help

Figure 2-15. *A New Java Class dialog*

3. Enter the new class name in the Class Name field. If you accessed this dialog by selecting a package in the IDE, the Package field is pre-filled with the selected package in the IDE. If you accessed this dialog by selecting a project, this field is blank; you need to enter the package name for the new class. You can enter the package name of your choice irrespective of how you access this dialog.

4. Click the Finish button when you are done. The new class with an empty body will be added to the IDE.

Customizing Project Properties

NetBeans lets you customize several properties for your Java project using the Project Properties dialog. You can access the dialog by selecting the project and choosing the Properties menu item from the right-clicked menu. The Project Properties dialog for the TestApp is shown in Figure 2-16.

Figure 2-16. *The Project Properties dialog for the TestApp*

On the left side of the dialog is the list of categories of properties. When you select a property category, the details are displayed on the right side. The following are brief descriptions of each property category:

- **Sources:** It is used set source code-related properties, for example, source folder, format, profile, encoding, etc. under the Sources category. The Profile property is new in Java 8. It lets you select a compact profile compact1, compact2, compact3, or full JRE. The default is full JRE. When you select a compact profile, the IDE will restrict you from using the API outside of that compact profile. The Includes/Excludes button lets you include and exclude fields from the project. Use this button when you want to keep some files in the project, but do not want to compile them, for example, the files may not be compiled as they are not complete.

- **Libraries**: Among several properties, it lets you set two important properties: Java platform and CLASSPATH. Clicking the Manage Platforms button opens the Java Platform Manager dialog where you can select an existing platform or add a new platform. Use the Add Project, Add Library, and Add JAR/Folder buttons to add projects, pre-defined set of JAR files, and JAR/Folder to the CLASSPATH. This CLASSPATH is used to compile and run your Java project. Note that the Java classes that you add to your project using the IDE are automatically added to the CLASSPATH. The CLASSPATH is set for the project only for the NetBeans IDE.

- **Build**: It lets you set properties for several subcategories. Under the Compiling subcategory, you can set compiler-related options. You can choose to compile the source code when it is saved or you can choose to compile the source code yourself using the menu options in the IDE. Under the Packaging subcategory, you can set options for packaging your class files. The Deployment subcategory lets you choose native packing options for your project. The Documenting subcategory lets you set options for generating Java documentation for the project.

- **Run**: This category lets you set properties that are used to run the project. You can set the Java platform, JVM arguments. Using the category, you can set main class for your project.

Opening an Existing NetBeans Project

It is assumed that you have downloaded the source code for this book. The source code contains a NetBeans 8.0 project. To open the project, follow these steps.

1. Choose the Open Project menu item under the File menu. An Open Project dialog is displayed.

2. Navigate to the folder that contains the unzipped downloaded source code. The project BeginningJavaFundamentals is displayed, as shown in Figure 2-17.

Figure 2-17. *Opening the NetBeans Java project for the source code for this book*

3. Select the project and click the Open Project button. The project is opened the project in the IDE. Use the Project or Files tabs on the left to browse the source code for all chapters in this book.

Behind the Scenes

This section will answer some general questions related to compiling and running Java programs. For example, why do we compile Java source code to bytecode format before running it? What is Java platform? What is a JVM and how does it work? The detailed discussion of these topics is beyond the scope of this book. Please refer to the JVM specification for detailed discussion on any topic related to the JVM functionality. The JVM specification is available online at http://docs.oracle.com/javase/specs.

Let's look at a simple daily life example. Suppose there is a Frenchman who can understand and speak only French and he has to communicate with three other persons: an American, a German, and a Russian, and these three only know one language (English, German, and Russian, respectively). How will the Frenchman communicate to the other three? There are many ways to solve this problem.

- The Frenchman may learn all three languages.

- The Frenchman may hire a translator who knows all four languages.

- The Frenchman may hire three translators who know French-English, French-German, and French-Russian.

There are numerous other possible solutions to this problem. Let's consider the similar problem in the context of running a Java program. The Java source code is compiled into bytecode. The same bytecode needs to be run without any modification to all operating systems. Designers of Java language chose the third option, which is to have a translator for each operating system. The job of the translator is to translate the bytecode into machine code, which is native to the operating system running the translated code. The translator is called a Java Virtual Machine (JVM). You need to have a JVM for each operating system. Figure 2-18 is a pictorial view of how the JVM acts as a translator between bytecode (class file) and different operating systems.

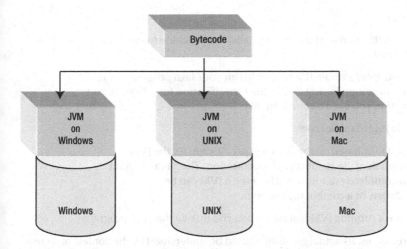

Figure 2-18. *A JVM as a translator between bytecode and an operating system*

A Java program compiled into bytecode format has two advantages:

- You do not need to recompile your source code if you want to run it on another machine with a different operating system. It is also called platform independence in Java. It is also known as "write once, run anywhere" for Java code.

- If you are running a Java program over a network, the program runs faster because of the compact size of the bytecode format, which results in less loading time over the network.

In order to run a Java program over the network, the size of the Java code must be compact enough to be transported over the network faster. The class file, which is generated by a Java compiler in bytecode format, is very compact. This is one of the advantages of compiling the Java source code in bytecode format.

The second important advantage of using bytecode format is that it is architecture-neutral. By bytecode format being architecture-neutral, it means if you compile the Java source code on a specific host system, say, Windows, the generated class file does not have any mention or effects that it was generated on Windows. If you compile the same Java source code on two different host systems, for example, Windows and UNIX, both class files will be the same.

The class file in bytecode format cannot be directly executed on a host system because it does not have any host system-specific direct instructions. In other words, we can say that bytecode is not a machine language for any specific host system. Now, the question is who understands the bytecode and who translates it into underlying host system specific language? The JVM performs this job. The bytecode is the machine language for the JVM. If you compile Java source code to generate a class file on Windows, you can run the same class file on UNIX if you have a Java platform (JVM and Java API collectively are known as the Java platform) available on the machine running on UNIX. You do not need to recompile your source code to generate a new class file for UNIX, because the JVM running on UNIX can understand the bytecode you generated on Windows. This is how the concept of "write once, run anywhere" is implemented for a Java program.

The Java platform, also called Java runtime system, consists of two things:

- The Java virtual machine (JVM)

- The Java Application Programming Interface (Java API)

The term "JVM" is used in three contexts:

- *The JVM specification*: It is the specification or standard of an abstract machine for which a Java compiler can generate bytecode.

- *The concrete realization of the JVM specification*: If you want to run your Java program, you need to have a real JVM, which is developed using the abstract specification for a JVM. To run the Java program in previous section you used a command like

```
C:\javaprograms>java com.jdojo.intro.Welcome
```

  Here, java is a program developed fully based on the abstract specification for the JVM. Therefore, it is the concrete realization of the abstract JVM specification. The java program (or JVM) has been implemented completely in software. However, a JVM can be implemented in software or hardware, or a combination of both.

- *A running JVM instance*: You have a running JVM instance when you invoke the java program.

This book uses the term JVM for all three cases. Its actual meaning should be understood by the context of its use.

One of the jobs a JVM performs is to execute the bytecode and generate a machine-specific instruction set for the host system. A JVM has a classloader and an execution engine. The classloader reads the content of a class file when required and loads it into memory. The job of the execution engine is to execute the bytecode.

A JVM is also called a Java Interpreter. Often, the term "Java Interpreter" is misleading, particularly to those programmers who have just started learning the Java language. By the term "Java Interpreter," they conclude that the execution engine of a JVM interprets the bytecodes one at a time, and so Java must be very slow. The name "Java Interpreter" for a JVM has nothing to do with the technique the execution engine uses to execute the bytecode. The actual technique, which the execution engine may opt to execute the bytecode, depends on the specific implementation of the JVM. Some execution engines types are interpreter, just-in-time compiler, and adaptive optimizer. In its simplest kind, which is interpreter, the execution engine interprets the bytecodes one at a time, and therefore, it is slower. In its second kind, which is the just-in-time compiler, it compiles the whole code for a method in the underlying host machine language for the first time that method is called. Then it reuses the compiled code the next time the same method is called. This kind of execution engine is faster compared with the first kind, but requires more memory to cache the compiled code. In adaptive optimizer technique, it does not compile and cache the whole bytecode; rather it does so only for the most heavily used part of the bytecode.

What is an API (application programming interface)? An API is a specific set of methods made available by an operating system or by an application to the programmers for its direct use. In the previous sections, you created the Welcome class in the com.jdojo.intro package, which declared a method main, which accepts an array of String as an argument and returns nothing (indicated by keyword void). If you expose all these pieces of information about the created package, class and method, and make it available to other programmers for use, your method main in the Welcome class is a typical, though trivial, example of an API. Generally, when we use the term "API" we mean a set of methods that are available to the programmer for use. Now it is easy to understand what the Java API means. The Java API is the set of all classes and other components that are available to programmers for use while writing Java source code. In your Welcome class example, you have already used one Java API. You used it inside the body of the main method to print the message on the console. The code, which used the Java API, is

```
System.out.println("Welcome to the Java world");
```

You did not declare any method named println in your code. This method was made available to the JVM at runtime through Java API, which is the part of Java Platform. Broadly speaking, Java API can be classified in two categories: Core API and Extension API. Every JDK must support the Core API. Examples of Core Java APIs are Java runtimes (e.g., Applets, AWT, I/O, etc.), JFC, JDBC, etc. Java Extension APIs are JavaMail, JNDI (Java naming and Directory Interface), JavaHelp, etc. Java 8 includes JavaFX 8 API as an extension API. The process of compiling and running a Java program is depicted in Figure 2-19.

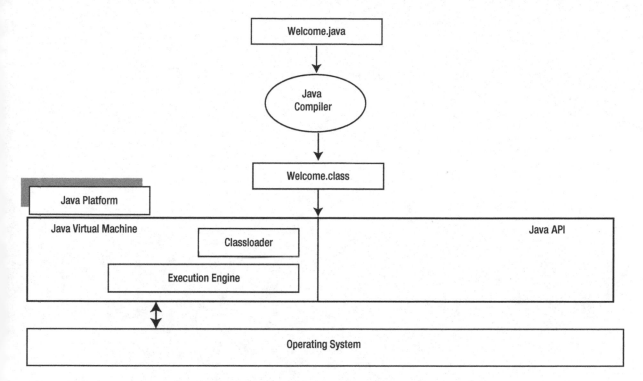

Figure 2-19. *All components involved in compiling and running a Java program*

Summary

Java programs are written in plain text format using a text editor or IDE. The Java source code is also known as a compilation unit and it is stored in a file with a .java extension. Several integrated development environments (IDEs) for Java, such as NetBeans, are freely available in the market. Using an IDE to develop Java applications reduces the time and effort involved.

A Java program is compiled into a class file using a Java compiler. The class file contains bytecode. The Java compiler that comes with the JDK is called javac. The compiled code is run by a JVM. The JDK installs a JVM that can be run as a java command. Both javac and java commands are located in the JDK_HOME\bin directory, where JAVA_HOME is the installation directory for the JDK.

CHAPTER 3

■ ■ ■

Data Types

In this chapter, you will learn:

- What data types are
- What identifiers are and detailed rules to declare them
- The difference between primitive and reference data types
- How to declare variables of a data type
- How to assign a value to a variable
- Detailed descriptions of all primitive data types in Java
- What literals of a data type are
- What casting is and when it is needed
- Binary representation of integers and floating-point numbers
- Different rounding modes for floating-point numbers
- How Java implements IEEE floating-point standards

What Is a Data Type?

A data type (or simply a type) is defined in terms of three components:

- A set of values (or data objects)
- A set of operations that can be applied to all values in the set
- A data representation, which determines how the values are stored

A programming language provides some predefined data types, which are known as built-in data types. A programming language may also let programmers define their own data types, which are known as user-defined data types.

A data type that consists of an atomic, indivisible value, and that is defined without the help of any other data types, is known as a primitive data type. User-defined data types are defined in terms of primitive data types and other user-defined data types. Typically, a programming language does not let the programmers extend or redefine primitive data types.

Java provides many built-in primitive data types, such as int, float, boolean, char, etc. For example, the three components that define the int primitive data type in Java are as follows:

- An int data type consists of a set of all integers between   -2,147,483,648 and 2,147,483,647.

- Operations such as addition, subtraction, multiplication, division, comparison, and many more are defined for the int data type.

- A value of the int data type is represented in 32-bit memory in 2's compliment form.

All three components of the int data type are predefined by the Java language. Developers cannot extend or redefine the definition of the int data type in Java. You can give a name to a value of the int data type as

```
int employeeId;
```

This statement states that employeeId is a name (technically called an identifier) that can be associated with one value from the set of values that defines values for the int data type. For example, you can associate integer 1969 to the name employeeId using an assignment statement like

```
employeeId = 1969;
```

What Is an Identifier?

An identifier in Java is a sequence of characters of unlimited length. The sequence of characters includes all Java letters and Java digits, the first of which must be a Java letter. Java uses the Unicode character set. A Java letter is a letter from any language that is represented by Unicode character set. For example, A-Z, a-z, _ (underscore), and $ are considered Java letters from the ASCII character set range of Unicode. Java digits include 0-9 ASCII digits and any Unicode character that denotes a digit in a language. Spaces are not allowed in an identifier.

In fact, an identifier is a technical term for a name. Therefore, an identifier is simply the name given to a class, method, variable, etc. in a Java program. The name, Welcome, of our Java class is an example of an identifier. The names of variables num1, num2, and str1 used in our examples are also identifiers. All characters used in an identifier are important, as is their case. The names welcome, Welcome, and WELCOME are three different identifiers. There are three important things to remember about identifiers in Java:

- There is no limit on the number of characters used in an identifier. An identifier can be as small as one character long (for example, i, j, k) or as big as you want.

- Characters used in an identifier are drawn from the Unicode character set, not only from the ASCII character set.

- Identifiers are case sensitive. For example, num and Num are two different identifiers.

Examples of valid identifiers are as follows:

```
num1                // Can use a-z and 0-9 and start with a letter
kn                  // Only letters
_abc                // Can start with an underscore
_                   // Can have only one letter, which is an underscore
sum_of_two_numbers  // Can have letters and underscores
Outer$Inner         // Can have a-z, A-Z and $
$var                // Can also start with $
```

Examples of invalid identifiers are as follows:

```
2num      // Cannot start with a number
my name   // Cannot have a space
num1+num2 // Cannot have + sign
num1-num2 // Cannot have hyphen or minus sign
```

Java defines a list of words called keywords. Keywords are words that have predefined meanings in Java and they can only be used in the contexts defined by the Java language. Keywords in Java cannot be used as identifiers. The complete list of Java keywords is listed in Table 3-1.

Table 3-1. *List of Keywords and Reserved Words in Java*

abstract	continue	for	new	switch
assert	default	goto	package	synchronized
boolean	do	if	private	this
break	double	implements	protected	throw
byte	else	import	public	throws
case	enum	instanceof	return	transient
catch	extends	int	short	try
char	final	interface	static	void
class	finally	long	strictfp	volatile
const	float	native	super	while

The two keywords, const and goto, are not currently used in Java. They are reserved keywords and they cannot be used as identifiers.

In addition to all the keywords, three words, true, false, and null, cannot be used as identifiers; true and false are boolean literals (or boolean constants) and null is a reference literal.

Data Types in Java

Before we start discussing all data types available in Java, let's take a simple example of adding two numbers. Suppose your friend asks you to add two numbers. The procedure to add two numbers goes as follows.

1. Your friend tells you the first number. You listen to him and your brain records the number at a particular location in your memory. Of course, you do not know where the number is exactly stored in your brain's memory.

2. Your friend tells you the second number, you listen to him, and again, your brain records it at a particular location in your memory.

3. Now, your friend asks you to add the two numbers. Your brain comes into action again. It recalls (or reads) the two numbers, adds them, and you tell your friend the sum of the two numbers.

Now, if your friend wants you to tell him the difference of the same two numbers, he does not need to tell you those two numbers again. This is because these two numbers are stored in your memory, and your brain can recall and use them again. However, whether your brain can perform addition of those two numbers depends on many factors, for example, how big those two numbers are; whether your brain can memorize (or store) those big numbers; whether your brain is trained to do addition, etc. The process of adding two numbers also depends on the type of these two numbers. Your brain will use different logic to add them depending on whether two numbers are whole numbers (e.g. 10 and 20), real numbers (e.g. 12.4 and 19.1), or the mix of whole and real numbers (e.g. 10 and 69.9). The entire process takes place in your brain without you noticing it (maybe because you are so accustomed to doing these additions). However, when you want to do any kind of manipulation on numbers or any other types of values in a Java program, you need to specify the details about the values you want to manipulate and the procedure for manipulating those values.

Let's discuss the same example of adding two numbers in a Java program. The first thing you need to tell Java is the type of the two numbers you want to add. Let's assume that you want to add two integers, 50 and 70. When you added two numbers by yourself, your brain gave each number a name (maybe as the first number and the second number). You did not notice the naming of those numbers by your brain. However, in a Java program, you have to explicitly give names (also known an identifier) to both numbers. Let's name the two numbers as num1 and num2, respectively. The following two lines in a Java program indicate the fact that there are two integers, num1 and num2:

```
int num1;
int num2;
```

The int keyword is used to indicate that the name that follows represents an integer value, for example, 10, 15, 70, 1000, etc. When the above two lines of code are executed, Java allocates two memory locations and associates the name num1 with the first memory location and the name num2 with the second memory location. The memory states after the execution have been depicted in Figure 3-1 as Memory State – I.

Figure 3-1. *Memory states in the process of adding two numbers*

These memory locations are called variables. The names num1 and num2 are associated with these two memory locations. Strictly speaking, num1 and num2 are two names associated with two memory locations. However, roughly speaking, you say

- num1 and num2 are two variables, or

- num1 and num2 are two variables of int data type, or

- num1 and num2 are two int variables.

Because you have declared num1 and num2 variables of int data type, you cannot store a real number, such as 10.51, at these memory locations. The following piece of code stores 50 in num1 and 70 in num2:

```
num1 = 50;
num2 = 70;
```

The memory states after execution of the above two lines of code have been depicted in Figure 3-1 as Memory State-II. Now, you want to add the two numbers. Before you add them, you must allocate another memory location, which will hold the result. You name this memory location as num3 and the following piece of code performs these tasks:

```
int num3;           // Allocates the memory location num3
num3 = num1 + num2;  // Computes sum and store the result in num3
```

The memory states after execution of the above two lines of code are depicted in Figure 3-1 as Memory State-III. The two lines above can be combined into one:

```
int num3 = num1 + num2;
```

A variable has three properties:

- A memory location to hold the value

- The type of the data stored at the memory location

- A name (also called identifier) to refer to the memory location

The data type of the variable also determines the range of the values that the memory location can hold. Therefore, the amount of memory allocated for a variable depends on its data type. For example, 32 bits of memory is allocated for a variable of the int data type. In this example, each variable (num1, num2, and num3) uses 32 bits of memory.

Java supports two kinds of data types:

- Primitive data type

- Reference data type

A variable of the primitive data type holds a value whereas a variable of the reference data type holds the reference to an object in memory. I will discuss one of the reference data types available in Java, String, in this section. String is a class defined in the Java library and you can use it to manipulate text (sequence of characters). You declare a reference variable str of String type as

```
String str;
```

Before you assign the reference of an object to a reference variable, you need to create an object. You create an object using the new operator. You can create an object of the String class with a text "Hi" as follows:

```
// Creates a String object and assigns the reference of the object to str
str = new String("Hi");
```

What happens when this code is executed? First, memory is allocated and the name of the variable str is associated with that memory location, as shown in Figure 3-2. This process is the same as declaring a primitive data type variable. The second piece of code creates a String object in memory with text "Hi" and stores the reference (or memory address) of the String object into the variable str. This fact is shown in the second half of Figure 3-2 by using an arrow pointing from the variable str to the object in memory.

Figure 3-2. *Memory states using reference variables assignments*

You can also assign the reference of an object stored in one reference variable to another reference variable. In such cases, both reference variables refer to the same object in memory. This can be achieved as follows:

```
// Declares String reference variable str1 and str2
String str1;
String str2;

// Assigns the reference of a String object "Hello" to str1
str1 = new String("Hello");

// Assigns the reference stored in str1 to str2
str2 = str1;
```

There is a reference constant (also known as reference literal) null, which can be assigned to any reference variable. If null is assigned to a reference variable, it means that the reference variable is not referring to any object in memory. The null reference literal can be assigned to str2.

```
str2 = null;
```

The memory states after execution of all of the above statements are depicted in Figure 3-3.

Figure 3-3. *Memory states using null in the reference variables assignments*

A String object is created using the new operator. However, strings are used so often that there is a shortcut to create a string object. All string literals, a sequence of characters enclosed in double quotes, are treated as String objects. Therefore, instead of using the new operator to create a String object, you can use string literals like so:

```
// Assigns the reference of a String object with text "Hello" to str1
String str1 = "Hello";

// Assigns the reference of a String object with text "Hello" to str1
String str1 = new String ("Hello");
```

■ **Tip**   There is a subtle difference between the above two statements, which assign a String object to str1 with the same text "Hello". I will discuss the difference when I cover the String class in detail Chapter 11.

Primitive Data Types in Java

Java has eight primitive data types. They are byte, short, int, long, char, float, double, and boolean. They are divided into two categories: boolean data type and numeric data type. The numeric data type can be further subdivided into integral and floating-point types. All primitive data types and their categories are shown in Figure 3-4.

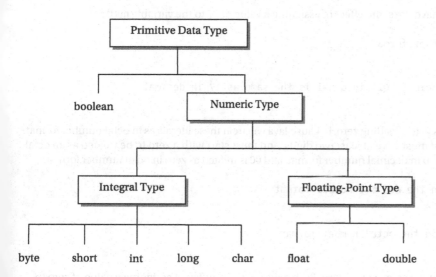

Figure 3-4. List of primitive data types in Java

Integral Data Types

An integral data type is a numeric data type whose values are integers. Java offers five integral data types: byte, short, int, long, and char. All integral data types are described in detail in the sections to follow.

The int Data Type

The int data type is a 32-bit signed Java primitive data type. A variable of the int data type takes 32 bits of memory. Its valid range is -2,147,483,648 to 2,147,483,647 (-2^{31} to $2^{31} - 1$). All whole numbers in this range are known as integer literals (or integer constants). For example, 10, -200, 0, 30, 19, etc. are integer literals of int. An integer literal can be assigned to an int variable, say num1, like so:

```
int num1 = 21;
```

Integer literals can also be expressed in

- Decimal number format
- Octal number format
- Hexadecimal number format
- Binary number format

When an integer literal starts with a zero and has at least two digits, it is considered to be in the octal number format. The following line of code assigns a decimal value of 17 (021 in octal) to num1:

```
// 021 is in octal number format, not in decimal
int num1 = 021;
```

The following two lines of code have the same effect of assigning a value of 17 to the variable num1:

```
// No leading zero - decimal number format
int num1 = 17;

// Leading zero - octal number format. 021 in octal is the same as 17 in decimal
int num1 = 021;
```

Be careful when using int literals with a leading zero, because Java will treat these literals as in octal number format. Note that an int literal in octal format must have at least two digits, and must start with a zero to be treated as an octal number. The number 0 is treated as zero in decimal number format, and 00 is treated as zero in octal number format.

```
// Assigns zero to num1, 0 is in the decimal number format
int num1 = 0;

// Assigns zero to num1, 00 is in the octal number format
int num1 = 00;
```

Note that both 0 and 00 represent the same value, zero. Both have the same effect of assigning a value of zero to the variable num1.

All int literals in the hexadecimal number format start with 0x or 0X, that is, zero immediately followed by an uppercase or lowercase X, and they must contain at least one hexadecimal digit. Note that hexadecimal number format uses 16 digits, 0-9 and A-F (or a-f). The case of the letters A to F does not matter. The following are the examples of using int literals in hexadecimal format:

```
int num1 = 0x123;
int num2 = 0xdecafe;
int num3 = 0x1A2B;
int num4 = 0X0123;
```

An int literal can also be represented using the binary number format. All int literals in the binary number format start with 0b or 0B, that is, zero immediately followed by an uppercase or lowercase B. The following are examples of using int literals in the binary number format:

```
int num1 = 0b10101;
int num2 = 0b00011;
int num3 = 0b10;
int num4 = 0b00000010;
```

The following assignments assign the same decimal number 51966 to an int variable num1 in all four different formats:

```
num1 = 51966;                // Decimal format
num1 = 0145376;              // Octal format, starts with a zero
num1 = 0xCAFE;              // Hexadecimal format, starts with 0x
num1 = 0b1100101011111110;  // Binary format starts with 0b
```

Java has a class named Integer (note the upper case I in Integer), which defines two constants to represent maximum and minimum values for the int data type, Integer.MAX_VALUE and Integer.MIN_VALUE. For example,

```
int max = Integer.MAX_VALUE; // Assigns maximum int value to max
int min = Integer.MIN_VALUE; // Assigns minimum int value to min
```

The long Data Type

The long data type is a 64-bit signed Java primitive data type. It is used when the result of calculations on whole numbers may exceed the range of the int data type. Its range is -9,223,372,036,854,775,808 to 9,223,372,036,854,775,807 (-2^{63} to 2^{63} - 1). All whole numbers in the range of long are called integer literals of long type.

51 is an integer literal. What is its data type: int or long? An integer literal of type long always ends with L (or lowercase l). This book uses L to mark the end of an integer literal of the long type, because l (lowercase L) is often confused with 1 (digit one) in print. The following are examples of using a integer literal of long type:

```
long num1 = 0L;
long num2 = 401L;
long mum3 = -3556L;
long num4 = 89898L;
long num5 = -105L;
```

■ **Tip**   25L is an integer literal of long type whereas 25 is an integer literal of int type.

Integer literals of long type can also be expressed in octal, hexadecimal, and binary formats. For example,

```
long num1;
num1 = 25L;        // Decimal format
num1 = 031L;       // Octal format
num1 = 0X19L;      // Hexadecimal format
num1 = 0b11001L;   // Binary format
```

When a long literal is assigned to a variable of type long, the Java compiler checks the value being assigned and makes sure that it is in the range of the long data type; otherwise it generates a compile time error. For example

```
// One more than maximum positive value for long. This will generate a compiler error
long num1 = 9223372036854775808L;
```

Because the int data type has a lower range than long data type, the value stored in an int variable can always be assigned to a long variable.

```
int num1 = 10;
long num2 = 20; // OK to assign int literal 20 to a long variable num2
num2 = num1;    // OK to assign an int to a long
```

The assignment from int to long is valid, because all values that can be stored in an int variable can also be stored in a long variable. However, the reverse is not true. You cannot simply assign the value stored in a long variable to an int variable. There is a possibility of value overflow. For example,

```
int num1 = 10;
long num2 = 2147483655L;
```

If you assign the value of num2 to num1 as

```
num1 = num2;
```

the value stored in num2 cannot be stored in num1, because the data type of num1 is int and the value of num2 falls outside the range that the int data type can handle. To guard against making such errors inadvertently, Java does not allow you to write code like

```
// A compile-time error. long to int assignment is not allowed in Java
num1 = num2;
```

Even if the value stored in a long variable is well within the range of the int data type, the assignment from long to int is not allowed, as shown in the following example:

```
int num1 = 5;
long num2 = 25L;
```

```
// A compile-time error. Even if num2's value 25 which is within the range of int.
num1 = num2;
```

If you want to assign the value of a long variable to an int variable, you have to explicitly mention this fact in your code, so that Java makes sure you are aware that there may be data overflow. You do this using "cast" in Java, like so:

```
num1 = (int)num2; // Now it is fine because of the "(int)" cast
```

By writing (int)num2, you are instructing Java to treat the value stored in num2 as an int. At runtime, Java will use only the 32 least significant bits of num2, and assign the value stored in those 32 bits to num1. If num2 has a value that is outside the range of the int data type, you would not get the same value in num1.

Java has a class Long (note the upper case L in Long), which defines two constants to represent maximum and minimum values of long data type, Long.MAX_VALUE and Long.MIN_VALUE.

```
long max = Long.MAX_VALUE;
long min = Long.MIN_VALUE;
```

The byte Data Type

The byte data type is an 8-bit signed Java primitive integer data type. Its range is -128 to 127 (-2^7 to $2^7 - 1$). This is the smallest integer data type available in Java. Generally, byte variables are used when a program uses a large number of variables whose values fall in the range -128 to 127 or when dealing with binary data in a file or over the network. Unlike int and long literals, there are no byte literals. However, you can assign any int literal that falls in the range of byte to a byte variable. For example,

```
byte b1 = 125;
byte b2 = -11;
```

If you assign an int literal to a byte variable and the value is outside the range of the byte data type, Java generates a compiler error. The following piece of code will produce a compiler error:

```
// An error. 150 is an int literal outside -128 to 127
byte b3 = 150;
```

Note that you can only assign an int literal between -128 and 127 to a byte variable. However, this does not imply that you can also assign the value stored in an int variable, which is in the range of -128 to 127, to a byte variable. The following piece of code will generate a compiler error, because it assigns the value of an int variable, num1, to a byte variable, b1:

```
int num1 = 15;

// OK. Assignment of int literal (-128 to 127) to byte.
byte b1 = 15;

// A compile-time error. Even though num1 has a value of 15, which is in the range -128 and 127.
b1 = num1;
```

Java does not allow you to assign the value of a variable of a higher range data type to the variable of a lower range data type because there is a possible loss of precision in making such an assignment. To make such an assignment from int to byte, you must use a cast, as you did in the case of the long-to-int assignment. The assignment of num1 to b1 can be rewritten as follows:

```
b1 = (byte)num1; // Ok
```

After this cast from int to byte, the Java compiler would not complain about the int-to-byte assignment. If num1 holds a value that cannot be correctly represented in the 8-bit byte variable b1, the higher order bits (9th to 32nd) of num1 are ignored and the value represented in the lower 8 bits is assigned b1. In such a case of int-to-byte assignment, the value assigned to the destination byte variable may not be the same as the value of the source int variable if the value of the source variable falls outside the range of byte data type.

However, irrespective of the value in the source int variable, the destination byte variable will always have a value between -128 and 127. Like int, since long is also a bigger data type than byte, you need to use explicit cast if you want to assign the value of a long variable to a byte variable. For example,

```
byte b4 = 10;
long num3 = 19L;

b4 = (byte)num3;  // OK because of cast
b4 = 19L;         // Error. Cannot assign long literal to byte
b4 = (byte)19L;   // OK because of cast
```

It is true that both 19 and 19L represent the same number. However, to the Java compiler, they are different. 19 is an int literal, that is, its data type is int, whereas 19L is a long literal, that is, its data type is long.

Java has a class Byte (note the upper case B in Byte), which defines two constants to represent maximum and minimum values of the byte data type, Byte.MAX_VALUE and Byte.MIN_VALUE.

```
byte max = Byte.MAX_VALUE;
byte min = Byte.MIN_VALUE;
```

The short Data Type

The short data type is a 16-bit signed Java primitive integer data type. Its range is -32768 to 32767 (or -2^{15} to $2^{15} - 1$). Generally, short variables are used when a program uses a large number of variables whose values fall in the range of the short data type or when dealing with data in a file, which can be easily handled using short data type. Unlike int and long literals, there is no short literal. However, you can assign any int literal that falls in the range of short (-32768 to 32767) to a short variable. For example,

```
short s1 = 12905;  // ok
short s2 = -11890;  // ok
```

The value of a byte variable can always be assigned to a short variable because the range of the byte data type falls within the range of the short data type. All other rules for assignment of a value from an int or long variable to a short variable are same as that for the byte variable. The following snippet of code illustrates the assignment of byte, int, and long values to short variables:

```
short s1 = 15;  // ok
byte b1 = 10;   // ok
s1 = b1;        // ok

int num1 = 10;    // ok
s1 = num1;        // A compile-time error
s1 = (short)num1; // ok because of cast from int to short
s1 = 35000;       // A compile-time error of an int literal outside the short range

long num2 = 555L; // ok
s1 = num2;        // A compile-time error
s1 = (short)num2; // ok because of the cast from long to short
s1 = 555L;        // A compile-time error
s = (short)555L;  // ok because of the cast from long to short
```

Java has a class called Short (note the upper case S in Short), which defines two constants to represent maximum and minimum values of short data type, Short.MAX_VALUE and Short.MIN_VALUE.

```
short max = Short.MAX_VALUE;
short min = Short.MIN_VALUE;
```

The char Data Type

The char data type is a 16-bit unsigned Java primitive data type. It represents a Unicode character. Note that char is an unsigned data type. Therefore, a char variable cannot have a negative value. The range of the char data type is 0 to 65535, which is the same as the range of the Unicode set. A character literal represents a value of the char data type. A character literal in Java can be expressed in the following formats:

- A character enclosed in single quotes
- As a character escape sequence
- As a Unicode escape sequence
- As an octal escape sequence

A character can be expressed by enclosing it in single quotes. The following snippet of code assigns values to char variables using this form:

```
char c1 = 'A';
char c2 = 'L';
char c3 = '5';
char c4 = '/';
```

Recall that a sequence of characters enclosed in double quotes is a String literal. A String literal cannot be assigned to a char variable, even if the String literal consists of only one character. In fact, the assignment of a String literal to a char variable is not allowed because of the rule that a value of a reference data type cannot be assigned to a variable of a primitive data type. All String literals represent objects of String class in Java and hence they are of reference data type, whereas character literals represent a value of the char primitive data type.

```
char c1 = 'A';    // OK
String s1 = 'A';  // An error. Cannot assign a char 'A' to a String s1
String s2 = "A";  // OK. "A" is a String assigned to a String variable
String s3 = "ABC"; // OK. "ABC" is a String literal
char c2 = "A";    // An error. Cannot assign a String "A" to char c2
char c4 = 'AB';   // An error. A character literal must contain only one character
```

A character literal can also be expressed as a character escape sequence. A character escape sequence starts with a backslash immediately followed by a character, and both are enclosed in single quotes. There are eight predefined character escape sequences as listed in Table 3-2.

Table 3-2. *List of Character Escape Sequences*

Character Escape Sequence	Description
'\n'	A linefeed
'\r'	A carriage return
'\f'	A form feed
'\b'	A backspace
'\t'	A tab
'\\'	A backslash
'\"'	A double quote
'\''	A single quote

A character literal expressed in the form of a character escape sequence consists of two characters—a backslash and a character following the backslash. However, they represent only one character. There are only eight character escape sequences in Java. You cannot define your own character escape sequences.

```
char c1 = '\n'; // Assigns a linefeed to c1
char c2 = '\"'; // Assigns double quote to c2
char c3 = '\a'; // A compile-time error. Invalid character escape sequence
```

A character literal can also be expressed as a Unicode escape sequence in the form '\uxxxx', Here, \u (a backslash immediately followed by a lowercase u) denotes the start of the Unicode escape sequence, and xxxx represents exactly four hexadecimal digits. The value represented by xxxx is the Unicode value for the character. The character 'A' has the Unicode value of 65. The value 65 in decimal can be represented in hexadecimal as 41. So, the character 'A' can be expressed in Unicode escape sequence as '\u0041'. The following snippet of code assigns the same character 'A' to the char variables c1 and c2:

```
char c1 = 'A';
char c2 = '\u0041';  // Same as c2 = 'A'
```

A character literal can also be expressed as an octal escape sequence in the form '\nnn'. Here, n is an octal digit (0-7). The range for the octal escape sequence is '\000' to '\377'. The octal number 377 is the same as the decimal number 255. Therefore, using octal escape sequence, you can represent characters whose Unicode code range from 0 to 255 decimal integers.

A Unicode character set (code range 0 to 65535) can be represented as a Unicode escape sequence ('\uxxxx'). Why does Java have another octal escape sequence, which is a subset of Unicode escape sequence? The octal escape sequences exist to represent characters for compatibility with other languages that use 8-bit unsigned chars to represent a character. Unlike a Unicode escape sequence, where you are always required to use four hexadecimal digits, in an octal escape sequence you can use one, two, or three octal digits. Therefore, an octal escape sequence may take on a form '\n', '\nn', or '\nnn', where n is one of the octal digits 0, 1, 2, 3, 4, 5, 6, and 7. Some examples of an octal escape sequence are as follows:

```
char c1 = '\52';
char c2 = '\141';
char c3 = '\400'; // A compile-time error. Octal 400 is out of range
char c4 = '\42';
char c5 = '\10';  // Same as '\n'
```

You can also assign an int literal to a char variable if int literal falls in the range 0-65535. When you assign an int literal to a char variable, the char variable represents the character whose Unicode code is equal to the value represented by that int literal. The Unicode code for the character 'a' (lowercase A) is 97. The decimal value 97 is represented as 141 in octal and 61 in hexadecimal. You can represent the Unicode character 'a' in three different forms in Java: 'a', '\141', and '\u0061'. You can also use int literal 97 to represent the Unicode character 'a'.

```
char c1 = 97; // Same as c1 = 'a'; c1 = '\141'; or, c1 = '\u0061';
```

A byte variable takes 8 bits and a char variable takes 16 bits. Even if the byte data type has smaller range than the char data type, you cannot assign a value stored in a byte variable to a char variable. The reason is that byte is a signed data type whereas char is an unsigned data type. If the byte variable has a negative value, say -15, it cannot be stored in a char variable without losing the precision. In such a case, you need to use an explicit cast. The following snippet of code illustrates possible cases of assignments from char to other integral data type and vice versa:

```
byte b1 = 10;
short s1 = 15;
int num1 = 150;
long num2 = 20L;
char c1 = 'A';

// byte and char
b1 = c1;          // An error
b1 = (byte)c1;    // Ok
c1 = b1;          // An error
c1 = (char)b1;    // Ok

// short and char
s1 = c1;          // An error
s1 = (short)c1;   // Ok
c1 = s1;          // An error
c1 = (char)s1;    // Ok

// int and char
num1 = c1;        // Ok
num1 = (int)c1;   // Ok. But, cast is not required. Use num1 = c1
c1 = num1;        // An error
c1 = (char)num1;  // Ok
c1 = 255;         // Ok. 255 is in the range of 0-65535
c1 = 70000;       // An error. 70000 is out of range 0-65535
c1 = (char)70000; // Ok. But, will lose the original value

// long and char
num2 = c1;        // Ok
num2 = (long)c1;  // Ok. But, cast is not required. Use num2 = c1
c1 = num2;        // An error
c1 = (char)num2;  // Ok
c1 = 255L;        // An error. 255L is a long literal
c1 = (char)255L;  // Ok. But use c1 = 255 instead
```

The boolean Data Type

The boolean data type has only two valid values: `true` and `false`. These two values are called boolean literals. You can use boolean literals as

```
boolean done; // Declares a boolean variable named done
done = true;  // Assigns true to done
```

One important point to note is that a boolean variable cannot be cast to any other data type and vice versa. Java does not specify the size of the boolean data type. Its size is left up to the JVM implementation. Typically, a value of a boolean data type is stored internally in a byte.

Floating-Point Data Types

A number that contains a fractional part is known as a real number, for example, 3.25, 0.49, -9.19, etc. A computer stores every number, real or integral, in binary format, which consists of only 0s and 1s. Therefore, it is necessary to convert a real number to its binary representation before it can be stored. It must be converted back to a real number after its binary representation is read. When a real number is converted to its binary representation, the computer must also store the position of the decimal point within the number. There are two strategies to store a real number in computer memory.

- Store only the binary representation of the number and assume that there are always a fixed number of digits before and after the point. A point is called a decimal point in the decimal representation of a number and a binary point in the binary representation. The type of representation in which the position of the point is always fixed in a number is known as fixed-point number format.

- Store the binary representation of the real number and the position of the point in the real number. Since the number of digits before and after the point can vary in this kind of representation of the real number, we say that the point can float. This kind of representation is called a floating-point format.

Floating-point representations are slower and less accurate compared to fixed-point representations. However, floating-point representations can handle a larger range of numbers with the same computer memory as compared to that of fixed-point representations.

Java supports the floating-point number format. It is important to note that not all real numbers have exact binary representations, and therefore they are represented as floating-point approximations. Java uses the IEEE 754 Floating-Point standard to store real numbers. IEEE is acronym for the Institute of Electrical and Electronic Engineers. Java has two floating-point Numeric data types:

- `float`
- `double`

The float Data Type

The `float` data type uses 32 bits to store a floating-point number in the IEEE 754 standard format. A floating-point number represented in 32 bits according to the IEEE 754 standard is also known as a single-precision floating-point number. It can represent a real number as small as 1.4×10^{-45} and as big as 3.4×10^{38} (approx.) in magnitude. The range includes only the magnitude. It could be positive or negative. Here, 1.4×10^{-45} is the smallest positive number greater than zero that can be stored in a `float` variable.

All real numbers that end with f or F are called float literals. A float literal can be expressed in the following two formats:

- Decimal number format
- Scientific notation

Examples of float literals in decimal number format are as follows:

```
float f1 = 8F;
float f2 = 8.F;
float f3 = 8.0F;
float f4 = 3.51F;
float f5 = 0.0F;
float f6 = 16.78f;
```

Real number 3.25 is also written using exponential forms such as 32.5×10^{-1} or 0.325×10^{1}. In Java, such real numbers can be represented as float literals using scientific notation. In scientific notation, the number 32.5×10^{-1} is written as 32.5E-1. As a float literal, it can be written as 32.5E-1F or 32.5E-1f. All of the following float literals denote the same real number 32.5:

```
3.25F
32.5E-1F
0.325E+1F
0.325E1F
0.0325E2F
0.0325e2F
3.25E0F
```

The float data type defines two zeros: +0.0F (or 0.0F) and -0.0F. However, for the comparison purposes, both +0.0F and -0.0F are considered equal.

The float data type defines two infinities: positive infinity and negative infinity. For example, the result of the dividing 2.5F by 0.0F is a float positive infinity whereas the result of dividing 2.5F by -0.0F is a float negative infinity.

Results of some of the operations on float are not defined. For example, dividing 0.0F by 0.0F is indeterminate. Indeterminate results are represented by a special value of the float data type called NaN (Not-a-Number). Java has a Float class (Note the upper case F in Float), which defines three constants that represent positive infinity, negative infinity, and NaN of the float data type. Table 3-3 lists these three float constants and their meanings. The table also lists two constants, which represent the maximum and minimum (greater than zero) float values that can be stored in a float variable.

Table 3-3. *float Constants Defined in the float Class*

float Constants	Meaning
Float.POSITIVE_INFINITY	Positive infinity of type float
Float.NEGATIVE_INFINITY	Negative infinity of type float
Float.NaN	Not a Number of type float
Float.MAX_VALUE	The largest positive value that can be represented in a float variable. This is equal to 3.4×10^{38} (approx.).
Float.MIN_VALUE	The smallest positive value greater than zero that can be represented in a float variable. This is equal to 1.4×10^{-45}.

The value of all integral types (int, long, byte, short, and char) can be assigned to a variable of the float data type without using an explicit cast. The following are some examples of using the float data type:

```
int num1 = 15000;
float salary = num1;          // Ok. int variable to float
salary = 12455;               // Ok. int literal to float
float bigNum = Float.MAX_VALUE; // Assigns maximum float value
bigNum = 1226L;               // Ok, a long literal to float
float justAChar = 'A';        // Ok. Assigns 65.0F to justAChar

// Ok. Assigns positive infinity to the fInf variable
float fInf = Float.POSITIVE_INFINITY;

// Ok. Assigns Not-a-Number to fNan variable
float fNan = Float.NaN;

// A compile-time error. Cannot assign a float literal to a float variable
// greater than the maximum value of float(3.4E38F approx)
float fTooBig = 3.5E38F;

// A compile-time error. Cannot assign a float literal to a float variable less
// than the minimum value (greater than zero) of float 1.4E-45F
float fTooSmall = 1.4E-46F;
```

A float value must be cast before it is assigned to a variable of any integral data type int, long, byte, short, or char.

```
int num1 = 10;
float salary = 10.0F;
num1 =  salary;       // An error. Cannot assign float to int
num1 = (int)salary;  // Ok
```

Most floating-point numbers are approximation of their corresponding real numbers. The assignment of int and long to float may result in loss of precision. Consider the following piece of code:

```
int num1 = 1029989998; // Stores an integer in num1
float num2 = num1;     // Assigns the value stored in num1 to num2
int num3 = (int)num2;  // Assigns the value stored in num2 to num3
```

You expect that the value stored in num1 and num3 should be same. However, they are not the same because the value stored in num1 cannot be stored exactly in a floating-point format in the float variable num2. Not all floating-point numbers have an exact representation in binary format. This is the reason that num1 and num3 are not equal. Please refer to the section "Binary Representation of Floating-Point Numbers" for more details.

The double Data Type

The double data type uses 64 bits to store a floating-point number in the IEEE 754 standard format. A floating-point number represented in 64 bits according to IEEE 754 standard is also known as a double-precision floating-point number. It can represent a number as small as 4.9×10^{-324} and as big as 1.7×10^{308} (approx.) in magnitude. The range includes only magnitude. It could be positive or negative. Here, 4.9×10^{-324} is the smallest positive number greater than zero that can be stored in a double variable.

All real numbers are called double literals. A double literal may optionally end with d or D, for example, 19.27d. However, the suffix d or D is optional in double literals. That is, both 19.27 and 19.27d represent the same double literal. This book uses double literals without the suffix d or D. A double literal can be expressed in the following two formats:

- Decimal number format

- Scientific notation

Examples of double literals in decimal number format are as follows:

```
double d1 = 8D
double d2 = 8.;
double d3 = 8.0;
double d4 = 8.D;
double d5 = 78.9867;
double d6 = 45.0;
```

■ **Tip**   8 is an int literal whereas 8D, 8., and 8.0 are double literals.

Like a float literal, you can also use scientific notation to express double literals.

```
double d1 = 32.5E-1;
double d2 = 0.325E+1;
double d3 = 0.325E1;
double d4 = 0.0325E2;
double d5 = 0.0325e2;
double d6 = 32.5E-1D;
double d7 = 0.325E+1d;
double d8 = 0.325E1d;
double d9 = 0.0325E2d;
```

Like the float data type, the double data type defines two zeros, two infinities, and a NaN. They are represented by constants in the Double class. Table 3-4 lists these constants and their meanings. Table 3-4 also lists two constants, which represent the maximum and minimum (greater than zero) double values that can be represented in a double variable.

Table 3-4. *double Constants in the Double Class*

double Constants	Meaning
Double.POSITIVE_INFINITY	Positive infinity of type double
Double.NEGATIVE_INFINITY	Negative infinity of type double
Double.NaN	Not a Number of type double
Double.MAX_VALUE	The largest positive value that can be represented in a double variable. This is equal to 1.7×10^{308} (approx.)
Double.MIN_VALUE	The smallest positive value greater than zero that can be represented in a double variable. This is equal to 4.9×10^{-324}.

The value of all integral types (int, long, byte, short, char) and float can be assigned to a variable of the double data type without using an explicit cast.

```
int num1 = 15000;
double salary = num1;          // Ok. int to double assignment
salary = 12455;                // Ok. int literal to double
double bigNum = Double.MAX_VALUE; // Assigns the maximum double value
bigNum = 1226L;                // Ok, long literal to double
double justAChar = 'A';        // Ok. Assigns 65.0 to justAChar

// Ok. Assigns positive infinity to dInf variable
double dInf = Double.POSITIVE_INFINITY;

// Ok. Assigns Not-a-Number to dNan variable
double dNan = Double.NaN;

// A compile-time error. Cannot assign a double literal to a double variable
// greater than the maximum value of double (1.7E308 approx)
double dTooBig = 1.8E308;

// A compile-time error. Cannot assign a double literal to a double variable
// less than the minimum value (greater than zero) of double 4.9E-324
double dTooSmall = 4.9E-325;
```

A double value must be cast to the integral type before it is assigned to a variable of any integral data type (int, long, byte, short, or char).

```
int num1 = 10;
double salary = 10.0;
num1 = salary;       // A compile-time error. Cannot assign double to int
num1 = (int)salary; // Now Ok.
```

Underscores in Numeric Literals

Beginning with Java 7, you can use any number of underscores between two digits in numeric literals. For example, an int literal 1969 can be written as 1_969, 19_69, 196_9, 1___969, or any other forms using underscores between two digits. The use of underscores is also allowed in octal, hexadecimal, and binary formats. Big numbers are harder to read without any punctuation marks (e.g., a comma as a thousand-separator). Use of underscores in big numbers makes them easier to read. The following examples show the valid uses of underscores in numeric literals:

```
int x1 = 1_969;             // Underscore in deciaml format
int x2 = 1__969;            // Multiple consecutive underscores
int x3 = 03_661;            // Underscore in octal literal
int x4 = 0b0111_1011_0001; // Underscore in binary literal
int x5 = 0x7_B_1;           // Underscores in hexadecimal literal
byte b1 = 1_2_7;            // Underscores in decimal format
double d1  = 1_969.09_19;  // Underscores in double literal
```

Underscores are allowed in numeric literals only between digits. This means that you cannot use underscores in the beginning or end of a numeric literal. You cannot use underscores with prefixes such as 0x for hexadecimal format and 0b for binary format, and suffixes such as L for long literal and F for float literal. The following examples show the invalid uses of underscores in numeric literals:

```
int y1 = _1969;        // An error. Underscore in the beginning
int y2 = 1969_;        // An error. Underscore in the end
int y3 = 0x_7B1;       // An error. Underscore after prefix 0x
int y4 = 0_x7B1;       // An error. Underscore inside prefix 0x
long z1 = 1969_L;      // An error. Underscore with suffix L
double d1 = 1969_.0919; // An error. Underscore before decimal
double d1 = 1969._0919; // An error. Underscore after decimal
```

■ **Tip**   You can write the int literal 1969 in octal format as 03661. The zero in the beginning of an int literal in the octal format is considered a digit, not a prefix. It is allowed to use underscores after the first zero in an int literal in octal format. You can write 03661 as 0_3661.

Java Compiler and Unicode Escape Sequence

Recall that any Unicode character in a Java program can be expressed in the form of a Unicode escape sequence. For example, the character 'A' can be replaced by '\u0041'. The Java compiler first converts every occurrence of a Unicode escape sequence to a Unicode character. A Unicode escape sequence starts with \u followed by four hexadecimal digits. '\\u0041' is not a Unicode escape sequence. To make uxxxx a valid part of a Unicode escape sequence, it must be preceded by odd number of backslashes, because two contiguous backslashes (\\) represent one backslash character. Therefore, "\\u0041" represents a 6-character string composed of '\', 'u', '0', '0', '4', and '1'. However, "\\\u0041" represents a two-character string ("\A").

Sometimes, inappropriate use of Unicode escape sequence in Java source code may result in a compile-time error. Consider the following declaration of a char variable:

```
char c = '\u000A';
```

The programmer intends to initialize the variable c with a linefeed character whose Unicode escape sequence is \u000A. When this piece of code is compiled, the Java compiler will convert \u000A into an actual Unicode character and this piece of code will be split into two lines as follows:

```
char c = '
    ';  // After the actual linefeed is inserted
```

Since a character literal cannot continue in two lines, the above piece of code generates a compile-time error. The correct way to initialize the variable c is to use the character escape sequence \n as shown:

```
char c = '\n'; // Correct
```

In character and String literals, the linefeed and carriage return should always be written as \n and \r, respectively, not as \u000A and \u000D. Even a line of comment may generate a compiler error if you do not use the linefeed and carriage return characters correctly. Suppose you commented the above wrong declaration of the char variable, as shown:

```
// char c = '\u000A';
```

Even if this line is a comment line, it will generate a compiler error. The comment will be split into two lines before compilation, like so:

```
// char c = '
';
```

The second line, which contains, ';, causes the compiler error. The multi-line comment syntax would not generate a compiler error in such a case.

```
/* char c = '\u000A'; */
```

would be converted to

```
/* char c = '
'; */
```

which is a valid multi-line comment.

A Short Break

I have finished discussing all primitive data types available in Java. In the following section, I will discuss the general concepts of binary numbers and their use in representing different types of values in Java. If you have a computer science background, you may skip this section.

The program in Listing 3-1 shows how to declare variables of different data types using literals. It also prints the values for some constants in the Double class. Java 8 has added the Double.BYTES constant that contains the number of bytes used by a double variable.

Listing 3-1. Using Primitive Data Types

```
// NumTest.java
package com.jdojo.datatype;

public class NumTest {
        public static void main(String[] args) {
                int anInt = 100;
                long aLong = 200L;
                byte aByte = 65;
                short aShort = -902;
                char aChar = 'A';
                float aFloat = 10.98F;
                double aDouble = 899.89;

                // Print values of the variables
                System.out.println("anInt = " + anInt);
                System.out.println("aLong = " + aLong);
                System.out.println("aByte = " + aByte);
                System.out.println("aShort = " + aShort);
                System.out.println("aChar = " + aChar);
                System.out.println("aFloat = " + aFloat);
                System.out.println("aDouble = " + aDouble);
```

```
            // Print some double constants
            System.out.println("Max double = " + Double.MAX_VALUE);
            System.out.println("Min double = " + Double.MIN_VALUE);
            System.out.println("Positive infinity for double = " + Double.POSITIVE_INFINITY);
            System.out.println("Negative infinity for double = " + Double.NEGATIVE_INFINITY);
            System.out.println("Not-a-Number for double = " + Double.NaN);
            System.out.println("Double takes " + Double.BYTES + " bytes");
        }
}
```

```
anInt = 100
aLong = 200
aByte = 65
aShort = -902
aChar = A
aFloat = 10.98
aDouble = 899.89
Max double = 1.7976931348623157E308
Min double = 4.9E-324
Positive infinity for double = Infinity
Negative infinity for double = -Infinity
Not-a-Number for double = NaN
double takes 8 bytes
```

Binary Representation of Integers

Computers use the binary number system to work with data. All data in a binary system is stored using 1's and 0's. Characters 1 and 0 are called bits (short for binary digit). They are the smallest units of information a computer can work with. A group of 8 bits is called a byte or octet. Half a byte (i.e. a group of four bits) is called a nibble. A computer uses data bus, a pathway, to send data from one part of the computer system to another. How much information can be moved from one part to another at one time depends on the bit-width of the data bus. The bit-width of the data bus on a particular computer is also known as word-size, and information contained in one word-size is simply referred to as a word. Therefore, a word may refer to 16-bit or 32-bit or another bit-width depending on computer's architecture. The long and double data types in Java take 64 bits. On a computer with a word-size of 32 bits, these two data types are not treated atomically. For example, to write a value in a variable of long data type two write actions are performed, one for each 32-bit half.

A decimal number can be converted to binary format using the following steps:

- Divide the decimal number successively by 2

- After each division, record the remainder. This will be 1 or 0.

- Continue the above two steps until the result of the division is 0 (zero)

- The binary number is formed by writing digits in the remainder column from bottom to top.

For example, the binary representation of decimal number 13 can be computed as shown in Table 3-5.

Table 3-5. *Decimal-to-Binary Conversion*

Number	Divided by 2	Result	Remainder
13	13/2	6	1
6	6/2	3	0
3	3/2	1	1
1	1/2	0	1

The binary representation of decimal number 13 is 1101. A byte variable in Java occupies one byte. The value 13 in a byte variable is stored as 00001101. Note that four zeros are added in front of the binary representation 1101 because a byte variable always occupies 8 bits irrespective of the value that it contains. The rightmost bit in a byte or a word is known as the least significant bit (LSB) and the leftmost bit as the most significant bit (MSB). The MSB and LSB for the binary representation of 13 are shown in Figure 3-5.

Figure 3-5. *MSB and LSB in a binary number*

Each bit in a binary number is assigned a weight, which is a power of 2. A binary number can be converted to its decimal equivalent by multiplying each bit in the binary number by its weight and adding them up. For example, 1101 in binary can be converted to its decimal equivalent as follows:

$$(1101)_2 = 1 \times 2^0 + 0 \times 2^1 + 1 \times 2^2 + 1 \times 2^3$$
$$= 1 + 0 + 4 + 8$$
$$= (13)_{10}$$

Java stores the negative integral numbers in 2's complement form. Let's discuss the complement of a number in a given number system. Every number system has a base, also known radix. For example, 10 is the radix for the decimal number system, 2 is for the binary number system, and 8 is for the octal number system. We will use the symbol R for radix. Every number system defines two types of complements:

- Diminished radix complement (also known as (R-1)'s complement)
- Radix complement (also known as R's complement)

Therefore, for the decimal number system, we have 9's complement and 10's complement; for the octal number system, we have 7's and 8's complements, and for the binary number system, we have 1's and 2's complements.

Diminished Radix Complement

Let N be a number in a number system with radix R and n is the total number of digits in the number N. The diminished radix complement or (R-1)'s complement of the number N is defined as $(R^n-1) - N$.

In the decimal number system, the 9's complement of a number is $(10^n - 1) - N$. Since 10^n consists of 1 followed by n zeros, (10^n-1) consists of n 9s. Therefore, 9's complement of a number can be computed simply by subtracting each digit in the number from 9. For example, 9's complement of 5678 is 4321 and 9's complement of 894542 is 105457.

In binary number system, the 1's complement of a binary number is given by (2^n-1) - N. Since 2^n in binary number system consists of 1 followed by n zeros, (2^n-1) consists of n 1s. For example, 1's complement of 10110 (here, n is 5) can be computed as $(2^5 -1)$ - 10110, which is 11111 - 10110 (2^5-1) is 31, which is 11111 in binary.

The 1's complement of a binary number can be computed simply by subtracting each digit in the number from 1. A binary number consists of 0s and 1s. When you subtract 1 from 1, you get 0, and when you subtract 0 from 1, you get 1. Therefore, 1's complement of a binary number can be computed just by inverting the bits of the number, that is, by changing 1 to 0 and 0 to 1. For example, 1's complement of 10110 is 01001 and 1's complement of 0110001 is 1001110.

In a number system, (R-1)'s complement of a number is computed by subtracting each digit of the number from the maximum digit value of that number system. For example, the maximum digit value in an octal number system is 7, and therefore, 7's complement of an octal number is computed by subtracting each digit of that number from 7. For a hexadecimal number system, the maximum digit value is 15 represented by F. For example, 7's complement of 56072 octal number is 21705; 15's complement of 6A910F hexadecimal number is 956EF0.

Radix Complement

Let N be a number in a number system of radix R, and n is the total number of digits in the number N. The radix complement or R's complement of the number N is defined as R^n - N. For N = 0, the R's complement is defined as zero.

It is evident from the definition of R's and (R-1)'s complements that R's complement of a number is computed by adding 1 to (R-1)'s complement of that number. Therefore, 10's complement of a decimal number is obtained by adding 1 to its 9's complement, and 2's complement of a binary number is obtained by adding 1 to its 1's complement. Therefore, 2's complement of 10110 is 01001 + 1, which is 01010. By carefully looking at the procedure to compute 2's complement of a binary number, you can observe it can be computed just by looking at the binary number. The simple procedure to compute 2's complement of a binary number can be described as follows:

- Start from the right end of the binary number.

- Write down all digits unchanged up to the first 1 bit.

- Subsequently invert the bits to get the 2's complement of the binary number.

For example, let's compute 2's complement of 10011000. Start from the right end and write down all digits unchanged up to the first 1 bit. Since the fourth digit from right is 1, you will write first four digits unchanged, which is 1000. Now, invert the bits starting from fifth bit from right, which will give 01101000. The procedure is illustrated in Figure 3-6.

Figure 3-6. Computing 2's complement of a binary number

All negative integers (byte, short, int, and long) are stored as their 2's complements in memory. Let's consider two byte variables in Java.

```
byte bPos = 13;
byte bNeg = -13;
```

The bPos is stored in memory as 00001101. The 2's complement of 00001101 is computed as 11110011. Therefore, bNeg, which is -13, is stored as 11110011, as shown in Figure 3-7.

bPos   00001101
           ↑

Sign bit 0 denotes a positive number

bNeg   11110011
          ↑

     Sign bit 1 denotes a negative number

Figure 3-7. *Storing the number 13 in 2's complement forms*

Binary Representation of Floating-Point Numbers

Any binary floating-point system can represent only a finite number of floating-point values in exact form. All other values must be approximated by the closest representable value. The IEEE 754-1985 is the most widely accepted floating-point standard in the computer industry, and it specifies the format and the method to represent binary floating-point numbers. The goal of the IEEE standard, which is designed for engineering calculations, is to maximize accuracy (to get as close as possible to the actual number). Precision refers to the number of digits that you can represent. The IEEE standard attempts to balance the number of bits dedicated to the exponent with the number of bits used for the fractional part of the number, to keep both accuracy and precision within acceptable limits. This section describes IEEE 754-1985 standard for binary floating-point format in general and points out how Java supports this standard.

A floating-point number has four parts:

- Sign

- Significand (also known as mantissa)

- Base (also known as radix)

- Exponent

The floating-point number 19.25 can be represented with all its four parts as

```
+19.25 x 10⁰
```

Here, the sign is + (positive), the significand is 19.25, the base is 10, and the exponent is 0.

The number 19.25 can also be represented in many other forms, as shown below. I will omit the positive sign of the number, that is, +19.25 will be written as 19.25.

```
19.25 x 10⁰
1.925 x 10¹
0.1925 x 10²
192.5 x 10⁻¹
1925 x 10⁻²
```

Therefore, a floating-point number can be represented an infinite number of ways. A floating-point number represented in base 10 is said to be in normalized form if its significand satisfies the following rule:

```
0.1 <= significand < 1
```

According to this rule, the representation 0.1925 x 10^2 is the normalized form of 19.25. The floating-point number 19.25 (base 10) can be written as 10011.01 in binary form (base 2). The floating-point number 19.25 can be rewritten in many different binary forms. Some of the alternate binary representations of decimal 19.25 are as follows:

```
10011.01 x 2⁰
1001.101 x 2¹
100.1101 x 2²
1.001101 x 2⁴
100110.1 x 2⁻¹
1001101 x 2⁻²
```

Note that in binary form the base is 2. When the binary point is shifted to the left by one digit, the exponent is incremented by one. When the binary point is shifted to the right by one digit, the exponent is decremented by one. A floating-point number in a binary form is normalized if its significand satisfies the following condition:

```
1 <= significand < 2
```

If the significand of a binary floating-point number is of the form 1.bbbbbbb..., where b is a bit (0 or 1), the binary floating-point number is said to be in normalized form. Therefore, 1.001101 x 2^4 is the normalized form of binary floating-point number 10011.01. In other words, a normalized binary floating-point number starts with a bit 1, immediately followed by a binary point.

The floating-point numbers, which are not normalized, are called denormalized floating-point numbers. A denormalized floating-point number is also called denormal or subnormal. All floating-point numbers cannot be represented in a normalized form. There could be two reasons for this.

- The number does not contain any bit as 1. An example of this is 0.0. Since 0.0 does not have any bit set as 1, it cannot be represented in the normalized form.

- Computers use a fixed number of bits to store the sign, significand, and exponent of a binary floating-point number. If the exponent of a binary floating-point number is the minimum exponent allowed by the computer storage format and the significand is less than 1, such a binary floating-point number cannot be normalized before storing it in computer. For example, suppose that -126 is the minimum exponent value that can be stored in a given storage format for a binary floating-point number. If the binary floating-point number is 0.01101 x 2^{-126}, this number cannot be normalized. The normalized form of this number will be 1.101 x 2^{-128}. However, the given storage format allows minimum exponent as -126 (I have assumed number -126 for this example). Therefore, the exponent -128 (-128 < -126) cannot be stored in the given storage format and that is why 0.01101 x 2^{-126} cannot be stored in the normalized form.

Why do we need to normalize a binary floating-point number before storing it in memory? The following are the advantages of doing this:

- The normalized representation is unique.

- Because the binary point in a binary floating-point number can be placed anywhere in the number, you must store the position of binary point along with the number. By normalizing the number, you always place the binary point after the first 1 bit, and therefore, you need not store the position of the binary point. This saves memory and time to store one extra piece of information.

- Two normalized binary floating-point numbers can be compared easily by comparing their signs, significands, and exponents.

- In a normalized form, the significand can use all its storage bits to store significant digits (bits). For example, if you allocate only five bits to store the significand, for the number 0.0010110×2^{10} only 0.00101 part of the significand will be stored. However, if you normalize this number as 1.0110×2^7, the significand can be stored fully in five bits.

- In a normalized form, the significand always starts with a 1 bit, which can be omitted while storing the significand. When reading back, you can add the leading 1 bit. This omitted bit is called the "hidden bit" and it provides one extra bit of precision.

The IEEE 754 -1985 standard defines the four floating-point formats as follows:

- 32-bit single-precision floating-point format

- 64-bit double-precision floating-point format

- Single-extended floating-point format

- Double-extended floating-point format

Java uses IEEE 32-bit single-precision floating-point format to store the values of float data type. It uses 64-bit double-precision floating-point format to store the values of double data type.

I will discuss only IEEE 32-bit single-precision floating-point format. The difference between single-precision floating-point format and other formats are the total number of bits used to store the binary floating-point numbers and the distribution of number of bits among sign, exponent, and significand. The difference among different IEEE formats will be shown at the end of the discussion.

32-bit Single-Precision Floating-Point Format

The 32-bit single-precision floating-point format uses 32 bits to store a binary floating-point number. A binary floating-point number is of the following form:

Sign * Significand * $2^{Exponent}$

Since the base is always 2, this format does not store the value of the base. The 32 bits are distributed as follows:

- 1 bit to store the sign

- 8 bits to store the exponent

- 23 bits to store the significand

The layout for the single-precision floating-point format is shown in Table 3-6.

Table 3-6. *IEEE Single-Precision Format Layout*

1-bit Sign	8-bit Exponent	23-bit Significand
s	eeeeeeee	fffffffffffffffffffffff

Sign

IEEE single-precision floating-point format uses 1 bit to store the sign of the number. A 0 sign bit indicates a positive number and 1 sign bit indicates a negative number.

Exponent

The exponent takes 8 bits. The exponent can be positive or negative. The range of the exponent value that can be stored in 8-bit is -127 to 128. There must be a mechanism to represent the sign of the exponent. Note that the 1-bit sign field in the layout shown in Table 3-7 stores the sign of the floating-point number, not the sign of the exponent. To store the sign of the exponent, you can use the sign-magnitude method, where 1 bit is used to store the sign and the remaining 7 bits store the magnitude of the exponent. You can also use 2's complement method to store the negative exponent as is used to store integers. However, IEEE does not use either of these two methods for storing the exponent. IEEE uses the biased representation of the exponent to store the exponent value.

What is a bias and what is a biased exponent? A bias is a constant value, which is 127 for IEEE 32-bit single-precision format. The bias value is added to the exponent before storing it in memory. This new exponent, after adding a bias, is called a biased exponent. The biased exponent is computed as follows:

```
Biased Exponent = Exponent + Bias
```

For example, 19.25 can be written in normalized binary floating-point format as 1.001101×2^4. Here, the exponent value is 4. However, the exponent value stored in memory will be a biased exponent, which will be computed as follows:

```
Biased Exponent = Exponent + Bias
                = 4 + 127 (Single-precision format)
                = 131
```

For 1.001101×2^4, 131 will be stored as the exponent. When reading back the exponent of a binary floating-point number, you must subtract the bias value for that format to get the actual exponent value.

Why does IEEE use biased exponent? The advantage of using a biased exponent is that positive floating-point numbers can be treated as integers for comparison purposes.

Suppose E is the number of bits used to store the exponent value in a given floating-point format. The value of the bias for that format can be computed as

```
Bias = 2^(E - 1) - 1
```

The exponent ranges from -127 to 128 for the single-precision format. Therefore, the biased exponent ranges from 0 to 255. Two extreme exponent values (-127 and 128 for unbiased, and 0 and 255 for biased) are used to represent special floating-point numbers, such as zero, infinities, NaNs and denormalized numbers. The exponent range of -126 to 127 (biased 1 to 254) is used to represent normalized binary floating-point numbers.

Significand

IEEE single-precision floating-point format uses 23 bits to store the significand. The number of bits used to store the significand is called the precision of that floating-point format. Therefore, you might have guessed that the precision of floating-point numbers stored in the single-precision format is 23. However, this is not true. But first I need to discuss the format in which the significand is stored before I conclude about the precision of this format.

The significand of a floating-point number is normalized before it is stored in memory. The normalized significand is always of the form 1.fffffffffffffffffffffff. Here, an f denotes a bit 0 or 1 for the fractional part of significand. Because the leading 1 bit is always present in the normalized form of significand, you need not store the leading 1 bit. Therefore, while storing the normalized significand, you can use all 23 bits to store the fractional part of the significand. In fact, not storing the leading 1 bit of a normalized significand gives you one extra bit of precision. This way, you represent 24 digits (1 leading bit + 23 fraction bits) in just 23 bits. Thus, for normalized significand the precision of a floating-point number in IEEE single-precision format is 24.

```
Actual Significand: 1.ffffffffffffffffffffffff (24 digits)
Stored Significand:   ffffffffffffffffffffffff (23 digits)
```

If you always represent the significand of a binary floating-point number in normalized form, there is a gap around zero on the number line. The minimum number in magnitude that can be represented in IEEE single-precision format can be computed as follows:

- *Sign*: It can be 0 or 1, denoting a pocsitive or negative number. For this example, let's assume the sign bit as 0 to indicate a positive number.

- *Exponent*: The minimum exponent value is -126. Recall that the exponent values -127 and 128 are reserved to represent special floating-point numbers. The minimum biased exponent will be -126 + 127 = 1. The binary representation of the biased exponent 1 in 8-bit is 00000001.

- *Significand*: The minimum value of significand in the normalized form will consist of the leading 1 bit and all 23 fraction bits set to 0 as 1.00000000000000000000000.

If you combine the binary representation of a normalized floating-point number with the minimum possible values for the exponent and significand, the actual number stored in the computer will look like the one shown in Table 3-7.

Table 3-7. Minimum Possible Normalized Number

Sign	Exponent	Significand
0	00000001	00000000000000000000000
1-bit	8-bit	23-bit

The value of the minimum floating-point number in decimal is 1.0×2^{-126}. Therefore, 1.0×2^{-126} is the first representable normalized number after zero, leaving a gap around zero on the number line.

If you store only normalized floating-point numbers using IEEE single-precision format, all numbers less than 1.0×2^{-126} in magnitude must be rounded to zero. This will cause a serious problem when dealing with tiny numbers in a program. In order to store numbers smaller than 1.0×2^{-126} the numbers must be denormalized.

Special Floating-Point Numbers

This section describes special floating-point numbers and their representations in the IEEE single-precision format.

Signed Zeros

The IEEE floating-point format allows for two zeros, +0.0 (or 0.0) and -0.0. Zero is represented by the minimum exponent value -127 for the single-precision format. The significand is 0.0 for zero. Since the sign bit can be 0 or 1, there are two zeros: +0.0 and -0.0. The binary representations of zeros in the single-precision format are shown in Table 3-8.

Table 3-8. Binary Representations of Positive and Negative Zeros in the Single-Precision Format

Number	Sign	Exponent	Significand
0.0	0	00000000	00000000000000000000000
-0.0	1	00000000	00000000000000000000000

For comparison purposes, +0.0 and -0.0 are considered equal. Therefore, the expression 0.0 == -0.0 always returns true.

Why does IEEE define two zeros if they are considered equal? The sign of zero is used to determine the result of an arithmetic expression involving multiplication and division. The result of 3.0 * 0.0 is a positive zero (0.0), whereas the result of 3.0 * (-0.0) is a negative zero (-0.0). For a floating-point number num with the values ±Infinity, the relation 1/(1/num) = num holds true only because of two signed zeros.

Signed Infinities

The IEEE floating-point format allows for two infinities: positive infinity and negative infinity. The sign bit represents the sign of infinity. The maximum exponent value 128 (the biased exponent 255) for the single-precision format and zero significand represents infinity. The maximum biased value 255 can be represented in 8-bit with all bits set to 1 as 11111111. The binary representations of infinities in single-precision format are shown in Table 3-9.

Table 3-9. *Binary Representations of Positive and Negative Infinities in the Single-Precision Format*

Number	Sign	Exponent	Significand
+Infinity	0	11111111	00000000000000000000000
-Infinity	1	11111111	00000000000000000000000

NaN

NaN stands for "Not-a-Number." NaN is the result of arithmetic operations that do not have meaningful results, such as dividing zero by zero, the square root of a negative number, adding -Infinity to +Infinity, etc.

NaN is represented by maximum exponent value (128 for single-precision format) and non-zero significand. The sign bit is not interpreted for NaN. What happens when NaN is one of the operands in an arithmetic expression? For example, what is the result of NaN + 100? Should the execution of an arithmetic expression involving NaNs be stopped or continued? There are two types of NaNs:

- Quiet NaN
- Signaling NaN

A quiet NaN, when encountered as an operand in an arithmetic expression, quietly (i.e. without raising any trap or exception) produces another quiet NaN as the result. In case of a quiet NaN, the expression NaN + 100 will result in another quiet NaN. The most significant bit in the significand is set to 1 for a quiet NaN. Table 3-10 shows a binary representation of a quiet NaN. In the table, s and b indicate a 0 or 1 bit.

Table 3-10. *A Binary Representation of a Quiet NaN*

Number	Sign	Exponent	Significand
Quiet NaN	s	11111111	1bbbbbbbbbbbbbbbbbbbbbb

When a signaling NaN is encountered as an operand in an arithmetic expression, an invalid operation exception is signaled and a quiet NaN is delivered as the result. Signaling NaNs are generally used to initialize the uninitialized variables in a program, so when variables are not initialized before they are used, errors can be signaled. The most significant bit of the significand is set to 0 for a signaling NaN. Table 3-11 shows a binary representation of a signaling NaN. In the table, s and b indicate a 0 or 1 bit.

Table 3-11. *A Binary Representation of a Quiet NaN*

Number	Sign	Exponent	Significand
Signaling NaN	s	11111111	0bbbbbbbbbbbbbbbbbbbbbbb

■ **Tip** IEEE defines $2^{24} - 2$ distinct NaNs for the single-precision format and $2^{53} - 2$ distinct NaNs for the double-precision format. However, Java has only one NaN for the float data type and one NaN for the double data type. Java always uses a quiet NaN.

Denormals

When the biased exponent is 0 and the significand is non-zero, it denotes a denormalized number. Table 3-12 shows the bits pattern to represent denormalized numbers in the single-precision format.

Table 3-12. *The Bits Pattern for a Denormalized Single-Precision Floating-Point Number*

Sign	Exponent	Significand
s	000000000	fffffffffffffffffffffff

In Table 3-12, s denotes a sign bit, which can be 0 for a positive number and 1 for a negative number. The exponent bits are all zeros. At least one of the bits in the significand is denoted 1. The decimal value of the denormalized number is computed as shown:

$(-1)^s$ * 0.fffffffffffffffffffffff * 2^{-126}

Suppose you want to store a number 0.25 x 2^{-128} in the single-precision format. If you write this number in normalized form after converting 0.25 in binary, it will be 1.0 x 2^{-130}. However, the minimum exponent allowed for single-precision format is -126. Therefore, this number cannot be stored in normalized form in single-precision format. The exponent is kept as -126 and the binary point is shifted to the left, resulting in denormalized form as 0.0001 x 2^{-126}. The number is stored as shown in Table 3-13.

Table 3-13. *Bits Pattern for a Denormalized Number 1.0 * 2^{-130}*

Number	Sign	Exponent	Significand
0.0001 x 2^{-126}	0	00000000	00010000000000000000000

It seems that for the number 0.0001 x 2^{-126}, the biased exponent should be computed as -126 + 127 = 1 and the exponent bits should be 00000001. However, this is not true. For denormalized numbers, the exponent is stored as all 0 bits; when reading it back, it is interpreted as -126. This is so because you need to distinguish between normalized and denormalized numbers when reading back floating-point numbers, and for all denormalized numbers, there is no leading 1-bit in their significands. The denormalized numbers fill the gap around zero on the number line, which would have been there if you had stored only normalized numbers.

Rounding Modes

Not all real numbers can be exactly represented in binary floating-point format in finite number of bits. Therefore, real numbers that cannot be exactly represented in a binary floating-point format must be rounded. There are four rounding modes:

- Round toward zero
- Round toward positive infinity
- Round toward negative infinity
- Round toward nearest

Rounding Toward Zero

This rounding mode is also called truncation or chop mode. In this rounding mode, the total number of bits (or digits) that is retained from the original number is the same as the number of bits available to store the floating-point number in the given format. The rest of bits are ignored. This rounding mode is called "rounding toward zero" because it has the effect of making the rounded result closer to zero. Some examples of rounding towards zero are shown in Table 3-14.

Table 3-14. *Examples of Rounding Towards Zero*

Original Number	Available Number of Binary Points	Rounded Number
1.1101	2	1.11
-0.1011	2	-0.10
0.1010	2	0.10
0.0011	2	0.00

Rounding Toward Positive Infinity

In this rounding mode, numbers are rounded to a value closer to the positive infinity. Some examples of rounding towards positive infinity are shown in Table 3-15.

Table 3-15. *Examples of Rounding Towards Positive Infinity*

Original Number	Available Number of Binary Points	Rounded Number
1.1101	2	10.00
-0.1011	2	-0.10
0.1010	2	0.11
0.0011	2	0.01

Rounding Toward Negative Infinity

In this rounding mode, numbers are rounded to a value closer to the negative infinity. Some examples of rounding towards negative infinity are shown in Table 3-16.

Table 3-16. *Examples of Rounding Towards Negative Infinity*

Original Number	Available Number of Binary Points	Rounded Number
1.1101	2	1.11
-0.1011	2	-0.11
0.1010	2	0.10
0.0011	2	0.00

Rounding Toward Nearest

In this rounding mode, the rounded result is the nearest representable floating-point number. In case of a tie, that is, if there are two representable floating-point numbers that are equally near to the original number, the result is the one that has its least significant bit as zero. In other words, in case of a tie, the rounded result is the even number. The system, which implements IEEE floating-point standards, has this mode as the default rounding mode. The IEEE standard states that the system should also allow users to select one of the other three rounding modes. Java uses this mode as the default rounding mode for floating-point numbers. Java does not allow users (that is, programmers) to select any other rounding modes. Some examples of rounding towards nearest are shown in Table 3-17.

Table 3-17. *Examples of Rounding Towards Nearest*

Original Number	Available Number of Binary Points	Rounded Number
1.1101	2	1.11
-0.1011	2	-0.11
0.1010	2	0.10
0.0011	2	0.01

IEEE Floating-Point Exceptions

The IEEE floating-point standard defines several exceptions that occur when the result of a floating-point operation is unacceptable. Exceptions can be ignored, in which case some default action is taken, such as returning a special value. When trapping is enabled for an exception, an error is signaled whenever that exception occurs. Floating-point operations can lead to any of the following five types of floating point exceptions:

- Division by zero exception
- Invalid operation exception
- Overflow exception
- Underflow exception
- Inexact exception

Division by Zero Exception

A division by zero exception occurs when a non-zero number is divided by a floating-point zero. If no trap handler is installed, infinity of appropriate sign is delivered as the result.

Invalid Operation Exception

An invalid operation exception occurs when the operand is invalid for an operation being performed. If no trap handler is installed, a quiet NaN is delivered as the result. The following are some of the operations that raise an invalid exception:

- Square root of a negative number
- Division of zero by zero or of infinity by infinity
- Multiplication of zero and infinity
- Any operation on a signaling NaN
- Subtracting infinity from infinity
- When a quiet NaN is compared with the > or < relational operators

Overflow Exception

An overflow exception occurs when the result of a floating-point operation is too large in magnitude to fit in the intended destination format. For example, when you multiply Float.MAX_VALUE by 2 and try to store the result in a float variable. If no trap handler is installed, the result to be delivered depends on the rounding mode and the sign of the intermediate result.

- If the rounding mode is rounding toward zero, the result of overflow is the largest finite number that can be represented in that format. The sign of the result is same as the sign of the intermediate result.
- If the rounding mode is rounding toward positive infinity, the negative overflow results in the most negative finite number for that format and the positive overflow results in the most positive finite number for that format.
- If the rounding mode is rounding toward negative infinity, the negative overflow results in negative infinity and the positive overflow results in the most positive finite number for that format.
- If the rounding mode is rounding toward nearest, the overflow results in infinity. The sign of the result is same as the sign of the intermediate result.

However, if trap handler is installed, the result delivered to the trap handler in case of overflow is determined as follows: the infinitely precise result is divided by 2^t and rounded before delivering it to the trap handler. The value of t is 192 for single-precision format, 1536 for double-precision format, and $3 \times 2^{n-1}$ for extended format, where n is the number of bits used to represent the exponent.

Underflow Exception

The underflow exception occurs when the result of an operation is too small to be represented as a normalized float in its format. If trapping is enabled, the floating-point-underflow exception is signaled. Otherwise, the operation results in a denormalized float or zero. Underflow can be abrupt or gradual. If the result of an operation is less than the minimum value that can be represented in normalized form in the format, the result could be delivered as zero or a denormalized number. In case of an abrupt underflow, the result is zero. In case of a gradual underflow, the result is a denormalized number. The IEEE default is gradual underflow (denormalized numbers). Java supports gradual underflow.

Inexact Exception

The inexact exception is signaled if the rounded result of an operation is not identical to the infinitely precise result. Inexact exceptions are quite common. 1.0/3.0 is an inexact operation. Inexact exceptions also occur when the operation overflows without an overflow trap.

Java and IEEE Floating-Point Standards

Java follows a subset of the IEEE-754 standard. The following are some of the differences between the IEEE floating-point standard and their Java implementations:

- Java does not signal the IEEE exceptions.

- Java has no signaling NaN.

- Java uses the rounding toward nearest mode to round the inexact results. However, Java rounds towards zero when converting a floating value to an integer. Java does not provide the user-selectable rounding modes for floating-point computations: up, down, or towards zero.

- IEEE defines $(2^{24} - 2)$ NaNs for single-precision format and $(2^{53} - 2)$ NaNs for double-precision format. However, Java defines only one NaN for each of these two formats.

Table 3-18 lists the parameters for different IEEE formats.

Table 3-18. *Parameters for the IEEE Formats*

	Width in Bits	Exponent Width in bits	Precision	Maximum Exponent	Minimum Exponent	Exponent Bias
Single-precision	32	8	24	127	-126	127
Double-precision	64	11	53	1023	-1022	1023
Single-extended	>= 43	>= 11	>= 32	>= 1023	<= -1022	Unspecified
Double-extended	>= 79	>= 15	>= 64	>= 16383	<= -16382	Unspecified

Little-Endian and Big-Endian

These two terms are related to the direction of bytes in a word within CPU architecture. Computer memory is referenced by addresses that are positive integers. It is "natural" to store numbers with the least significant byte coming before the most significant byte in the computer memory. Sometimes computer designers prefer to use a reversed order version of this representation. The "natural" order, where less significant byte comes before more significant byte in memory, is called little-endian. Many vendors like IBM, CRAY, and Sun preferred the reverse order that, of course, is called big-endian. For example, the 32-bit hex value 0x45679812 would be stored in memory as follows:

```
Address         00  01  02  03
-------------------------------
Little-endian   12  98  67  45
Big-endian      45  67  98  12
```

Difference in endian-ness can be a problem when transferring data between two machines. Table 3-19 lists some vendors, their `float` type, and the endian-ness on their machines.

Table 3-19. *Vendors, Float Types, and Endian-ness*

Vendor	Float Type	Endian-ness
ALPHA	DEC/IEEE	Little-endian
IBM	IBM	Big-endian
MAC	IEEE	Big-endian
SUN	IEEE	Big-endian
VAX	DEC	Little-endian
PC	IEEE	Little-endian

Everything in Java binary format files is stored in big-endian order. This is sometimes called network order. This means that if you use only Java, all files are done the same way on all platforms: Mac, PC, UNIX, etc. You can freely exchange binary data electronically without any concerns about endian-ness. The problem comes when you must exchange data files with some program not written in Java that uses little-endian order, most commonly a program written in C. Some platforms use big-endian order internally (Mac, IBM 390); some uses little-endian order (Intel). Java hides that internal endian-ness from you.

Summary

Every value in Java has a data type. Java supports two kinds of data types: primitive data types and reference data types. Primitive data types represent atomic, indivisible values. Java has eight Numeric data types: `byte`, `short`, `int`, `long`, `float`, `double`, `char`, and `boolean`. Literals of primitive data types are constants. Reference data types represent references of objects in memory. Java is a statically typed programming language. That is, it checks the data types of all values at compile time.

CHAPTER 4

■ ■ ■

Operators

In this chapter, you will learn:

- What operators are

- The different types of operators available in Java

- Operator precedence, which determines the order in which operators are evaluated when multiple operators are used in the same expression

What Is an Operator?

An operator is a symbol that performs a specific kind of operation on one, two, or three operands, and produces a result. The type of the operator and its operands determines the kind of operation performed on the operands and the type of the result produced. Operators in Java can be categorized based on two criteria:

- The number of operands they operate on

- The type of operation they perform on the operands

There are three types of operators based on the number of operands. An operator is called a unary, binary, or ternary operator based on the number of operands. If an operator takes one operand, it called a unary operator; if it takes two operands, it called a binary operator; if it takes three operands, it called a ternary operator.

A unary operator can use postfix or prefix notation. In the postfix notation, the unary operator appears after its operand.

```
operand operator  // Postfix notation
```

For example,

```
num++; // num is an operand and ++ is a unary Java operator
```

In a prefix notation, the unary operator appears before its operand.

```
operator operand  // Prefix notation
```

For example,

```
++num;  // ++ is a Java unary operator and num is an operand
```

A binary operator uses infix notation. The operator appears in between the two operands.

```
operand1 operator operand2  // Infix notation
```

For example,

```
10 + 15;  // 10 is operand1, + is a binary operator, and 15 is operand2
```

Like a binary operator, a ternary operator uses infix notation.

```
operand1 operator1 operand2 operator2 operand3 // Infix notation
```

Here, operator1 and operator2 make a ternary operator.
For example,

```
/* isSunday is the first operand, ? is the first part of ternary operator, holiday is the second
operand, : is the second part of ternary operator, noHoliday is the third operand
*/
isSunday ? holiday : noHoliday;
```

An operator is called an arithmetic operator, a relational operator, a logical operator, or a bitwise operator, depending on the kind of operation it performs on its operands. Java has a big list of operators. This chapter discusses most of the Java operators. Some of the operators will be discussed in later chapters.

Assignment Operator (=)

An assignment operator (=) is used to assign a value to a variable. It is a binary operator. It takes two operands. The value of the right-hand operand is assigned to the left-hand operand. The left-hand operand must be a variable. For example,

```
int num;
num = 25;
```

Here, num = 25 uses the assignment operator =. In this example, 25 is the right-hand operand. num is the left-hand operand, which is a variable of type int.

Java ensures that the value of the right-hand operand of the assignment operator is assignment compatible to the data type of the left-hand operand. Otherwise, a compile-time error occurs. In case of reference variables, you may be able to compile the source code and get a runtime error if the object represented by the right-hand operand is not assignment compatible to the reference variable as the left-hand operand. For example, the value of type byte, short, and char are assignment compatible to int data type, and hence the following snippet of code is valid:

```
byte b = 5;
char c = 'a';
short s = -200;
int i = 10;
i = b; // Ok. byte b is assignment compatible to int i
i = c; // Ok. char c is assignment compatible to int i
i = s; // Ok. short s is assignment compatible to int i
```

However, long to int and float to int assignments are not compatible and hence the following snippet of code generates compile-time errors:

```
long big = 524L;
float f = 1.19F;
int i = 15;
i = big; // A compile-time error. long to int, assignment incompatible
i = f;   // A compile-time error. float to int, assignment incompatible
```

In such a case where the right-hand operand's value is not assignment compatible with the left-hand variable's data type, the value of the right-hand operand must be cast to appropriate type. The above pieces of invalid code, which use assignment operators, can be rewritten with cast as follows:

```
i = (int)big; // Ok
i = (int)f;   // Ok
```

An expression is a series of variables, operators, and method calls, constructed according to the syntax of the Java programming language that evaluates to a single value. For example, num = 25 is an expression. The expression, which uses the assignment operator, also has a value. The value of the expression is equal to the value of the right-hand operand. Consider the following piece of code, assuming that num is an int variable:

```
num = 25;
```

Here, num = 25 is called an expression and num = 25; is called a statement. The expression num = 25 does two things.

- Assigns the value 25 to the variable num.

- Produces a value 25, which is equal to the value of the right-hand operand of the assignment operator.

The second effect (producing a value) of using the assignment operator in an expression may seem strange at this point. You may wonder what happens to the value 25 produced by the expression num = 25. Do you ever use the value returned by an expression? The answer is yes. You do use the value returned by an expression. Consider the following expression, which uses chained assignment operators, assuming that num1, and num2 are int variables:

```
num1 = num2 = 25;
```

What happens when the above piece of code is executed? First, the part of the expression num2 = 25 is executed. As mentioned earlier, there will be two effects of this execution:

- It will assign a value of 25 to num2.

- It will produce a value of 25. In other words, you can say that after assigning the value 25 to num2, the expression num2 = 25 is replaced by a value 25, which changes the main expression num1 = num2 = 25 to num1 = 25.

Now, the expression num1 = 25 is executed and the value 25 is assigned to num1 and the value produced, which is 25, is ignored. This way, you can assign the same value to more than one variable in a single expression. There can be any number of variables used in such a chained assignment expression. For example,

```
num1 = num2 = num3 = num4 = num5 = num6 = 219;
```

Suppose that there are two int variables, num1 and num2. The following assignment, num1 = num2, assigns the value 200 stored in num2 to num1:

```
int num1 = 100; // num1 is 100
int num2 = 200; // num2 is 200
num1 = num2; // num1 is 200. num2 is 200
num2 = 500;  // num2 is 500. num1 is still 200
```

When you say num1 = num2, the value stored in num2 is copied to num1, and both num1 and num2 maintain their own copy of the same value 200. Later on, when num2 = 500 is executed, the value of only num2 changes to 500. But the value of num1 remains the same: 200. Now, suppose there are two reference variable, ref1 and ref2, which refer to two different objects of the same class. If you write

```
Object ref1 = new Object(); // An object
Object ref2 = new Object(); // An object
ref1 = ref2;
```

the effect of the expression ref1 = ref2 is that both reference variables, ref1 and ref2, now refer to the same object in memory: the object that was being referred to by ref2. After this assignment, both reference variables, ref1 and ref2, are equally capable of manipulating the object. The changes made to the object in memory by reference variable ref1 will be observed by ref2 also and vice versa. The chapter on classes and objects discusses more about reference variable assignments.

Declaration, Initialization, and Assignment

Before a variable of any type is used in a Java program, it must be declared and must have a value assigned to it. Suppose you want to use an int variable named num1. First, you must declare it.

```
int num1; // Declaration of a variable num1
```

A value can be assigned to a variable after it is declared or at the time of declaration itself. When a value is assigned to a variable after it has been declared, it is known as assignment. The following piece of code declares an int variable num2 and assigns 50 to it:

```
int num2;   // Declaration of a variable num2
num2 = 50;  // Assignment
```

When a value is assigned to a variable at the time of declaration itself, it is known as initialization. The following code declares an int variable num3 and initializes it to a value 100:

```
int num3 = 100; // Declaration of variable num3 and its initialization
```

You can declare more than one variable of the same type in one declaration by separating each variable name by a comma.

```
// Declaration of three variables num1, num2 and num3 of type int
int num1, num2, num3;
```

You can also declare more than one variable in one declaration, and initialize some or all.

```
// Declaration of variables num1, num2 and num3. Initialization of only num1 and num3
int num1 = 10, num2, num3 = 200;

// Declaration and initialization of variables num1, num2 and num3
int num1 = 10, num2 = 20, num3 = 30;
```

Java will not let you use a variable unless it has been assigned a value either through the process of initialization or assignment. Java implicitly initializes variables declared in a particular context. Variables declared in other contexts must be initialized, or assigned a value, before they are used, if Java does not initialize them implicitly. I will discuss the implicit initialization of a variable by Java in the chapter on classes and objects. It is a good programming practice to initialize a variable at the time of its declaration.

Arithmetic Operators

Table 4-1 lists all arithmetic operators in Java. All operators listed in Table 4-1 can only be used with numeric type operands. That is, both operands to arithmetic operators must be one of types byte, short, char, int, long, float, and double. These operators cannot have operands of boolean primitive type and reference type. The following sections describe arithmetic operators in detail.

Table 4-1. *List of Arithmetic Operators in Java*

Operators	Description	Type	Usage	Result
+	Addition	Binary	2 + 5	7
-	Subtraction	Binary	5 - 2	3
+	Unary plus	Unary	+5	Positive five. Same as 5
-	Unary minus	Unary	-5	Negative of five
*	Multiplication	Binary	5 * 3	15
/	Division	Binary	5 / 2	2
			6 / 2	3
			5.0 / 2.0	2.5
			6.0 / 2.0	3.0
%	Modulus	Binary	5 % 3	2
++	Increment	Unary	num++	Evaluates to the value of num, increments num by 1.
--	Decrement	Unary	num--	Evaluates to the value of num, decrements num by 1.
+=	Arithmetic compound-assignment	Binary	num += 5	Adds 5 to the value of num and assigns the result to num. If num is 10, the new value of num will be 15.

(continued)

Table 4-1. (*continued*)

Operators	Description	Type	Usage	Result
-=	Arithmetic compound assignment	Binary	num -= 3	Subtracts 3 from the value of num and assigns the result to num. If num is 10, the new value of num will be 7.
*=	Arithmetic compound assignment	Binary	num *= 15	Multiplies 15 to the value of num and assigns the result to num. If num is 10, the new value of num will be 150.
/=	Arithmetic compound assignment	Binary	num /= 5	Divides the value of num by 5 and assigns the result to num. If num is 10, the new value of num will be 2.
%=	Arithmetic compound assignment	Binary	num %= 5	Calculates the remainder of num divided by 5 and assigns the result to num. If num is 12, the new value of num will be 2.

Addition Operator (+)

The addition operator (+) is used in the form

```
operand1 + operand2
```

The addition arithmetic operator (+) is used to add two numeric values represented by the two operands, for example, 5 + 3 results in 8. The operands may be any numeric literals, numeric variables, numeric expressions, or method calls. Every expression involving the addition operator has a data type. The data type of the expression is determined according to one of the four rules:

- If one of the operands is the data type double, the other operand is converted to the double data type and the whole expression is of type double. Otherwise,

- If one of the operands is the data type float, the other operand is converted to the float data type and the whole expression is of type float. Otherwise,

- If one of the operands is the data type long, the other operand is converted to the long data type and the whole expression is of type long. Otherwise,

- If none of the above three rules applies, all operands are converted to int, provided they are not already of type int, and the whole expression is of type int.

These rules have some important implications. Let's consider a byte variable b1, which is assigned a value of 5, as shown in the following piece of code:

```
byte b1;
b1 = 5;
```

You get a compile-time error when you try to assign the same value 5 to a byte variable b1, as shown in the following snippet of code:

```
byte b1;
byte b2 = 2;
byte b3 = 3;
b1 = b2 + b3; // A compile-time error. Trying to assign 5 to b1
```

Why does the above snippet of code result in a compile-time error? Do the expressions b1 = 5 and b1 = b2 + b3 not have the same effect of assigning 5 to the variable b1? Yes, the effect would be the same. However, the rules that govern the assignment operation are different in two cases. In the expression b1 = 5, the assignment is governed by the rule that any int literal between -128 and 127 can be assigned to a byte variable. Because 5 is between -128 and 127, the assignment of b1 = 5 is valid. The second assignment, b1 = b2 + b3, is governed by the fourth rule for the determination of the data type of an arithmetic expression, which uses addition operator. Because both operands in the expression b2 + b3 are of byte types, the operands b2 and b3 are first converted to the int data type, and then the expression b2 + b3 becomes of the int type. Because the data type of b1 is byte, which is smaller than the int data type of the expression b2 + b3, the assignment b1 = b2 + b3 (that is, int to byte) is not compatible, and that is the reason it generates an error. In such a case, you need to cast the result of the right-hand expression to the data type of the left-hand operand.

```
b1 = (byte)(b2 + b3); // Ok now
```

Beginners may try to write the above statement of code like so:

```
b1 = (byte) b2 + b3; // An error again
```

The two expressions (byte)(b2 + b3) and (byte)b2 + b3 are not the same. In the expression (byte) (b2 + b3), first b2 and b3 are promoted to int data type, and then an addition is performed, which results in a value 5 of the int data type. Then, the int value 5 is cast to byte and assigned to b1.

In the expression (byte)b2 + b3, first, b2 is cast to byte. Note that this cast is redundant since b2 is already of type byte; both b2 and b3 are promoted to int data type; and the whole expression of (byte)b2 + b3 is of type int. Since int to byte assignment is not permitted, the expression would not compile.

The error produced by the second expression, (byte) b2 + b3, raises an interesting question. Why did Java not first compute b2 + b3 in (byte)b2 + b3 and then applied (byte) to the result? Because there were two operations to be done, one being the cast to byte and another being the addition of b2 and b3, Java did the cast on b2 first and the addition second. The decision to perform the cast first followed by the addition was not arbitrary. Each operator in Java has a precedence order. The operator, which has higher precedence, is evaluated first before the operators having lower precedence order. The cast operator has higher precedence than the addition operator. This is the reason that (byte)b2 was evaluated first in (byte)b2 + b3. You can always override the precedence of operators using parentheses; note how I overrode the precedence of the cast operator by using parentheses in expression (byte)(b2 + b3). Let's consider another example.

```
byte b1;
b1 = 3 + 2; // Will this line of code compile?
```

Will the expression b1 = 3 + 2 compile? If you apply the fourth rule for determining the data type of this expression, it should not compile because 3 and 2 are int literals. The expression 3 + 2 is of type int. Because int is not assignment compatible to byte, the expression b1 = 3 + 2 should give an error. However, this assumption is wrong and the expression b1 = 3 + 2 will compile fine. In this case, the assignment proceeds as follows: the operands 3 and 2 are constants, so their values are known at compile time. Therefore, the compiler computes the result of the expression 3 + 2 at the time of compilation and replaces 3 + 2 by its result, 5. The expression b1 = 3 + 2 is replaced by b1 = 5 by the compiler. Now you can see why Java didn't give any errors for this expression. Because the int literal 5 is in the range of -128 to 127, b1 = 5 is a valid assignment according to the rule of assignment of int literal to a byte variable. However, if you try to write an expression as b1 = 127 + 10, certainly it would not compile because the result of 127 + 10 is 137 and is thus out of range for a byte data type.

Here are the final words on the data type conversion of the operands and the determination of the type of the expression involving the addition operator.

```
var = operand1 + operand2;
```

If operand1 and operand2 are compile-time constants, the result of operand1 + operand2 determines whether the above assignment is valid. If the result of operand1 + operand2 is in the range for the data type of the variable var, the above expression will compile. Otherwise, a compile-time error is generated. If either operand1 or operand2 is a variable (that is, the value of either operand1 or operand2 cannot be ascertained at compile time), the data type of the expression is determined according to one of the four rules discussed in the beginning of this section. The following are examples of correct and incorrect use of the addition operator. The comments along with the code indicate whether the user is correct.

```
byte b1 = 2;
byte b2 = 3;
short s1 = 100;
int i = 10;
int j = 12;
float f1 = 2.5F;
double d1 = 20.0;

b1 = 15 + 110; // Ok. 125 is in the range -128 and 127

// An error. i is promoted to int and i + 5 is of the data type int.
// int to byte assignment is not permitted
b1 = i + 5;

b1 = (byte)(i + 5); // OK

// An error. s1 is promoted to int and s1 + 2 is of the data type int.
// int to byte assignment is not permitted
b1 = s1 + 2;

// An error. b2 is promoted to float and f1 + b2 is of the data type float.
// float to byte assignment is not permitted
b1 = f1 + b2;

// An error. f1 is promoted to double and f1 + d1 is of the data type double
b1 = f1 + d1;

// Ok. i is promoted to float and i + f1 is of the data type float
f1 = i + f1;

// An error. i is promoted to double and i + d1 is of data type double.
// double to float assignment is not permitted
f1 = i + d1;

f1 = (float)(i + d1); // OK
```

```
// An error. 2.0 and 3.2 are of the type double. The result of 2.0 + 3.2 is 5.2,
// which is also of the type double. double to float assignment is not permitted.
f1 = 2.0 + 3.2;

// Ok. 2.0F and 3.2F are of the type float. The result of 2.0F + 3.2F,
// which is 5.2F, is of the type float.
f1 = 2.0F + 3.2F;

// Ok. j is promoted to float and f1 + j is of the data type float.
// float to double assignment is permitted.
d1 = f1 + j;
```

Subtraction Operator (-)

The subtraction operator (-) is used in the form

```
operand1 - operand2
```

The subtraction operator is used to compute the difference of two numbers, for example 5 - 3 results in 2. All rules that I discussed about the numeric data conversion of the operands and the determination of the data type of the expression involving the addition operator are also applicable for an expression involving subtraction operator. The following are some examples of using the subtraction operator:

```
byte b1 = 5;
int i = 100;
float f1 = 2.5F;
double d1 = 15.45;

// Ok. 200 - 173 will be replaced by 27.
// b1 = 27 is ok, because 27 is in the range -128 and 127
b1 = 200 - 173;

// An error. i - 27 is of the type int. int to byte assignment is not allowed
b1 = i - 27;

b1 = (byte)(i -27);  // OK
```

Multiplication Operator (*)

The multiplication operator (*) is used in the form

```
operand1 * operand2
```

The multiplication operator is used to compute the product of two numbers, for example, 7 * 3 results in 21. All rules that I discussed about the numeric data conversion of the operands and the determination of the data type of the expression involving the addition operator are also applicable for an expression involving the multiplication operator. The following are some examples of using the multiplication operator:

```
byte b2 = 5;
int i2 = 10;
float f2 = 2.5F;
double d2 = 15.45;
```

107

```
// Ok. 20 * 6 will be replaced by 120
// b2 = 120 is ok, because 120 is in the range -128 and 127
b2 = 20 * 6;

// An error. i2 * 12 is of the type int. int to byte assignment is not allowed.
b2 = i2 * 12;

b2 = (byte)(i2 * 12); // OK

// Ok. i2 * b2 is of the type int and int to float assignment is allowed
f2 = i2 * b2;

// Error. d2 * i2 is of type double and double to float assignment is not allowed
f2 = d2 * i2;

f2 = (float)(d2 * i2); // Ok
```

Division Operator (/)

The division operator (/) is used in the form

```
operand1 / operand2
```

The division operator is used to compute the quotient of two numbers, for example 5.0/2.0 results in 2.5. All the rules I discussed about the numeric data conversion of the operands and the determination of the data type of the expression involving the addition operator are also valid for an expression involving the division operator.

There are two types of division:

- Integer division
- Floating-point division

If both the operands of the division operator are integers, that is, byte, short, char, int, or long, the usual division operation is carried out and the result is truncated towards zero to represent an integer. For example, if you write an expression 5/2, the division yields 2.5; the fractional part 0.5 is ignored; and the result is 2. The following examples illustrate the integer division:

```
int num;
num = 5/2; // Assigns 2 to num
num = 5/3; // Assigns 1 to num
num = 5/4; // Assigns 1 to num
num = 5/5; // Assigns 1 to num
num = 5/6; // Assigns 0 to num
num = 5/7; // Assigns 0 to num
```

In all of the above examples, the value assigned to the variable num is an integer. The result is an integer in all cases not because the data type of variable num is int. The result is integer because both the operands of the division operator are integers. Because the data types of both operands are int, the whole expression 5/3 is of type int. Because the fractional portion (e.g. 0.5, 0.034) cannot be stored in an int data type, the fractional portion is ignored and the result is always an integer. If either or both of the operands of the division operator are float or double type, floating-point division is performed and the result is not truncated. For example,

```
float f1;

// 15.0F and 4.0F are of float type. So, the expression 15.0F/4.0F is of the type float.
// The result 3.75F is assigned to f1.
f1 = 15.0F/4.0F;

// 15 is of type int and 4.0F is of type float. The expression 15/4.0F is of type float.
// The result 3.75F is assigned to f1.
f1 = 15/4.0F;

// An error. 15.0 is of the type double and 4.0F is of the type float.
// The expression 15.0/4.0F is of type double. The result 3.75 is of the
// type double and cannot be assigned to f1.
f1 = 15.0/4.0F;

f1 = (float)(15.0/4.0F); // Ok. 3.75F is assigned to f1

// 15 and 4 are of the type int. The expression 15/4 is of type int.
// An integer division is performed. The result 3 is assigned to f1,
// because int to float assignment is allowed
f1 = 15/4;
```

What happens when you try to divide a number (integer or floating-point) by 0 (zero)? The result of dividing a number by zero depends on the type of division. If an integer division is performed on the number, dividing by zero results in a runtime error. If you write expression 3/0 in a Java program, it compiles fine, but it gives error when it is executed at runtime. For example,

```
int i = 2;
int j = 5;
int k = 0;
i = j/k;  // A runtime error. Divide by zero
i = 0/0;  // A runtime error. Divide by zero
```

If either operand of the division operator is a floating-point number, a floating-point division is performed and the result of dividing the number by zero is not an error. If the dividend (in 7/2, 7 is the dividend and 2 is the divisor) is a non-zero number in a floating-point divide-by-zero operation, the result is either positive infinity or a negative infinity. If the dividend is a floating-point zero (e.g. 0.0 or 0,0F), the result is NaN. For example,

```
float f1 = 2.5F;
double d1 = 5.6;

f1 = 5.0F/0.0F;    // Float.POSITIVE_INFINITY is assigned to f1
f1 = -5.0F/0.0F;   // Float.NEGATIVE_INFINITY is assigned to f1
f1 = -5.0F/-0.0F;  // Float.POSITIVE_INFINITY is assigned to f1
f1 = 5.0F/-0.0F;   // Float.NEGATIVE_INFINITY is assigned to f1
d1 = 5.0/0.0;      // Double.POSITIVE_INFINITY is assigned to d1
d1 = -5.0/0.0;     // Double.NEGATIVE_INFINITY is assigned to d1
d1 = -5.0/-0.0;    // Double.POSITIVE_INFINITY is assigned to d1
d1 = 5.0/-0.0;     // Double.NEGATIVE_INFINITY is assigned to d1
```

```
// 5.0F is of the type float and 0 is of the type int. 5.0F/0 is of type float.
// Float.POSITIVE_INFINITY is assigned to f1
f1 = 5.0F/0;

// A compile-time error. 5.0F is of the type float and 0.0 is of the type double
// 5.0F/0.0 is of the type double. double to float assignment is not allowed.
f1 = 5.0F/0.0;

f1 = (float)(5.0F/0.0); // f1 is assigned Float.POSITIVE_INFINITY
f1 = 0.0F/0.0F;  // Assigns Float.NaN to f1
d1 = 0.0/0.0;    // Assigns Double.NaN to d1
d1 = -0.0/0.0;   // Assigns Double.NaN to d1
```

Modulus Operator (%)

The modulus operator (%) is used in the form

```
operand1 % operand2
```

The modulus operator is also known as the remainder operator. The modulus operator performs a division on the left-hand operand by its right-hand operand and returns the remainder of the division, for example, 7%5 evaluates to 2. All rules about the numeric data conversion of the operands and the determination of the data type of the expression involving the addition operator are also applicable for expressions involving the modulus operator. Because the use of the modulus operator involves a division operation, there are some special rules to determine the result of a modulus operation.

If both operands of the modulus operator are integers, the following rules are applied to compute the result.

Rule #1

It is a runtime error if the right-hand operand is zero. For example,

```
int num;
num = 15 % 0; // A runtime error
```

Rule #2

If the right-hand operand is not zero, the sign of the result is the same as the sign of the left-hand operand. For example,

```
int num;
num = 15 % 6;    // Assigns 3 to num
num = -15 % 6;   // Assigns -3 to num
num = 15 % -6;   // Assigns 3 to num
num = -15 % -6;  // Assigns -3 to num because left-hand operand is -15, which is negative
num = 5 % 7;     // Assigns 5 to num
num = 0 % 7;     // Assigns 0 to num
```

If either operand of the modulus operator is a floating-point number, the following rules are applied to compute the result.

Rule #1

The operation never results in an error even if the right-hand operand is a floating-point zero.

Rule #2

The result is NaN if either operand is NaN. For example,

```
float f1;
double d1;
f1 = Float.NaN % 10.5F;     // Assigns Float.NaN to f1
f1 = 20.0F % Float.NaN;     // Assigns Float.NaN to f1
f1 = Float.NaN % Float.NaN; // Assigns Float.NaN to f1

// A compile-time error. The expression is of the type double.
// double to float assignment is not allowed
f1 = Float.NaN % Double.NaN;

d1 = Float.NaN % Double.NaN; // Assigns Double.NaN to d1
```

Rule #3

If the right-hand operand is zero, the result is NaN. For example,

```
float f1;
f1 = 15.0F % 0.0F; // Assigns Float.NaN to f1
```

Rule #4

If the left-hand operand is infinity, the result is NaN. For example,

```
float f1;
f1 = Float.POSITIVE_INFINITY % 2.1F; // Assigns Float.NaN to f1
```

Rule #5

If none of the above rules apply, the modulus operator returns the remainder of the division of the left-hand operand and the right-hand operand. The sign of the result is the same as the sign of the left-hand operand. For example,

```
float f1;
double d1;
f1 = 15.5F % 6.5F; // Assigns 2.5F to f1
d1 = 5.5 % 15.65;  // Assigns 5.5 to d1
d1 = 0.0 % 3.78;   // Assigns 0.0 to d1
d1 = 85.0 % Double.POSITIVE_INFINITY;  // Assigns 85.0 to d1
d1 = -85.0 % Double.POSITIVE_INFINITY; // Assigns -85.0 to d1
d1 = 85.0 % Double.NEGATIVE_INFINITY;  // Assigns 85.0 to d1
d1 = -85.0 % Double.NEGATIVE_INFINITY; // Assigns -85.0 to d1
```

Unary Plus Operator (+)

The unary plus operator (+) is used in the form

+operand

The operand must be a primitive numeric type. If the operand is of the byte, short, or char type, the unary plus operator promotes it to int type. Otherwise, there is no effect of using this operator. For example, if there is an int variable num, which has a value of 5, +num still has the same value of 5. The following example illustrates its use:

```
byte b1 = 10;
byte b2 = +5;

b1 = b2;  // Ok. byte to byte assignment

// A compile-time error. b2 is of the type byte. But, use of the unary plus operator on
// b2 promoted its type to int. Therefore, +b2 is of the type int.
// int (+b2) to byte (b1) assignment is not allowed.
b1 = +b2;

b1 = (byte) +b2; // Ok
```

Unary Minus Operator (-)

The unary minus operator (-) is used in the form

-operand

The unary minus operator arithmetically negates the value of its operand. The operand must be a primitive numeric type. If the type of the operand is byte, short, or char, it promotes the operand to the int type. The following example illustrates its use:

```
byte b1 = 10;
byte b2 = -5;

b1 = b2;  // Ok. byte to byte assignment

// A compile-time error. b2 is of the type byte. But, use of unary minus operator (-) on
// b2 promoted its type to int. Therefore, -b2 is of type int.
// int (-b2) to byte (b1) assignment is not allowed.
b1 = -b2;

b1 = (byte) -b2; // Ok
```

Compound Arithmetic Assignment Operators

Each of the five basic arithmetic operators (+, -, *, /, and %) has a corresponding compound arithmetic assignment operator. These operators can be explained better with an example. Suppose you have two variables, num1 and num2.

```
int num1 = 100;
byte num2 = 15;
```

If you want to add the value of num1 to num2, you would write code as

```
num2 = (byte)(num2 + num1);
```

You need to cast the result of num2 + num1 to byte because the data type of the expression is int. The same effect can be rewritten using the compound arithmetic operator (+=), as follows:

```
num2 += num1; // Adds the value of num1 to num2
```

A compound arithmetic assignment operator is used in the following form:

```
operand1 op= operand2
```

Here, op is one of the arithmetic operators (+, -, *, /, and %). operand1 and operand2 are of primitive numeric data types, where operand1 must be a variable. The above expression is equivalent to the following expression:

```
operand1 = (Type of operand1) (operand1 op operand2)
```

For example,

```
int i = 100;
i += 5.5; // Assigns 105 to i
```

is equivalent to

```
i = (int)(i + 5.5); // Assigns 105 to i
```

There are two advantages of using the compound arithmetic assignment operators.

- The operand1 is evaluated only once. For example, in i += 5.5, the variable i is evaluated only once, whereas in i = (int) (i + 5.5), the variable i is evaluated twice.

- The result is automatically cast to the type of operand1 before assignment. The cast may result in a narrowing conversion or an identity conversion. In the above example, the cast is a narrowing conversion. The expression i + 5.5 is of the type double and the result of this expression is cast to int. So, the result of double 105.5 is converted to int 105. If you write an expression like i += 5, the equivalent expression will be i = (int)(i + 5). Because the type of the expression i + 5 is already int, the casting the result to int again is an identity conversion.

The compound assignment operator += can also be applied to String variables. In such cases, the operand1 must be of type String and the operand2 may be of any type including boolean. For example,

```
String str1 = "Hello";
str1 = str1 + 100;  // Assigns "Hello100" to str1
```

can be rewritten as

```
str1 += 100; // Assigns "Hello100" to str1
```

■ **Tip**   Of the compound operators, only the += operator can be used with a String left-hand operand.

The following are examples of using the compound assignment operators. In the examples, each use of a compound assignment operator is independent of the effects of its previous uses. In all cases, it has been assumed that the values of the variables remain the same, as the values assigned to them at the time of their declarations.

```
int i = 110;
float f = 120.2F;
byte b = 5;
String str = "Hello";
boolean b1 = true;

i += 10;  // Assigns 120 to i

// A compile-time error. boolean type cannot be used with +=
// unless left-hand operand (here i) is a String variable
i += b1;

i -= 15;  // Assigns 95 to i. Assuming i was 110
i *= 2;   // Assigns 220 to i. Assuming i was 110
i /= 2;   // Assigns 55 to i. Assuming i was 110
i /= 0;   // A runtime error . Division by zero error
f /= 0.0; // Assigns Float.POSITIVE_INFINITY to f
i %= 3;   // Assigns 2 to i. Assuming i is 110

str += " How are you?"; // Assigns "Hello How are you?" to str
str += f;  // Assigns "Hello120.2" to str. Assuming  str was "Hello"
b += f;    // Assigns 125 to b. Assuming b was 5, f was 120.2
str += b1; // Assigns "Hellotrue" to str. Assuming str was "Hello"
```

Increment (++) and Decrement (--) Operators

The increment operator (++) is used with a variable of numeric data type to increment its value by 1, whereas the decrement operator (--) is used to decrement the value by 1. In this section, I will discuss only the increment operator. The same discussion applies to the decrement operator with the only difference being it will decrement the value by 1 instead of increment it by 1.

Suppose you declare an int variable called i.

```
int i = 100;
```

To increment the value of i by 1, you can use one of the four following expressions:

```
i = i + 1; // Assigns 101 to i
i += 1;    // Assigns 101 to i
i++;       // Assigns 101 to i
++i;
```

The increment operator ++ can also be used in a more complex expression as

```
int i = 100;
int j = 50;
j = i++ + 15;  // Assigns 115 to j and i becomes 101
```

The expression i++ + 15 is evaluated as follows:

- The value of i is evaluated and the right-hand expression becomes 100 + 15.

- The value of i in memory is incremented by 1. So, at this stage the value of the variable i in memory is 101.

- The expression 100 + 15 is evaluated and the result 115 is assigned to j.

There are two kinds of increment operators:

- Post-fix increment operator, for example, i++

- Pre-fix increment operator, for example, ++i

When ++ appears after its operand, it is called a post-fix increment operator. When ++ appears before its operand, it is called a pre-fix increment operator. The only difference in post-fix and pre-fix increment operators is the order in which it uses the current value of its operand and the increment in its operand's value. The post-fix increment uses the current value of its operand first, and then increments the operand's value, as you saw in the expression j = i++ + 15. Because i++ uses a post-fix increment operator, first the current value of i is used to compute the value of expression i++ + 15 (e.g. 100 + 15). The value assigned to j is 115. And then the value of i is incremented by 1.

The result would be different if the above expression is rewritten using a pre-fix increment operator.

```
int i = 100;
int j = 50;
j = ++i + 15;  // i becomes 101 and assigns 116 to j
```

In this case, the expression ++i + 15 is evaluated as follows:

- Because ++i uses a pre-fix increment operator, first the value of i is incremented in memory by 1. Therefore, the value of i is 101.

- The current value of i, which is 101, is used in the expression and the expression becomes 101 + 15.

- The expression 101 + 15 is evaluated and the result 116 is assigned to j.

Note that after evaluation of both expressions i++ + 15 and ++i + 15, the value of i is the same, which is 101. However, the values assigned to j differ. If you are using the increment operator ++ in a simple expression as in i++ or ++i, you cannot observe any difference in using a post-fix or pre-fix operator.

Here is a puzzle for Java beginners. The puzzle includes the use of the increment operator as follows:

```
int i = 15;
i = i++; // What will be the value of i after this assignment?
```

What will be the value of i after i = i++ is executed? If your guess is 16, you are wrong. Here is the explanation of how the expression is evaluated.

- i++ is evaluated. Because i++ uses a post-fix increment operator, the current value of i is used in the expression. The current value of i is 15. The expression becomes i = 15.

- The value of i is incremented by 1 in memory as the second effect of i++. At this point, the value of i is 16 in memory.

- The expression i = 15 is evaluated and the value 15 is assigned to i. The value of the variable i in memory is 15 and that is the final value. In fact, variable i observed a value 16 in the previous step, but this step overwrote that value with 15. Therefore, the final value of the variable i after i = i++ is executed will be 15, not 16.

In the above example, the order of operations is important. It is important to note that in case of i++ the value of the variable i is incremented as soon as the current value of i is used in the expression. To make this point clearer, consider the following example:

```
int i = 10;
i = i++ + i;   // Assigns 21 to i
i = 10;
i = ++i + i++; // Assigns 22 to i
```

There are also post-fix and pre-fix decrement operators (e.g. i--, --i). The following are examples of using post-fix and pre-fix decrement operators:

```
int i = 15;
int j = 16;
i--;
--i;
i = 10;
i = i--;       // Assigns 10 to i
i = 10;
j = i-- + 10;  // Assigns 20 to j and 9 to i
i = 10;
j = --i + 10;  // Assigns 19 to j and 9 to i
```

There are two important points to remember about the use of increment and decrement operators.

- The operand of the increment and decrement operators must be a variable. For example, the expression 5++ is incorrect because ++ is being used with a constant.

- The result of the expression using ++ or -- operator is a value, not a variable. For example, i++ evaluates to a value, so you cannot use i++ as the left-hand of an assignment operator or where a variable is required.

String Concatenation Operator (+)

The + operator is overloaded. An operator is said to be overloaded if it is used to perform more than one function. So far, you have seen its use as an arithmetic addition operator to add two numbers. It can also be used to concatenate two strings. Two strings, such as "abc" and "xyz", can be concatenated using the + operator as "abc" + "xyz" to produce new string "abcxyz". The following is another example of a string concatenation:

```
String str1 = "Hello,";
String str2 = " Alekhya";
String str3 = str1 + str2; // Assigns "Hello, Alekhya" to str3
```

The string concatenation operator is also used to concatenate a primitive and a reference data type value to a string. I will discuss only concatenation of string and primitive data types in this section. When either operand of the + operator is a string, it performs string concatenation. When both operands of + are numeric, it performs number addition. Consider the following snippet of code:

```
int num = 26;
String str1 = "Alphabets";
String str2 = num + str1; // Assigns "26Alphabets" to str2
```

When the expression num + str1 is executed, the + operator acts as a string concatenation operator because its right-hand operand, str1, is a String. Before num and str1 are concatenated, num is replaced by its string representation, which is "26". Now, the expression becomes "26" + str1, which results in "26Alphabets". Table 4-2 lists the string representation of the values of the primitive data types.

Table 4-2. *String Representations of the Values of Primitive Data Types*

Data Type	Value	String Representation
int, short, byte, long	1678	"1678"
	0	"0"
char	'A'	"A"
	'\u0041' (Unicode escape sequence)	"A"
boolean	true	"true"
	false	"false"
float	2.5	"2.5"
	0.0F	"0.0"
	-0.0F	"-0.0"
	Float.POSITIVE_INFINITY	"Infinity"
	Float.NEGATIVE_INFINITY	"-Infinity"
	Float.NaN	"NaN"

(continued)

117

Table 4-2. (*continued*)

Data Type	Value	String Representation
double	89.12	"89.12"
	0.0	"0.0"
	-0.0	"-0.0"
	Double.POSITIVE_INFINITY	"Infinity"
	Double.NEGATIVE_INFINITY	"-Infinity"
	Double.NaN	"NaN"

If a String variable contains the null reference, the concatenation operator uses a string "null". The following examples illustrate the use of string representations of the values of primitive data types in string concatenation:

```
boolean b1 = true;
boolean b2 = false;
int num = 365;
double d = -0.0;
char c = 'A';
String str1;
String str2 = null;

str1 = b1 + " friends";  // Assigns "true friends" to str1
str1 = b2 + " identity"; // Assigns "false identity" to str1

// Assigns "null and void" to str1. Because str2 is null, it is replaced
// by a string "null" by the concatenation operator
str1 = str2 + " and void";

str1 = num + " days"; // Assigns "365 days" to str1
str1 = d + " zero";    // Assigns "-0.0 zero" to str1

str1 = Double.NaN + " is absurd"; // Assigns "NaN is absurd" to str1

str1 = c + " is a letter"; // Assigns "A is a letter" to str1
str1 = "This is " + b1;     // Assigns "This is true" to str1

// Assigns "Beyond Infinity" to str1
str1 = "Beyond " + Float.POSITIVE_INFINITY
```

It may be confusing to determine the result of an expression that uses more than one + operator and strings. What will be the result of the expression 12 + 15 + " men"? Will the result be "1215 men" or "27 men"? The key to finding the correct answer is to find which + is an arithmetic operator and which + is a string concatenation operator.

If both the operands are numeric, the + operator performs addition. If either operand is a string, the + operator performs string concatenation. The execution of an expression proceeds from left to right unless overridden by using parentheses. In the expression 12 + 15 + " men", the first + from the left performs addition on 12 and 15, which results in 27. After that, the expression reduces to 27 + " men". Now, the + operator performs a string concatenation because the right-hand operand, " men", is a string and it results in "27 men".

Consider the following piece of code:

```
int num1 = 12;
int num2 = 15;
String str1 = " men";
String str2;
```

You want to create a string of "1215 men" using the three variables (num1, num2, and str1) and the + operator. You want to assign the result to str2. The following is a first attempt:

```
str2 = num1 + num2 + str1;
```

This statement will assign "27 men" to str2.

Another solution is to place num2 + str1 in parentheses.

```
str2 = num1 + (num2 + str1); // Assigns "1215 men" to str2
```

The expression in parentheses is evaluated first. The expression (num2 + str1) is evaluated first to reduce the expression to num1 + "15 men", which in turn will evaluate to "1215 men".

Another option is to place an empty string in the beginning of the expression.

```
str2 = "" + num1 + num2 + str1; // Assigns "1215 men" to str1
```

In this case, "" + num1 is evaluated first, and it results in "12", which reduces the expression to "12" + num2 + str1. Now "12" + num2 is evaluated, which results in "1215". Now the expression is reduced to "1215" + " men", which results in a string "1215 men".

You may also place an empty string between num1 and num2 in the expression to get the same result.

```
str2 = num1 + "" + num2 + str1; // Assigns "1215 men" to str2
```

Sometimes the string concatenation is trickier than you think. Consider the following piece of code:

```
int num = 15;
boolean b = false;
String str1 = "faces";
String str2 = b + num + str1; // A compile-time error
```

The last line in this snippet of code will generate a compile-time error. What is wrong with the statement? You were expecting a string of "false15faces" to be assigned to str2, weren't you? Let's analyze the expression b + num + str1. Is the first + operator from left an arithmetic operator or a string concatenation operator? For a + operator to be a string concatenation operator, it is necessary that at least one of its operands is a string. Since neither b nor num is a string, the first + operator from the left in b + num + str1 is not a string concatenation operator. Is it an arithmetic addition operator? Its operands are of type boolean (b) and int (num). You have learned that an arithmetic addition operator (+) cannot have a boolean operand. The presence of a boolean operand in the expression b + num caused the compile-time error. A boolean cannot be added to a number. However, the + operator works on a boolean as a string concatenation operator if another operand is a string. To correct the above compile-time error, you can rewrite the expression in a number of ways, as shown:

```
str2 = b + (num + str1);    // Ok. Assigns "false15faces" to str2
str2 = "" + b + num + str1; // Ok. Assigns "false15faces" to str2
str2 = b + "" + num + str1; // Ok. Assigns "false15faces" to str2
```

You use the `println()` and `print()` methods to print a message on the standard output, as follows:

```
System.out.println("Prints a new line at the end of text");
System.out.print("Does not print a new line at the end of text");
```

If you use the `System.out.println()` method to print text to the console, after printing the text, it also prints a new line character at the end of the text. The only difference between using the `println()` and `print()` is that the former prints a new line at the end of the text, whereas the latter does not. The `println()` and `print()` methods are overloaded. Until now, you have seen their use only with string arguments. You can pass any Java data type argument to these two methods. The following snippet of code illustrates how to pass Java primitive types as arguments to these methods:

```
int num = 156;

// Prints 156 on the console
System.out.println(num);

// Prints Value of num = 156 on the console
System.out.println("Value of num = " + num);

// Prints a new line character on the console
System.out.println();
```

Listing 4-1 contains a complete program to demonstrate the use of arithmetic operators and the string concatenation operator.

Listing 4-1. An Example of Using Java Operators

```java
// ArithOperator.java
package com.jdojo.operator;

class ArithOperator {
        public static void main ( String[] args ) {
                int num = 120;
                double realNum = 25.5F;
                double veryBigNum = 25.8 / 0.0;
                double garbage = 0.0 / 0.0;
                boolean test = true;

                // Print the value of num
                System.out.println ("num = " + num);

                // Print the value of realNum
                System.out.println ("realNum = " + realNum);

                // Print the value of veryBigNum
                System.out.println ("veryBigNum = " + veryBigNum);

                // Print the value of garbage
                System.out.println ("garbage = " + garbage);
```

```
// Print the value of test
System.out.println ("test = " + test);

// Print the maximum value of int type
System.out.println ("Maximum int = " + Integer.MAX_VALUE);

// Print the maximum value of double type
System.out.println ("Maximum double = " + Double.MAX_VALUE);

// Print the sum of two numbers
System.out.println ("12.5 + 100 = " + (12.5 + 100));

// Print the difference of two numbers
System.out.println ("12.5 - 100 = " + (12.5 - 100));

// Print the multiplication of two numbers
System.out.println ("12.5 * 100 = " + (12.5 * 100));

// Print the result of division
System.out.println ("12.5 / 100 = " + (12.5 / 100));

// Print the result of modulus
System.out.println ("12.5 % 100 = " + (12.5 % 100));

// Print the result of string concatenation
System.out.println ("\"abc\" + \"xyz\" = " + "\"" + ("abc" + "xyz") + "\"");

        }
}
```

```
num = 120
realNum = 25.5
veryBigNum = Infinity
garbage = NaN
test = true
Maximum int = 2147483647
Maximum double = 1.7976931348623157E308
12.5 + 100 = 112.5
12.5 - 100 = -87.5
12.5 * 100 = 1250.0
12.5 / 100 = 0.125
12.5 % 100 = 12.5
"abc" + "xyz" = "abcxyz"
```

Relational Operators

All relational operators are binary operators. That is, they take two operands. The result produced by a relational operator is always a Boolean value true or false. Table 4-3 lists the relational operators available in Java.

Table 4-3. *List of Relational Operators in Java*

Operators	Meaning	Type	Usage	Result
==	Equal to	Binary	3 == 2	false
!=	Not equal to	Binary	3 != 2	true
>	Greater than	Binary	3 > 2	true
>=	Greater than or equal to	Binary	3 >= 2	true
<	Less than	Binary	3 < 2	false
<=	Less than or equal to	Binary	3 <= 2	false

Equality Operator (==)

The equality operator (==) is used in the form

```
operand1 == operand2
```

The equality operator is used to test two operands for equality. It uses the following rules:

- Both operands must be either primitive type or reference type. Mixed operands types are not allowed. Mixing the operands types results in a compile-time error.

- For primitive operands, it returns true if the both operands represent the same value; otherwise, it returns false. If both operands must be either numeric or boolean. A mix of numeric and boolean types is not allowed.

- For reference operands, it returns true if the both operands refer to the same object in memory; otherwise it returns false.

Suppose there is an int variable i.

```
int i = 10;
```

Now, i == 10 will test whether i is equal to 10 or not. Because i is equal to 10, the expression i == 10 will evaluate to true.

Let's consider another example.

```
int i;
int j;
int k;
boolean b;

i = j = k = 15;    // Assign 15 to i, j, and k
b = (i == j == k); // A compile-time error
```

In this example, you tried to test whether the three variables i, j and k have the same value, and the expression (i == j == k) resulted in an error. Why did you get the error? The expression (i == j == k) is evaluated as follows:

- First, i == j is evaluated in expression i == j == k. Since both i and j have the same value, which is 15, the expression i == j returns true.

- The first step reduced the expression i == j == k to true == k. This is an error because the operands of == operator are of boolean and int types. You cannot mix boolean and numeric types operands with the equality operator.

The following rules apply when the operands of the equality operator are floating-point types.

Rule #1

Both negative zero (-0.0) and positive zero (0.0) are considered equal. Recall that -0.0 and 0.0 are stored differently in memory.

```
double d1 = 0.0;
double d2 = -0.0;
boolean b = (d1 == d2); // Assigns true to b
```

Rule #2

A positive infinity is equal to another positive infinity. A negative infinity is equal to another negative infinity. However, a positive infinity is not equal to a negative infinity.

```
double d1 = Double.POSITIVE_INFINITY;
double d2 = Double.NEGATIVE_INFINITY;
boolean b1 = (d1 == d2); // Assigns false to b1
boolean b2 = (d1 == d1); // Assigns true to b2
```

Rule #3

If either operand is NaN, the equality test returns false.

```
double d1 = Double.NaN;
double d2 = 5.5;
boolean b = (d1 == d2); // Assigns false to b
```

Note that even if both the operands are NaN, the equality operator will return false.

```
d1 = Double.NaN;
d2 = Double.NaN;
b = (d1 == d2); // Assigns false to b
```

How do you test whether the value stored in a float or double variable is NaN? If you write the following piece of code to test for the value of a double variable d1 being NaN, it will always return false:

```
double d1 = Double.NaN;
boolean b = (d1 == Double.NaN); // Assigns false to b. Incorrect way
```

Float and Double classes have an isNaN() method, which accepts a float and a double argument, respectively. It returns true if the argument is NaN, Otherwise, it returns false. For example, to test if d1 is NaN, the above expression can be rewritten as shown:

```
double d1 = Double.NaN;

// Assigns true to b. Correct way to test for a NaN value
b = Double.isNaN(d1);
```

You should not use == operator to test two strings for equality. For example,

```
String str1 = new String("Hello");
String str2 = new String("Hello");
boolean b;

b = (str1 == str2); // Assigns false to b
```

The new operator always creates a new object in memory. Therefore, str1 and str2 refer to two different objects in memory and this is the reason that str1 == str2 evaluates to false. It is true that both String objects in memory have the same text. Whenever == operator is used with reference variables, it always compares the references of the objects its operands are referring to. To compare the text represented by the two String variables str1 and str2, you should use the equals() method of the String class, as shown:

```
// Assigns true to b because str1 and str2 have the same text of "Hello"
b = str1.equals(str2);

// Assigns true to b because str1 and str2 have the same text of "Hello"
b = str2.equals(str1);
```

I will discuss more about strings comparison in the chapter on Strings.

Inequality Operator (!=)

The inequality operator (!=) is used in the form

```
operand1 != operand2
```

The inequality operator returns true if operand1 and operand2 are not equal. Otherwise, it returns false. The rules for the data types of the operands of inequality (!=) operator are the same that of equality operator (==).

```
int i = 15;
int j = 10;
int k = 15;
boolean b;
b = (i != j); // Assigns true to b
b = (i != k); // Assigns false to b
b = (true != true);  // Assigns false to b
b = (true != false); // Assigns true to b
b = (false != true); // Assigns true to b
```

If either operand is NaN (float or double), inequality operator returns true. If d1 is a floating-point variable (double or float), d1 == d1 returns false and d1 != d1 returns true if and only if d1 is NaN.

Greater Than Operator (>)

The greater than operator (>) is used in the form

```
operand1 > operand2
```

The greater than operator returns true if the value of operand1 is greater than the value of operand2. Otherwise, it returns false. The greater than operator can be used only with primitive numeric data types. If either of the operand is NaN (float or double), it returns false.

```
int i = 10;
int j = 15;
double d1 = Double.NaN;
boolean b;

b = (i > j); // Assigns false to b
b = (j > i); // Assigns true to b

// A compile-time error. > cannot be used with boolean operands
b = (true > false);

b = ( d1 > Double.NaN ); // Assigns false to b

String str1 = "Hello";
String str2 = "How is Java?";

// A compile-time error. > cannot be used with reference type operands str1 and str2
b = (str1 > str2);
```

If you want to test if the number of characters in String str1 is greater than that of str2, you should use the length() method of the String class. The length() method of String class returns the number of characters in the string. For example,

```
i = str1.length(); // Assigns 5 to i. "Hello" has 5 characters
b = (str1.length() > str2.length()); // Assigns false to b
b = (str2.length() > str1.length()); // Assigns true to b
```

Greater Than or Equal to Operator (>=)

The greater than or equal to operator (>=) is used in the form

```
operand1 >= operand2
```

The greater than or equal to operator returns true if the value of operand1 is greater than or equal to the value of operand2. Otherwise, it returns false. The greater than or equal to operator can be used only with primitive numeric data types. If either of the operands is NaN (float or double), the greater than or equal to operator returns false.

```
int i = 10;
int j = 10;
boolean b;
b = (i >= j);  // Assigns true to b
b = (j >= i);  // Assigns true to b
```

Less Than Operator (<)

The less than operator (<) is used in the form

```
operand1 < operand2
```

The less than operator returns true if operand1 is less than operand2. Otherwise, it returns false. The operator can be used only with primitive numeric data types. If either operand is NaN (float or double), the less than operator returns false.

```
int i = 10;
int j = 15;
double d1 = Double.NaN;
boolean b;
b = (i < j);  // Assigns true to b
b = (j < i);  // Assigns false to b

// A compile-time error. < cannot be used with boolean operands
b = (true < false);

b = (d1 < Double.NaN); // Assigns false to b
```

Less Than or Equal to Operator (<=)

The less than or equal to operator (<=) is used in the form

```
operand1 <= operand2
```

The less than or equal to operator returns true if the value of operand1 is less than or equal to the value of operand2. Otherwise, it returns false. The operator can be used only with primitive numeric data types. If either of the operand is NaN (float or double), the less than or equal to operator returns false.

```
int i = 10;
int j = 10;
int k = 15;
boolean b;

b = (i <= j);  // Assigns true to b
b = (j <= i);  // Assigns true to b
b = (j <= k);  // Assigns true to b
b = (k <= j);  // Assigns false to b
```

Boolean Logical Operators

Table 4-4 lists Boolean logical operators available in Java. All Boolean logical operators can be used only with boolean operand(s). Subsequent sections will explain the usage of these operators in detail.

Table 4-4. *List of Boolean Logical Operators*

Operators	Meaning	Type	Usage	Result
!	Logical NOT	Unary	!true	false
&&	Short-circuit AND	Binary	true && true	true
&	Logical AND	Binary	true & true	true
||	Short-circuit OR	Binary	true || false	true
|	Logical OR	Binary	true | false	true
^	Logical XOR(Exclusive OR)	Binary	true ^ true	false
&=	AND assignment	Binary	test &= true	
|=	OR assignment	Binary	test |= true	
^=	XOR assignment	Binary	test ^= true	

Logical NOT Operator (!)

The logical NOT operator (!) is used in the form

!operand

The operator returns true if the operand is false, and false if the operand is true.

```
boolean b;
b = !true;       // Assigns false to b
b = !false;      // Assigns true to b

int i = 10;
int j = 15;
boolean b1 = true;
b = !b1;       // Assigns false to b
b = !(i > j); // Assigns true to b, because i > j returns false
```

Suppose you want to change the value of a boolean variable b to true if its current value is false, and to false if its current value is true. This can be achieved as shown:

```
b = !b; // Assigns true to b if it was false and false if it was true
```

Logical Short-Circuit AND Operator (&&)

The logical short-circuit AND operator (&&) is used in the form

operand1 && operand2

The operator returns true if both operands are true. If either operand is false, it returns false. It is called a short-circuit AND operator because if operand1 (the left-hand operand) evaluates to false, it returns false without evaluating operand2 (the right-hand operand).

```
int i = 10;
int j = 15;
boolean b = (i > 5 && j > 10);  // Assigns true to b
```

In this expression, i > 5 is evaluated first and it returns true. Because the left hand operand evaluated to true, the right hand operand was also evaluated. The right-hand operand, j > 10, is evaluated, which also returns true. Now, the expression is reduced to true && true. Because both operands are true, the final result is true.

Consider another example.

```
int i = 10;
int j = 15;
boolean b = (i > 20 && j > 10);  // Assigns false to b
```

The expression i > 20 returns false. The expression reduces to false && j > 10. Because the left-hand operand is false, the right-hand operand, j > 10, is not evaluated and && returns false. However, there is no way to prove in the above example that the right-hand operand, which is j > 10, was not evaluated.

Let's consider another example to prove this point. I have already discussed the assignment operator (=). If num is a variable of type int, num = 10 returns a value 10.

```
int num = 10;
boolean b = ((num = 50) > 5); // Assigns true to b
```

Note the use of parentheses in this example. In the expression ((num = 50) > 5), the expression, (num = 50), is executed first. It assigns 50 to num and returns 50, reducing the expression to (50 > 5), which in turn returns true. If you use the value of num after the expression num = 50 is executed, its value will be 50.

Keeping this point in mind, consider the following snippet of code:

```
int i = 10;
int j = 10;
boolean b = (i > 5 && ((j = 20) > 15));

System.out.println("b = " + b);
System.out.println("i = " + i);
System.out.println("j = " + j);
```

This piece of code will print

```
b = true
i = 10
j = 20
```

Because the left-hand operand, which is i > 5, evaluated to true, the right-hand of operand ((j = 20) > 15) was evaluated and the variable j was assigned a value 20. If you change the above piece of code so the left-hand operand evaluates to false, the right-hand operand would not be evaluated and the value of j will remain 10. The changed piece of code is as follows:

```
int i = 10;
int j = 10;

// ((j = 20) > 5) is not evaluated because i > 25 returns false
boolean b = (i > 25 && ((j = 20) > 15));
```

128

```
System.out.println ("b = " + b);
System.out.println ("i = " + i);
System.out.println ("j = " + j); // Will print j = 10
```

The above piece of code will print

```
b = false
i = 10
j = 10
```

Logical AND Operator (&)

The logical AND operator (&) is used in the form

```
operand1 & operand2
```

The logical AND operator returns true if both operands are true. If either operand is false, it returns false. The logical AND operator (&) works the same way as the logical short-circuit AND operator (&&), except for one difference. The logical AND operator (&) evaluates its right-hand operand even if its left-hand operand evaluates to false.

```
int i = 10;
int j = 15;
boolean b;

b = (i > 5 & j > 10);          // Assigns true to b
b = (i > 25 & ((j = 20) > 15)); // ((j = 20) > 5) is evaluated even if i > 25 returns false
System.out.println ("b = " + b);
System.out.println ("i = " + i);
System.out.println ("j = " + j); // Will print j = 20
```

The above piece of code will print

```
b = false
i = 10
j = 20
```

Logical Short-Circuit OR Operator (||)

The logical short-circuit OR operator (||) is used in the form

```
operand1 || operand2
```

The logical short-circuit OR operator returns true if either operand is true. If both operands are false, it returns false. It is called a short-circuit OR operator because if operand1 evaluates to true, it returns true without evaluating operand2.

```
int i = 10;
int j = 15;
boolean b = (i > 5 || j > 10); // Assigns true to b
```

In the above expression, i > 5 is evaluated first, and it returns true. Because the left-hand operand evaluated to true, the right hand operand is not evaluated, and the expression (i > 5 || j > 10) returns true.

Consider another example.

```
int i = 10;
int j = 15;
boolean b = (i > 20 || j > 10); // Assigns true to b
```

The expression i > 20 returns false. The expression reduces to false || j > 10. Because the left-hand operand to || is false, the right-hand operand, j > 10, is evaluated, which returns true and the entire expression returns true.

Logical OR Operator (|)

The logical OR operator (|) is used in the form

```
operand1 | operand2
```

The logical OR operator returns true if either operand is true. If both operands are false, it returns false. The logical OR operator works the same way as the logical short-circuit OR operator, except for one difference. The logical OR operator evaluates its right-hand operand even if its left-hand operand evaluates to true.

```
int i = 10;
int j = 15;
boolean b = (i > 5 | j > 10); // Assigns true to b
```

The expression i > 5 is evaluated first and it returns true. Even if the left-hand operand, i > 5, evaluates to true, the right-hand operand, j > 15, is still evaluated, and the whole expression (i > 5 | j > 10) returns true.

Logical XOR Operator (^)

The logical XOR operator (^) is used in the form

```
operand1 ^ operand2
```

The logical XOR operator returns true if operand1 and operand2 are different. That is, it returns true if one of the operands is true, but not both. If both operands are the same, it returns false.

```
int i = 10;
boolean b;

b = true ^ true;      // Assigns false to b
b = true ^ false;     // Assigns true to b
b = false ^ true;     // Assigns true to b
b = false ^ false;    // Assigns false to b
b = (i > 5 ^ i < 15); // Assigns false to b
```

Compound Boolean Logical Assignment Operators

There are three compound Boolean logical assignment operators. Note that Java does not have any operators like &&= and ||=. These operators are used in the form

```
operand1 op= operand2
```

The operand1 must be a boolean variable and op may be &, |, or ^. The above form is equivalent to writing

```
operand1 = operand1 op operand2
```

Table 4-5 shows the compound logical assignment operators and their equivalents.

Table 4-5. *Compound Logical Assignment Operators and Their Equivalents*

Expression	is equivalent to
operand1 &= operand2	operand1 = operand1 & operand2
operand1 |= operand2	operand1 = operand1	operand2
operand1 ^= operand2	operand1 = operand1 ^ operand2

With the &= operator, if both operands evaluate to true, &= returns true. Otherwise, it returns false.

```
boolean b = true;
b &= true;  // Assigns true to b
b &= false; // Assigns false to b
```

With the != operator, if either operand evaluates to true, != returns true. Otherwise, it returns false.

```
boolean b = false;
b |= true;  // Assigns true to b
b |= false; // Assigns false to b
```

With the ^= operator, if both operands evaluate to different values, that is, one of the operands is true but not both, ^= returns true. Otherwise, it returns false.

```
boolean b = true;
b ^= true;  // Assigns false to b
b ^= false; // Assigns true to b
```

Ternary Operator (? :)

Java has one conditional operator. It is called a ternary operator as it takes three operands. It is used in the form

```
boolean-expression ? true-expression : false-expression
```

The two symbols of "?" and ":" make the ternary operator. If the boolean-expression evaluates to true, it evaluates the true-expression; otherwise, it evaluates false-expression.

Suppose you have three integer variables: num1, num2, and minNum. You want to assign minNum the minimum of num1 and num2. You can use ternary operator to accomplish this.

```
int num1 = 50;
int num2 = 25;

// Assigns num2 to minNum, because num2 is less than num1
int minNum = (num1 < num2 ? num1 : num2);
```

Operator Precedence

Consider the following piece of code:

```
int result;
result = 10 + 8 / 2; // What will be the value assigned to result?
```

What will be the value assigned to the variable result after the last statement in this piece of code is executed? Will it be 9 or 14? It depends on the operation that is done first. It will be 9 if the addition 10 + 8 is performed first. It will be 14 if the division 8/2 is performed first. All expressions in Java are evaluated according to operator precedence hierarchy, which establishes the rules that govern the order in which expressions are evaluated. Operators with higher precedence are evaluated before the operators with lower precedence. If operators have the same precedence, the expression is evaluated from left to right. Multiplication, division, and remainder operators have higher precedence than addition and subtraction operators. Therefore, in the above expression, 8/2 is evaluated first, which reduces the expression to 10 + 4, which in turn results in 14.

Consider another expression.

```
result = 10 * 5 / 2;
```

The expression, 10 * 5 / 2, uses two operators: a multiplication operator and a division operator. Both operators have the same precedence. The expression is evaluated from left to right. First, the expression 10 * 5 is evaluated, and then the expression 50 / 2 is evaluated. The whole expression evaluates to 25. If you wanted to perform division first, you must use parentheses. Parentheses have the highest precedence, and therefore, the expression within parentheses is evaluated first. You can rewrite the above piece of code using parentheses.

```
result = 10 * (5 / 2); // Assigns 20 to result. Why?
```

You can also use nested parentheses. In nested parentheses, the innermost parentheses' expression is evaluated first. Table 4-6 lists Java operators in their precedence order. Operators in the same level have the same precedence. Table 4-6 lists some of the operators I have not discussed yet. I will discuss them later in this chapter or in other chapters. In the table, a lower the value in the level column indicates a higher precedence.

Table 4-6. *Java Operators and Their Precedence*

Level	Operator Symbol	Action Performed
1	++	Pre-or-post increment
	--	Pre-or-post decrement
	+, -	Unary plus, unary minus
	~	Bitwise complement
	!	Logical Not
	(type)	Cast
2	*, /, %	Multiplication, division, modulus
3	+, -	Addition, subtraction
	+	String concatenation
4	<<	Left shift
	>>	Signed right shift
	>>>	Unsigned right shift
5	<	Less than
	<=	Less than or equal
	>	Greater than
	>=	Greater than or equal
	instanceof	Type comparison
6	==	Equal in value
	!=	Not equal to
7	&	Bitwise AND
	&	Logical AND
8	^	Bitwise XOR
	^	Logical XOR
9	|	Bitwise OR
	|	Logical OR
10	&&	Logical short-circuit AND
11	||	Logical short-circuit OR
12	?:	Ternary
13	=	Assignment
	+=, -=, *=, /=, %=, <<=, >>=, >>>=, &=, |=,^=	Compound assignment

Bitwise Operators

A bitwise operator manipulates individual bits of its operands. Bitwise operators are listed in Table 4-7.

Table 4-7. *List of Bitwise Operators*

Operators	Meaning	Type	Usage	Result
&	Bitwise AND	Binary	25 & 24	24
|	Bitwise OR	Binary	25 | 2	27
^	Bitwise XOR	Binary	25 ^ 2	27
~	Bitwise complement (1's complement)	Unary	~25	-26
<<	Left shift	Binary	25 << 2	100
>>	Signed right shift	Binary	25 >> 2	6
>>>	Unsigned right shift	Binary	25 >>> 2	6
&=, !=, ^=, <<=, >>=, >>>=	Compound assignment Bitwise operators	Binary		

All bitwise operators work with only integers. The bitwise AND (&) operator operates on corresponding bits of its two operands and returns 1 if both bits are 1, and 0 otherwise. Note that the bitwise AND (&) operates on each bit of the respective operands, not on the operands as a whole. The following is the result of all bit combination using the bitwise AND (&) operator:

```
1 & 1 = 1
1 & 0 = 0
0 & 1 = 0
0 & 0 = 0
```

Consider the following piece of code in Java:

```
int i = 13 & 3;
```

The value of 13 & 3 is computed as follows. The 32 bits have been shown in 8-bit chunks for clarity. In memory, all 32 bits are contiguous.

```
13          00000000 00000000 00000000 00001101
3           00000000 00000000 00000000 00000011
---------------------------------------------
13 & 3 -    00000000 00000000 00000000 00000001 (Equal to decimal 1)
```

Therefore, 13 & 3 is 1, which is assigned to i in the above piece of code.

The bitwise OR (|) operates on corresponding bits of its operands and returns 1 if either bit is 1, and 0 otherwise. The following is the result of all bit combinations using bitwise OR (|) operator:

```
1 | 1 = 1
1 | 0 = 1
0 | 1 = 1
0 | 0 = 0
```

The value of 13 | 3 can be computed as follows. The result of 13 | 3 is 15.

```
13          00000000 00000000 00000000 00001101
3           00000000 00000000 00000000 00000011
---------------------------------------------
13 | 3   00000000 00000000 00000000 00001111 (Equal to decimal 15)
```

The bitwise XOR (^) operates on corresponding bits of its operands and returns 1 if only one of the bits is 1. Otherwise, it returns 0. The following is the result of all bit combinations using bitwise XOR (^) operator:

```
1 ^ 1 = 0
1 ^ 0 = 1
0 ^ 1 = 1
0 ^ 0 = 0
```

The value of 13 ^ 3 can be computed as follows. The result of 13 ^ 3 is 14.

```
13          00000000 00000000 00000000 00001101
3           00000000 00000000 00000000 00000011
---------------------------------------------
13 ^ 3   00000000 00000000 00000000 00001110 (Equal to decimal 14)
```

The bitwise NOT (~) operates on each bit of its operand. It inverts the bits, that is, 1 is changed to 0 and 0 is changed to 1. It is also called a bitwise complement operator. It computes 1's complement of its operand. The following is the result of all bit combinations using bitwise NOT (~) operator:

```
~1 = 0
~0 = 1
```

The value of ~13 can be computed as follows. The result of ~13 is -14.

```
13       00000000 00000000 00000000 00001101
---------------------------------------------
~13      11111111 11111111 11111111 11110010  (Equal to decimal -14)
```

The bitwise left shift operator (<<) shifts all the bits to the left by the number of bits specified as its right-hand operand. It inserts zeros at the lower-order bits. The effect of shifting 1 bit to left is same as multiplying the number by 2. Therefore, 9 << 1 will produce 18, whereas 9 << 2 produces 36. The procedure to compute 13 << 4 can be depicted as shown in Figure 4-1.

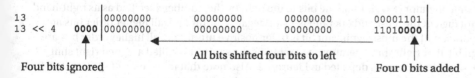

Figure 4-1. *Computing 13 << 4*

What is the result of 13 << 35? You might have guessed zero. However, this is not true. In fact, only 32 bits are used to represent 13, because 13 is considered as int literal and int occupies 32 bits. You can shift all bits to the left only by 31 bits in an int. If the left-hand operand of bitwise left shift operator (<<) is int, only five lower order bits' value of the right-hand operand is used as the number of bits to shift. For example, in 13 << 35, the right-hand operand (35) can be represented in binary as follows:

00000000000000000000000000100011

The five lower order bits in 35 are 00011, which is equal to 3. Therefore, when you write 13 << 35, it is equivalent to writing 13 << 3. For all positive right-hand operands of the bitwise left shift operator, you can take the modulus of the right-hand operand with 32, which would be the final number of bits to shift. Therefore, 13 << 35 can be considered as 13 << (35 % 32) which is the same as 13 << 3. If the left-hand operand is long, the value of the first six lower order bits of the right-hand operand is used as the number of bits to shift.

```
long  val = 13;
long result;
result = val << 35;
```

Since val is a long variable, the six lower order bits of 35, which are 100011, will be used as the number to shift. Figure 4-2 shows the steps used to compute 13 >> 4 and -13 >> 4.

Figure 4-2. *Computing 13 >> 4 and -13 >> 4*

The bitwise signed right shift operator (>>) shifts all the bits to the right by the number specified as its right-hand operand. If the most significant digit of the left-hand operand is 1 (for negative numbers), all higher order bits are filled with 1s after the shift operation. If the most significant bit is 0 (for positive numbers), all higher order bits are filled with 0s. Because the sign bit after right shift operation (>>) remains the same, it is called a signed right shift operator. For example, 13 >> 4 results in zero, as depicted in Figure 4-2. Also note that in the case of -13 >> 4 all four higher order bits are filled with 1s because in -13, the most significant digit is 1. The result of -13 >> 4 is -1.

The unsigned right shift operator (>>>) works the same as the signed right shift operator (>>), except for one difference. It always fills the higher order bits with zero. The result of 13 >>> 4 is zero whereas the result of -13 >>> 4 is 268435455, as shown below. There is no unsigned left shift operator.

```
13           00000000 00000000 00000000  00001101
13 >>> 4     00000000 00000000 00000000  00000000 1101

-13          11111111 11111111 11111111  11110011
-13 >>> 4    00001111 11111111 11111111  11111111 0011
```

A compound bitwise assignment operator is used in the following form:

```
operand1 op= operand2
```

Here, op is one of the bitwise operators of &, |, ^, <<, >>, and >>>. operand1 and operand2 are of primitive integral data type where operand1 must be a variable. The above expression is equivalent to the following expression:

```
operand1 = (Type of operand1) (operand1 op operand2)
```

Assuming that there are two int variables, i and j, Table 4-8 lists the equivalent expression for compound bitwise assignment operators.

Table 4-8. *List of Compound Bitwise Assignment Operators*

Expression	is equivalent to
i &= j	i = i & j
i |= j	i = i | j
i ^= j	i = i ^ j
i <<= j	i = i << j
i >>= j	i = i >> j
i >>>= j	i = i >>> j

Summary

An operator is a symbol that is used to perform some type of computation on its operands. Java contains a rich set of operators. Operators are categorized as unary, binary, or ternary based on the number of operands they take. They are categorized as arithmetic, relational, logical, etc. based on the operation they perform on their operands.

An operator is called overloaded if it can be used in multiple contexts to perform different types of computations. Java contains a + operator that is overloaded. It is used as an arithmetic addition operator as well as a string concatenation operator. Unlike C++, Java does not let developers overload operators in programs.

CHAPTER 5

■ ■ ■

Statements

In this chapter, you will learn:

- What statements are in Java
- About the different types of statements available in Java, for example, control flow statements, loop statements, and so on.

What Is a Statement?

A statement specifies an action in a Java program, such as assigning the sum of x and y to z, printing a message to the standard output, writing data to a file, etc.

Types of Statements

Statements in Java can be broadly classified into three categories:

- Declaration statement
- Expression statement
- Control flow statement

Declaration Statement

A declaration statement is used to declare a variable. You have already been using this type of statement. For example,

```
int num;
int num2 = 100;
String str;
```

Expression Statement

An expression with a semicolon at the end is called an expression statement. However, not all Java expressions can be converted to expression statements by appending a semicolon to them. If i and j are two int variables, i + j is an arithmetic expression. However, i + j; (i + j with a semicolon) is not a valid expression statement. Only the following four kinds of expressions can be converted to expression statements by appending a semicolon to them:

- Increment and decrement expressions. For example,

```
num++;

++num;

num--;

--num;
```

- Assignment expressions. For example,

```
num = 100;

num *= 10;
```

- Object creation expressions. For example,

```
new String("This is a text");
```

  Note that this statement creates a new object of the String class. However, the new object's reference is not stored in any reference variable. Therefore, this statement is not very useful. In some cases, however, you can use such an object creation statement.

- Method invocation expressions

  You invoke the method println() to print a message on console. When you use the println() method without semicolon at the end, it is an expression. When you add a semicolon at the end of the method call, it becomes a statement. For example,

```
System.out.println("This is a statement");
```

Control Flow Statement

By default, all statements in a Java program are executed in the order they appear in the program. However, you can change the order of execution using control flow statements. Sometimes you may want to execute a statement or a set of statements only if a particular condition is true. Sometimes you may want to execute a set of statements repeatedly for a number of times or as long as a particular condition is true. All of these are possible in Java using control flow statements; if and for statements are examples of control flow statements.

A Block Statement

A block statement is a sequence of zero or more statements enclosed in braces. A block statement is generally used to group together several statements, so they can be used in a situation that requires you to use a single statement. In some situations, you can use only one statement. If you want to use more than one statement in those situations, you can create a block statement by placing all your statements inside braces, which would be treated as a single statement. You can think of a block statement as a compound statement that is treated as one statement. The following are examples of block statements:

```
{ // Start of a block statement. Block statement starts with {
        int num1 = 20;
        num1++;

} // End of the block statement. Block statement ends with }

{
  // Another valid block statement with no statements inside
}
```

All the variables declared in a block statement can only be used within that block. In other words, you can say that all variables declared in a block have local scope. Consider the following piece of code:

```
// Declare a variable num1
int num1;

{ // Start of a block statement
        // Declares a variable num2, which is a local variable for this block
        int num2;

        // num2 is local to this block, so it can be used here
        num2 = 200;

        // We can use num1 here because it is declared outside and before this block
        num1 = 100;
} // End of the block statement

// A compile-time error. num2 has been declared inside a block and
// so it cannot be used outside that block
num2 = 50;
```

You can also nest a block statement inside another block statement. All the variables declared in the enclosing blocks (outer blocks) are available to the enclosed blocks (inner blocks). However, the variables declared in the enclosed inner blocks are not available in enclosing outer blocks. For example,

```
// Start of the outer block
{
        int num1 = 10;

        // Start of the inner block
        {
                // num1 is available here because we are in an inner block
                num1 = 100;
                int num2 = 200; // Declared inside the inner block
                num2 = 678;     // OK. num2 is local to inner block
        }
        // End of the inner block
```

```
        // A compile-time error. num2 is local to the inner block.
        // So, it cannot be used outside the inner block.
        num2 = 200;
}
// End of the outer block
```

One important thing to remember about nested block statement is that you cannot define a variable with the same name inside an inner block if a variable with the same name has already been defined in the outer block. This is because the variables declared in the outer block can always be used inside the inner block and if you declare a variable with the same name inside the inner block, there is no way for Java to differentiate between these two variables inside the inner block. The following snippet of code is incorrect:

```
int num1 = 10;
{
        // A compile-time error. num1 is already in scope. Cannot redeclare num1
        float num1 = 10.5F;

        float num2 = 12.98F; // OK

        {
                // A compile-time error. num2 is already in scope. You can use
                // num2 already define in the outer block, but cannot redeclare it.
                float num2;
        }
}
```

The if-else Statement

The format of an if-else statement is

```
if (condition)
        statement1
else
        statement2
```

The condition must be a Boolean expression. That is, it must evaluate to true or false. If the condition evaluates to true, statement1 is executed. Otherwise, statement2 is executed. The else part is optional. You may write a statement as

```
if (condition)
        statement1
```

Suppose there are two int variables, num1 and num2. You want to add 10 to num2 if num1 is greater than 50. Otherwise, you want to subtract 10 from num2. You can write this logic using an if-else statement.

```
if (num1 > 50)
        num2 = num2 + 10;
else
        num2 = num2 - 10;
```

The execution of this if-else statement is shown in Figure 5-1.

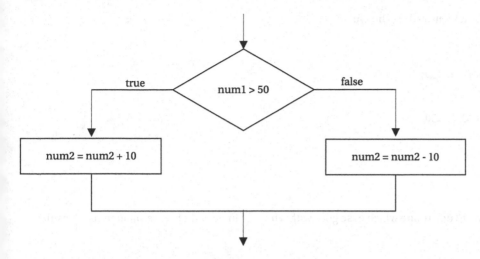

Figure 5-1. *Execution of an if-else statement*

Suppose you have three int variables, num1, num2, and num3. You want to add 10 to num2 and num3 if num1 is greater than 50. Otherwise, you want to subtract 10 from num2 and num3. You may try the following snippet of code, which is incorrect:

```
if (num1 > 50)
        num2 = num2 + 10;
        num3 = num3 + 10;
else
        num2 = num2 - 10;
        num3 = num3 - 10;
```

The snippet of code will generate a compiler error. What is wrong with this code? You can place only one statement between if and else in an if-else statement. This is the reason that the statement num3 = num3 + 10; caused a compile-time error. In fact, you can always associate only one statement with the if part in an if-else statement or in a simple if statement. This is also true for the else part. In the above piece of code, only num2 = num2 - 10; is associated with the else part; the last statement, num3 = num3 - 10;, is not associated with the else part. You want to execute two statements when num1 is greater than 50 or not. In this case, you need to bundle two statements into one block statement, like so:

```
if (num1 > 50) {
        num2 = num2 + 10;
        num3 = num3 + 10;
}
else {
        num2 = num2 - 10;
        num3 = num3 - 10;
}
```

The if-else statement can be nested, as shown:

```
if (num1 > 50) {
        if (num2 < 30) {
                num3 = num3 + 130;
        }
        else {
                num3 = num3 - 130;
        }
}
else {
        num3 = num3 = 200;
}
```

Sometimes it is confusing to determine which else goes with which if in nested if-else statements. Consider the following piece of code:

```
int i = 10;
int j = 15;

if (i > 15)
if (j == 15)
        System.out.println("Thanks");
else
        System.out.println("Sorry");
```

What will be the output when this snippet of code is executed? Will it print "Thanks" or "Sorry" or nothing? If you guessed that it would not print anything, you already understand if-else association.

You can apply a simple rule to figure out which else goes with which if in an if-else statement. Start with the "else" and move up. If you do not find any other "else," the first "if" you find goes with the "else" you started with. If you find one "else" in moving up before you find any "if," the second "if" goes with the "else" you started with, and so on. In the above piece of code, starting with "else" the first "if" you find is "if (j == 15)" and so the "else" goes with this "if." The above piece of code can be rewritten as follows:

```
int i = 10;
int j = 15;

if (i > 15) {
        if (j == 15) {
                System.out.println("Thanks");
        }
        else {
                System.out.println("Sorry");
        }
}
```

Because i is equal to 10, the expression i > 15 will return false and hence the control would not enter the if statement at all. Therefore, there would not be any output.

Note that the condition expression in an if statement must be of the boolean type. Therefore, if you want to compare two int variables, i and j, for equality, your if statement must look like the following:

```
if (i == j)
        statement
```

You cannot write an if statement like this:

```
if (i = 5) /* A compile-time error */
        statement
```

This if statement will not compile because i = 5 is an assignment expression and it evaluates to an int value 5. The condition expression must return a Boolean value: true or false. Therefore, an assignment expression cannot be used as a condition expression in an if statement, except when you are assigning a Boolean value to a boolean variable, like so:

```
boolean b;
if (b = true) /* Always returns true */
        statement
```

Here, the assignment expression b = true always returns true after assigning true to b. In this case, the use of the assignment expression in if statement is allowed because the data type of expression b = true is boolean.

You can use the ternary operator in place of simple if-else statement. Suppose, if a person is male, you want to set the title to "Mr." and if not, to "Ms.". You can accomplish this using an if-else statement and also using a ternary operator, like so:

```
String title = "";
boolean isMale = true;

// Using an if-else statement
if (isMale)
        title = "Mr.";
else
        title = "Ms.";

// Using a ternary operator
title = (isMale ? "Mr." : "Ms.");
```

You can see the difference in using the if-else statement and the ternary operator. The code is compact using the ternary operator. However, you cannot use a ternary operator to replace all if-else statements. You can use the ternary operator in place of the if-else statement only when the if and else parts in the if-else statement contain only one statement and both statements return the same type of values. Because the ternary operator is an operator, it can be used in expressions. Suppose you want to assign the minimum of i and j to k. You can do this in the following declaration statement of the variable k:

```
int i = 10;
int j = 20;
int k = (i < j ? i : j); // Using a ternary operator in initialization
```

The same can be achieved using an if-else statement, as shown:

```
int i = 10;
int j = 20;
int k;

if (i < j)
        k = i;
else
        k = j;
```

Another difference in using a ternary operator and an `if-else` statement is that you can use an expression, which uses a ternary operator as an argument to a method. However, you cannot use an `if-else` statement as an argument to a method. Suppose you have a `calc()` method that accepts an `int` as an argument. You have two integers, `num1` and `num2`. If you want to pass the minimum of the two integers to the `calc()` method, you would write the code as shown:

```
// Use of an if-else statement
if (num1 < num2)
        calc(num1);
else
        calc(num2);

// Use of a ternary operator
calc(num1 < num2 ? num1 : num2)
```

Suppose you want to print the message "k is 15" if the value of an `int` variable k is equal to 15. Otherwise, you want to print the message "k is not 15". You can print the message using a ternary operator writing one line of code as follows:

```
System.out.println(k == 15 ? "k is 15" : "k is not 15");
```

The switch Statement

The general form of a `switch` statement is

```
switch (switch-expression) {
        case label1:
                statements

        case label2:
                statements

        case label3:
                statements

        default:
                statements
}
```

The `switch-expression` must evaluate to a type: `byte`, `short`, `char`, `int`, `enum`, or `String`. The `enum` type (shorthand for enumerated type) was introduced in Java 5. Please refer to the chapter on enums for details on how to use an enum type in a `switch` statement. Java 7 added support for the `String` type in a `switch` statement. Please refer to Chapter 11 for details on how to use strings in a `switch` statement. The `label1`, `label2`, etc. are compile-time constant expressions whose values must be in the range of the type of the `switch-expression`. A `switch` statement is evaluated as follows:

- The `switch-expression` is evaluated.

- If the value of the `switch-expression` matches a `case` label, the execution starts from the matched `case` label and executes all statements until the end of the `switch` statement.

- If the value of the `switch-expression` does not match a `case` label, execution starts at the statement following the optional `default` label and continues until the end of the `switch` statement.

For example,

```java
int i = 10;
switch (i) {
        case 10: // Found the match
                System.out.println("Ten"); // Execution starts here
        case 20:
                System.out.println("Twenty");
        default:
                System.out.println ("No-match");
}
```

```
Ten
Twenty
No-match
```

The value of i is 10. The execution starts at the first statement following case 10: and falls through case 20: and default labels executing the statements under these labels. If you change the value of i to 50, there would not be any match in case labels and the execution would start at the first statement after the default label, which will print "No-match". The following example illustrates this logic:

```java
int i = 50;
switch (i) {
        case 10:
                System.out.println("Ten");
        case 20:
                System.out.println("Twenty");
        default:
                System.out.println("No-match"); /* Execution starts here */
}
```

```
No-match
```

The default label may not be the last label to appear in a switch statement and is optional. For example,

```java
int i = 50;
switch (i) {
        case 10:
                System.out.println("Ten");
        default:
                System.out.println("No-match"); // Execution starts here
        case 20:
                System.out.println("Twenty");

}
```

```
No-match
Twenty
```

Because the value of i is 50, which does not match any of the case labels, the execution starts at the first statement after default label. The control falls through the subsequent label case 20: and executes the statement following this case label, which prints "Twenty". Generally, you want to print "Ten" if the value of i is 10 and "Twenty" if the value of i is 20. If the value of i is not 10 and 20, you want to print "No-match". This is possible using a break statement inside switch statement. When a break statement is executed inside a switch statement, the control is transferred outside the switch statement. For example,

```
int i = 10;
switch (i) {
        case 10:
                System.out.println("Ten");
                break; // Transfers control outside the switch statement
        case 20:
                System.out.println("Twenty");
                break; // Transfers control outside the switch statement
        default:
                System.out.println("No-match");
                break; // Transfers control outside the switch statement. It is not necessary.
}
```

```
Ten
```

Note the use of the break statement in the above snippet of code. In fact, the execution of a break statement inside a switch statement stops the execution of the switch statement and transfers control to the first statement, if any, following the switch statement. In the above snippet of code, the use of a break statement inside the default label is not necessary because the default label is the last label in the switch statement and the execution of the switch statement will stop after that anyway. However, it is recommended to use a break statement even inside the last label to avoid errors if additional labels are added later.

The value of the constant expressions used as the case labels must be in the range of the data type of switch-expression. Keeping in mind that the range of the byte data type in Java is -128 to 127, the following code would not compile because the second case label is 150, which is outside the range of the byte data type:

```
byte b = 10;
switch (b) {
        case 5:
                b++;
        case 150: // A compile-time error. 150 is greater than 127
                b--;
        default:
                b = 0;
}
```

Two case labels in a switch statement cannot be the same. The following piece of code would not compile because case label 10 is repeated:

```
int num = 10;
switch (num) {
        case 10:
                num++;
        case 10: // A compile-time error. Duplicate case label 10
                num--;
        default:
                num = 100;
}
```

It is important to note that the labels for each case in a switch statement must be a compile-time constant. That is, the value of the labels must be known at compile time. Otherwise, a compile-time error occurs. For example, the following code would not compile:

```
int num1 = 10;
int num2 = 10;
switch (num1) {
        case 20:
                System.out.println("num1 is 20");
        case num2: // A Compile-time error. num2 is a variable and cannot be used as a label
                System.out.println("num1 is 10");
}
```

You might say that you know the value of num2 is 10 when the switch statement will be executed. However, all variables are evaluated at runtime. The values of variables are not known at compile time. Therefore, the case num2: causes the compiler error. This is necessary because Java makes sure at compile time itself that all case labels are within the range of the data type of the switch-expression. If they are not, the statements following those case labels will never get executed at runtime.

■ **Tip**   The default label is optional. There can be at most one default label in a switch statement.

A switch statement is a clearer way of writing an if-else statement when the condition-expression in an if-else statement compares the value of the same variable for equality. For example, the following if-else and switch statements accomplish the same thing:

```
// Using an if-else statement
if (i == 10)
        System.out.println("i is 10");
else if (i == 20)
        System.out.println("i is 20");
elsc
        System.out.println("i is neither 10 nor 20");
```

```
// Using a switch statement
switch (i) {
        case 10:
                System.out.println("i is 10");
                break;
        case 20:
                System.out.println("i is 20");
                break;
        default:
                System.out.println("i is neither 10 nor 20");
}
```

The for Statement

A for statement is an iteration statement (also called a for-loop statement), which is used to loop through a statement for a number of times based on some conditions. The general form of a for-loop statement is

```
for (initialization; condition-expression; expression-list)
        Statement
```

The initialization, condition-expression, and expression-list are separated by a semicolon. A for-loop statement consists of four parts:

- Initialization

- Condition-expression

- Statement

- Expression-list

First, the initialization part is executed; then, the condition-expression is evaluated. If the condition-expression evaluates to true, the statement associated with the for-loop statement is executed. After that, all expressions in the expression-list are evaluated. The condition-expression is evaluated again, and if it evaluates to true, statement associated with the for-loop statement is executed and then the expression-list, and so on. This loop of execution is repeated until the condition-expression evaluates to false. The execution of a for-loop statement is depicted in Figure 5-2.

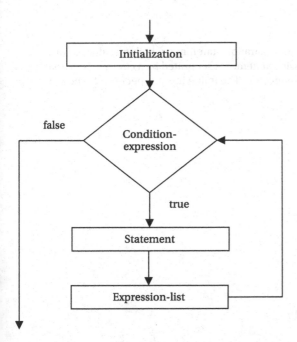

Figure 5-2. *Execution of a for statement*

For example, the following for-loop statement will print all integers between 1 and 10, inclusive:

```
for(int num = 1; num <= 10; num++)
        System.out.println(num);
```

First, int num = 1 is executed, which declares an int variable num and initializes it to 1. It is important to note that variables declared in the initialization part of the for-loop statement can only be used within that for-loop statement. Then, condition-expression (num <= 10) is evaluated, which is 1 <= 10. It evaluates to true for the first time. Now, the statement associated with the for-loop statement is executed, which prints the current value of num. Finally, the expression in the expression-list, num++, is evaluated, which increments the value of num by 1. At this point, the value of num becomes 2. The condition-expression 2 <= 10 is evaluated, which returns true, and the current value of num is printed. This process continues until the value of num becomes 10 and it is printed. After that, num++ sets the value of num to 11, and the condition-expression 11 <= 10 returns false, which stops the execution of the for-loop statement.

All three parts (initialization, condition-expression, and expression-list) in a for-loop statement are optional. Note that the fourth part, the statement, is not optional. Therefore, if you do not have a statement to execute in a for-loop statement, you must use an empty block statement or a semicolon in place of a statement. A semicolon that is treated as a statement is called an empty statement or a null statement. An infinite loop using a for-loop statement can be written as follows:

```
for( ; ; ) { /* An infinite loop */
}
```

Or

```
for( ; ; ); /* An infinite loop. Note a semicolon as a statement */
```

A detailed discussion of each part of a for-loop statement follows.

Initialization

The initialization part of a for-loop statement can have a variable declaration statement, which may declare one or more variables of the same type, or it can have a list of expression statements separated by a comma. Note that the statements used in the initialization part do not end with a semicolon. The following snippet of code shows the initialization part in a for-loop statement:

```
// Declares two variables i and j of the same type int
for(int i = 10, j = 20; ; );

// Declares one double variable salary
for(double salary = 3455.78F; ; );

// Attempts to declare two variables of different types
for(int i = 10, double d1 = 20.5; ; ); /* An error */

// Uses an expression i++
int i = 100;
for(i++; ; );     // OK

// Uses an expression to print a message on the console
for(System.out.println("Hello"); ; );   // OK

// Uses two expressions: to print a message and to increment num
int num = 100;
for(System.out.println("Hello"), num++; ; );
```

You can declare a new variable in the initialization part of a for-loop statement. However, you cannot re-declare a variable that is already in scope.

```
int i = 10;
for (int i = 0; ; ); // An error. Cannot re-declare i
```

You can reinitialize the variable i in the for-loop statement, as shown:

```
int i = 10; // Initialize i to 10
i = 500; // Value of i changes here to 500

/* Other statements go here... */

for (i = 0; ; ); // Reinitialize i to zero inside the for-loop loop
```

Condition-expression

The condition-expression must evaluate to a Boolean value of true or false. Otherwise, a compiler error occurs. The condition-expression is optional. If it is omitted, a Boolean value of true is assumed as a condition-expression, which results in an infinite loop unless a break statement is used to stop the loop. The following two for-loop statements result in infinite loops and they are the same:

Infinite loop I

```
for( ; ; ); // Implicitly condition-expression is true
```

Infinite loop II

```
for( ; true; ); // Explicit true is used here
```

A break statement is used to stop the execution of a for-loop statement. When a break statement is executed, the control is transferred to the next statement, if any, after the for-loop statement. You can rewrite the for-loop statement to print all integers between 1 and 10 using a break statement.

```
for(int num = 1;   ; num++) {       // No condition-expression
        System.out.println(num); // Print the number
        if (num == 10) {
                break; // Break out of loop when i is 10
        }
}
```

This for-loop statement prints the same integers as the previous for-loop statement did. However, the latter is not recommended because you are using a break statement instead of using the condition-expression to break out of the loop. It is good programming practice to use a condition-expression to break out of a for loop.

Expression-list

The expression-list part is optional. It may contain one or more expressions separated by a comma. You can use only expressions that can be converted to a statement by appending a semicolon at the end. Please refer to the discussion on the expression statement in the beginning of this chapter for more details. You can rewrite the same example of printing all integers between 1 and 10 as follows:

```
for(int num = 1; num <= 10; System.out.println(num), num++);
```

Note that this for-loop statement uses two expressions in the expression-list, which are separated by a comma. A for-loop statement gives you more power to write compact code.

You can rewrite the above for-loop statement as follows to make it more compact and accomplish the same task:

```
for(int num = 1; num <= 10; System.out.println(num++));
```

Note that you combined the two expressions in the expression-list into one. You used num++ as the argument to the println() method, so it prints the value of num first, and then increments its value by 1. Can you predict the output of the above for-loop statement if you replace num++ by ++num?

You can also use nested for-loop statements, that is, for-loop statements inside another for-loop statement. Suppose you want to print a 3x3 (read as three by three) matrix.

```
11      12      13
21      22      23
31      32      33
```

The code to print the 3x3 matrix can be written as

```java
// Outer for-loop statement
for(int i = 1; i <= 3; i++) {
        // Inner for-loop statement
        for(int j = 1; j <= 3; j++) {
                System.out.print(i + "" + j);

                // Prints a tab after each column value
                System.out.print("\t");
        }

        System.out.println(); // Prints a new line
}
```

The above piece of code can be explained using the following steps.

1. The execution starts in the initialization part (int i = 1) of the outer for-loop statement where i is initialized to 1.

2. The condition-expression for the outer for-loop statement (i <= 3) is evaluated for i equal to 1, which is true.

3. The statement part of the outer for loop starts with an inner for-loop statement.

4. Now j is initialized to 1.

5. The condition-expression for the inner for-loop statement (j <= 3) is evaluated for j equal to 1, which is true.

6. The block statement associated with the inner for-loop statement is executed, which prints 11 and a tab.

7. The expression-list of the inner for-loop statement (j++) is executed, which increments the value of j to 2.

8. The condition expression for the inner for-loop statement (j <= 3) is evaluated for j equal to 2, which is true.

9. The block statement associated with the inner for-loop statement is executed, which prints 12 and a tab. At this stage the printed text is

    11   12

10. The expression-list of the inner for-loop statement (j++) is executed, which increments the value of j to 3.

11. The condition-expression for the inner for-loop statement (j <= 3) is evaluated for j equal to 3, which is true.

12. The block statement associated with the inner for-loop statement is executed, which prints 13 and a tab. At this stage the printed text is

    11   12   13

13. The expression-list of the inner for-loop statement (j++) is executed, which increments the value of j to 4.

14. The condition expression for the inner for-loop statement (j <= 3) is evaluated for j equal to 4, which is false. At this point, the inner for loop is finished.

15. The last statement of the block statement for outer for-loop statement, which is System.out.println(), is executed, which prints a system-dependent line separator.

16. The expression-list of the outer for-loop statement (i++) is executed, which increment the value if i to 2.

17. Now, the inner for-loop statement is started afresh with the value of i equal to 2. This sequence of steps is also executed for i equal to 3. When i becomes 4, the outer for-loop statement exits, and at this point, the printed matrix will be

11	12	13
21	22	23
31	32	33

Note that this snippet of code also prints a tab character at the end of every row and a new line after the last row, which are not necessary. One important point to note is that the variable j is created every time the inner for-loop statement is started and it is destroyed when the inner for-loop statement exits. Therefore, the variable j is created and destroyed three times. You cannot use the variable j outside the inner for-loop statement because it has been declared inside the inner for-loop statement and its scope is local to that inner for-loop statement. Listing 5-1 contains the complete code for the discussion in this section. The program makes sure not to print extra tabs and new line characters.

Listing 5-1. Using a for Loop to Print a 3x3 Matrix

```java
// PrintMatrix.java
package com.jdojo.statement;

public class PrintMatrix {
    public static void main(String[] args) {
        for(int i = 1; i <= 3; i++) {
            for(int j = 1; j <= 3; j++) {
                System.out.print(i + "" + j);

                // Print a tab, except for the last number in a row
                if (j < 3) {
                    System.out.print("\t");
                }
            }

            // Print a new line, except after the last line
            if (i < 3) {
                System.out.println();
            }
        }
    }
}
```

11	12	13
21	22	23
31	32	33

The for-each Statement

Java 5 introduced an enhanced for loop, which is called a for-each loop. It is used for iterating over elements of arrays and collections. This section is included here to complete the list of statements that lets you loop through a group values. Please refer to the chapters on arrays and collections for more detailed explanation of the for-each loop. The general syntax for a for-each loop is as follows:

```
for(Type element : a_collection_or_an_array) {
        // This code will be executed once for each element in the collection/array.
        // Each time this code is executed, the element variable holds the reference
        // of the current element in the collection/array
}
```

The following snippet of code prints all elements of an int array numList:

```
int[] numList = {10, 20, 30, 40};
for(int num : numList) {
        System.out.println(num);
}
```

```
10
20
30
40
```

The while Statement

A while statement is another iteration (or, loop) statement, which is used to execute a statement repeatedly as long as a condition is true. A while statement is also known as a while-loop statement. The general form of a while-loop statement is

```
while (condition-expression)
        Statement
```

The condition-expression must be a boolean expression and the statement can be a simple statement or a block statement. The condition-expression is evaluated first. If it returns true, the statement is executed. Again, the condition-expression is evaluated. If it returns true, the statement is executed. This loop continues until the condition-expression returns false. Unlike the for-loop statement, the condition-expression in a while-loop statement is not optional. For example, to make a while statement infinite loop, you need to use the boolean literal true as the condition-expression.

```
while (true)
        System.out.println ("This is an infinite loop");
```

In general, a for-loop statement can be converted to a while-loop statement. However, not all for-loop statements can be converted to a while-loop statement. The conversion between a for-loop and a while-loop statement is shown below.

A for-loop statement:

```
for (initialization; condition-expression; expression-list)
        Statement
```

Equivalent while-loop Statements:

```
Initialization
while (condition-expression) {
        Statement
        Expression-list
}
```

You can print all integers between 1 and 10 using a while-loop as shown:

```
int i = 1;
while (i <= 10) {
        System.out.println(i);
        i++;
}
```

The above code can also be rewritten as

```
int i = 0;
while (++i <= 10) {
        System.out.println(i);
}
```

or

```
int i = 1;
while (i <= 10) {
        System.out.println(i++);
}
```

A break statement is used to exit the loop in a while-loop statement. You can rewrite the above example using a break statement as follows. Note that the following piece of code is written only to illustrate the use of a break statement in a while-loop; it is not a good example of using a break statement.

```
int i = 1;
while (true) {    // Cannot exit the loop from here
        if (i <= 10) {
                System.out.println(i);
                i++;
        }
        else {
                break; // Exit the loop
        }
}
```

The do-while Statement

The do-while statement is another loop statement. It is similar to the while-loop statement with one difference. The statement associated with a while loop statement may not be executed even once if the condition-expression evaluates to false for the first time. However, the statement associated with a do-while statement is executed at least once. The general form of a do-while statement is

```
do
        Statement
while (condition-expression);
```

Note that the do-while statement ends with a semicolon. The condition-expression must be a boolean expression. The statement can be a simple statement or a block statement. The statement is executed first. Then the condition-expression is evaluated. If it evaluates to true, the statement is executed again. This loop continues until the condition-expression evaluates to false. Like in a for loop and a while loop, a break statement may be used to exit a do-while loop. A do-while loop can compute the sum of integers between 1 and 10 as shown:

```
int i = 1;
int sum = 0;
do {
        sum = sum + i; // Better to use sum += i
        i++;
}
while (i <= 10);

// Print the result
System.out.println("Sum = " + sum);
```

```
Sum = 55
```

The break Statement

A break statement is used to exit from a block. There are two forms of the break Statements:

- Unlabeled break statement
- Labeled break statement

An example of an unlabeled break statement is

```
break;
```

An example of a labeled break statement is

```
break label;
```

You have already seen the use of the unlabeled break statement inside switch, for-loop, while-loop, and do-while statements. It transfers control out of a switch, for-loop, while-loop, and do-while statement in which it appears. In case of nested statements of these four kinds, if an unlabeled break statement is used inside the inner statement, it transfers control only out of the inner statement, not out of the outer statement. Suppose you want to print the lower half of the 3x3 matrix as shown:

```
11      21      22
31      32      33
```

To print only the lower half of the 3x3 matrix, you can write the following snippet of code:

```java
for(int i = 1; i <= 3; i++) {
        for(int j = 1; j <= 3; j++) {
                System.out.print ( i + "" + j);
                if (i == j) {
                        break; // Exit the inner for loop
                }
                System.out.print("\t");
        }
        System.out.println();
}
```

The break statement has been used inside the inner for-loop statement. When the value of the outer loop counter (i) becomes equal to the value of the inner loop counter (j), the break statement is executed, and the inner loop exits. If you want to exit from the outer for-loop statement from inside the inner for-loop statement, you have to use a labeled break statement. A label in Java is any valid Java identifier followed by a colon. The following are some valid labels in Java:

```
label1:
alabel:
Outer:
Hello:
IamALabel:
```

Now use a labeled break statement in the above example and see the result.

```java
outer:  // Defines a label named outer
for(int i = 1; i <= 3; i++ ) {
        for(int j = 1; j <= 3; j++ ) {
                System.out.print(i + "" + j);
                if (i == j) {
                        break outer;  // Exit the outer for loop
                }
                System.out.print("\t");
        }
        System.out.println();
} // The outer label ends here
```

The output of the above snippet of code will be 11. Why did it print only one element of the 3x3 matrix? This time you have used a labeled break statement inside the inner for-loop statement. When i == j evaluates to true for the first time, the labeled break statement is executed. It transfers control out of the block, which has been labeled as outer. Note that the outer label appears just before the outer for-loop statement. Therefore, the block associated with the label outer is the outer for-loop statement. A labeled statement can be used not only inside switch, for-loop, while-loop, and do-while statements. Rather it can be used with any type of a block statement. The following is a trivial example of a labeled break Statements:

```
blockLabel:
{
        int i = 10;
        if (i == 5) {
                break blockLabel; // Exits the block
        }

        if (i == 10) {
                System.out.println("i is not five");
        }
}
```

One important point to remember about a labeled break statement is that the label used with the break statement must be the label for the block in which that labeled break statement is used. The following snippet of code illustrates an incorrect use of a labeled break Statements:

```
lab1:
{
        int i = 10;
        if (i == 10)
                break lab1; // Ok. lab1 can be used here
}

lab2:
{
        int i = 10;
        if (i == 10)
                // A compile-time error. lab1 cannot be used here because this block is not
                // associated with lab1 label. We can use only lab2 in this block
                break lab1;
}
```

The continue Statement

A continue statement can only be used inside the for-loop, while-loop, and do-while statements. There are two forms of the continue Statements:

- Unlabeled continue statement
- Labeled continue statement

An example of an unlabeled continue statement is

```
continue;
```

An example of a labeled continue statement is

```
continue label;
```

When a continue statement is executed inside a for loop, the rest of the statements in the body of the loop are skipped and the expressions in the expression-list are executed. You can print all odd integers between 1 and 10 using a for-loop statement, as shown:

```
for (int i = 1; i < 10; i += 2) {
        System.out.println(i);
}
```

In this for-loop statement, you increment the value of i by 2 in the expression-list. You can rewrite the above for-loop statement using a continue statement, as shown in Figure 5-3.

```
for(int i = 1; i < 10; i++) {
        if (i % 2 == 0) {
                continue;
        }
        System.out.println(i);
}
```

Figure 5-3. *Using a continue statement inside a for-loop statement*

The expression i % 2 returns zero for the values of i that are multiple of 2, and the expression i % 2 == 0 returns true. In such cases, the continue statement is executed and the last statement, System.out.println(i), is skipped. The increment statement i++ is executed after the continue statement is executed. The above snippet of code is certainly not the best example of using a continue statement; however, it serves the purpose of illustrating its use.

When an unlabeled continue statement is executed inside a while loop or do-while loop, the rest of the statements in the loop is skipped and the condition-expression is evaluated for the next iteration. For example, the snippet of code in Figure 5-4 will print all odd integers between 1 and 10, using a continue statement inside a while loop.

```
int i = 1;
while (i < 10) {
        if (i % 2 == 0) {
                i++;
                continue;
        }
        System.out.println(i);
        i++;
}
```

Figure 5-4. *Using a continue statement inside a while-loop statement*

The main difference in using a `continue` statement inside a `for` loop and a `while` loop is the place where the control is transferred. Inside a `for` loop, control is transferred to the expression-list, and in a `while` loop, the control is transferred to the condition-expression. This is why a `for`-loop statement cannot always be converted to a `while`-loop statement without modifying some logic.

An unlabeled `continue` statement always continues the innermost `for` loop, `while` loop, and `do-while` loop. If you are using nested loop statements, you need to use a labeled `continue` statement to continue in the outer loop. For example, you can rewrite the snippet of code that prints lower half of the 3x3 matrix using a `continue` statement as shown:

```
outer: // The label "outer" starts here
for(int i = 1; i <= 3; i++) {
        for(int j = 1; j <= 3; j++) {
                System.out.print(i + "" + j);
                System.out.print("\t");
                if (i == j) {
                        System.out.println(); // Print a new line
                        continue outer; // Continue the outer loop
                }

        }
} // The label "outer" ends here
```

An Empty Statement

An empty statement is a semicolon by itself. An empty statement does nothing. If an empty statement does not do anything, why do we have it? Sometimes a statement is necessary as part of the syntax of a construct. However, you may not need to do anything meaningful. In such cases, an empty statement is used. A `for` loop must have a statement associated with it. However, to print all integers between 1 and 10 you can only use initialization, condition-expression, and expression-list parts of a `for`-loop statement. In this case, you do not have a statement to associate with the `for`-loop statement. Therefore, you use an empty statement in this case, as shown:

```
for(int i = 1; i <= 10; System.out.println(i++))
; // This semicolon is an empty statement for the for loop
```

Sometimes an empty statement is used to avoid double negative logic in the code. Suppose noDataFound is a boolean variable. You may write a snippet of code as shown:

```
if (noDataFound)
        ; // An empty statement
else {
        // Do some processing
}
```

The above `if-else` statement can be written without using an empty statement, like so:

```
if (!noDataFound) {
        // Do some processing
}
```

It is a personal choice, which of the above piece of code to use. Finally, note that if you type two or more semicolons where only one was required, it would not cause any errors, because each extra semicolon is considered as an empty statement. For example,

```
i++;  // Ok. Here, semicolon is part of statement
i++;; // Still Ok. The second semicolon is considered as empty statement.
```

You cannot use an empty statement where a statement is not allowed. For example, when only one statement is allowed, adding an extra empty statement will cause an error, as shown in the following snippet of code. It associates two statements, i++; and an empty statement (;), to an if statement, where only one statement is allowed.

```
if (i == 10)
        i++;; // A compile-time error. Cannot use two statements before an else statement
else
        i--;
```

Summary

A statement in a Java program specifies an action. Statements in Java can be broadly classified in three categories: declaration statements, expression statements, and control flow statements. A declaration statement is used to declare variables. An expression statement is used to evaluate an expression. A control flow statement controls the order in which other statements are executed. Control flow statements include if, if-else and looping statements. A looping statement executes a block of statements repeatedly until some condition becomes false. Java provides four looping statements: for loop, for-each loop, while loop, and do-while loop. A break statement is used to transfer control outside of a block statement or a loop. A continue statement is used to ignore executing the remaining code for a loop and continue with the next iteration. Java has an empty statement, too, which is simply a semicolon by itself.

■ ■ ■

Classes and Objects

In this chapter, you will learn:

- What classes are in Java

- How to declare classes in Java

- How to declare class members such as fields and methods and their access levels

- How to create objects of a class

- How to declare import statements in a compilation unit

- The meaning of the pronouns this and super in a Java program

- Different parameter passing mechanisms in general, and then, the parameter passing mechanisms in Java

- What constructors of a class are and how to use them

- Initializers of a class

- Declaring final variables, classes, and methods

- How to declare and use varargs parameters

- What generic classes are and how to use them

What Is a Class?

Classes are the basic units of programming in the object-oriented paradigm. In the chapter on writing java programs, you looked at some elementary aspects of a class in Java, for example, using the class keyword to declare a class, declaring the main() method to run a class, etc. This chapter explains how to declare and use a class in detail.

Let's start with a simple example of a class in the real world to build the technical concept of a class in Java. When you look around, you see a number of objects, such as books, computers, keyboards, tables, chairs, humans, etc. Each object that you see belongs to a class. Ask yourself a simple question, "Who am I?" Your obvious answer would be: I am a human. What do you mean by saying that you are a human being? You mean that a human class exists in the world and you are one of the instances ("being") of that class. You also understand that other humans (other instances of the human class) also exist, who are similar but not the same to you. Both you and your friend, being instances of the same human class, have the same properties, such as name, gender, height, weight, and behaviors, such as the ability to think, talk, walk, etc. However, the properties and behaviors differ for you and your friend in value, quality, or both. For example, you both have a name and the ability to talk. However, your name may be Richard and your friend's name may be Greg. You may talk slowly whereas your friend may talk fast. If you want to prepare a model for you and your friend to examine your behaviors, there are two choices.

- You can list all properties and behaviors for you and your friend separately and examine them separately as if there is no connection between you and your friend.

- You can list the properties and behaviors for you and your friend that are in common and then examine them as properties and behavior for an entity without naming you and your friend. This model assumes that all listed properties and behaviors will be present in an entity (without naming it) though they may vary from entity to entity. You may want to list all properties and behaviors for you and your friend as properties and behavior of a class, say human, and treat you and your friend as two different instances of that human class. Essentially, you have grouped together entities (e.g., you and your friend) with similar properties and behaviors, and called that group a class. Then you will treat all objects (again, you and your friend) as instances of that class.

The first approach treats each object as a separate entity. In the second approach, objects are classified based on similarity of properties and behaviors where an object always belongs to a class; the class becomes the essential part of programming. To determine any property or behavior of an object, you need to look up its class definition. For example, you are an object of the human class. Can you fly? This question can be answered by going through a series of steps. First, you need to answer the question "What class do you belong to?" The answer is that you belong to the human class. Does the human class define a flying behavior? The answer is no. Because you are an instance of the human class that does not define the flying behavior, you cannot fly. If you look carefully at the way you arrived at the answer, you would find that the question is asked on an object (you), but the answer was provided by the class (human) to which the object belongs.

Classes are essential, and they are basic parts of programs in object-oriented programming. They are used as templates to create objects. Let's discuss how to define a class. A class in Java may consist of five components:

- Fields

- Methods

- Constructors

- Static initializers

- Instance initializers

Fields and methods are also known as members of the class. Classes and interfaces can also be members of a class. This chapter focuses only on fields and methods. I will discuss classes and interfaces as class members in Chapter 2 of *Beginning Java Language Features* (ISBN: 978-1-4302-6658-7). A class can have zero or more class members.

Constructors are used to create objects of a class. You must have at least one constructor for a class. Initializers are used to initialize fields of a class. You can have zero or more initializers of static or instance types. The rest of this chapter will discuss how to declare and use the different components of a class.

Declaring a Class

The general syntax for declaring a class in Java is

```
<<modifiers>> class <<class name>> {
    // Body of the class goes here
}
```

Here, <<modifiers>> are keywords that associate special meanings to the class declaration. A class declaration may have zero or more modifiers. The keyword class is used to declare a class. The <<class name>> is a user-defined name of the class, which should be a valid identifier. Each class has a body, which is specified inside a pair of braces ({}). The body of a class contains its different components, for example, fields, methods, etc. The following snippet of code defines a class named Human with an empty body. Note that here the Human class does not use any modifiers.

```
// Human.java
class Human {
        // Empty body for now
}
```

Declaring Fields in a Class

Fields of a class represent properties (also called attributes) of objects of that class. Suppose every object of human class has two properties: a name and a gender. The human class should include declarations of two fields: one to represent name and one to represent gender.

The fields are declared inside the body of the class. The general syntax to declare a field in a class is

```
<<modifiers>> class <<class name>> {
        // A field declaration
        <<modifiers>> <<data type>> <<field name>> = <<initial value>>;
}
```

A field declaration can use zero or more modifiers. The data type of the field precedes its name. Optionally, you can also initialize each field with a value. If you do not want to initialize a field, its declaration should end with a semicolon after its name.

With the declaration of two fields, name and gender, the declaration of the Human class will look as shown:

```
// Human.java
class Human {
        String name;
        String gender;
}
```

■ **Tip**   It is a convention (not a rule or a requirement) in Java to start a class name with an uppercase letter and capitalize the subsequent words, for example, Human, Table, ColorMonitor, etc. The name of fields and methods should start with a lowercase letter and the subsequent words should be capitalized, for example, name, firstName, maxDebitAmount, etc.

The Human class declares two fields: name and gender. Both fields are of the String type. Every instance (or object) of the Human class will have a copy of these two fields.

Sometimes a property belongs to the class itself, not to any particular instance of that class. For example, the count of all humans is not a property of any specific human. Rather, it belongs to the human class itself. The existence of the count of human is not tied to any specific instance of the human class, even though each instance of the human class contributes to the value of the count property. Only one copy of the class property exists irrespective of the number of instances that exists for the class. However, a separate copy of the instance property exists for each instance of a class. For example, a separate copy of the name and the gender properties exist for each instance of the Human class. You always specify name and gender of a human. However, even if there is no instance of the Human class, you can say that the count of the Human class instances is zero.

Java lets you declare two types of fields for a class:

- Class fields

- Instance fields

Class fields are also known as class variables. Instance fields are also known as instance variables. In the above snippet of code, name and gender are two instance variables of the Human class. Java has a different way to declare class variables. All class variables must be declared using the static keyword as a modifier. The declaration of the Human class in Listing 6-1 adds a count class variable.

Listing 6-1. Declaration of a Human Class with One Class Variable and Two Instance Variables

```
// Human.java
package com.jdojo.cls;

class Human {
        String name;         // An instance variable
        String gender;       // An instance variable
        static long count;   // A class variable because of the static modifier
}
```

■ **Tip**   A class variable is also known as a static variable. An instance variable is also known as a non-static variable.

Creating Instances of a Class

The following is the general syntax to create an instance of a class:

```
new <<Call to Class Constructor>>;
```

The new operator is followed by a call to the constructor of the class whose instance is being created. The new operator creates an instance of a class by allocating the memory on heap. The following statement creates an instance of the Human class:

```
new Human();
```

Here, Human() is a call to the constructor of the Human class. Did you add any constructor to your Human class? No. You have not added any constructor to your Human class. You have added only three fields to it. How can you use a constructor for a class that you have not added? When you do not add a constructor to a class, the Java compiler adds one for you. The constructor that is added by the Java compiler is called a default constructor. The default constructor accepts no arguments. The name of the constructor of a class is the same as the class name. I will discuss constructors in detail later in this chapter.

What happens when an instance of a class is created? The new operator allocates memory for each instance field of the class. Recall that class variables are not allocated memory when an instance of the class is created. Figure 6-1 depicts an instance of the Human class in memory.

Figure 6-1. *An instance of the Human class in memory created by the new Human() instance creation expression*

The figure shows that memory is allocated for instance variables name and gender. You can create as many instances of the Human class as you want. Each time you create an instance of the Human class, Java runtime allocates memory for name and gender instance variables. How much memory is allocated for an instance of the Human class? The simple answer is that you do not know exactly how much memory is used by an instance of a class. In fact, you do not need to know how much memory is needed to create an instance of a class. The Java runtime takes care of memory allocation as well as deallocation automatically for you.

Now, you want to move a step forward and want to assign values to name and gender instance variables for the newly created instance of the Human class. Can you assign values to name and gender instance variables of the newly created instance of the Human class? The answer is no. You cannot access name and gender instance variables, even though they exist in memory. To access instance variables of an instance of a class, you must have its reference (or handle). The expression new Human() creates a new instance of the Human class in memory. The newly created instance is like a balloon filled with Helium gas left in the air. When you release a Helium-filled balloon in the air, you lose control of the balloon. If you attach a string to the balloon before releasing it in the air, you can control the balloon using the string. Similarly, if you want to have control (or access) to an instance of a class, you must store the reference of that instance in a reference variable. You control a balloon with a string; you control a television with a remote controller. The type of controlling device depends on the type of the object that you want to control. Similarly, you need to use different types of reference variables to refer to (or to handle, or to work with) instances of different classes.

The name of a class defines a new reference type in Java. A variable of a specific reference type can store the reference of an instance of the same reference type in memory. Suppose you want to declare a reference variable, which will store a reference of an instance of the Human class. You will declare the variable as shown:

```
Human jack;
```

Here, Human is the class name, which is also a reference type, and jack is a variable of that type. In other words, jack is a reference variable of Human type. The jack variable can be used to store a reference of an instance of the Human class.

The new operator allocates the memory for a new instance of a class and returns the reference (or the indirect pointer) to that instance. You need to store the reference returned by the new operator in a reference variable.

```
jack = new Human();
```

Note that jack itself is a variable and it will be allocated memory separately. The memory location for the jack variable will store the reference of the memory location of the newly created instance of the Human class. Figure 6-2 depicts the memory state when reference variable jack is declared and when an instance of the Human class is created and its reference is assigned to the jack variable.

Figure 6-2. *Memory states when a reference variable is declared and when a reference variable is assigned the reference of an instance of a class*

You can think of the jack variable as a remote controller for a Human instance in memory. You can refer to the Human instance in memory using the jack variable. I will discuss how to use a reference variable in the next section. You can also combine the above two statements into one.

```
Human jack = new Human();
```

The null Reference Type

Every class in Java defines a new reference type. Java has a special reference type called null type. It has no name. Therefore, you cannot define a variable of the null reference type. The null reference type has only one value defined by Java, which is the null literal. It is simply null. The null reference type is assignment compatible with any other reference type. That is, you can assign a null value to a variable of any reference type. Practically, a null value stored in a reference type variable means that the reference variable is referring to no object. You can think of storing a null to a reference variable as a string with no balloon attached to it, where balloon is a valid object and string is a reference variable. For example, you can write code like

```
// Assign null value to john
Human john = null;  // john is not referring to any object
john = new Human(); // Now, john is referring to a valid Human object
```

You can use a null literal with comparison operators to check for equality and inequality.

```
if (john == null) {
        // john is referring to null. Cannot use john for anything
}

if (john != null) {
        // Do something with john
}
```

Note that null is a literal of null type. Java does not let you mix reference types and primitive types. You cannot assign null to a primitive type variable. The following assignment statement will generate a compilation time error:

```
// A compile-time error. A reference type value, null, cannot be assigned to
// a primitive type variable num
int num = null;
```

Because null (or any reference type value) cannot be assigned to a primitive type variable, Java compiler does not allow you to compare a primitive value to a null value. The following comparison will generate a compilation time error. In other words, you can compare a reference type with reference types, and a primitive type with primitive types.

```
int num = 0;

// A compile-time error. Cannot compare a primitive type to a reference type
if (num == null) {
}
```

■ **Tip**   Java has a special reference type that is called null type. The null type does not have a name. The null type has a literal value, which is represented by `null`. The null type is assignment compatible with all other reference types. You can assign any reference type variable a `null` value. You can cast `null` value to any reference type. It is to be emphasized that `null` is a literal value of "null reference type," not a keyword.

Using Dot Notation to Access Fields of a Class

Dot notation is used to refer to instance variables. The general form of the dot notation syntax is

```
<<Reference Variable Name>>.<<Instance Variable Name>>
```

For example, you use `jack.name` to refer to the name instance variable of the instance to which the `jack` reference variable is referring. If you want to assign a value to the name instance variable, you can use

```
jack.name = "Jack Parker";
```

The following statement assigns the value of the name instance variable to a `String` variable aName:

```
String aName = jack.name;
```

How do you refer to class variables? You have two ways to refer to a class variable using dot notation.

- You can refer to a class variable using the name of the class.

  ```
  <<Class Name>>.<<Class Variable Name>>
  ```

  For example, you can use `Human.count` to refer to the count class variable of the Human class. To assign a new value, say 101, to the count class variable you can write

  ```
  Human.count = 101;
  ```

  To read the value of the count class variable into a variable called population, you can use

  ```
  long population = Human.count;
  ```

- You can also use a reference variable to refer to the class variable of a class. For example, you can use `jack.count` to refer to the count class variable of the Human class. You can use the following statement to assign value, say 101, to the count class variable:

  ```
  jack.count = 101;
  ```

  The following statement reads the value of the count class variable into a variable called population:

  ```
  long population = jack.count;
  ```

  Both of the above statements assume that jack is a reference variable of Human type and it refers to a valid Human instance.

■ **Tip** You can use the class name or a reference variable of the class type to refer to a class variable. Since the class variable belongs to the class and it is shared by all instances of the class, it is logical to refer to it using the class name. However, you always use a reference variable of a class type to refer to the instance variables.

It is time to see the use of fields in the Human class. Listing 6-2 has a complete program that demonstrates how to access class variables and instance variables of a class.

Listing 6-2. A Test Class to Demonstrate How to Access (Read/Write) Class Variables and Instance Variables of a Class

```java
// FieldAccessTest.java
package com.jdojo.cls;

class FieldAccessTest {
        public static void main(String[] args) {
                // Create an instance of Human class
                Human jack = new Human();

                // Increase count by one
                Human.count++;

                // Assign values to name and gender
                jack.name = "Jack Parker";
                jack.gender = "Male";

                // Read and print the values of name, gender and count
                String jackName = jack.name;
                String jackGender = jack.gender;
                long population = Human.count;

                System.out.println("Name: " + jackName);
                System.out.println("Gender: " + jackGender);
                System.out.println("Population: " + population);

                // Change the name
                jack.name = "Jackie Parker";

                // Read and print the changed name
                String changedName = jack.name;
                System.out.println("Changed Name: " + changedName);
        }
}
```

```
Name: Jack Parker
Gender: Male
Population: 1
Changed Name: Jackie Parker
```

The following statement needs some explanation:

```
// Increase count by one
Human.count++;
```

It uses the increment operator (++) on the count class variable. After the count class variable is incremented by 1, you read and print its value. The output shows that after incrementing its value by 1, its value becomes 1. It means that its value was zero before the Human.count++ statement was executed. However, you have never set its value to zero. Its declaration was as follows:

```
static long count;
```

When the count class variable was declared as shown above, it was initialized to zero by default. All fields of a class (class variables and instance variables) are initialized to a default value, if you do not assign an initial value to them. I will discuss the initialization of fields of a class in detail in the next section.

Default Initialization of Fields

All fields of a class, static as well as non-static, are initialized to a default value. The default value of a field depends on its data type.

- A numeric field (byte, short, char, int, long, float, and double) is initialized to zero.

- A boolean field is initialized to false.

- A reference type field is initialized to null.

According to the above rules, the fields of the Human class will be initialized as follows:

- The count class variable is initialized to zero because it is of numeric type. This is the reason, Human.count++ evaluated to 1 (0 + 1 = 1) as shown in the output of Listing 6-2.

- The name and gender instance variables are of String type. String is a reference type. They are initialized to null. Recall that a copy of the name and gender fields exists for every object of the Human class, and each copy of name and gender is initialized to null.

If you consider the above default initialization of the fields of the Human class, it behaves as if you have declared the Human class as shown below. This declaration of the Human class and the one as shown in Listing 6-1 are the same.

```
class Human {
        String name = null;
        String gender = null;
        static long count = 0;
}
```

Listing 6-3 demonstrates the default initialization of fields. The DefaultInit class includes only instance variables. The class fields are initialized with the same default value as the instance fields. If you declare all fields of the DefaultInit class as static, the output will be the same.

Listing 6-3. Default Initialization of Class Fields

```java
// DefaultInit.java
package com.jdojo.cls;

class DefaultInit {
        byte b;
        short s;
        int i;
        long l;
        float f;
        double d;
        boolean bool;
        String str;

        public static void main(String[] args) {
                // Create an object of DefaultInit class
                DefaultInit obj = new DefaultInit();

                // Print the default values for all instance variables
                System.out.println("byte is initialized to " + obj.l);
                System.out.println("short is initialized to " + obj.s);
                System.out.println("int is initialized to " + obj.i);
                System.out.println("long is initialized to " + obj.l);
                System.out.println("float is initialized to " + obj.f);
                System.out.println("double is initialized to " + obj.d);
                System.out.println("boolean is initialized to " + obj.bool);
                System.out.println("String is initialized to " + obj.str);
        }
}
```

```
byte is initialized to 0
short is initialized to 0
int is initialized to 0
long is initialized to 0
float is initialized to 0.0
double is initialized to 0.0
boolean is initialized to false
String is initialized to null
```

Access Level Modifiers for a Class

In Listing 6-1, you created the Human class in the com.jdojo.cls package. You used the Human class in Listing 6-2 to create its object in the FieldAccessTest class, which is in the same package as the Human class. You had no problem in compiling and running the following statement in Listing 6-2:

```java
Human jack = new Human();
```

Let's create a class `ClassAccessTest` in the `com.jdojo.common` package. Note that the package for the `ClassAccessTest` class is different from the package for the Human class. The code for the `ClassAccessTest` class is

```
// ClassAccessTest.java
package com.jdojo.common;

public class ClassAccessTest {
        public static void main(String[] args) {
                Human jack;
        }
}
```

The code for the `ClassAccessTest` class is very simple. It does only one thing—declares a reference variable of Human type in its `main()` method. Compile the `ClassAccessTest` class. Oops! You got a compilation time error.

```
"ClassAccessTest.java": cannot find symbol; symbol  : class Human, location: class com.jdojo.common.
ClassAccessTest at line 6, column 5
```

If you read the error carefully, the compiler is complaining about the type Human in the following variable declaration:

```
Human jack;
```

The compiler is stating that it could not find the definition of the term Human. What is wrong in the `ClassAccessTest` class with the `jack` variable declaration? When you refer to a class by its simple name, the compiler looks for that class declaration in the same package where the referring class is. In your case, the referring class `ClassAccessTest` is in the `com.jdojo.common` package and it uses the simple name, Human, to refer to the Human class. Therefore, the compiler looks for the Human class in the `com.jdojo.common` package. The compiler is looking for a `com.jdojo.common.Human` class, which you do not have. This is the reason why you received the error.

By using the simple name Human in `ClassAccessTest`, you meant to refer to the Human class in the `com.jdojo.cls` package, not in the `com.jdojo.common` package. If you had the Human class in the `com.jdojo.common` package, your code for `ClassAccessTest` would have compiled. Let's assume that you do not have a `com.jdojo.common.Human` class and you want to fix the compilation time error. You can fix it by using the fully qualified name of the Human class, like so:

```
// ClassAccessTest.java
package com.jdojo.common;

public class ClassAccessTest {
  public static void main(String[] args) {
    com.jdojo.cls.Human jack;
  }
}
```

Now compile the `ClassAccessTest` class. Oops! You got a compilation time error again. However, this time, the error is different.

```
"ClassAccessTest.java": com.jdojo.cls.Human is not public in com.jdojo.cls; cannot be accessed from
outside package at line 6, column 24
```

This time, the compiler is not saying that it does not understand the Human type. It is saying that it knows what com.jdojo.cls.Human type is; however, it is accessible only inside the com.jdojo.cls package in which it has been declared. In other words, the Human type is not accessible inside the com.jdojo.common package. Here comes the concept of the access level for a class.

When you declare a class, you can also specify whether the class can be accessed (or used, or referred to) from any package in the application, or only from within the package in which it has been declared. For example, you can specify in the declaration of the Human class whether it can be accessed only from within the com.jdojo.cls package or from any package including the com.jdojo.common package. The general syntax specifying access-level for a class is

```
<<access level modifier>>class <<class name>> {
        // Body of the class goes here
}
```

There are only two valid values for <<access level modifier>>in a class declaration: no value and public.

- No value: It is the same as the absence of <access level modifier>>. It is also known as package-level access. If a class has package-level access, it can be accessed only within the package in which it has been declared. The Human class in Listing 6-1 has package-level access. This is the reason that you were able to use (or access) the Human class in the FieldAccessTest class in Listing 6-2. Note that the Human class and the FieldAccessTest class are in the same package and both have package-level access. Therefore, they can refer to each other. The Human class is in the com.jdojo.cls package and it has package-level access. Therefore, it cannot be accessed from any other package, for example, com.jdojo.common. This is the reason that you received the compilation time error when you tried to compile the ClassAccessTest class.

- public: A class with a public access level modifier can be accessed from any package in the application. If you want the Human class to be accessible from any package (e.g. com.jdojo. common), you need to declare it as public.

Let's redefine the Human class as shown in Listing 6-4. This time, you have specified its access level as public, so it is accessible from any package.

Listing 6-4. Redefined Human Class with the Public Access Level Modifier

```
// Human.java
package com.jdojo.cls;

public class Human {
        String name;        // Instance variable
        String gender;      // Instance variable
        static long count;  // Class variable
}
```

Recompile the Human class, and then compile the ClassAccessTest class. This time, the ClassAccessTest class compiles without any errors.

■ **Tip**   What does it mean when I state that a class is accessible from a package? A class defines a new reference type. A reference type can be used to declare a variable. When a class is accessible in a package, the class name can be used as a reference type, for example, to declare a variable, in the code that resides in that package.

Import Declarations

You learned two rules in the previous section:

- You must declare a class public to use it in a package other than the package in which it is declared.

- You need to use the fully qualified name of a class to use it in a package other than the one in which it is declared. A class can be referred to using its simple name in the package in which it is declared.

There is no alternative to the first rule. That is, a class must be declared public if it needs to be accessible from outside its package.

There is another way to deal with the second rule. You can refer to a class by its simple name outside its package by using an import declaration. An import declaration is used to import a class into a compilation unit from outside the package of the compilation unit. Technically speaking, an import declaration is used to import any type into a compilation unit, not just a class. Import declarations appear just after the package declaration and before the first type declaration. Figure 6-3 shows the place where import declarations appear. You can have multiple import declarations in a compilation unit.

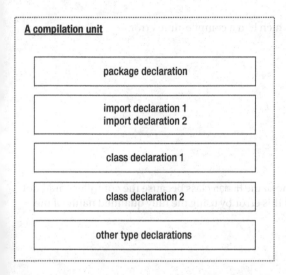

Figure 6-3. *The structure of a compilation unit in Java*

This section mentions importing only class types. However, the same rules apply for importing any other types, for example, interface types, annotation types, or enum types. Because I have covered only class types up to this point, I will not mention any other types in this discussion.

There are two types of import declarations:

- Single-type import declaration

- Import-on-demand declaration

Single-Type Import Declaration

A single-type import declaration is used to import a single type (e.g. a class) from a package. It is of the form

```
import <<fully qualified name of a type>>;
```

The following import declaration imports the Human class from the com.jdojo.cls package:

```
import com.jdojo.cls.Human;
```

A single-type import declaration imports only one type from a package. If you want to import more than one type (e.g. three classes) from a package (or from different packages), you need to use a separate import declaration for each type. The following import declarations import Class11 from pkg1 package, Class21 and Class22 from pkg2 package, and Class33 from pkg3 package:

```
import pkg1.Class11;
import pkg2.Class21;
import pkg2.Class22;
import pkg3.Class33;
```

Let's revisit the com.jdojo.common.ClassAccessTest class, which had a compile-time error.

```
// ClassAccessTest.java
package com.jdojo.common;

public class ClassAccessTest {
        public static void main(String[] args) {
                Human jack;
        }
}
```

You received a compiler error when you used the simple name of the Human class because the compiler could not find a Human class in the com.jdojo.common package. You resolved this error by using the fully qualified name of the Human class, like so:

```
// ClassAccessTest.java
package com.jdojo.common;

public class ClassAccessTest {
        public static void main(String[] args) {
                com.jdojo.cls.Human jack; // Uses full qualified name for the Human class
        }
}
```

You have another way to resolve this error, which is by using a single-type-import declaration. You can import the com.jdojo.cls.Human class to its simple name. The modified ClassAccessTest class declaration is as follows:

```
// ClassAccessTest.java - Modified version
package com.jdojo.common;

import com.jdojo.cls.Human; // Import the Human class
```

```
public class ClassAccessTest {
        public static void main(String[] args) {
                Human jack; // Use simple name of the Human class
        }
}
```

The modified version of the ClassAccessTest class compiles fine. When the compiler comes across the simple name of the Human class in the statement, like

```
Human jack;
```

it goes through all import declarations to resolve the simple name to a fully qualified name. When it tries to resolve the simple name Human, it finds the import declaration, import com.jdojo.cls.Human, which imports the Human class. It assumes that you intended to use the com.jdojo.cls.Human class when you used the simple name Human in the above statement. The compiler replaces the above statement with the following statement:

```
com.jdojo.cls.Human jack;
```

■ **Tip**   Import declarations let you use the simple name of a type in your code, thus making your code more readable. When you compile your code, the compiler replaces the simple name of a type with its fully qualified name. It uses import declarations for converting simple names of the types to their fully qualified names. It is to be emphasized that using import declarations in your Java program does not affect the size of your compiled code or runtime performance. Using import declarations is just a way to use the simple names of classes in your source code.

There are many subtle points to remember while using import declarations. I will discuss them shortly.

Import-on-Demand Declaration

Sometimes you may need to import multiple types from the same package. You need to use as many single-type-import declarations as the number of types you need to import from the package. An import-on-demand declaration is used to import multiple types from a package using one import declaration. The syntax for an import-on-demand declaration is

```
import <<package name>>.*;
```

Here, the package name is followed by a dot and an asterisk (*). For example, the following import-on-demand declaration imports all types (that includes all classes) from com.jdojo.cls package:

```
import com.jdojo.cls.*;
```

Sometimes the use of an asterisk in an import-on-demand declaration leads to wrong assumption about the types that are imported. Suppose there are two classes, C1 and C2. They are in packages p1 and p1.p2, respectively. That is, their fully qualified names are p1.C1 and p1.p2.C2. You may write an import-on-demand declaration as

```
import p1.*;
```

thinking that it will import both classes, p1.C1 and p1.p2.C2. This assumption is wrong. The declaration

```
import p1.*;
```

imports all types only from p1 package. It will not import the p1.p2.C2 class because the C2 class is not in the p1 package; rather it is in the p2 package, which is a sub-package of p1. The asterisk at the end of an import-on-demand declaration means all types only from the specified package. The asterisk does not mean sub-packages and types inside those sub-packages. Sometimes programmers attempt to use multiple asterisks in an import-on-demand declaration thinking that it will import types from all sub-packages too.

```
import p1.*.*; // A compile-time error
```

The above import-on-demand declaration results in a compiler error because it uses multiple asterisks. It does not follow the syntax for an import-on-demand declaration. In an import-on-demand declaration, the declaration must end with a dot followed by one and only one asterisk.

If you want to import both classes C1 and C2, you need to use two import-on-demand declarations.

```
import p1.*;
import p1.p2.*;
```

You can rewrite the code for the ClassAccessTest class using an import-on-demand declaration.

```
// ClassAccessTest.java - Modified version uses import-on-demand
package com.jdojo.common;

// Import all types from the com.jdojo.cls package incuding the Human class
import com.jdojo.cls.*;

public class ClassAccessTest {
        public static void main(String[] args) {
                Human jack; // Use simple name of the Human class
        }
}
```

When the compiler tries to resolve the simple name Human in the above code, it will use an import-on-demand declaration to see if a Human class exists in com.jdojo.cls package. In fact, the asterisk in the import declaration will be replaced by Human and then the compiler checks if the com.jdojo.cls.Human class exists. Suppose you have two classes in the com.jdojo.cls package named Human and Table. The following code will compile with one import-on-demand declaration:

```
// ClassAccessTest.java - Modified version uses import-on-demand
package com.jdojo.common;

// Import all types from com.jdojo.cls package including Human and Table classes
import com.jdojo.cls.*;

public class ClassAccessTest {
        public static void main(String[] args) {
                Human jack; // Use simple name of the Human class
                Table t1;   // Use simple name of the Table class
        }
}
```

The one import-on-demand declaration in the above code has the same effect as the following two single-type-import declarations:

```
import com.jdojo.cls.Human; // Import Human class
import com.jdojo.cls.Table; // Import Table class
```

Which type of import declaration is better to use in your Java program: single-type import or import-on-demand? It is simple to use the import-on-demand declaration. However, it is not readable. Let's look at the following code, which compiles fine. Assume that class A and B are not in the com.jdojo.cls package.

```
// ImportOnDemandTest.java
package com.jdojo.cls;

import p1.*;
import p2.*;

public class ImportOnDemandTest {
        public static void main(String[] args) {
                A a; // Declare a variable of class A type
                B b; // Declare a variable of class B type
        }
}
```

Can you tell, by looking at the above code, the fully qualified names of the classes A and B? Is class A in the package p1 or p2? It is impossible to tell just by looking at the code the package to which classes A and B belong because you have used import-on-demand declarations. Let's rewrite the above code using two single-type-import declarations.

```
// ImportOnDemandTest.java
package com.jdojo.cls;

import p1.A;
import p2.B;

public class ImportOnDemandTest {
        public static void main(String[] args) {
                A a; // Declare a variable of class A type
                B b; // Declare a variable of class B type
        }
}
```

By looking at the import declarations, you can now tell that class A is in the package p1 and class B is in the package p2. A single-type import declaration makes it easy for readers to know which class is being imported from which package. It also makes it easy to know the number and name of the classes used from other packages in your program. This book uses single-type import declaration in all examples, except in examples where I discuss import-on-demand declarations.

Even though you are advised to use single-type-import declaration in your programs, you need to know some tricky uses and implications of using both single-type import and import-on-demand declarations in the same program. Subsequent sections will discuss them in detail.

Import Declarations and Type Search Order

Import declarations are used to resolve simple names of types to their fully qualified names during compilation. The compiler uses predefined rules to resolve the simple names. Suppose the following statement appears in a Java program that uses a simple name A:

```
A var;
```

The Java compiler must resolve the simple name A to its fully qualified name during the compilation process. It searches for a type referenced in a program in the following order:

- The current compilation unit
- Single-type import declarations
- Types declared in the same package
- Import-on-demand declarations

The above list of type search is not complete. If a type has nested types, the nested type is searched before looking in the current compilation unit. I will defer the discussion of nested types until inner classes are discussed in Chapter 2 of the book Beginning Java Language Features (ISBN: 978-1-4302-6658-7).

Let's discuss the rules for a type search using some examples. Suppose you have a Java source file (a compilation unit) B.java whose content is as follows. Note that the file B.java contains declarations for two classes A and B.

```
// B.java
package p1;

class B {
    A var;
}

class A {
    // Code goes here
}
```

Class B refers to class A with its simple name when it declares an instance variable var of type A. When the B.java file is compiled, the compiler will look for a type with the simple name A in the current compilation unit (B.java file). It will find a class declaration whose simple name is A in the current compilation unit. The simple name A will be replaced with its fully qualified name p1.A. Note that both classes A and B are declared in the same compilation unit, and therefore they are in the same package, p1. The class B definition will be changed as follows by the compiler:

```
package p1;

class B {
        p1.A var; // A has been replaced by p1.A by the compiler
}
```

Suppose you want to use class A from package p2 in the previous example. That is, there is a class p2.A and you want to declare the instance variable var of type p2.A in class B instead of p1.A. Let's try to solve it by importing class p2.A using a single-type-import declaration, like so:

```
// B.java - Includes a new import declaration
package p1;

import p2.A;

class B {
        A var; // We want to use p2.A when you use A
}

class A {
        // Code goes here
}
```

When you compile the modified B.java file, you will get the following compilation error:

```
"B.java": p1.A is already defined in this compilation unit at line 2, column 1
```

What is wrong with the modified source code? When you remove the single-type-import declaration from it, it compiles fine. It means it is the single-type import declaration that is causing the error. Before you resolve this compiler error, you need to learn about a new rule about single-type import declarations. The rule is

> *It is a compile time error to import more than one type with the same simple name using multiple single-type-import declarations.*

Suppose you have two classes, p1.A and p2.A. Note that both classes have the same simple name A placed in two different packages. According to the above rules, if you want to use the two classes, p1.A and p2.A, in the same compilation unit, you cannot use two single-type-import declarations.

```
// Test.java
package pkg;

import p1.A;
import p2.A; // A compile-time error

class Test {
        A var1; // Which A to use p1.A or p2.A?
        A var2; // Which A to use p1.A or p2.A?
}
```

The reason behind this rule is that the compiler has no way to know which class (p1.A or p2.A) to use when you use simple name A in the code. Java might have solved this issue by using the first imported class or last imported class, which might have been error prone. Java decided to nip the problem in the bud by giving you a compiler error when you import two classes with the same simple names, so you cannot make silly mistakes like this and end up spending hours resolving them.

Let's go back to the problem of importing the p2.A class in a compilation unit, which already declares a class A. The following code produces a compile-time error:

```
// B.java - Includes a new import declaration
package p1;

import p2.A;

class B {
        A var1; // We want to use p2.A when you use A
}

class A {
        // Code goes here
}
```

You have used only one single-type import declaration, not two, in the above code. Why did you get an error? When you declare more than one class in the same compilation unit, most likely they are closely related and they would refer to each other. You need to think as if Java imports each of the classes declared in the same compilation unit using a single-type import declaration. You can think of the above code being transformed by Java as shown:

```
// B.java - Includes a new import declaration
package p1;

import p1.A; // Think of it being added by Java
import p1.B; // Think of it being added by Java
import p2.A;

class B {
        A var; // We want to use p2.A when you use A
}

class A {
        // Code goes here
}
```

Can you now see the problem? The class A has been imported twice, once by Java and once by you, and this is the reason for the error. How do you refer to p2.A in your code anyway? It is simple. Use the fully qualified name p2.A whenever you want to use p2.A in your compilation unit.

```
// B.java - Uses fully qualified name p2.A in class B
package p1;

class B {
    p2.A var; // Use fully qualified name of A
}
class A {
    // Code goes here
}
```

■ Tip   It is a compile-time error to import a type using a single-type-import declaration into a compilation unit, if a type with the same simple name exists in the same compilation unit.

Let's resolve the compiler error with the code that needs to use classes from different packages with the same simple name. The code is as follows:

```java
// Test.java
package pkg;

import p1.A;
import p2.A; // A compile-time error

class Test {
        A var1; // Which A to use p1.A or p2.A?
        A var2; // Which A to use p1.A or p2.A?
}
```

You can resolve the error using one of the two following methods:

- Remove both import declarations and always use the fully qualified name of class A.

    ```java
    // Test.java
    package pkg;

    class Test {
            p1.A var1; // Use p1.A
            p2.A var2; // Use p2.A
    }
    ```

- Use only one import declaration to import class A from one package, say p1, and use the fully qualified name of class A from other package p2.

    ```java
    // Test.java
    package pkg;

    import p1.A;

    class Test {
            A var1;     // Refers to p1.A
            p2.A var2; // Uses the fully qualified name p2.A
    }
    ```

■ Tip   If you want to use multiple classes in a compilation unit with the same simple name, but from different packages, you can import a maximum of one class. For the rest of the classes, you must use the fully qualified name. You have the option of using the fully qualified name for all classes.

Let's discuss some of the rules about using import-on-demand declarations. The compiler uses the import-on-demand declarations in resolving a simple name of a type after it has used all other means to resolve the simple name. It is valid to import a class with the same simple name using a single-type import declaration as well as an import-on-demand declaration. In such a case, the single-type import declaration is used. Suppose you have three Classes and objects: p1.A, p2.A, and p2.B. Suppose you have a compilation unit as follows:

```java
// C.java
package p3;

import p1.A;
import p2.*;

class C {
        A var; // Will always use p1.A (not p2.A)
}
```

In the above code, class A has been imported twice: once using simple type import declaration from package p1, and once using import-on-demand declaration from package p2. The simple name A is resolved to p1.A because a single-type import declaration always takes precedence over an import-on-demand declaration. Once the compiler finds a class using a single-type import declaration, it stops the search there without looking for that class using any import-on-demand declarations.

Let's change the import declarations in the above code to use import-on-demand declarations, as follows:

```java
// C.java
package p3;

import p1.*;
import p2.*;

class  C {
        A var; // An error. Which A to use p1.A or p2.A?
}
```

Compilation of class C generates an error.

```
"C.java": reference to A is ambiguous, both class p2.A in p2 and class p1.A in p1 match at line 8,
column 5
```

The error message is loud and clear. When the compiler finds a class using an import-on-demand declaration, it continues searching for the class in all import-on-demand declarations. If it finds the class with the same simple name using multiple import-on-demand declarations, it generates an error. You can resolve the above compiler error in several ways:

- Use two single-type-import declarations.

- Use one single-type import and one import-on-demand declaration.

- Use fully qualified names for both classes.

Below is a list of some more rules about import declarations.

- Duplicate single-type import and import-on-demand declarations are ignored. The following code is valid:

```
// D.java
package p4;

import p1.A;
import p1.A; // Ignored. A duplicate import declaration.
import p2.*;
import p2.*; // Ignored. A duplicate import declaration.

class D {
      // Code goes here
}
```

- It is legal, though not needed, to import classes from the same package using single-type import declarations or import-on-demand declaration. The following code imports class F from the same package p5. Note that all classes declared in the same package are automatically imported by Java. In such a case, the import declaration is ignored.

```
// E.java
package p5;

import p5.F; // Will be ignored

class E {
      // Code goes here
}

// F.java
package p5;

import p5.*; // Will be ignored

class F {
      // Code goes here
}
```

Automatic Import Declarations

You have been using the String class and the System class by their simple names and you never cared to import them in any of your programs. The fully qualified names of these classes are java.lang.String and java.lang.System. Java always imports all types declared in the java.lang package automatically. Think of the following import-on-demand declaration being added to your source code before compilation:

```
import java.lang.*;
```

This is the reason that you were able to use the simple names of String and System classes in your code without importing them. You can use any types from the java.lang package by their simple names in your programs.

It is not an error to use an import declaration to import types from java.lang package. They will be simply ignored by the compiler. The following code will compile without errors:

```
package p1;

import java.lang.*;   // Will be ignored because it is automatically done for you

public class G {
        String anythingGoes; // Refers to java.lang.String
}
```

You need to be careful when using the simple name of a type, which is the same as a type that is defined in the java.lang package. Suppose you declare a p1.String class.

```
// String.java
package p1;

public class String {
    // Code goes here
}
```

Suppose you have a Test class in the same package, p1.

```
// Test.java
package p1;

public class Test {
        // Which String class will be used: p1.String or java.lang.String
        String myStr;
}
```

Which String class is referred in the Test class: p1.String or java.lang.String? It will refer to p1.String, not java.lang.String, because the package of the compilation unit (which is p1 in this case) is searched before any import declarations to resolve the simple names of types. The compiler finds the String class in package p1. It will not search java.lang package for the String class. If you want to use the java.lang.String class in the above code, you must use its fully qualified name, as shown:

```
// Test.java
package p1;

public class Test {
        java.lang.String s1; // Use java.lang.String
        p1.String s2;        // Use p1.String
        String s3;           // Will use p1.String
}
```

Static Import Declarations

A static import declaration does what its name suggests. It imports static members (static variables/methods) of a type into a compilation unit. You learned about static variable (or class variable) in previous sections. I will discuss static methods in the next section.

A static import declaration also comes in two flavors: single-static import and static-import-on-demand. A single-static import declaration imports one static member from a type. A static-import-on-demand declaration imports all static members of a type. The general syntax of static import declaration is as follows:

Single-static-import declaration:

```
import static <<package name>>.<<type name>>.<<static member name>>;
```

Static-import-on-demand declaration:

```
import static <<package name>>.<<type name>>.*;
```

You have been printing messages in the standard output using the System.out.println() method. System is a class in java.lang package that has a static variable named out. When you use System.out, you are referring to that static variable out of the System class. You can use a static import declaration to import the out static variable from the System class as follows:

```
import static java.lang.System.out;
```

Your program now does not need to qualify the out variable with the System class name as System.out. Rather, it can use the name out to mean System.out in your program. The compiler will use the static import declaration to resolve the name out to System.out.

Listing 6-5 demonstrates how to use a static import declaration. It imports the out static variable of the System class. Note that the main() method uses out.println() method, not System.out.println(). The compiler will replace the out.println() call with the System.out.println() call.

Listing 6-5. Using Static Import Declarations

```java
// StaticImportTest.java
package com.jdojo.cls;

import static java.lang.System.out;

public class StaticImportTest {
        public static void main(String[] args) {
                out.println("Hello static import!");
        }
}
```

Hello static import!

■ **Tip** An import declaration imports a type name and it lets you use the type's simple name in your program. What an import declaration does with a type, a static import declaration does with a static member of a type. A static import declaration lets you use the name of a static member (static variable/method) of a type without qualifying it with the type name.

Let's look at another example of using static import declarations. The Math class in the java.lang package has many utility constants and static methods. For example, it has a class variable named PI, whose value is equal to 22/7 (the pi in mathematics). If you want to use any of the static variables or methods of the Math class, you will need to qualify them with the class name Math. For example, you would refer to the PI static variable as Math.PI and the sqrt() method as Math.sqrt(). You can import all static members of the Math class using the following static-import-on-demand declaration:

```
import static java.lang.Math.*;
```

Now you can use the name of the static member without qualifying them with the class name Math. Listing 6-6 demonstrates using the Math class by importing its static members.

Listing 6-6. Using Static Imports to Import Multiple Static Members of a Type

```java
// StaticImportTest2.java
package com.jdojo.cls;

import static java.lang.System.out;
import static java.lang.Math.*;

public class StaticImportTest2 {
        public static void main(String[] args) {
                double radius = 2.9;
                double area = PI * radius * radius;

                out.println("Value of PI is: " + PI);
                out.println("Radius of circle: " + radius);
                out.println("Area of circle: " + area);
                out.println("Square root of 2.0: " + sqrt(2.0));
        }
}
```

```
Value of PI is: 3.141592653589793
Radius of circle: 2.9
Area of circle: 26.420794216690158
Square root of 2.0: 1.4142135623730951
```

The following are some important rules about static import declaration.

Static Import Rule #1

If two static members with the same simple name are imported, one using single-static import declaration and other using static-import-on-demand declaration, the one imported using single-static import declaration takes precedence. Suppose there are two classes, p1.C1 and p2.C2. Both classes have a static method called m1. The following code will use p1.C1.m1() method because it is imported using the single-static import declaration:

```java
// Test.java
package com.jdojo.cls;

import static p1.C1.m1; // Imports C1.m1() method
import static p2.C2.*;  // Imports C2.m1() method too
```

```
public class Test {
        public static void main(String[] args) {
                m1();    // C1.m1() will be called
        }
}
```

Static Import Rule #2

Using single-static-import declaration to import two static members with the same simple name is not allowed. The following static import declarations generate an error because both of them import the static member with the same simple name of m1:

```
import static p1.C1.m1;
import static p1.C2.m1; // An error
```

Static Import Rule #3

If a static member is imported using a single-static import declaration and there exists a static member in the same class with the same name, the static member in the class is used. The following is the code for two classes, p1.A and p2.Test:

```
// A.java
package p1;

public class A {
        public static void test() {
                System.out.println("p1.A.test()");
        }
}
```

```
// Test.java
package p2;

import static p1.A.test;

public class Test {
        public static void main(String[] args) {
                test(); // Will use p2.Test.test() method, not p1.A.test() method
        }

        public static void test() {
                System.out.println("p2.Test.test()");
        }
}
```

```
p2.Test.test()
```

The Test class imports the static method test() from class p1.A using a single-static import declaration. The Test class also defines a static method test(). When you use the simple name, test, to call the test() method in the main() method, it refers to p2.Test.test() method, not the one imported by the static import.

There is a hidden danger in using static import declarations in such cases. Suppose you did not have a test() static method in the p2.Test class. In the beginning, the test() method call will call p1.A.test() method. Later, you add a test() method in the Test class. Now the test() method call will start calling p2.Test.test(), which will introduce a hard-to-find bug in your program.

■ **Tip** It may seem that static imports help you use simple names of static members to make the program simpler to write and read. Sometimes static imports may introduce subtle bugs in your program, which may be hard to debug. You are advised not use static imports at all, or only in very rare circumstances.

Declaring Methods of a Class

A method in a class defines the behavior of the objects of that class or the behavior of the class itself. A method is a named block of code. The method can be invoked to execute its code. The code that invokes the method is called the caller of the method. Optionally, a method may accept input values from the caller and it may return a value to the caller. The list of input values is known as parameters. A method may have zero parameters. If a method has zero parameters, you say that method does not have any parameters or method does not take any parameters. A method is always defined inside the body of a class. To keep the sample code simple, I will show a method as an isolated block of code in this section. I will show a method inside a class body when I discuss a complete example.

The general syntax for a method declaration is of the form

```
<<modifiers>> <<return type>> <<method name>> (<<parameters list>>) <<throws clause>> {
        // Body of the method goes here
}
```

Here, <<modifiers>> is an optional list of modifiers; <<return type>> is the data type of the value returned from the method; <<method name>> is the name of the method. The method name is followed by a pair of opening and closing parentheses. Optionally, you can specify one or more parameters to the method within the parentheses. Multiple parameters are separated by a comma. The closing parenthesis may optionally be followed by a throws clause. Finally, you specify the code for the method inside opening and closing braces.

Note that four parts in a method declaration are mandatory: the return type, method name, a pair of opening and closing parentheses, and a pair of opening and closing braces. Let's discuss each part in a method declaration in detail. I will discuss modifiers in various sections of this chapter and subsequent chapters in this book. I will discuss the throws clause in the chapter on exception handling.

The following is an example of a method: it is named add; it takes two parameters of type int named n1 and n2, and it returns their sum:

```
int add(int n1, int n2) {
        int sum = n1 + n2;
        return sum;
}
```

The return type of a method is the data type of the value that the method will return when it is invoked. It could be a primitive data type (for example, int, double, boolean, etc.) or a reference type (for example, Human, String, etc.). Sometimes, a method does not return a value to its caller. The keyword void is used as the return type if a method does not return any value to the caller. In the above example, the add method returns the sum of two integers, which will be an integer. This is the reason that its return type is specified as int.

The method name must be a valid Java identifier. Conventionally, a Java method starts with a lowercase and subsequently a word cap is used. For example, getName, setName, getHumanCount, and createHuman are valid method names. AbCDeFg is also a valid method name; it just doesn't follow standard conventions.

A method may take input values from its caller. A parameter is used to take an input value from the caller. A parameter consists of two parts: a data type and a variable name. In fact, a method parameter is a variable declaration. The variables are used to hold the input values that are passed from the method's caller. A comma is used to separate two parameters of a method. In the above example, the add method declares two parameters, n1 and n2. Both parameters are of the int data type. When the add method is called, the caller must pass two int values. The first value passed from the caller is stored in n1, and the second value passed from the caller is stored in n2. The parameters n1 and n2 are also known as formal parameters.

A method is uniquely identified by its signature in a particular context. The signature of a method is the combination of its name and its parameter's number, types, and order. Modifiers, return types, and parameter names are not part of the signature. Table 6-1 lists some examples of method declarations and their signatures. Most often, you will have situations where you need to understand whether two methods have the same signature. It is very important to understand that the type and order of the method's parameters are part of its signature. For example, double add(int n1, double d1) and double add(double d1, int n1) have different signatures because the order of their parameters differs even though the number and types of parameters are the same.

Table 6-1. *Examples of Method's Declarations and Their Signatures*

Method Declaration	Method Signature
int add(int n1, int n2)	add(int, int)
int add(int n3, int n4)	add(int, int)
public int add(int n1, int n2)	add(int, int)
public int add(int n1, int n2) throws OutofRangeException	add(int, int)
void process(int n)	process(int)
double add(int n1, double d1)	add(int, double)
double add(double d1, int n1)	add(double, int)

■ **Tip** The signature of a method uniquely identifies the method within a class. It is not allowed to have more than one method in a class with the same signature.

Finally, the code for the method is specified in the method's body, which is enclosed in braces. Executing the code for a method is also called "calling a method" or "invoking a method." A method is invoked using its name with the values for its parameters, if any, within parentheses. To call your add method, you need to use the following statement:

```
add(10, 12);
```

The above call to the add method passes 10 and 12 as the values for parameters n1 and n2, respectively. The two values, 10 and 12, that are used to call the add method are called actual parameters. Java copies the actual parameters to the formal parameters before it executes the code inside the body of the method. In the above call to the add method, 10 will be copied in n1, and 12 will be copied in n2. You can refer to the formal parameter names as variables having actual parameter values inside the method's body. You can see n1 and n2 being treated as variables in the following statement in the add method:

```
int sum = n1 + n2;
```

A return statement is used to return a value from a method. It starts with the return keyword. If a method returns a value, the return keyword must be followed by an expression, which evaluates to the value being returned. If the method does not return a value, its return type is specified as void. If the method's return type is void, the method does not have to include a return statement. If a method with a void return type wants to include a return statement, the return keyword must not be followed by any expression; the return keyword is immediately followed by a semicolon to mark the end of the statement. Here are the two flavors of the return statement:

```
// If a method returns a value, <<an expression>>must evaluate to a data type,
// which is assignment compatible with the specified return type of the method
return <<an expression>>;
```

or

```
// If method's return type is void
return;
```

What does a return statement do? As its name suggests, it returns the control to the caller of the method. If it has an expression, it evaluates the expression and returns the value of the expression to the caller. If a return statement does not have an expression, it simply returns the control to its caller. A return statement is the last statement that is executed in a method's body. You can have multiple return statements in a method's body. However, at most, only one return statement may be executed for a method call.

The add method returns the sum of two of its parameters. How do you capture the returned value of a method? A method call itself is an expression whose data type is the return type of the method and it evaluates to the returned value from the method. For example, if you write a statement like

```
add(10, 12);
```

add(10, 12) is an expression and its data type is int. At runtime, it will be evaluated to an int value of 22, which is the value returned from the add method. To capture the value of a method call, you can use the method call expression anywhere you can use a value. For example, the following snippet of code assigns the value returned from the add method to a variable call sum:

```
int sum = add(10, 12); // sum variable will be assigned 22
```

Now turn your attention to a method, which does not return a value. You specify void as the return type for such a method. Let's consider the following method declaration for a method printPoem;

```
void printPoem() {
        System.out.println("Strange fits of passion have I known:");
        System.out.println("And I will dare to tell,");
        System.out.println("But in the lover's ear alone,");
        System.out.println("What once to me befell.");
}
```

The printPoem method specifies void as its return type, which means that it does not return a value to its caller. It does not specify any parameters, which means it does not accept any input values from its caller. If you need to call the printPoem method, you need to write the following statement:

```
printPoem();
```

■ **Note**   When I refer to a method in any discussion in this book, I use the method name followed by a pair of opening and closing parentheses. For example, I will refer to the add method as add() and printPoem method as printPoem(). Sometimes, I need to refer to the formal parameters of the method to make the meaning of the method clear. In those cases, I may just use the data type of the formal parameters, for example, add(int, int), to refer to the add(int n1, int n2) method. No matter what convention I use to refer to a method in the discussion, the context of its use will make the meaning clear.

Since the printPoem() method does not return any value, you cannot use a call to this method as part of any expression where a value is expected. For example, the following statement results in a compiler error:

```
int x = printPoem(); // A compile-time error
```

When a method's return type is void, it is not necessary to use a return statement because you do not have a value to return from the method. Recall that a return statement does two things: evaluates its expression, if any, and returns the control to the caller by ending the execution in the method's body. Even if you do not return a value from a method, you can still use a return statement simply to end the execution of the method. Let's add a parameter to the printPoem method to allow the caller to pass the stanza number that it wants to print. The modified method declaration is as follows:

```
void printPoem(int stanzaNumber) {
        if (stanzaNumber < 1 || stanzaNumber > 2) {
                System.out.println("Cannot print stanza #" + stanzaNumber);
                return; // End the method call
        }

        if (stanzaNumber == 1) {
                System.out.println("Strange fits of passion have I known:");
                System.out.println("And I will dare to tell,");
                System.out.println("But in the lover's ear alone,");
                System.out.println("What once to me befell.");
        }
        else if (stanzaNumber == 2) {
                System.out.println("When she I loved looked every day");
                System.out.println("Fresh as a rose in June,");
                System.out.println("I to her cottage bent my way,");
                System.out.println("Beneath an evening-moon.");
        }
}
```

The modified `printPoem()` method knows how to print stanza #1 and #2. If its caller passes a stanza number outside this range, it prints a message and ends the method call. This is accomplished by using a `return` statement in the first `if` statement. You could have written the above `printPoem()` method without writing any return statement as follows:

```
void printPoem(int stanzaNumber) {
        if (stanzaNumber == 1) {
                /* Print stanza #1 */
        }
        else if (stanzaNumber == 2) {
                /* Print stanza #2 */
        }
        else {
                System.out.println("Cannot print stanza #" + stanzaNumber);
        }
}
```

The compiler will force you to include a `return` statement in the body of a method that specifies a return type in its declaration. However, if the compiler determines that a method has specified a return type, but it always ends its execution abnormally, for example, by throwing an exception, you do not need to include a `return` statement in the method's body. For example, the following method declaration is valid. Do not worry about the `throw` and `throws` keywords at this time; I will cover them in Chapter 9.

```
int aMethod() throws Exception {
        throw new Exception("Do not call me...");
}
```

Local Variables

A variable declared inside a method, a constructor, or a block is called a local variable. I will discuss constructors shortly. A local variable declared in a method exists only for the duration the method is being executed. Because a local variable exists only for a temporary duration, it cannot be used outside the method, the constructor, or the block in which it is declared. The formal parameters for a method are treated as local variables. They are initialized with the actual parameter values when the method is invoked, and before the method's body is executed. You need to observe the following rules about the usage of local variables.

Rule #1

Local variables are not initialized by default. Note that this rule is the opposite of the rule for instance/class variable's initialization. When an instance/class variable is declared, it is initialized with a default value. Consider the following partial definition of an `add()` method:

```
int add(int n1, int n2) {
        int sum;
        /* What is the value of sum? We do not know because it is not initialized yet */

        /* More code goes here... */
}
```

Rule #2

This rule is an offshoot of the first rule. A local variable cannot be accessed in the program until it is assigned a value. The following snippet of code will generate a compiler error because it tries to print the value of the local variable, sum, before it is assigned a value. Note that Java runtime has to read (or access) the value of the sum variable before it prints the value.

```
int add(int n1, int n2) {
        int sum;

        // A compile-time error. Cannot read sum because it is not assigned a value yet.
        System.out.println(sum);
}
```

The following snippet of code will compile fine because the local variable sum is initialized before it is read:

```
int add(int n1, int n2) {
        int sum = 0 ;
        System.out.println(sum); // Ok. Will print 0
}
```

Rule #3:

A local variable can be declared anywhere in the body of a method. However, it must be declared before it is used. The implication of this rule is that you do not need to declare all local variables at the start of the method body. It is a good practice to declare a variable closer to its use.

Rule #4

A local variable hides the name of an instance variable and a class variable with the same name. Let's discuss this rule in detail. Every variable, irrespective of its type, has a scope. Sometimes the scope of a variable is also known as its visibility. The scope of a variable is the part of the program where the variable can be referred to with its simple name. The scope of a local variable declared in a method is the part of the method body that follows the variable declaration. The scope of a local variable declared in a block is the rest of the block that follows the variable declaration. The scope of the formal parameters of a method is the entire body of the method. It means that the name of the formal parameters of a method can be used throughout the body of that method. For example,

```
int sum(int n1, int n2) {
        // n1 and n2 can be used here
}
```

The scope of an instance variable and a class variable is the entire body of the class. For example, the instance variable n1 and the class variable n2 can be referred to with its simple name anywhere in the class NameHidingTest1, as shown:

```
class NameHidingTest1 {
        int n1 = 10;          // An instance variable
        static int n2 = 20;   // A class variable

        // m1 is a method
        void m1() {
                // n1 and n2 can be used here
        }

        int n3 = n1; // n1 can be used here
}
```

What happens when two variables, say one instance variable and one local variable, are in scope in the same part of a program? Let's consider the following code for the NameHidingTest2 class:

```
class NameHidingTest2 {
        int n1 = 10;   // An instance variable

        /// m1 is a method
        void m1() {
                int n1 = 20; // A local variable

                /* Both, instance variable n1 and local variable n1, are in scope here */

                int n2 = n1; // What value is assigned to n2 - 10 or 20?
        }

        /* Only instance variable n1 is in scope here */

        int n3 = n1; // n3 is assigned 10 from the instance variable n1
}
```

When the m1() method is executed in the above code, what value will be assigned to the variable n2? Note the class declares an instance variable with the name n1, and the method m1() also declares a local variable with the name n1. The scope of the instance variable n1 is the entire class body that includes the body of the m1() method. The scope of the local variable n1 is the entire body of the m1() method. When the statement

```
int n2 = n1;
```

is executed inside the m1() method, two variables with the same name n1 are in scope: one has a value of 10 and one has a value of 20. Which n1 does the above statement refer to: n1 the instance variable, or n1 as the local variable? When a local variable has the same name as the name of a class field, an instance/class variable, the local variable name hides the name of the class field. This is known as name hiding. In the above case, the local variable name n1 hides the name of the instance variable n1 inside the m1() method. The above statement will refer to the local variable n1, not the instance variable n1. Therefore, n2 will be assigned a value of 20.

■ **Tip**   A local variable with the same name as a class field hides the name of the class field. In other words, when a local variable as well as a class field with the same name are in the scope, the local variable takes precedence.

The following code for the class NameHidingTest3 clarifies the scenario when a local variable comes into scope:

```
public class NameHidingTest3 {
        int n1 = 10;   // An instance variable n1

        public void m1() {

                /* Only the instance variable n1 is in scope here */

                int n2 = n1; // Assigns 10 to n2
```

```
        /* Only the instance variable n1 is in scope here. The local variable n2
           is also in scope here, which you are ignoring for our discussion for now */

        int n1 = 20; /* A local variable n1 */

        /* Both, instance variable n1 and local variable n1 are in scope here.
           We are ignoring n2 for now. */

        int n3 = n1; // Assigns 20 to n3
    }
}
```

The above code assigns the value of the n1 variable to n2 inside the m1() method. You have not declared the local variable n1 at the time you assigned the value of n1 to n2. At this time, only the instance variable n1 is in scope. When you assign n1 to n3, at that time both instance variable n1 and local variable n1 are in scope. The values assigned to n2 and n3 depend on the name-hiding rule. When two variables with the same names are in scope, the local variable is used.

Does it mean that you cannot declare an instance/class variable and a local variable with the same name and use both at the same time? The answer is no. You can declare an instance/class variable and a local variable with the same name. The only thing you need to know is how to refer to the instance/class variable if its name is hidden by a local variable. You will learn about referring to the hidden instance/class variables in the next section.

Instance Method and Class Method

In the previous sections, I discussed two types of class fields: instance variables and class variables. A class can have two types of methods: instance methods and class methods. Instance methods and class methods are also called non-static methods and static methods, respectively.

An instance method is used to implement behavior for the instances (also called objects) of the class. An instance method can only be invoked in the context of an instance of the class.

A class method is used to implement the behavior for the class itself. A class method always executes in the context of a class.

The static modifier is used to define a class method. The absence of the static modifier in a method declaration makes the method an instance method. The following are examples of declaring some static and non-static methods:

```
// A static or class method
static void aClassMethod() {
        // method's body goes here
}

// A non-static or instance method
void anInstanceMethod() {
        // method's body goes here
}
```

Recall that a separate copy of an instance variable exist for each instance of a class, whereas only one copy of a class variable exists, irrespective of the existence of the number of instances (possibly zero) of the class.

When a static method of a class is called, an instance of that class may not exist. Therefore, it is not allowed to refer to instance variables from inside a static method. Class variables exist as soon as the class definition is loaded into memory. The class definition is always loaded into memory before the first instance of a class is created. Note that it is not necessary to create an instance of a class to load its definition into memory. JVM guarantees that all class variables of a class exist before any instances of the class. Therefore, you can always refer to a class variable from inside an instance method.

■ **Tip**   A class method (or static method) can refer to only class variables (or static variables) of the class. An instance method (non-static method) can refer to class variables as well as instance variables of the class.

Listing 6-7 demonstrate the types of class fields that are accessible inside a method.

Listing 6-7. Accessing Class Fields from Static and Non-static Methods

```java
// MethodType.java
package com.jdojo.cls;

public class MethodType {
        static int m = 100; // A static variable
        int n = 200;        // An instance variable

        // Declare a static method
        static void printM() {

                /* We can refer to only static variable m in this method
                    because you are inside a static method */

                System.out.println("printM() - m = " + m);

                /* System.out.println("printM() - n = " + n); */ /* A compile-time error */
        }

        // Declare an instance method
        void printMN() {
                /* We can refer to both static and instance variables m and n in this method */
                System.out.println("printMN() - m = " + m);
                System.out.println("printMN() - n = " + n);
        }
}
```

The MethodType class declares m as a static variable and n as a non-static variable. It declares printM() as a static method and printMN() as an instance method. Inside the printM() method, you can refer to only static variable m because a static method can refer to only static variables. If you uncomment the commented statement inside the printM() method, the code will not compile because a static method will attempt to access a non-static variable n. The printMN() method is a non-static method and it can access both static variable m and non-static variable n. Next, you would like to invoke the printM() and printMN() methods of the MethodType class. The next section discusses how to invoke a method.

Invoking a Method

Executing the code in the body of a method is called invoking (or calling) a method. Instance methods and class methods are invoked differently. An instance method is invoked on an instance of the class using dot notation.

```
<<instance reference>>.<<instance method name>>(<<actual parameters>>)
```

Note that you must have a reference to an instance of a class before calling an instance method of that class. For example, you can write the following snippet of code to invoke the printMN() instance method of the MethodType class listed in Listing 6-7:

```
// Create an instance of MethodType class and
// store its reference in mt reference variable
MethodType mt = new MethodType();

// Invoke the printMN() instance method using the mt reference variable
mt.printMN();
```

To invoke a class method, you use dot notation with the class name. The following snippet of code invokes the printM() class method of the MethodType class:

```
// Invoke the printM() class method
MethodType.printM();
```

Whatever belongs to a class also belongs to all instances of that class. You can also invoke a class method using a reference of an instance of that class.

```
MethodType mt = new MethodType();
mt.printM(); // Call the class method using an instance mt
```

Which is a better way to invoke a class method: using the class name or using an instance reference? Both ways do the same job. However, using the class name to invoke a class method is more intuitive than using an instance reference. This book uses a class name to invoke a class method, except for the purpose of demonstrating that you can also use an instance reference to invoke a class method. Listing 6-8 demonstrates how to invoke an instance method and a class method of a class. Note that the output shows the same result when you invoke the class method printM() using the class name or an instance reference.

Listing 6-8. Examples of Invoking Instance Methods and Class Methods of a Class

```java
// MethodTypeTest.java
package com.jdojo.cls;

public class MethodTypeTest {
        public static void main(String[] args) {
                // Create an instance of the MethodTYpe class
                MethodType mt = new MethodType();

                System.out.println("Invoking instance method...");

                // Invoke the instance method
                mt.printMN();

                System.out.println("Invoking class method on class name...");
```

```
                    // Invoke the class method using the class name
                    MethodType.printM();

                    System.out.println("Invoking class method on an instance...");

                    // Invoke the class method using the instance reference
                    mt.printM();
            }
}
```

```
Invoking instance method...
printMN() - m = 100
printMN() - n = 200
Invoking class method on class name...
printM() - m = 100
Invoking class method on an instance...
printM() - m = 100
```

The Special main() Method

You learned about declaring a method in a class in the previous section. Let's discuss the main() method that you have been using to run your classes. The main() method declaration is as follows:

```
public static void main(String[] args) {
        // Method body goes here
}
```

Two modifiers, public and static, are used in the declaration of the main() method. The public modifier makes it accessible from anywhere in the application as long as the class in which it is declared is accessible. The static modifier makes it a class method, so it can be invoked using a class name. Its return type is void, which means it does not return a value to its caller. Its name is main and it accepts one parameter of type String array (String[]). Note that you have been using args as the name of its parameter. However, you can use any parameter name you wish. For example, you can declare the main method as public static void main(String[] myParameters), which is the same as declaring the main method as shown above. Whatever parameter name you choose, you will need to use the same name in the body of the method if you need to refer to the parameter passed to this method.

What is special about the declaration of a main() method in a class? You run a Java application by passing a class name to the java command. For example, you would use the following command to run the MethodTypeTest class:

```
java com.jdojo.cls.MethodTypeTest
```

When the above command is executed, the JVM (the java command essentially starts a JVM) finds and loads the MethodType class definition in memory. Then, it looks for a method declaration, which is declared as public and static, returns void, and has a method argument as String array. If it finds the main() method declaration, the JVM invokes the method. If it does not find the main() method, it does not know where to start the application and it throws an error stating that no main() method was found.

Why do you need to declare the main() method as static? The main() method serves as the entry point for a Java application. It is invoked by the JVM when you run a class. The JVM does not know how to create an instance of a class. It needs a standard way to start a Java application. Specifying all details about the main() method and making it static provides the JVM a standard way to start a Java application. By making the main() method static, the JVM can invoke it using the class name, which is passed on the command line.

What will happen if you do not declare the main() method as static? If you do not declare the main() method as static, it will be treated as an instance method. The code will compile fine. However, you will not be able to run the class, which has its main() method declared as an instance method.

Can you have more than one main() method in a class? The answer is yes. You can have multiple methods in a class, which can be named main as long as they do not have the same signature. The following declaration for the MultipleMainMethod class, which declares three main() methods, is valid. The first main() method, which is declared as public static void main(String[] args), may be used as the entry point to the Test class. The other two main() methods have no special significance as far as the JVM is concerned.

```
// MultipleMainMethod.java
package com.jdojo.cls;

public class MultipleMainMethods {
    public static void main(String[] args) {
        /* May be used as the application entry point */
    }

    public static void main(String[] args, int a) {
        /* Another main() method */
    }

    public int main() {
        /* Another main() method */
        return 0;
    }
}
```

Is it required for each class in Java to have a main() method? The answer is no. It is required that you declare a public static void main(String[] args) method in a class if you want to run that class. If you have a Java application, you will need to have a main() method in at least one class so you can start you application by running that class. All other classes that are used in the application, but are not used to start the application, do not need to have a main() method.

Can you invoke the main() method in your code? Or, can it be invoked only by the JVM? The main() method is invoked by JVM when you run a class. Apart from that, you can treat the main() method as any other class method. Programmers have a general (and wrong) impression that the main() method can only be invoked by a JVM. However, that is not true. It is true that the main() method is generally (but not necessarily) invoked by a JVM to start a Java application. However, it does not have to be invoked (at least theoretically) only by a JVM. Here is an example that shows how the main() method can be invoked like any other class method. Listing 6-9 has the definition of a MainTest1 class, which declares a main() method. Listing 6-10 has the definition of a MainTest2 class, which declares a main() method.

Listing 6-9. A MainTest1 Class, Which Declares a main() Method

```java
// MainTest1.java
package com.jdojo.cls;

public class MainTest1 {
        public static void main(String[] args) {
                System.out.println("Inside main() method of the MainTest1 class.");
        }
}
```

Listing 6-10. A MainTest2 Class, Which Declares a main() Method, Which in Turn Calls the main() Method of the MainTest1 Class

```java
// MainTest2.java
package com.jdojo.cls;

public class MainTest2 {
        public static void main(String[] args) {
                MainTest1.main(args);
        }
}
```

```
Inside main() method of the MainTest1 class.
```

The main() method of the MainTest2 class invokes the main() method of the MainTest1 class using the following code:

```java
MainTest1.main(null);
```

Note that the main() method of the MainTest1 class accepts a String array as a parameter and the above statement passes null as the actual value for that parameter. I will discuss arrays in detail in the chapter on arrays. You run the MainTest2 class as

```
java com.jdojo.cls.MainTest2
```

The JVM will invoke the main() method of the MainTest2 class, which in turn invokes the main() method of the MainTest1 class. The output in Listing 6-10 confirms this. You can also let the JVM invoke the main() method of the MainTest1 class by running the MainTest1 class as

```
java com.jdojo.cls.MainTest1
```

■ **Tip** The main() method in a class, which is declared as public static void main(String[] args), has a special meaning only when the class is run by the JVM. It serves as an entry point for the Java application. Otherwise, the main() method is treated the same as any other class methods.

What Is this?

Java has a keyword called this. It is a reference to the current instance of a class. It can be used only in the context of an instance. It can never be used in the context of a class because it means the current instance, and no instance exists in the context of a class.

The keyword this is used in many contexts. I will cover most of its uses in this chapter, not necessarily in this section. However, you need to note that when it appears in Java code, it means the current instance of the class for which the code is being executed.

Let's consider the following snippet of code that declares a class ThisTest1:

```java
public class ThisTest1 {
        int varA = 555;
        int varB = varA;       // Assign value of varA to varB
        int varC = this.varA; // Assign value of varA to varC
}
```

The ThisTest1 class declares three instance variables: varA, varB, and varC. The instance variable varA is initialized to 555. The instance variable varB is initialized to the value of varA, which is 555. The instance variable varC is initialized to the value of varA, which is 555. Note the difference in initialization expressions for varB and varC. I used unqualified varA when I initialized varB. I used this.varA when I initialized varC. However, the effect is the same. Both varB and varC are initialized with the value of varA. When I use this.varA, it means the value of varA for the current instance, which is 555. In this simple example, it was not necessary to use the keyword this. In the above case, the unqualified varA refers to the varA for the current instance. However, there are some cases where you must use the keyword this. I will discuss such cases shortly.

Since the use of the keyword this is illegal in the context of a class, you cannot use it when you initialize a class variable, like so:

```java
// Would not compile
public class ThisTest2 {
        static int varU = 555;
        static int varV = varU;
        static int varW = this.varU; // A compile-time error
}
```

When you compile the code for the class ThisTest2, you receive the following compiler error:

"ThisTest2.java": non-static variable this cannot be referenced from a static context at line 4, column 21

The compiler error is loud and clear that you cannot use the keyword this in a static context. Note that static and non-static words are synonymous with "class" and "instance" terms in Java. Static context is the same as class context and non-static context is the same as instance context. The above code can be corrected by removing the qualifier this from the initialization expression for varW, as follows:

```java
public class CorrectThisTest2 {
        static int varU = 555;
        static int varV = varU;
        static int varW = varU; // Ok
}
```

You can also qualify a class variable with a class name, as shown in the CorrectThisTest3 class:

```
public class CorrectThisTest3 {
        static int varU = 555;
        static int varV = varU;
        static int varW = CorrectThisTest3.varU;
}
```

■ **Tip**   Most of the time you can use the simple name of instance and class variables within the class in which they are declared. You need to qualify an instance variable with the keyword this and a class variable with the class name only when the instance variable or the class variable is hidden by another variable with the same name.

Let's consider the following snippet of code for the ThisTest3 class:

```
public class ThisTest3 {
        int varU = 555;
        static int varV = varU; // A compile-time error
        static int varW = varU; // A compile-time error
}
```

When you compile the ThisTest3 class, you will receive the following error:

```
"ThisTest3.java": non-static variable varU cannot be referenced from a static context at line 3,
column 21
"ThisTest3.java": non-static variable varU cannot be referenced from a static context at line 4,
column 21
```

The compiler error is the same in kind, although differently phrased, compared to the compiler error that you received for the ThisTest2 class. Last time, it complained about using the keyword this. This time, it complained about using the instance variable varU. Both the keyword this and the varU exist in the context of an instance. They do not exist in the context of a class. Whatever exists in the context of an instance cannot be used in the context of a class. However, whatever exists in the context of a class can always be used in the context of an instance. The instance variable declaration and initialization occurs in the context of an instance. In the ThisTest3 class, varU is an instance variable and it exists only in the context of an instance. The varV and varW in ThisTest3 class are class variables and they exist only in the context of a class. This is the reason that the compiler complained.

Let's consider the code for the ThisTest4 class, shown in Listing 6-11. It declares an instance variable, num, and an instance method, printNum(). In the printNum() instance method, it prints the value of the instance variable num. In its main() method, it creates an instance of the ThisTest4 class and invokes the printNum() method on it. The output of the ThisTest4 class shows the expected result.

Listing 6-11. An Example of Using the Simple Name of an Instance Variable in an Instance Method

```
// ThisTest4.java
package com.jdojo.cls;

public class ThisTest4 {
        int num = 1982; // An instance variable
```

```
        void printNum() {
                System.out.println("Instance variable num: " + num);
        }

        public static void main(String[] args) {
                ThisTest4 tt4 = new ThisTest4();
                tt4.printNum();
        }
}
```

```
Instance variable num: 1982
```

Let's modify the printNum() method of the ThisTest4 class so it accepts an int parameter. Let's name the parameter num. Listing 6-12 has the modified code for the printNum() method as part of the ThisTest5 class.

Listing 6-12. Variables Name Hiding

```java
// ThisTest5.java
package com.jdojo.cls;

public class ThisTest5 {
        int num = 1982; // An instance variable

        void printNum(int num) {
                System.out.println("Parameter num: " + num);
                System.out.println("Instance variable num: " + num);
        }

        public static void main(String[] args) {
                ThisTest5 tt5 = new ThisTest5();
                tt5.printNum(1969);
        }
}
```

```
Parameter num: 1969
Instance variable num: 1969
```

The output of the ThisTest5 class indicates that the printNum() method is using its parameter num when you use the simple name num inside its body. This is an example of name hiding, where the local variable (method parameter is considered a local variable) num hides the name of the instance variable num inside the printNum() method's body. In the printNum() method, the simple name num refers to its parameter num, not the instance variable num. In this case, you must use the keyword this to qualify the num variable if you want to refer to the num instance variable inside the printNum() method. Using this.num is the only way you can refer to the instance variable from inside the printNum() method, as long you keep the parameter name as num. Another way is to rename the parameter to something other than num, for example, numParam or newNum. Listing 6-13 shows how to use the keyword this to refer to the num instance variable inside the printNum() method.

Listing 6-13. Using the this Keyword to Refer to an Instance Variable Whose Name Is Hidden by a Local Variable

```
// ThisTest6.java
package com.jdojo.cls;

public class ThisTest6 {
        int num = 1982; // An instance variable

        void printNum(int num) {
                System.out.println("Parameter num: " + num);
                System.out.println("Instance variable num: " + this.num);
        }

        public static void main(String[] args) {
                ThisTest6 tt6 = new ThisTest6();
                tt6.printNum(1969);
        }
}
```

```
Parameter num: 1969
Instance variable num: 1982
```

The output of ThisTest6 shows the expected result. If you do not want to use the keyword this, you can rename the parameter of the printNum() method, like so:

```
void printNum(int numParam) {
        System.out.println("Parameter num: " + numParam);
        System.out.println("Instance variable num: " + num);
}
```

Once you rename the parameter to something other than num, the num instance variable is no longer hidden inside the body of the printNum() method, and therefore you can refer to it using its simple name.

You can use the keyword this to refer to the instance variable num inside the printNum() method even if it is not hidden as shown below. However, using the keyword this in the following case is a matter of choice, not a requirement.

```
void printNum(int numParam) {
        System.out.println("Parameter num: " + numParam);
        System.out.println("Instance variable num: " + this.num);
}
```

In the previous example, you saw that use of the keyword this is necessary to access instance variables when the instance variable name is hidden. You can avoid using the keyword this in such circumstances by renaming the variable that hides the instance variable name, or renaming the instance variable itself. Sometimes it is easier to keep the variable names the same, as they represent the same thing. This book uses the convention of using the same name for instance variables and local variables if they represent the same thing in the class. For example, the following code is very common:

```
public class Student {
        private int id; // An instance variable
```

```java
    public void setId(int id) {
            this.id = id;
    }

    public int getId() {
            return this.id;
    {
}
```

The Student class declares an instance variable id. In its setId() method, it also names the parameter id, and uses this.id to refer to the instance variable. It also uses this.id to refer to the instance variable id in its getId() method. Note that there is no name hiding occurring in the getId() method and you could use the simple name id, which means the instance variable id.

I will discuss the use of the keyword this again in this chapter and subsequent chapters. Table 6-2 lists the parts of a class, the context in which they occur, and the permitted use of the keyword this, the instance variable, and the class variable. I have not yet covered all parts of a class that are listed in Table 6-2. I will cover them shortly in this chapter.

Table 6-2. *The Context Type and Allowed Use of the Keyword this, an Instance Variable, and a Class Variable*

Part of a Class	Context	Can use this keyword?	Can use instance variable?	Can use class variable?
Instance variable initialization	Instance	Yes	Yes	Yes
Class variable initialization	Class	No	No	Yes
Instance initializer	Instance	Yes	Yes	Yes
Class initializer (Also called static initializer)	Class	No	No	Yes
Constructor	Instance	Yes	Yes	Yes
Instance method (Also called non-static method)	Instance	Yes	Yes	Yes
Class method (Also called static method)	Class	No	No	Yes

The keyword this is a final (a constant is called final in Java because Java uses the final keyword to declare a constant) reference to the current instance of the class in which it appears. Because it is final, you cannot change its value. Because this is a keyword, you cannot declare a variable named this. The following code will generate a compiler error:

```java
public class ThisError {
        void m1() {
                // An error. Cannot name a variable this
                int this = 10;

                // An error. Cannot assign a value to this because it is a constant.
                this = null;
        }
}
```

You can also use the keyword this to qualify an instance method name, although it is never required. The following snippet of code shows the m1() method invoking the m2() method using the keyword this. Note that both methods are instance methods and they could use the simple name to invoke each other.

```
public class ThisTestMethod {
        void m1() {
                // Invoke the m2() method
                this.m2(); // same as "m2();"
        }

        void m2() {
                // do something
        }
}
```

Access Levels for Class Members

I have covered access levels for a class, which can be public or default (or package level). This section discusses access levels for class members: fields and methods. The access level for a class member determines what area of the program can access (use or refer to) it. One of the following four access level modifiers can be used for a class member:

- public

- private

- protected

- Default or package-level access

Three out of the four types of access levels for a class member are specified using one of the three keywords: public, private, or protected. The fourth type is called the default access level (or package-level access), and it is specified by using no access modifiers. That is, the absence of any of the three access level modifiers, public, private, or protected, specifies package-level access.

If a class member is declared as public using the public keyword, it can be accessed from anywhere in Java code, provided the class itself is accessible.

If a class member is declared as private using the private keyword, it can be accessed only within the body of the declaring class, and nowhere else.

If a class member is declared as protected using the protected keyword, it can be accessed from the same package or from descendants of the class, even if the descendants are in a different package. I will discuss the protected access level in detail in the chapter on inheritance.

If you do not use any access level modifier for a class member, it has package-level access. A class member with a package-level access can be accessed from the same package.

Access levels for a class member can be listed from the most restrictive to the least restrictive as private, package-level, protected, and public. Table 6-3 summarizes the four access levels for a class member.

Table 6-3. *List of Access Levels for Class Members*

Access Level for Class Member	Accessibility
private	Only within the same class
package-level	In the same package
protected	Same package or descendant in any package
public	Everywhere

The following is a sample class that declares many class members with different access levels:

```java
// AccessLevelSample.java
package com.jdojo.cls;

// Class AccessLevelSample has public access level
public class AccessLevelSample {
        private int num1;    // private access level
        int num2;            // package-level access
        protected int num3; // protected access level
        public int num4;    // public access level

        public static int count = 1; // public access level

        // m1() method has private access level
        private void m1() {
                // Code goes here
        }

        // m2() method has package-level access
        void m2() {
                // Code goes here
        }

        // m3() method has protected access level
        protected void m3() {
                // Code goes here
        }

        // m4() method has public access level
        public void m4() {
                // Code goes here
        }

        // doSomething() method has private access level
        private static void doSometing() {
                // Code goes here
        }
}
```

Note that access levels can be specified for both instance and static members of a class. It is a convention to specify the access level modifier as the first modifier in the declaration. If you declare a static field for a class that is public, you should use the public modifier first, and then the static modifier, as a convention. For example, both of the following declarations for an instance variable num, are valid:

```java
// Declaration #1
public static int num; // Conventionally used

// Declaration #2
static public int num; // Technically correct, but Conventionally not used.
```

Let's discuss some examples of using the access level modifiers for class members, and their effects. Consider the code for the AccessLevel class shown in Listing 6-14.

Listing 6-14. An AccessLevel Class with Class Members Having Different Access Levels

```java
// AccessLevel.java
package com.jdojo.cls;

public class AccessLevel {
        private int v1 = 100;
        int v2 = 200;
        protected int v3 = 300;
        public int v4 = 400;

        private void m1() {
                System.out.println("Inside m1():");
                System.out.println("v1 = " + v1 + ", v2 = " + v2 +
                                    ", v3 = " + v3 + ", v4 = " + v4);
        }

        void m2() {
                System.out.println("Inside m2():");
                System.out.println("v1 = " + v1 + ", v2 = " + v2 +
                                    ", v3 = " + v3 + ", v4 = " + v4);
        }

        protected void m3() {
                System.out.println("Inside m3():");
                System.out.println("v1 = " + v1 + ", v2 = " + v2 +
                                    ", v3 = " + v3 + ", v4 = " + v4);
        }

        public void m4() {
                System.out.println("Inside m4():");
                System.out.println("v1 = " + v1 + ", v2 = " + v2 +
                                    ", v3 = " + v3 + ", v4 = " + v4);
        }
}
```

The class has four instance variables called v1, v2, v3, and v4 and four instance methods called m1(), m2(), m3(), and m4(). Four different access level modifiers have been used for instance variables and instance methods. I have chosen to use instance variables and methods in this example; the same access level rules apply to class variables and class methods. The code for the AccessLevel class compiles without any errors. Note that no matter what the access level for a class member is, it is always accessible inside the class in which it is declared. This can be verified by the fact that you have accessed (read their values) all instance variables, which have different access levels, inside all four methods.

Let's consider the AccessLevelTest1 class shown in Listing 6-15.

Listing 6-15. A Test Class Loated in the Same Package as the AccessLevel Class

```java
// AccessLevelTest1.java
package com.jdojo.cls;

public class AccessLevelTest1 {
        public static void main(String[] args) {
                AccessLevel al = new AccessLevel();

                // int a = al.v1; /* A compile-time error */
                int b = al.v2;
                int c = al.v3;
                int d = al.v4;

                System.out.println("b = " + b + ", c = " + c + ", d = " + d);

                //al.m1(); /* A compile-time error */
                al.m2();
                al.m3();
                al.m4();

                /* Modify the values of instance variables */
                al.v2 = 20;
                al.v3 = 30;
                al.v4 = 40;

                System.out.println("\nAfter modifying v2, v3 and v4");

                al.m2();
                al.m3();
                al.m4();
        }
}
```

```
b = 200, c = 300, d = 400
Inside m2():
v1 = 100, v2 = 200, v3 = 300, v4 = 400
Inside m3():
v1 = 100, v2 = 200, v3 = 300, v4 = 400
Inside m4():
v1 = 100, v2 = 200, v3 = 300, v4 = 400

After modifying v2, v3 and v4
Inside m2():
v1 = 100, v2 = 20, v3 = 30, v4 = 40
Inside m3():
v1 = 100, v2 = 20, v3 = 30, v4 = 40
Inside m4():
v1 = 100, v2 = 20, v3 = 30, v4 = 40
```

The AccessLevel and AccessLevelTest1 classes are in the same package. AccessLevelTest1 can access all class members of the AccessLevel class, except the ones declared private. You cannot access the instance variable v1 and the instance method m1() of the AccessLevel class from the AccessLevelTest1 class because their access level is private. If you uncomment the two statements in the AccessLevelTest1 class, which attempts to access the private instance variable v1 and the private instance method m1()of the AccessLevel class, you would receive the following compiler error:

```
"AccessLevelTest1.java": v1 has private access in com.jdojo.cls.AccessLevel at line 7, column 16
"AccessLevelTest1.java": m1() has private access in com.jdojo.cls.AccessLevel at line 12, column 8
```

The AccessLevelTest1 class reads the values of the instance variables of the AccessLevel class, as well as modifies them. You must note one thing: even though you cannot access the private instance variable v1 and the private method m1() of the AccessLevel class from the AccessLevelTest1 class, you are able to print the value of the private instance variable v1 as shown in the output.

An access level modifier for a class member specifies who can access them directly. If a class member is not accessible directly, it might be accessible indirectly. In this example, the instance variable v1 and the instance method m1() are not directly accessible from outside the AccessLevel class; however, they may be indirectly accessible from outside. Indirect access to an inaccessible class member is usually given by providing another method, which is accessible from outside.

Suppose you want the outside world to read and modify the value of the otherwise inaccessible private instance variable v1. You need to add two public methods, getV1() and setV1(), to the AccessLevel class; these two methods will read and modify the value of the v1 instance variable. Your modified AccessLevel class would look as follows:

```java
public class AccessLevel {
        private int v1;

        /* Other code goes here */

        public int getV1() {
                return this.v1;
        }

        public void setV1(int v1) {
                this.v1 = v1;
        }
}
```

Now, even if the private instance variable v1 is not directly accessible from outside, it is made indirectly accessible through the public methods getV1() and setV1(). Let's consider another test class as shown in Listing 6-16.

Listing 6-16. A Test Class Located in a Different Package from the AccessLevel Class

```java
// AccessLevelTest2.java
package com.jdojo.cls.p1;

import com.jdojo.cls.AccessLevel;

public class AccessLevelTest2 {
        public static void main(String[] args) {
                AccessLevel al = new AccessLevel();
```

```
                  //int a = al.v1; /* A compile-time error */
                  //int b = al.v2; /* A compile-time error */
                  //int c = al.v3; /* A compile-time error */
                  int d = al.v4;

                  System.out.println("d = " + d);

                  //al.m1(); /* A compile-time error */
                  //al.m2(); /* A compile-time error */
                  //al.m3(); /* A compile-time error */
                  al.m4();

                  /* Modify the values of instance variables */
                  //al.v2 = 20;   /* A compile-time error */
                  //al.v3 = 30;   /* A compile-time error */
                  al.v4 = 40;

                  System.out.println("After modifying v4...");
                  //al.m2();   /* A compile-time error */
                  //al.m3();   /* A compile-time error */
                  al.m4();
       }
}
```

```
d = 400
Inside m4():
v1 = 100, v2 = 200, v3 = 300, v4 = 400
After modifying v4...
Inside m4():
v1 = 100, v2 = 200, v3 = 300, v4 = 40
```

Note the AccessLevelTest2 class in the com.jdojo.cls.p1 package, which is different from the com.jdojo.cls package in which the AccessLevel class exists. The code for the AccessLevelTest2 class is similar to the code for the AccessLevelTest1 class, except for the fact that most of the statements have been commented. Note that you need to use an import statement to import the AccessLevel class from the com.jdojo.cls package so you can use its simple name inside the main() method. In the AccessLevelTest1 class, it was not necessary to import the AccessLevel class because they are in the same package. The AccessLevelTest2 class can access only the public members of the AccessLevel class because it is in a different package than the AccessLevel class. This is the reason that the uncommented statements access only the public instance variable v4 and the public method m4(). Note that even if only the v4 instance variable is accessible, you are able to print the values of v1, v2, and v3 as well, by accessing them indirectly through the public method m4().

Let's consider a trickier situation. See Listing 6-17.

Listing 6-17. A Class with Package-level Access Having a Public Instance Variable

```
// AccessLevel2.java
package com.jdojo.cls;

class AccessLevel2 {
        public static int v1 = 600;
}
```

Note that there is no access level modifier used for the AccessLevel2 class, which gives it a package-level access by default. That is, the AccessLevel2 class is accessible only within the com.jdojo.cls package. The AccessLeve2 class is simple. It declares only one member, which is the public static variable v1.

Let's consider the class AccessLevelTest3 shown in Listing 6-18, which is in a different package than the class AccessLevel2.

Listing 6-18. A Test Class That Attempts to Access a Public Member of a Class with a Package-level Access

```
// AccessLevelTest3.java
package com.jdojo.cls.p1;

import com.jdojo.cls.AccessLevel2; // A compile-time error

public class AccessLevelTest3 {
        public static void main(String[] args) {
                int a = AccessLevel2.v1; // A compile-time error
        }
}
```

The AccesssLeveTest3 class attempts to access the public static variable v1 of the AccessLevel2 class, which generates a compiler error. Did I not say that a class member with public access level is accessible from anywhere? Yes. I did say that. Here is the catch. Suppose you have some money in your pocket and you declare that your money is public. Therefore, anyone can have your money. However, you hide yourself so that no one can have access to you. How can anyone access your money unless you become accessible to him first? This is the case with the AccessLevel2 class and its public static variable v1. Compare the AccessLevel2 class with yourself, and its public static variable v1 with your money. The AccessLevel2 class has package-level access. Therefore, only the code within its package (com.jdojo.cls) can access its name. Its static variable v1 has the access level of public, which means any code can access it from any package. The static variable v1 belongs to the AccessLevel2 class. Unless the AccessLevel2 class itself is accessible, its static variable v1 cannot be accessed, even though it has been declared public. The import statement in Listing 6-18 will also generate a compiler error for the reason that the AccessLevel2 class is not accessible outside its package com.jdojo.cls.

■ **Tip** You must consider the access level of both the class and its member to determine whether a class member is accessible. The access level of a class member may make it accessible to a part of a program. However, that part of a program can access the class member only if the class itself, to which the member belongs, is also accessible.

Access Level—A Case Study

A class member can have one of the four access levels: private, protected, public, or package-level. Which access level should be used with a class member? The answer depends on the member type and its purpose. Let's discuss an example of a bank account. Suppose you create a class Account to represent a bank account.

```
// Account.java
package com.jdojo.cls;

public class Account {
        public double balance;
}
```

A bank account holds the balance in the account. The above definition of the Account class does just that. In the real world, a bank account can hold many more pieces of information, for example, account number, account holder name, address, etc. Let's keep the Account class simple so you can focus on the discussion of access levels. It allows its every instance to hold a numeric value in its balance instance variable. If you want to create an instance of the Account class and manipulate its balance, it will look like this:

```
// Create an account object
Account ac = new Account();

// Change the balance to 1000.00
ac.balance = 1000.00;

// Change the balance to 550.29
ac.balance = 550.29;
```

This snippet of code can be executed anywhere in a Java application because both the Account class and its balance instance variable are public. However, in the real world, no one would let his bank account be manipulated like this. For example, a bank may require you to have a minimum balance of zero in your account. With the above implementation, nothing stops you from executing the following statement, which reduces the balance in an account to a negative number:

```
// Set a negative balance
ac.balance = -440.67;
```

In object-oriented programming, as a rule of thumb, the pieces of information that define the state of an object should be declared private. All instance variables of a class constitute the state of objects of that class. Therefore, they should be declared private. If code outside a class is needed to have access to a private instance variable, the access should be given indirectly, by providing a method. The method should have an appropriate access level, which will allow only intended client code to access it. Let's declare the balance instance variable as private. The modified code for the Account class is as follows:

```
// Account.java
package com.jdojo.cls;

public class Account {
        private double balance;
}
```

With the modified Account class, you can create an object of the Account class anywhere in a Java application.

```
// Create an account object
Account ac = new Account();
```

However, you cannot access the balance instance variable of the Account object unless you write the code inside the Account class itself. The following code is valid only if the code is written inside the Account class because the private instance variable balance cannot be accessed from outside the Account class:

```
// Change the balance
ac.balance = 188.37;
```

The modified version of the Account class is not acceptable in this form because you can create an account, but you cannot read or manipulate its balance. The Account class must provide some interface for the outside world to access and manipulate its balance in a controlled way. For example, if you have money and want to share it with the outside world, you do not show the money to everyone and ask him to take it directly. Rather, anyone who wants your money needs to ask you (send you a message), and then you give him your money according to certain situations. In other words, money is your private possession and you let other access it in a controlled way by making them ask you for that money, instead of letting them just take money directly from your pocket. Similarly, you want others to view the balance of an account, credit money to an account, and debit money from an account. However, all these actions should happen through an Account object, rather than manipulating the balance of an account object directly.

Java lets you send a message to an object by using instance methods. An object can receive a message from the outside world and it can respond differently to the same message depending on its internal state. For example, when all your money is gone and someone asks you for money, you can respond by saying that you do not have any money. However, you responded to the same message (give me money) differently (by giving the money) when you had money.

Let's declare three public methods in the Account class that will serve as an interface to the outside world who wants to access and manipulate the balance of an account.

- A getBalance() method will return the balance of an account.

- A credit() method will deposit a specified amount to an account.

- A debit() method will withdraw a specified amount from an account.

- Both credit() and debit() methods will return 1 if the transaction is successful and -1 if the transaction fails.

Listing 6-19 has the code for the modified Account class.

Listing 6-19. A Modified Version of the Account Class with a Private Instance Variable and Public Methods

```
// Account.java
package com.jdojo.cls;

public class Account {
        private double balance;

        public double getBalance() {
                // Return the balance of this account
                return this.balance;
        }

        public int credit(double amount) {
                // Make sure credit amount is not negative, NaN or infinity
                if (amount < 0.0 || Double.isNaN(amount) || Double.isInfinite(amount)) {
                        System.out.println("Invalid credit amount: " + amount);
                        return -1;
                }

                // Credit the amount
                System.out.println("Crediting amount: " + amount);
                this.balance = this.balance + amount;
                return 1;
        }
```

```java
    public int debit(double amount) {
        // Make sure the debit amount is not negative, NaN or infinity */
        if (amount < 0.0 || Double.isNaN(amount) || Double.isInfinite(amount)) {
            System.out.println("Invalid debit amount: " + amount);
            return -1;
        }

        // Make sure a minimum balance of zero is maintained
        if (this.balance < amount) {
            System.out.println("Insufficient fund. Debit attempted: " + amount);
            return -1;
        }

        // Debit the amount
        System.out.println("Debiting amount: " + amount);
        this.balance = this.balance - amount;
        return 1;
    }
}
```

The class has a private instance variable and public methods that let the outside world access and modify the private instance variable. The public methods are acting like protective covers for the private instance variable. They let the outside world read or modify the private instance variable in a controlled way. For example, you cannot credit a negative amount, and a minimum of zero balance must be maintained.

Let's test your modified Account class. The test code is shown in Listing 6-20. It creates an object of the Account class and attempts various operations on it using its public methods. The results are shown in the output, which indicates that this is an improved Account class that protects an account object from being manipulated incorrectly. You can also note that making the instance variables private and allowing access to them through public methods lets you enforce your business rules. If you expose the instance variables, you cannot enforce any business rules that control its valid values because anyone can modify it without any restrictions.

Listing 6-20. A Test Class to Test the Account Class Behavior

```java
// AccountTest.java
package com.jdojo.cls;

public class AccountTest {
    public static void main(String[] args) {
        Account ac = new Account();
        double balance = ac.getBalance();
        System.out.println("Balance = " + balance);

        // Credit and debit some amount
        ac.credit(234.78);
        ac.debit(100.12);

        balance = ac.getBalance();
        System.out.println("Balance = " + balance);

        // Attempt to credit and debit invalid amounts
        ac.credit(-234.90);
        ac.debit(Double.POSITIVE_INFINITY);
```

```
            balance = ac.getBalance();
            System.out.println("Balance = " + balance);

            // Attempt to debit more than the balance
            ac.debit(2000.00);

            balance = ac.getBalance();
            System.out.println("Balance = " + balance);
    }
}
```

```
Balance = 0.0
Crediting amount: 234.78
Debiting amount: 100.12
Balance = 134.66
Invalid credit amount: -234.9
Invalid debit amount: Infinity
Balance = 134.66
Insufficient fund. Debit attempted: 2000.0
Balance = 134.66
```

One important point to keep in mind when you design a class is its maintainability. Keeping all instance variables private and allowing access to them through public methods makes your code ready for future changes. Suppose you started with a zero minimum balance for an account. You have deployed the Account class in the production environment and it is being used in many places in the application. Now, you want to implement a new business rule that states that every account must have a minimum balance of 100. It is easy to make this change. Just change the code for the debit() method and you are done. You do not need to make any changes to the client code that is calling the debit() method of the Account class. Note that you need a little more work on the Account class to fully enforce the rule of a minimum balance of 100. When an account is created, the balance is zero by default. To enforce this new minimum balance rule at the time an account is created, you will need to know about constructors of a class. I will discuss constructors later in this chapter.

Another option for the access level for the balance instance variable in the Account class is to give it a package-level access. Recall that a package-level access is given to a class member by using no access modifier in its declaration. If the balance instance variable has package-level access, it is a little better than giving it public access because it is not accessible from everywhere. However, it can be accessed and manipulated directly by the code inside the same package in which the Account class has been declared. We all understand that letting any code access the balance instance variable directly from outside the Account class is not acceptable. Additionally, if you declare the method of the Account class to have package-level access, it can be used only inside the same package in which the Account class has been declared. You want objects of the Account class to be manipulated from anywhere in the application using its methods. Therefore, you cannot declare the methods or the instance variable of the Account class to have package-level access. When do you declare a class and/or a class member to have package-level access? Typically, package-level access is used for a class and its members when the class has to serve as a helper class or internal implementation for other classes in a package.

When do you use a private access level for class members? You have already seen the benefits of using the private instance variables for the Account class. The private access level for instance variables provides data hiding, where the internal state of the object is protected from outside access. An instance method for a class defines a behavior for its objects. If a method is used only internally within a class, and no outside code has any business knowing about it, the method should have a private access level. Let's go back to your Account class. You have used the same logic to validate the amount passed to the credit() and debit() methods. You can move the code that validates the amount to a `private` method, `isValidAmount()`,which is used internally by the Account class. It checks if an amount being used for credit or debit is not a negative number, not a NaN, and not infinity. These three criteria for a number to be a valid number apply only to the Account class, and no other class needs to be using them. This is the reason you need to declare this method `private`. Declaring it `private` has another advantage. In the future, you may make a rule that you must credit or debit a minimum of 10 from any account. At that time, you could just change the `private` `isValidAmount()` method and you are done. If you had made this method `public`, it would affect all the client code, which was using it to validate an amount. You may not want to change the criteria for a valid amount globally. To keep the effect of a change localized in a class, when the business rules change, you must implement a method as private. You can implement this logic in your Account class as follows (only changed code is shown):

```java
// Account.java
package com.jdojo.cls;

public class Account {
    /* Other code goes here */

    public int credit(double amount) {
        // Make sure credit amount is valid
        if (!this.isValidAmount(amount, "credit")) {
            return -1;
        }
        /* Other code goes here */
    }

    public int debit(double amount) {
        // Make sure debit amount is valid
        if (!this.isValidAmount(amount, "debit")) {
            return -1;
        }
        /* Other code goes here */
    }

    // Use a private method to validate credit/debit amount
    private boolean isValidAmount(double amount, String operation) {
        // Make sure amount is not negative, NaN or infinity
        if (amount < 0.0 || Double.isNaN(amount) || Double.isInfinite(amount)) {
            System.out.println("Invalid " + operation + " amount: " + amount);
            return false;
        }
        return true;
    }
}
```

Note that you might have implemented the `credit()` method (`debit()` method as well) in a simpler way using the following logic:

```java
if (amount >= 0) {
    this.balance - this.balance + amount;
    return 1;
}
```

```
else {
        /* print error here */
        return -1;
{
```

You could use the simpler logic to implement the credit() method, which checks if the amount is valid, instead of checking if the amount is invalid. I did not use this logic because I wanted to demonstrate in the same example how to use a private method. Sometimes one writes more code to drive home a point in a discussion.

Now you are left with the protected access level modifier. When do you declare a class member protected? A class member with the protected access level can be accessed in the same package and in the descendant class, even if the descendant class is not in the same package. I will discuss how to create a descendant class and the use of the protected access level in the chapter on inheritance.

Parameter Passing Mechanisms

This section discusses different ways of passing parameters to a method that are used in different programming languages. I will not discuss anything that is specific to Java in this section. The syntax or symbols used in this section may not be supported by Java. This section is important to programmers in understanding the memory states in the process of a method call. If you are an experienced programmer, you may skip this section. The next section will discuss the parameter passing mechanisms in Java.

The following are some of the mechanisms to pass parameters to a method:

- Pass by value

- Pass by constant value

- Pass by reference

- Pass by reference value

- Pass by result

- Pass by result value

- Pass by name

- Pass by need

A variable has three components: a name, a memory address (or a location), and data. The name of a variable is a logical name that is used in a program to refer to its memory address. Data is stored at the memory address that is associated with the variable name. The data stored at the memory address is also known as the value of the variable. Suppose you have an int variable id whose value is 785, which is stored at the memory address 131072. You may declare and initialize the id variable as follows:

```
int id = 785;
```

You can visualize the relationship between the variable name, its memory address, and the data stored at the memory address as depicted in Figure 6-4.

Variable name   Memory address   Value stored at the address

Figure 6-4. Relationship between a variable name, its memory address, and data

In Figure 6-4, you see that the actual data of the variable id is stored at the memory address. You can also store a data at a memory address, which is not the actual value for the variable; rather it is the memory address of the location where the actual value is stored. In this case, the value stored at the first memory address is a reference to the actual data stored at some other memory address, and such a value is known as a reference or a pointer. If a variable stores the reference to some data, it is called a reference variable.

Contrast the phrases "a variable" and "a reference variable." A variable stores the actual data itself at its memory location. A reference variable stores the reference (or memory address) of the actual data. Figure 6-5 depicts the difference between a variable and a reference variable. Here, idRef is a reference variable and id is a variable. Both variables are allocated memory separately. The actual value of 785 is stored at the memory location of id variable, which is 131072. However, the memory location (262144) of idRef stores the address of the id variable (or address or memory location, where 785 is stored). You can get to the value 785 in memory using either variable. The operation to get the actual data that a reference variable refers to is called dereferencing.

Figure 6-5. Difference between a variable and a reference variable

A method (also called function or procedure in some programming languages) can optionally accept parameters from its caller. A method's parameters allow data sharing between the caller context and the method context. Many mechanisms are in practice to pass the parameters to a method. The following sections discuss some of the commonly used parameter passing mechanisms.

Pass By Value

Pass by value is the simplest parameter passing mechanism to understand. However, it is not necessarily the most efficient and the easiest to implement in all situations. When a method is called, the values of the actual parameters are copied to the formal parameters. When the method execution starts, two copies of the value exist in memory: one copy for the actual parameter and one copy for the formal parameter. Inside the method, the formal parameter operates on its own copy of the value. Any changes made to the value of the formal parameter do not affect the value of the actual parameter.

Figure 6-6 depicts the memory state when a method is called using the pass by value mechanism. It is to be emphasized that once the formal parameter gets its value, which is a copy of the actual parameter, the two parameters have nothing to do with each other. The formal parameter is discarded at the end of the method call. However, the actual parameter persists in memory after the method call ends. How long the actual parameter persists in memory depends on the context of the actual parameter.

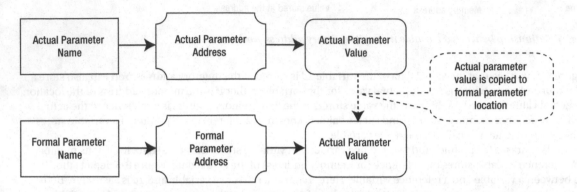

Figure 6-6. *Memory states for actual and formal parameters when a method is called*

Let's consider the following code for the `increment()` method, which accepts an `int` parameter and increments it by 2:

```
// Assume that num is passed by value
void increment(int num) {
        /* #2 */
        num = num + 2;
        /* #3 */
}
```

Suppose you call the `increment()` method with the following snippet of code:

```
int id = 57;
/* #1 */
increment(id);
/* #4 */
```

Four points of executions in the code are labeled as #1, #2, #3, and #4. Table 6-4 describes the memory states for the actual parameter and the formal parameter, before, after, and when the `increment()` method is invoked. Note that the formal parameter `num` no longer exists in memory at #4.

Table 6-4. *Description of Memory States for Actual and Formal Parameters When the increment() Method is Called and the Parameter is Passed by Value*

Point of Execution	Memory State of Actual Parameter id	Memory State of Formal Parameter num
#1	The id variable exists in memory and its value is 57.	The num variable does not exist at this point.
#2	The id variable exists in memory and its value is 57.	The formal parameter, num, has been created in memory. The value of the actual parameter id has been copied to the address associated with the num variable. At this point, num holds the value of 57.
#3	The id variable exists in memory and its value is 57.	At this point, num holds value of 59.
#4	The id variable exists in memory and its value is 57.	The formal parameter, num, does not exist in memory at this point because the method call is over.

All local variables, including formal parameters, are discarded when a method invocation is over. You can observe that incrementing the value of the formal parameter inside the increment() method was practically useless because it can never be communicated back to the caller environment. If you want to send back one value to the caller environment, you can use a return statement in the method body to do that. The following is the code for the smartIncrement() method, which returns the incremented value to the caller:

```
// Assume that num is passed by value
int smartIncrement(int num) {
    num = num + 2;
    return num;
}
```

You will need to use the following snippet of code to store the incremented value that is returned from the method in the id variable:

```
int id = 57;
id = smartIncrement(id);  // Store the returned value in id
/* At this point id has a value of 59 */
```

Note that pass by value lets you pass multiple values from the caller environment to the method using multiple parameters. However, it lets you send back only one value from the method. If you just consider the parameters in a method call, pass by value is a one-way communication. It lets you pass information from the caller to the method using parameters. However, it does not let you pass back information to the caller through the parameters. Sometimes you may want to send multiple values from a method to the caller's environment through the parameters. In those cases, you need to consider different ways to pass parameters to the method. The pass by value mechanism is of no help in such situations.

A method that is used to swap two values does not work when the parameters are passed by values. Consider the following code for a classical swap() method:

```
// Assume that x and y are passed by value
void swap(int x, int y) {
        int temp = x;
        x = y;
        y = temp;
}
```

You can call the above swap() method using the following snippet of code:

```
int u = 75;
int v = 53;
swap(u, v);
/*At this point, u and v will be still 75 and 53, respectively */
```

By this time, you should be able to figure out why the values of u and v were not swapped when they were passed to the swap() method. When the swap() method was called, the values of u and v were copied to the locations of the x and y formal parameters, respectively. Inside the swap() method, the values of the formal parameters x and y were swapped and the values of actual parameters u and v were not touched at all. When the method call was over, the formal parameters x and y were discarded.

The advantages of using pass by value are as follows:

- It is easy to implement.

- If the data being copied is a simple value, it is faster.

- The actual parameters are protected from any side effects when they are passed to the method.

The disadvantages of using pass by value are as follows:

- If the actual parameter is a complex data, such as a large object, it may be difficult, if not impossible, to copy the data to another memory location.

- Copying a large amount of data takes memory space and time, which may slow down the method call.

Pass By Constant Value

Pass by constant value is essentially the same mechanism as pass by value with one difference that the formal parameters are treated as constants, and hence, they cannot be changed inside the method's body. The values of actual parameters are copied to the formal parameters as is done in pass by value. You can only read the value of formal parameters inside the method's body if they are passed by constant value.

Pass By Reference

It is important that you do not confuse the phrases "reference" and "pass by reference." A "reference" is a piece of information (typically a memory address) that is used to get to the actual data stored at some other location. "Pass by reference" is a mechanism to pass information from a caller's environment to a method using formal parameters.

In pass by reference, the memory address of the actual parameter is passed and the formal parameter is mapped (or associated) with the memory address of the actual parameter. This technique is also known as aliasing, where multiple variables are associated with the same memory location. The formal parameter name is an alias for the actual parameter name. When a person has two names, no matter which of the two names you use, you refer to the same person. Similarly, when a parameter is passed by reference, no matter which name you use in the code (the actual parameter name or the formal parameter name), you are referring to the same memory location and hence the same data.

In pass by reference, if the formal parameter is modified inside the method, the actual parameter sees the modification instantaneously. Figure 6-7 depicts the memory state for actual and formal parameters when a parameter to a method is passed by reference.

Figure 6-7. *Memory states of actual and formal parameters when the parameters are passed by reference*

Many books use the phrase "pass by reference." However, they do not mean the one we are discussing in this section. They really mean "pass by reference value," which I will discuss in the next section. Note that in pass by reference, you do not allocate separate memory for the formal parameter. Rather, you just associate the formal parameter name to the same memory location of the actual parameter.

Let's do your increment() method call exercise again. This time, you assume that the num parameter is passed by reference.

```
// Assume that num is passed by reference
void increment(int num) {
        /* #2 */
        num = num + 2;
        /* #3 */
}
```

You will call the increment() method with the following snippet of code:

```
int id = 57;
/* #1 */
increment(id);
/* #4 */
```

Table 6-5 describes the memory states for the actual parameter and formal parameter, before, after, and during the increment() method's invocation. Note that at #4, the formal parameter num no longer exists in memory and still the actual parameter id has the value of 59 after the method call is over.

227

Table 6-5. *Description of Memory States for Actual and Formal Parameters When the increment() Method Is Called and the Parameter Is Passed by Reference*

Point of Execution	Memory State of Actual Parameter id	Memory State of Formal Parameter num
#1	The id variable exists in memory and its value is 57.	The num variable does not exist at this point.
#2	The *id* variable exists in memory and its value is 57.	The formal parameter's name, num, has been associated with the memory address of actual parameter id. At this point, num refers to value of 57, which is exactly the same as what id refers to.
#3	The id variable exists in memory and its value is 59. Inside the method, you used the formal parameter named num to increment the value by 2. However, id and num are two names for the same memory location and therefore, the value of id is also 59.	At this point, num holds value of 59.
#4	The id variable exists in memory and its value is 59.	The formal parameter named num does not exist in memory at this point because method call is over.

Pass by reference allows you to have two-way communication between the caller environment and the called method. You can pass multiple parameters by reference to a method and the method can modify all parameters. All modifications to formal parameters are reflected back to the caller's environment instantaneously. It lets you share multiple pieces of data between the two environments.

The classical swap() method example works when its parameters are passed by reference. Consider the following swap() method's definition:

```
// Assume that x and y are passed by reference
void swap(int x, int y) {
        int temp = x;
        x = y;
        y = temp;
}
```

You can call the above swap() method using the following snippet of code:

```
int u = 75;
int v = 53;
swap(u, v);
/* At this point, u and v will be 53 and 75, respectively. */
```

Let's consider the following snippet of code for a method name getNumber():

```
// Assume that x and y are passed by reference
int getNumber(int x, int y) {
        int x = 3;
        int y = 5;
        int sum = x + y;
        return sum;
}
```

Suppose you call the getNumber() method as follows:

```
int w = 100;
int s = getNumber(w, w);
/* What is value of s at this point: 200, 8, 10 or something else? */
```

When the getNumber() method returns, what value will be stored in the variable s? Note that both parameters to the getNumber() method are passed by reference and you pass the same variable, w, for both parameters in your call. When the getNumber() method starts executing, the formal parameters x and y are aliases to the same actual parameter w. When you use w, x, or y, you are referring to the same data in memory. Before adding x and y, and storing the result in the sum local variable, the method sets the value of y to 5, which makes w, x, and y all have a value of 5. When x and y are added inside the method, both x and y refer to the value 5. The getNumber() method returns 10.

Let's consider another call to the getNumber() method as a part of an expression, as follows:

```
int a = 10;
int b = 19;
int c = getNumber(a, b) + a;
/* What is value of c at this point? */
```

It is little trickier to guess the value of c in the above snippet of code. You will need to consider the side effect of the getNumber() method call on the actual parameters. The getNumber() method will return 8, and it will also modify the value of a and b to 3 and 5, respectively. A value of 11 (8 + 3) will be assigned to c. Consider the following statement in which you have changed the order of the operands for the addition operator:

```
int a = 10;
int b = 19;
int d =  a + getNumber(a, b);
/* What is value of d at this point? */
```

The value of d will be 18 (10 + 8). The local value of 10 will be used for a. You need to consider the side effects on actual parameters by a method call if the parameters are passed by reference. You would have thought that expressions getNumber(a, b) + a and a + getNumber(a, b) would give the same results. However, when the parameters are passed by reference, the result may not be the same, as I have explained above.

The advantages of using pass by reference are as follows:

- It is more efficient, compared to pass by value, as actual parameters values are not copied.

- It lets you share more than one piece of values between the caller and the called method environments.

The disadvantages of using pass by reference are as follows:

- It is potentially dangerous if the modification made to the actual parameters inside the called method is not taken into consideration by the caller.

- The program logic is not simple to follow because of the side effects on the actual parameters through formal parameters.

Pass By Reference Value

The mechanism of passing parameters to a method using a pass by reference value is different from that of pass by reference. However, both mechanisms have the same effects. In the pass by reference value, the reference of the actual parameter is copied to the formal parameter. The formal parameter uses a dereferencing mechanism to access the actual parameter's value. The modification made by the formal parameters inside the method is immediately visible to the actual parameters, as is the case in pass by reference. Figure 6-8 depicts the memory states for the actual and formal parameters when the pass by reference value mechanism is used.

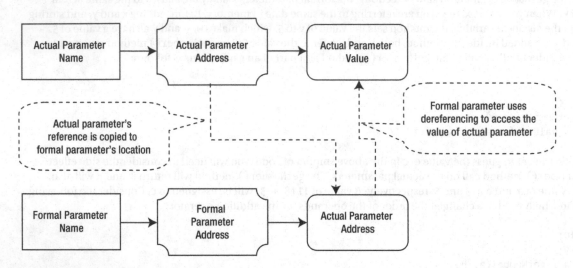

Figure 6-8. *Memory states for actual and formal parameters when a method call is made using pass by reference value mechanism*

There is an important difference between pass by reference and pass by reference values. In a pass by reference value, the reference of the actual parameter is copied to the formal parameter as part of the method call. However, you can change the formal parameter to refer to a different location in memory inside the method, which will not make the actual parameter refer to the new location in memory. Once you change the reference stored in the formal parameter, any changes made to the value stored at the new location will not change the value of the actual parameter.

The discussions and examples referring to the side effects and memory states for pass by reference also apply to the pass by reference value mechanism. Most of the programming languages simulate the pass by reference mechanism using pass by reference value.

Pass by Constant Reference Value

Pass by constant reference value is essentially the same as pass by reference value with one difference. The formal parameter is treated as a constant inside the method body. That is, the formal parameter holds the copy of the reference held by the actual parameter throughout the execution of the method. The formal parameter cannot be modified inside the method's body to hold reference of data other than what the actual parameter is referencing.

Pass by Result

You can think of pass by result as the opposite of pass by value. In pass by value, the value of the actual parameter is copied to the formal parameter. In pass by result, the value of the actual parameter is not copied to the formal parameter. The formal parameter is considered an uninitialized local variable when the method execution starts. During the method execution, the formal parameter is assigned a value. At the end of the method execution, the value of the formal parameter is copied back to the actual parameter.

Figure 6-9 depicts the memory state for the actual and formal parameters when the pass by result mechanism of parameter passing is used.

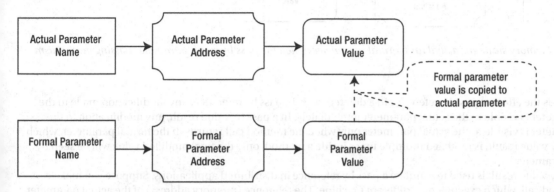

Figure 6-9. Memory states for actual and formal parameters when the pass by result parameter passing mechanism is used

Sometimes the formal parameters are also known as OUT parameters when the pass by result mechanism is used. They are called OUT parameters because they are used to *copy out* a value from the method to the caller's environment. Likewise, formal parameters are sometimes known as IN parameters if they uses the pass by value mechanism because they are used to *copy in* the value of the actual parameter.

Pass by Value Result

Also known as pass by copy-restore, this is a combination of pass by value and pass by result (hence the name "pass by value result"). It is also known as the IN-OUT way of passing parameters. When a method is called, the value of the actual parameter is copied to the formal parameter. During the execution of the method, the formal parameter operates on its own local copy of data. When the method call is over, the value of the formal parameter is copied back to the actual parameter. This is the reason that it is also called pass by copy-restore. It copies the value of the actual parameter in the beginning of the method call and restores the value of formal parameter in the actual parameter at the end of the method call. Figure 6-10 depicts the memory state of actual and formal parameters when the pass by value result mechanism is used to pass parameters.

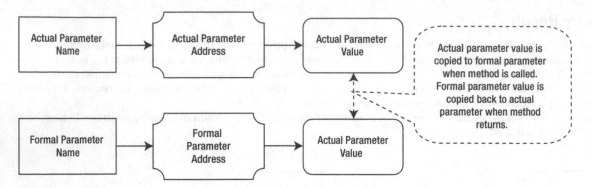

Figure 6-10. *Memory states for actual and formal parameters when the pass by result parameter passing mechanism is used*

It achieves the effect of pass by reference in a different way. In pass by reference, any modification made to the formal parameter is visible to the actual parameter immediately. In a pass by value result, any modification to the formal parameter is visible to the actual parameter only when the method call returns. If the formal parameter, which uses a pass by value result, is modified multiple times inside a method, only the final modified value will be seen by the actual parameter.

A pass by value result is used to simulate a pass by reference in distributed applications. Suppose you make a remote method call, which executes on a different machine. The reference (memory address) of the actual parameter, which exists in one machine, will not make any sense in the machine on which the remote method is executed. In such cases, the client application sends a copy of the actual parameter to the remote machine. The value copied to the formal parameter is on the remote machine. The formal parameter operates on the copy. When the remote method call returns, the value of the formal parameter on the remote machine is copied back to the actual parameter on the client machine. This gives the client code the functionality of passing parameters by reference to remote methods that run on another machine.

Pass By Name

Typically, the actual parameter expression is evaluated before its value/reference is passed to a method. In pass by name, the actual parameter's expressions are not evaluated when a method is called. The formal parameter's name inside the body of the method is substituted textually with the expressions of their corresponding actual parameters. Actual parameters are evaluated each time they are encountered during the execution of the method and they are evaluated in the caller's context, not the method's context. If there is a name conflict between the local variables in the method and the actual parameter expression during substitution, the local variables are renamed to give every variable a unique name.

Pass by name is implemented using thunks. A thunk is a piece of code that computes and returns the value of an expression in a specific context. A thunk is generated for each actual parameter and its reference is passed to the method. At each use of a formal parameter, a call to thunk is made, which evaluates the actual parameter in the caller context.

The advantage of pass by name is that the actual parameters are never evaluated unless they are used in the method. This is also known as lazy evaluation. Contrast it with the pass by value mechanism, where actual parameters are always evaluated before they are copied to the formal parameter. This is called eager evaluation. The disadvantage of pass by name is that the actual parameters are evaluated every time the corresponding formal parameters are used inside the method's body. It is also harder to follow the logic of a method if it uses the pass by name formal parameter, which can also have side effects.

Consider the following declaration for a method squareDivide():

```
int squareDivide(int x, int y) {
        int z =  x * x/y * y;
        return z;
}
```

Consider the following snippet of code that calls the squareDivide() method:

```
squareDivide((4+4), (2+2));
```

You can visualize the execution of the above call as if you have written the squareDivide() method as follows. Note that the actual argument expressions of (2+2) and (4+4) are evaluated multiple times inside the method's body.

```
int squareDivide() {
    int z = (4+4)*(4+4)/(2+2)*(2+2);
    return z;
}
```

Pass by Need

Pass by need is similar to pass by name with one difference. In pass by name, actual parameters are evaluated each time they are used in the method. In pass by need, the actual parameters are evaluated only once upon their first use. When a thunk for an actual parameter is called for the first time, it evaluates the actual parameter expression, caches the value and returns it. When the same thunk is called again, it simply returns the cached value, rather than re-evaluating the actual parameter expression again.

Parameter Passing Mechanisms in Java

Java supports two kinds of data types: primitive data type and reference data type. A primitive data type is a simple data structure and it has only one value associated with it. A reference data type is a complex data structure and it represents an object. A variable of a primitive data type stores the value directly at its memory address. Suppose you have an int variable id. Further suppose it has been assigned a value of 754 and its memory address is 131072.

```
int id = 754;
```

Figure 6-11 shows the memory state of the id variable.

Variable name   Memory address   Value stored at the address

Figure 6-11. *The memory state for an id variable when its value is 754*

The value 754 is directly stored at the memory address 131072, which is associated with the id variable name. What happens if you execute the following statement, which assigns a new value of 351 to the id variable?

```
id = 351;
```

When a new value 351 is assigned to the id variable, the old value of 754 is replaced with the new value at the memory address as shown in Figure 6-12.

Variable name   Memory address   Value stored at the address

Figure 6-12. *The memory state for an id variable when a new value of 351 is assigned to it*

Things are different when you work with objects and reference variables. Let's consider the declaration of a Car class as shown in Listing 6-21. It has three instance variables: model, year, and price, which have been given initial values of "Unknown", 2000, and 0.0, respectively.

Listing 6-21. Car Class with Three Public Instance Variables

```java
// Car.java
package com.jdojo.cls;

public class Car {
        public String model = "Unknown";
        public int year    = 2000;
        public double price = 0.0;
}
```

When you create an object of a reference type, the object is created on the heap and it is stored at a specific memory address. Let's create an object of the Car class as follows:

```java
new Car();
```

Figure 6-13 shows the memory state when the above statement is executed to create a Car object. You probably assumed that the memory address where the object is stored is 262144. Notice that when an object is created, memory is allocated for all of its instance variables and they are initialized. In this case, model, year, and price of the new Car object have been initialized properly, as shown in the figure.

Memory address   Object stored at the address

Figure 6-13. *Memory state when a Car object is created using the new Car() statement*

At this point, there is no way to refer to the newly created Car object from a Java program even though it exists in memory. The new operator (as used in new Car()) returns the memory address of the object it creates. In your case, it will return 262144. Recall that the memory address of the data (the Car object, in your case) is also called as reference of that data. From now onwards you will say that the new operator in Java returns a reference to the object it creates instead of saying that it returns the memory address of the object. Both mean the same thing. However, Java uses the term "reference," which has a more generic meaning than "memory address." In order to access the newly created Car object, you must store its reference in a reference variable. Recall that a reference variable stores the reference to some data, which is stored somewhere else. All variables that you declare of reference type are reference variables in Java. A reference variable in Java can store a null reference, which means that it refers to nothing. Consider the following snippet of code that performs different things on reference variables:

```
Car myCar = null;    /* #1 */
myCar = new Car();   /* #2 */
Car xyCar = null;    /* #3 */
xyCar = myCar;       /* $4 */
```

When the statement labeled #1 is executed, memory is allocated for myCar reference variable, say at memory address 8192. The null value is a special value, typically a memory address of zero, which is stored at the memory address of the myCar variable. Figure 6-14 depicts the memory state for the myCar variable when it is assigned a null reference.

Figure 6-14. *Memory state for the myCar variable, when the "Car myCar = null" statement is executed*

The execution of statement labeled #2 is a two-step process. First, it executes the new Car() part of the statement to create a new Car object. Suppose the new Car object is allocated at memory address of 9216. The new Car() expression returns the reference of the new object, which is 9216. In the second step, the reference of the new object is stored in myCar reference variable. The memory state for the myCar reference variable and the new Car object after the statement labeled #2 is executed is shown in Figure 6-15. Note that the memory address of the new Car object (9216) and the value of the myCar reference variable match at this point. You do not need to worry about the numbers used in this example for memory addresses; I just made up some numbers to drive home the point of how the memory addresses are used internally. Java does not let you access the memory address of an object or a variable. Java lets you access/modify the state of objects through reference variables.

The reference variable, myCar, stores reference of Car object

Car object

Figure 6-15. *Memory states for the myCar reference variable and the new Car object when the myCar = new Car() statement is executed*

The statement labeled #3 is similar to the statement labeled #1. The memory state for the xyCar reference variable is shown in Figure 6-16, assuming that 10240 is the memory address for the xyCar reference variable.

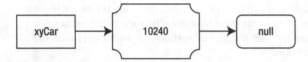

Figure 6-16. *Memory state of xyCar reference variable*

It is interesting to note the memory state when the statement labeled #4 is executed. The statement reads as follows:

```
xyCar = myCar;  /* #4 */
```

Recall that a variable name has two things associated with it: a memory address and a value stored at that memory address. The memory address (or location) is also known as its lvalue whereas the value stored at its memory address is also called rvalue. When a variable is used to the left of an assignment operator (xyCar in statement labeled #4), it refers to its memory address. When a variable is used to the right of assignment operator (myCar in statement labeled #4), it refers to its value (rvalue) stored at its memory address. The statement labeled #4 can be read as follows:

```
xyCar = myCar; /* #4 */
At lvalue of xyCar store rvalue of myCar;        /* #4 - another way */
At memory address of xyCar store value of myCar /* #4 - another way */
```

Therefore, when you execute the statement xyCar = myCar, it reads the value of myCar, which is 9216, and stores it at the memory address of xyCar. The reference variable myCar stores a reference to a Car object. An assignment like xyCar = myCar does not copy the object to which myCar refers. Rather, it copies the value stored in myCar (a reference to the Car object) to xyCar. When the assignment xyCar = myCar is complete, the reference variables of myCar and xyCar have reference to the same Car object in memory. At this point, only one Car object exists in memory. Figure 6-17 shows the memory state when statement labeled #4 is executed.

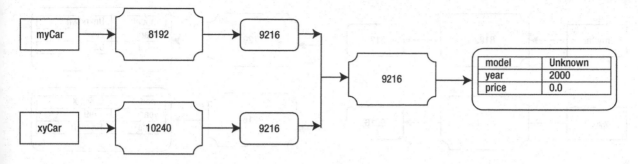

Figure 6-17. *Memory state showing myCar and xyCar referencing the same Car object in memory*

At this time, you can use reference variables myCar or xyCar to access the Car object in memory. The following snippet of code will access the same object in memory:

```
myCar.model = "Civic LX"; /* Use myCar to change model */
myCar.year  = 1999;       /* Use myCar to change year */
xyCar.price = 16000.00;   /* Use xyCar to change the price */
```

After executing the above three statements, model, year, and price will be changed for the Car object and the memory state will look as shown in Figure 6-18.

Figure 6-18. *Memory state showing myCar and xyCar referencing the same Car object in memory after myCar and xyCar have been used to change the state of the Car object*

At this point, two reference variables myCar and xyCar and one Car object exist in memory. Both reference variables are referencing the same Car object. Let's execute the following statement and label it as #5:

```
myCar = new Car(); /* #5 */
```

The above statement will create a new Car object in memory with initial values for its instance variables and assign the reference of the new Car object to the myCar reference variable. The xyCar reference variable still references the Car object it was referencing before. Suppose the new Car object has been allocated at memory address 5120. The memory state for two reference variables myCar and xyCar and two Car objects is shown in Figure 6-19.

Figure 6-19. *Memory state of reference variables myCar and xyCar and two Car objects*

Let's make one more change and set the xyCar reference variable to null as shown:

```
xyCar = null; /* #6 */
```

Figure 6-20 shows the memory state after statement #6 is executed.

Figure 6-20. *Memory state of reference variables myCar and xyCar and two Car objects after xyCar has been assigned a null reference*

Now the xyCar reference variable stores a null reference and it no longer refers to any Car object. The Car object with Civic LX model is not being referenced by any reference variable. You cannot access this Car object at all in your program because you do not have a reference to it. In Java terminology, the Car object with the Civic LX model is not reachable. When an object in memory is not reachable, it becomes eligible for garbage collection. Note that the Car object with the Civic LX model is not destroyed (or deallocated) immediately after xyCar is set to null. It stays in memory until the garbage collector runs and makes sure that it is not reachable. Please refer to the chapter on garbage collection for more details on how an object's memory is deallocated.

I have covered enough background about variables types and how they work in Java. It is time to discuss the parameter passing mechanism in Java. In brief, we can state

All parameters in Java are passed by value.

This brief statement causes a lot of confusion. Does it mean that when a parameter is a reference type, a copy of the object the actual parameter refers to is made and assigned to the formal parameter? It is important to elaborate on the phrase "All parameters in Java are passed by value" with examples. Even veteran Java programmers have problems understanding the parameter passing mechanism in Java. To be more elaborate, Java supports the following four types of parameter passing mechanisms:

- Pass by value

- Pass by constant value

- Pass by reference value

- Pass by constant reference value

Note that all four ways of passing parameters in Java includes the word "value." This is the reason that many books on Java summarize them as "Java passes all parameters by value." Please refer to the previous section for more details for the above-mentioned four types of parameter passing mechanisms.

The first two types, pass by value and pass by constant value, apply to parameters of primitive data types. The last two types, pass by reference value and pass by constant reference value, apply to the parameters of reference type.

When a formal parameter is of a primitive data type, the value of the actual parameter is copied to the formal parameter. Any changes made to the formal parameter's value inside the method's body will change only the copy of the formal parameter and not the value of the actual parameter. Now you can tell that swap() method to swap two primitive values will not work in Java. Listing 6-22 demonstrates that swap() method cannot be written in Java because primitive type parameters are passed by value. The output shows that the x and y formal parameters of the swap() method receive the values of a and b. The values of x and y are swapped inside the method, which does not affect the values of actual parameters a and b at all.

Listing 6-22. An Incorrect Attempt to Write a swap() Method to Swap Values of Two Primitive Types in Java

```java
// BadSwapTest.java
package com.jdojo.cls;

public class BadSwapTest {
    public static void swap(int x, int y) {
        System.out.println("#2: x = " + x + ", y = " + y);

        int temp = x;
        x = y;
        y = temp;

        System.out.println("#3: x = " + x + ", y = " + y);
    }

    public static void main(String[] args) {
        int a = 19;
        int b = 37;

        System.out.println("#1: a = " + a + ", b = " + b);

        // Call the swap() method to swap values of a and b
        BadSwapTest.swap(a, b);

        System.out.println("#4: a = " + a + ", b = " + b);
    }
}
```

```
#1: a = 19, b = 37
#2: x = 19, y = 37
#3: x = 37, y = 19
#4: a = 19, b = 37
```

A primitive type parameter is passed by value. However, you can modify the value of the formal parameter inside the method without affecting the actual parameter value. Java also lets you use pass by constant value. In this case, the formal parameter cannot be modified inside the method. The formal parameter is initialized with the value of the actual parameter by making a copy of the actual parameter and then it is a constant value, which can only be read. You need to use the final keyword in the formal parameter declaration to indicate that you mean to pass the parameter by constant value. Any attempt to change the value of a parameter, which uses pass by constant value, results in a compiler error. Listing 6-23 demonstrates how to use the pass by constant value mechanism to pass the parameter x to the test() method. Any attempt to change the value of the formal parameter x inside the test() method will result in a compiler error. If you uncomment the "x = 10;" statement inside the test() method, you would get the following compiler error:

```
Error(10):  final parameter x may not be assigned
```

You have passed two parameters, x and y, to the test() method. The parameter y is passed by value, and hence it can be changed inside the method. This can be confirmed by looking at the output.

Listing 6-23. An Example of Pass by Constant Value

```java
// PassByConstantValueTest.java
package com.jdojo.cls;

public class PassByConstantValueTest {
        // x uses pass by constant value and y uses pass by value
        public static void test(final int x, int y) {
                System.out.println("#2: x = " + x + ", y = " + y);

                /* Uncommenting following statement will generate a compile-time error */
                // x = 79; /* Cannot change x. It is passed by constant value */

                y = 223; // Ok to change y

                System.out.println("#3: x = " + x + ", y = " + y);
        }

        public static void main(String[] args) {
                int a = 19;
                int b = 37;
                System.out.println("#1: a = " + a + ", b = " + b);
                PassByConstantValueTest.test(a, b);
                System.out.println("#4: a = " + a + ", b = " + b);
        }
}
```

```
#1: a = 19, b = 37
#2: x = 19, y = 37
#3: x = 19, y = 223
#4: a = 19, b = 37
```

Let's discuss the parameter passing mechanism for reference type parameters. Java lets you use the pass by reference value and pass by constant reference value mechanisms to pass reference type parameters to a method. When a parameter is passed by reference value, the reference stored in the actual parameter is copied to the formal parameter. When the method starts executing, both the actual parameter and the formal parameter refer to the same object in memory. If the actual parameter has a null reference, the formal parameter will contain the null reference. You can assign a reference to another object to the formal parameter inside the method's body. In this case, the formal parameter starts referencing the new object in memory and the actual parameter still references the object it was referencing before the method call. Listing 6-24 demonstrates the pass by reference mechanism in Java. It creates a Car object inside the main() method and stores the reference of the Car object in myCar reference variable.

```
// Create a Car object and assign its reference to myCar
Car myCar = new Car();
```

It modifies the model, year, and price of the newly created Car object using myCar reference variable.

```
// Change model, year and price of Car object using myCar
myCar.model = "Civic LX";
myCar.year  = 1999;
myCar.price = 16000.0;
```

The message labeled #1 in the output shows the state of the Car object. The myCar reference variable is passed to the test() method using the following call:

```
PassByReferenceValueTest.test(myCar);
```

Since the type of the formal parameter xyCar in the test() method is Car, which is a reference type, Java uses the pass by reference value mechanism to pass the value of the myCar actual parameter to the xyCar formal parameter. When the test(myCar) method is called, Java copies the reference of the Car object stored in the myCar reference variable to the xyCar reference variable. When the execution enters the test() method's body, myCar and xyCar reference the same object in memory. At this time, there is only one Car object in memory and not two. It is very important to understand that the test(myCar) method call did not make a copy of the Car object referenced by the myCar reference variable. Rather, it made a copy of the reference (memory address) of the Car object referenced by the myCar reference variable, which is the actual parameter, and copied that reference to the xyCar reference variable, which is the formal parameter. The fact that both myCar and xyCar reference the same object in memory is indicated by the message labeled #2 in the output, which is printed using the xyCar formal parameter inside the test() method.

Now you create a new Car object and assign its reference to the xyCar formal parameter inside the test() method.

```
// Let's make xyCar refer to a new Car object
xyCar = new Car();
```

At this point, there are two Car objects in memory. The xyCar formal parameter references the new Car object and not the one whose reference was passed to the method. Note that the actual parameter myCar still references the Car object that you created in the main() method. The fact that the xyCar formal parameter references the new Car object is indicated by the message labeled #3 in the output. When the test() method call returns, the main() method prints details of the Car object being referenced by the myCar reference variable. See Listing 6-24.

Listing 6-24. An Example of a Pass by Reference Value

```java
// PassByReferenceValueTest.java
package com.jdojo.cls;

public class PassByReferenceValueTest {
    public static void main(String[] args) {
        // Create a Car object and assign its reference to myCar
        Car myCar = new Car();

        // Change model, year and price of Car object using myCar
        myCar.model = "Civic LX";
        myCar.year  = 1999;
        myCar.price = 16000.0;

        System.out.println("#1: model = " + myCar.model +
                           ", year = "   + myCar.year +
                           ", price = "  + myCar.price);

        PassByReferenceValueTest.test(myCar);

        System.out.println("#4: model = " + myCar.model +
                           ", year = "   + myCar.year +
                           ", price = "  + myCar.price);
    }

    public static void test(Car xyCar) {
        System.out.println("#2: model = " + xyCar.model +
                           ", year = "   + xyCar.year +
                           ", price = "  + xyCar.price);

        // Let's make xyCar refer to a new Car object
        xyCar = new Car();

        System.out.println("#3: model = " + xyCar.model +
                           ", year = "   + xyCar.year +
                           ", price = "  + xyCar.price);
    }
}
```

```
#1: model = Civic LX, year = 1999, price = 16000.0
#2: model = Civic LX, year = 1999, price = 16000.0
#3: model = Unknown, year = 2000, price = 0.0
#4: model = Civic LX, year = 1999, price = 16000.0
```

■ **Tip**   When a reference type parameter is passed to a method in Java, the formal parameter can access the object the same way the actual parameter can access the object. The formal parameter can modify the object by directly changing the values of the instance variables or by calling methods on the object. Any modification made on the object through the formal parameter is immediately visible through the actual parameter because both hold the reference to the same object in memory. The formal parameter itself can be modified to reference another object (or the `null` reference) inside the method.

If you do not want the method to change the reference type formal parameter to reference a different object than the one referenced by the actual parameter, you can use the pass by constant reference value mechanism to pass that parameter. If you use the keyword `final` in the reference type formal parameter declaration, the parameter is passed by constant reference value and the formal parameter cannot be modified inside the method. The following declaration of the test() method declares the xyzCar formal parameter as `final` and it is passed by constant reference value. The method attempts to change the xyzCar formal parameter by assigning a null reference to it and then by assigning a reference to a new Car objects. Both of these assignment statements will generate a compiler error:

```
// xyzCar is passed by constant reference value because it is declared final
void test(final Car xyzCar) {
        // Can read the object referenced by xyzCar
        String model = xyzCar.model;

        // Can modify object referenced by xyzCar
        xyzCar.year = 2001;

        /* Cannot modify xzyCar. That is, xyzCar must reference the object what the actual
           parameter is referencing at the time this method is called. You cannot even set it to
           null reference. */
        xyzCar = null;       // A compile-time error. Cannot modify xyzCar
        xyzCar = new Car(); // A compile-time error. Cannot modify xyzCar
}
```

Let's discuss one more example on parameter passing mechanism in Java. Consider the following code for the changeString() method:

```
public static void changeString(String s2) {
        /* #2 */
        s2 = s2 + " there";
        /* #3 */
}
```

Consider the following snippet of code that calls the changeString() method:

```
String s1 = "hi";
/* #1 */
changeString(s1);
/* #4 */
```

What will be the content of s1 at #4? String is a reference type in Java. At #1, s1 is referencing a String object whose content is "hi". When the changeString(s1) method is called, s1 is passed to s2 by reference value. At #2, s1 and s2 are referencing the same String object in memory whose content is "hi". When s2 = s2 + " there" statement is executed, two things happens. First, s2 + " there" expression is evaluated, which creates a new String object in memory with content of "hi there" returns its reference. The reference returned by the s2 + " there" expression is assigned to s2 formal parameter. At this time, there are two String objects in memory: one with the content of "hi" and another with the content of "hi there". At #3, the actual parameter s1 is referencing the String object with the content of "hi" and the formal parameter s2 is referencing the String object with content "hi there". When the changeString() method call is over, the formal parameter s2 is discarded. Note that the String object with content "hi there" still exists in memory after the changeString() method call is over. Only the formal parameter is discarded when a method call is over and not the object to which the formal parameter was referencing. At #4, the reference variable s1 still refers to the String object with content "hi". Listing 6-25 has the complete code that attempts to modify a formal parameter of String type.

Listing 6-25. Another Example of Pass by Reference Value Parameter Passing in Java

```java
// PassByReferenceValueTest2.java
package com.jdojo.cls;

public class PassByReferenceValueTest2 {
    public static void changeString(String s2) {
        System.out.println("#2: s2 = " + s2);
        s2 = s2 + " there";
        System.out.println("#3: s2 = " + s2);
    }

    public static void main(String[] args) {
        String s1 = "hi";
        System.out.println("#1: s1 = " + s1);
        PassByReferenceValueTest2.changeString(s1);
        System.out.println("#4: s1 = " + s1);
    }
}
```

```
#1: s1 = hi
#2: s2 = hi
#3: s2 = hi there
#4: s1 = hi
```

■ **Tip** A String object is immutable, meaning that its content cannot be changed after it is created. If you need to change the content of a String object, you must create a new String object with the new content.

Constructors

A constructor is a named block of code that is used to initialize an object of a class immediately after the object is created. The structure of a constructor looks similar to a method. However, the similarity between the two stops right there, in their looks. They are two different constructs and they are used for different purposes.

Declaring a Constructor

The general syntax for a constructor declaration is

```
<<Modifiers>> <<Constructor Name>>(<<parameters list>>) throws <<Exceptions list>> {
       // Body of constructor goes here
}
```

The declaration of a constructor starts with modifiers. A constructor can have its access modifier as `public`, `private`, `protected`, or package-level (no modifier). The constructor name is the same as the simple name of the class. The constructor name is followed by a pair of opening and closing parentheses, which may include parameters. Optionally, the closing parenthesis may be followed by the keyword `throws`, which in turn is followed by a comma-separated list of exceptions. I will discuss the use of the keyword `throws` in chapter 9. The body of the constructor where you place your code is enclosed in braces.

If you compare the syntax to declare a method with the syntax to declare a constructor, you will find that they are almost the same. It is suggested to keep the method declaration in mind when learning about constructor declaration because most of the things are similar.

The following code shows an example of declaring a constructor for a class Test. Figure 6-21 shows the anatomy of the constructor.

Figure 6-21. Anatomy of the constructor for the Test class

```
// Test.java
package com.jdojo.cls;

public class Test {
       public Test() {
               // Code goes here
       }
}
```

■ **Tip**   The name of a constructor must match the simple name, not the fully qualified name, of the class.

Unlike a method, a constructor does not have a return type. You cannot even specify void as a return type for a constructor. Consider the following declaration of a class Test2:

```
public class Test2 {
        // Below is a method, not a constructor.
        public void Test2() {
                // Code goes here
        }
}
```

Does the class Test2 declare a constructor? The answer is no. The class Test2 does not declare a constructor. Rather, what you may be looking at is a method declaration, which has the same name as the simple name of the class. It is a method declaration because it specifies a return type of void. Note that a method name could also be the same as the class name as shown above.

Just the name itself does not make a method or constructor. If the name of a construct is the same as the simple name of the class, it could be a method or a constructor. If it specifies a return type, it is a method. If it does not specify a return type, it is a constructor.

When do you use a constructor? You use a constructor with the new operator to initialize an instance (or an object) of a class just after the new instance is created. Sometimes the phrases "create" and "initialize" are used interchangeably in the context of a constructor. However, you need to be clear about the difference in creating and initializing an object. The new operator creates an object and a constructor initializes the object.

The following statement uses a constructor of the Test class to initialize an object of the Test class:

```
Test t = new Test();
```

Figure 6-22 shows the anatomy of the above statement. The new operator is followed by the call to the constructor. The new operator along with the constructor call, for example "new Test()", is called an instance (or object) creation expression. An instance creation expression creates an object in memory, executes the code in the body of the specified constructor, and finally, returns the reference of the new object.

Figure 6-22. *Anatomy of a constructor call with the new operator*

I have covered enough theories for declaring a constructor. It is time to see a constructor in action. Listing 6-26 has the code for a Cat class.

Listing 6-26. A Cat Class with a Constructor

```
// Cat.java
package com.jdojo.cls;

public class Cat {
        public Cat() {
                System.out.println("Meow...");
        }
}
```

The Cat class declares a constructor. Inside the constructor's body, it prints a message "Meow..." in the standard output. Listing 6-27 has the code for a CatTest class, which creates two Cat objects in its main() method. Note that you always use an object creation expression to create a new object of the Cat class. It is up to you to store the reference of the new object in a reference variable. The first Cat object is created and its reference is not stored. The second Cat object is created and its reference is stored in a reference variable c.

Listing 6-27. A Test Class That Creates Two of the Cat Objects

```
// CatTest.java
package com.jdojo.cls;

public class CatTest {
        public static void main(String[] args) {
                // Create a Cat object and ignore its reference
                new Cat();

                // Create another Cat object and store its reference in c
                Cat c = new Cat();
        }
}
```

```
Meow...
Meow...
```

Overloading a Constructor

A class can have more than one constructor. If a class has multiple constructors, they are called overloaded constructors. Since the name of the constructor must be the same as the simple name of the class, there is a need to differentiate one constructor from another. The rules for overloaded constructors are the same as for overloaded methods. If a class has multiple constructors, all of them must differ from the others in the number, order, or type of parameters. Listing 6-28 has the code for a Dog class, which declares two constructors. One constructor accepts no parameters and another accepts a String parameter.

Listing 6-28. A Dog Class with Two Constructors, One with No Parameter and One with a String Parameter

```java
// Dog.java
package com.jdojo.cls;

public class Dog {
        // Constructor #1
        public Dog() {
                System.out.println("A dog is created.");
        }

        // Constructor #2
        public Dog(String name) {
                System.out.println("A dog named " + name + " is created.");
        }
}
```

If a class declares multiple constructors, you can use any of them to create an object of that class. For example, the following two statements create two objects of the Dog class:

```java
Dog dog1 = new Dog();
Dog dog2 = new Dog("Cupid");
```

The first statement uses the constructor with no parameters and the second one uses the constructor with a String parameter. If you use a constructor with parameters to create an object, the actual parameter's order, type and number must match the formal parameter's order, type and number. Listing 6-29 has the complete code that creates two Dog objects using different constructors.

Listing 6-29. Testing the Constructors of the Dog Class

```java
// DogTest.java
package com.jdojo.cls;

public class DogTest {
        public static void main(String[] args) {
                Dog d1 = new Dog();            // Uses Constructor #1
                Dog d2 = new Dog ("Canis"); // Uses Constructor #2
        }
}
```

```
A dog is created.
A dog named Canis is created.
```

The output of running the DogTest class indicates that different constructors are called when two Dog objects are created in the main() method.

■ **Tip**   A constructor is called once per object creation expression. You can execute the code for one constructor only once in the process of an object creation. If the code for a constructor is executed N times, it means N number of objects of that class will be created and you must use N number of object creation expressions to do that. However, when an object creation expression calls a constructor, the called constructor may call another constructor from its body. I will cover this scenario where one constructor calls another later in this section.

Writing Code for a Constructor

So far, you have been writing trivial code in constructors. What kind of code should you write in a constructor? The purpose of a constructor is to initialize the instance variables of the newly created object. Inside a constructor, you should restrict yourself only to write code that initializes instance variables of the object. An object is not fully created when a constructor is called. The object is still in the process of creation. If you write some processing logic in a constructor assuming that a full blown object exists in memory, sometimes you may get unexpected results.

Let's create another class to represent a dog object. You will call this class SmartDog, as shown in Listing 6-30.

Listing 6-30. A SmartDog Class That Declares Two Constructors to Initialize Instance Variables Differently

```java
// SmartDog.java
package com.jdojo.cls;

public class SmartDog {
        private String name;
        private double price;

        public SmartDog() {
                // Initialize the name to "Unknown" and the price to 0.0
                this.name = "Unknown";
                this.price = 0.0;

                System.out.println("Using SmartDog() constructor");
        }

        public SmartDog(String name, double price) {
                // Initialize name and price instance variables
                // with the name and price parameters
                this.name = name;
                this.price = price;

                System.out.println("Using SmartDog(String, double) constructor");
        }

        public void bark() {
                System.out.println(name + " is barking...");
        }

        public void setName(String name) {
                this.name = name;
        }
```

```java
        public String getName() {
                return this.name;
        }

        public void setPrice(double price) {
                this.price = price;
        }

        public double getPrice() {
                return this.price;
        }

        public void printDetails(){
                System.out.print("Name: " + this.name );
                if (price > 0.0) {
                        System.out.println(", price: " + this.price );
                }
                else {
                        System.out.println(", price: Free" );
                }
        }
}
```

The SmartDog class looks a little bigger. However, its logic is very simple. The following are the main points in the SmartDog class that you need to understand:

- It declares two instance variables called name and price. The name instance variable stores the name of a smart dog. The price instance variable stores the price for which it can be sold.

- It declares two constructors. The first constructor has no parameters. It initializes the name and price instance variables to Unknown and 0.0, respectively. The second constructor accepts two parameters named name and price. It initializes the name and price instance variables to whatever values are passed for the two parameters. Note the use of the keyword this inside the constructors. The keyword this refers to the object for which the constructor's code is executing. The use of the keyword this is not necessary in the first constructor. However, you must use the keyword this to refer to instance variables in the second constructor because the names of the formal parameters hide the name of the instance variables.

- The two constructors initialize instance variables (or state of the object) in their bodies. They do not include any other processing logic.

- The instance method bark() prints a message on the standard output with the name of the smart dog who is barking.

- The setName() and getName() methods are used to set and get the name of the smart dog. The setPrice() and getPrice() methods are used to set and get the price of the smart dog.

- The printDetails() method prints the name and price of a smart dog. If the price for a smart dog is not set to a positive value, it prints the price as "Free".

Listing 6-31 has the code for a SmartDogTest class that demonstrates how the two constructors initialize the instance variables.

Listing 6-31. A Test Class to Demonstrate the Use of the SmartDog Class

```java
// SmartDogTest.java
package com.jdojo.cls;

public class SmartDogTest {
        public static void main(String[] args)  {
                // Create two SmartDog objects
                SmartDog sd1 = new SmartDog();
                SmartDog sd2 = new SmartDog("Nova", 219.2);

                // Print details about the two dogs
                sd1.printDetails();
                sd2.printDetails();

                // Make them bark
                sd1.bark();
                sd2.bark();

                // Change the name and price of Unknown dog
                sd1.setName("Opal");
                sd1.setPrice(321.80);

                // Print details again
                sd1.printDetails();
                sd2.printDetails();

                // Make them bark one more time
                sd1.bark();
                sd2.bark();
        }
}
```

```
Using SmartDog() constructor
Using SmartDog(String, double) constructor
Name: Unknown, price: Free
Name: Nova, price: 219.2
Unknown is barking...
Nova is barking...
Name: Opal, price: 321.8
Name: Nova, price: 219.2
Opal is barking...
Nova is barking...
```

Calling a Constructor from another Constructor

A constructor may call another constructor of the same class. Let's consider the following Test class. It declares two constructors; one accepts no parameters and one accepts an int parameter.

```
public class Test {
        Test() {
        }

        Test(int x) {
        }
}
```

Suppose you want to call the constructor with an int parameter from the constructor with no parameter. Your first attempt, which is wrong, would be as follows:

```
public class Test {
        Test() {
                // Call another constructor
                Test(103); // A compile-time error
        }

        Test(int x) {
        }
}
```

The above code does not compile. Java has a special way to call a constructor from another constructor. You must use the keyword this, as if it is the name of the constructor, to call a constructor from another constructor. The following code calls the constructor with an int parameter from the constructor with no parameter using the statement, "this(103);". This is another use of the keyword this.

```
public class Test {
        Test() {
                // Call another constructor
                this(103); // OK. Note the use of the keyword this.
        }

        Test(int x) {
        }
}
```

There are two rules about calling a constructor from another constructor. The rules ensure that one constructor is executed only once during the process of an object creation of a class.

- If a constructor calls another constructor, it must be the first executable statement in the constructor's body. This makes it easy for the compiler to check that a constructor has been called and it has been called only once. For example, the following code will generate a compiler error because a call to the constructor with int parameter this(k) is the second statement inside the constructor's body, not the first statement.

```
public class Test {
    Test() {
        int k = 10; // First statement
        this(k);    // Second statement. A compile-time error
    }

    Test(int x) {
    }
}
```

An attempt to compile the code for the above Test class will generate the following error message:

```
Error(4):  call to this must be first statement in constructor
```

- A constructor cannot call itself because it will result in a recursive call. In the following code for the Test class, both constructors attempt to call themselves:

```
public class Test {
    Test() {
        this();
    }

    Test(int x ) {
        this(10);
    }
}
```

An attempt to compile the above code will result in the following error. One error message is generated for each attempt to call the constructor itself.

```
Error(2):  recursive constructor invocation
Error(6):  recursive constructor invocation
```

Typically, you create overloaded constructors for a class when you have many ways to initialize an object of a class. Let's consider the SmartDog class shown in Listing 6-30. Two constructors give you two ways to initialize a new SmartDog object. The first one initializes the name and the price with default values. The second constructor lets you initialize name and price with the value supplied by the caller. Sometimes you may perform some logic to initialize the object inside a constructor. Letting you call another constructor from a constructor allows you to write such logic only once. You can make use of this feature for your SmartDog class, as shown:

```
// SmartDog.java
package com.jdojo.cls;

public class SmartDog {
    private String name;
    private double price;

    public SmartDog() {
        // Call another constructor with "Unknown" and 0.0 as parameters
        this("Unknown", 0.0);
```

```
                System.out.println("Using SmartDog() constructor");
        }

        public SmartDog(String name, double price) {
                // Initialize name and price to specified name and price
                this.name = name;
                this.price = price;

                System.out.println("Using SmartDog(String, double) constructor");
        }

        /* Rest of code remains the same */
}
```

Note that you changed the code only inside the constructor that accepts no parameters. Instead of setting the default values for name and price in the first constructor, you called the second constructor with the default values as parameters from the first one.

Using a return Statement Inside a Constructor

A constructor cannot have a return type in its declaration. It means a constructor cannot return any value. Recall that a return statement is of two types: one with a return expression and one without a return expression. The return statement without a return expression simply returns the control to the caller without returning any value. You can use a return statement without a return expression inside a constructor body. When a return statement in a constructor is executed, the control returns to the caller, ignoring the rest of the constructor's code.

The following code shows an example of using a return statement in a constructor. If the parameter x is a negative number, the constructor simply executes a return statement to end the call to the constructor. Otherwise, it performs some logic.

```
public class Test {
        public Test(int x) {
                if (x < 0) {
                        return;
                }

                /* Perform some logic here */
        }
}
```

Access Level Modifier for a Constructor

Access level for a constructor determines the part of the program that can use that constructor in an object creation expression to create an object of that class. You can specify one of the four access levels for a constructor: public, private, protected, and package-level. The following code declares four constructors for the Test class. A comment for each constructor explains its access level.

```
// Class Test has public access level
public class Test {
        // Constructor #1 - Package-level access
        Test() {
        }
```

```
    // Constructor #2 - public access level
    public Test(int x) {
    }

    // Constructor #3 - private access level
    private Test(int x, int y) {
    }

    // Constructor #4 - protected access level
    protected Test(int x, int y, int z){
    }
}
```

The effect of these access levels is the same as their effect for a method. A constructor with a public access level can be used in any part of the program. A constructor with private access level can be used only inside the same class in which it is declared. A constructor with protected access level can be used in any part of the program in the same package in which its class is declared and inside any descendant class in any package. A constructor with package-level access can be used inside the same package in which its class is declared.

You can specify public or package-level access level for a class. A class defines a new reference type, which you can use to declare a reference variable. The access level of a class determines in which part of the program the name of the class can be used. Usually, you use the name of a class in a cast or in a reference variable declaration as shown:

```
// Test class name is used to declare the reference variable t
Test t;

// Test class name is used to cast the reference variable xyz
Test t2 = (Test)xyz;
```

Let's discuss the different combinations of access levels for a class and its constructor, and its effects in a program. Consider the following code that declares a class T1 with public access level and it has a constructor, which also has a public access level:

```
// T1.java
package com.jdojo.cls.p1;

public class T1 {
    public T1() {
    }
}
```

Because the class T1 has a public access level, you can declare a reference variable of type T1 as shown below anywhere in the program:

```
// Code inside any package
T1 t;
```

Because the constructor for the class T1 has a public access level, you can use it in an object creation expression in any package.

```
// Code inside any package
new T1();
```

You can combine the above two statements into one in the code in any package.

```
// Code inside any package
T1 t = new T1();
```

Let's consider the following code for the class T2, which has a public access level and has a constructor with a private access level:

```
// T2.java
package com.jdojo.cls.p1;

public class T2 {
        private T2() {
        }
}
```

Because class T2 has a public access level, you can use its name to declare a reference variable in any package. The constructor for class T2 has a private access level. The implication of having a private constructor is that you cannot create an object of the T2 class outside the T2 class. Recall that a private method, field, or a constructor cannot be used outside the class in which it is declared. Therefore, the following code will not compile unless it appears inside the T2 class:

```
// Code outside the T2 class
new T2(); // A compile-time error
```

What is the use of the T2 class if you cannot create its object outside of the T2 class? Here are the possible situations where you can declare a constructor private, and still create and use objects of the class:

- A constructor is used to create an object of a class. You may want to restrict the number of objects for a class. The only way you can restrict the number of objects of a class is by having the full control of its constructors. If you declare all constructors of a class to have the private access level, you have full control over how the objects of that class will be created. Typically, you include one or more public static methods in that class, which create and/or return an object of that class. If you design a class so that only one object of the class may exist, it is called a singleton pattern. The following code is a version of the T2 class that is based on the singleton pattern. It declares a private static reference variable called instance, which holds the reference of the T2 class object. Note that the T2 class uses its own private constructor to create an object. Its public static getInstance() method returns the lone object of the class. More than one object of the T2 class cannot exist.

  ```
  // T2.java
  package com.jdojo.cls.p1;

  public class T2 {
          private static T2 instance = new T2();

          private T2() {
          }
  ```

```
        public static T2 getInstance() {
                return T2.instance;
        }
        /* Other code goes here */
}
```

You can use the T2.getInstance() method to get the reference of an object of the T2 class. Internally, the T2 class does not create a new object every time you call the T2.getInstance() method. Rather, it returns the same object reference for all calls to this method.

```
T2 t1 = T2.getInstance();
T2 t2 = T2.getInstance();
```

- Sometimes you want a class to have only static members. It may not make sense to create an object of such a class. For example, the java.lang.Math class declares its constructor private. The Math class contains static variables and static methods to perform numeric operations. It does not make sense to create an object of the Math class.

- You can also declare all constructors of a class private to prevent inheritance. Inheritance lets you define a class by extending the definition of another class. If you do not want anyone else to extend your class, one way to achieve this is to declare all constructors of your class private. Another way to prevent your class from being extended is to declare it final. I will discuss inheritance in detail in the chapter on inheritance.

Let's consider the class T3 whose constructor has protected access level as shown:

```
// T3.java
package com.jdojo.cls.p1;

public class T3 {
        protected T3() {
        }
}
```

A constructor with protected access level can be used anywhere in the same package or inside a descendant class in any package. The class T3 is in the com.jdojo.cls.p1 package. You can write the following statement anywhere in com.jdojo.cls.p1 package, which creates an object of the T3 class:

```
// Valid anywhere in the com.jdojo.cls.p1 package
new T3();
```

I will cover inheritance in detail later. However, to complete the discussion of a protected constructor, you will use inheritance in the example below. Things about inheritance will be clearer when I discuss it in the chapter on inheritance. You inherit (or extend) a class using the keyword extends. The following code creates a T3Child class by inheriting it from the T3 class:

```
// T3Child.java
package com.jdojo.cls.p2;

import com.jdojo.cls.p1.T3;
```

```java
public class T3Child extends T3 {
        public T3Child() {
                super(); // Ok. Calls T3() constructor, which is declared protected.
        }
}
```

The T3 class is called the parent class of the T3Child class. An object of a child class cannot be created until the object of its parent class is created. Note the use of the super() statement inside T3Child() constructor's body. The statement super() calls the protected constructor of the T3 class. I use the super keyword to call the parent class constructor as you use keyword this to call another constructor of the same class. You cannot call the protected constructor of T3 directly as

```java
new T3() ;
```

outside the com.jdojo.cls.p1 package.

Consider a T4 class with a constructor having package-level access. Recall that using no access level modifier gives package-level access.

```java
// T4.java
package com.jdojo.cls.p1;

public class T4 {
        // T4() has package-level access
        T4() {
        }
}
```

You can use T4's constructor to create its object anywhere in the com.jdojo.cls.p1 package. Sometimes you need a class that works as a helper class for other classes in a package. Objects of these classes need to be created only within the package. You can specify package-level access for constructors of such helper classes.

Default Constructor

The primary goal of declaring a class is to create an object of its type. You need a constructor to create an object of a class. The necessity to have a constructor for a class is so obvious that the Java compiler adds a constructor to your class if you do not declare one. The constructor that is added by the compiler is called the default constructor. The default constructor does not have any parameters. Sometimes the default constructor is also called a no-args constructor. The access level of the default constructor is the same as the access level of the class.

The classes that you have been working with are called top-level classes. You can also declare a class within another class, which is called an inner class. A top-level class can have public or package-level access. However, an inner class can have public, private, protected, or package-level access. The Java compiler adds a default constructor for a top-level class as well as for a nested class. A default constructor for a top-level class can have either public or package-level access depending on the access level of the class. However, a default constructor for an inner class can have access level of public, private, protected or package-level depending on its class access level.

Table 6-6 shows some examples of classes and the compiler adding a default constructor to them. When the compiler adds a default constructor, it also adds a statement super() to call the no-args constructor of the parent class. Sometimes the call to the parent's no-args constructor inside the default constructor may cause your class not to compile. Please refer to the chapter on inheritance for a complete discussion on this topic.

Table 6-6. *Examples of Classes for Which a Default Constructor Is Added by the Java Compiler*

Source Code for Your Class	Compiled Version of Your Class	Comments
| ```
public class Test {
}
``` | ```
public class Test {
    public Test() {
    }
}
``` | The compiler adds a default constructor with public access level. |
| ```
class Test {
}
``` | ```
class Test {
    Test() {
    }
}
``` | The compiler adds a default construct with package-level access. |
| ```
public class Test {
  Test() {
  }
}
``` | ```
public class Test {
  Test() {
  }
}
``` | The Test class already had a constructor. The compiler does not add any constructor. |
| ```
public class Test {
  public Test(int x) {
  }
}
``` | ```
public class Test {
  public Test(int x) {
  }
}
``` | The Test class already had a constructor. The compiler does not add any constructor. |
| ```
public class Test {
  private class Inner {
  }
}
``` | ```
public class Test {
  public Test() {
  }
  private class Inner {
    private Inner(){
    }
  }
}
``` | Test is a public top-level class and Inner is a private inner class. The compiler adds a public default constructor for the Test class and a private default constructor for the Inner class. |

■ **Tip** It is good programming practice to add a constructor explicitly to all your classes rather than letting the compiler add a default constructor for your classes. The story of constructors is not over yet. You will revisit constructors in the chapter on inheritance.

A static Constructor

Constructors are used in the context of the creating a new object; hence, it is consider part of the object context, not the class context. You cannot declare a constructor static. The keyword this, which is a reference to the current object, is available inside the body of a constructor as it is available inside the body of an instance method.

Instance Initialization Block

You have seen that a constructor is used to initialize an instance of a class. An instance initialization block, also called instance initializer, is also used to initialize objects of a class. Why does Java provide two constructs to perform the same thing? Not all classes in Java can have a constructor. Are you surprised to learn that not all classes can have constructors? I did not mention this fact during the discussion on constructors. Briefly, I mentioned inner classes, which are different from top-level classes. I will discuss one more type of class in Chapter 2 of *Beginning Java Language Features* (ISBN: 978-1-4302-6658-7) called an anonymous class. As the name suggests, an anonymous class does not have a name. Recall that a constructor is a named block of code whose name is the same as the simple name of the class. Because an anonymous class cannot have a name, it cannot have a constructor either. How will you initialize an object of an anonymous class? You can use an instance initializer to initialize an object of an anonymous class. The use of an instance initializer to initialize an object is not limited only to anonymous classes. Any type of class can use it to initialize its object.

An instance initializer is simply a block of code inside the body of a class, but outside any methods or constructors. Recall that a block of code is a sequence of legal Java statements enclosed within braces. An instance initializer does not have a name. Its code is simply placed inside an opening brace and a closing brace. The following snippet of code shows how to declare an instance initializer for the Test class. Note that an instance initializer is executed in instance context and the keyword this is available inside the instance initializer.

```java
public class Test {
        private int num;

        // An instance initializer
        {
                this.num = 101;

                /* Other code for the instance initializer goes here */
        }

        /* Other code for Test class goes here */
}
```

You can have multiple instance initializers for a class. All of them are executed automatically in textual order for every object you create. Code for all instance initializers are executed before any constructor. Listing 6-32 demonstrates the sequence in which the constructor and instance initializers are executed.

Listing 6-32. Example of Using an Instance Initializer

```java
// InstanceInitializer.java
package com.jdojo.cls;

public class InstanceInitializer {
        {
                System.out.println("Inside instance initializer 1.");
        }

        {
                System.out.println("Inside instance initializer 2.");
        }
```

```
        public InstanceInitializer() {
                System.out.println("Inside no-args constructor.");
        }

        public static void main(String[] args) {
                InstanceInitializer ii = new InstanceInitializer();
        }
}
```

```
Inside instance initializer 1.
Inside instance initializer 2.
Inside no-args constructor.
```

■ **Tip** An instance initializer cannot have a `return` statement. It cannot throw checked exceptions unless all declared constructors list those checked exceptions in their `throws` clause; an exception to this rule is made in the case of an anonymous class because it does not have a constructor; an instance initializer of an anonymous class may throw checked exceptions.

static Initialization Block

A static initialization block is also known as a `static` initializer. It is similar to an instance initialization block. It is used to initialize a class. In other words, you can initialize class variables inside a `static` initializer block. An instance initializer is executed once per object whereas a static initializer is executed only once for a class when the class definition is loaded into JVM. To differentiate it from an instance initializer, you need to use the `static` keyword in the beginning of its declaration. You can have multiple static initializers in a class. All static initializers are executed in textual order in which they appear, and execute before any instance initializers. Listing 6-33 demonstrates when a static initializer is executed.

Listing 6-33. An Example of Using a static Initializer in a Class

```
// StaticInitializer.java
package com.jdojo.cls;

public class StaticInitializer {
        private static int num;

        // An instance initializer
        {
                System.out.println("Inside instance initializer.");
        }

        // A static initializer. Note the use of the keyword static below.
        static {
                num = 1245;
                System.out.println("Inside static initializer.");
        }
```

```java
        // Constructor
        public StaticInitializer() {
                System.out.println("Inside constructor.");
        }

        public static void main(String[] args) {
                System.out.println("Inside main() #1. num: " + num);

                // Declare a reference variable of the class
                StaticInitializer si;

                System.out.println("Inside main() #2. num: " + num);

                // Create an object
                new StaticInitializer();

                System.out.println("Inside main() #3. num: " + num);

                // Create another object
                new StaticInitializer();
        }
}
```

```
Inside static initializer.
Inside main() #1. num: 1245
Inside main() #2. num: 1245
Inside instance initializer.
Inside constructor.
Inside main() #3. num: 1245
Inside instance initializer.
Inside constructor.
```

The output may be confusing at first. It shows that the static initializer has executed even before the first message is displayed in the main() method. You get the output when you run the StaticInitializer class using the following command:

```
java com.jdojo.cls.StaticInitializer
```

The java command must load the definition of the StaticInitializer class before it can execute its main() method. When the definition of the StaticInitializer class is loaded into memory, at that time the class is initialized and its static initializer is executed. This is the reason that you see the message from the static initializer before you see the message from the main() method. Note that instance initializer is called twice because you create two objects of the StaticInitializer class.

■ **Tip** A static initializer cannot throw checked exceptions and it cannot have a return statement.

The final Keyword

The final keyword is used in many contexts in a Java program. It takes on different meanings in different contexts. However, as its name suggests, its primary meaning is the same in all contexts. Its primary meaning is

> *The construct with which the final keyword is associated does not allow modifying or replacing its original value or definition.*

If you remember the primary meaning of the final keyword, it will help you understand its specialized meaning in a specific context. The final keyword can be used in the following three contexts:

- A variable declaration
- A class declaration
- A method declaration

In this section, you will discuss the use of the final keyword only in the context of a variable declaration. The chapter on inheritance discusses its use in the context of class and method declarations in detail. In this section, I will briefly describe its meaning in all three contexts.

If a variable is declared final, it can be assigned a value only once. That is, the value of a final variable cannot be modified once it has been set. If a class is declared final, it cannot be extended (or subclassed). If a method is declared final, it cannot be redefined (overridden or hidden) in the subclasses of the class that contains the method.

Let's discuss the use of the final keyword in a variable declaration. In this discussion, a variable declaration means the declaration of a local variable, a formal parameter of a method/constructor, an instance variable, and a class variable. To declare a variable as final, you need to use the final keyword in the variable's declaration. The following snippet of code declares four final variables: YES, NO, MSG, and act:

```
final int YES = 1;
final int NO = 2;
final String MSG = "Good-bye";
final Account act = new Account();
```

You can set the value of a final variable only once. Attempting to set the value of a final variable the second time will generate a compilation time error.

```
final int x = 10;
int y = 101 + x; // Reading x is ok

// A compilation time error. Cannot change value of the final variable x once it is set
x = 17;
```

There are two ways to initialize a final variable:

- You can initialize it at the time of its declaration.
- You can defer its initialization until a later time.

Until what time you can defer the initialization of a final variable depends on the variable type. However, you must initialize the final variable before it is read for the first time.

If you do not initialize a final variable at the time of its declaration, such a variable is known as a blank final variable.

```
final int multiplier; // A blank final variable

/* Do something here... */

// Set the value of multiplier first time
multiplier = 3;

// Ok to read the multiplier variable
int value = 100 * multiplier;
```

Let's go through examples of each type of variable and how to declare them final.

final Local Variables

You can declare a local variable final. If you declare a local variable as a blank final variable, you must initialize it before using. You will receive a compilation time error if you try to change the value of the final local variable the second time. The following snippet of code uses final and blank final local variables in the test() method. Comments in the code explain what you can do with final variables in the code.

```
public static void test() {
        int x = 4;         // A variable
        final int y = 10; // A final variable. Cannot change y here onward
        final int z;       // A blank final variable

        // We can read x and y, and modify x
        x = x + y;

        /* We cannot read z here because it is not initialized yet */

        /* Initialize the blank final variable z */
        z = 87;

        /* Can read z now. Cannot change z here onwards */

        x = x + y + z;

        /* Perform other logic here... */
}
```

final Parameters

You can also declare a formal parameter final. A formal parameter is initialized automatically with the value of the actual parameter when the method or the constructor is invoked. Therefore, you cannot change the value of a final formal parameter inside the method's or the constructor's body. The following snippet of code shows the final formal parameter x for the test2() method:

```
public void test2(final int x) {
        /* Can read x, but cannot change it */
        int y = x = 11;

        /* Perform other logic here... */
}
```

final Instance Variables

You can declare an instance variable final and blank final. An instance variable is a part of an object's state. A final instance variable specifies part of the object's state that does not change after the object is created. A blank final instance variable must be initialized when an object is created. The following rules apply for initializing a blank final instance variable:

- It must be initialized in one of the instance initializers or all constructors. The following rules expand on this rule.

- If it is initialized in an instance initializer, it should not be initialized again in any other instance initializers or constructors.

- If it is not initialized in any of the instance initializers, the compiler makes sure it is initialized only once, when any of the constructors is invoked. This rule can be broken into two sub-rules. As a rule of thumb, a blank final instance must be initialized in all constructors. If you follow this rule, a blank final instance variable will be initialized multiple times if a constructor calls another constructor. To avoid multiple initialization of a blank final instance variable, it should not be initialized in a constructor if the first call in the constructor is a call to another constructor, which initializes the blank final instance variable.

The above rules for initializing a blank final instance variable may seem complex. However, it is simple to understand if you remember only one rule that a blank final instance variable must be initialized once and only once when any of the constructors of the class is invoked. All of the above-described rules are to ensure that this rule is followed.

Let's consider different scenarios of initializing final and blank final instance variables. We do not have anything to discuss about final instance variable as follows where x is a final instance variable for the Test class:

```java
public class Test {
    private final int x = 10;
}
```

The final instance variable x has been initialized at the time of its declaration and its value cannot be changed afterwards.

The following code shows a Test2 class with a blank final instance variable y:

```java
public class Test2 {
    private final int y; // A blank final instance variable
}
```

Attempting to compile theTest2 class generates an error because the blank final instance variable y is never initialized. Note that the compiler will add a default constructor for the Test2 class, but it will not initialize y inside the constructor. The following code for the Test2 class will compile because it initializes y in an instance initializer:

```java
public class Test2 {
    private final int y;

    {
        y = 10; // Initialized in an instance initializer
    }
}
```

The following code would not compile because it initializes y more than once inside two instance initializers:

```
public class Test2 {
        private final int y;

        {
                y = 10; // Initialized y for the first time
        }

        {
                y = 10; // An error. Initializing y again
        }
}
```

The above code may seem legal to you. However, it is not legal because two instance initializers are initializing y, even though both of them sets y to the same value 10. The rule is about number of times a blank final instance variable should be initialized, irrespective of the value being used for its initializations. Since all instance initializers are executed when an object of the Test2 class is created, y will be initialized twice, which is not legal.

The following code for the class Test2 with two constructors would compile:

```
public class Test2 {
        private final int y;
        public Test() {
                y = 10; // Initialize y
        }

        public Test(int z) {
                y = z; // Initialize y
        }
}
```

The above code initializes the blank final instance variable y in both constructors. It may seem that y is being initialized twice—once in each constructor. Note that y is an instance variable and one copy of y exists for each object of the Test2 class. When an object of the Test2 class is created, it will use one of the two constructors, not both. Therefore, for each object of the Test2 class, y is initialized only once.

Below is the modified code for the Test2 class, which presents a tricky situation. Both constructors initialize the blank final instance variable y. The tricky part is that the no-args constructor calls another constructor.

```
public class Test2 {
        private final int y;

        public Test() {
                this(20); // Call another constructor
                y = 10;   // Initialize y
        }

        public Test(int z) {
                y = z; // Initialize y
        }
}
```

The above code for the Test2 class would not compile. The compiler generates an error message, which reads as *variable y might already have been assigned*. Let's consider creating an object of the Test2 class as

```
Test2 t = new Test2(30);
```

There is no issue in creating an object of the Test2 class by invoking the one-arg constructor. The blank final instance variable y is initialized only once. Let's create an object of the Test2 class.

```
Test2 t2 = new Test2();
```

When the no-args constructor is used, it calls the one-arg constructor, which initializes y to 20. The no-args constructor initializes y again to 10, which is the second time initialization for y. For this reason, the above code for the Test2 class would not compile. You need to remove the initialization of y from no-args constructor and the code would compile. The following is the modified code for the Test2 class that would compile:

```
public class Test2 {
    private final int y;

    public Test() {
        this(20); // Another constructor will initialize y
    }

    public Test(int z) {
        y = z; // Initialize y
    }
}
```

final Class Variables

You can declare a class variable final and blank final. You must initialize a blank final class variable in one of the static initializers. If you have more than one static initializer for a class, you must initialize all the blank final class variables only once in one of the static initializers.

The following code for the Test3 class shows how to deal with a final class variable. It is customary to use all uppercase letters to name final class variables. It is also a way to define constants in Java programs. The Java class library has numerous examples where it defines public static final variables to use them as constants.

```
public class Test3 {
    public static final int YES = 1;
    public static final int NO = 2;
    public static final String MSG;

    static {
        MSG = "I am a blank final static variable";
    }
}
```

final Reference Variables

Any type of variable (primitive and reference) can be declared final. The primary meaning of the final keyword is the same in both cases. That is, the value stored in a final variable cannot be changed once it has been set. I will look at the final reference variable in a little more detail in this section. A reference variable stores the reference of an object. A final reference variable means that once it references an object (or null), it cannot be modified to reference another object. Consider the following statement:

```
final Account act = new Account();
```

Here, act is a final reference variable of the Account type. It is initialized at the time of its declaration. At this time, act is referencing an object in memory.

Now, you cannot make the act variable to reference another object in memory. The following statement generates a compilation time error:

```
act = new Account(); // A compile-time error. Cannot change act
```

A common misconception arises in this case. Mistakenly, programmers believe that the Account object that is referenced by the act reference variable cannot be changed. The declaration statement of the act reference variable as final has two things.

- act is a reference variable, which is final,

- There is an Account object in memory whose reference is stored in the act variable.

It is the act reference variable that cannot be changed, not the Account object it is referencing. If the Account class allows you to change the state of its object, you can change the state using the act variable. The following are valid statements, which modify the balance instance variable of the Account object:

```
act.deposit(2001.00); // Modifies state of the Account object
act.debit(2.00);       // Modifies state of the Account object
```

If you do not want an object of a class to be modified after it is created, you need to include that logic in the class design. The class should not let any of its instance variables be modified after the object is created. Such objects are called immutable objects.

Compile-time vs. Runtime final Variables

You use final variables to define constants. This is the reason that final variables are also called constants. If the value of a final variable can be computed by the compiler at compile-time, such a variable is a compile-time constant. If the value of a final variable cannot be computed by the compiler, it is a runtime final variable. The values of all blank final variables are not known until runtime. References are not computed until runtime. Therefore, all blank final variables and final reference variables are runtime constants.

Java performs an optimization when you use compile-time constants in an expression. It replaces the use of the compile-time constant with the actual value of the constant. Suppose you have a Constants class as shown below. It declares a MULTIPLIER static final variable.

```
public class Constants {
        public static final int MULTIPLIER = 12;
}
```

Consider the following statement:

```
int x = 100 * Constants.MULTIPLIER;
```

When you compile the above statement, the compiler will replace Constants.MULTIPLIER with its value 12 and your statement is compiled as

```
int x = 100 * 12;
```

Now, 100 * 12 is also a compile-time constant expression. The compiler will replace it with its value 1200 and your original statement will be compiled as

```
int x = 1200;
```

There is one downside of this compiler optimization. If you change the value of the MULTIPLIER final variable in the Constants class, you must recompile all the classes that refer to the Constants.MULTIPLIER variable. Otherwise, they will continue using the old value of the MULTIPLIER constant that existed when they were compiled last time.

What is a varargs Method?

The term "varargs" is shorthand for "variable-length arguments." The varargs feature was introduced in Java 5. It lets you declare a method or constructor that accepts a variable number of arguments (or parameters). I will use only the term "method" in our discussion. However, the discussion also applies to constructors.

The number of arguments a method accepts is called its arity. A method that accepts variable-length arguments is called a variable-arity method or varargs method. What does a varargs method look like? Let's discuss how a non-varargs method works before you look at a varargs method.

Consider the following code for a MathUtil class that declares a max() method. The method has two parameters. It computes and returns the maximum of its two arguments.

```java
public class MathUtil {
        public static int max(int x, int y) {
                int max = x;
                if (y > max) {
                        max = y;
                }
                return max;
        }
}
```

There is nothing extraordinary going on in the MathUtil class or in its max() method. Suppose you want to compute the maximum of two integers, say 12 and 18; you would invoke the max() method as so:

```
int max = MathUtil.max(12, 18);
```

When the above statement is executed, 18 will be assigned to the variable max. Suppose you want to compute the maximum of three integers. You might come up with the following logic:

```
int max = MathUtil.max(MathUtil.max(70, 9), 30);
```

The above logic works fine. It computes the maximum of two integers, and then computes the maximum of the two and the third integer. Suppose you want to compute maximum of ten integers. You might repeat the above logic and that will work, although the code may not be readable. You need a better way of doing this.

Let's try overloading the max() method, so it accepts three integer arguments. Here is the newer version of the MathUtil class, called MathUtil2:

```java
public class MathUtil2 {
        public static int max(int x, int y) {
                int max = x;
                if (y > max) {
                        max = y;
                }
                return max;
        }

        public static int max(int x, int y, int z) {
                int max = x;
                if (y > max) {
                        max = y;
                }

                if (z > max) {
                        max = z;
                }
                return max;
        }
}
```

You can compute maximum of two and three integers as

```java
int max1 = MathUtil2.max(12, 18);
int max2 = MathUtil2.max(10, 8, 18);
```

Adding a max() method with three int arguments did solve the problem temporarily. The real problem still remains. You will have to add a max() method with all possible number of integer arguments. You would agree that no programmer wants to write a max() method where he will have to keep adding a newer version.

Before Java 5, when the number of arguments of a method was not known at design time, you would declare the method argument as an array of int, as shown below. I will discuss arrays in detail in chapter 15.

```java
public class MathUtil3 {
        public static int max(int[] num) {
                /* Must check for zero element in num here */
                int max = Integer.MIN_VALUE;
                for(int i = 0; i < num.length; i++) {
                        if (num[i] > max) {
                                max = num[i];
                        }
                }
                return max;
        }
}
```

You can write the following snippet of code that will compute the maximum of two and three integers using the MathUtil3.max() method:

```
int[] num1 = new int[] {10, 1};
int max1 = MathUtil3.max(num1);

int[] num2 = new int[] {10, 8, 18} ;
int max2 = MathUtil3.max(num2);
```

You can pass an arbitrary number of integers to the MathUtil3.max() method. In a sense, you have a way to pass an arbitrary number of arguments to a method. What bothers programmers is the way the method needs to be called when its argument type is an array. You must create an array object and package the values of all its elements when you need to call the method with an array argument. The issue here is not the code inside the max(int[] num) method. Rather, it is the client code that calls this method.

Varargs comes to the rescue. Let's declare a max() method, which can accept any number of integer arguments including zero arguments. The beauty of a varargs method is in the simpler client code that calls the method. So, how do you declare a varargs method? All you need to do is to add an ellipsis (or triple-dot like ...) after the data type of the method's argument. The following snippet of code shows a max() method declaration with one variable-length argument, num, which is of the int data type. Note the placement of ellipsis after the data type int.

```
public static int max(int... num) {
    // Code goes here
}
```

Adding whitespaces before and after ellipsis is optional. All of the following varargs method declarations are valid. They use different whitespaces before and after the ellipsis.

```
public static int max(int... num)   // A space after
public static int max(int ... num) // A space before and after
public static int max(int...num)    // No space before and after
public static int max(int ...
num) // A space before and a newline after
```

A varargs method can have more than one argument. The following snippet of code shows that aMethod() accepts three arguments, one of which is a variable-length argument:

```
public static int aMethod(String str, double d1, int...num) {
    // Code goes here
}
```

There are two restrictions for a varargs method:

- A varargs method can have a maximum of one variable-length argument. The following declaration for m1() method is invalid because it declares two variable-length arguments, n1 and n2:

  ```
  // Invalid declaration
  void m1(String str, int...n1, int...n2) {
      // Code goes here
  }
  ```

- The variable-length argument of a varargs method must be the last argument in the argument list. The following declaration for m2() method is invalid because the variable-length argument n1 is not declared as the last argument:

```
// Invalid declaration
void m2(int...n1, String str) {
    // Code goes here
}
```

You can fix the above declaration by moving argument n1 to the last, like so:

```
void m2(String str, int...n1) {
    // Code goes here
}
```

Let's rewrite the max() method to make it a varargs method, as shown:

```
public class MathUtil4 {
    public static int max(int...num) {
        int max = Integer.MIN_VALUE;
        for(int i = 0; i < num.length; i++) {
            if (num[i] > max) {
                max = num[i];
            }
        }
        return max;
    }
}
```

You almost always have a loop inside a varargs method that processes the list of arguments for the variable-length argument. The length property gives you the number of values that were passed for the variable-length argument. For example, num.length in the max() varargs method will give you the number of integers that were passed to the method. To get the nth value in the variable-length argument, you need to use varArgsName[n-1]. For example, num[0], num[1], and num[n-1] will contain the first, second, and nth value passed in for the num variable-length argument. If you just want to process all values passed in for a variable-length argument, you can use a simpler loop, a foreach loop, which was introduced to Java 5. You can rewrite the code for max() method using foreach loop as follows:

```
public static int max2(int...num) {
    int max = Integer.MIN_VALUE;
    for(int currentNumber : num) {
        if (currentNumber > max) {
            max = currentNumber;
        }
    }
    return max;
}
```

The body of the MathUtil4.max() method is exactly the same as if the num argument is declared as an int array. You are right in thinking so. The Java compiler implements a variable-length argument of a method using an array. The above declaration of the MathUtil4.max() method is changed by the compiler. The declaration part max(int...num) is changed to max(int[] num) when you compile the code. What benefit do you get using a variable-length argument? The benefit of using a variable-length argument in a method comes from the elegant way of calling the method. You can call the MathUtil4.max() method as follows:

```
int max1 = MathUtil4.max(12, 8);
int max2 = MathUtil4.max(10, 1, 30);
```

You can use zero or more arguments for a variable-length argument in a method. The following code is a valid call to the max() method:

```
int max = MathUtil4.max(); // Passing no argument is ok
```

What will be returned by calling the MathUtil4.max() method with no argument? If you look at the method's body, it will return Integer.MIN_VALUE, which is -2147483648. Practically, a call to the max() method without at least two arguments is not a valid call. You must check for invalid number of arguments when a method is a varargs method. You do not get a problem of invalid number of arguments for non-varargs methods because the compiler will force you to use the exact number of arguments. The following declaration of the max() method will force its caller to pass at least two integers:

```
// Argumenets n1 and n2 are mandatory
public static int max(int n1, int n2, int... num) {
        // Code goes here
}
```

The compiler will treat the first two arguments, n1 and n2, as mandatory and the third argument, num, as optional. Now, you can pass two or more integers to the max() method. Listing 6-34 shows the final, complete code for the max() method.

Listing 6-34. A Utility Class to Compute the Maximum of Some Specified Integers Using a Varargs Method

```
// MathUtil5.java
package com.jdojo.cls;

public class MathUtil5 {
        public static int max(int n1, int n2, int... num) {
                // Initialize max to teh maximu of n1 and n2
                int max = (n1 > n2 ? n1 : n2);

                for(int i = 0; i < num.length; i++) {
                        if (num[i] > max) {
                                max = num[i];
                        }
                }
                return max;
        }
}
```

```
        public static void main(String[] args) {
                System.out.println("max(7, 9) = " + MathUtil5.max(7, 9));
                System.out.println("max(70, 19, 30) = " + MathUtil5.max(70, 19, 30));
                System.out.println("max(-7, -1, 3) = " + MathUtil5.max(-70, -1, 3));
        }
}
```

```
max(7, 9) = 9
max(70, 19, 30) = 70
max(-7, -1, 3) = 3
```

You can pass any number of integers when you call the MathUtil5.max() method. All of the following statements are valid:

```
int max1 = MathUtil5.max(12, 8);         // will return 12
int max2 = MathUtil5.max(10, 1, 30);     // will return 30
int max3 = MathUtil5.max(11, 3, 7, 37);  // will return 37
```

If you call the MathUtil5.max() method with no arguments or one argument, the compiler will generate an error.

```
int max1 = MathUtil5.max();     // A compile-time error
int max2 = MathUtil5.max(10);   // A compile-time error
```

Overloading a Varargs Method

The same overloading rules for methods also apply to a varargs method. You can overload a method with a variable-length argument as long as the parameters for the methods differ in type, order, or number. For example, the following is a valid example of an overloaded max() method:

```
public class MathUtil6 {
        public static int max(int x, int y) {
                // Code goes here
        }

        public static int max(int...num) {
                // Code goes here
        }
}
```

Consider the following snippet of code, which calls the overloaded method MathUtil6.max() with two arguments:

```
int max = MathUtil6.max(12, 13); // which max() will be called?
```

The MathUtil6 class has two max() methods. One method accepts two int parameters and another accepts a variable-length int parameter. In the above case, Java will call the max(int x, int y). Java first attempts to find a method declaration using an exact match for the number of parameters. If it does not find an exact match, it looks for a match using variable-length parameters.

■ **Tip**   If a varargs method is overloaded, Java uses the more specific version of the method instead of using a varargs method. Java uses varargs method as the last resort to resolve a method call.

Sometimes a call to an overloaded varargs method may cause confusion to the Java compiler. The overloading of the method itself may be valid. However, the call to it may cause an issue. Consider the following snippet of code for the MathUtil7 class, which is a valid example of method overloading:

```java
public class MathUtil7 {
        public static int max(int...num) {
                // Code goes here
        }

        public static int max(double...num) {
                // Code goes here
        }
}
```

Which version of the max() method will be called when the following statement is executed?

```java
int max = MathUtil7.max(); // Which max() to call?
```

The above statement will generate a compilation time error stating that the call to MathUtil7.max() is ambiguous. Java allows you to pass zero or more values for a variable-length argument. In the above statement, both methods max(int...num) and max(double...num) qualify for the MathUtil7.max() call. The compiler cannot decide which one to call. You may find many other instances where a call to an overloaded varargs method results in an ambiguous method call and the compiler will generate an error. The error message will guide you to the offending code.

Varargs Methods and the main() Method

Recall that if you want to run a class, you need to declare a main() method in it with a String array as its argument. The signature for the main() method must be main(String[] args). A varargs method is implemented by Java compiler using an array. If your method signature is m1(XXX...args), it is changed to m1(XXX[] args) by the compiler. Now you can declare the main() method of your class using the older notation that uses a String array or using a newer notation that uses a varargs. The following declaration of main() method for the Test class is valid. You will be able to run the Test class using the java command.

```java
public class Test {
        public static void main(String...args)  {
                System.out.println("Hello from varargs main()...");
        }
}
```

Generic Classes

Abstraction and polymorphism are at the heart of object-oriented programming. Defining a variable is an example of abstraction where the variable hides the actual values. Defining a method hides the details of its implementation logic, which is another form of abstraction. Defining parameters for a method is part of polymorphism that allows the method to work on different types of value or objects.

Java 5 added a new feature called generics that allows for writing true polymorphic code in Java. Using generics, you can write code without knowing the type of the objects you code operates on. It lets you create generic classes, constructors, and methods.

A generic class is defined using formal type parameters. Formal type parameters are a list of comma-separated variable names placed in angle-brackets (<>) after the class name in the class declaration. The following snippet of code declares a class Wrapper that takes one formal type parameter:

```
public class Wrapper<T>  {
        // Code for the Wrapper class goes here
}
```

The parameter has been given a name T. What is T at this point? The answer is that you do not know. All you know at this point is that T is a type variable, which could be any reference type in Java, such as String, Integer, Double, etc. The formal type parameter value is specified when the Wrapper class will be used. The classes that take formal type parameter are also known as parameterized classes.

You can declare a variable of the Wrapper<T> class specifying the String type as the value for its formal type parameter as shown below. Here, String is the actual type parameter.

```
Wrapper<String> stringWrapper;
```

Java lets you use a generic class without specifying the formal type parameters. This is allowed for backward compatibility. You can also declare a variable of the Wrapper<T> class as shown:

```
Wrapper aRawWrapper;
```

When a generic class is used without specifying the actual type parameters, it is known as raw type. The above declaration used the Wrapper<T> class as a raw type as it did not specify the value for T.

■ **Tip**   The actual type parameter for a generic class, if specified, must be a reference type, for example, String, Human, etc. Primitive types are not allowed as the actual type parameters for a generic class.

A class may take more than one formal type parameter. The following snippet of code declares a Mapper class that takes two formal parameters, T and R:

```
public class Mapper<T, R>  {
        // Code for the Mapper class goes here
}
```

You can declare variable of the Mapper<T, R> class as follows:

```
Mapper<String, Integer> mapper;
```

Here, the actual type parameters are String and Integer.

It is customary, not a requirement, to give one-character names to the formal type parameters, for example, T, R, U, V, etc. Typically, T stands for "Type," R for "Return," etc. One-character names make the code more readable. However, nothing stops you from declaring a generic class as follows, which has four formal type parameters named MyType, YourType, Hello, and WhoCares.

```
public class Fun<MyType, YourType, Hello, WhoCares> {
        // Code for the Mapper class goes here
}
```

Java will compile the above code, but readers of your code will complain for sure!

The formal type parameters are available inside the class body to be used as types. Listing 6-35 declares a generic class Wrapper<T>.

Listing 6-35. Declaring a Generic Class Wrapper<T>

```
// Wrapper.java
package com.jdojo.cls;

public class Wrapper<T> {
        private T obj;

        public Wrapper(T obj) {
                this.obj = obj;
        }

        public T get() {
                return obj;
        }

        public void set(T obj) {
                this.obj = obj;
        }
}
```

The Wrapper<T> class uses the formal type parameter to declare instance variable obj to declare a formal parameter for its constructor and set() method, and as a return type for the get() method.

You can create an object of the generic type by specifying the actual type parameter for the constructor as follows:

```
Wrapper<String> w1 = new Wrapper<String>("Hello");
```

Most of the time, the compiler can infer the actual type parameter for the constructor. In those cases, you can omit the actual type parameter. In the following assignment statement, the compiler will infer the actual type parameter for the constructor as String:

```
Wrapper<String> w1 = new Wrapper<>("Hello");
```

Once you have declared a variable of the generic class, you can think of the formal type parameter as the specified actual type parameter for all practical purposes. Now, you can think that, for w1, the get() method of the Wrapper<T> class returns a String.

```
String s1= w1.get();
```

The program in Listing 6-36 shows how to use the generic Wrapper<T> class.

Listing 6-36. Using a Generic Class in Your Code

```java
// WrapperTest.java
package com.jdojo.cls;

public class WrapperTest {
        public static void main(String[] args) {
                Wrapper<String> w1 = new Wrapper<>("Hello");
                String s1 = w1.get();
                System.out.println("s1=" + s1);

                w1.set("Testing generics");
                String s2 = w1.get();
                System.out.println("s2=" + s2);

                w1.set(null);
                String s3 = w1.get();
                System.out.println("s3=" + s3);
        }
}
```

```
s1=Hello
s2=Testing generics
s3=null
```

This is just the tip of the iceberg when it comes to what generics offer in Java. To understand generics completely, you must cover other topics, such as inheritance, first. Generics are covered fully in the book *Beginning Java 8 Language Features* (ISBN: 978-1-4302-6658-7).

Summary

Classes are the basic building blocks in object-oriented programming. A class represents a reference type in Java. Classes serve as templates to create objects of their types. A class consists of four parts: fields, initializers, constructors, and methods. Fields represents the state of objects of the class. Initializers and constructors are used to initialize fields of the class. The new operator is used to create objects of a class. Methods represent the behavior of the objects of the class.

Fields and methods are known as members of the class. Constructors are not considers members of the class. Fields, methods, and constructors of a class and the class itself have an access level. There are four types of access levels: public, private, protected, and package-level. The presence of the keyword public, private, and protected in defining them gives them public, private, and protected access level, respectively. Absence of any of these keywords specifies the package-level access. A top-level class can have either public of package level access. Methods and constructors can have any one of the four types of access levels.

Import statements in a compilation unit are used to import types from other packages. They allow using the simple names of types of other packages. The compiler uses the import statements to resolve the simple names to fully qualified names. Static import statements are used to import static member of types from other packages.

Different mechanisms to pass parameters to methods and constructors exist. Java uses pass by value and pass by constant value mechanisms to pass parameters of primitive data types. Pass by reference value and pass by constant reference value are used to pass parameters of reference types.

You can define a class and its members `final`. If something is `final` it means its definition or value, whatever it represents, cannot be modified. `final` variables are used to define constants in Java. Compile-time constants are constants whose values are known when the program is compiled. Runtime constants are constants whose values are not known until the program is run.

Varargs parameters are used to define parameters for methods and constructors where they can take variable number of parameters.

Java allows you to write true polymorphic code using generics in which code is written in terms of formal type parameters.

CHAPTER 7

■ ■ ■

The Object and Objects Classes

In this chapter, you will learn

- About the hierarchical class structure in Java
- About the Object class being the superclass of classes
- How to use methods of the Object class with detailed examples
- How to reimplement methods of the Object class in your class
- How to check two objects for equality
- The difference between immutable and mutable objects
- How to use the utility methods of the Objects class to deal with null values gracefully

The Object Class

Java has an Object class in the java.lang package. All Java classes, those that are included in the Java class libraries and those that you create, extend the Object class directly or indirectly. All Java classes are a subclass of the Object class and the Object class is the superclass of all classes. Note that the Object class itself does not have a superclass.

Classes in Java are arranged in a tree-like hierarchical structure, where the Object class is at the root (or top). I will discuss class hierarchy in detail in the chapter on inheritance. I will discuss some details of the Object class in this chapter.

There are two important rules about the Object class. I will not explain the reasons behind these rules here. The reasons why you could do these things with the Object class will be clear after you read the chapter on inheritance.

Rule #1

A reference variable of the Object class can hold a reference of an object of any class. As any reference variable can store a null reference, so can a reference variable of the Object type. Consider the following declaration of a reference variable obj of the Object type:

```
Object obj;
```

You can assign a reference of any object in Java to obj. All of the following statements are valid:

```
// Can assign the null reference
obj = null;
```

```
// Can assign a reference of an object of the Object class
obj = new Object();

// Can assign a reference of an object of the Account class
Account act = new Account();
obj = act;

// Can assign a reference of object of any class. Assume that the AnyClass class exists
obj = new AnyClass();
```

The opposite of the above rule is not true. You cannot assign a reference of an object of the Object class to a reference variable of any other type. The following statement is not valid:

```
Account act = new Object(); // A compile-time error
```

Sometimes, you may store the reference of an object of a specific type, say Account type, in a reference variable of the Object type, and later you would like to assign the same reference back to a reference variable of the Account type. You can do so by using a cast as shown:

```
Object obj2 = new Account();
Account act = (Account)obj2; // Must use a cast
```

Sometimes you may not be sure that a reference variable of the Object class holds a reference to an object of a specific type. In those situations, you need to use the instanceof operator to test. The left operand of the instanceof operator is a reference variable and its right operand is a class name. If its left operand is a reference of its right operand type, it returns true. Otherwise, it returns false. Please refer to the chapter on inheritance for more detailed discussion on the instanceof operator.

```
Object obj;
Cat c;

/* Do something here and store a reference in obj... */

if (obj instanceof Cat) {
        // If we get here, obj holds a reference of a Cat for sure
        c = (Cat)obj;
}
```

You will need to make use of this rule when you have a method that takes an Object as a parameter. You can pass a reference of any object for the parameter of the Object class. Consider the following snippet of code that shows a method declaration:

```
public void m1(Object obj) {
    // Code goes here
}
```

You can call m1() in a number of different ways:

```
m1(null);            // Pass null reference
m1(new Object());    // Pass a reference of an object of the Object class
m1(new AnyClass());  // Pass a reference of an object of the AnyClass class
```

Rule #2

The Object class has nine methods, which are available to be used in all classes in Java. We can put the methods into two categories.

Methods in the first category have been implemented in the Object class. You are supposed to use them as they have been implemented. You cannot reimplement (the technical term for reimplement is override) these methods in any class you create. Their implementation is final. Methods that fall into this category are getClass(), notify(), notifyAll(), and wait().

Methods in the second category have a default implementation in the Object class. You can customize their implementations by reimplementing them in your classes. Methods that fall into this category are toString(), equals(), hashCode(), clone(), and finalize().

A Java programmer must understand the proper use of all of the methods in the Object class. I will discuss them in detail, except the notify(), notifyAll(), and wait() methods. These methods are used in thread synchronization. They will be discussed in a separate chapter on threads in the book *Beginning Java Language Features* (ISBN: 978-1-4302-6658-7). Table 7-1 lists all methods in the Object class with a brief description. The "Yes" in the "Implemented" column indicates that the Object class has implementation for the method, which can be used without writing any code. The "No" in this column means that you need to implement the method before using it. The "Yes" in the "Customizable" column indicates that you can reimplement the method to customize it. The "No" in this column indicates that the Object class has implemented the method and its implementation is final.

Table 7-1. *List of Methods in the Object Class with Their Brief Description*

Method	Implemented	Customizable	Description
public String toString()	Yes	Yes	It returns a string representation of an object. Typically, it is used for debugging purpose.
public boolean equals(Object obj)	Yes	Yes	It is used to compare two objects for equality.
public int hashCode()	Yes	Yes	It returns a hash code (an integer) value of an object.
protected Object clone() throws CloneNotSupportedException	No	Yes	It is used to make a copy of an object.
protected void finalize() throws Throwable	No	Yes	It is called by the garbage collector before an object is destroyed.
public final Class getClass()	Yes	No	It returns a reference to the Class object of the object.
public final void notify()	Yes	No	Notifies one thread in the wait queue of the object.
public final void notifyAll()	Yes	No	Notifies all threads in the wait queue of the object.
public final void wait() throws InterruptedException public final void wait(long timeout) throws InterruptedException public final void wait (long timeout, int nanos) throws InterruptedException	Yes	No	Makes a thread wait in the wait queue of the object with or without a timeout.

To reimplement a method of the Object class, you need to declare the method the same way as it has been declared in the Object class, and then write your own code in its body. There are more rules to reimplement a method. I will cover all rules in Chapter 16 on inheritance. You can reimplement the toString() method of the Object class in your class, say Test, as shown:

```
public class Test {
    /* Reimplement the toString() method of the Object class */
    public String toString() {
        return "Here is a string";
    }
}
```

I will discuss six methods of the Object class in detail in the sections to follow.

What Is the Class of an Object?

Every object in Java belongs to a class. You define a class in source code, which is compiled into a binary format (usually a class file with the *.class* extension). Before a class is used at runtime, its binary representation is loaded into JVM. Loading the binary representation of a class into JVM is handled by an object called a class loader. Typically, multiple class loaders are used in a Java application to load different types of classes. A class loader is an instance of the class java.lang.ClassLoader. Java lets you create your own class loader by extending the ClassLoader class. Typically, you do not need to create your own class loaders. The Java runtime will use its built-in class loaders to load your classes.

A class loader reads the binary format of the class definition into JVM. The binary class format may be loaded from any accessible location, for example, a local file system, a network, a database, etc. Then, it creates an object of the java.lang.Class class, which represents the binary representation of the class in JVM. Note the uppercase C in the class name java.lang.Class. The binary format of a class definition may be loaded multiple times in the JVM by different class loaders. A class inside a JVM is identified by the combination of its fully qualified name and its class loader. Typically, the binary definition of a class is loaded only once in a JVM.

■ **Tip** You can think of an object of the Class class as a runtime descriptor of the source code of a class. Your source code for a class is represented by an object of the Class class at runtime.

The getClass() method of the Object class returns the reference of the Class object. Since the getClass() method is declared and implemented in the Object class, you can use this method on a reference variable of any type. The following snippet of code shows how to get the reference of the Class object for a Cat object:

```
Cat c = new Cat();
Class catClass = c.getClass();
```

The Class class is generic and its formal type parameter is the name of the class that is represented by its object. You can rewrite the above statement using generics, like so:

```
Class<Cat> catClass = c.getClass();
```

By default, the class definition is loaded only once, and there is only one Class object per Java class. You are not considering those cases where you have written code to load the same class more than once. If you use the getClass() method on different objects of the same class, you will get the reference of the same Class object. Consider the following snippet of code:

```
Cat c2 = new Cat();
Cat c3 = new Cat();

Class catClass2 = c2.getClass();
Class catClass3 = c3.getClass();
```

Here, c2 and c3 are two objects of the same Cat class. Therefore, c2.getClass() and c3.getClass() return the reference of the same Class object, which represents the Cat class in the JVM. The expression catClass2 == catClass3 will evaluate to true.

The Class class has many useful methods. I discuss most of its methods in Chapter 3 of the book *Beginning Java Language Features*. You can use its getName() method to get the fully qualified name of the class. You can use its getSimpleName() to get the simple name of the class. For example,

```
String fullName = catClass.getName();
String simpleName = catClass.getSimpleName();
```

■ **Tip** Not all classes in an application are loaded into JVM when the application starts. A class is loaded and a corresponding Class object is created when the application uses the class for the first time.

Computing Hash Code of an Object

A hash code is an integer value that is computed for a piece of information using an algorithm. A hash code is also known as a hash sum, a hash value, or simply a hash. The algorithm to compute an integer from a piece of information is called a hash function.

The definition of a hash code involves three things:

- A piece of information
- An algorithm
- An integer value

You have a piece of information. You apply an algorithm to it to produce an integer value. The integer value that you get is the hash code for the piece of information you had. If you change the piece of information or the algorithm, the computed the hash code may or may not change. Figure 7-1 depicts the process of computing the hash code.

Figure 7-1. *Process of computing a hash code*

Computing a hash code is a one-way process. Getting the original piece of information from a hash code is not an easy task and it is not the goal of the hash code computation either.

The piece of information that could be used to generate a hash code could be an arbitrary sequence of bytes, characters, numbers, or a combination of them. For example, you may want to compute the hash code for a string "Hello".

What does a hash function look like? A hash function may be as simple as the following function, which returns the integer zero for all input data:

```
int myHashFunction(your input data) {
        return 0;  // Always return zero
}
```

The above hash function fits the definition of a hash function although it is not a practically good one. Writing a good hash function is not an easy task. You need to consider a number of things about the input data before you can write a good hash function.

Why would you need a hash code? It is needed for efficient retrieval of data associated with it when the data is stored in a hash based collection (or container). Before data is stored in a container, its hash code is computed, and then it is stored at a location (also called a bucket), which is based on its hash code. When you want to retrieve the data, its hash code is used to find its location in the container, making the retrieval of the information faster. It is worth noting that an efficient retrieval of data using hash code is based on distribution of the hash code values over a range. If the hash codes that are generated are not uniformly distributed, the retrieval of data may not be efficient. In the worst case, the retrieval of data may be as bad as a linear search through all elements stored in the container. If you use a hash function as shown above, all elements in the container will be stored in the same bucket, which will require searching through all elements. Using a good hash function so that it gives you uniformly distributed hash codes is critical in implementing an efficient hash based container for fast data retrieval.

What is the use of hash codes in Java? Java uses hash codes for the same reason described above—to efficiently retrieve data from hash based collections. If the objects of your class are not used as keys in a hash based collection, for example, in a Hashtable, HashMap, etc., you need not even worry about hash codes for your objects at all.

You can compute hash code for an object in Java. In case of an object, the pieces of information that will be used to compute the hash code are the pieces of information that make up the state of the object. Java designers considered the hash code for an object so important that they provided a default implementation to compute the hash code for an object in the Object class.

The Object class has a hashCode() method that returns an int, which is the hash code of the object. The default implementation of this method computes the hash code of an object by converting the memory address of the object into an integer. Since the hashCode() method is defined in the Object class, it is available in all classes in Java. However, you are free to override the implementation in your class. Here are the rules that you must follow when you override the hashCode() method in your class. Suppose there are two object references, x and y.

- If x.equals(y) returns true, x.hashCode() must return an integer, which is equal to y.hashCode(). That is, if two objects are equal using the equals() method, they must have the same hash codes.

- If x.hashCode() is equal to y.hashCode(), it is not necessary that x.equals(y) returns true. That is, if two objects have the same hash codes using the hashCode() method, they do not have to be equal using the equals() method.

- If the hashCode() method is called on the same object multiple times in the same execution of a Java application, the method must return the same integer value. The hashCode() and equals() methods are closely tied. If your class overrides any of these two methods, it must override both for the objects of your class to work correctly in hash-based collections. Another rule is that you should use only those instance variables to compute the hash code for an object, which are also used in the equals() method to check for equality.

If your class is mutable, you should not be using objects of your class as keys in hash-based collections. If the object has been used as a key changes after their use, you will not be able to locate the object in the collection because locating an object in a hash based collection is based on its hash code. In such cases, you will have stranded objects in the collection.

How should you implement a hashCode() method for a class? Here are some guidelines to write the logic for the hashCode() method for your class, which is reasonable for most of the purposes:

- Start with a prime number, say 37.

```
int hash = 37;
```

- Compute the hash code value for each instance variable of primitive data types separately using the following logic. Note that you need to use only those instance variables in the hash code computation, which are also part of the equals() method logic. Let's store the result of this step in an int variable code. Let's assume that value is the name of the instance variable.

  For byte, short, int, and char data types, use their integer value as

  ```
  code = (int)value;
  ```

  For long data type, use the XOR for two halves of 64-bit as

  ```
  code = (int)(value ^ (value >>>32));
  ```

  For float data type, convert its floating-point values to an equivalent integer value using

  ```
  code = Float.floatToIntBits(value)
  ```

  For double data type, convert its floating-point value to long using the doubleToLongBits() method of the Double class and then convert the long value to an int value using the procedure as described above for the long data type.

  ```
  long longBits = Double.doubleToLongBits(value);
  code = (int)(longBits ^ (longBits >>>32));
  ```

  For boolean data type, use 1 for true and 0 for false.

  ```
  code = (value ? 1 : 0)
  ```

- For a reference instance variable, use 0 if it is null. Otherwise, call its hashCode() method to get its hash code. Suppose ref is the name of the reference variable.

  ```
  code = (ref == null ? 0: ref.hashCode());
  ```

  Compute the hash code using the following formula. Using 59 in the formula is an arbitrary decision. Any other prime number, say 47, will work fine.

  ```
  hash = hash * 59 + code;
  ```

- Repeat the above three steps for all instance variables you want to include in your hashCode() computation.

- Finally, return the value contained in the hash variable from your hashCode() method.

The above method is one of the many ways, not the only way, to compute hash code of an object in Java. Consult a good textbook on computing hash codes if you need a stronger hash function. All primitive wrapper classes and String class override the hashCode() method to provide reasonably good implementations of hash functions.

■ **Tip**   Java 7 added a utility class java.lang.Objects. It contains a hash() method that computes the hash code for any number of values of any type. From Java 7, you are advised to use the Objects.hash() method to compute the hash code of an object. Please refer to "The Objects Class" section later in this chapter for more details.

Listing 7-1 contains the code for a Book class. It shows one of the possible implementations of the hashCode() method.

Listing 7-1. A Book Class That Reimplements the hashCode() Method

```java
// Book.java
package com.jdojo.object;

public class Book {
        private String title;
        private String author;
        private int pageCount;
        private boolean hardCover;
        private double price;

        /* Other code goes here */

        /* Must implement the equals() method too. */

        public int hashCode() {
                int hash = 37;
                int code = 0;

                // Use title
                code = (title == null ? 0 : title.hashCode());
                hash = hash * 59 + code;

                // Use author
                code = (author == null ? 0 : author.hashCode());
                hash = hash * 59 + code;

                // Use pageCount
                code = pageCount;
                hash = hash * 59 + code;

                // Use hardCover
                code = (hardCover ? 1 : 0);
                hash = hash * 59 + code;
```

```
                // Use price
                long priceBits = Double.doubleToLongBits(price);
                code = (int)(priceBits ^ (priceBits >>>32));
                hash = hash * 59 + code;

                return hash;
        }
}
```

The class has five instance variables: title, author, pageCount, hardcover, and price. The implementation uses all five instance variables to compute the hash code for a Book object. You must also implement the equals() method for the Book class, which must use all the five instance variables to check if two Book objects are equal. You need to make sure that the equals() method and the hashCode() method use the same set of instance variables in their logic. Suppose you add one more instance variable to the Book class. Let's call it ISBN. Because ISBN identifies a book uniquely, you might use only the ISBN instance variable to compute its hash code and to compare for equality with another Book object. In this case, it will be sufficient to use only one instance variable to compute the hash code and check for equality.

There are some misconceptions about the hash code of an object in Java. Developers think that the hash code uniquely identifies an object and it must be a positive integer. However, they are not true. The hash code does not identify an object uniquely. Two distinct objects may have the same hash codes. A hash code does not have to be only a positive number. It could be any integer value, positive as or negative. There is also confusion about the usage of hash codes. They are used solely for the purpose of efficient retrieval of data from a hash-based collection. If your objects are not used as keys in hash based collections and you do not override the equals() method in your class, you do not need to worry about reimplementing the hashCode() method in your class at all. Most likely, it will be overriding the equals() method that will prompt you to override the hashCode() method for your class. If you do not override and provide correct implementation of hashCode() and equals() methods in your class at the same time, the objects of your class would not behave properly in hash-based collections. The Java compiler or the Java runtime will never give you any warnings or errors about the incorrect implementations of these two methods in your class.

Comparing Objects for Equality

Every object in the universe is different from all other objects, and every object in a Java program is different from all other objects. All objects have a unique identity. The memory address at which an object is allocated can be treated as its identity, which will make it always unique. Two objects are the same if they have the same identity (or reference in Java terminology). Consider the following snippet of code:

```
Object obj1;
Object obj2;

/* Do something... */
if (obj1 == obj2) {
        /* obj1 and obj2 are the same object based on identity */
}
else {
        /* obj1 and obj2 are different objects based on identity */
}
```

The above code uses identity comparison to test for equality of obj1 and obj2. It compares the references of two objects to test whether they are equal.

Sometimes you want to treat two objects as equal if they have the same state based on some or all of their instance variables. If you want to compare two objects of your class for equality based on criteria other than their references (identities), your class needs to reimplement the equals() method of the Object class. The default implementation of the equals() method in the Object class compares the references of the object being passed as the parameter and the object on which the method is called. If the two references are equal, it returns true. Otherwise, it returns false. In other words, the equals() method in the Object class performs identity based comparison for equality. The implementation of the method is as follows. Recall that the keyword this inside an instance method of a class refers to the reference of the object on which the method is called.

```
public boolean equals(Object obj) {
        return (this == obj);
}
```

Consider the following snippet of code. It compares some Point objects using the equality operator (==), which always compares the references of its two operands. It also uses the equals() method of the Object class to compare the same two references. The output shows that the result is the same. Note that your Point class does not contain an equals() method. When you call the equals() method on a Point object, the equals() method's implementation of the Object class is used.

```
Point pt1 = new Point(10, 10);
Point pt2 = new Point(10, 10);
Point pt3 = new Point(12, 19);
Point pt4 = pt1;

System.out.println("pt1 == pt1: " + (pt1 == pt1));
System.out.println("pt1.equals(pt1): " + pt1.equals(pt1));

System.out.println("pt1 == pt2: " + (pt1 == pt2));
System.out.println("pt1.equals(pt2): " + pt1.equals(pt2));

System.out.println("pt1 == pt3: " + (pt1 == pt3));
System.out.println("pt1.equals(pt3): " + pt1.equals(pt3));

System.out.println("pt1 == pt4: " + (pt1 == pt4));
System.out.println("pt1.equals(pt4): " + pt1.equals(pt4));
```

```
pt1 == pt1: true
pt1.equals(pt1): true
pt1 == pt2: false
pt1.equals(pt2): false
pt1 == pt3: false
pt1.equals(pt3): false
pt1 == pt4: true
pt1.equals(pt4): true
```

In practice, two points are considered the same if they have the same (x, y) coordinates. If you want to implement this rule of equality for your Point class, you must reimplement the equals() method as shown in Listing 7-2.

Listing 7-2. A SmartPoint Class That Reimplements equals() and hashCode() Methods

```java
// SmartPoint.java
package com.jdojo.object;

public class SmartPoint {
        private int x;
        private int y;

        public SmartPoint(int x, int y) {
                this.x = x;
                this.y = y;
        }

        /* Reimplement the equals() method */
        public boolean equals(Object otherObject) {
                // Are the same?
                if (this == otherObject) {
                        return true;
                }

                // Is otherObject a null reference?
                if (otherObject == null) {
                        return false;
                }

                // Do they belong to the same class?
                if (this.getClass() != otherObject.getClass()) {
                        return false;
                }

                // Get the reference of otherObject in a SmartPoint variable
                SmartPoint otherPoint = (SmartPoint)otherObject;

                // Do they have the same x and y co-ordinates
                boolean isSamePoint = (this.x == otherPoint.x && this.y == otherPoint.y);

                return isSamePoint;
        }

        /* Reimplement hashCode() method of the Object class,
           which is a requirement when you reimplement equals() method */
        public int hashCode() {
                return (this.x + this.y);
        }
}
```

You call your new class SmartPoint. Java advises to reimplement hashCode() and equals() methods together if any one of them is reimplemented in your class. The Java compiler would not complain if you reimplement the equals() method and not the hashCode() method. However, you will get unpredictable results when you use the objects of your class in hash-based collections.

The only requirement for a hashCode() method is that if the m.equals(n) method returns true, m.hashCode() must return the same value as n.hashCode(). Because your equals() method uses (x, y) coordinates to test for equality, you return the sum of x and y coordinates from the hashCode() method, which fulfills the technical requirement. Practically, you need to use a better hashing algorithm to compute the hash value.

You have written a few lines of codes in the equals() method of the SmartPoint class. Let's go through the logic one by one. First, you need to check if the object passed is the same as the object on which the method is called. If two objects are the same, you consider them equal by retuning true. This is accomplished by the following code:

```
// Are they the same?
if (this == otherObject) {
        return true;
}
```

If the parameter being passed is null, the two objects cannot be the same. Note that the object on which the method is called can never be null because you cannot call a method on a null reference. Java runtime will throw runtime exception when an attempt is made to call a method on a null reference. The following code makes sure that you are comparing two non-null objects:

```
// Is otherObject a null reference?
if (otherObject == null) {
        return false;
}
```

The parameter type of the method is Object. This means that any type of object reference can be passed. For example, you can use apple.equals(orange), where apple and orange are references to an Apple object and an Orange object, respectively. In your case, you want to compare only a SmartPoint object to another SmartPoint object. To make sure that the objects being compared are of the same class, you need the following code. If someone calls the method with a parameter that is not a SmartPoint object, it returns false.

```
// Do they have the same class?
if (this.getClass() != otherObject.getClass()) {
        return false;
}
```

At this point, you are sure that someone is trying to compare two non-null SmartPoint objects that have different identity (references). Now you would like to compare the (x, y) coordinates of two objects. To access the x and y instance variables of the otherObject formal parameter, you must cast it to a SmartPoint object. The following statement does it:

```
// Get the reference of otherObject in a SmartPoint variable
SmartPoint otherPoint = (SmartPoint)otherObject;
```

At this point, it is just the matter of comparing the values of x and y instance variables of the two SmartPoint objects. If they are the same, you consider two objects equal by returning true. Otherwise, two objects are not equal and you return false. This is accomplished by the following code:

```
// Do they have the same x and y co-ordinates
boolean isSamePoint = (this.x == otherPoint.x && this.y == otherPoint.y);
return isSamePoint;
```

It is time to test your reimplementation of the equals() method in the SmartPoint class. Listing 7-3 is your test class. You can observe in the output that you have two ways of comparing two SmartPoint objects for equality. The equality operator (==) compares them based on identity and the equals() method compares them based on values of the (x, y) coordinates. Note that if (x, y) coordinates are the same for two SmartPoint objects, the equals() method returns true.

Listing 7-3. A Test Class to Demonstrate the Difference Between Identity and State Comparisons

```java
// SmartPointTest.java
package com.jdojo.object;

public class SmartPointTest {
    public static void main(String[] args)  {
        SmartPoint pt1 = new SmartPoint(10, 10);
        SmartPoint pt2 = new SmartPoint(10, 10);
        SmartPoint pt3 = new SmartPoint(12, 19);
        SmartPoint pt4 = pt1;

        System.out.println("pt1 == pt1: " + (pt1 == pt1));
        System.out.println("pt1.equals(pt1): " + pt1.equals(pt1));

        System.out.println("pt1 == pt2: " + (pt1 == pt2));
        System.out.println("pt1.equals(pt2): " + pt1.equals(pt2));

        System.out.println("pt1 == pt3: " + (pt1 == pt3));
        System.out.println("pt1.equals(pt3): " + pt1.equals(pt3));

        System.out.println("pt1 == pt4: " + (pt1 == pt4));
        System.out.println("pt1.equals(pt4): " + pt1.equals(pt4));
    }
}
```

```
pt1 == pt1: true
pt1.equals(pt1): true
pt1 == pt2: false
pt1.equals(pt2): true
pt1 == pt3: false
pt1.equals(pt3): false
pt1 == pt4: true
pt1.equals(pt4): true
```

There are some specifications for implementing the equals() method in your class, so your class will work correctly when used with other areas (e.g. hash-based collections) of Java. It is the responsibility of the class designer to enforce these specifications. If your class does not conform to these specifications, the Java compiler or Java runtime will not generate any errors. Rather, objects of your class will behave incorrectly. For example, you will add your object to a collection, but you may not be able to retrieve it. Here are specifications for the equals() method's implementation. Assume that x, y, and z are non-null references of three objects.

- *Reflexivity*: It should be reflexive. The expression x.equals(x) should return true. That is, an object must be equal to itself.

- *Symmetry*: It should be symmetric. If x.equals(y) returns true, y.equals(x) must return true. That is, if x is equal to y, y must be equal to x.

- *Transitivity*: It should be transitive. If x.equals(y) returns true and y.equals(z) returns true, x.equals(z) must return true. That is, if x is equal to y and y is equal to z, x must be equal to z.

- *Consistency*: It should be consistent. If x.equals(y) returns true, it should keep returning true until the state of x or y is modified. If x.equals(y) returns false, it should keep returning false until the state of x or y is modified.

- *Comparison with null reference*: An object of any class should not be equal to a null reference. The expression x.equals(null) should always return false.

- *Relationship with hashCode() method*: If x.equals(y) returns true, x.hashCode() must return the same value as y.hashCode(). That is, if two objects are equal according to the equals() method, they must have the same hash code values returned from their hashCode() methods. However, the opposite may not be true. If two objects have the same hash codes, that does not imply that they must be equal according to the equals() method. That is, if x.hashCode() is equal to y.hashCode(), that does not imply that x.equals(y) will return true.

Your SmartPoint class satisfies all six rules for equals() and hashCode() methods. It was fairly easy to implement the equals() method for the SmartPoint class. It has two primitive type instance variables and you used both of them in comparison for equality.

There are no rules as to how many of instance variables should be used to compare for equality of two objects of a class. It all depends on the use of the class. For example, if you have an Account class, the account number itself may be sufficient in your case to compare for the equality of two Account objects. However, make sure you use the same instance variables in the equals() method to compare for equality and in the hashCode() method to compute hash code value. If your class has reference instance variables, you may call their equals() methods from inside the equals() method of your class. Listing 7-4 shows how to use a reference instance variable comparison inside the equals() method.

Listing 7-4. Overriding the equals() and hsshCode() Methods in a Class

```java
// SmartCat.java
package com.jdojo.object;

public class SmartCat {
        private String name;

        public SmartCat(String name) {
                this.name = name;
        }

        /* Reimplement the equals() method */
        public boolean equals(Object otherObject) {
                // Are they the same?
                if (this == otherObject) {
                        return true;
                }
```

```
        // Is otherObject a null reference?
        if (otherObject == null) {
                return false;
        }

        // Do they belong to the same class?
        if (this.getClass() != otherObject.getClass()) {
                return false;
        }

        // Get the reference of otherObject is a SmartCat variable
        SmartCat otherCat = (SmartCat)otherObject;

        // Do they have the same names
        boolean isSameName = (this.name == null? otherCat.name == null
                                        :this.name.equals(otherCat.name) );

        return isSameName;
    }

    /* Reimplement the hashCode() method, which is a requirement
       when you reimplement equals() method */
    public int hashCode() {
            return (this.name == null? 0 : this.name.hashCode());
    }
}
```

The SmartCat class has a name instance variable, which is of the type String. The String class has its own version of the equals() method implementation that compares two strings character by character. The equals() method of the SmartCat class calls the equals() method on the name instance variables to check if two names are equal. Similarly, it makes use of the hashCode() method's implementation in the String class in its hashCode() method.

String Representation of an Object

An object is represented by its state, which is the combination of values of all its instance variables at a point in time. Sometimes it is helpful, usually in debugging, to represent an object in a string form. What should be in the string that represents an object? The string representation of an object should contain enough information about the state of the object in a readable format. The toString() method of the Object class lets you write your own logic to represent the object of your class in a string. The Object class provides a default implementation of the toString() method. It returns a string in the following format:

```
<<fully qualified class name>>@<<hash code of object in hexadecimal>>
```

Consider the following snippet of code and its output. You may get a different output.

```
// Create two objects
Object obj = new Object();
IntHolder intHolder = new IntHolder(234);

// Get string representation of objects
String objStr = obj.toString();
String intHolderStr = intHolder.toString();
```

```
// Print the string representations
System.out.println(objStr);
System.out.println(intHolderStr);
```

```
java.lang.Object@360be0
com.jdojo.object.IntHolder@45a877
```

Note that your IntHolder class does not have a toString() method. Still, you were able to call the toString() method using the intHolder reference variable because all methods in the Object class are available in all classes automatically.

You may notice that the string representation that is returned from toString() method for IntHolder object is not so useful. It does not give you any clues about the state of the IntHolder object. Let's reimplement the toString() method in your IntHolder class. You will call the new class SmartIntHolder. What should your toString() method return? An object of SmartIntHolder represents an integer value. It would be fine just to return the stored integer value as a string. You can convert an integer value, say 123, into a String object using the valueOf() static method of the String class as

```
String str = String.valueOf(123); // str contains "123" as a string
```

Listing 7-5 has the complete code for your SmartIntHolder class.

Listing 7-5. Reimplementing toString() Method of the Object Class in the SmartIntHolder Class

```
// SmartIntHolder.java
package com.jdojo.object;

public class SmartIntHolder {
        private int value;

        public SmartIntHolder(int value) {
                this.value = value;
        }

        public void setValue(int value) {
                this.value = value;
        }

        public int getValue() {
                return value;
        }

        /* Reimplement toString() method of the Object class */
        public String toString() {
                // Return the stored value as a string
                String str = String.valueOf(this.value);
                return str;
        }
}
```

The following snippet of code shows you how to use the toString() method of the SmartIntHolder class:

```
// Create an object of the SmartIntHolder class
SmartIntHolder intHolder = new SmartIntHolder(234);
String intHolderStr = intHolder.toString();
System.out.println(intHolderStr);

// Change the value in SmartIntHolder object
intHolder.setValue(8967);
intHolderStr = intHolder.toString();
System.out.println(intHolderStr);
```

```
234
8967
```

There is no special technical requirement for reimplementing the toString() method in your class. You need to make sure it is declared public, its return type is String, and it does not take any parameters. The returned string should be human readable text to give an idea about the state of the object at the time the method is called. It is recommended to reimplement the toString() method of the Object class in every class you create.

Suppose you have a Point class to represent a 2D point as shown in Listing 7-6. A Point holds the x and y coordinates of a point. An implementation of the toString() method in the Point class may return a string of the form (x, y), where x and y are the coordinates of the point.

Listing 7-6. A Point Class Whose Object Represents a 2-D Point

```
// Point.java
package com.jdojo.object;

public class Point {
        private int x;
        private int y;

        public Point(int x, int y) {
                this.x = x;
                this.y = y;
        }

        /* Reimplement toString() method of the Object class */
        public String toString() {
                String str = "(" + x + ", " + y + ")";
                return str;
        }
}
```

The toString() method of a class is very important, and Java provides you with easy ways to use it. Java calls the toString() method of an object automatically for you in situations when it needs a string representation of the object. Two such situations that are worth mentioning:

- A string concatenation expression involving a reference of an object

- A call to System.out.print() and System.out.println() methods with an object reference as a parameter

When you concatenate a string and an object like

```
String str = "Hello" + new Point(10, 20);
```

Java calls the toString() method on the Point object and concatenate the returned value to the "Hello" string. The above statement will assign a "Hello(10, 20)" string to the str variable. The above statement is the same as the following one:

```
String str = "Hello" + new Point(10, 20).toString();
```

You use the string concatenation operator (+) to concatenate data of different types. First, Java gets the string representations of all data before concatenating them. Calling the toString() method of an object automatically for you in a concatenation expression helps you save some typing. If the object reference that is used in concatenation is a null reference, Java uses a "null" string as the string representation.

The following snippet of code makes the call to the toString() method on object references clear. You may observe that the result is the same when you use the object's reference by itself or you call its toString() method in a string concatenation expression. Similarly, when you use System.out.println(pt), Java automatically calls the toString() method on the pt reference variable.

```
Point pt = new Point(10, 12);

String str1 = "Test " + pt;
String str2 = "Test " + pt.toString();

// str1 and str 2 will have the same content
System.out.println(pt);
System.out.println(pt.toString());
System.out.println(str1);
System.out.println(str2);
```

```
(10, 12)
(10, 12)
Test (10, 12)
Test (10, 12)
```

The following snippet of code shows the effect of using a null reference in a string concatenation expression and in the System.out.println() method call. Note that you cannot use pt.toString() when pt is holding a null reference. The call to any method on a null reference will generate a runtime exception.

```
// Set pt to null
Point pt = null;
String str3 = "Test " + pt;
System.out.println(pt);
System.out.println(str3);
//System.out.println(pt.toString()); /* Will generate a runtime exception */
```

```
null
Test null
```

Cloning Objects

Java does not provide an automatic mechanism to clone (make a copy) an object. Recall that when you assign a reference variable to another reference variable, only the reference of the object is copied, not the content of the object. Cloning an object means copying the content of the object bit by bit. If you want objects of your class to be cloned, you must reimplement the clone() method in your class. Once you reimplement the clone() method, you should be able to clone objects of your class by calling the clone() method. The declaration of the clone() method in the Object class is as follows:

```
protected Object clone() throws CloneNotSupportedException
```

You need to observe few things about the declaration of the clone() method.

- It is declared protected. Therefore, you will not be able to call it from the client code. The following code is not valid:

  ```
  Object obj = new Object();
  Object clone = obj.clone(); // Error. Cannot access protected clone() method
  ```

  This means you need to declare the clone() method public in your class if you want the client code to clone objects of your class.

- Its return type is Object. It means you will need to cast the returned value of the clone() method. Suppose MyClass is cloneable. Your cloning code will look as

  ```
  MyClass mc = new MyClass();
  MyClass clone = (MyClass)mc.clone(); // Need to use a cast
  ```

You do not need to know any internal details about an object to clone it. The clone() method in the Object class has all the code that is needed to clone an object. All you need is to call it from the clone() method of your class. It will make a bitwise copy of the original object and return the reference of the copy.

The clone() method in the Object class throws a CloneNotSupportedException. It means when you call the clone() method of the Object class, you need to place the call in a try-catch block, or rethrow the exception. You will learn more about the try-catch block in Chapter 9. You have the option not to throw a CloneNotSupportedException from the clone() method of your class. The following snippet of code is placed inside the clone() method of your class, which calls the clone() method of the Object class using the super keyword:

```
YourClass obj = null;
try {
        // Call clone() method of the Object class using super.clone()
        obj = (YourClass)super.clone();
}
catch (CloneNotSupportedException e) {
        e. printStackTrace();
}

return obj;
```

One important thing that you must do is add an "implements Cloneable" clause in your class declaration. Cloneable is an interface declared in the java.lang package. You will learn about interface in Chapter 17. For now, just add this clause in your class declaration. Otherwise, you will get a runtime error when you call the clone() method on the objects of your class. Your class declaration must look like

```
public class MyClass implements Cloneable {
     // Code for your class goes here
}
```

Listing 7-7 has the complete code for a DoubleHolder class. It overrides the clone() method of the Object class. The comments in the clone() method explains what the code is doing. The clone() method of DoubleHolder class does not have a throws clause as the clone() method of the Object class has. When you override a method, you have an option to drop the throws clause that is declared in the superclass.

Listing 7-7. A DoubleHolder Class with Cloning Capability

```
// DoubleHolder.java
package com.jdojo.object;

public class DoubleHolder implements Cloneable {
     private double value;

     public DoubleHolder(double value) {
          this.value = value;
     }

     public void setValue(double value) {
          this.value = value;
     }

     public double getValue() {
          return this.value;
     }

     public Object clone() {
          DoubleHolder copy = null;
          try {
               // Call the clone() method of the Object class, which will do a
               // bit-by-bit copy and return the reference of the clone
               copy = (DoubleHolder) super.clone();
          }
          catch (CloneNotSupportedException e) {
               // If anything goes wrong during cloning, print the error details
               e.printStackTrace();
          }
          return copy;
     }
}
```

Once your class implements the clone() method correctly, cloning an object of your class is as simple as calling its clone() method. The following snippet of code shows how to clone an object of the DoubleHolder class. Note that you must use cast to cast the returned reference from the dh.clone() method call to the DoubleHolder type.

```
DoubleHolder dh = new DoubleHolder(100.00);
DoubleHolder dhClone = (DoubleHolder) dh.clone();
```

At this point, there are two separate objects of the DoubleHolder class. The dh variable references the original object and dhClone variable references the cone of the original object. The original as well as the cloned object hold the same value of 100.00. However, they have separate copies of the value. If you change the value in the original object, for example, dh.setValue(200), the value in the cloned object remains unchanged. Listing 7-8 shows how to use the clone() method to clone an object of the DoubleHolder class. The output proves that once you clone an object, there are two separate objects in memory.

Listing 7-8. A Test Class to Demonstrate Object Cloning

```
// CloningTest.java
package com.jdojo.object;

public class CloningTest {
        public static void main(String[] args) {
                DoubleHolder dh = new DoubleHolder(100.00);

                // Clone dh
                DoubleHolder dhClone = (DoubleHolder)dh.clone();

                // Print the values in original and clone
                System.out.println("Original:" + dh.getValue());
                System.out.println("Clone :" + dhClone.getValue());

                // Change the value in original and clone
                dh.setValue(200.00);
                dhClone.setValue(400.00);

                // Print the values in original and clone again
                System.out.println("Original:" + dh.getValue());
                System.out.println("Clone :" + dhClone.getValue());
        }
}
```

```
Original:100.0
Clone :100.0
Original:200.0
Clone :400.0
```

From Java 5, you need not specify the return type of the clone() method in your class as the Object type. You can specify your class as the return type in the clone() method declaration. This will not force the client code to use a cast when it call the clone() method of your class. The following snippet of code shows the changed code for the DoubleHolder class, which will compile only in Java 5 or later. It declares DoubleHolder as the return type of the clone() method and uses a cast in the return statement.

```java
// DoubleHolder.java
package com.jdojo.object;

public class DoubleHolder implements Cloneable {
        /* The same code goes here as before... */

        public DoubleHolder clone() {
                Object copy = null;
                /* The same code goes here as before... */

                return (DoubleHolder)copy;
        }
}
```

With the above declaration for the clone() method, you can write code to clone an object as follows. Note that no cast is needed anymore.

```java
DoubleHolder dh = new DoubleHolder(100.00);
DoubleHolder dhClone = dh.clone();// Clone dh. No cast is needed
```

An object may be composed of another object. In such cases, two objects exist in memory separately—a contained object and a container object. The container object stores the reference of the contained object. When you clone the container object, the reference of the contained object is cloned. After cloning is performed, there are two copies of the container object; both of them have references to the same contained object. This is called a shallow cloning because references are copied, not the objects. The clone() method of the Object class makes only shallow cloning, unless you code it otherwise. Figure 7-2 shows the memory state of a compound object, where an object contains a reference of another object. Figure 7-3 shows the memory state when the compound object is cloned using a shallow cloning. You may notice that in shallow cloning the contained object is shared by the original compound object and the cloned compound object.

Figure 7-2. *A compound object. The container object stores a reference of another object (Contained object)*

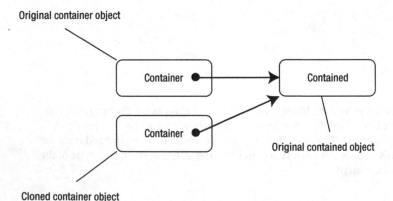

Figure 7-3. *Memory state after the container object is cloned using a shallow cloning*

When the contained objects are copied rather than their references during cloning of a compound object, it is called deep cloning. You must clone all the objects referenced by all reference variables of an object to get a deep cloning. A compound object may have multiple levels of chaining of contained objects. For example, the container object may have a reference of another contained object, which in turn has a reference of another contained object and so on. Whether you will be able to perform a deep cloning of a compound object depends on many factors. If you have a reference of a contained object, it may not support cloning and in that case, you have to be content with shallow cloning. You may have a reference of a contained object, which itself is a compound object. However, the contained object supports only shallow cloning, and in that case again, you will have to be content with shallow cloning. Let's look at examples of shallow and deep cloning.

If the reference instance variables of an object store references to immutable objects, you do not need to clone them. That is, if the contained objects of a compound object are immutable, you do not need to clone the contained objects. In this case, shallow copy of the immutable contained objects is fine. Recall that immutable objects cannot be modified after they are created. An immutable object's references can be shared by the multiple objects without any side effects. This is one of the benefits of having immutable objects. If a compound object contains some references to mutable objects and some to immutable objects, you must clone the referenced mutable objects to have a deep copy.

Listing 7-9 has code for a ShallowClone class.

Listing 7-9. A ShallowClone Class That Supports Shallow Cloning

```java
// ShallowClone.java
package com.jdojo.object;

public class ShallowClone implements Cloneable {
        private DoubleHolder holder = new DoubleHolder(0.0);

        public ShallowClone(double value) {
                this.holder.setValue(value);
        }

        public void setValue(double value) {
                this.holder.setValue(value);
        }

        public double getValue() {
                return this.holder.getValue();
        }

        public Object clone() {
                ShallowClone copy = null;
                try {
                        copy = (ShallowClone)super.clone();
                }
                catch (CloneNotSupportedException e) {
                        e.printStackTrace();
                }
                return copy;
        }
}
```

An object of the ShallowClone class is composed of an object of the DoubleHolder class. The code in the clone() method of the ShallowClone class is the same as for the clone() method of the DoubleHolder class. The difference lies in the type of instance variables that are used for the two classes. The DoubleHolder class has an instance variable of primitive type double, whereas the ShallowClone class has an instance variable of the reference type DoubleHolder. When the ShallowClone class calls the clone() method of the Object class (using super.clone()), it receives a shallow copy of itself. That is, it shares the DoubleHolder object used in its instance variable with its clone.

Listing 7-10 has test cases to test an object of the ShallowClone class and its clone. The output shows that after you make a clone, changing the value through the original object also changes the value in the cloned object. This is so because the ShallowClone object stores the value in another object of the DoubleHolder class, which is shared by both the cloned and the original objects.

Listing 7-10. A Test Class to Demonstrate the Shallow Copy Mechanism

```
// ShallowCloneTest.java
package com.jdojo.object;

public class ShallowCloneTest {
    public static void main(String[] args)  {
        ShallowClone sc = new ShallowClone(100.00);
        ShallowClone scClone = (ShallowClone)sc.clone();

        // Print the value in original and clone
        System.out.println("Original:" + sc.getValue());
        System.out.println("Clone :" + scClone.getValue());

        // Change the value in original and it will change the value
        // for clone too because we have done shallow cloning
        sc.setValue(200.00);

        // Print the value in original and clone
        System.out.println("Original:" + sc.getValue());
        System.out.println("Clone :" + scClone.getValue());
    }
}
```

```
Original:100.0
Clone :100.0
Original:200.0
Clone :200.0
```

In a deep cloning, you need to clone all objects referenced by all reference instance variables of an object. You must perform a shallow cloning before you can perform a deep cloning. The shallow cloning is performed by calling the clone() method of the Object class. Then you will need to write code to clone all reference instance variables. Listing 7-11 has code for a DeepClone class, which performs a deep cloning.

Listing 7-11. A DeepClone Class That Performs Deep Cloning

```java
// DeepClone.java
package com.jdojo.object;

public class DeepClone implements Cloneable {
        private DoubleHolder holder = new DoubleHolder(0.0);

        public DeepClone(double value) {
                this.holder.setValue(value);
        }

        public void setValue(double value) {
                this.holder.setValue(value);
        }

        public double getValue() {
                return this.holder.getValue();
        }

        public Object clone() {
                DeepClone copy = null;
                try {
                        copy = (DeepClone)super.clone();

                        // Need to clone the holder reference variable too
                        copy.holder = (DoubleHolder)this.holder.clone();
                }
                catch (CloneNotSupportedException e) {
                        e.printStackTrace();
                }

                return copy;
        }
}
```

If you compare the code in the clone() method of the ShallowClone and DeepClone classes, you will find that for deep cloning you had to write only one extra line of code.

```java
// Need to clone the holder reference variable too
copy.holder = (DoubleHolder)this.holder.clone();
```

What will happen if the DoubleHolder class is not cleanable? In that case, you would not be able to write the above statement to clone the holder instance variable. You could have cloned the holder instance variable as follows:

```java
// Need to clone the holder reference variable too
copy.holder = new DoubleHolder(this.holder.getValue());
```

The goal is to clone the holder instance variable and it does not have to be done by calling its clone() method. Listing 7-12 shows how your DeepClone class works. Compare its output with the output of the ShallowCloneTest class to see the difference.

Listing 7-12. A Test Class to Test Deep Cloning of Objects

```java
// DeepCloneTest.java
package com.jdojo.object;

public class DeepCloneTest {
        public static void main(String[] args) {
                DeepClone sc = new DeepClone(100.00);
                DeepClone scClone = (DeepClone)sc.clone();

                // Print the value in original and clone
                System.out.println("Original:" + sc.getValue());
                System.out.println("Clone :" + scClone.getValue());

                // Change the value in original and it will not change the value
                // for clone because we have done deep cloning
                sc.setValue(200.00);

                // Print the value in original and clone
                System.out.println("Original:" + sc.getValue());
                System.out.println("Clone :" + scClone.getValue());
        }
}
```

```
Original:100.0
Clone :100.0
Original:200.0
Clone :100.0
```

■ **Tip**   Using the `clone()` method of the `Object` class is not the only way to make a clone of an object. You can use other methods to clone an object. You may provide a copy constructor, which accepts an object of the same class and creates a clone of that object. You may provide a factory method in your class, which may accept an object and returns its clone. Another way to clone an object is to serialize it and then deserialized it. Serializing and deserializing objects is covered in Chapter 7 in *Beginning Java Language Features*.

Finalizing an Object

Sometimes an object uses resources that need to be released when the object is destroyed. Java provides you with a way to perform resource release or some other type of cleanup, when an object is about to be destroyed. In Java, you create objects, but you cannot destroy objects. The JVM runs a low priority special task called garbage collector to destroy all objects that are no longer referenced. The garbage collector gives you a chance to execute your cleanup code before an object is destroyed.

The `Object` class has a `finalize()` method, which is declared as follows:

```java
protected void finalize() throws Throwable { }
```

The finalize() method in the Object class does not do anything. You need to override the method in your class. The finalize() method of your class will be called by the garbage collector before an object of your class is destroyed. Listing 7-13 has code for the Finalize class. It overrides the finalize() method of the Object class and prints a message on the standard output. You can perform any cleanup logic in this method. The code in the finalize() method is also called finalizer.

Listing 7-13. A Finalize Class That Overrides the finalize() Method of the Object Class

```java
// Finalize.java
package com.jdojo.object;

public class Finalize {
    private int x;

    public Finalize(int x) {
        this.x = x;
    }

    public void finalize() {
        System.out.println("Finalizing " + this.x);

        /* Perform any cleanup work here... */
    }
}
```

The garbage collector calls the finalizer for each object only once. Running a finalizer for an object does not necessarily mean that the object will be destroyed immediately after the finalizer finishes. A finalizer is run when the garbage collector determines that no reference exists for the object. However, an object may pass its own reference to some other part of the program when its finalizer is run. This is the reason that the garbage collector checks one more time after it runs an object's finalizer to make sure that no references exists for that object and then it destroys (de-allocates memory) the object. The order in which finalizers are run and the time at which they are run are not specified. It is not even guaranteed that a finalizer will run at all. This makes it undependable for a programmer to write cleanup logic in the finalize() method. There are better ways to perform cleanup logic, for example, using a try-finally block. It is suggested not to depend on the finalize() method in your Java program to clean up resources uses by an object.

Listing 7-14 contains code to test the finalizers for your Finalize class. You may get a different output when you run this program.

Listing 7-14. A Test Class to Test Finalizers

```java
// FinalizeTest.java
package com.jdojo.object;

public class FinalizeTest {
    public static void main(String[] args) {
        // Create many objects, say 20000 objects.
        for(int i = 0; i < 20000; i++) {
            new Finalize(i);
        }
    }
}
```

```
Finalizing 15247
Finalizing 15248
Finalizing 15246
```

The program creates 20,000 objects of the Finalize class without storing their references. It is important that you do not store the references of the objects you create. As long as you hold the reference of an object, it will not be destroyed and its finalizer will not be run. You can see from the output that only three objects got a chance to run their finalizers before the program finished. You may get no output at all or a different output. If you do not get any output, you can try by increasing the number of objects to create. The garbage collector will destroy objects when it feels it is running low in memory. You may need to create more objects to trigger garbage collection, which in turn will run finalizers of your objects.

Immutable Objects

An object whose state cannot be changed after it is created is called an immutable object. A class whose objects are immutable is called an immutable class. If an object's state can be changed (or mutated) after it has been created, it is called a mutable object, and its class is called a mutable class.

Before I go into details of creating and using immutable objects, let's define the word "immutability." Instance variables of an object define the state of an object. There are two views of an object's state: internal and external. The internal state of the object is defined by the actual values of its instance variables at a point in time. The external state of the object is defined by the values that the users (or clients) of the object see at a point in time. When we state that an object is immutable, we must be specific about which state of the object we mean to be immutable: internal state, external state, or both.

Typically, when we use the phrase "an immutable object" in Java, we mean external immutability. In external immutability, an object may change its internal state after its creation. However, the change in its internal state is not visible to external users. The users do not see any changes in its state after its creation. In internal immutability, the state of an object does not change after it is created. If an object is internally immutable, it is also externally immutable. I will discuss examples of both.

Immutable objects have several advantages over mutable objects. An immutable object can be shared by different areas of a program without worrying about its state changes. Testing an immutable class is easy. An immutable object is inherently thread-safe. You do not have to synchronize access to your immutable object from multiple threads since its state does not change. Please refer to the chapter on threads in the book *Beginning Java Language Features* for more details on thread synchronization. An immutable object does not have to be copied and passed to another area of the program in the same Java application because its state does not change. You can just pass its reference and that serves as a copy. Its reference can be used to access its content. Avoiding copying is a big performance advantage as it saves both time and space.

Let's start with a mutable class whose object's state can be modified after it is created. Listing 7-15 has code for an IntHolder class.

Listing 7-15. An Example of a Mutable Class Whose Object's State Can Be Changed After Creation

```java
// IntHolder.java
package com.jdojo.object;

public class IntHolder {
        private int value;

        public IntHolder(int value) {
                this.value = value;
        }
```

```java
        public void setValue(int value) {
                this.value = value;
        }

        public int getValue() {
                return value;
        }
}
```

The value instance variable defines the state of an IntHolder object. You create an object of the IntHolder class as shown:

```java
IntHolder holder = new IntHolder(101);
int v = holder.getValue(); // will return 101
```

At this time, the value instance variable holds 101, which defines its state. You can get and set the instance variable using the getter and setter.

```java
// Change the value
holder.setValue(505);
int w = holder.getValue(); // will return 505
```

At this point, the value instance variable has changed from 101 to 505. That is, the state of the object has changed. The change in state was facilitated by the setValue() method. Objects of the IntHolder class are examples of mutable objects.

Let's make the IntHolder class immutable. All you need to do is to remove the setValue() method from it to make it an immutable class. Let's call your immutable version of the IntHolder class as IntWrapper, as shown in Listing 7-16.

Listing 7-16. An Example of an Immutable Class

```java
// IntWrapper.java
package com.jdojo.object;

public class IntWrapper {
        private final int value;

        public IntWrapper(int value) {
                this.value = value;
        }

        public int getValue() {
                return value;
        }
}
```

This is how you create an object of the IntWrapper class:

```java
IntWrapper wrapper = new IntWrapper(101);
```

At this point, the wrapper object holds 101 and there is no way to change it. Therefore, the IntWrapper class is an immutable class and its objects are immutable objects. You might have noticed that two changes were made to the IntHolder class to convert it to the IntWrapper class. The setValue() method was removed and the value instance variable was made final. In this case, it was not necessary to make the value instance variable final. The use of the final keyword makes your intention clear to the reader of the class and it protects the value instance variable from being changed inadvertently. It is good practice (use it as a rule of thumb) to declare all instance variables that define the immutable state of an object final so the Java compiler will enforce the immutability during compile time. The objects of IntWrapper class are immutable internally as well as externally. There is no way to change its state once it is created.

Let's create a variant of the IntWrapper class, which will be externally immutable but internally mutable. Let's call it IntWrapper2. It is listed in Listing 7-17.

Listing 7-17. An Example of an Externally Immutable and Internally Mutable Class

```java
// IntWrapper2.java
package com.jdojo.object;

public class IntWrapper2 {
        private final int value;
        private int halfValue = Integer.MAX_VALUE;

        public IntWrapper2(int value) {
                this.value = value;
        }

        public int getValue() {
                return value;
        }

        public int getHalfValue() {
                // Compute half value if it is not already computed
                if (this.halfValue == Integer.MAX_VALUE) {
                        // Cache the half value for future use
                        this.halfValue = this.value / 2;
                }
                return this.halfValue;
        }
}
```

IntWrapper2 adds another instance variable called halfValue, which will hold the half value of the value that is passed to the constructor. It is a trivial example. However, it serves the purpose to explain what you mean by externally and internally immutable objects. Suppose (just for the sake of this discussion) that computing half of an integer is a very costly process and you do not want to compute it in the constructor of the IntWrapper2 class, especially if nobody every asks for it. The halfValue instance variable is initialized to the maximum integer value, which works as a flag that it is not computed yet. You have added a getHalfValue() method, which checks if you have already computed the half value. For the first time, it will compute the half value and cache it in halfValue instance variable. From the second time onward, it will simply return the cached value.

The question is, "Is an IntWrapper2 object immutable?" The answer is yes and no. It is internally mutable. However, it is externally immutable. Once it is created, its client will see the same return value from the getValue() and getHalfValue() methods. However, its state (halfValue to be specific) changes once in its lifetime when the getHalfValue() method is called for the first time. However, this change is not visible to the users of the object. This method returns the same value on all subsequent calls. Objects like IntWrapper2 are called immutable objects. Recall that typically an immutable object means externally immutable.

The String class in the Java class library is an example of an immutable class. It uses the caching technique discussed for the IntWrapper2 class. The String class computes hash code for its content when its hashCode() method is called for the first time and caches the value. Thus, a String object changes its state internally, but not for its client. You will not come across the phrase "A String object in Java is externally immutable and internally mutable." Rather, you will come across the phrase "A String object in Java is immutable." You should understand that it means String objects are at least externally immutable.

Listing 7-18 shows a tricky situation where an attempt has been made to create an immutable class. The IntHolderWrapper class has no method that can directly let you modify the value stored in its valueHolder instance variable. It seems to be an immutable class.

Listing 7-18. An Unsuccessful Attempt to Create an Immutable Class

```java
// IntHolderWrapper.java
package com.jdojo.object;

public class IntHolderWrapper {
        private final IntHolder valueHolder;

        public IntHolderWrapper(int value) {
                this.valueHolder = new IntHolder(value);
        }

        public IntHolder getIntHolder() {
                return this.valueHolder;
        }

        public int getValue() {
                return this.valueHolder.getValue();
        }
}
```

Listing 7-19 has a test class to test the immutability of the IntHolderWrapper class.

Listing 7-19. A Test Class to Test Immutability of the IntHolderWrapper Class

```java
// BadImmutableTest.java
package com.jdojo.object;

public class BadImmutableTest {
        public static void main(String[] args) {
                IntHolderWrapper ihw = new IntHolderWrapper(101);

                int value = ihw.getValue();
                System.out.println("#1 value = " + value);

                IntHolder holder = ihw.getIntHolder();
                holder.setValue(207);

                value - ihw.getValue();
                System.out.println("#2 value = " + value);
        }
}
```

```
#1 value = 101
#2 value = 207
```

The output shows that the IntHolderWrapper class is mutable. Two calls to its getValue() method return different values. The culprit is its getIntHolder() method. It returns the instance variable valueHolder, which is a reference variable. Note that the valueHolder instance variable represents an object of the IntHolder class, which makes up the state of an IntHolderWrapper object. If the object that valueHolder reference variable references is changed, the state of IntHolderWrapper is changed, too. Since the IntHolder object is mutable, you should not return its reference to the client from the getIntHolder() method. The following two statements change the state of the object from the client code:

```
IntHolder holder = ihw.getIntHolder(); /* Got hold of instance variable */
holder.setValue(207); /* Change the state by changing the instance variable's state */
```

Note that the designer of the IntHolderWrapper class missed the point when he returned the valueHolder reference, that even though there is no direct way to change the state of the IntHolderWrapper class, it can be changed indirectly.

How do you correct the problem? The solution is easy. In the getIntHolder() method, make a copy of the valueHolder object and return the reference of the copy instead of the instance variable itself. This way, if the client changes the value, it will be changed only in client's copy, not in the copy held by IntHolderWrapper object. Listing 7-20 has the correct immutable version of the IntHolderWrapper class, which you call IntHolderWrapper2.

Listing 7-20. A Modified, Immutable Version of the IntHolderWrapper Class

```java
// IntHolderWrapper2.java
package com.jdojo.object;

public class IntHolderWrapper2 {
        private final IntHolder valueHolder;

        public IntHolderWrapper2(int value) {
                this.valueHolder = new IntHolder(value);
        }

        public IntHolder getIntHolder() {
                // Make a copy of valueHolder
                int v = this.valueHolder.getValue();
                IntHolder copy = new IntHolder(v);

                // Return the copy instead of the original
                return copy;
        }

        public int getValue() {
                return this.valueHolder.getValue();
        }
}
```

Creating an immutable class is a little trickier than it seems. I have covered some of the cases in this section. Here is another case where you need to be careful. Suppose you have designed an immutable class that has a reference type instance variable. Suppose it accepts the initial value of its reference type instance variable in one of its constructors. If the instance variable's class is a mutable class, you must make a copy of the parameter passed to its constructor and store the copy in the instance variable. The client code that passes the object's reference in the constructor may change the state of this object through the same reference later. Listing 7-21 shows how to implement the second constructor for the IntHolderWrapper3 class correctly. It has the incorrect version of the implementation for the second constructor commented.

Listing 7-21. Using a Copy Constructor to Correctly Implement an Immutable Class

```
// IntHolderWrapper3.java
package com.jdojo.object;

public class IntHolderWrapper3 {
        private final IntHolder valueHolder;

        public IntHolderWrapper3(int value) {
                this.valueHolder = new IntHolder(value);
        }

        public IntHolderWrapper3(IntHolder holder) {
                // Must make a copy of holder parameter
                this.valueHolder = new IntHolder(holder.getValue());

                /* Following implementation is incorrect. Client code will be able to change the
                    state of the object using holder reference later */
                //this.valueHolder = holder; /* do not use it */
        }

        /* Rest of the code goes here... */
}
```

The Objects Class

Java 7 added a new utility class Objects in the java.util package for working with objects. It consists of all static methods. Most of the methods of the Objects class deal with null values gracefully. Java 8 has added few more utility methods to the class. The following is the list of methods in the class. Their descriptions follow the list.

- `<T> int compare(T a, T b, Comparator<? super T> c)`
- `boolean deepEquals(Object a, Object b)`
- `boolean equals(Object a, Object b)`
- `int hash(Object... values)`
- `int hashCode(Object o)`
- `boolean isNull(Object obj)`
- `boolean nonNull(Object obj)`

- `<T> T requireNonNull(T obj)`
- `<T> T requireNonNull(T obj, String message)`
- `<T> T requireNonNull(T obj, Supplier<String> messageSupplier)`
- `String toString(Object o)`
- `String toString(Object o, String nullDefault)`

The `compare()` method is used to compare two objects for sorting purpose. It returns 0 if both arguments are identical. Otherwise, it returns the value of `c.compare(a, b)`. It returns 0 if both arguments are `null`.

The `deepEquals()` method is used to check if two objects are deeply equal. It returns `true` if both arguments are deeply equal. Otherwise, it returns `false`. It returns `true` if both arguments are `null`.

The `equals()` method compares two objects for equality. It returns `true` if both arguments are equal. Otherwise, it returns `false`. It returns `true` if both arguments are `null`.

The `hash()` method generates a hash code for all specified objects. It can be used to compute the hash code for an object, which is based on the multiple instance fields. If a single object reference is passed to this method, the returned hash code value is not equal to the hash code value returned from the object's `hashCode()` method. If `obj` is an object reference, `obj.hashCode()` is not equal to `Objects.hash(obj)`.

The `hashCode()` method returns the hash code value of the specified object. If the argument is `null`, it returns 0.

The `isNull()` method returns `true` if the specified object is `null`. Otherwise, it returns `false`. You can also check whether an object is null using the comparison operator `==`, for example, `obj == null` returns true of `obj` is null. The `isNull()` method is added in Java 8. It exists to be used as a method reference (`Objects::isNull`) in lambda expressions. Lambda expressions are discussed in the book *Beginning Java Language Features*.

The `nonNull()` method performs the check opposite of what the `isNull()` method does. It is added in Java8 to be used in lambda expression as a method reference (`Objects::nonNull`).

The `requireNonNull(T obj)` method checks if the argument is not `null`. If the argument is `null`, it throws a `NullPointerException`. This method is designed for validating parameters of methods and constructors. Notice the formal type parameter `<T>` in the method's declaration. It is a generic method. Any type of object is passed. Its return type is the same as the type of the passed object. The method is overloaded. The second version of the method lets you specify the message for the `NullPointerException` that is thrown when the argument is `null`. The third version of the method takes a `Supplier<String>` as the second argument. This is added in Java 8. It defers the creation of the message until the null check is performed. If the argument is `null`, the `get()` method of the `Supplier<String>` is called to get the error message that is used in `NullPointerException`. Use the third argument if you want to add the timestamp in your error message.

The `toString()` method returns a "null" string if the argument is `null`. For a non-null argument, it returns the value returned by calling the `toString()` method on the argument. The second version of the method lets you specify the default retuned string when the argument is null.

Listing 7-22 demonstrates how to use some of the methods of the `Objects` class. The program uses a lambda expression to create a `Supplier<String>` object. Lambda expressions are discussed in Chapter 5 in book *Beginning Java Language Features*. You may get a different output when you run the program.

Listing 7-22. A Test Class to Demonstrate the Use of the Methods of the Objects Class

```
// ObjectsTest.java
package com.jdojo.object;

import java.time.Instant;
import java.util.Objects;
import java.util.function.Supplier;
```

```java
public class ObjectsTest {
        public static void main(String[] args) {
                // Compute hash code for two integers, a char, and a string
                int hash = Objects.hash(10, 8900, '\u20b9', "Hello");
                System.out.println("Hash Code is " + hash);

                // Test for equality
                boolean isEqual = Objects.equals(null, null);
                System.out.println("null is equal to null: " + isEqual);

                isEqual = Objects.equals(null, "XYZ");
                System.out.println("null is equal to XYZ: " + isEqual);

                // toString() method test
                System.out.println("toString(null) is " + Objects.toString(null));
                System.out.println("toString(null, \"XXX\") is " + Objects.toString(null, "XXX"));

                // Testing requireNonNull(T obj, String message)
                try {
                        printName("Doug Dyer");
                        printName(null);
                }
                catch (NullPointerException e) {
                        System.out.println(e.getMessage());
                }

                // requireNonNull(T obj, Supplier<String> messageSupplier)
                try {
                        // Using a lambda expression to create a Supplier<String> object.
                        // The Supplier returns a timestamped message.
                        Supplier<String> messageSupplier = () -> "Name is required. Error generated
                            on " + Instant.now();
                        printNameWithSuplier("Babalu", messageSupplier);
                        printNameWithSuplier(null, messageSupplier);
                }
                catch (NullPointerException e) {
                        System.out.println(e.getMessage());
                }
        }

        public static void printName(String name) {
                // Test name for not null. Generate a NullPointerException if it is null.
                Objects.requireNonNull(name, "Name is required.");

                // Print the name if the above statement dod not throw an exception
                System.out.println("Name is " + name);
        }
}
```

```java
        public static void printNameWithSuplier(String name, Supplier<String> messageSupplier) {
                // Test name for not null. Generate a NullPointerException if it is null.
                Objects.requireNonNull(name, messageSupplier);

                // Print the name if the above statement dod not throw an exception
                System.out.println("Name is " + name);
        }
}
```

```
Hash Code is 79643668
null is equal to null: true
null is equal to XYZ: false
toString(null) is null
toString(null, "XXX") is XXX
Name is Doug Dyer
Name is required.
Name is Babalu
Name is required. Error generated on 2014-01-18T06:02:43.713Z
```

Summary

Classes in Java are arranged in a tree-like hierarchy. Classes in the tree have a superclass-subclass relationship. The Object class is at the root of the class hierarchy. It is the superclass of all classes in Java. The Object class is in the java.lang package. The Object class contains methods that are automatically available in all classes. Some methods have been implemented and some not. Classes can also reimplement some methods in the Object class. A reference variable of the Object class can store the reference of any reference type in Java.

Java 7 added a utility class Objects in the java.util package. The class contains convenience methods to compute hash codes for objects. Most of the methods in this class exist to deal with null value gracefully. Java 8 has added some additional methods to this class for the new lambda language feature.

CHAPTER 8

■ ■ ■

Wrapper Classes

In this chapter, you will learn:

- About the wrapper classes and how to use them
- How primitive values are automatically boxed into wrapper objects when needed
- How wrapper objects are automatically unboxed into primitive values when needed

Wrapper Classes

In previous chapters, you learned that primitive and reference types are not assignment compatible. You cannot even compare a primitive value with an object reference. Some parts of the Java library work only with objects; for example, collections in Java work only with objects. You cannot create a list of primitive values, such as 1, 3, 8, and 10. You will need to wrap the primitive values into objects before you can store them in a list or set.

The assignment incompatibility between primitive values and reference values has existed in Java since its first release. The Java library provided eight classes in the java.lang package to represent each of the eight primitive types. These classes are called wrapper classes as they wrap a primitive value in an object. Table 8-1 lists the primitive types and their corresponding wrapper classes. Notice the names of the wrapper classes. Following the Java convention for naming classes, they start with an uppercase letter.

Table 8-1. *List of Primitive Types and Their Corresponding Wrapper Classes*

Primitive Type	Wrapper Class
byte	Byte
short	Short
int	Integer
long	Long
float	Float
double	Double
char	Character
boolean	Boolean

All wrapper classes are immutable. They provide two ways to create their objects:

- Using constructors
- Using the valueOf() factory methods

Each wrapper class, except Character, provides at least two constructors: one takes a value of the corresponding primitive type and another takes a String. The Character class provides only one constructor that takes a char. The following snippet of code creates objects of some wrapper classes:

```
// Creates an Integer object from an int
Integer intObj1 = new Integer(100);

// Creates an Integer object from a String
Integer intObj2 = new Integer("1969");

// Creates a Double object from a double
Double doubleObj1 = new Double(10.45);

// Creates a Double object from a String
Double doubleObj2 = new Double("234.60");

// Creates a Character object from a char
Character charObj1 = new Character('A');

// Creates a Boolean object from a boolean
Boolean booleanObj1 = new Boolean(true);

// Creates Boolean objects from Strings
Boolean booleanTrue = new Boolean("true");
Boolean booleanFalse = new Boolean("false");
```

Another way to create objects of wrapper classes is to use their valueOf() methods. The valueOf() methods are static. The following snippet of code creates objects of some wrapper classes using their valueOf() methods:

```
Integer intObj1 = Integer.valueOf(100);
Integer intObj2 = Integer.valueOf("1969");
Double doubleObj1 = Double.valueOf(10.45);
Double doubleObj2 = Double.valueOf("234.60");
Character charObj1 = Character.valueOf('A');
```

■ **Note**   Use of this method to create objects for integer numeric values (byte, short, int, and long) is preferred over constructors as this method caches some objects for reuse. The wrapper classes for these primitive types cache wrapper objects for primitive values between -128 and 127. For example, if you call Integer.valueOf(25) multiple times, the reference of the same Integer object from the cache is returned. However, when you call new Integer(25) multiple times, a new Integer object is created for each call.

Listing 8-1 demonstrates the difference in using constructors and valueOf() methods for the Integer wrapper class.

Listing 8-1. The Difference Between Using Constructors and valueOf() Method to Create Integer Objects

```java
// CachedWrapperObjects.java
package com.jdojo.wrapper;

public class CachedWrapperObjects {
    public static void main(String[] args) {
        System.out.println("Using the constructor:");

        // Create two Integer objects using constructors
        Integer iv1 = new Integer(25);
        Integer iv2 = new Integer(25);
        System.out.println("iv1 = iv1 = " + iv1 + ", iv2 = " + iv2);

        // Compare iv1 and iv2 references
        System.out.println("iv1 == iv2: " + (iv1 == iv2));

        // Let's see if they are equal in values
        System.out.println("iv1.equals(iv2): " + iv1.equals(iv2));

        System.out.println("\nUsing the valueOf() method:");

        // Create two Integer objects using the valueOf()
        Integer iv3 = Integer.valueOf(25);
        Integer iv4 = Integer.valueOf(25);
        System.out.println("iv3 = " + iv3 + ", iv4 = " + iv4);

        // Compare iv3 and iv4 references
        System.out.println("iv3 == iv4: " + (iv3 == iv4));

        // Let's see if they are qual in values
        System.out.println("iv3.equals(iv4): " + iv3.equals(iv4));
    }
}
```

```
Using the constructor:
iv1 = 25, iv2 = 25
iv1 == iv2: false
iv1.equals(iv2): true

Using the valueOf() method:
iv3 = 25, iv4 = 25
iv3 == iv4: true
iv3.equals(iv4): true
```

Notice that iv1 and iv2 are references to two different objects, as iv1 == iv2 returns false. However, iv3 and iv4 are references to the same object, as iv3 == iv4 returns true. Of course, all iv1, iv2, iv3, and iv4 represent the same primitive value of 25 as indicated by the returned value from the equals() method. Typically, programs use smaller integer literals. If you are wrapping bigger integers, the valueOf() method creates a new object every time it is called.

■ **Tip** The new operator always creates a new object. If you do not need new objects of the primitive values, use the valueOf() factory method of the wrapper class instead of using the constructors. The equals() methods in the wrapper classes have been reimplemented to compare the wrapped primitive values in wrapper objects, not their references.

Numeric Wrapper Classes

Byte, Short, Integer, Long, Float, and Double classes are numeric wrapper classes. They are all inherited from the Number class. The Number class is declared abstract. You cannot create an object of the Number class. However, you can declare reference variables of the Number class. You can assign an object reference of any of the six numeric wrapper classes to a reference of the Number class.

The Number class contains six methods. They are named xxxValue() where xxx is one of the six primitive data types (byte, short, int, long, float, and double). The return type of the methods is the same as xxx. That is, the byteValue() method returns a byte, the intValue() method returns an int, etc. The following snippet shows how to retrieve different primate type values from a numeric wrapper object:

```
// Creates an Integer object
Integer intObj = Integer.valueOf(100);

// Gets byte from Integer
byte b = intObj.byteValue();

// Gets double from Integer
double dd = intObj.doubleValue();
System.out.println("intObj = " + intObj);
System.out.println("byte from intObj = " + b);
System.out.println("double from intObj = " + dd);

// Creates a Double object
Double doubleObj = Double.valueOf("329.78");

// Gets different types of primitive values from Double
double d = doubleObj.doubleValue();
float f = doubleObj.floatValue();
int i = doubleObj.intValue();
long l = doubleObj.longValue();

System.out.println("doubleObj = " + doubleObj);
System.out.println("double from doubleObj = " + d);
System.out.println("float from doubleObj = " + f);
System.out.println("int from doubleObj = " + i);
System.out.println("long from doubleObj = " + l);
```

```
intObj = 100
byte from intObj = 100
double from intObj = 100.0
doubleObj = 329.78
double from doubleObj = 329.78
float from doubleObj = 329.78
int from doubleObj = 329
long from doubleObj = 329
```

Java 8 has added some methods like sum(), max(), and min() in some of the numeric wrapper classes such as Integer, Long, Float, and Double. For example, Integer.sum(10, 20) simply returns the result of 10 + 20. At first, you might think, "Did the wrapper class designers not have any useful things to do instead of adding these trivial methods? Did we forget using the addition operator + to add two numbers, so we will use the Integer.sum(10, 20)?" Your assumption is wrong. These methods have been added for a greater purpose. They are not intended to be used as Integer.sum(10, 20). Their references are used in lambda expressions working with collections. I cover them in the lambda expression discussion in the book *Beginning Java Language Features* (ISBN 978-1-4302-6658-7).

Your program may receive numbers as strings. You may want to obtain primitive values or wrapper objects from those strings. Sometimes the integer values in a string may be encoded in different bases (also called radix), for example, decimal, binary, hexadecimal, etc. Wrapper classes help in working with strings containing primitive values.

- Use the valueOf() methods to convert strings into wrapper objects.

- Use the parseXxx() methods to convert strings into primitive values.

The Byte, Short, Integer, Long, Float, and Double classes contain parseByte(), parseShort(), parseInt(), parseLong(), parseFloat() and parseDouble() methods to parse strings into primitive values, respectively.

The following snippet of code converts a string containing an integer in binary format into an Integer object and an int value:

```
String str = "01111111";
int radix = 2;

// Creates an Integer object from the string
Integer intObject = Integer.valueOf(str, radix);

// Extracts the int value from the string
int intValue = Integer.parseInt(str, 2);

System.out.println("str = " + str);
System.out.println("intObject = " + intObject);
System.out.println("intValue = " + intValue);
```

```
str = 01111111
intObject = 127
intValue = 127
```

All numeric wrapper classes contain several useful constants. Their MIN_VALUE and MAX_VALUE constants represent the minimum and maximum values that can be represented by their corresponding primitive type. For example, Byte.MIN_VALUE constant is -128 and Byte.MAX_VALUE constant is 127, which are the minimum and maximum value that can be stored in a byte. They also have a SIZE constant that represents the size in bits that a variable of the corresponding primitive type occupies. For example, Byte.SIZE is 8 and Integer.SIZE is 32.

Typically, you receive strings from external sources, for example, a file. If strings cannot be converted to numbers, wrapper classes will throw a NumberFormatException. It is common to place the string parsing logic inside a try-catch block and handle the exceptions.

The following snippet of code attempts to parse two strings into double values. The first string contains a valid double and the second one an invalid double. A NumberFormatException is thrown when the parseDouble() method is called to parse the second string.

```
String str1 = "123.89";
try {
        double value1 = Double.parseDouble(str1);
        System.out.println("value1 = " + value1);
}
catch (NumberFormatException e) {
        System.out.println("Error in parsing " + str1);
}

String str2 = "78H.90"; // An invalid double
try {
        double value2 = Double.parseDouble(str2);
        System.out.println("value2 = " + value2);
}
catch (NumberFormatException e) {
    System.out.println("Error in parsing " + str2);
}
```

```
value1 = 123.89
Error in parsing 78H.90
```

■ **Note** The java.math package contains BigDecimal and BigInteger classes. They are used to hold big decimal and integer numbers, which do not fit into the primitive types double and long. These classes are mutable and they are typically not called wrapper classes. Use them if you perform computations on big numbers and you do not want to lose intermediate values that exceed the standard primitive type range.

The Character Wrapper Class

An object of the Character class wraps a char value. The class contains several constants and methods that are useful while working with characters. For example, it contains isLetter() and isDigit() methods to check if a character is a letter and digit. The toUpperCase() and toLowerCase() methods convert a character to uppercase and lowercase. It is worth exploring the API documentation for this class. The class provides a constructor and a factory valueOf() method to create objects from a char. Use the factory method for better performance. The charValue() method returns the char that the object wraps. The following snippet of code shows how to create Character objects and how to use some of their methods:

```
// Using the constructor
Character c1 = new Character('A');
```

```
// Using the factory method - preferred
Character c2 = Character.valueOf('2');
Character c3 = Character.valueOf('ñ');

// Getting the wrapped char values
char cc1 = c1.charValue();
char cc2 = c2.charValue();
char cc3 = c3.charValue();

System.out.println("c1 = " + c1);
System.out.println("c2 = " + c2);
System.out.println("c3 = " + c3);

// Using some Character class methods on c1
System.out.println("isLowerCase c1  = " + Character.isLowerCase(cc1));
System.out.println("isDigit c1  = " + Character.isDigit(cc1));
System.out.println("isLetter c1  = " + Character.isLetter(cc1));
System.out.println("Lowercase of c1  = " + Character.toLowerCase(cc1));

// Using some Character class methods on c2
System.out.println("isLowerCase c2  = " + Character.isLowerCase(cc2));
System.out.println("isDigit c2  = " + Character.isDigit(cc2));
System.out.println("isLetter c2  = " + Character.isLetter(cc2));
System.out.println("Lowercase of c2  = " + Character.toLowerCase(cc2));

System.out.println("Uppercase of c3  = " + Character.toUpperCase(cc3));
```

```
c1 = A
c2 = 2
c3 = ñ
isLowerCase c1  = false
isDigit c1  = false
isLetter c1  = true
Lowercase of c1  = a
isLowerCase c2  = false
isDigit c2  = true
isLetter c2  = false
Lowercase of c2  = 2
Uppercase of c3  = Ñ
```

The Boolean Wrapper Class

An object of the Boolean class wraps a boolean. The Boolean.TRUE and Boolean.FALSE are two constants of the Boolean type to represent boolean true and false values. You can create a Boolean object using the constructors or the valueOf() factory method. When parsing a string, this class treats "true" (ignoring the case of all characters) as the true and any other strings as the false. Use the valueOf() method of this class to create a Boolean object as much as possible because it returns Boolean.TRUE or Boolean.FALSE constant instead of creating new objects. The following snippet of code shows how to use the Boolean class. The variable name in each statement indicates the type of boolean value (true or false) represented in the Boolean object.

```
// Using constructors
Boolean b11True = new Boolean(true);
Boolean b21True = new Boolean("true");
Boolean b31True = new Boolean("tRuE");
Boolean b41False = new Boolean("false");
Boolean b51False = new Boolean("how is this"); // false

// Using the factory methods
Boolean b12True = Boolean.valueOf(true);
Boolean b22True = Boolean.valueOf("true");
Boolean b32True = Boolean.valueOf("tRuE");
Boolean b42False = Boolean.valueOf("false");
Boolean b52False = Boolean.valueOf("how is this"); // false

// Getting a boolean value from a Boolean object
boolean bbTrue = b12True.booleanValue();

// Parsing strings to boolean values
boolean bTrue = Boolean.parseBoolean("true");
boolean bFalse = Boolean.parseBoolean("This string evaluates to false");

// Using constants
Boolean bcTrue    = Boolean.TRUE;
Boolean bcFalse = Boolean.FALSE;

// Printing some Boolean objects
System.out.println("bcTrue = " + bcTrue);
System.out.println("bcFalse = " + bcFalse);
```

```
bcTrue = true
bcFalse = false
```

Unsigned Numeric Operations

Java does not support unsigned primitive integer data types. The byte, short, int, and long are signed data types. For a signed data type, half of the range of values is used for storing positive number and half for negative numbers, as one bit is used to store the sign of the value. For example, a byte takes 8 bits; its range is -128 to 127. If you were to store only positive numbers in a byte, its range would have been 0 to 255.

Java 8 has not added any new unsigned integer data types. Rather, it has added some static methods in wrapper classes that support operations treating the bits in the signed values as if they are unsigned integers.

The Byte class contains two static methods:

- `int toUnsignedInt(byte x)`

- `long toUnsignedLong(byte x)`

The methods convert the specified byte argument into an int and a long as if the byte stores an unsigned value. If the specified byte argument is zero or a positive number, the converted int and long values will be the same as the argument value. If the argument is a negative number, the converted number will be $2^8 + x$. For example, for an input of 10, the returned value will be 10, and for an input of -10, the returned value will be $2^8 + (-10)$, which is 246. Negative numbers are stored in 2's complement form. The value -10 will be stored as 11110110. The most significant bit 1 indicates that it is a negative number. The 2's complement of the first 7 bits (1110110) would be 001010, which is 10 in decimal. If you consider the actual bits, 11110110, in a byte as an unsigned integer, its value is 246 (128 + 64 + 32 + 16 + 0 + 4 + 2 + 0). The following snippet of code shows how to get the value stored in a byte as an unsigned integer:

```
byte b = -10;
int x = Byte.toUnsignedInt(b);
System.out.println("Signed value in byte = " + b);
System.out.println("Unsigned value in byte = " + x);
```

```
Signed value in byte = -10
Unsigned value in byte = 246
```

The Short class contains the same two methods as the Byte class, except they take a short as an argument and convert it to an int and a long.

The Integer class contains the following static methods to support unsigned operations and conversions:

- int compareUnsigned(int x, int y)

- int divideUnsigned(int dividend, int divisor)

- int parseUnsignedInt(String s)

- int parseUnsignedInt(String s, int radix)

- int remainderUnsigned(int dividend, int divisor)

- long toUnsignedLong(int x)

- String toUnsignedString(int i)

- String toUnsignedString(int i, int radix)

Notice that the Integer class does not contain addUnsigned(), subtractUnsigned(), and multiplyUnsigned() methods as the three operation are bitwise identical on two signed and two unsigned operands. The following snippet of code shows the division operation on two int variables as if their bits represent unsigned values:

```
// Two negative ints
int x = -10;
int y = -2;

// Performs signed division
System.out.println("Signed x = " + x);
System.out.println("Signed y = " + y);
System.out.println("Signed x/y = " + (x/y));

// Performs unsigned division by treating x and y holding unsigned values
long ux = Integer.toUnsignedLong(x);
long uy = Integer.toUnsignedLong(y);
int uQuotient = Integer.divideUnsigned(x, y);
System.out.println("Unsigned x = " + ux);
System.out.println("Unsigned y = " + uy);
System.out.println("Unsigned x/y = " + uQuotient);
```

```
Signed x = -10
Signed y = -2
Signed x/y = 5
Unsigned x = 4294967286
Unsigned y = 4294967294
Unsigned x/y = 0
```

The Long class contains methods to perform unsigned operations. The methods are similar to the ones in the Integer class. Note that you cannot convert the value stored in a long to an unsigned value as you would need a bigger storage than provided by the long data type to do so, but long is the biggest integer data type provided by Java. This is the reason that the Byte and Short classes have toUsignedInt() and toUnSignedLong() methods, as int and long are bigger than byte and short. In fact, to store the value of a signed data type X as an unsigned value in a signed data type Y, the size of the data type Y needs to be at least twice as big as that of X. Following this storage requirement, there is a toUnsignedLong() method in the Integer class, but no such method exist in the Long class.

Autoboxing and Unboxing

AutoBoxing and unboxing are features added in Java 5 to work with primitive data types and their corresponding wrapper classes. They are implemented completely in the compiler. Before we define autoboxing/unboxing, let's discuss an example. The example is trivial, but it serves the purpose of demonstrating the pain you had to go through before Java 5, when you were working with conversion between primitive types to their wrapper objects and vice-versa.

Suppose you have a method that accepts two int values, adds them, and returns an int value. You might say, "What is the big deal about this method?" It should be as simple as the following:

```
// Only method code is shown
public static int add(int a, int b) {
        return a + b;
}
```

The method can be used as

```
int a = 200;
int b = 300;
int result = add(a, b); // result will get a value of 500
```

And you are right that there is no big deal about this method at all. Let's add a bit of a twist to the logic. Think about the same method working with Integer objects instead of int values. Here is the code for the same method:

```
public static Integer add(Integer a, Integer b) {
        int aValue = a.intValue();
        int bValue = b.intValue();
        int resultValue = aValue + bValue;
        Integer result = new Integer(resultValue);

        return result;
}
```

Did you notice the complexity that is involved when you changed the same method to use Integer objects? You had to perform three things to add two int values in the Integer objects.

- Unwrap the methods arguments, a and b, from Integer objects to int values using their intValue() method.

```
int aValue = a.intValue();
int bValue = b.intValue();
```

- Perform an addition of two int values.

```
int resultValue = aValue + bValue;
```

- Wrap the result into a new Integer object and return the result.

```
Integer result = Integer.valueOf(resultValue);
return result;
```

Listing 8-2 has the complete code to demonstrate the use of the add() method.

Listing 8-2. Adding Two int Values Using Integer Objects

```java
// MathUtil.java
package com.jdojo.wrapper;

public class MathUtil {
        public static Integer add(Integer a, Integer b) {
                int aValue = a.intValue();
                int bValue = b.intValue();
                int resultValue = aValue + bValue;
                Integer result = Integer.valueOf(resultValue);
                return result;
        }

        public static void main(String[] args) {
                int iValue = 200;
                int jValue = 300;
                int kValue; /* will hold result as int */

                // Box iValue and jValue into Integer objects
                Integer i = Integer.valueOf(iValue);
                Integer j = Integer.valueOf(jValue);

                // Store returned value of the add() method in an Integer object k
                Integer k = MathUtil.add(i, j);

                // Unbox Integer object's int value into kValue int variable
                kValue = k.intValue();
```

```
            // Display the result using int variables
            System.out.println(iValue + " + " + jValue + " = " + kValue);
        }
}
```

```
200 + 300 = 500
```

Note the amount of code needed just to add two int values. Wrapping/unwrapping an int value to an Integer and vice versa is just a pain for Java developers. Java designers realized it (though too late) and they automated this wrapping and unwrapping process for you.

The automatic wrapping from a primitive data type (byte, short, int, long, float, double, char and boolean) to its corresponding wrapper object (Byte, Integer, Long, Float, Double, Character and Boolean) is called autoboxingThe reverse, unwrapping from wrapper object to its corresponding primitive data type, is called unboxing.

With autoboxing/unboxing, the following code is valid:

```
Integer n = 200; // Boxing
int a = n;       // Unboxing
```

The compiler will replace the above statement with the following:

```
Integer n = Integer.valueOf(200);
int a = n.intValue();
```

The code in the main() method of the MathUtil class listed in Listing 8-2 can be rewritten as follows. The boxing and unboxing are done for you automatically.

```
int iValue = 200;
int jValue = 300;
int kValue = MathUtil.add(iValue, jValue);
System.out.println(iValue + " + " + jValue + " = " + kValue);
```

■ **Tip** Autoboxing/unboxing is performed when you compile the code. The JVM is completely unaware of the boxing and unboxing performed by the compiler.

Beware of Null Values

Autoboxing/unboxing does save you from writing additional lines of codes. It also makes your code look neater. However, it does come with some surprises. One of the surprises is getting a NullPointerException where you would not expect it to happen. Primitive types cannot have a null value assigned to them, whereas reference types can have a null value. The boxing and unboxing happens between primitive types and reference types. Look at the following snippet of code:

```
Integer n = null; // n can be assigned a null value
int a = n;        // will throw NullPointerException at run time
```

In this snippet of code, suppose you do not control the assignment of null to n. You might get a null Integer object as a result of a method call, for example, int a = getSomeValue(), where getSomeValue() returns an Integer object. A NullPointerException in such places may be a surprise for you. However, it will happen, because int a = n is converted to int a = n.intValue() and n is null in this case. This surprise is the part of the advantage you get from autoboxing/unboxing and you need to just be aware of it.

Overloaded Methods and Autoboxing/Unboxing

You have a few surprises when you call an overloaded method and want to rely on autoboxing/unboxing feature. Suppose you have two methods in a class.

```
public void test(Integer iObject) {
        System.out.println("Integer=" + iObject);
}

public void test(int iValue) {
        System.out.println("int=" + iValue);
}
```

Suppose you make two calls to the test() method.

```
test(101);
test(new Integer(101));
```

Which of the following will be the output?

```
int=101
Integer=101
```

or

```
Integer=101
int=101
```

The rule for a method invocation that uses autoboxing/unboxing follows a two-step process.

1. If the actual argument being passed is a primitive type (as in test(10)),

    a. Try to find a method with the primitive type argument. If there is no exact match, try widening the primitive type to find a match.

    b. If the previous step fails, box the primitive type and try to find a match.

2. If the actual argument being passed is a reference type (as in test(new Integer(101)),

    a. Try to find a method with the reference type argument. If there is match, call that method. In this case, a match does not have to be exact. It should follow the subtype and super type assignment rule.

    b. If the previous step fails, unbox the reference type to the corresponding primitive type and try to find an exact match, or widen the primitive type and find a match.

If you apply these rules to the above snippet of code, it will print

```
int=101
Integer=101
```

Suppose you have two `test()` methods.

```
public void test(Integer iObject) {
  System.out.println("Integer=" + iObject);
}

public void test(long iValue) {
  System.out.println("long=" + iValue);
}
```

What will be printed if you use the following code?

```
test(101);
test(new Integer(101));
```

It will print

```
long=101
Integer=101
```

The first call of `test(101)` will try to find an exact match for an `int` argument. It does not find a method `test(int)`, so it widens the `int` data type, finds a match `test(long)`, and calls this method.

Suppose you have two `test()` methods.

```
public void test(Long lObject) {
  System.out.println("Long=" + lObject);
}

public void test(long lValue) {
  System.out.println("long=" + lValue);
}
```

What will be printed if you execute the following code?

```
test(101);
test(new Integer(101));
```

It will print

```
long=101
long=101
```

Are you surprised by looking at the above output? Apply the rules that I have listed and you will find that the above output followed those rules. The call to test(101) is clear because it widens 101 from int to long and executes the test(long) method. To call test(new Integer(101)), it looks for a method test(Integer) and it does not find one. Note that a reference type is never widened. That is, an Integer is never widened to Long. Therefore, it unboxes the Integer to int and looks for test(int) method, which it does not find. Now, it widens the int and finds test(long) and executes it.

I have one more surprise. Consider the following two test() methods:

```
public void test(Long lObject) {
        System.out.println("Long=" + lObject);
}

public void test(Object obj) {
        System.out.println("Object=" + obj);
}
```

What will be printed when you execute the following code?

```
test(101);
test(new Integer(101));
```

This time, you will get the following output:

```
Object=101
Object=101
```

Does it make sense? Not really. Here is the explanation. When it calls test(101), it has to box int to an Integer, because there is no match for test(int), even after widening the int value. So, test(101) becomes test(Integer.valueOf(101)). Now it does not find any test(Integer) either. Note that Integer is a reference type and it inherits the Number class, which in turn inherits the Object class. Therefore, an Integer is always an Object, and Java allows you to assign an object of subtype (Integer) to a variable of supertype (Object). This is the reason that the test(Object) is called in this case. The second call, test(new Integer(101)), works the same way. It tries for test(Integer) method. When it does not find it, the next match for it is test(Object) based on the subtype and supertype assignment rule for reference types.

Comparison Operators and AutoBoxing/Unboxing

I will discuss comparison operations ==, >, >=, <, <=. Only == (logical equality operator) can be used with both reference type and primitive types. The other operators must be used only with primitive types.

Let's discuss the easy ones (>, >=, < and <=) first. If a numeric wrapper object is used with these comparison operators, it must be unboxed and the corresponding primitive type used in the comparison. Consider the following snippet of code:

```
Integer a = 100;
Integer b = 100;
System.out.println("a : " + a);
System.out.println("b : " + b);
System.out.println("a > b: " + (a > b));
```

```
System.out.println("a >= b: " + (a >= b));
System.out.println("a < b: " + (a < b));
System.out.println("a <= b: " + (a <= b));
```

```
a : 100
b : 100
a > b: false
a >= b: true
a < b: false
a <= b: true
```

There is no surprise in the above output. If you mix the two types, reference and primitive, with these comparison operators, you still get the same results. First, the reference type is unboxed and a comparison with the two primitive types takes place. For example,

```
if (101 > new Integer(100)) {
        // Do something
}
```

is converted to

```
if(101 <= (new Integer(100)).intValue()) {
        // Do something
}
```

Now, let's discuss the == operator and the autoboxing rules. If both operands are primitive types, they are compared as primitive types using a value comparison. If both operands are reference types, their references are compared. In these two cases, no autoboxing/unboxing takes place. When one operand is a reference type and another is a primitive type, the reference type is unboxed to a primitive type and a value comparison takes place. Let's see examples of each type.

Consider the following snippet of code. It is an example of using both primitive type operands for the == operator.

```
int a = 100;
int b = 100;
int c = 505;
System.out.println(a == b); // will print true
System.out.println(a == c); // will print false
```

Consider the following snippet of code:

```
Integer aa = new Integer(100);
Integer bb = new Integer(100);
Integer cc = new Integer(505);
System.out.println(aa == bb); // will print false
System.out.println(aa == cc); // will print false
```

In this snippet of code, no autoboxing/unboxing takes place. Here, aa == bb and aa == cc compare the references of aa, bb and cc, not their values. Every object created with the new operator has a unique reference.

Now, here's a surprise: consider the following snippet of code. This time you are relying on autoboxing.

```
Integer aaa = 100; // Boxing - Integer.valueOf(100)
Integer bbb = 100; // Boxing - Integer.valueOf(100)
Integer ccc = 505; // Boxing - Integer.valueOf(505)
Integer ddd = 505; // Boxing - Integer.valueOf(505)
System.out.println(aaa == bbb); // will print true
System.out.println(aaa == ccc); // will print false
System.out.println(ccc == ddd); // will print false
```

You used aaa, bbb, ccc, and ddd as reference types. How is aaa == bbb true whereas ccc == ddd false? All right. This time, there is no surprise coming from the autoboxing feature. Rather, it is coming from the Integer. valueOf() method. For all values between –128 and 127, the Integer class caches Integer object references. The cache is used when you call its valueOf() method. For example, if you call Integer.valueOf(100) twice, you get the reference of the same Integer object from the cache that represents the int value of 100. However, if you call Integer.valueOf(n), where n is outside the range –128 to 127, a new object is created for every call. This is the reason that aaa and bbb have the same reference from the cache, whereas ccc and ddd have different references. Byte, Short, Character and Long classes also cache object references for values in the range –128 to 127.

Collections and Autoboxing/Unboxing

Autoboxing/unboxing helps you work with collections. Collections work only with reference types. You cannot use primitive types in collections. If you want to store primitive types in a collection, you must wrap the primitive value before storing it, and unwrap it after retrieving it. Suppose you have a List and you want to store integers in it. This is how you would do it:

```
List list = new ArrayList();
list.add(new Integer(101));
Integer a = (Integer)list.get(0);
int aValue = a.intValue();
```

You are back to square one. The add() and get() methods of the List interface work with Object type, and you had to resort to wrapping and unwrapping the primitive types again. The autoboxing/unboxing may help you in wrapping the primitive type to a reference type, and the above code may be rewritten as

```
List list = new ArrayList();
list.add(101); // Autoboxing will work here
Integer a = (Integer)list.get(0);
int aValue = a.intValue();
/*int aValue = list.get(0); */ // autounboxing won't compile
```

Because the return type of the get() method is Object, the last statement in this snippet of code would not work. Note that unboxing happens from a primitive wrapper type (such as Integer) to its corresponding primitive type (such as int). If you try to assign an Object reference type to an int primitive type, the autounboxing does not happen. In fact, your code would not even compile, because Object to int conversion is not allowed.

Try the following code:

```
List<Integer> list = new ArrayList<>();
list.add(101); // autoboxing will work
int aValue = list.get(0); // autounboxing will work, too
```

All collection classes are generic classes. They declare formal type parameters. Specifying the Integer type in angle brackets (<Integer>), while creating the List object, tells the compiler that the List will hold object of only Integer type. This gives the compiler freedom to wrap and unwrap your primitive int values while you work with the List object. Please refer to the chapter on generics in the book *Beginning Java Language Features* (ISBN 978-1-4302-6658-7) for more details.

Summary

For each primitive data type, Java provides a class to represent values of the primitive data type as objects. Java does not support unsigned primitive numeric data types and unsigned numeric operations. Java 8 added limited support for unsigned operations on primitive data types by adding some methods in the wrapper classes.

Java does not allow mixing of primitive type and reference type values in the same expression. It is inconvenient to convert the primitive values to their wrapper objects and vice versa. Java 5 added support for automatically converting the primitive values to wrapper objects and vice versa depending on the context. This feature is called autoboxing/unboxing. For example, it allows assigning an integer 25 to a reference of the Integer object; the compiler automatically boxes the integer 25 in a wrapper object using the expression Integer.valueOf(25).

CHAPTER 9

■ ■ ■

Exception Handling

In this chapter, you will learn

- About error handling in Java using exceptions
- How to use `try-catch` blocks to handle exceptions
- How to use `finally` blocks to clean up resources
- The different between checked and unchecked exceptions
- How to create a new exception type and use it in your code
- How to use auto-closeable resources using a `try-catch-resources` block
- How to access the stack frames of a thread

What Is an Exception?

An exception is a condition that may arise during the execution of a Java program when a normal path of execution is not defined. For example, a Java program may encounter a numeric expression that attempts to divide an integer by zero. Such a condition may occur during the execution of the following snippet of code:

```
int x = 10, y = 0, z;
z = x/y; // Divide-by-zero
```

The statement z = x/y attempts to divide x by y. Because y is zero, the result of x/y is not defined in Java. Note that dividing a floating-point number by zero, for example 9.5/0.0, is defined and it is infinity. In generic terms, the abnormal condition, such as dividing an integer by zero, can be phrased as follows:

An error occurs when a Java program attempts to divide an integer by zero.

The Java programming language describes the above error condition differently. In Java, it is said

An exception is thrown when a Java program attempts to divide an integer by zero.

Practically, both statements mean the same thing. They mean that an abnormal condition in a program has occurred.

What happens after the abnormal condition occurs in a program? You need to handle such an abnormal condition in the program. One of the ways to handle it is to check for all possibilities that may lead to an abnormal condition, before performing the action. You may rewrite the above code as follows:

```
int x = 10, y = 0, z;
if (y == 0) {
```

```
        // Report the abnormal/error condition here
}
else {
        // Perform division here
        z = x/y;
}
```

You may observe that this snippet of code does two things: it handles the error condition and performs the intended action. It mixes the code for performing error handling and the action. One line of code (z = x/y) has bloated to at least five lines of code. This is a simple example. You may not fully realize the real problem when the error handling code is mixed with the actual code performing actions.

To make this problem clear, let's consider another example. Suppose you want to write Java code that will update an employee's salary. An employee's records are stored in a database. The pseudocode might look as follows:

```
Connect to the database
Fetch the employee record
Update the employee salary
Commit the changes
```

The actual code would perform the above-mentioned four actions. Any of the four actions may result in an error. For example, you may not be able to connect to the database because the database is down; you may not be able to commit the changes because of some validations failed. You need to perform error checking after an action is performed and before the subsequent action is started. The pseudocode with error checking may look as follows:

```
// Connect to the database
if (connected to the database successfully) {
        // Fetch the employee record
        if (employee record fetched) {
                // Update the employee salary
                if (update is successful) {
                        // Commit the changes
                        if (commit was successful ) {
                                // Employee salary was saved successfully
                        }
                        else {
                                // An error. Save failed
                        }
                }
                else {
                        //An error. Salary could not be updated
                }
        }
        else {
                // An error. Employee record does not exist
        }
}
else {
        // An error. Could not connect to the database
}
```

Notice that when you added error handling to your four lines of pseudocode, the code bloated to over twenty lines. The worst thing about the above code is that the code that performs the action has been cluttered with error-handling code. It has also introduced many nested if-else statements resulting in spaghetti code.

In the last two examples, you saw that the way of handling errors that uses if-else statements is not elegant and maintainable. Java has a better way to handle errors: by separating the code that performs actions from the code that handles errors. In Java, we use the phrase "exception" instead of "error" to indicate an abnormal condition in a program; the phrase "exception handling" is used instead of the phrase "error handling." In general, we say that an error occurs and you handle it. In Java, we say that an exception is thrown and you catch it. This is the reason that *exception handling* is also called *catching an exception*. The code that handles the exception is known as an *exception handler*. You could rewrite the above pseudocode using Java syntax (not full-fledged Java code, though) as follows:

```
try {
        // Connect to the database
        // Fetch employee record
        // Update employee salary
        // Commit the changes
}
catch(DbConnectionException e1){
        // Handle DB Connection exception here
}
catch(EmpNotFoundException e2){
        // Handle employee not found exception here
}
catch(UpdateFailedException e3){
        // Handle update failed exception here
}
catch(CommitFailedException e4){
        // Handle commit failed exception here
}
```

You do not need to understand the above pseudocode fully. I will discuss the details shortly. You need to observe the structure of the code, which allows for separation of the code that performs actions from the code that handles exceptions. The code that performs the actions is placed inside a try block and the code that handles the exception is placed inside a catch block. You will observe that this code is much better in terms of elegance and maintainability compared to the previous attempt in which you had to write many if-else statements to achieve the same.

■ **Tip**   In Java, an exception is thrown and caught. Catching an exception is the same as handling the exception. The code that performs the action may throw an exception and the code that handles the exception catches the thrown exception. This style of exception handling allows you to separate the code that performs actions from the code that handles the exceptions that may arise while performing the actions.

An Exception Is an Object

How does the exception handling part of the code know about the exception that occurs in another part of the code? When an exception occurs, Java creates an object with all pieces of information about the exception (e.g., type of exception, line number in the code where the exception occurred, etc.) and passes it to the appropriate exception handling code. The term "exception" is used to mean one of two things—the exceptional condition and the Java object to represent the exceptional condition. The meaning of the term will be clear from the context.

When we talk about throwing an exception, we are talking about three things.

- Occurrence of an exceptional condition

- Creation of a Java object to represent the exceptional condition

- Throwing (or passing) the exception object to the exception handler

The throwing of an exception is the same as passing an object reference to a method. Here, you may imagine the exception handler as a method that accepts a reference of an exception object. The exception handler catches the exception object and takes appropriate action. You can think of catching an exception by the exception handler as a method call without the return, where the exception object's reference is the actual parameter to the method. Java also lets you create your own object that represents an exception and then throw it.

■ **Tip**   An exception in Java is an object that encapsulates the details of an error.

Using a try-catch Block

Before I discuss the try-catch block, let's write a Java program that attempts to divide an integer by zero, as shown in Listing 9-1.

Listing 9-1. A Java Program Attempting to Divide an Integer by Zero

```
// DivideByZero.java
package com.jdojo.exception;

public class DivideByZero {
        public static void main(String[] args) {
                int x = 10, y = 0, z;
                z = x/y;
                System.out.println("z = " + z);
        }
}
```

```
Exception in thread "main" java.lang.ArithmeticException: / by zero
        at com.jdojo.exception.DivideByZero.main(DivideByZero.java:7)
```

Is the output of Listing 9-1 what you were expecting? It indicates an exception has occurred when you ran the DivideByZero class. The output contains four pieces of information:

- It includes the name of the thread in which the exception occurred. The name of the thread is "main". You can learn about threads and the name of a thread in detail in the chapter on threads in the book *Beginning Java Language Features* (ISBN 978-1-4302-6658-7).

- It includes the type of the exception that has occurred. The type of an exception is indicated by the name of the class of the exception object. In this case, java.lang.ArithmeticException is the name of the class of the exception. The Java runtime creates an object of this class and passes its reference to the exception handler.

- It includes a message that describes the exceptional condition in the code that caused the error. In this case, the message is "/ by zero" (read "divide by zero").

- It includes the location where the exception occurred. The second line in the output indicates that the exception has occurred inside the main() method of the com.jdojo.exception. DivideByZero class. The source code is contained in the DivideByZero.java file. The line number in the source code that caused the exception is 7.

You may notice that in just two lines of output the Java runtime has printed enough pieces of information to help you track down the error in your code.

When z = x/y at line 7 is executed, the Java runtime detects the exceptional condition, which is an attempt to divide an integer by zero. It creates a new object of the class ArithmeticException with all relevant pieces of information about the exception, and then throws (or passes) this object to an exception handler. Who caught (or handled) the exception in this case? You did not specify any exception handler in the code. In fact, you do not even know how to specify an exception handler at this point. Because you did not specify an exception handler in this case, the Java runtime handled the exception for you. Does the Java runtime handle all exceptions that are thrown in a Java program? The answer is yes. The Java runtime handles all exceptions in a Java program. However, It handles an exception only when you do not handle it yourself.

If an exception occurs and the Java runtime does not find a programmer-defined exception handler to handle it, such an exception is called an *uncaught exception*. All uncaught exceptions are handled by the Java runtime. Because an uncaught exception is always handled by the Java runtime, why should you even worry about providing any exception handler in your program? This is an interesting point. Why do you need to worry about doing something that would be done by the Java runtime for you? If you are too lazy to clean up your own mess (handling your own error condition), there is bad news for you. You should not expect too much from the Java runtime. You may not like the way the runtime handles exceptions for you. It catches the uncaught exception, prints the error stack on the standard error, and halts your Java application. In other words, if you let the Java runtime handle all your exceptions, your program stops executing at the point where the exception occurs. Is this what you want to do? The answer would be no. Sometimes, after you handle the exception, you may want to proceed with executing the rest of your program rather than halting the program. When you ran the DivideByZero class, the expression x/y in the statement z = x/y resulted in an exception. Java did not finish executing the statement z=x/y. Sometimes this situation is phrased as "The statement z=x/y finished abnormally." The runtime handled the exception, but it stopped executing the whole program. This is the reason that you do not see the output of the following statement in your program:

```
System.out.println("z = " + z);
```

Now you know that letting the runtime handle your exception is not always a good idea. If you want to handle exceptions yourself, you need to place your code in a try block. A try block looks like the following:

```
try {
    // Code for the try block goes here
}
```

A try block starts with the keyword try, followed by an opening brace and a closing brace. The code for the try block is placed inside the opening and the closing braces.

A try block cannot be used just by itself. It must be followed by one or more catch blocks, or one finally block, or a combination of both. To handle an exception that might be thrown by the code inside a try block, you need to use a catch block. One catch block can be used to handle multiple types of exceptions. For now, I'll focus on handling only one type of exception in a catch block; I'll cover how to handle multiple exceptions in a catch block in a separate section.

The syntax for a catch block is similar to the syntax for a method.

```
catch (ExceptionClassName parameterName) {
    // Exception handling code goes here
}
```

Note that a catch block's declaration is exactly like a method declaration. It starts with the keyword catch, followed by a pair of parentheses. Within the parentheses, you declare a parameter, as you do in a method. The parameter type is the name of the exception class that it is supposed to catch. The parameterName is a user-given name. Parentheses are followed by an opening brace and a closing brace. The exception handling code is placed within the braces. When an exception is thrown, the reference of the exception object is copied to the parameterName. You can use the parameterName to get information from the exception object. It behaves exactly like a formal parameter of a method.

You can associate one or more catch blocks to a try block. The general syntax for a try-catch block is as follows. The following snippet of code shows a try block, which has three catch blocks associated with it. You can associate as many catch blocks to a try block as you want.

```java
try {
        // Your code that may throw an exception goes here
}
catch (ExceptionClass1 e1){
        // Handle exception of ExceptionClass1 type
}
catch (ExceptionClass2 e2){
        // Handle exception of ExceptionClass2 type
}
catch (ExceptionClass3 e3){
        // Handle exception of ExceptionClass3 type
}
```

Let's use a try-catch block to handle the possible divide by zero exception in your code. Listing 9-2 has the complete code.

Listing 9-2. Handling an Exception Using a try-catch Block

```java
// DivideByZeroWithTryCatch.java
package com.jdojo.exception;

public class DivideByZeroWithTryCatch {
        public static void main(String[] args) {
                int x = 10, y = 0, z;
                try {
                        z = x / y;
                        System.out.println("z = " + z);
                }
                catch(ArithmeticException e) {
                        // Get the description of the exception
                        String msg = e.getMessage();

                        // Print a custom error message
                        System.out.println("An error has occurred. The error is: " + msg);
                }

                System.out.println("At the end of the program.");
        }
}
```

```
An exception has occurred. The error is: / by zero
At the end of the program.
```

The output of Listing 9-2 is nicer than that of Listing 9-1. It tells you exactly what happened when the program was executed. Notice that the program did not terminate when the exception occurred because you handled the exception. The program executed the last statement that printed the "At the end of the program" message.

Transfer of Control

You need to understand very precisely the flow of control when an exception is thrown in a try block. First, the Java runtime creates an object of the appropriate class to represent the exception that has occurred. The first catch block following the try block is checked. If the exception object can be assigned to the parameter for the catch block, the parameter of the catch block is assigned the reference of the exception object, and the control is transferred to the body of the catch block. When the catch block finishes executing its body, the control is transferred to the point following the try-catch block. It is very important to note that after executing the catch block the control is not transferred back to the try block. Rather, it is transferred to the code that follows the try-catch block. If a try block has many catch blocks associated with it, a maximum of one catch block is executed. Figure 9-1 shows the transfer of control in a typical Java program when an exception occurs in a try block.

```
Some statements go here...
try {
        try-statement-1;
        try-statement-2;
        try-statement-3;
}
catch(Exception1 e1) {
        catch-statement-11;
        catch-statement-12;
}
catch(Exception2 e2) {
        catch-statement-21;
        catch-statement-22;
}
catch(Exception3 e3) {
        catch-statement-31;
        catch-statement-32;
}

statement-1;
more statements go here...
```

Figure 9-1. *Transfer of control when an exception occurs in a try block*

You assume that when try-statement-2 is executed, it throws an exception of type Exception2. When the exception is thrown, the control is transferred to the second catch block, and catch-statement-21 and catch-statement-22 are executed. After catch-statement-22 is executed, control is transferred outside the try-catch block, and statement-1 starts executing. It is very important to understand that try-statement-3 is never executed when try-statement-2 throws an exception. Among three catch blocks, a maximum of one will be executed when a statement inside the try block throws an exception.

Exception Class Hierarchy

The Java class library contains many exception classes. Figure 9-2 shows a few exception classes. Note that the Object class does not belong to the family of exception classes. It is shown in the figure as an ancestor of the Throwable class in the inheritance hierarchy.

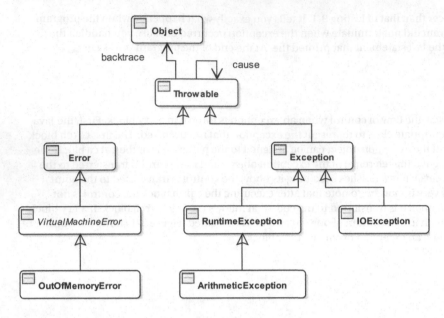

Figure 9-2. A few classes in the exception class hierarchy

The exception class hierarchy starts at the java.lang.Throwable class. Recall that the Object class is the superclass for all classes in Java. It is also the superclass of the Throwable class. This is the reason that the figure shows the Object class at the top of the class hierarchy. It is to be emphasized that the Java exception class family starts at the Throwable class, not at the Object class.

When an exception is thrown, it must be an object of the Throwable class, or any of its subclasses. The parameter of the catch block must be of type Throwable, or one of its subclasses, such as Exception, ArithmeticException, IOException, etc. The following catch blocks are not valid catch blocks because their parameters are not a Throwable or a subclass of Throwable:

```
// A compile-time error. The Object class is not a throwable class.
catch(Object e1) {
}
```

```
// A compile-time error. The String class is not a throwable class.
catch(String e1) {
}
```

The following catch blocks are valid because they specify throwable types as a parameter, which are the Throwable class or its subclasses:

```
// Throwable is a valid exception class
catch(Throwable t) {
}
```

```
// Exception is a valid exception class because it is a subclass of Throwable
catch(Exception e) {
}

// IOException class is a valid exception class because it is a subclass of Throwable
catch(IOException t) {

}

// ArithmeticException is a valid exception class because it is a subclass of Throwable
catch(ArithmeticException t) {
}
```

You can also create your own exception classes by inheriting your classes from one of the exception classes. Figure 9-2 shows only a few of the hundreds of exception classes that are available in the Java class library. I will discuss how to inherit a class from another class in Chapter 16 on inheritance. I will present an example of a user-defined exception class later in this chapter.

Arranging Multiple catch Blocks

A reference variable of the Object class can refer to any type of object. Assuming AnyClass is a class, the following is a valid statement:

```
Object obj = new AnyClass();
```

The rule behind the above assignment is that the reference of an object of a class can be assigned to a reference variable of its own type or its superclass. Because the Object class is the superclass (direct or indirect) of all classes in Java, it is valid to assign a reference of any object to a reference variable of the Object class. This assignment rule is not limited to just a reference variable of the Object class. It is applicable to any object. It is stated as

> *A reference variable of class T can refer to an object of class S if S is the same as T or S is a subclass of T. The following statements are always valid in Java assuming S is a subclass of T:*
> ```
> T t1 = new T();
> T t2 = new S();
> ```

You can see that the above rule implies that any object's reference can be stored in a reference variable of the Object type. I will elaborate on this rule in Chapter 7.

Let's apply this assignment rule to the exception class hierarchy. Because the Throwable class is the superclass of all exception classes, a reference variable of the Throwable class can refer to an object of any exception class. All of the following statements are valid:

```
Throwable e1 = new Exception();
Throwable e2 = new IOException();
Throwable e3 = new RuntimeException();
Throwable e4 = new ArithmeticException();
```

With this rule of assignment in mind, let's consider the following try-catch block:

```
try {
        statement1;
        statement2; // Exception of class MyException is thrown here
        statement3;
}
catch (Exception1 e1) {
        // Handle Exception1
}
catch(Exception2 e2) {
        // Handle Exception2
}
```

When the above snippet of code is executed, statement2 throws an exception of the MyException type. Suppose the runtime creates an object of MyException as follows:

```
new MyException();
```

Now the runtime selects the appropriate catch block, which can catch the exception object. It starts looking for the appropriate catch clock sequentially starting from the first catch block that is associated with the try block. The process to check if a catch block can handle an exception is very simple. Take the parameter type and parameter name of the catch block and place them to the left of an assignment operator and place the exception object that is thrown to the right. If the statement thus formed is a valid Java statement, that catch block will handle the exception. Otherwise, the runtime will repeat this check with the next catch block.

To check if the first catch block can handle the MyException in the above snippet of code, Java will form the following statement:

```
// Catch parameter declaration = thrown exception object reference
Exception1 e1 = new MyException();
```

The above statement is a valid Java statement only if the MyException class is a subclass of the Exception1 class, or MyException and Exception1 are the same class. If the above statement is valid, the runtime will assign the reference of the MyException object to e1, and then execute the code inside the first catch block. If the above statement is not a valid statement, the runtime will apply the same check for the second catch block by using the following statement:

```
// Catch parameter declaration = thrown exception object reference
Exception2 e2 = new MyException();
```

If the above statement is valid, the MyException object is assigned to e2 and the body of the catch block is executed. If the above statement is not valid, the runtime did not find a matching catch block for the exception thrown in the try block, and then a different execution path is chosen, which I will discuss shortly.

Typically, you add a catch block after a try block for every type of exception that can be thrown from the try block. Suppose there is a try block and it can throw three kinds of exceptions, which are represented by three classes, Exception1, Exception2, and Exception3. Suppose Exception1 is the superclass of Exception2, and Exception2 is the superclass of Exception3. The class hierarchy for the three exception classes is shown in Figure 9-3.

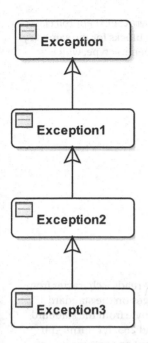

Figure 9-3. *The class hierarchy for Exception1, Exception2, and Exception3 exception classes*

Consider the following try-catch block:

```
try {
        // Exception1, Exception2 or Exception 3 could be thrown here
}
catch (Exception1 e1) {
        // Handle Exception1
}
catch (Exception2 e2) {
        // Handle Exception2
}
catch (Exception3 e3) {
        // Handle Exception3
}
```

If you try to apply the steps to find an appropriate catch block, the above snippet of code would always execute the first catch block, irrespective of the type of exception thrown (Exception1, Exception2, or Exception3) from the try block. This is because Exception1 is the direct/indirect superclass of Exception2 and Exception3. The above snippet of code shows a logical mistake made by the developer. The Java compiler is designed to handle this kind of logical mistake that you might make and it generates a compile-time error. You must apply the following rule for arranging multiple catch blocks for a try block:

Multiple catch blocks for a try block must be arranged from the most specific exception type to the most generic exception type. Otherwise, a compile-time error occurs. The first catch block should handle the most specific exception type and the last the most generic exception type.

The following snippet of code uses a valid sequence of multiple catch blocks. The ArithmeticException class is a subclass of the RuntimeException class. If both of these exceptions are handled in catch blocks for the same try block, the most specific type, which is ArithmeticException, must appear before the most generic type, which is RuntimeException.

```
try {
        // Do something, which might throw Exception
}
catch(ArithmeticException e1) {
        // Handle ArithmeticException first
}
catch(RuntimeException e2) {
        // Handle RuntimeException after ArithmeticException
}
```

Checked and Unchecked Exceptions

Before I start discussing checked and unchecked exceptions, let's look at a Java program that reads a character from the standard input. You have been using the System.out.println() method to print messages on the standard output, which is typically the console. You can use the System.in.read() method to read a byte from the standard input, which is typically the keyboard. It returns the value of the byte as an int between 0 and 255. It returns –1 if the end of input is reached. The following is the code that reads a byte from the standard input and returns it as a character. It assumes that the language you are using has all alphabets whose Unicode values are between 0 and 255. The readChar() method has the main code. To read a character from the standard input, you will need to use the ReadInput.readChar() method.

```
// ReadInput.java
package com.jdojo.exception;

public class ReadInput {
        public static char readChar() {
                char c = '\u0000';
                int input = System.in.read();
                if (input != -1) {
                        c = (char)input;
                }
                return c;
        }
}
```

Try to compile the ReadInput class. Oops! The compiler could not compile ReadInput class. It generated the following error message:

```
"ReadInput.java": unreported exception java.io.IOException; must be caught or declared to be thrown at line 7, column 31
```

The compiler error is pointing to line 7 in the source code:

```
int input = System.in.read();
```

There is something missing in this statement. The compiler error also tells you that there is an uncaught exception, which must be caught or declared. You know about catching an exception using a try-catch block. However, you probably do not understand how to declare an exception. You will learn about declaring an exception in the next section.

The System.in.read() method call may throw a java.io.IOException. The compiler error is telling you to place this method call in a try-catch block, so you can handle the exception. If you do not catch this exception, you need to include in the declaration of the readChar() method that it might throw a java.io.IOException. You learned in the previous sections that the runtime handles all uncaught exceptions. So why can't the Java runtime handle java.io.IOException in this case? Here comes the concept of checked and unchecked exceptions. You need to learn about checked and unchecked exception types to fully understand the compiler error.

Three kinds of exceptional conditions may occur in a Java program:

- In the first category are exceptions that have a higher potential to occur, and you can handle them. For example, when you read from a file, it is more likely that an I/O error may occur. It is better to handle these kinds of exceptions in your program. Classes in the exception class hierarchy (refer to Figure 9-2), which are subclasses of the Exception class, including the Exception class itself and excluding RuntimeException and all its subclasses, fall into this category. If a method or constructor may throw an exception of this category, you must take an appropriate action to handle that exception in your code that calls the method or constructor. What is that "appropriate action" that you need to take to handle these kinds of exceptions? You may take one of the following two actions:

  - You can place the code that can throw the exception in a try-catch block. One of the catch blocks must be capable of handling the type of exception that may be thrown.

  - You can specify in the calling method/constructor declaration that it may throw an exception. You accomplish this by using a throws clause in the method/constructor declaration.

- In the second category are the exceptions that may occur during the course of the execution of a Java program, and there is little you can do to handle it. For example, you will receive a java.lang.OutOfMemeoryError exception when the runtime is out of memory. You cannot do anything to recover from an out of memory error. It is better for you to let the application crash, and then look at ways to manage the memory more efficiently in your program. Classes in the exception class hierarchy (refer to Figure 9-2), which are subclasses of the Error class, and the Error class itself, fall into this category of exception. If a piece of code may throw an exception of this category, the compiler does not insist on taking an action on your part. If an exception of this kind is thrown at runtime, the runtime will handle it for you by displaying a detailed error message and halting the application.

- In the third category are exceptions that may occur at runtime, and you may be able to recover from the exceptional condition if you handle them yourself. There are numerous exceptions in this category. However, if you feel that it is more likely that an exception of this kind may be thrown, you should handle it in your code. If you attempt to handle them by using try-catch blocks, your code tends to get cluttered. Classes in the exception class hierarchy (refer to Figure 9-2), which are subclasses of the RuntimeException class, and the RuntimeException class itself, fall into this category of exception. If a piece of code may throw an exception of this category, the compiler does not insist on taking an action on your part. If an exception of this kind is thrown at runtime, the runtime will handle it for you by displaying a detailed error message and halting the program.

Exceptions in the first category are known as checked exceptions. The Throwable class also falls under checked exceptions. The Throwable class, the Exception class, and subclasses of the Exception class, excluding the RuntimeException class and its subclasses, are called checked exceptions. They are called checked exceptions because the compiler checks that they are handled in the code.

All exceptions that are not checked exceptions are called unchecked exceptions. The Error class, all subclasses of the Error class, the RuntimeException class, and all its subclasses are unchecked exceptions. They are called unchecked exceptions because the compiler does not check if they are handled in the code. However, you are free to handle them. The program structure for handling a checked or an unchecked exception is the same. The difference between them is in the way the compiler forces (or does not force) you to handle them in the code.

Let's fix the compiler error for the ReadInput class. Now you know that java.io.IOException is a checked exception and the compiler will force you to handle it. You will handle it by using a try-catch block. Listing 9-3 shows the code for the ReadInput class. This time, you have handled the IOException in its readChar() method and the code will compile fine.

Listing 9-3. A ReadInput Class Whose readChar() Method Reads One Character from the Standard Input

```java
// ReadInput.java
package com.jdojo.exception;

import java.io.IOException;

public class ReadInput {
    public static char readChar() {
        char c = '\u0000';
        int input = 0;
        try {
            input = System.in.read();
            if (input != -1) {
                c = (char)input;
            }
        }
        catch (IOException e) {
            System.out.print("IOException occurred while reading input.");
        }
        return c;
    }
}
```

How do you use the ReadInput class? You can use it the same way you use other classes in Java. You need to call the ReadInput.readChar() static method if you want to capture the first character entered by the user. Listing 9-4 has code that shows how to use the ReadInput class. It prompts the user to enter some text. The first character of the entered text is shown on the standard output.

Listing 9-4. A Program to Test the ReadInput Class

```java
// ReadInputTest.java
package com.jdojo.exception;

public class ReadInputTest {
    public static void main(String[] args) {
        System.out.print("Enter some text and press Enter key: ");
        char c = ReadInput.readChar();
        System.out.println("First character you entered is: " + c);
    }
}
```

```
Enter some text and press Enter key: Hello
First character you entered is: H
```

Checked Exception - Catch or Declare

If a piece of code may throw a checked exception, you must do one of the following:

- Handle the checked exception by placing the piece of code inside a try-catch block.

- Specify in your method/constructor declaration that it throws the checked exception.

The call to the System.in.read() method in the readChar() method of the ReadInput class (see Listing 9-3) throws a checked exception of the IOException type. You applied the first option in this case and handled the IOException by placing the call to the System.in.read() method in a try-catch block

Let's assume that you are writing a method m1() for a class that has three statements. Suppose three statements may throw checked exceptions of types Exception1, Exception2, and Exception3, respectively.

```
// Will not compile
public void m1() {
        statement-1; // May throw Exception1
        statement-2; // May throw Exception2
        statement-3; // May throw Exception3
}
```

You cannot compile the code for the m1() method in the above form. You must either handle the exception using a try-catch block or include in its declaration that it may throw the three checked exceptions. If you want to handle the checked exceptions in the m1() method's body, your code may look as follows:

```
public void m1() {
        try {
                statement-1; // May throw Exception1
                statement-2; // May throw Exception2
                statement-3; // May throw Exception3
        }
        catch(Exception1 e1) {
                // Handle Exception1 here
        }
        catch(Exception2 e2) {
                // Handle Exception2 here
        }
        catch(Exception3 e3) {
                // Handle Exception3 here
        }
}
```

The above code assumes that when one of the three exceptions is thrown, you do not want to execute the remaining statements.

If you want to use different logic, you might need more than one try-catch block. For example, if your logic states that you must attempt to execute all three statements, even if the previous statement throws an exception, your code would look as follows:

```
public void m1() {
        try {
                statement-1; // May throw Exception1
        }
        catch(Exception1 e1) {
                // Handle Exception1 here
        }

        try {
                statement-2; // May throw Exception2
        }
        catch(Exception2 e2) {
                // Handle Exception2 here
        }

        try {
                statement-3; // May throw Exception3
        }
        catch(Exception3 e3) {
                // Handle Exception3 here
        }
}
```

The second way to get rid of the compiler error is to specify in the m1() method's declaration that it throws three checked exceptions. This is accomplished by using a throws clause in the m1() method's declaration. The general syntax for a throws clause is

```
<<modifiers>> <<return type>> <<method name>>(<<params>>) throws <<List of Exceptions>> {
        // Method body goes here
}
```

The keyword throws is used to specify a throws clause. The throws clause is placed after the closing parenthesis of the method's parameters list. The throws keyword is followed by a comma-separated list of exception types. Recall that an exception type is nothing but the name of a Java class, which is in the exception class hierarchy. You can specify a throws clause in the declaration of the m1() method as follows:

```
public void m1() throws Exception1, Exception2, Exception3 {
        statement-1; // May throw Exception1
        statement-2; // May throw Exception2
        statement-3; // May throw Exception3
}
```

You can also mix the two options in the same method when a piece of code throws more than one checked exception. You can handle some of them using a try-catch block, and declare some of them using a throws clause in method's declaration. The following code handles Exception2 using a try-catch block and uses a throws clause to declare exceptions Exception1 and Exception3:

```
public void m1() throws Exception1, Exception3 {
        statement-1; // May throw Exception1

        try {
                statement-2; // May throw Exception2
        }
        catch(Exception2 e){
                // Handle Exception2 here
        }

        statement-3; // May throw Exception3
}
```

Let's get back to the ReadInput class example. Listing 9-3 fixed the compiler error by adding a try-catch block. Let's now use the second option: include a throws clause in the readChar() method's declaration. Listing 9-5 has another version of the ReadInput class, which is called ReadInput2.

Listing 9-5. Using a throws Clause in a Method's Declaration

```
// ReadInput2.java
package com.jdojo.exception;

import java.io.IOException;

public class ReadInput2 {
        public static char readChar() throws IOException {
                char c = '\u0000';
                int input = 0;
                input = System.in.read();
                if (input != -1) {
                        c = (char)input;
                }
                return c;
        }
}
```

The following code for the ReadInput2Test class tests the readChar() method of the ReadInput2 class:

```
// ReadInput2Test.java
package com.jdojo.exception;

public class ReadInput2Test {
        public static void main(String[] args) {
                System.out.print("Enter some text and then press Enter key: ");
                char c = ReadInput2.readChar();
                System.out.print("The first character you entered is: " + c);
        }
}
```

Now, compile the ReadInput2Test class. Oops! Compiling the ReadInput2Test class generates the following error:

Error(6,11): unreported exception: class java.io.IOException; must be caught or declared to be thrown

The compiler error may not be very clear to you at this point. The readChar() method of the ReadInput2 class declares that it may throw an IOException. The IOException is a checked exception. Therefore, the following piece of code in the main() method of ReadInput2Test may throw a checked IOException:

```
char c = ReadInput2.readChar();
```

Recall the rules about handling the checked exceptions, which I mentioned in the beginning of this section. If a piece of code may throw a checked exception, you must use one of the two options: place that piece of code inside a try-catch block to handle the exception, or specify the checked exception using a throws clause in the method's or constructor's declaration. Now, you must apply one of the two options for the ReadInput2.readChar() method's call in the main() method. Listing 9-6 uses the first option and places the call to ReadInput2.readChar() method inside a try-catch block. Note that you have placed three statements inside the try block, which is not necessary. You needed to place inside the try block only the code that may throw the checked exception.

Listing 9-6. A Program to Test the ReadInput2.readChar() Method

```java
// ReadInput2Test2.java
package com.jdojo.exception;

import java.io.IOException;

public class ReadInput2Test2 {
    public static void main(String[] args) {
        char c = '\u0000';
        try {
            System.out.print("Enter some text and then press Enter key:");
            c = ReadInput2.readChar();
            System.out.println("The first character you entered is: " + c);
        }
        catch(IOException e) {
            System.out.println("Error occurred while reading input.");
        }
    }
}
```

You can also use the second option to fix the compiler error. Listing 9-7 has the code using the second option.

Listing 9-7. A Program to Test the ReadInput2.readChar() Method

```java
// ReadInput2Test3.java
package com.jdojo.exception;

import java.io.IOException;

public class ReadInput2Test3 {
    public static void main(String[] args) throws IOException {
        char c = '\u0000';
        System.out.print("Enter some text and then press Enter key: ");
        c = ReadInput2.readChar();
        System.out.print("The first character you entered is: " + c);
    }
}
```

The program includes a throws clause with an IOException for the main() method. Can you run the ReadInput2Test3 class as you have been running other classes using the java command? Yes. You can run the ReadInput2Test3 class the same way you run other classes in Java. The requirement to run a class is that it should include a main() method, which is declared as public static void main(String[] args). The requirement does not specify anything about a throws clause. A main() method, which is used to run a class as a starting point, may or may not contain a throws clause.

Suppose you run the ReadInput2Test3 class and the call to the System.in.read() method in the readChar() method of the ReadInput2 class throws an IOException. How will the IOException be handled and what will handle it? When an exception is thrown in a method body, the runtime checks if the code throwing the exception is inside a try-catch block. If the exception throwing code is inside a try-catch block, the Java runtime looks for the catch block that can handle the exception. If it does not find a catch block that can handle the exception, or the method call is not inside a try-catch block, the exception is propagated up the method call stack. That is, the exception is passed to the caller of the method. In your case, the exception is not handled in the readChar() method of the ReadInput2 class. Its caller is the piece of code in the main() method of the ReadInput2Test2 class. In this case, the same exception is thrown at the point where the ReadInput2.readChar() method call is made inside the ReadInput2Test2.main() method. The runtime applies the same checks to handle the exception. If you run the ReadInput2Test2 class and an IOException is thrown, the runtime finds that the call to ReadInput2.readChar() is inside a try-catch block, which can handle the IOException. Therefore, it will transfer the control to the catch block, which handles the exception, and the program continues in the main() method of the ReadInput2Test2 class. It is very important to understand that the control does not go back to the ReadInput2.readChar() method after it throws an exception and the exception is handled inside the ReadInput2Test2.main() method.

When you run the ReadInput2Test3 class, the call to the ReadInput2.readChar() method is not inside a try-catch block. In this case, the Java runtime will have to propagate the exception up the method call stack. The main() method is the beginning of the method call stack for a Java application. This is the method where all Java applications start. If the main() method throws an exception, the runtime handles it. Recall that if the runtime handles an exception for you, it prints the call stack details on the standard error and exits the application.

Recall that a catch block with an exception type can handle an exception of the same type, or any of its subclass type. For example, a catch block with Throwable exception type is capable of handling all types of exceptions in Java, because the Throwable class is the superclass of all exception classes. This concept is also applicable to the throws clause. If a method throws a checked exception of Exception1 type, you can mention Exception1 type in its throws clause or any of the superclasses of Exception1. The reasoning behind this rule is that if the caller of the method handles an exception that is the superclass of Exception1, the same handler can also handle Exception1.

■ **Tip** The Java compiler forces you to handle a checked exception either by using a try-catch block or by using a throws clause in the method or constructor declaration. If a method throws an exception, it should be handled somewhere in the call stack. That is, if a method throws an exception, its caller can handle it, or its caller's caller can handle, and so on. If an exception is not handled by any callers in the call stack, it is known as an uncaught exception (or an unhandled exception). An uncaught exception is finally handled by the Java runtime, which prints the exception stack trace on the standard error and exits the Java application. A different behavior may be specified for uncaught exceptions in a thread. Please refer to the chapter on threads in the book *Beginning Java Language Features* (ISBN 978-1-4302-6658-7) for more details on how to specify an exception handler for a thread.

The compiler is very particular about checked exceptions being handled by programmers. If the code in a try block cannot throw a checked exception and its associated catch blocks catch checked exceptions, the compiler will generate an error. Consider the following code, which uses a try-catch block. The catch block specifies an IOException, which is a checked exception. However, the corresponding try block does not throw an IOException.

```java
// CatchNonExistentException.java
package com.jdojo.exception;

import java.io.IOException;

// Will not compile
public class CatchNonExistentException {
    public static void main(String[] args) {
        int x = 10, y = 0, z = 0;
        try {
            z = x / y;
        }
        catch(IOException e) {
            // Handle exception
        }
    }
}
```

When you compile the code for the CatchNonExistentException class, you would get the following compiler error:

```
Error(12):  exception java.io.IOException is never thrown in body of corresponding try statement
```

The error message is self-explanatory. It states that IOException is never thrown in the try block. Therefore, the catch block must not catch it.

One way to fix the above compiler error is to remove the try-catch block altogether. The following is another interesting way (but not a good way) to mention a generic catch block:

```java
// CatchNonExistentException2.java
package com.jdojo.exception;
```

```java
// Will compile fine
public class CatchNonExistentException2 {
    public static void main(String[] args) {
        int x = 10, y = 0, z = 0;
        try {
            z = x / y;
        }
        catch(Exception e) {
            // Handle the exception
        }
    }
}
```

Exception is also a checked exception type in Java as is IOException. If a catch block should not catch a checked exception unless it is thrown in the corresponding try block, how does the code for CatchNonExistentException2 compile fine? Should it not generate the same compiler error? At first thought, you are right. It should fail compilation for the same reason the CatchNonExistentException class failed. There are two checked exceptions classes that are exceptions to this rule. Those two exception classes are Exception and Throwable. The Exception class is the superclass of IOException and other exceptions, which are checked exceptions. It is also the superclass of RuntimeException and all subclasses of RuntimeException, which are unchecked exceptions. Recall the rule that a superclass exception type can also handle a subclass exception type. Therefore, you can use the Exception class to handle checked exceptions as well as unchecked exceptions. The rule of checking for catch blocks for un-thrown exceptions applies only to checked exceptions. Exception and Throwable classes in a catch block can handle checked as well as unchecked exceptions because they are superclasses of both types. This is the reason that the compiler will let you use these two checked exception types in a catch block, even though the associated try block does not throw any checked exceptions.

■ **Tip**   All rules about the compiler check for exceptions being handled or thrown are applicable only to checked exceptions. Java does not force you to handle the unchecked exceptions in your code. However, you are free to handle them as you feel appropriate to do so.

Checked Exceptions and Initializers

You cannot throw a checked exception from a static initializer. If a piece of code in a static initializer throws a checked exception, it must be handled using a try-catch block inside the initializer itself. The static initializer is called only once for a class, and the programmer does not have a specific point in code to catch it. This is the reason that a static initializer must handle all possible checked exceptions that it may throw.

```
public class Test {
        static {
                // Must use try-catch blocks to handle all checked exceptions
        }
}
```

The rule is different for instance initializers. An instance initializer is called as part of a constructor call for the class. It may throw checked exceptions. However, all those checked exceptions must be included in the throws clause of all constructors for that class. This way, the compiler can make sure all checked exceptions are taken care of by programmers when any of the constructors are called. The following code for the Test class assumes that the instance initializer throws a checked exception of a CException type. The compiler will force you to add a throws clause with CException to all constructors of Test.

```
public class Test {
        // Instance initializer
        {
                // Throws a checked exception of type CException
        }

        // All constructors must specify that they throw CException
        // because the instance initializer throws CException
        public Test() throws CException {
                // Code goes here
        }
```

```
        public Test(int x) throws CException {
                // Code goes here
        }

        // Rest of the code goes here
}
```

You must handle the CException when you create an object of the Test class using any of its constructors as

```
Test t = null;
try {
        t = new Test();
}
catch (CException e) {
        // Handle exception here
}
```

If you do not handle the CException using a try-catch block, you must use a throws clause to specify that the method or constructor that uses the constructor of the Test class may throw CException.

If an instance initializer throws a checked exception, you must declare a constructor for your class. The compiler will add a default constructor to your class if you do not add one. However, the compiler will not add a throws clause to the default constructor, which will break the above rule. The following code will not compile:

```
public class Test123 {
        {
                // May throw CException, which is a checked exception.
        }
}
```

When the Test123 class is compiled, the compiler adds a default constructor, and the class Test123 will look as follows:

```
public class Test123 {
        {
                // May throw CException, which is a checked exception.
        }

        public Test123() {
                // An empty body. The compiler did not add a throws clause.
        }
}
```

Note that the default constructor, which was added by the compiler, does not contain a throws clause to include CException, which is thrown by the instance initializer. This is the reason that the Test123 class will not compile. To make the Test123 class compile, you must add at least one constructor explicitly and use a throws clause to specify that it may throw CException.

Throwing an Exception

A Java exception is not something that is always thrown by the runtime. You can also throw an exception in your code using a throw statement. The syntax for a throw statement is

```
throw <<A throwable object reference>>;
```

Here, throw is a keyword, which is followed by a reference to a throwable object. A throwable object is an instance of a class, which is a subclass of the Throwable class, or the Throwable class itself. The following is an example of a throw statement, which throws an IOException:

```
// Create an object of IOException
IOException e1 = new IOException("File not found");

// Throw the IOException
throw e1;
```

Recall that the new operator returns the reference of the new object. You can also create a throwable object and throw it in one statement.

```
// Throw an IOException
throw new IOException("File not found");
```

The same rules for handling exceptions apply when you throw an exception in your code. If you throw a checked exception, you must handle it by placing the code in a try-catch block, or by using a throws clause in the method or constructor declaration that contains the throw statement. These rules do not apply if you throw an unchecked exception.

Creating an Exception Class

You can also create your own exception classes. They must extend (or inherit from) an existing exception class. I will cover how to extend a class in detail in Chapter 16 on inheritance. This section will discuss the necessary syntax to extend a class. The keyword extends is used to extend a class.

```
<<Class Modifiers>>class <<Class Name>>extends <<Superclass Name>> {
        // Body for <<Class Name>>goes here
}
```

Here, <<Class Name>>is your exception class name and <<Superclass Name>>is an existing exception class name, which is extended by your class.

Suppose you want to create a MyException class, which extends the java.lang.Exception class. The syntax would be as follows:

```
public class MyException extends Exception {
        // Body for MyException class goes here
}
```

How does the body of an exception class look? An exception class is like any other classes in Java. Typically, you do not add any methods to your exception class. Many useful methods that can be used to query an exception object's state are declared in the Throwable class and you can use them without re-declaring them. Typically, you include four constructors to your exception class. All constructors will call the corresponding constructor of its superclass using the super keyword. Listing 9-8 shows the code for a MyException class with four constructors.

Listing 9-8. A MyException Class That Extends the Exception Class

```java
// MyException.java
package com.jdojo.exception;

public class MyException extends Exception {
        public MyException() {
                super();
        }

        public MyException(String message) {
                super(message);
        }

        public MyException(String message, Throwable cause) {
                super(message, cause);
        }

        public MyException(Throwable cause) {
                super(cause);
        }
}
```

The first constructor creates an exception with null as its detailed message. The second constructor creates an exception with a detailed message. The third and fourth constructors let you create an exception by wrapping another exception with/without a detailed message.

You can throw an exception of type MyException.

```java
throw new MyException("Your message goes here");
```

You can use the MyException class in a throws clause in a method/constructor declaration or as a parameter type in a catch block.

```java
import com.jdojo.exception.MyException;
...
public void m1() throws MyException {
        // Code for m1() body goes here
}

try {
        // Code for the try block goes here
}
catch(MyException e) {
        // Code for the catch block goes here
}
```

Table 9-1 shows some of the commonly used methods of the Throwable class. Note that the Throwable class is the superclass of all exception classes in Java. All of the methods shown in this table are available in all exception classes.

Table 9-1. *A Partial List of Methods of the Throwable Class*

Method	Description
Throwable getCause()	This method was added in Java 1.4. It returns the cause of the exception. If the cause of the exception is not set, it returns null.
String getMessage()	It returns the detailed message of the exception.
StackTraceElement[] getStackTrace()	This method was added in Java 1.4. It returns an array of stack trace elements. Each element in the array represents one stack frame. The first element of the array represents the top of the stack and the last element of the array represents the bottom of the stack. The top of the stack is the method/constructor where the exception object is created. The object of StackTraceElement class holds information such as class name, method name, file name, line number, etc.
Throwable initCause(Throwable cause)	It was added in Java 1.4. There are two ways to set an exception as the cause of an exception. One way is to use the constructor, which accepts the cause as a parameter. Another way is to use this method.
void printStackTrace()	It prints the stack trace on the standard error stream. The output prints the description of the exception object itself as the first line and then the description of each stack frame. Printing stack trace for an exception is very useful for the debugging purpose.
void printStackTrace(PrintStream s)	It prints the stack trace to the specified PrintStream object.
void printStackTrace(PrintWriter s)	It prints the stack trace to the specified PrintWriter object.
String toString()	It returns a short description of the exception object. The description of an exception object contains the name of the exception class and the detail message.

Listing 9-9 demonstrates the use of the printStackTrace() method for an exception class. The main() method calls the m1() method, which in turn calls the m2() method. The stack frame for this call starts with the main() method, which will be at the bottom of the stack. The top of the stack contains the m2() method. The output shows that the printStackTrace() method prints the stack information from top to bottom. Each stack frame contains the name of the class, the method name, the source file name, and the line number. The first line of the printStackTrace() method prints the class name of the exception object with a detailed message.

Listing 9-9. Printing the Stack Trace of an Exception

```
// StackTraceTest.java
package com.jdojo.exception;

public class StackTraceTest {
    public static void main(String[] args) {
        try {
            m1();
        }
        catch(MyException e) {
            e.printStackTrace(); // Print the stack trace
        }
    }
```

```
        public static void m1() throws MyException {
                m2();
        }

        public static void m2() throws MyException {
                throw new MyException("Some error has occurred.");
        }
}
```

```
com.jdojo.exception.MyException: Some error has occurred.
        at com.jdojo.exception.StackTraceTest.m2(StackTraceTest.java:20)
        at com.jdojo.exception.StackTraceTest.m1(StackTraceTest.java:16)
        at com.jdojo.exception.StackTraceTest.main(StackTraceTest.java:7)
```

Listing 9-9 demonstrates how to print the stack trace of an exception on the standard error. Sometimes you may need to save the stack trace in a file or in a database. You may need to get the stack trace information as a string in a variable. Another version of the printStackTrace() method lets you do this. Listing 9-10 shows how to use the printStackTrace(PrintWriter s) method to print the stack trace of an exception object to a String object. The program is the same as Listing 9-9 with one difference. It stores the stack trace in a string and then prints that string on the standard output. The method getStackTrace() writes the stack trace to a string and returns that string. Please refer to the chapter on input/output in the book *Beginning Java Language Features* (ISBN 978-1-4302-6658-7) for more details on how to use the StringWriter and PrintWriter classes.

Listing 9-10. Writing Stack Trace of an Exception to a String

```java
// StackTraceAsStringTest.java
package com.jdojo.exception;

import java.io.StringWriter;
import java.io.PrintWriter;

public class StackTraceAsStringTest {
        public static void main(String[] args) {
                try {
                        m1();
                }
                catch(MyException e) {
                        String str = getStackTrace(e);

                        // Print the stack trace to the standard output
                        System.out.println(str);
                }
        }

        public static void m1() throws MyException {
                m2();
        }
```

```
        public static void m2() throws MyException {
                throw new MyException("Some error has occurred.");
        }

        public static String getStackTrace(Throwable e) {
                StringWriter strWriter = new StringWriter();
                PrintWriter printWriter = new PrintWriter(strWriter);
                e.printStackTrace(printWriter);

                // Get the stack trace as a string
                String str = strWriter.toString();

                return str;
        }
}
```

```
com.jdojo.exception.MyException: Some error has occurred.
        at com.jdojo.exception.StackTraceAsStringTest.m2(StackTraceAsStringTest.java:25)
        at com.jdojo.exception.StackTraceAsStringTest.m1(StackTraceAsStringTest.java:21)
        at com.jdojo.exception.StackTraceAsStringTest.main(StackTraceAsStringTest.java:10)
```

The finally Block

You have seen how to associate one or more catch blocks to a try block. A try block can also have zero or one finally block. A finally block is never used by itself. It is always used with a try block. The syntax for using a finally block is

```
finally {
        // Code for finally block goes here
}
```

A finally block starts with the keyword finally, which is followed by an opening brace and a closing brace. The code for a finally block is placed inside the braces.

There are two possible combinations of try, catch, and finally blocks: try-catch-finally or try-finally. A try block may be followed by zero or more catch blocks. A try block can have a maximum of one finally block. A try block must have either a catch block, a finally block, or both. The syntax for a try-catch-finally block is

```
try {
        // Code for try block goes here
}
catch(Exception1 e1) {
        // Code for catch block goes here
}
finally {
        // Code for finally block goes here
}
```

The syntax for a try-finally block is

```
try {
        // Code for try block goes here
}
finally {
        // Code for finally block goes here
}
```

When you use a `try-catch-finally` block, your intention is to execute the following logic:

Try executing the code in the try. If the code in the `try` block throws any exception, execute the matching catch block. Finally, execute the code in the `finally` block no matter how the code in the try and catch blocks finish executing.

When you use a `try-finally` block, your intention is to execute the following logic:

Try executing the code in the try block. When the code in the try block finishes, execute the code in the finally block.

■ **Tip** A `finally` block is guaranteed to be executed no matter what happens in the associated `try` and/or `catch` block. There are two exceptions to this rule: the `finally` block may not be executed if the thread that is executing the `try` or `catch` block dies, or a Java application may exit, for example, by calling `System.exit()` method, while executing the `try` or `catch` block.

Why do you need to use a `finally` block? Sometimes you want to execute two sets of statements, say `set-1` and `set-2`. The condition is that `set-2` should be executed no matter how the statements in `set-1` finish executing. For example, statements in `set-1` may throw an exception or may finish normally. You may be able to write the logic, which will execute `set-2` after `set-1` is executed, without using a `finally` block. However, the code may not look clean. You may end up repeating the same code multiple places and writing spaghetti `if-else` statements. For example, `set-1` may use constructs, which make the control jump from one point of the program to another. It may use constructs like break, continue, return, throw, etc. If `set-1` has many points of exit, you will need to repeat the call to `set-2` before exiting at many places. It is difficult and ugly to write logic that will execute `set-1` and `set-2`. The `finally` block makes it easy to write this logic. All you need to do is to place `set-1` code in a `try` block and the `set-2` code in a `finally` block. Optionally, you can also use `catch` blocks to handle exceptions that may be thrown from `set-1`. You can write Java code to execute `set-1` and `set-2` as follows:

```
try {
        // Execute all statements in set-1
}
catch(MyException e1) {
        // Handle any exceptions here that may be thrown by set-1
}
finally {
        // Execute statements in set-2
}
```

If you structure your code to execute `set-1` and `set-2` as shown above, you get cleaner code with guaranteed execution of `set-2` after `set-1` is executed.

Typically, you use a `finally` block to write cleanup code. For example, you may obtain some resources in your program that must be released when you are done with them. A `try-finally` block lets you implement this logic. Your code structure would look as follows:

```
try {
        // Obtain and use some resources here
}
finally {
        // Release the resources that were obtained in the try block
}
```

You write `try-finally` blocks frequently when you write programs that perform database transactions and file input/output. You obtain and use a database connection in the `try` block and release the connection in the `finally` block. When you work with a database-related program, you must release the database connection, which you obtained in the beginning, no matter what happens to the transaction. It is similar to executing statements in `set-1` and `set-2` as described above. Listing 9-11 demonstrates the use of a `finally` block in four different situations.

Listing 9-11. Using a finally Block

```java
// FinallyTest.java
package com.jdojo.exception;

public class FinallyTest {
        public static void main(String[] args) {
                int x = 10, y = 0, z;
                try {
                        System.out.println("Before dividing x by y.");
                        z = x / y;
                        System.out.println("After dividing x by y.");
                }
                catch (ArithmeticException e) {
                        System.out.println("Inside catch block - 1.");
                }
                finally {
                        System.out.println("Inside finally block - 1.");
                }

                System.out.println("-------------------------------");

                try {
                        System.out.println("Before setting z to 2449.");
                        z = 2449;
                        System.out.println("After setting z to 2449.");
                }
                catch (Exception e) {
                        System.out.println("Inside catch block - 2.");
                }
                finally {
                        System.out.println("Inside finally block - 2.");
                }
```

```
                System.out.println("-------------------------------");

            try {
                    System.out.println("Inside try block - 3.");
            }
            finally {
                    System.out.println("Inside finally block - 3.");
            }

                System.out.println("-----------------------------");

            try {
                    System.out.println("Before executing System.exit().");
                    System.exit(0);
                    System.out.println("After executing System.exit().");
            }
            finally {
                    // This finally block will not be executed
                    // because application exits in try block
                    System.out.println("Inside finally block - 4.");
            }
        }
    }
}
```

```
Before dividing x by y.
Inside catch block - 1.
Inside finally block - 1.
-----------------------------
Before setting z to 2449.
After setting z to 2449.
Inside finally block - 2.
-----------------------------
Inside try block - 3.
Inside finally block - 3.
-----------------------------
Before executing System.exit().
```

The first try-catch-finally block attempts to perform a divide-by-zero operation on an integer. The expression x/y throws an ArithmeticException and control is transferred to the catch block. The finally block is executed after the catch block finishes. Note that the second message in the try block is not printed because once an exception is thrown, the control jumps to the nearest matching catch block and the control never goes back to the try block again.

The second try-catch-finally block is an example where the try block finishes normally (without throwing an exception). After the try block finishes, the finally block is executed.

The third try-finally block is simple. The try block finishes normally, and then the finally block is executed.

The fourth try-finally block demonstrates an exceptional case when a finally block is not executed. The try block exits the application by executing the System.exit() method. The application stops executing when the System.exit() method is called without executing the associated finally block.

Rethrowing an Exception

An exception that is caught can be rethrown. You may want to rethrow an exception for different reasons. One of the reasons could be to take an action after catching it, but before propagating it up the call stack. For example, you may want to log the details about the exception and then rethrow it to the client. Another reason is to hide the exception type/location from the client. You are not hiding the exceptional condition itself from the client. Rather, you are hiding the type of the exceptional condition. You may want to hide the actual exception type from clients for two reasons:

- The client may not be ready to handle the exception that is thrown, or

- The exception that is thrown does not make sense to the client.

Rethrowing an exception is as simple as using a throw statement. The following code snippet catches the exception, prints its stack trace, and rethrows the same exception. When the same exception object is rethrown, it preserves the details of the original exception.

```
try {
        // Code that might throw MyException
}
catch(MyException e) {
        e.printStackTrace(); // Print the stack trace

        // Rethrow the same exception
        throw e;
}
```

When an exception is thrown from a catch block, another catch block in the same group is not searched to handle that exception. If you want to handle the exception thrown from a catch block, you need to enclose the code that throws the exception inside another try-catch block. Another way to handle it is to enclose the whole try-catch block inside another try-catch block. The following snippet of code shows the two ways of arranging nested try-catch to handle Exception1 and Exception2. The actual arrangement of nested try-catch depends on the situation at hand. If you do not enclose the code that may throw an exception inside a try block or the try block does not have a matching associated catch block that can catch the exception, the runtime will propagate the exception up the call stack provided the method is defined with a throws clause.

```
// #1 - Arranging nested try-catch
try {
        // May throw Exception1
}
catch(Exception1 e1) {
        // Handle Exception1 here

        try {
                // May throw Exception2
        }
        catch(Exception2 e2) {
                // Handle Exception2 here
        }
}
```

```
/* #2 - Arranging nested try-catch */
try {
        try {
                // May throw Exception1
        }
        catch(Exception1 e1) {
                // Handle Exception1 here

                // May throw Exception2
        }
}
catch(Exception2 e2) {
        // Handle Exception2 here
}
```

The following snippet of code shows how to catch an exception of one type and rethrow an exception of another type:

```
try {
        // Code that might throw a MyException
}
catch(MyException e) {
        e.printStackTrace(); // Print the stack trace

        // Rethrow another type of exception
        throw new RuntimeException(e.getMessage());
}
```

The catch block catches the MyException, prints its stack trace, and rethrows a RuntimeException. In the process, it loses the details of the original exception that was thrown. When the RuntimeException is created, it packages the information of stack frames from the point where it was created. The client gets the information about the rethrown RuntimeException from the point it was created, not about the original MyException. In the above code, you have hidden both the type and the location of the original exception from the client.

You can also rethrow another type of exception and use the original exception as the cause of the rethrown exception. It is as if the new exception is a wrapper for the original exception. You can set the cause of an exception using one of the constructors of the new exception type that accepts a cause as a parameter. You can also use the initCause() method to set the cause of the exception. The following snippet of code rethrows a RuntimeException setting MyException as its cause:

```
try {
        // Code that might throw a MyException
}
catch(MyException e) {
        e.printStackTrace(); // Print the stack trace

        // Rethrow a new exception using original exception as its cause
        throw new RuntimeException(e.getMessage(), e);
}
```

You also have the option just to hide the location of the exception from the client when you rethrow an exception. The fillInStackTrace() method of the Throwable class fills in the stack trace information to an exception object from the point where this method is called. You need to call this method on the exception you catch and want to rethrow to hide the location of the original exception. The following snippet of code shows how to rethrow an exception by hiding the location of the original exception:

```
try {
        // Code that might throw MyException
}
catch(MyException e) {
        // Re-package the stack frames in the exception object
        e.fillInStackTrace();

        // Rethrow the same exception
        throw e;
}
```

Listing 9-12 demonstrates how to rethrow an exception by hiding the location of the original exception. The MyException is thrown inside the m2() method. The m1() method catches the exception, refills the stack trace, and rethrows it. The main() method receives the exception as if the exception was thrown inside m1(), not inside m2().

Listing 9-12. Rethrowing an Exception to Hide the Location of the Original Exception

```
// RethrowTest.java
package com.jdojo.exception;

public class RethrowTest {
        public static void main(String[] args) {
                try {
                        m1();
                }
                catch(MyException e) {
                        // Print the stack trace
                        e.printStackTrace();
                }
        }

        public static void m1() throws MyException {
                try {
                        m2();
                }
                catch(MyException e) {
                        e.fillInStackTrace();
                        throw e;
                }
        }

        public static void m2() throws MyException {
                throw new MyException("An error has occurred.");
        }
}
```

```
com.jdojo.exception.MyException: An error has occurred.
        at com.jdojo.exception.RethrowTest.m1(RethrowTest.java:20)
        at com.jdojo.exception.RethrowTest.main(RethrowTest.java:7)
```

Analysis of Rethrown Exceptions

Java 7 improved the mechanism of rethrowing exceptions. Consider the following snippet of code for a method declaration:

```java
public void test() throws Exception {
    try {
        // May throw Exception1, or Exception2
    }
    catch (Exception e) {
        // Rethrow the caught exception
        throw e;
    }
}
```

The try block may throw Exception1 or Exception2. The catch block specifies Exception as its parameter and it rethrows the exception it catches. Prior to Java 7, the compiler sees the catch block throwing an exception of Exception type and it insisted that, in the throws clause, the test() method must specify that it threw an exception of the Exception type or the supertype of the Exception type.

Because the try block can throw exceptions of only Exception1 and Exception2 types, the catch block will rethrow an exception that is always of these two types. Java 7 performs this analysis when an exception is rethrown. It lets you specify the throws clause of the test() method accordingly. In Java 7, you can specify more specific exception types, Exception1 and Exception2, in the test() method's throws clause, as follows:

```java
public void test() throws Exception1, Exception2 {
    try {
        // May throw Exception1, Exception2 or Exception3
    }
    catch (Exception e) {
        // Rethrow the caught exception
        throw e;
    }
}
```

Throwing too Many Exceptions

There is no limit on the number of exception types that a method/constructor can list in its throws clause. However, it is better to keep the number low. The client that uses a method has to deal with all the exceptions that the method may throw in one way or another. It is also important to keep in mind that a method should not throw a new type of exception once it has been designed, implemented, and released to public. If a method starts throwing a new type of exception after its public release, all client code that call this method must change. It indicates poor design if a method throws too many exceptions or a new exception is added after its public release. You can avoid these issues with your method by catching all lower-level exceptions inside your method and rethrowing a higher-level exception. The exception that you throw may contain the lower-level exception as its cause. Consider the following snippet of code for a method m1() that throws three exceptions (Exception1, Exception2, and Exception3):

```java
public void m1() throws Exception1, Exception2, Exception3 {
    // Code for m1() method goes here
}
```

You can redesign the m1() method to throw only one exception, say MyException, as follows:

```
public void m1() throws MyException {
      try {
              // Code for m1() method goes here
      }
      catch(Exception1 e1){
              throw new MyException("Msg1", e1);
      }
      catch(Exception2 e2){
              throw new MyException("Msg2", e1);
      }
      catch(Exception3 e3){
              throw new MyException("Msg3", e1);
      }
}
```

The redesigned method throws only one exception, which is of type MyException. The detailed message for the exception is specific to the lower-level exception that is thrown and caught inside the method. The lower-level exception is also propagated to the client as the cause of the higher-level exception. If the m1() method needs to throw a new exception in the future, you can still fit the new exception in the old design. You need to add a catch block to catch the new exception and rethrow MyException. This design keeps the throws clause of the m1() method stable. It also allows for more exception types to be included in its body in future.

■ **Tip**   Do not throw a generic exception from your method, such as Throwable, Exception, Error, RuntimeException, etc. Do not specify a generic exception type in a catch block. The purpose of exception throwing or handling is to know exactly the error condition that occurred and take appropriate action. It helps you to understand the cause of an error by giving specific error messages to users. Generating a specific error message is possible only when you handle exceptions using specific exception types.

Accessing the Stack of a Thread

The stack is an area of memory that is used to store temporary data. It uses last-in, first-out (LIFO) style to add and remove data. A stack resembles a stack in everyday life, such as a stack of books. The bottom of the stack has the first book that was placed on it. The top of the stack has the last book that was placed on it. When a book has to be removed from the stack, the last book that was placed on the stack will be removed first. This is the reason a stack is also called last-in, first-out memory. Figure 9-4 shows the arrangement of a stack.

Figure 9-4. *Memory arrangement in a stack*

The figure shows three books placed on a stack. Book-1 was placed first, Book-2 second, and Book-3 third. Book-3, which is added last onto the stack, represents the top of the stack. Book-1, which is added first onto the stack, represents the bottom of the stack. Adding an element to a stack is called a *push* operation and removing an element from a stack is called a *pop* operation. Initially, a stack is empty and the first operation is the push operation. When a stack is being discarded, it must perform an equal number of push and pop operations so it is empty again.

Each thread in Java is allocated a stack to store its temporary data. A thread stores the state of a method invocation onto its stack. The state of a Java method comprises the parameters' values, local variables, any intermediate computed values, and the method's return value, if any. A Java stack consists of stack frames. Each frame stores the state of one method invocation. A new frame is pushed onto a thread's stack for a method invocation. The frame is popped from a thread's stack when the method completes.

Suppose a thread starts at the m1() method. The m1() method calls the m2() method, which in turn calls the m3() method. Figure 9-5 shows the frames on the stack of a thread when methods m1(), m2(), and m3() are called. Note that the figures shows the frames when the method m3() is called from the method m2(), which in turn is called from the method m1().

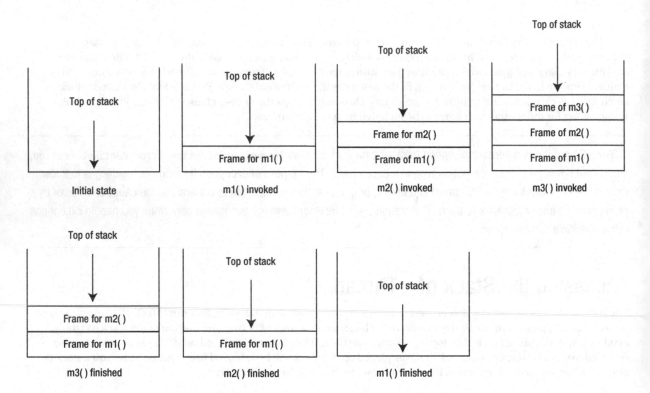

Figure 9-5. *State of the stack of a thread when methods m1(), m2(), and m3() are called*

You can get some pieces of information about the stack of a thread at a specific point in time. Note that the state of a thread's stack is always changing as the program executes. Therefore, you get a snapshot of the stack of a thread as it existed at the time you requested it. An object of the java.lang.StackTraceElement class represents a stack frame. You can query four pieces of information about a stack frame: class name, file name, method name, and line number. To get the stack information, you need to call the getStackTrace() method of a Throwable object. It returns an array of StackTraceElement objects. The first element of the array represents the top stack frame. The last element of the array represents the bottom stack frame. When you create an object of the Throwable class (or any exception class in Java), it captures the stack of the thread that is executing.

Listing 9-13 demonstrates how to get to the stack frames of a thread. A Throwable object captures the stack of the thread at the point it is created. If you have a Throwable object and want to capture the snapshot of the stack of a thread at a different point where the Throwable object was created, you can call the fillInStackTrace() method of the Throwable class. It captures the current state of stack for the current thread at the point you call this method.

Listing 9-13. A Sample Program That Prints the Details of the Stack Frames of a Thread

```java
// StackFrameTest.java
package com.jdojo.exception;

public class StackFrameTest {
    public static void main(String[] args) {
        m1();
    }

    public static void m1() {
        m2();
    }

    public static void m2() {
        m3();
    }

    public static void m3() {
        // Create a Throwable object that will hold the stack state
        // at this point for the thread that executes the following statement
        Throwable t = new Throwable();

        // Get the stack trace elements
        StackTraceElement[] frames = t.getStackTrace();

        // Print details about the stack frames
        printStackDetails(frames);
    }

    public static void printStackDetails(StackTraceElement[] frames) {
        System.out.println("Frame count: " + frames.length);

        for (int i = 0; i < frames.length; i++) {
            // Get frame details
            int frameIndex = i; // i = 0 means top frame
            String fileName = frames[i].getFileName();
            String className = frames[i].getClassName();
            String methodName = frames[i].getMethodName();
            int lineNumber = frames[i].getLineNumber();

            // Print frame details
            System.out.println("Frame Index: " + frameIndex);
            System.out.println("File Name: " + fileName);
            System.out.println("Class Name: " + className);
            System.out.println("Method Name: " + methodName);
```

```
                        System.out.println("Line Number: " + lineNumber);
                        System.out.println("--------------------------");
                }
        }
}
```

```
Frame count: 4
Frame Index: 0
File Name: StackFrameTest.java
Class Name: com.jdojo.exception.StackFrameTest
Method Name: m3
Line Number: 21
--------------------------
Frame Index: 1
File Name: StackFrameTest.java
Class Name: com.jdojo.exception.StackFrameTest
Method Name: m2
Line Number: 14
--------------------------
Frame Index: 2
File Name: StackFrameTest.java
Class Name: com.jdojo.exception.StackFrameTest
Method Name: m1
Line Number: 10
--------------------------
Frame Index: 3
File Name: StackFrameTest.java
Class Name: com.jdojo.exception.StackFrameTest
Method Name: main
Line Number: 6
--------------------------
```

Now that you have access to the stack frames of a thread, you may want to know what you can do with this information. The information about a thread's stack lets you know the location in the program where the code is executing. Typically, you log this information for debugging purposes. If you compare the output of the printStackTrace() method with the output of Listing 9-13, you would observe that they are similar, except that they print the same information in different formats.

The try-with-resources Block

Java 7 added a new construct called try-with-resources. Before Java 7, when you worked with a resource, such as a file, a SQL statement, etc., you had to use a finally block and write a few lines of boilerplate code to close the resource. Prior to Java 7, the typical code, to work with a resource, would look as follows:

```
AnyResource aRes;
try {
        aRes = create the resource...;
        // Work with the resource here
}
```

```
finally {
        // Let us try to close the resource
        try {
                if (aRes != null) {
                        aRes.close(); // Close the resource
                }
        }
        catch(Exception e) {
                e.printStackTrace();
        }
}
```

With the new try-with-resources construct in Java 7, the above code can be written as

```
try (AnyResource aRes = create the resource...) {
        // Work with the resource here. The resource will be closed automatically.
}
```

Wow! You were able to write the same logic in just three lines of code using a try-with-resource construct in Java 7, when it used to take sixteen lines of code. The try-with-resources construct automatically closes the resources when the program exits the construct. A try-with-resource construct may have one or more catch blocks and/or a finally block.

On the surface, the try-with-resources construct is as simple as it seems in the above example. However, it comes with some subtleties that I need to discuss in detail.

You can specify multiple resources in a try-with-resources block. Two resources must be separated by a semicolon. The last resource must not be followed by a semicolon. The following snippet of code shows some usage of try-with-resources to use one and multiple resources:

```
try (AnyResource aRes1 = getResource1()) {
        // Use aRes1 here
}

try (AnyResource aRes1 = getResource1();
        AnyResource aRes2 = getResource2()) {
        // Use aRes1 and aRes2 here
}
```

The resources that you specify in a try-with-resources are implicitly final. You can declare the resources final, even though it is redundant to do so.

```
try (final AnyResource aRes1 = getResource1()) {
        // Use aRes1 here
}
```

A resource that you specify in a try-with-resources must be of the type java.lang.AutoCloseable. Java 7 added the AutoCloseable interface, which has a close() method. When the program exits the try-with-resources block, the close() method of all the resources is called automatically. In the case of multiple resources, the close() method is called in the reverse order in which the resources are specified.

Consider a MyResource class as shown in Listing 9-14. It implements the AutoCloseable interface and provides implementation for the close() method. If the exceptionOnClose instance variable is set to true, its close() method throws a RuntimeException. Its use() method throws a RuntimeException if the level is zero or less. Let's use the MyResource class to demonstrate various rules in using the try-with-resources block.

Listing 9-14. An AutoCloseable Resource Class

```java
// MyResource.java
package com.jdojo.exception;

public class MyResource implements AutoCloseable {
        private int level;
        private boolean exceptionOnClose;

        public MyResource(int level, boolean exceptionOnClose) {
                this.level = level;
                this.exceptionOnClose = exceptionOnClose;
                System.out.println("Creating MyResource. Level = " + level);
        }

        public void use() {
                if (level <= 0) {
                        throw new RuntimeException("Low in level.");
                }
                System.out.println("Using MyResource level " + this.level);
                level--;
        }

        @Override
        public void close() {
                if (exceptionOnClose) {
                        throw new RuntimeException("Error in closing");
                }
                System.out.println("Closing MyResource...");
        }
}
```

Listing 9-15 shows a simple case of using a MyResource object in a try-with-resources block. The output demonstrates that the try-with-resources block automatically calls the close() method of the MyResource object.

Listing 9-15. A Simple Use of MyResource Object in a try-with-resources Block

```java
// SimpleTryWithResource.java
package com.jdojo.exception;

public class SimpleTryWithResource {
        public static void main(String[] args) {
                // Create and use a resource of MyResource type.
                // Its close() method will be called automatically */
                try (MyResource mr = new MyResource(2, false)) {
                        mr.use();
                        mr.use();
                }
        }
}
```

```
Creating MyResource. Level = 2
Using MyResource level 2
Using MyResource level 1
Closing MyResource...
```

When a resource is being closed automatically, an exception may be thrown. If a try-with-resources block completes without throwing an exception and the call to the close() method throws the exception, the runtime reports the exception thrown from the close() method. If a try-with-resources block throws an exception and the call to the close() method also throws an exception, the runtime suppresses the exception thrown from the close() method and reports the exception thrown from the try-with-resources block. The following snippet of code demonstrates this rule:

```java
// Create a resource of MyResource type with two levels, which can throw exception on closing
// and use it thrice so that its use() method throws an exception
try (MyResource mr = new MyResource (2, true) ) {
        mr.use();
        mr.use();
        mr.use(); // Will throw a RuntimeException
}
catch(Exception e) {
        System.out.println(e.getMessage());
}
```

```
Creating MyResource. Level = 2
Using MyResource level 2
Using MyResource level 1
Low in level.
```

The third call to the use() method throws an exception. In the above snippet of code, the automatic close() method call will throw a RuntimeException because you pass true as the second argument when you create the resource. The output shows that the catch block received the RuntimeException that was thrown from the use() method, not from the close() method.

You can retrieve the suppressed exceptions by using the getSuppressed() method of the Throwable class. The method was added in Java 7. It returns an array of Throwable objects. Each object in the array represents a suppressed exception. The following snippet of code demonstrates the use of the getSuppressed() method to retrieve the suppressed exceptions:

```java
try (MyResource mr = new MyResource (2, true) ) {
        mr.use();
        mr.use();
        mr.use(); // Throws an exception
}
catch(Exception e) {
        System.out.println(e.getMessage());

        // Display messages of supressed exceptions
        System.out.println("Suppressed exception messages are...");
        for(Throwable t : c.getSuppressed()) {
                System.out.println(t.getMessage());
        }
}
```

```
Creating MyResource. Level = 2
Using MyResource level 2
Using MyResource level 1
Low in level.
Suppressed exception messages are...
Error in closing
```

A Multi-Catch Block

Java 7 added support for a multi-catch block to handle multiple types of exceptions in a catch block. Suppose you want to catch three exceptions: Exception1, Exception2, and Exception3. Prior to Java 7, your code would look as follows:

```
try {
        // Code that may throw Exception1, Exception2, or Exception3
}
catch (Exception1 e1){
        // Handle Exception1
}
catch (Exception2 e2){
        // Handle Exception2
}
catch (Exception3 e3){
        // Handle Exception3
}
```

Prior to Java 7, each exception must be handled in a separate catch block. This sometimes resulted in code duplication when multiple exceptions were handled in the same way. Sometimes, instead of using a separate catch block to catch multiple exceptions, a programmer would use one catch block and specify the parameter of a more generic exception type.

```
try {
        // Code that may throw Exception1, Exception2 or Exception3
}
catch (Throwable t){
        // Handle any exception
}
```

Java 7 addresses both issues:

- The deficiency in Java language that did not let a programmer handle multiple exceptions in one catch block

- The laziness of programmers of using a generic exception type to handle multiple exceptions in a catch block

Java 7 added support for catching multiple exceptions using a multi-catch block. You can specify multiple exceptions types in a multi-catch block. Multiple exceptions are separated by a vertical bar (|). In Java 7, the above code can be written as follows:

```
try {
        // May throw Exception1, Exception2, or Exception3
}
catch (Exception1 | Exception2 | Exception3  e) {
        // Handle Exception1, Exception2, and Exception3
}
```

In a multi-catch block, it is not allowed to have alternative exceptions that are related by subclassing. For example, the following multi-catch block is not allowed, because Exception1 and Exception2 are subclasses of Throwable:

```
try {
        // May throw Exception1, Exception2, or Exception3
}
catch (Exception1 | Exception2 | Throwable  e) {
        // Handle Exceptions here
}
```

The above snippet of code will generate the following compiler error:

```
error: Alternatives in a multi-catch statement
cannot be related by subclassing
                catch (Exception1 | Exception2 | Throwable  e) {
                                                  ^
   Alternative Exception1 is a subclass of alternative Throwable
1 error
```

Summary

An exception is the occurrence of an abnormal condition in a Java program where a normal path of execution is not defined. Java lets you separate the code that performs the actions from the code that handles exceptions that may occur when the actions are performed.

Use a try-catch block to place your action-performing code in the try block and exception-handling code in the catch block. A try block may also have a finally block, which is typically used to clean up resources used in the try block. You can have a combination of try-catch, try-catch-finally, or try-finally blocks. Java 7 added supported for a try-with-resources block that comes in handy to close resources automatically.

There are two types of exceptions: checked exceptions and unchecked exceptions. The compiler makes sure that all checked exceptions are handled in the program or the program declares them in a throws clause. Handling or declaring unchecked exceptions is optional.

■ ■ ■

Assertions

In this chapter, you will learn:

- What an assertion is in Java

- How to use assertions in Java programs

- How to enable and disable assertions

- How to check the status of an assertion

What Is an Assertion?

The literal meaning of assertion is to state something in a strong, confident, and forceful way. When you assert "something," you believe that "something" to be true. Note that asserting "something" does not make that "something" always true. It simply means that chances are very high (or you are confident) that "something" is true. Sometimes you may be wrong and that "something" may be false, even if you assert it to be true.

The meaning of an assertion in Java is similar to its literal meaning. It is a statement in a Java program. It lets programmers assert a condition to be true at a specific point in the program. Consider the following snippet of code, which has two statements with one comment in between:

```
int x = 10 + 15;
/* We assert that value of x is 25 at this point */
int z = x + 12;
```

The first statement uses two hard-coded integer values, 10 and 15, and assigns their sum to the variable x. You can assert that the value of variable x is 25 after the first statement is executed. Note the use of comments to make the assertion in the above case. What is the probability that the value of x will be other than 25 in the above code? You may think that the probability of x having a value other than 25 is zero. It means your assertion will be true all the time. So, what was the point in adding a comment, which asserts that the value of x is 25, when it is obvious by just looking at the code? In programming, what seems obvious at one time may not be obvious at other times.

Consider the following snippet of code assuming that a getPrice() method exists:

```
int quantity = 15;
double unitPrice = getPrice();
/* We assert that unitPrice is greater than 0.0 at this point */
double totalPrice = quantity * unitPrice;
```

In this code, you have made an assertion that the value of the variable unitPrice will be greater than 0.0 after the second statement is executed. What is the probability that the value of unitPrice will be greater than 0.0 after the second statement is executed? It is difficult to answer this question by just looking at the code. However, you assume, for the above code to work correctly, that your assertion "the value of unitPrice is greater than 0.0" must be true. Otherwise, your code will indicate a serious bug in the getPrice() method. It may be obvious for a customer that the price for an item will be always greater than zero. However, it is not so obvious to a programmer, because he has to depend on the correct implementation of the getPrice() method. If the getPrice() method has a bug, the programmer's assertion will be false. If the programmer's assertion is false, he needs to know about the failure of his assertion, and he needs to take action to fix the bug. If his assertion was false, he would not want to proceed with the price computations. He would want to halt the price computation as soon as his assertion fails. You have used a comment to state your assertion. A comment is not executable code. Even if the value of unitPrice is not greater than zero, your comment is not going to report this error condition or halt the program. You need to use the assertion facility in such cases to receive a detailed error message and halt the program.

You can make an assertion in Java using an assert statement. The syntax for an assert statement comes in two forms:

```
// Form #1
assert booleanAssertionExpression;
```

```
// Form #2
assert booleanAssertionExpression : errorMessageExpression;
```

An assert statement starts with the assert keyword, which is followed by a boolean assertion expression that is the condition that a programmer believes to be true. If the assertion expression evaluates to true, no action is taken. If the assertion expression evaluates to false, the runtime throws a java.lang.AssertionError.

The second form of the assert statement syntax allows you to specify a custom error message expression when the assertion error is thrown. The assertion condition and the custom message are separated by a colon. The errorMessageExpression does not have to be a string. It could an expression that may evaluate to any data type, except the void data type. The runtime will convert the result of the error message expression to string. You can rewrite the code shown previously to take advantage of the assert statement, like so:

```
int x = 10 + 15;
assert x == 25; // Uses the first form of the assert statement
int z = x + 12;
```

Here you replaced the comment with an assert statement. All you need to specify is the condition you assert (or believe) to be true. You used the first form of the assert statement. You did not use any custom message when your assertion fails. When the assertion fails, the Java runtime provides you with all details such as line number, source code, file name, etc. about the error.

In most cases, the first form of the assert statement is sufficient. If you think some values from the program at the time of error may help you diagnose the problem better, you should use the second form of the assert statement. Suppose you want to print the value of x when the assertion fails. You could use the following snippet of code:

```
int x = 10 + 15;
assert x == 25: "x = " + x; // Uses the second form of the assert statement
int z = x + 12;
```

If you want just the value of x and nothing else, you can use the following snippet of code:

```
int x = 10 + 15;
assert x == 25: x; // Uses the second form of the assert statement
int z = x + 12;
```

Note that the errorMessageExpression in the second form of assert statement could be of any data type excluding void. The above snippet of code provides x as the value of errorMessageExpression, which evaluates to an int. The runtime will use the string representation of the value of x when it throws an AssertionError.

At this point, you may be tempted to test the assert statement. Let's discuss some more details before you compile and run Java classes with the assert statement. However, you will use Java code with an assert statement, as shown in Listing 10-1.

Listing 10-1. A Simple Test Class to Test the Assert Statement

```java
// AssertTest.java
package com.jdojo.assertion;

public class AssertTest {
    public static void main(String[] args) {
        int x = 10 + 15;
        assert x == 100:"x = " + x; // should throw an AssertionError
    }
}
```

The code for the AssertTest class is simple. It assigns a value of 25 to the variable x and asserts that the value of x should be 100. When you run the AssertTest class, you expect that it would always throw an AssertionError.

Testing Assertions

It is time to see assert statement in action. Try to run the AssertTest class using the following command:

```
java com.jdojo.assertion.AssertTest
```

This command finishes without any output. Did you not expect an error message on the standard output? Is your assertion x == 100 not false? The value of x is 25, not 100. You need to perform one more step before you can see the assert statement in action.

Try the following command to run the AssertTest class:

```
java -ea com.jdojo.assertion.AssertTest
```

This command generates the following output:

```
Exception in thread "main" java.lang.AssertionError: x = 25
        at com.jdojo.assertion.AssertTest.main(AssertTest.java:7)
```

An AssertionError was generated with "x = 25" as the error message when you ran the AssertTest class. This is what happens when an assertion fails in your code. The Java runtime throws an AssertionError. Because you used the second form of the assert statement in your code, the error message also contains your custom assertion message, which prints the value of x. Note that the assertion error, by default, contains the line number and the source code file name where the assertion fails. The above error message states that the assertion failed at line 7 in the AssertFile.java source file.

So what is the magic behind using the -ea switch with the java command? By default, assert statements are not executed by the Java runtime. In other words, the assertion is disabled by default. You must enable the assertion when you run your class, so your assert statements are executed. The -ea switch enables the assertion at runtime. This is the reason that you received the expected error message when you used the -ea switch to run the AssertTest class. I will discuss enabling/disabling assertion in detail in the next section.

Enabling/Disabling Assertions

The goal in using assertions is to detect logic errors in programs. Typically, assertions should be enabled in development and test environments. Assertions help programmers find the location and type of problems in code quickly. Once an application is tested, it is very unlikely that the assertions will fail. Java designers kept in mind the performance penalty that you may incur by using assertions in production environment. This is the reason that assertions are disabled at runtime by default. Although it is not desirable to enable assertions in a production environment, you have options to do so.

Java provides command-line options (or switches) to enable assertions at runtime at various levels. For example, you have options to enable assertions in all user-defined classes, all system classes, all classes in a package and its subpackages, just for one class, etc. Table 10-1 lists all switches that you can use on the command line to enable/disable assertions at runtime.

Table 10-1. *Command-Line Switches to Enable/Disable Assertions at Runtime*

Command-Line Switch	Description
-enableassertions or -ea	Used to enable assertions at runtime for system classes as well as user-defined classes. You can pass an argument to this switch to control the level at which assertions are enabled.
-disableassertions or -da	Used to disable assertions at runtime for system classes as well as user-defined classes. You can pass an argument to this switch to control the level at which assertions are disabled.
-enablesystemassertions or -esa	Used to enable assertions in all system classes. You cannot pass any arguments to this switch.
-disablesystemassertions or -dsa	Used to disable assertions in all system classes. You cannot pass any arguments to this switch.

Two switches, -ea and –da, let you control the enabling and disabling of assertions at various levels. You can pass an argument to these switches to control the level at which assertions should be enabled or disabled. Note that you cannot pass any arguments to –esa and –dsa switches. They enable and disable assertions in all system classes. If you pass an argument to the –ea or –da switch, the switch and the argument must be separated by a colon, as shown below. Table 10-2 lists the possible arguments that can be used with these switches.

```
-ea:argument
-da:argument
```

Table 10-2. *List of Arguments That Can Be Passed to –ea and –da Switches*

Argument for –ea and –da switches	Description
(no argument)	Enables or disables assertions in all user-defined classes. Note that to enable/disable assertions in all system classes you need to use –esa and –dsa switches with no argument, respectively.
packageName...	Note the three dots after the packageName. It enables/disables assertions in the specified packageName and any of its subpackages. It can also be used to enable/disable assertions in system packages.
...	This argument value is three dots. It enables/disables assertions in the unnamed package in the current working directory.
className	Enables/disables assertions in the specified className. It can also be used to enable/disable assertions in system classes.

The following are examples of using assertion switches with different arguments. All examples assume that you are enabling assertions when you are running the com.jdojo.assertion.AssertTest class. The examples show you only how to enable assertions. By default, all assertions are disabled.

```
/* Enable assertions in all system classes */
java -esa com.jdojo.assertion.AssertTest

/* Enable assertions in all user-defined classes */
java -ea com.jdojo.assertion.AssertTest

/* Enable assertions in com.jdojo package and its sub-packages */
java -ea:com.jdojo… com.jdojo.assertion.AssertTest

/* Enable assertions in the unnamed package in the current directory */
java -ea:… com.jdojo.assertion.AssertTest

/* Enable assertions in com.jdojo.assertion.AssertTest class */
java -ea:com.jdojo.assertion.AssertTest com.jdojo.assertion.AssertTest
```

You can use multiple –ea or –da switches in one command to achieve finer granularity in enabling/disabling assertions. All switches are processed from left to right in the order they are specified.

```
/* Enable assertions in p1 package and all its sub-packages and disable assertion for p1.p2.MyClass
*/
java -ea:p1... -da:p1.p2.MyClass com.jdojo.assertion.AssertTest
```

■ **Tip** Assertions for a class are enabled or disabled when a class is loaded. The assertion status for a class cannot be changed after it is set. There is one exception to this rule. If an assert statement is executed before a class has been initialized, the Java runtime executes it as if assertions are enabled. This situation arises when two classes refer to each other in their static initializers by calling the constructors or the methods of another class.

Using Assertions

Confusion may arise as to when to use assertions in a program. An assertion is implemented in Java by adding a new class, `java.lang.AssertionError`, into the existing exception class hierarchy. Sometimes programmers mistake an assertion as another exception. This may be true when you just look at the class hierarchy and you may say that it is just another class in the existing exception class hierarchy. However, the similarity between exceptions and assertions stops right there in the class hierarchy. The main difference lies in the reason behind their usage. An exception is used to handle a user's error and business rules implementation. If it is possible to recover from exceptional conditions, you want to recover from them and proceed with the application. An assertion is used to detect programming errors made by programmers. You do not want to recover from a programming error and proceed with the application. Assertions are used to verify that what a programmer assumes about his program at a specific point in his code is true. You should never use an assertion to handle a user's error or to validate data, because assertions are not meant to be enabled in the production environment.

Assertions should not be used to validate data arguments for `public` methods. The following snippet of code is for a `credit()` method of the `BankAccount` class, which uses assertion to validate the amount being credited:

```
// An incorrect implementation
public void credit(double amount) {
        assert amount > 0.0 : "Invalid credit amount: " + amount;
        // Other code goes here
}
```

The code for the `credit()` method depends on enabling an assertion to validate the amount of credit to an account. Most likely, the assertion will be disabled in the production environment, which will allow a credit of even a negative number. Such validations for a `public` method's arguments should be performed using exceptions, as shown:

```
// A correct implementation
public void credit(double amount) {
        if (amount <=  0.0) {
                throw new IllegalArgumentException("Invalid credit amount:" + amount);
        }
        // Other code goes here
}
```

You can use assertions to validate a method's arguments for a non-public method. A non-public method cannot be called by clients directly. If a method's parameters for a non-public method are incorrect, it indicates the programmer's errors and use of assertions is appropriate.

You should not use an assertion that has side effects, such as an assertion that modifies the state of an object. Consider the following snippet of code in a method assuming that `reComputeState()` alters the state of the object of the class:

```
assert reComputeState();
```

When this `assert` statement is executed, it will alter the state of the object. The subsequent interaction with the object depends on its altered state. If the assertions are disabled, this code will not execute and the object will not behave properly.

You can use assertions to implement class invariants. Class invariants are conditions that always hold true about the values that determine the state of an object of a class. Class invariants may not be true for brief moments when an object is transitioning from one state to another. Suppose you have a BankAccount class with four instance variables: name, dob, startDate, and balance. The following class invariants must be true for a BankAccount object:

- The name on the account must not be null.

- The dob on the account must not be null and must not be a date in future.

- The startDate on the account must not be null.

- The startDate on the account must not be before dob.

- The balance on the account must be greater than zero.

You can pack all these conditions checks in one method, say validAccount() method.

```
private boolean validAccount() {
        boolean valid = false;

        // Check for class invariants here. Return true if it is true. Otherwise, return false.
        return valid;
}
```

You can use the following assertion in methods and constructors to make sure that the class invariants are enforced. You assume that the toString() method of the BankAccount class returns enough pieces of information to help programmers debug the error.

```
assert validAccount(); this.tostring();
```

You can use the above assert statement in the beginning of every method and before you return from the method. You do not need to check for class invariants inside a method if it does not modify the object's state. You should use it only at the end in a constructor because class invariants will not hold when the constructor starts executing.

Checking for Assertion Status

How do you know in your program if assertions are enabled? It is easy to check for the assertion status using an assert statement. Consider the following snippet of code:

```
boolean enabled = false;
assert enabled = true;
/* Check the value of enabled here */
```

This code uses the first form of the assert statement. Note that it uses the assignment operator (=), not the equality comparison operator (==) in the expression enabled = true. The expression will assign true to the enabled variable and it will evaluate to true. Note that the enabled variable has been initialized to false. If assertion is enabled, the enabled variable will have a value of true after the assert statement is executed. If assertion is disabled, the variable enabled will have a value of false. Therefore, checking for the value of the enabled variable after the assert statement will give you a clue whether assertions are enabled for your class. Listing 10-2 shows the complete code for checking if assertions are enabled for the AssertionStatusTest class. Note that assertion can be enabled or disabled on a class basis, too. If assertions are enabled for a specific class, it does not guarantee that it is also enabled for all other classes.

Listing 10-2. A Program to Check Whether Assertion is Enabled

```java
// AssertionStatusTest.java
package com.jdojo.assertion;

public class AssertionStatusTest {
    public static void main(String[] args)  {
        boolean enabled = false;
        assert enabled = true;
        if (enabled) {
            System.out.println("Assertion is enabled.");
        }
        else {
            System.out.println("Assertion is disabled.");
        }
    }
}
```

Summary

Assertions are a feature of the Java language that let you assert in your program for some conditions to hold. The keyword assert is used to write an assert statement. Assertions are used for detecting logical errors in a program and they are typically enabled in development and testing environments. Assertions can be enabled and disabled for packages and classes. They should not be used to validate user's inputs or business rules. Assertions do not replace exceptions. Rather they complement each other.

CHAPTER 11

■ ■ ■

Strings

In this chapter, you will learn:

- What a String object is
- How to create String objects
- How to use String literals
- How to manipulate Strings
- How to use Strings in a switch statement
- How to use StringBuilder and StringBuffer objects to work with mutable strings

What is a String?

A sequence of zero or more characters is known as a string. In Java programs, a string is represented by an object of the java.lang.String class. The String class is immutable. That is, the contents of a String object cannot be modified after it has been created. The String class has two companion classes, java.lang.StringBuilder and java.lang. StringBuffer. The StringBuilder class was introduced in Java 5. The companion classes are mutable. You should use them when the contents of your string can be modified.

String Literals

A string literal consists of a sequence of zero or more characters enclosed in double quotes. All string literals are objects of the String class. Examples of string literals are

```
""                        // An Empty string
"Hello"                   // A string literal consisting of 5 characters
"Just a string literal"   // A string literal consisting of 21 characters
```

Multiple string literals can be used to compose a single string literal.

```
// Composed of two string literals "Hello" and "Hi". It represents one string literal "HelloHi"
"Hello" + "Hi"
```

A string literal cannot be broken into two lines.

```
"He
llo"         // Cannot continue "He in this line. A compiler error
```

If you want to break "Hello" in two lines, you must break it using the string concatenation operator (+), as shown:

```
"He" +
"llo"
```

or

```
"He"
+ "llo"
```

Another example of a multi-line string literal is shown below. The entire text represents a string literal.

```
"This is a big string literal" +
" and it will continue in several lines." +

" It is also valid to insert multiple new lines as we did here. " +
"Adding more than one line in between two string literals " +
"is a feature of Java Language syntax, " +
" not of string literal."
```

Escape Sequence Characters in String Literals

A string literal is composed of characters. It is valid to use all escape sequence characters to form a string literal. For example, to include a line feed and a carriage return characters in a string literal you will use \n and \r, as shown:

```
"\n"      // A string literal with a line feed
"\r"      // A string literal with a carriage return
"\n\r"    // A string literal with a line feed and a carriage return
"First line.\nSecond line." // An embedded line feed
"Tab\tSeparated\twords"  // Embedded tab escape characters
"Double quote \" is here"  // An embedded double quote in string literal
```

Unicode Escapes in String Literals

A character can also be represented as a Unicode escape in the form \uxxxx, where an x is a hexadecimal digit (0-9 or A-F). In a string literal, the character 'A', the first uppercase English letter, can also be written as '\u0041', for example, Apple and \u0041pple are treated the same in Java. Line feed and carriage return escape characters can also be represented in Unicode escape character as '\u000A' and '\u000D', respectively. You cannot use Unicode escapes to embed a line feed and a carriage return characters in string literals. In other words, you cannot replace '\n' with '\u000A' and '\r' with '\u000D' in a string literal. Why? The reason is that Unicode escapes are processed in the very beginning of the compilation process resulting in the conversion of '\u000A' and '\u000D' into a real line feed, and a carriage return, respectively. This violates the rule that a string literal cannot be continued in two lines. For example, in the early stages of compilation "Hel\u000Alo" is translated into the following, which is an invalid string literal and generates a compiler error:

```
"Hel
lo"
```

■ **Tip**   It is a compile-time error to use Unicode escapes \u000A and \u000D in a string literal to represent a line feed and a carriage return, respectively. You must use the escape sequences of \n and \r instead.

What is a CharSequence?

A CharSequence is an interface in the java.lang package. I discuss interfaces in *Beginning Java Language Features* (ISBN 978-1-4302-6658-7). For now, you can think of a CharSequence as an object that represents a readable sequence of characters. String, StringBuffer, and StringBuilder, to name a few, are instances of CharSequence. They provide read-only methods to read some properties and the content of the sequence of characters represented by them. In the API documentation for the String class, you will see arguments of many methods declared as CharSequence. You can always pass a String, a StringBuilder, or a StringBuffer where a CharSequence is required.

Creating String Objects

The String class contains many constructors that can be used to create a String object. The default constructor lets you create a String object with an empty string as its content. For example, the following statement creates an empty String object and assigns its reference to the emptyStr variable:

```
String emptyStr = new String();
```

The String class contains a constructor, which takes another String object as an argument.

```
String str1 = new String();
String str2 = new String(str1); // Passing a String as an argument
```

Now str1 represents the same sequence of characters as str2. At this point, both str1 and str2 represent an empty string. You can also pass a string literal to this constructor.

```
String str3 = new String("");
String str4 = new String("Have fun!");
```

After these two statements are executed, str3 will refer to a String object, which has an empty string (a sequence of zero characters) as its content, and str4 will refer to a String object, which has "Have fun!" as its content.

Length of a String

The String class contains a length() method that returns the number of characters in the String object. Note that the length() method returns the number of characters in the string, not the number of bytes used by the string. The return type of the method length() is int. Listing 11-1 demonstrates how to compute the length of a string. The length of an empty string is zero.

Listing 11-1. Knowing the Length of a String

```
// StringLength.java
package com.jdojo.string;

public class StringLength {
        public static void main (String[] args) {
                // Create two string objects
                String str1 = new String() ;
                String str2 = new String("Hello") ;

                // Get the length of str1 and str2
                int len1 = str1.length();
                int len2 = str2.length();

                // Display the length of str1 and str2
                System.out.println("Length of \"" + str1 + "\" = " + len1);
                System.out.println("Length of \"" + str2 + "\" = " + len2);
        }
}
```

```
Length of "" = 0
Length of "Hello" = 5
```

String Literals Are String Objects

All string literals are objects of the String class. The compiler replaces all string literals with a reference to a String object. Consider the following statement:

```
String str1 = "Hello";
```

When this statement is compiled, the compiler encounters the string literal "Hello", and it creates a String object with "Hello" as its content. For all practical purposes, a string literal is the same as a String object. Wherever you can use the reference of a String object, you can also use a String literal. All methods of the String class can be used with String literals directly. For example, to compute the length of String literals, you can write

```
int len1 =  "".length();      // len1 is equal to 0
int len2 =  "Hello".length(); // len2 is equal to 5
```

String Objects Are Immutable

String objects are immutable. That is, you cannot modify the content of a String object. This leads to an advantage that strings can be shared without worrying about them getting modified. For example, if you need two objects of the String class with the identical content (the same sequence of characters), you can create one String object and you can use its reference at both places. Sometimes the immutability of strings in Java is misunderstood, typically by beginners. Consider the following piece of code:

```
String str;
str = new String("Just a string");
str = new String("Another string");
```

Here, str is a reference variable that can refer to any String object. In other words, str can be changed and it is mutable. However, the String object, which str refers to, is always immutable. This scenario is depicted in Figure 11-1 and Figure 11-2.

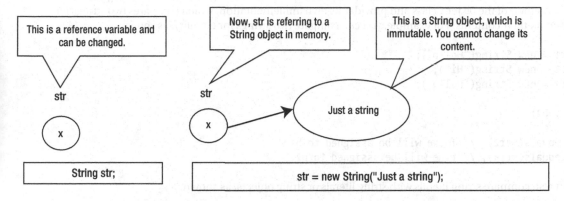

Figure 11-1. *A String reference variable and a String object*

Figure 11-2. *Assigning a different String object reference to a String variable*

If you do not want str to refer to any other String object after it has been initialized, you can declare it final, like so:

```
final String str = new String("str cannot refer to other object");
str = new String("Let us try"); // A compile-time error. str is final
```

■ **Tip**   It is the String object in memory that is immutable, not the reference variable of the String type. If you want a reference variable to refer to the same String object in memory all the time, you must declare the reference variable final.

Comparing Two Strings

You may want to compare the sequence of characters represented by two String objects. The String class overrides the equals() method of the Object class and provides its own implementation, which compares two strings for equality based on their contents. For example, you can compare two strings for equality, as shown:

```
String str1 = new String("Hello");
String str2 = new String("Hi");
String str3 = new String("Hello");

boolean b1, b2;

b1 = str1.equals(str2); // false will be assigned to b1
b2 = str1.equals(str3); // true will be assigned to b2
```

You can also compare string literals with string literals or string objects, as shown:

```
b1 = str1.equals("Hello");   // true will be assigned to b1
b2 = "Hello".equals(str1);   // true will be assigned to b2
b1 = "Hello".equals("Hi");   // false will be assigned to b1
```

Recall that the == operator always compares the references of two objects in memory. For example, str1 == str2 and str1 == str3 will return false, because str1, str2 and str3 are references of three different String objects in memory. Note that the new operator always returns a new object reference.

If you want to compare two strings based on the Unicode values of their characters, you can use the compareTo() method. Its signature is

```
public int compareTo(String anotherString)
```

It returns an integer, which can be 0 (zero), a positive integer, or a negative integer. It compares the Unicode values of the corresponding characters of two strings. If any two characters differ in their Unicode values, the method returns the difference between the Unicode values of those two characters. For example, "a".compareTo("b") will return –1. The Unicode value is 97 for a and 98 for b. It returns the difference 97 – 98, which is –1. The following are examples of string comparisons:

```
"abc".compareTo("abc") will return 0
"abc".compareTo("xyz") will return -23 (value of 'a' - 'x')
"xyz".compareTo("abc") will return 23 (value of 'x' - 'a')
```

It is very important to note that the compareTo() method compares two strings based on the Unicode values of their characters. The comparison may not be the same as the dictionary order comparison. This is fine for English and some other languages in which the Unicode values for characters are in the same order as the dictionary order of characters. This method should not be used to compare two strings in languages where the dictionary order of characters may not be the same as their Unicode values. To perform language-based string comparisons, you should use the compare() method of the java.text.Collator class instead. Please refer the "Locale-Insensitive String Comparison" section in this chapter to learn how to use java.text.Collator class.

The program shown in Listing 11-2 demonstrates the string comparisons.

Listing 11-2. Comparing Strings

```java
// StringComparison.java
package com.jdojo.string;

public class StringComparison {
        public static void main(String[] args) {
                String apple = new String("Apple") ;
                String orange = new String("Orange") ;

                System.out.println(apple.equals(orange));
                System.out.println(apple.equals(apple));
                System.out.println(apple == apple);
                System.out.println(apple == orange);
                System.out.println(apple.compareTo(apple));
                System.out.println(apple.compareTo(orange));
        }
}
```

```
false
true
true
false
0
-14
```

String Pool

Java maintains a pool of all string literals in order to minimize the memory usage and for better performance. It creates a String object in the string pool for every string literal it finds in a program. When it encounters a string literal, it looks for a string object in the string pool with the identical content. If it does not find a match in the string pool, it creates a new String object with that content and adds it to the string pool. Finally, it replaces the string literal with the reference of the newly created String object in pool. If it finds a match in the string pool, it replaces the string literal with the reference of the String object found in the pool.

Let's discuss this scenario with an example.

```java
String str1 = new String("Hello");
```

When Java encounters the string literal "Hello" in the program, it tries to find a match in the string pool. If there is no String object with the content "Hello" in the string pool, a new String object with "Hello" content is created and added to the string pool. The string literal "Hello" will be replaced by the reference of that new String object in the string pool. Because you are using the new operator, Java will create another string object on the heap. Therefore, two String objects will be created in this case. Consider the following code:

```
String str1 = new String("Hello");
String str2 = new String("Hello");
```

How many String objects will be created by this code? Suppose when the first statement is executed, "Hello" was not in the string pool. Therefore, the first statement will create two String objects. When the second statement is executed, the string literal "Hello" will be found in the string pool. This time, "Hello" will be replaced by the reference of the already existing object in the pool. However, Java will create a new String object because you are using the new operator in the second statement. The above two statements will create three String objects assuming that "Hello" was not there in the string pool. If "Hello" was already in the string pool when these statements started executing, only two String objects will be created.

Consider the following statements:

```
String str1 = new String("Hello");
String str2 = new String("Hello");
String str3 = "Hello";
String str4 = "Hello";
```

What will be the value returned by str1 == str2? It will be false because the new operator always creates a new object in memory and returns the reference of that new object.

What will be the value returned by str2 == str3? It will be false again. This needs a little explanation. Note that the new operator always creates a new object. Therefore, str2 has a reference to a new object in memory. Because "Hello" has already been encountered while executing the first statement, it exists in the string pool and str3 refers to the String object with content "Hello" in the string pool. Therefore, str2 and str3 refer to two different objects and str2 == str3 returns false.

What will be the value returned by str3 == str4? It will be true. Note that "Hello" has already been added to the string pool when the first statement was executed. The third statement will assign a reference of a String object from the string pool to str3. The fourth statement will assign the same object reference from the string pool to str4. In other words, both str3 and str4 are referring to the same String object in the string pool. The == operator compares the two references; therefore, str3 == str4 returns true.

Consider another example.

```
String s1 = "Have" + "Fun";
String s2 = "HaveFun";
```

Will s1 == s2 return true? Yes, it will return true. When a String object is created in a compile-time constant expression, it is also added to the string pool. Since "Have" + "Fun" is a compile-time constant expression, the resulting string, "HaveFun", will be added to the string pool. Therefore, s1 and s2 will refer to the same object in the string pool.

All compile-time constant string literals are added to the string pool. Consider the following examples to clarify this rule:

```
final String constStr = "Constant";   // constStr is a constant
String varStr = "Variable";           // varStr is not a constant

// "Constant is pooled" will be added to the string pool
String s1 = constStr + " is pooled";
```

```
// Concatenated string will not be added to the string pool
String s2 = varStr + " is not pooled";
```

After executing the above snippet of code, "Constant is pooled" == s1 will return true, whereas "Variable is not pooled" == s2 will return false.

■ **Tip** All string literals and string literals resulting from compile-time constant expressions are added to the string pool.

You can add a String object to the string pool using its intern() method. The intern() method returns the reference of the object from string pool if it finds a match. Otherwise, it adds a new String object to the string pool and returns the reference of the new object. For example, in the previous snippet of code, s2 refers to a String object, which has the content "Variable is not pooled". You can add this String object to the string pool by writing

```
// Will add the content of s2 to the string pool and return the reference
// of the string object from the pool
s2 = s2.intern();
```

Now "Variable is not pooled" == s2 will return true because you have already called the intern() method on s2 and its content has been pooled.

■ **Tip** The String class maintains a pool of strings internally. All string literals are added to the pool automatically. You can add your own strings to the pool by invoking the intern() method on the String objects. You cannot access the pool directly. There is no way to remove string objects from the pool, except exiting and restarting the app.

String Operations

This section describes some of the frequently used operations on String objects.

Getting the Character at an Index

You can use the charAt() method to get a character at a particular index from a String object. The index starts at zero as depicted in Table 11-1.

Table 11-1. *Index of a Character in a String Object*

Index ->	0	1	2	3	4
Character ->	H	E	L	L	O

Note that the index of the first character H is 0 (zero), the second character E is 1, and so on. The index of the last character O is 4, which is equal to the length of the string "Hello" minus 1.

The following snippet of code will print the index value and the character at each index in a string of "HELLO":

```
String str = "HELLO";

// Get the length of string
int len = str.length();

// Loop through all characters and print their indexes
for (int i = 0; i < len; i++) {
        System.out.println(str.charAt(i) + " has index " + i);
}
```

```
H has index 0
E has index 1
L has index 2
L has index 3
O has index 4
```

Testing Strings for Equality

If you want to compare two strings for equality ignoring their cases, you can use the equalsIgnoreCase() method. If you want to perform a case-sensitive comparison for equality, you need to use the equals() method instead as previously described.

```
String str1 = "Hello";
String str2 = "HELLO";

if (str1.equalsIgnoreCase(str2)) {
        System.out.println ("Ignoring case str1 and str2 are equal");
}
else {
        System.out.println("Ignoring case str1 and str2 are not equal");
}

if (str1.equals(str2)) {
        System.out.println("str1 and str2 are equal");
}
else {
        System.out.println("str1 and str2 are not equal");
}
```

```
Ignoring case str1 and str2 are equal
str1 and str2 are not equal
```

Testing a String to be Empty

Sometimes you need to test whether a `String` object is empty. The length of an empty string is zero. There are three ways to check for an empty string:

- Use the `isEmpty()` method.
- Use the `equals()` method.
- Get the length of the `String` and check if it is zero.

The following snippet of code shows how to use the three methods:

```
String str1 = "Hello";
String str2 = "";

// Using the isEmpty() method
boolean empty1 = str1.isEmpty(); // Assigns false to empty1
boolean empty2 = str2.isEmpty(); // Assigns true to empty1

// Using the equals() method
boolean empty3 = "".equals(str1); // Assigns false to empty3
boolean empty4 = "".equals(str2); // Assigns true to empty4

// Comparing length of the string with 0
boolean empty5 = str1.length() == 0; // Assigns false to empty5
boolean empty6 = str2.length() == 0; // Assigns true to empty6
```

Which of the above methods is the best? The first method may seem more readable as the method name suggests what is intended. However, the second method is preferred as it handles the comparison with `null` gracefully. The first and third methods throw a `NullPointerException` if the string is `null`. The second method returns false when the string is `null`, for example, `"".equals(null)` returns `false`.

Changing the Case

To convert the content of a string to lower and upper case, you can use the `toLowerCase()` and the `toUpperCase()` methods, respectively. For example, `"Hello".toUpperCase()` will return the string `"HELLO"`, whereas `"Hello".toLowerCase()` will return the string `"hello"`.

Recall that `String` objects are immutable. When you use the `toLowerCase()` or `toUpperCase()` method on a `String` object, the content of the original object is not modified. Rather, Java creates a new `String` object with the identical content as the original `String` object with the cases of the original characters changed. The following snippet of code creates three `String` objects:

```
String str1 = new String("Hello"); // str1 contains "Hello"
String str2 = str1.toUpperCase();  // str2 contains "HELLO"
String str3 = str1.toLowerCase();  // str3 contains "hello"
```

Searching for a String

You can get the index of a character or a string within another string using the indexOf() and lastIndexOf() methods. For example,

```
String str = new String("Apple");

int index;
index = str.indexOf('p');       // index will have a value of 1
index = str.indexOf("pl");      // index will have a value of 2
index = str.lastIndexOf('p');   // index will have a value of 2
index = str.lastIndexOf("pl");  // index will have a value of 2
index = str.indexOf("k");       // index will have a value of -1
```

The indexOf() method starts searching for the character or the string from the start of the string and returns the index of the first match. The lastIndexOf() method matches the character or the string from the end and returns the index of the first match. If the character or string is not found in the string, these methods return –1.

Representing Values as Strings

The String class has an overloaded valueOf() static method. It can be used to get the string representation of the values of any primitive data type or any object. For example,

```
String s1 = String.valueOf('C');  // s1 has "C"
String s2 = String.valueOf("10"); // s2 has "10"
String s3 = String.valueOf(true); // s3 has "true"
String s4 = String.valueOf(1969); // s4 has "1969"
```

Getting a Substring

You can use the substring() method to get a sub-part of a string. This method is overloaded. One version takes the start index as the parameter and returns a substring beginning at the start index to the end of string. Another version takes the start index and the end index as parameters. It returns the substring beginning at the start index and one less than the end index. For example,

```
String s1 = "Hello".substring(1);    // s1 has "ello"
String s2 = "Hello".substring(1, 4); // s2 has "ell"
```

Trimming a String

You can use the trim() method to remove all leading and trailing whitespaces and control characters from a string. In fact, the trim() method removes all leading and trailing characters from the string, which have Unicode value less than \u0020 (decimal 32). For example,

- "   hello   ".trim() will return "hello"
- "hello   ".trim() will return "hello"
- "\n   \r \t   hello\n\n\n\r\r" will return "hello"

Note that the trim() method removes only leading and trailing whitespaces. It does not remove any whitespace or control characters if they appear in the middle of the string. For example,

- " he\nllo   ".trim() will return "he\nllo" because \n is inside the string.

- "h ello".trim() will return "h ello" because the space is inside the string.

Replacing Part of a String

The replace() method takes an old character and a new character as arguments. It returns a new String object by replacing all occurrences of the old character by the new character. For example,

```
String oldStr = new String("tooth");

// o in oldStr will be replaced by e. newStr will contain "teeth"
String newStr = oldStr.replace('o', 'e');
```

Matching Start and End of a String

The startsWith() checks if the string starts with the specified argument, whereas endsWith() checks if the string ends with the specified string argument. Both methods return a boolean value.

```
String str = "This is a Java program";

// Test str, if it starts with "This"
if (str.startsWith("This")){
        System.out.println("String starts with This");
}
else {
        System.out.println("String does not start with This");
}

// Test str, if it ends with "program"
if (str.endsWith("program")) {
        System.out.println("String ends with program");
}
else {
        System.out.println("String does not end with program");
}
```

```
String starts with This
String ends with program
```

Splitting and Joining Strings

It is often useful to split a string around a specified delimiter and join multiple strings into one string using a specified delimiter.

Use the split() method to split a string into multiple strings. Splitting is performed using a delimiter. The split() method returns an array of String. You will learn about arrays in Chapter 15. However, you will use it in this section just to complete the operations of strings.

■ **Note** The split() method takes a regular expression that defines a pattern as a delimiter. I will discuss regular expressions in Chapter 14.

```
String str = "AL,FL,NY,CA,GA";

// Split str using a comma as the delimiter
String[] parts = str.split(",");

// Print the the string and its parts
System.out.println(str);

for(String part : parts) {
        System.out.println(part);
}
```

```
AL,FL,NY,CA,GA
AL
FL
NY
CA
GA
```

Java 8 adds a static join() method to the String class that joins multiple strings into one string. It is overloaded.

- String join(CharSequence delimiter, CharSequence... elements)
- String join(CharSequence delimiter, Iterable<? extends CharSequence> elements)

The first version takes a delimiter and a sequence of strings to be joined. The second version takes a delimiter and an Iterable, for example, a List or Set. The following snippet of code uses the first version to join some strings:

```
// Join some strings using a comma as the delimiter
String str = String.join(",", "AL", "FL", "NY", "CA", "GA");
System.out.println(str);
```

```
AL,FL,NY,CA,GA
```

Strings in a switch Statement

I discussed the switch statement in Chapter 5. Java 7 added support for strings in a switch statement. The switch-expression uses a String type. If the switch-expression is null, a NullPointerException is thrown. The case labels must be String literals. You cannot use String variables in the case labels. The following is an example of using a String in a switch statement, which will print "Turn on" on the standard output:

```
String status = "on";
switch(status) {
        case "on":
                System.out.println("Turn on"); // Will execute this
                break;
        case "off":
                System.out.println("Turn off");
                break;
        default:
                System.out.println("Unknown command");
                break;
}
```

The switch statement for strings compares the switch-expression with case labels as if the equals() method of the String class has been invoked. In the above example, status.equals("on") will be invoked to test if the first case block should be executed. Note that the equals() method of the String class performs a case-sensitive string comparison. It means that the switch statement that uses strings is case-sensitive.

The following switch statement will print "Unknown command" on the standard output, because the switch-expression "ON" in uppercase will not match the first case label "on" in lowercase.

```
String status = "ON";
switch(status) {
        case "on":
                System.out.println("Turn on");
                break;
        case "off":
                System.out.println("Turn off");
                break;
        default:
                System.out.println("Unknown command"); // Will execute this
                break;
}
```

As good programming practice, you need to do the following two things before executing a switch statement with strings:

- Check if the switch-expression for the switch statement is null. If it is null, do not execute the switch statement.

- If you want to perform a case-insensitive comparison in a switch statement, you need to convert the switch-expression to lowercase or uppercase and use lowercase or uppercase in the case labels accordingly.

You can rewrite the above switch statement example as shown in Listing 11-3, which takes care of the above two suggestions.

Listing 11-3. Using Strings in a switch Statement

```java
// StringInSwitch.java
package com.jdojo.string;

public class StringInSwitch {
        public static void main(String[] args) {
                operate("on");
                operate("off");
                operate("ON");
                operate("Nothing");
                operate("OFF");
                operate(null);
        }

        public static void operate(String status) {
                // Check for null
                if (status == null) {
                        System.out.println("status cannot be null.");
                        return;
                }

                // Convert to lowercase
                status = status.toLowerCase();

                switch (status) {
                        case "on":
                                System.out.println("Turn on");
                                break;
                        case "off":
                                System.out.println("Turn off");
                                break;
                        default:
                                System.out.println("Unknown command");
                                break;
                }
        }
}
```

```
Turn on
Turn off
Turn on
Unknown command
Turn off
status cannot be null.
```

Testing a String for Palindrome

If you are an experienced programmer, you may skip this section. This is meant to serve as a simple exercise for beginners.

A palindrome is a word, a verse, a sentence, or a number that reads the same in forward and backward directions. For example, "Able was I ere I saw Elba" and 1991 are examples of palindromes. Let's write a method that will accept a string as an argument and test if that string is a palindrome. The method will return true if the string is a palindrome. Otherwise, it will return false. You will use some methods of the String class that you learned in the previous sections. The following is the description of the steps to be performed inside the method.

Assume that the number of characters in the input string is n. You need to compare the character at indexes 0 and (n-1), 1 and (n -2), 2 and (n - 3), and so on. Note that if you continue the comparison, in the end, you will compare the character at the index (n-1) with the character at index 0, which you have already compared in the beginning. You need to compare the characters only halfway through. If all comparisons for equality returns true, the string is a palindrome.

The number of characters in a string may be odd or even. Comparing characters only halfway works in both cases. The middle of a string varies depending on whether the length of the string is odd or even. For example, the middle of the string "FIRST" is the character R. What is the middle character in the string "SECOND"? You can say there is no middle character in it as its length is even. For this purpose, it is interesting to note that if the number of characters in the string is odd, you do not need to compare the middle character with any other character.

You need to continue the character comparison up to the half of the string length if the number of characters in the string is even, and up to half of the string *length minus one* if the number of characters is odd. You can get the numbers of comparisons to be done in both the cases by dividing the length of the string by 2. Note that the length of a string is an integer and if you divide an integer by 2, the integer division will discard the fraction part, if any, which will take care of cases with an odd number of characters. Listing 11-4 has the complete code.

Listing 11-4. Testing a String for a Palindrome

```java
// Palindrome.java
package com.jdojo.string;

public class Palindrome {
    public static void main(String[] args) {
        String str1 = "hello";
        boolean b1 = Palindrome.isPalindrome(str1);
        System.out.println(str1 + " is a palindrome: " + b1 );

        String str2 - "noon";
        boolean b2 = Palindrome.isPalindrome(str2);
        System.out.println(str2 + " is a palindrome: " + b2 );
    }

    public static boolean isPalindrome(String inputString) {
        // Check for null argument.
        if (inputString == null) {
            throw new IllegalArgumentException("String cannot be null.");
        }

        // Get the length of string
        int len = inputString.length();

        // In case of an empty string and one character strings,
        // we do not need to do any comparisions.
        // They are always palindromes.
```

```
            if (len <= 1) {
                    return true;
            }

            // Convert the string into uppercase,
            // so we can make the comparisons case insensitive
            String newStr = inputString.toUpperCase();

            // Initialize the result variable to true
            boolean result = true;

            // Get the number of comparisons to be done
            int counter = len / 2;

            // Do the comparison
            for (int i = 0; i < counter; i++) {
                    if (newStr.charAt(i)!= newStr.charAt(len - 1 - i)) {
                            // It is not a palindrome
                            result = false;

                            // Exit the loop
                            break;
                    }
            }

            return result;
        }
}
```

```
hello is a palindrome: false
noon is a palindrome: true
```

StringBuilder and StringBuffer

StringBuilder and StringBuffer are companion classes for the String class. Unlike a String, they represent a mutable sequence of characters. That is, you can change the content of StringBuilder and StringBuffer without creating a new object. You might wonder why two classes exist to represent the same thing—a mutable sequence of characters. The StringBuffer class has been part of the Java library since the beginning whereas the StringBuilder class was added in Java 5. The difference between the two lies in thread safety. StringBuffer is thread-safe and StringBuilder is not thread-safe. Most of the time, you do not need thread safety and using StringBuffer in those cases has a performance penalty. This is the reason that StringBuilder was added later. Both classes have the same methods, except that all methods in StringBuffer are synchronized. I will discuss only StringBuilder in this section. Using StringBuffer in your code would be just a matter of changing the class name.

■ **Tip** Use StringBuilder when no thread safety is needed, for example, manipulating a sequence of characters in a local variable in a method or constructor. Otherwise, use StringBuffer. Thread safety and synchronization are described in Chapter 8 in *Beginning Java Language Features* (ISBN 978-1-4302-6658-7).

You can use objects of the StringBuilder class, instead of the String class, in situations where content of a string changes frequently. Recall that because of the immutability of the String class, string manipulations using a String object result in many new String objects, which in turn degrade the performance. A StringBuilder object can be thought of as a modifiable string. It has many methods to modify its contents.

The StringBuilder class contains four constructors:

- StringBuilder()

- StringBuilder(CharSequence seq)

- StringBuilder(int capacity)

- StringBuilder(String str)

The no-args constructor creates an empty StringBuilder with a default capacity of 16.

The second constructor takes a CharSequence object as an argument. It creates a StringBuilder object, whose content is the same as the specified CharSequence.

The third constructor takes an int as argument; it creates an empty StringBuilder object whose initial capacity is the same as the specified argument. The capacity of a StringBuilder is the number of characters it can hold without allocating more space. The capacity gets adjusted automatically when additional space is needed.

The fourth constructor takes a String and creates a StringBuilder that has the same content as the specified String. The following are some examples of creating StringBuilder objects:

```
// Create an empty StringBuilder with a default initial capacity of 16 characters
StringBuilder sb1 = new StringBuilder();

// Create a StringBuilder from of a string
StringBuilder sb2 = new StringBuilder("Here is the content");

// Create an empty StringBuilder with 200 characters as the initial capacity
StringBuilder sb3 = new StringBuilder(200);
```

The append() method lets you add text to the end of the StringBuilder. It is overloaded. It takes many types of arguments. Please refer to the API documentation for the class for the complete list of all overloaded append() methods. It has other methods, for example, insert() and delete(), that let you modify its content, too.

The StringBuilder class has two properties: length and capacity. At a given point in time, their values may not be the same. Its length refers to the length of its content whereas its capacity refers to the maximum number of characters it can hold without going for new memory to be allocated. Its length can be, at most, equal to its capacity. The length() and capacity() methods return its length and capacity, respectively. For example,

```
StringBuilder sb = new StringBuilder(200);  // Capacity:200, length:0
sb.append("Hello");                          // Capacity:200, length:5
int len = sb.length();                       // len is assigned 5
int capacity = sb.capacity();                // capacity is assigned 200
```

Capacity of a StringBuilder is controlled by the runtime, whereas its length is controlled by the content you place in it. The runtime adjusts the capacity as its content is modified.

You can get the content of a StringBuilder as a String by using its toString() method.

```
// Create a String object
String s1 = new String("Hello");

// Create a StringBuilder from of the String object s1
StringBuilder sb = new StringBuilder(s1);
```

```
// Append " Java" to the StringBuilder's content
sb.append(" Java"); // Now, sb contains "Hello Java"

// Get a String from the StringBuilder
String s2 = sb.toString(); // s2 contains "Hello Java"
```

Unlike String, StringBuilder has a setLength() method, which takes its new length as an argument. If the new length is greater than the old length, the extra positions are filled with null characters (a null character is \u0000). If the new length is less than the old length, its content is truncated to fit in the new length.

```
// Length is 5
StringBuilder sb = new StringBuilder("Hello");

// Now the length is 7 with last two characters as null character '\u0000'
sb.setLength(7);

// Now the length is 2 and the content is "He"
sb.setLength(2);
```

The StringBuilder class has a reverse() method, which replaces its contents with the same sequence of characters, but in reverse order.

Listing 11-5 illustrates the use of some of the methods of the StringBuilder class.

Listing 11-5. Using a StringBuilder Object

```
// StringBuilderTest.java
package com.jdojo.string;

public class StringBuilderTest {
        public static void main(String[] args) {
                // Create an empty StringNuffer
                StringBuilder sb = new StringBuilder();
                printDetails(sb);

                // Append "blessings"
                sb.append("blessings");
                printDetails(sb);

                // Insert "Good " in the beginning
                sb.insert(0, "Good ");
                printDetails(sb);

                // Delete the first o
                sb.deleteCharAt(1);
                printDetails(sb);

                // Append " be with you"
                sb.append(" be with you");
                printDetails(sb);

                // Set the length to 3
                sb.setLength(3);
                printDetails(sb);
```

```
                // Reverse the content
                sb.reverse();
                printDetails(sb);
        }

        public static void printDetails(StringBuilder sb) {
                System.out.println("Content: \"" + sb + "\"");
                System.out.println("Length: " + sb.length());
                System.out.println("Capacity: " + sb.capacity());

                // Print an empty line to separate results
                System.out.println();
        }
}
```

```
Content: ""
Length: 0
Capacity: 16

Content: "blessings"
Length: 9
Capacity: 16

Content: "Good blessings"
Length: 14
Capacity: 16

Content: "God blessings"
Length: 13
Capacity: 16

Content: "God blessings be with you"
Length: 25
Capacity: 34

Content: "God"
Length: 3
Capacity: 34

Content: "doG"
Length: 3
Capacity: 34
```

String Concatenation Operator (+)

You will often use the + operator to concatenate a strings, and a primitive type value or an object to another string. For example,

```
String str = "X" + "Y" + 12.56;
```

If concatenation were performed by creating intermediate string objects, the concatenation operation would create a big overhead. To optimize the string concatenation operation, the compiler replaces the string concatenation by a statement, which uses a StringBuilder. Because a StringBuilder object is modifiable, only one StringBuilder object needs to be created. The compiler replaces the above statement with the following one:

```
String str = new StringBuilder().append("X").append("Y").append(12.56).toString();
```

Note the use of the toString() method at the end of this statement. It is used to convert the final content of a StringBuilder to a String. It is also important to note that such cascaded method calls are possible because the append() method of StringBuilder returns a reference to itself.

Language-Sensitive String Comparison

The String class compares strings based on the Unicode values of their characters. Sometimes you may want to compare strings based on the dictionary order instead.

Use the compare() method of the java.text.Collator class to perform language-sensitive (dictionary order) string comparisons. The method takes two strings to be compared as arguments. It returns 0 if two strings are the same, 1 if the first string comes after the second, and -1 if the first string comes before the second. Listing 11-6 illustrates the use of the Collator class.

Listing 11-6. Language-Sensitive String Comparisons

```
// CollatorStringComparison.java
package com.jdojo.string;

import java.text.Collator;
import java.util.Locale;

public class CollatorStringComparison {
    public static void main(String[] args) {
        // Create a Locale object for US
        Locale USLocale = new Locale("en", "US");

        // Get collator instance for US
        Collator c = Collator.getInstance(USLocale);
        String str1 = "cat";
        String str2 = "Dog";

        int diff = c.compare(str1, str2);

        System.out.print("Comparing using Collator class: ");
        print(diff, str1, str2);
```

```
            System.out.print("Comparing using String class: ");
            diff = str1.compareTo(str2);
            print(diff, str1, str2);
    }

    public static void print(int diff, String str1, String str2) {
            if (diff > 0) {
                    System.out.println(str1 + " comes after " + str2);
            }
            else if (diff < 0) {
                    System.out.println(str1 + " comes before " + str2);
            }
            else {
                    System.out.println(str1 + " and " + str2 + " are the same.");
            }
    }
}
```

```
Comparing using Collator class: cat comes before Dog
Comparing using String class: cat comes after Dog
```

The program also shows the comparison of the same two strings using the String class. Note that the word "cat" comes before the word "Dog" in the dictionary order. The Collator class uses their dictionary orders to compare them. However, the String class compares the Unicode value of the first character of "cat", which is 99, and the first character of "Dog", which is 68. Based on these two values, the String class determines that "Dog" comes before "cat". The output confirms the two different ways of comparing strings.

Summary

In this chapter, you learned about String, StringBuilder, and StringBuffer classes. A String represents an immutable sequence of characters whereas a StringBuilder and StringBuffer represent a mutable sequence of characters. StringBuilder and StringBuffer work the same way, except the latter is thread-safe and the former is not.

The String class provides several methods to operate on its content. Whenever you obtain a part of the content from a String, a new String object is created. The String class compares two strings based on the Unicode values of their characters. Use java.text.Collator class to compare strings in dictionary order. From Java 7 and on, you can use strings in a switch statement.

CHAPTER 12

■■■

Dates and Times

In this chapter, you will learn

- What the new Date-Time API is

- About the design principles behind the Date-Time API

- About the evolution of timekeeping, time zones, and Daylight Saving Time

- About the ISO-8601 standard for date, time, and date-time keeping

- How to represent date, time, and date-time using the Date-Time API classes and how to query, adjust, format, and parse them

- How to use the legacy Date-Time API

- How to interoperate between the legacy and new Date-Time APIs

The Date-Time API

Java 8 introduced a new Date-Time API to work with date and time. In this chapter, I will refer to the date- and time-related classes available before Java 8 as the legacy Date-Time API. The legacy Date-Time API includes classes like Date, Calendar, GregorianCalendar, etc. They are in the java.util and java.sql packages. The Date class has existed since the inception of JDK; others were added in JDK 1.1.

Why did we need a new Date-Time API? The simple answer is that the designers of the legacy Date-Time API did not get it right in two attempts. To list a few of the problems, some of the issues with the legacy Date-Time API are

- A date always had two components: a date and a time. If you needed just a date without any time information, you had no choice. Developers used to set the time to midnight in a date object to represent a date-only date, which was incorrect for several reasons. The same argument is valid for storing only time.

- A datetime was simply stored as the number of milliseconds elapsed since January 1, 1970 midnight UTC.

- Manipulating dates were as complex as you can think; the year field in a Date object was stored as an offset from 1900; months ran from 0 to 11, not from 1 to 12, as humans are used to conceptualizing them.

- Legacy Date-Time classes were mutable and therefore not thread-safe.

Is the third time the charm? Here is a third attempt to provide a correct, powerful, and extensible Date-Time API. At least, so we say at the time of this writing! The new API is not a free ride, however. It has a steep learning curve if you want to use its full potential. It consists of about 80 classes. Do not worry about the big number of classes. They have been carefully designed and named. Once you understand the thoughts behind its design, it's relatively easy to figure out the name of a class and the methods that you need to use in a particular situation. As a developer, you need to understand about 15 classes to use the new Date-Time API effectively in your daily programming.

Design Principles

Before you start learning the details of the new Date-Time API, you will need to understand a few basic concepts about dates and times. The new Date-Time API is based on ISO-8601 date-time standards. A Java date-time framework named Joda-Time inspired the new API. If you have used Joda-Time before, you will be able to learn the new Date-Time API quickly. You can find the details of the Joda-Time project at http://joda-time.sourceforge.net.

The new API makes a distinction between how dates and times are used by machines and humans. Machines deal with time as continual ticks as a single incrementing number measured in seconds, milliseconds, etc. Humans use a calendar system to deal with time in terms of year, month, day, hour, minute, and second. The Date-Time API has a separate set of classes to deal with machine-based time and calendar-based human time. It lets you convert machine-based time to human-based time and vice versa.

The legacy Date-Time API has been around for over 15 years. It is very likely that you will encounter legacy date-time classes while working with existing applications. The legacy date-time classes have been retrofitted to work seamlessly with the new classes. When you write new code, use the new Date-Time API classes. When you receive objects of legacy classes as input, convert the legacy objects into new date-time objects, and use the new Date-Time API.

The new Date-Time API consists of mostly immutable classes. Because the new API is extensible, you are advised to create immutable classes, whenever possible, to extend the API. An operation on a date-time object creates a new date-time object. This pattern makes it easy to chain method calls.

Classes in the Date-Time API do not provide public constructors. They allow you to create their objects by providing static factory methods named of(), ofXxx(), and from(). The new API uses a well-defined naming convention for naming methods. Each class in the API has several methods. Knowing the method-naming convention lets you find the right method for your purpose easily. I will discuss the method-naming convention shortly in a separate section.

A Quick Example

Let's look at an example of working with dates and times using the new Date-Time API. An instance of the LocalDate class represents a local date without a time; an instance of the LocalTime class represents a local time without a date; an instance of the LocalDateTime class represents a local date and time; an instance of the ZonedDateTime class represents date and time with a time zone.

A LocalDate and a LocalTime are also called partials as they do not represent an instance on the timeline; they are not aware of changes in Daylight Saving Time. A ZonedDateTime represents a point in time in a given time zone that can be converted to an instant on the timeline; it is aware of Daylight Saving Time. For example, adding four hours to a LocalTime of 1 AM will give you another LocalTime of 5 AM irrespective of the date and location. However, if you add four hours to a ZonedDateTime representing 1 AM on March 9, 2014 in the Chicago/America time zone, it will give you 6 AM time on March 9, 2014 in the same time zone, as the clock is moved forward by one hour at 2 AM on that day because of Daylight Saving Time. Airline applications use instances of the ZonedDateTime class to store departure time and arrival time of flights.

In the Date-Time API, classes representing date, time, and datetime have a now() method that returns the current date, time, or datetime, respectively. The following snippet of code creates date-time objects representing a date, a time, and a combination of them with and without a time zone:

```
LocalDate dateOnly = LocalDate.now();
LocalTime timeOnly = LocalTime.now();
LocalDateTime dateTime = LocalDateTime.now();
ZonedDateTime dateTimeWithZone = ZonedDateTime.now();
```

A LocalDate is not time zone-aware. It will be interpreted differently in different time zones at the same moment of time. A LocalDate object is used for storing a date value when the time and time zone are not important to give a meaning to the date value, such as a birth date, the publication date of a book, etc.

You can specify the components of a datetime object using the static factory method of(). The following snippet of code creates a LocalDate by specifying the year, month, and day components of a date:

```
// Create a LocalDate representing January 12, 1968
LocalDate myBirthDate = LocalDate.of(1968, JANUARY, 12);
```

■ **Tip** A LocalDate stores a date-only value without a time and time zone. When you obtain a LocalDate using the static method now(), the system default time zone is used to get the date value.

Listing 12-1 shows how to get the current date, time, datetime, and datetime with the time zone. It also shows how to construct a date from year, month of year, and day of month. You may get a different output as it prints the current values for date and time.

Listing 12-1. Obtaining Current Date, Time, and Datetime, and Constructing a Date

```
// CurrentDateTime.java
package com.jdojo.datetime;

import java.time.LocalDate;
import java.time.LocalTime;
import java.time.LocalDateTime;
import java.time.ZonedDateTime;
import static java.time.Month.JANUARY;

public class CurrentDateTime {
        public static void main(String[] args) {
                // Get current date, time, and datetime
                LocalDate dateOnly = LocalDate.now();
                LocalTime timeOnly = LocalTime.now();
                LocalDateTime dateTime = LocalDateTime.now();
                ZonedDateTime dateTimeWithZone = ZonedDateTime.now();

                System.out.println("Current Date: " + dateOnly);
                System.out.println("Current Time: " + timeOnly);
                System.out.println("Current Date and Time: " + dateTime);
                System.out.println("Current Date, Time, and Zone: " + dateTimeWithZone);
```

```
        // Construct a birth date and time from date-time components
        LocalDate myBirthDate = LocalDate.of(1968, JANUARY, 12);
        LocalTime myBirthTime = LocalTime.of(7, 30);
        System.out.println("My Birth Date: " + myBirthDate);
        System.out.println("My Birth Time: " + myBirthTime);
    }
}
```

```
Current Date: 2014-01-02
Current Time: 13:36:43.474
Current Date and Time: 2014-01-02T13:36:43.474
Current Date, Time, and Zone: 2014-01-02T13:36:43.474-06:00[America/Chicago]
My Birth Date: 1968-01-12
My Birth Time: 07:30
```

The program uses four classes to get a local date, a time, a datetime, and a datetime with a time zone. In the legacy Date-Time API, you could have gotten a similar result using only the `Calendar` class.

The Date-Time API is pretty comprehensive. It spans about 80 classes and about 1,000 methods. It lets you represent and manipulate dates and times using different scales and different calendar systems. Several local standards and one universal standard (ISO-8601) have been in use for timekeeping. To take full advantage of the Date-Time API, you need to understand the history of timekeeping. The next few sections will give you a brief overview of different ways to measure time using calendar systems and ISO-8601 date and time standards. If you have a good understanding of these topics, you may skip these sections and continue from the "Exploring the New Date-Time API" section.

Evolution of Timekeeping

A scale is used to measure the quantity of physical things such as length of a string in meters, weight of a person in pounds, volume of water in liters, etc. Here, meters, pounds, and liters are units of measurement on a particular scale.

How do we measure time? Time is not a physical thing. To measure time, we link it to a periodic physical phenomenon, for example, swinging of a pendulum, rotation of earth on its axis, revolution of earth around the sun, oscillations of an electromagnetic signal associated with a quantum transition between two energy levels in an atom, etc. Thus, a time scale is an arrangement of events to define the duration of time.

In ancient times, events such as sunrise and sunset, which are generated because of the rotation of Earth on its axis, were used as a time scale; the unit of the time scale was day. Duration between two consecutive sunrises counted as one day.

As the human civilization progressed, devices for timekeeping were developed. Some of those were

- A sundial based on the position of the sun

- A mechanical clock based on periodic movement of a pendulum

- Finally, an atomic clock based on the properties of the caesium-133 atom

A clock is a timekeeping device that consists of two components: a frequency standard and a counter. The frequency standard in a clock is a component to obtain equally spaced periodic events to measure the length of a desired time interval. The counter (also called an accumulator or adder) counts the number of occurrences of the periodic event. For example, in a pendulum clock, the occurrence of a complete cycle of a pendulum indicates a time interval of one second, gears count the number of seconds, and the face of the clock displays the time. Even in ancient times, there was the concept of two-part clocks for timekeeping. The rotation of Earth provided the first component of the clock in terms of the periodic events of sunrise and sunset; a calendar provided the second component of the clock to count days, months, and years.

Based on Earth's rotation on its axis, several time scales, known as Universal Time (UT), have been used. Earth motion, around its axis and the sun, is irregular. Because of the irregularities in Earth motion, the length of the day from day to day and the number of the fractional days in a year from year to year vary. A solar day (also called an apparent or true solar day) is the length of time measured by observing two consecutive passings of the sun at local noon. If you use a perfect clock to observe the sun at a local meridian at noon every day, you would find that, throughout the year, position of the sun in the sky varies about four degrees (about 16 minutes in time) East-West of the local meridian. This implies that, on a particular day during a year, there could be up to 16 minutes difference between the time when it is noon shown by the clock and when the sun passes the local meridian. The difference between the clock time and the sun time, which arises because of the tilt of the earth rotation axis relative to its orbital plane and its elliptical orbit around the sun, is known as the equation of time. The time that is measured using the solar day is called apparent solar time.

The time obtained by applying corrections to the solar time to account for the equation of time is known as Universal Time Zero (UT0) or mean solar time. The midnight at prime meridian (zero degree longitude), which passes through Greenwich, England, is defined as 00 hours for UT0. The second is defined as 1/86400 of a mean solar day.

The wobbling of Earth relative to its axis of rotation is known as polar motion. UT0 corrected for polar motion yields another time scale, which is called UT1. Earth's rotational speed is not uniform. UT1 corrected for the seasonal variation in the rotational speed of Earth yields another time scale, which is called UT2.

The irregular spin rate of Earth led to another time scale known as Ephemeris Time (ET). ET was based on the period of one revolution of Earth around the sun and motion of other celestial bodies. On ET scale, the ephemeris second was defined as the fraction 1/31556925.9747 of the tropical year for 1900 January 0 at 12 hours ephemeris time. ET was replaced by Terrestrial Dynamical Time (TDT) and Barycentric Dynamical Time (TDB) in early 1980s.

The International Atomic Time (also known as TAI, for the French name Temps Atomique International) scale is an atomic time scale. The atomic second, the unit of time in the TAI scale, is defined as the duration of 9192631770 periods of the radiation corresponding to the transition between the two hyperfine levels of the ground state of the cesium-133 atom. In 1967, the definition of the atomic second became the definition of the International System of Units (SI) second. The International Bureau of Weights and Measures (BIPM) is the official timekeeper of atomic time. There are 65 laboratories with over 230 atomic clocks contributing to the TAI scale. Each clock contributing to TAI is assigned a weighting factor based on its performance. The weighted average of all the contributing atomic clocks gives TAI.

Why do we use many atomic clocks to measure TAI? One clock may fail and stop measuring time. Even atomic clocks are affected by environmental changes. To avoid such failures and inaccuracies, several atomic clocks are used to track TAI.

On January 1, 1972, Coordinated Universal Time (UTC) was adopted as the official time scale for the world for all civil purposes. UTC and atomic clocks run at the same rate. As BIPM counts the seconds on TAI scale, astronomers continue to measure time using the rotation of earth on its axis. Astronomical time is compared to UTC, and if they differ by more than 0.9 seconds, a leap second is added or subtracted to UTC to keep the time scales UT0 and UTC as close as possible. International Earth Rotation Service (IERS) makes the decision to introduce a leap second to UTC.

At any time, UTC differs from TAI by an integral number of seconds. The relation between UTC and TAI may be given as follows:

```
UTC = TAI - (algebraic sum of leap seconds)
```

As of July 1, 2012, 35 leap seconds have been added to UTC. So far, no leap second has been subtracted from UTC. Therefore, on July 1, 2012 and until another leap second is introduced, UTC and TAI are related as follows:

```
UTC = TAI - 35
```

You might think, because we have been adding leap seconds to UTC, UTC should be ahead of TAI. That is not true. Adding a leap second to UTC makes that hour on UTC scale 61 seconds long instead of 60 seconds. TAI is a continuous time scale; it keeps ticking all the time. When UTC completes the 61st second of the hour, TAI has moved to the first second in the next hour. Thus, UTC lags TAI when a leap second is added to it. Similar logic, but in reverse order, applies when a leap second is subtracted from UTC. If, at any time in future, the leap seconds added to and subtracted from UTC become equal, UTC and TAI will read the same time.

UTC represents the time of day at the prime meridian (zero degree longitude) on Earth, which passes through Greenwich, England. UTC is based on a 24-hour clock with the day starting at 00 hours midnight. UTC is also known as Zulu time. The ISO-8601 standard uses the letter Z as the UTC of day designator; for example, the UTC of day 19 minutes and 23 seconds past 15 hours is written as 15:19:23Z.

You're not done with UTC yet! I will discuss two more versions of UTC: Simplified UTC and UTC with Smoothed Leap Seconds (UTC-SLS).

Humans are used to understanding a solar day in terms of a 24-hour period: each hour consisting of 60 minutes and each minute consisting of 60 seconds. A solar day consists of 86400 seconds. On the UTC scale, a solar day may also consist of 86399 or 86401 seconds because of a leap second. For easier understanding for the common user, most computer systems ignore the leap seconds on the UTC scale. The UTC scale that ignores the leap seconds is called a simplified-UTC scale.

■ **Tip** To meet expectations of most users, the new Java Date-Time API uses simplified UTC, where leap seconds are ignored, making all days having the same number of 86400 seconds.

When the leap second is added or subtracted in UTC, it creates a gap or overlap of one second in the time scale at the end of the day. UTC-SLS is a proposed standard for handling a UTC leap second. Instead of introducing a leap second at the end of a day, UTC-SLS proposes to perform a smooth adjustment of 1 second over last 1000 seconds of the day by changing the rate of the clock by 0.1%. On a day when a leap second is added to UTC, UTC-SLS will make the last 1000 seconds of that day 1001 milliseconds long; thus, reducing the rate of the UTC-SLS clock from 23:43:21 to 24:00:00 by 0.1%. On a day when a leap second is added to UTC, UTC-SLS will make the last 1000 seconds of that day as 999 milliseconds long; thus, increasing the rate of the UTC-SLS clock from 23:43:19 to 24:00:00 by 0.1%.

Finally, there are proposals to have universal and monotonous civil time by getting rid of the leap seconds from UTC. Some have also proposed to replace the UTC leap seconds by leap hours!

Time Zones and Daylight Saving Time

When it was midnight of April 20, 2012 UTC, what local time was it in New Delhi, India and Chicago, USA? It was 5:30 in the morning of April 20, 2012 in New Delhi, India, and 7:00 in the evening of April 19, 2012 in Chicago, USA. How do we determine local time at a place? Wouldn't it be nice to have only one time for the entire world? If it is midnight UTC, it is midnight everywhere in the world. Maybe this would have been a good idea in the past as human minds are capable of getting used to new ideas over time through practice. Local time in a region is set such that a day starts at 00 hours, which is midnight. Therefore, 00 hours is midnight in New Delhi as well as Chicago.

Geographically, the world may be divided into 24 longitudinal bands, each covering a 15-degree range of longitude starting at the prime meridian; each band represents a one-hour time zone. The area covered by a time zone will observe the same time.

Humans are divided more politically than geographically. In this world, our political differences always override the geographical similarity! Sometimes an imaginary border separating two countries or states makes people observe different times on each side of the border.

In practice, time zones have been divided based on political regions: countries and regions within countries. Local time in each time zone is an offset from UTC. The offset, the difference in UTC and local time in a time zone, is called a zone offset. The regions east of the prime meridian use a positive zone offset. A negative zone offset is used for regions west to the prime meridian. The zone offset is expressed in hours and minutes such as +5:30 hours, -10:00 hours, etc. For example, India uses a zone offset of +5:30 hours; therefore, you can add 5 hours and 30 minutes to UTC to get Indian local time. You may think that the value for a zone offset is fixed for a time zone. Alas, we, the civilized and advanced humans, were so simple in timekeeping!

Some countries have more than one time zone. For example, USA has five time zones: Alaska, Pacific, Mountain, Central, and Eastern; India has only one time zone. In USA, when the local time in Mobile, Alabama (Central time zone) is 7:00 AM, it is 5:00 AM local time in Los Angeles, California (Pacific Time zone). Every part of India, because of only one time zone, observes the same time.

The zone offset for some time zones vary in a year. For example, in Chicago, USA (called Central time zone), the zone offset is -5:00 hours in summer and -6:00 hours in winter. Most countries use a fixed zone offset. For example, India uses a +5:30 hours fixed zone offset. The rules for a time zone, governing the time when the zone offset changes, and by how much it changes, are decided by government. These rules are known as time zone rules.

The zone offset ranges between +14:00 hours to -12:00 hours. If there are only 24 hours in a day, how do we have +14 as a zone offset? The range, +14 to -12, makes it a 26 hours day! Note that some countries consist of several small islands situated far apart on two sides of the International Date Line making them a day apart. This posed problems in official communication among the islands of these countries as they observed only four common weekdays. They extended the zone offset beyond 12:00, thus moving the International Date Line for their country, to keep the whole country on one side of the International Date Line. Examples of countries using +13:00 and +14:00 hours of zone offsets are Kiribati (pronounced as kirbas), Samoa, and Tokelau.

Daylight Saving Time is used to make better use of the daylight in the evening by moving the clocks forward (usually by one hour) in spring. Clocks are set back by the same amount of time in fall. The period of the year during which DST is observed is called summer; the other part of the year is called winter. Not all countries observe DST. The government of a country decides whether the country (or only some locations within a country) observes DST; if it does, government decides the dates and times to move the clocks forward and backward. For example, zones observing DST in the United States of America moved the clocks one hour forward at 2:00 AM local time on March 11, 2012, thus creating a gap of one hour. Note that on March 11, 2012, the local time between 2:00 AM and 3:00 AM did not exist in those zones in the USA. In fall, when clocks are moved back, a time overlap of the equal amount is created. India and Thailand are two among several countries that do not observe DST. DST changes the zone offset of the DST observing locations from UTC twice a year.

Calendar Systems

Humans use calendars to work with time. The time units used in calendars are year, month, day, hour, minute, and second. In this sense, a calendar is a system of tracking time, past and future, for humans in a meaningful way for social, political, legal, religious, etc. purposes.

Typically, a calendar system does not keep track of the time of day; it works in terms of day, month, and year. Broadly speaking, in a calendar, a day is based on the rotation of earth on its axis, month on the revolution of the moon around Earth, and year on the revolution of Earth around the sun. Sometimes, a calendar system is based on week, which is based on a non-astronomical cycle.

Throughout the history of humankind, different civilizations have been known to use different calendar systems. Most of the ancient calendar systems have been based on astronomical cycles generated by solar motion, lunar motion, or both, thus giving rise to three types of calendrical systems: solar, lunar, and lunisolar calendars.

A solar calendar is designed to align with a tropical year (also called a solar year), which is the mean interval between the vernal equinox. An equinox occurs twice a year when the center of the sun is in the same plane as the equator of earth. The term "equinox" means equal night; on an equinox, day and night are almost of the same length. A vernal equinox occurs during spring around March 21; an autumnal equinox occurs during autumn around September 22. The Gregorian calendar, which is the most used calendar worldwide for civil purposes, is an example of a solar calendar.

A lunar calendar is based on lunar phase cycle. It is not aligned to a tropical year. In a year, it drifts by 11 to 12 days from a tropical year. A lunar calendar takes about 33 years to catch up with a tropical year, to drift again for another 33 years. A lunar month, which is also called a synodic month, is the interval of time between new moons that is equal to 29 days, 12 hours, 44 minutes, and 2.8 seconds. The Islamic calendar is an example of a lunar calendar.

A lunisolar calendar computes months based on lunar phase cycle like a lunar calendar. However, it intercalates, in a 2-year or 3-year period, a month to keep itself aligned with a tropical year. The Buddhist, Hindu lunisolar, Chinese, Hebrew calendars are some examples of lunisolar calendars.

The Julian Calendar

The Julian calendar is a solar calendar introduced in the year -45 by Julius Caesar. It was widely used by the European civilization until year +1582 when the Gregorian calendar was introduced.

An ordinary year consists of 365 days. Every four years, a day is intercalated between February 28 and March 1, which is designated as February 29, to make the year 366 days, which is called a leap year. The year 0 (1 B. C.) is considered a leap year. The average length of a Julian calendar year is 365.25 days that is close to the length of a tropical year known in those days.

A year consists of 12 months. Months are fixed in lengths. Table 12-1 lists the order, name, and number of days in months in the Julian calendar.

Table 12-1. *Order, Name, and Number of Days in Months in Julian and Gregorian Calendars*

Order	Month Name	Number of Days
1	January	31
2	February	28 (29 in a leap year)
3	March	31
4	April	30
5	May	31
6	June	30
7	July	31
8	August	31
9	September	30
10	October	31
11	November	30
12	December	31

The Gregorian Calendar

The Gregorian calendar is the most widely used calendar in the world for civil purposes. It follows the rules of the Julian calendar for number of months in a year and number of days in months. However, it changed the rule for computing a leap year: a year is a leap year if it is exactly divisible by 4. A year exactly divisible by 100 is not a leap year unless it is also divisible by 400.

For example, 4, 8, 12, 400, and 800 are known as leap years, and 1, 2, 3, 5, 300, and 100 are known as common years. Year 0 (1 B. C.) is considered a leap year. With a new definition of a leap year, the average length of a year in the Gregorian calendar is 365.2425 days, which is very close to the length of a tropical year. The Gregorian calendar repeats every 400 years. If you save your paper calendar for year 2014, your nth great-grandchildren will be able to reuse it in year 2414!

The Gregorian calendar was introduced on Friday, October 15, 1582. The day before the Gregorian calendar started, it was Thursday, October 4, 1582 according to the existing Julian calendar. Note that the introduction of the Gregorian calendar left the cycle of weekdays unaffected; however, it left a discontinuity of 10 days between the two calendars that is called the cutover. Dates before the cutover are Julian dates, dates after the cutover are Gregorian dates, and dates during the cutover do not exist.

Gregorian calendar did not exist before October 15, 1582. How do we assign dates to the events before the start of the Gregorian calendar? The Gregorian calendar applied to the dates when it was not in effect is called a proleptic Gregorian calendar. Therefore, October 14, 1582 exists In a proleptic Gregorian calendar, which is the same as October 4, 1582 in the Julian calendar.

Why was the first day of the Gregorian calendar Friday, October 15, 1582, and not Friday, October 5, 1582? According to (Doggett, Calendars n.d.), in Julian calendar, the date of Easter, a Christian festival, was computed based on an assumption that March 21 is the date for vernal equinox. Later, it was realized that vernal equinox had been drifting from March 21; hence, the date of Easter drifts from the seasonal springtime. To keep the date of Easter synchronized with springtime, the adjustment of 10 days were made in the start date of the Gregorian calendar, so the vernal equinox in year 1583 and later occurs approximately on March 21.

■ **Tip**   The main difference between the Julian and Gregorian calendar is the rule for determining a leap year. The mean length of a year in the Gregorian calendar is closer to the length of the tropical year than that of in the Julian calendar.

ISO-8601 Standards for Datetime

The new Date-Time API has extensive support for ISO-8601 standards. This section is intended to present a brief and limited overview of the datetime components and their textual representations included in the ISO-8601 standards.

A datetime in ISO 8601 consists of three components: date, time, and zone offset that are combined in the following format:

```
[date]T[time][zone offset]
```

A date component consists of three calendar fields: year, month, and day. Two fields in a date are separated by a hyphen.

```
year-month-day
```

For example, 2012-04-30 represents the 30th day in April of year 2012.

Sometimes humans deal with dates that may not contain complete information to identify a specific day in a calendar. For example, December 25 makes sense as a Christmas day without specifying the year part of the date. To identify a specific Christmas day in a calendar, we must also specify the year. A date with some missing parts is known as a partial. 2012, 2012-05, -----05-29, etc. are examples of partials. ISO-8601 allows omitting parts in a date only from the right end. That is, it allows omitting day, or month and day. The Date-Time API allows three types of partials: year, year-month, and month-day.

Date and time components are separated by a character T. A time component consists of fields: hour, minute, and second. A colon separates two fields in a time component. A time is represented in the format

`hour:minute:second`

ISO-8601 uses a 24-hour timekeeping system. The hour element can be between 00 and 24. The hour 24 is used to denote the end of a calendar day. The value for the minute element ranges from 00 to 59. The second element may range from 00 to 60. The value 60 for the second element indicates a positive leap second. For example, 15:20:56 represents a local time of 20 minutes and 56 seconds past 15 hours after midnight. When reduced accuracy is allowed, second, or second and minute elements may be omitted from a time. For example, 15:19 and 07 denote 19 minutes past 15 hours, and 07 hours from midnight, respectively.

Midnight is the start of a calendar day. It is represented by 00:00:00 or 00:00. The start of a calendar day coincides with the end of the previous calendar day. Therefore, midnight of a calendar day may also be represented by 24:00:00 or 24:00.

When a date, time, or datetime is specified without a zone offset, it is considered a local date, time, or datetime, respectively. Examples of a local date, time, and datetime are 2012-05-01, 13:52:05, and 2012-05-01T13:52:05, respectively.

Using a zone offset, you can represent a time component relative to UTC of day. The zone offset represents a fixed difference between a local time and UTC. It starts with a plus or minus sign (+or -) followed by hour and minute elements, which are separated by a colon. Some examples of zone offset are +05:30, -06:00, +10:00, +5:30, etc. The character Z is used as a zone offset designator to denote the UTC time of day. For example, 10:20:40Z represents the UTC of day 20 minutes and 40 seconds past 10 in the morning; 12:20:40+2:00 represents a local time of day 20 minutes and 40 seconds past 12 in the afternoon, which is 2 hours ahead of UTC. Both times, 10:20:40Z and 12:20:40+2:00, represent the same point in time.

■ **Tip** ISO-8601 specifies standards for using a fixed zone offset from the UTC component in time representation. Recall that a zone offset may vary for time zones that observe Daylight Saving Time. In addition to ISO-8601 standards, the Date-Time API supports a variable zone offset as well.

An example of a datetime having all three components fully specified is the following:

`2012-05-01T16:30:00-06:00`

The above datetime represents May 1, 2012 30 minutes past 16 hours from midnight that is 6 hours behind UTC.

ISO-8601 includes standards for several other date- and time-related concepts such as instant, duration, period, time interval, etc. The Date-Time API provides classes whose objects directly represent most, but not all, ISO date and time concepts.

The toString() methods of all date and time classes in the Date-Time API return a textual representation of date and time in ISO formats. The API includes classes to let you format a date and time in non-ISO formats.

The ISO standards include formats for specifying an amount of time known as duration. ISO-8601 defines duration as a non-negative quantity. However, the Date-Time API also allows a negative quantity treated as duration. The ISO format for representing duration is as follows:

`PnnYnnMnnDTnnHnnMnnS`

In the above format, P is a duration designator; nn denotes a number; Y, M, D, H, M, and S denote year, month, day, hour, month, and second, respectively; T is a time designator that is present only if duration involves hour, minute, and second. The following are examples of textual representation of some durations. Inline comments describe the duration.

```
P12Y       // A duration of 12 years
PT15:30    // A duration of 15 hours and 30 minutes
PT20S      // A duration of 20 seconds
P4Y2MT30M  // A duration of 4 years 2 months and 30 minutes
```

■ **Tip**　The Date-Time API provides Duration and Period classes to deal with an amount of time. A Duration represents an amount of time on machine-scale timeline. A Period represents an amount of time on human-scale timeline.

Exploring the New Date-Time API

At first, exploring the Date-Time API is intimidating as it contains many classes with numerous methods. Learning the naming convention of methods will help understand the API tremendously. The Date-Time API has been designed carefully to keep the names of classes and their methods consistent and intuitive. Methods starting with the same prefix do the similar work. For example, a of() method in a class is used as a static factory method to create an object of that class.

All classes, interfaces, and enums for the Date-Time API are in the java.time package and four of its subpackages:

- java.time contains frequently used classes. LocalDate, LocalTime, LocalDateTime, ZonedDateTime, Period, Duration, and Instant classes are in this package. Classes in this package are based on ISO standards.

- java.time.chrono contains classes supporting non-ISO calendar systems, for example, Hijrah calendar, ThaiBuddhist calendar, etc.

- java.time.format contains classes for formatting and parsing dates and times.

- java.time.temporal contains classes for accessing components of dates and times. It also contains classes that acts like date-time adjusters.

- java.time.zone contains classes supporting time zones and zone rules.

The following sections explain the prefixes used in method names in the Date-Time API with their meanings and examples.

The ofXXX( ) Methods

Classes in the Date-Time API do not provide public constructors to create their objects. They let you create objects through static factory methods named ofXXX(). The following snippet of code shows how to create objects of the LocalDate class:

```
LocalDate ld1 = LocalDate.of(2012, 5, 2); // 2012-05-02
LocalDate ld2 = LocalDate.of(2012, Month.JULY, 4); // 2012-07-04
LocalDate ld3 = LocalDate.ofEpochDay(2002); // 1975-06-26
LocalDate ld4 = LocalDate.ofYearDay(2014, 40); // 2014-02-09
```

The from( ) Methods

A from() method is a static factory method, similar to an of() method, that is used to derive a datetime object from the specified argument. Unlike an of() method, a from() method requires data conversion on the specified argument.

To understand what a from() method does, think of it named as deriveFrom() method. Using a from() method, you derive a new datetime object from the specified argument. The following snippet of code shows how to derive a LocalDate from a LocalDateTime:

```
LocalDateTime ldt = LocalDateTime.of(2012, 5, 2, 15, 30); // 2012-05-02T15:30
LocalDate ld = LocalDate.from(ldt); // 2012-05-02
```

The withXXX( ) Methods

Most classes in the Date-Time API are immutable. They do not have setXXX() methods. If you want to change a field of a datetime object, for example, the year value in a date, you need to look for a method with a prefix like withXXX. A withXXX() method returns a copy of an object with the specified field changed.

Assume that you have a LocalDate object and you want to change its year. You need to use the withYear(int newYear) method of the LocalDate class. The following snippet of code shows how to obtain a LocalDate from another LocalDate with the year changed:

```
LocalDate ld1 = LocalDate.of(2012, Month.MAY, 2); // 2012-05-02
LocalDate ld2 = ld1.withYear(2014); // 2014-05-02
```

You can obtain a new LocalDate from an existing LocalDate by changing multiple fields by chaining the withXXX() method calls. The following snippet of code creates a new LocalDate from an existing LocalDate by changing the year and month:

```
LocalDate ld3 = LocalDate.of(2012, 5, 2); // 2012-05-02
LocalDate ld4 = ld3.withYear(2014).withMonth(7); // 2014-07-02
```

The getXXX( ) Methods

A getXXX() method returns the specified element of the object. For example, the getYear() method in the LocalDate object returns the year part of the date. The following snippet of code shows how to get year, month, and day from a LocalDate object:

```
LocalDate ld = LocalDate.of(2012, 5, 2);
int year = ld.getYear();        // 2012
Month month = ld.getMonth();    // Month.MAY
int day = ld.getDayOfMonth();   // 2
```

The toXXX( ) Methods

A toXXX() method converts an object to a related XXX type. For example, the toLocalDate() method in the LocalDateTime class returns a LocalDate object with the date in the object. Below are some examples of using toXXX() methods.

```
LocalDate ld = LocalDate.of(2012, 5, 2); // 2012-05-02

// Convert the date to epoch days. The epoch days is the number of days from
// 1970-01-01 to a date. A date before 1970-01-01 returns a negative integer.
long epochDays = ld.toEpochDay(); // 15462

// Convert a LocalDateTime to a LocalTime using the toLocalTime() method
LocalDateTime ldt = LocalDateTime.of(2012, 5, 2, 15, 50);
LocalTime lt = ldt.toLocalTime(); // 15:50
```

The atXXX( ) Methods

An atXXX( ) method lets you build a new datetime object from an existing datetime object by supplying some additional pieces of information. Contrast the use of an atXXX( ) method with that of a withXXX( ) method; the former lets you create a new type of object by providing additional information whereas the latter lets you create a copy of an object by changing its fields.

Suppose you have the date 2012-05-02. If you want to create a new date of 2012-07-02 (with month changed to 7), you would use a withXXX( ) method. If you want to create a datetime of 2012-05-02T15:30 (by adding time 15:30), you would use an atXXX( ) method. Some examples of using atXXX( ) methods are shown below.

```
LocalDate ld = LocalDate.of(2012, 5, 2);     // 2012-05-02
LocalDateTime ldt1 = ld.atStartOfDay();      // 2012-05-02T00:00
LocalDateTime ldt2 = ld.atTime(15, 30);      // 2012-05-02T15:30
```

The atXXX( ) methods supports the builder pattern. The following snippet of code shows how to use a builder pattern to build a local date:

```
// Use a builder pattern to build a date 2012-05-22
LocalDate d1 = Year.of(2012).atMonth(5).atDay(22);

// Use an of() factory method to build a date 2012-05-22
LocalDate d2 = LocalDate.of(2012, 5, 22);
```

The plusXXX( ) and minusXXX( ) Methods

A plusXXX( ) method returns a copy of an object by adding a specified value. For example, the plusDays(long days) method in the LocalDate class returns a copy of the LocalDate object by adding the specified number of days.

A minusXXX( ) method returns a copy of an object by subtracting a specified value. For example, the minusDays(long days) method in the LocalDate class returns a copy of the LocalDate object by subtracting the specified number of days.

```
LocalDate ld = LocalDate.of(2012, 5, 2); // 2012-05-02
LocalDate ld1 = ld.plusDays(5);          // 2012-05-07
LocalDate ld2 = ld.plusMonths(3);        // 2012-08-02
LocalDate ld3 = ld.plusWeeks(3);         // 2012-05-23
LocalDate ld4 = ld.minusMonths(7);       // 2011-10-02
LocalDate ld5 = ld.minusWeeks(3);        // 2012-04-11
```

The multipliedBy( ), dividedBy( ), and negated( ) Methods

Multiplication, division, and negation do not make sense on dates and times. They are applicable to the datetime types that denote an amount of time such as Duration and Period. Durations and periods can be added and subtracted. The Date-Time API supports negative durations and periods.

```
Duration d = Duration.ofSeconds(200); // PT3M20S (3 minutes and 20 seconds)
Duration d1 = d.multipliedBy(2);       // PT6M40S (6 minutes and 40 seconds)
Duration d2 = d.negated();             // PT-3M-20S (-3 minutes and -20 seconds)
```

Instants and Durations

A timeline (or a time axis) is a mathematical representation of the passage of time in terms of instantaneous events along a unique axis. A machine-scale timeline represents the passage of time as a single incrementing number as shown in Figure 12-1.

Figure 12-1. *A timeline representing the pasaage of machine-scale time*

An instant is a point representing a unique moment in time on a timeline. An epoch is an instant on a timeline that is used as a reference point (or the origin) to measure other instants.

An object of the Instant class represents an instant on the timeline. It uses a timeline to represent simplified UTC to a nanosecond precision. That is, the time interval (or duration) between two consecutive instants on the timeline is one nanosecond. The timeline uses 1970-01-01T00:00:00Z as the epoch. Instants after the epoch have positive values; instants before the epoch have negative values. The instant at the epoch is assigned a zero value.

There are different ways you can create an instance of the Instant class. Using its now( ) method, you can get the current instant using the system default clock.

```
// Get the current instant
Instant i1 = Instant.now();
```

You can obtain an instance of the Instant class using an amount of time in different units from the epoch. The following snippet of code creates an Instant object to represent 19 seconds from the epoch, which represents 1970-01-01T00:00:19Z:

```
// An instant: 19 seconds from the epoch
Instant i2 = Instant.ofEpochSecond(19);
```

An object of the Duration class represents an amount of time between two instants on the timeline. The Duration class supports a directed duration. That is, it allows a positive as well as negative duration. Figure 12-1 shows durations with arrows to signify that they are directed durations.

You can create an instance of the Duration class using one of its ofXXX() static factory methods.

```
// A duration of 2 days
Duration d1 = Duration.ofDays(2);

// A duration of 25 minutes
Duration d2 = Duration.ofMinutes(25);
```

■ **Tip** The toString() method of the Instant class returns a textual representation of the Instant in the ISO-8601 format yyyy-MM-ddTHH:mm:ss.SSSSSSSSSZ. The toString() method of the Duration class returns a textual representation of the duration in PTnHnMnS format, where n is the number of hours, minutes, or seconds.

What can you do with instants and durations? Typically, they are used for recording timestamps and elapsed time between two events. Two instants can be compared to know whether one occurs before or after other. You can add (and subtract) a duration to an instant to obtain another instant. Adding two durations results in another duration. Classes in the Date-Time API are Serializable. You can use Instant to store timestamps in databases.

Instant and Duration classes store second and nanosecond-of-second parts of their values separately. The Duration class has getSeconds() and getNano() methods, whereas the Instant class has getEpochSecond() and getNano() methods to get the two values. The following is an example of getting second and nanosecond of an Instant:

```
// Get the current instant
Instant i1 = Instant.now();

// Get seconds and nanoseconds
long seconds = i1.getEpochSecond();
int nanoSeconds = i1.getNano();

System.out.println("Current Instant: " + i1);
System.out.println("Seconds: " + seconds);
System.out.println("Nanoseconds: " + nanoSeconds);
```

```
(You will get a different output.)
Current Instant: 2014-01-03T17:01:32.261Z
Seconds: 1388768492
Nanoseconds: 261000000
```

Listing 12-2 demonstrates use of some operations that can be performed on instants and durations.

Listing 12-2. Using Instant and Duration Classes

```java
// InstantDurationTest.java
package com.jdojo.datetime;

import java.time.Duration;
import java.time.Instant;

public class InstantDurationTest {
        public static void main(String[] args) {
                Instant i1 = Instant.ofEpochSecond(20);
                Instant i2 = Instant.ofEpochSecond(55);
                System.out.println("i1:" + i1);
                System.out.println("i2:" + i2);

                Duration d1 = Duration.ofSeconds(55);
                Duration d2 = Duration.ofSeconds(-17);
                System.out.println("d1:" + d1);
                System.out.println("d2:" + d2);

                // Compare instants
                System.out.println("i1.isBefore(i2):" + i1.isBefore(i2));
                System.out.println("i1.isAfter(i2):" + i1.isAfter(i2));

                // Add and subtract durations to instants
                Instant i3 = i1.plus(d1);
                Instant i4 = i2.minus(d2);
                System.out.println("i1.plus(d1):" + i3);
                System.out.println("i2.minus(d2):" + i4);

                // Add two durations
                Duration d3 = d1.plus(d2);
                System.out.println("d1.plus(d2):" + d3);
        }
}
```

```
i1:1970-01-01T00:00:20Z
i2:1970-01-01T00:00:55Z
d1:PT55S
d2:PT-17S
i1.isBefore(i2):true
i1.isAfter(i2):false
i1.plus(d1):1970-01-01T00:01:15Z
i2.minus(d2):1970-01-01T00:01:12Z
d1.plus(d2):PT38S
```

Human-Scale Time

In the previous section, I discussed the use of Instant and Duration classes whose instances are more suited to dealing with machine-scale time. Humans deal with time in terms of fields such as year, month, day, hour, minute, and second. Recall the following format for specifying date and time in ISO-8601 format:

[date]T[time][zone offset]

The Date-Time API provides several classes, listed in Table 12-2, to represent all fields and their combinations of human-scale time. A Yes or No in the component column for a class indicates whether an instance of the class stores that component or not. I will discuss all of these classes in detail shortly.

Table 12-2. *Human-Scale Date and Time Classes and their Components*

Class Name	Date	Time	Zone Offset	Zone Rule
LocalDate	Yes	No	No	No
LocalTime	No	Yes	No	No
LocalDateTime	Yes	Yes	No	No
OffsetTime	No	Yes	Yes	No
OffsetDateTime	Yes	Yes	Yes	No
ZonedDateTime	Yes	Yes	Yes	Yes
ZoneOffset	No	No	Yes	No
ZoneId	No	No	Yes	Yes

The ZoneOffset Class

An instance of the ZoneOffset class represents a fixed zone offset from UTC time zone, for example, +05:30, -06:00, etc. It is a period of time that a time zone differs from the UTC.

A ZoneOffset is not aware of the changes in zone offset because of the observed Daylight Saving Time. The ZoneOffset class declares three constants:

- UTC
- MAX
- MIN

UTC is the time zone offset constant for UTC. MAX and MIN are the maximum and minimum supported zone offsets.

■ **Tip**   Z, not +00:00 or -00:00, is used as the zone offset designator for UTC time zone.

The ZoneOffset class provides methods to create its instances using a combination of hour, minute, and second. Listing 12-3 demonstrates how to create instances of the ZoneOffset class

Listing 12-3. Creating Instances of the ZoneOffset Class

```java
// ZoneOffsetTest.java
package com.jdojo.datetime;
import java.time.ZoneOffset;

public class ZoneOffsetTest {
        public static void main(String[] args) {
                // Create zone offset using hour, minute, and second
                ZoneOffset zos1 = ZoneOffset.ofHours(-6);
                ZoneOffset zos2 = ZoneOffset.ofHoursMinutes(5, 30);
                ZoneOffset zos3 = ZoneOffset.ofHoursMinutesSeconds(8, 30, 45);
                System.out.println(zos1);
                System.out.println(zos2);
                System.out.println(zos3);

                // Create zone offset using offset ID as a string
                ZoneOffset zos4 = ZoneOffset.of("+05:00");
                ZoneOffset zos5 = ZoneOffset.of("Z"); // Same as ZoneOffset.UTC
                System.out.println(zos4);
                System.out.println(zos5);

                // Print the values for zone offset constants
                System.out.println("ZoneOffset.UTC: "  + ZoneOffset.UTC);
                System.out.println("ZoneOffset.MIN: "  + ZoneOffset.MIN);
                System.out.println("ZoneOffset.MAX: "  + ZoneOffset.MAX);
        }
}
```

```
-06:00
+05:30
+08:30:45
+05:00
Z
ZoneOffset.UTC: Z
ZoneOffset.MIN: -18:00
ZoneOffset.MAX: +18:00
```

According to ISO-8601 standards, a zone offset may include hours and minutes, or hours only. The new Date-Time API also allows seconds in a zone offset. You can use the compareTo() method of the ZoneOffset class to compare a zone offset to another zone offset. Zone offsets are compared in descending order that is the order in which they occur in the time of the day, for example, a zone offset of +5:30 occurs before a zone offset of +5:00. ISO-8601 standards support zone offsets between -12:00 to +14:00. However, to avoid any problems in future if the zone offset gets extended, the Date-Time API supports zone offsets between -18:00 to +18:00.

The ZoneId Class

An instance of the ZoneId class represents a combination of a zone offset and the rules for changing the zone offset for observed Daylight Saving Time. Not all time zones observe Daylight Saving Time. To simplify your understanding about the ZoneId, you can think of it as

ZoneId = ZoneOffset + ZoneRules

■ **Tip** A ZoneOffset represents a fixed zone offset from UTC time zone whereas a ZoneId represents a variable zone offset. The variation, the time in the year when the zone offset is changed, and the amount of change, is controlled by time zone rules. The ZoneOffset class inherits from the ZoneId class.

A time zone has a unique textual ID, which can be specified in three formats:

- In this format, the zone ID is specified in terms of zone offset, which can be "Z", "+hh:mm:ss", or "-hh:mm:ss", for example, "+06:00".

- In this format, the zone ID is prefixed with "UTC", "GMT", or "UT" and followed by a zone offset, for example, "UTC+06:00".

- In this format, the zone ID is specified by using a region, for example, "America/Chicago".

Using the first two forms of Zone IDs, you create a ZoneId with a fixed zone offset. You can create a ZoneId using the of() factory method.

```
ZoneId usChicago = ZoneId.of("America/Chicago");
ZoneId bdDhaka = ZoneId.of("Asia/Dhaka");
ZoneId fixedZoneId = ZoneId.of("+06:00");
```

The ZoneId class provides access to all known time zone IDs. Its getAvailableZoneIds() static method returns a Set<String> containing all available zone Ids. Listing 12-4 shows how to print all zone IDs. A partial list of zone IDs is shown in the output.

Listing 12-4. Printing All Available Zone IDs

```
// PrintAllZoneIds.java
package com.jdojo.datetime;

import java.time.ZoneId;
import java.util.Set;

public class PrintAllZoneIds {
        public static void main(String[] args) {
                Set<String> zoneIds = ZoneId.getAvailableZoneIds();
                for (String zoneId: zoneIds) {
                        System.out.println(zoneId);
                }
        }
}
```

```
Asia/Aden
Africa/Cairo
Pacific/Honolulu
America/Chicago
Europe/Athens
...
```

A ZoneId object gives you access to zone rules for the time zone represented by the ZoneId. You can use the getRules() method of the ZoneId class to get an instance of the ZoneRules class to work with rules such as transitions for Daylight Saving Time, the zone offset for a specified datetime, the amount of daylight saving, etc. Typically, you will not use zone rules directly in your code. As a developer, you would use a ZoneId to create a ZonedDateTime, which is discussed shortly. The program in Listing 12-5 shows how to query the ZoneRules object to get information about the time offset and time changes for a ZoneId. The list of time transitions is very big and it is shown it partially in the output.

Listing 12-5. Knowing the Time Change Rules (the ZoneRules) for a ZoneId

```java
// ZoneRulesTest.java
package com.jdojo.datetime;

import java.time.LocalDateTime;
import java.time.ZoneId;
import java.time.ZoneOffset;
import java.time.zone.ZoneOffsetTransition;
import java.time.zone.ZoneRules;
import java.util.List;

public class ZoneRulesTest {
        public static void main(String[] args) {
                LocalDateTime now = LocalDateTime.now();
                System.out.println("Current Date Time: " + now);

                ZoneId fixedZoneId = ZoneId.of("+06:00");
                ZoneId bdDhaka = ZoneId.of("Asia/Dhaka");
                ZoneId usChicago = ZoneId.of("America/Chicago");

                // Print some zone rules for ZoneIds
                printDetails(fixedZoneId, now);
                printDetails(bdDhaka, now);
                printDetails(usChicago, now);
        }

        public static void printDetails(ZoneId zoneId, LocalDateTime now) {
                System.out.println("Zone ID: " + zoneId.getId());

                ZoneRules rules = zoneId.getRules();
                boolean isFixedOffset = rules.isFixedOffset();
                System.out.println("isFixedOffset(): " + isFixedOffset);
```

```
            ZoneOffset offset = rules.getOffset(now);
            System.out.println("Zone offset: " + offset);

            List<ZoneOffsetTransition> transitions = rules.getTransitions();
            System.out.println(transitions);
        }
}
```

```
Current Date Time: 2014-01-03T16:05:13.035
Zone ID: +06:00
isFixedOffset(): true
Zone offset: +06:00
[]
Zone ID: Asia/Dhaka
isFixedOffset(): false
Zone offset: +06:00
[Transition[Overlap at 1890-01-01T00:00+06:01:40 to +05:53:20], ..., Transition[Gap at
2009-06-19T23:00+06:00 to +07:00], Transition[Overlap at 2009-12-31T23:59+07:00 to +06:00]]
Zone ID: America/Chicago
isFixedOffset(): false
Zone offset: -06:00
[Transition[Overlap at 1883-11-18T12:09:24-05:50:36 to -06:00], ..., Transition[Gap at
2008-03-09T02:00-06:00 to -05:00], Transition[Overlap at 2008-11-02T02:00-05:00 to -06:00]]
```

Several organizations and groups provide a set of time zone rules as a database that contains the code and data for all time zones in the world. Each provider is given a unique group ID. One of the standard rules providers is a TZ database that is identified by TZDB group ID. Please refer to www.twinsun.com/tz/tz-link.htm for more details on the TZ database.

As the rules for a time zone change over time, a group provides multiple versions of rules data for different regions. Typically, a region represents a time zone where the time zone rules are the same. Each group has its own naming scheme for the versions and regions.

TZDB stores region names in a [area]/[city] format. Examples of some regions names are Africa/Tunis, America/Chicago, Asia/Kolkata, Asia/Tokyo, Europe/Istanbul, Europe/London, and Europe/Moscow.

The Date-Time API uses the TZDB as the default time zone rules provider. If you are using a region-based zone ID from the TZDB, use the region name as the zone id. The region name should be prefixed with the group ID of the provider in the form of "group~region" if a group other than TZDB is used for zone rules. For example, if you are using International Air Transport Association (IATA) provider, use "IATA~CHI" for the Chicago region. Please refer to the ZoneRulesProvider class in the java.time.zone package for more details on how to register your own zone rules provider.

Useful Datetime-Related Enums

Before I discuss classes that represent different combinations of date and time, it is worth discussing some enums representing constants for date and time components:

- Month
- DayOfWeek
- ChronoField
- ChronoUnit

Most of the time, you will use the constants in these enums directly as arguments to methods or receive them as return values from methods. Some enums include methods to compute useful date times values using the constant itself as input.

Representing Months

The Month enum has 12 constants to represents the 12 months of the year. The constant names are JANUARY, FEBRUARY, MARCH, APRIL, MAY, JUNE, JULY, AUGUST, SEPTEMBER, OCTOBER, NOVEMBER, and DECEMBER. Months are numbered sequentially from 1 to 12, January being 1 and December being 12. The Month enum provides some useful methods such as of() to get an instance of Month from an int value, from() to get the Month from any date object, getValue() to get the int value of the Month, etc.

For better readability, use an enum constant, if and when available in the Date-Time API, instead of an integer value. For example, for the month of July, use Month.JULY in your code, not integer 7. Sometimes the API provides two versions of a method: one takes the Month enum argument and another the int value of the month. An example of such methods is the static factory method of() method in the LocalDate class:

- static LocalDate of(int year, int month, int dayOfMonth)

- static LocalDate of(int year, Month month, int dayOfMonth)

Listing 12-6 demonstrates some uses of the Month enum.

Listing 12-6. Using the Month enum

```java
// MonthTest.java
package com.jdojo.datetime;

import java.time.LocalDate;
import java.time.Month;

public class MonthTest {
    public static void main(String[] args) {
        // Use Month.JULY as a method argument
        LocalDate ld1 = LocalDate.of(2012, Month.JULY, 1);

        // Derive a Month from a local date
        Month m1 = Month.from(ld1);

        // Create a Month from an int value 2
        Month m2 = Month.of(2);

        // Get the next month from m2
        Month m3 = m2.plus(1);

        // Get the Month from a local date
        Month m4 = ld1.getMonth();

        // Convert an enum constant to an int
        int m5 = m2.getValue();

        System.out.format("%s, %s, %s, %s, %d%n", m1, m2, m3, m4, m5);
    }
}
```

JULY, FEBRUARY, MARCH, JULY, 2

Representing the Day of Week

The DayOfWeek enum has seven constants to represent seven days of the week. The constants are MONDAY, TUESDAY, WEDNESDAY, THURSDAY, FRIDAY, SATURDAY, and SUNDAY. Its getValue() method returns an int value: 1 for Monday, 2 for Tuesday, and so on, which follows ISO-8601 standards. The DayOfWeek enum is in the java.time package. Below are some examples of using the DayOfWeek enum and its methods.

```
LocalDate ld = LocalDate.of(2012, 5, 10);

// Extract the day-of-week from a LocalDate
DayOfWeek dw1 = DayOfWeek.from(ld); // THURSDAY

// Get the int value of the day-of-week
int dw11 = dw1.getValue(); // 4

// Use the method of the LocalDate class to get day-of-week
DayOfWeek dw12 = ld.getDayOfWeek(); // THURSDAY

// Obtain a DayOfWeek instance using an int value
DayOfWeek dw2 = DayOfWeek.of(7); // SUNDAY

// Add one day to the day-of-week to get the next day
DayOfWeek dw3 = dw2.plus(1); // MONDAY

// Get the day-of-week two days ago
DayOfWeek dw4 = dw2.minus(2); // FRIDAY
```

Representing DateTime Fields

Most fields in datetime can be represented as a numeric value, for example, year, month, day, hour, etc. An instance of the TemporalField interface represents a field of datetime, for example, year, month-of-year, minutes-of-hour, etc. The ChronoField enum implements the TemporalField interface and provides several constants to represent fields in a datetime. The ChronoField enum contains a long list of constants. Some of them are as follows: AMPM_OF_DAY, CLOCK_HOUR_OF_AMPM, CLOCK_HOUR_OF_DAY, DAY_OF_MONTH, DAY_OF_WEEK, DAY_OF_YEAR, ERA, HOUR_OF_AMPM, HOUR_OF_DAY, INSTANT_SECONDS, MINUTE_OF_HOUR, MONTH_OF_YEAR, SECOND_OF_MINUTE, YEAR, YEAR_OF_ERA.

Typically, you use a TemporalField to get the value of the field from a datetime. All datetime classes have a get() method that returns an int value for the specified TemporalField. If the value for a field is too long for an int, use the companion getLong() method to get the value in a long.

Not all datetime classes support all type of fields. For example, a LocalDate does not support the MINUTE_OF_HOUR field. Use the isSupported() method of the datetime classes to check whether they support a specific type of field. Use the isSupportedBy() method of ChronoField to check if a field is supported by a datetime class.

■ **Tip** Constants for some datetime fields that are specific to the ISO-8601 calendar system are declared in the IsoFields class. For example, IsoFields.DAY_OF_QUARTER represents ISO-8601 based day-of-quarter.

The following snippet of code demonstrates how to use a ChronoField to extract a field value from a datetime and whether the datetime supported the field:

```
import java.time.LocalDate;
import java.time.LocalDateTime;
import java.time.temporal.ChronoField;
...
LocalDateTime now = LocalDateTime.now();
System.out.println("Current Date Time: " + now);
System.out.println("Year: " + now.get(ChronoField.YEAR));
System.out.println("Month: " + now.get(ChronoField.MONTH_OF_YEAR));
System.out.println("Day: " + now.get(ChronoField.DAY_OF_MONTH));
System.out.println("Hour-of-day: " + now.get(ChronoField.HOUR_OF_DAY));
System.out.println("Hour-of-AMPM: " + now.get(ChronoField.HOUR_OF_AMPM));
System.out.println("AMPM-of-day: " + now.get(ChronoField.AMPM_OF_DAY));

LocalDate today = LocalDate.now();
System.out.println("Current Date : " + today);
System.out.println("LocalDate supports year: " + today.isSupported(ChronoField.YEAR));
System.out.println("LocalDate supports hour-of-day: " + today.isSupported(ChronoField.HOUR_OF_DAY));

System.out.println("Year is supported by LocalDate: " + ChronoField.YEAR.isSupportedBy(today));
System.out.println("Hour-of-day is supported by LocalDate: " +
        ChronoField.HOUR_OF_DAY.isSupportedBy(today));
```

```
Current Date Time: 2014-03-01T10:15:24.918
Year: 2014
Month: 3
Day: 1
Hour-of-day: 10
Hour-of-AMPM: 10
AMPM-of-day: 0
Current Date : 2014-03-01
LocalDate supports year: true
LocalDate supports hour-of-day: false
Year is supported by LocalDate: true
Hour-of-day is supported by LocalDate: false
```

The value for the AMPM_OF_DAY field can be 0 or 1; 0 indicates AM and 1 indicates PM.

Representing the Units of Datetime Fields

Time is measured in units such as years, months, days, hours, minutes, seconds, weeks, etc. An instance of the TemporalUnit interface in the java.time.temporal package represents a unit of time. The ChronoUnit in the same package contains the following constants to represent units of time: CENTURIES, DAYS, DECADES, ERAS, FOREVER, HALF_DAYS, HOURS, MICROS, MILLENNIA, MILLIS, MINUTES, MONTHS, NANOS, SECONDS, WEEKS, and YEARS.

The ChronoUnit enum implements the TemporalUnit interface. Therefore, all constants in the enum are an instance of the TemporalUnit.

■ **Tip** Constants for some datetime units that are specific to the ISO-8601 calendar system are declared in the IsoFields class. For example, IsoFields.QUARTER_YEARS and IsoFields.WEEK_BASED_YEARS represent ISO-8601 based a quarter-year (3 months) and a week-based year (52 or 53 weeks), respectively. The ISO-8601 standard considers a seven day period as a week; a week starts on a Monday; the first calendar week of the year is the one that includes the first Thursday of the year; the first week of a year may start in the previous year and the last week of a year may end in the succeeding year. This may result in a 53 weeks in a year. For example, the first week of 2009 started on December 29, 2008 and the last week on December 29, 2009, making 2009 a 53 week year.

Datetime classes provide two methods, minus() and plus(). They take an amount of time and the unit of time to return a new datetime by subtracting and adding the specified time. Convenience methods such as minusDays(), minusHours(), plusDays(), plusHours(), etc. are also provided by the applicable classes to subtract and add time. The following snippet of code illustrates the use of the ChronoUnit enum constants with these methods:

```
import java.time.LocalDateTime;
import java.time.temporal.ChronoUnit;
...
LocalDateTime now = LocalDateTime.now();

// Get the date time 4 days ago
LocalDateTime ldt2 = now.minus(4, ChronoUnit.DAYS);

// Use the minusDays() method to get the same result
LocalDateTime ldt3 = now.minusDays(4);

// Get date and time 4 hours later
LocalDateTime ldt4 = now.plus(4, ChronoUnit.HOURS);

// Use the plusHours() method to get the same result
LocalDateTime ldt5 = now.plusHours(4);

System.out.println("Current Datetime: " + now);
System.out.println("4 days ago: " + ldt2);
System.out.println("4 days ago: " + ldt3);
System.out.println("4 hours after: " + ldt4);
System.out.println("4 hours after: " + ldt5);
```

```
Current Datetime: 2014-01-03T22:47:47.375
4 days ago: 2013-12-30T22:47:47.375
4 days ago: 2013-12-30T22:47:47.375
4 hours after: 2014-01-04T02:47:47.375
4 hours after: 2014-01-04T02:47:47.375
```

Local Date, Time, and Datetime

An instance of the LocalDate class represents a date without a time or time zone. Several methods in the class let you convert a LocalDate to other datetime objects and manipulate its fields (year, month, and day) to obtain another LocalDate. The following snippet of code creates some LocalDate objects:

```
// Get the current local date
LocalDate ldt1 = LocalDate.now();

// Create a local date May 10, 2012
LocalDate ldt2 = LocalDate.of(2012, Month.MAY, 10);

// Create a local date, which is 10 days after the epoch date 1970-01-01
LocalDate ldt3 = LocalDate.ofEpochDay(10); // 1970-01-11
```

The LocalDate class contains two constants, MAX and MIN, that are the maximum and minimum supported LocalDate respectively. The value for LocalDate.MAX is +999999999-12-31 and LocalDate.MIN is -999999999-01-01.

An instance of the LocalTime class represents a time without a date or time zone. Time is represented to a nanosecond precision. It contains MIN, MAX, MIDNIGHT, and NOON constants that represent time constants of 00:00, 23:59:59.999999999, 00:00, and 12:00, respectively. Several methods in this class let you create, manipulate, and compare times in different ways. The following snippet of code creates some LocalTime objects:

```
// Get the current local time
LocalTime lt1 = LocalTime.now();

// Create a local time 07:30
LocalTime lt2 = LocalTime.of(7, 30);

// Create a local time 07:30:50
LocalTime lt3 = LocalTime.of(7, 30, 50);

// Create a local time 07:30:50.000005678
LocalTime lt4 = LocalTime.of(7, 30, 50, 5678);
```

An instance of the LocalDateTime class represents a date and a time without a time zone. It provides several methods to create, manipulate, and compare datetimes. You can think of a LocalDateTime as a combination of LocalDate and LocalTime.

```
LocalDateTime = LocalDate + LocalTime
```

The following snippet of code creates some `LocalDateTime` objects:

```
// Get the current local datetime
LocalDateTime ldt1 = LocalDateTime.now();

// A local datetime 2012-05-10T16:14:32
LocalDateTime ldt2 = LocalDateTime.of(2012, Month.MAY, 10, 16, 14, 32);

// Construct a local datetime from a local date and a local time
LocalDate ld1 = LocalDate.of(2012, 5, 10);
LocalTime lt1 = LocalTime.of(16, 18, 41);
LocalDateTime ldt3 = LocalDateTime.of(ld1, lt1); // 2012-05-10T16:18:41
```

Please refer to the online API documentation for these classes for a complete list of methods. Make sure to read the "Exploring the New Date-Time API" section in this chapter before exploring the online API documentation. You will find over 60 methods just in one class, `LocalDateTime`. Without knowing the pattern behind those method names, looking at the API documentation for these classes will be overwhelming. Remember that you can achieve the same results using different methods in the API.

Listing 12-7 demonstrates some ways to create and perform operations on a local date, time, and datetime.

Listing 12-7. Using a Local Date, Time, and Datetime

```
// LocalDateTimeTest.java
package com.jdojo.datetime;

import java.time.LocalDate;
import java.time.LocalDateTime;
import java.time.LocalTime;
import java.time.Month;

public class LocalDateTimeTest {
        public static void main(String[] args) {
                // Create a local date and time
                LocalDate ld = LocalDate.of(2012, Month.MAY, 11);
                LocalTime lt = LocalTime.of(8, 52, 23);
                System.out.println("ld: " + ld);
                System.out.println("ld.isLeapYear(): " + ld.isLeapYear());
                System.out.println("lt: " + lt);

                // Create a local datetime from the local date and time
                LocalDateTime ldt = LocalDateTime.of(ld, lt);
                System.out.println("ldt: " + ldt);

                // Add 2 months and 25 minutes to the local datetime
                LocalDateTime ldt2 = ldt.plusMonths(2).plusMinutes(25) ;
                System.out.println("ldt2: " + ldt2);
```

```
                    // Derive the local date and time from teh localdatetime
                    LocalDate ld2 = LocalDate.from(ldt2);
                    LocalTime lt2 = LocalTime.from(ldt2);
                    System.out.println("ld2: " + ld2);
                    System.out.println("lt2: " + lt2);

        }
}
```

```
ld: 2012-05-11
ld.isLeapYear(): true
lt: 08:52:23
ldt: 2012-05-11T08:52:23
ldt2: 2012-07-11T09:17:23
ld2: 2012-07-11
lt2: 09:17:23
```

You can add years, months, and days to a LocalDate. What would be the result if you add one month to 2014-01-31? If the date-Time API simply adds the month to the month field, the result would be 2014-02-31, which is an invalid date. After adding the month, the result is checked if it is a valid date. If it is not a valid date, the day of month is adjusted to the last day of the month. In this case, the result would be 2014-02-28.

```
LocalDate ld1 = LocalDate.of(2014, Month.JANUARY, 31);
LocalDate ld2 = ld1.plusMonths(1);
System.out.println(ld1);
System.out.println(ld2);
```

```
2014-01-31
2014-02-28
```

If you add days to a LocalDate, the month and year fields are adjusted to keep the result a valid date.

```
LocalDate ld1 = LocalDate.of(2014, Month.JANUARY, 31);
LocalDate ld2 = ld1.plusDays(30);
LocalDate ld3 = ld1.plusDays(555);
System.out.println(ld1);
System.out.println(ld2);
System.out.println(ld3);
```

```
2014-01-31
2014-03-02
2015-08-09
```

How do you compute number of days, hours, etc. between two dates and times? The Date-Time API has different ways to compute the period between two dates and times. I will defer the discussion on such computations until the section "Period Between Two Dates and Times."

Offset Time and Datetime

An instance of the OffsetTime and OffsetDateTime classes represents a time and a datetime, respectively, with a fixed zone offset from UTC. An offset time and datetime have no knowledge of a time zone. Examples of an offset time and an offset datetime in the ISO-8601 format are 10:50:11+5:30 and 2012-05-11T10:50:11+5:30, respectively.

■ **Tip** There is no OffsetDate class. It was part of the initial design. Later, it was dropped.

The relationships between local and offset dates and times can be represented as follows:

```
OffsetTime = LocalTime + ZoneOffset
OffsetDateTime = LocalDateTime + ZoneOffset
```

Working with an offset time and datetime is similar to working with their local counterparts, except that you have to use a zone offset. You can always extract a LocalXxx from an OffsetXxx. An OffsetDateTime stores an instant on the timeline, and hence, conversion between OffsetDateTime and Instant is supported.

Listing 12-8 shows examples of creating offset time and datetime. When you get the current offset time and datetime using the now() method, the system default time zone is used to obtain the zone offset value. You will get a different output for current time and datetime.

Listing 12-8. Using Offset Dates, Times, and Datetimes

```java
// OffsetDateTimeTest.java
package com.jdojo.datetime;

import java.time.Instant;
import java.time.LocalDate;
import java.time.LocalTime;
import java.time.OffsetDateTime;
import java.time.OffsetTime;
import java.time.ZoneId;
import java.time.ZoneOffset;

public class OffsetDateTimeTest {
        public static void main(String[] args) {
                // Get the current offset time
                OffsetTime ot1 = OffsetTime.now();
                System.out.println("Current offset time: " + ot1);

                // Creete a zone offset +05:30
                ZoneOffset offset = ZoneOffset.ofHoursMinutes(5, 30);

                // Create an offset time
                OffsetTime ot2 = OffsetTime.of(16, 40, 28, 0, offset);
                System.out.println("An offset time: " + ot2);

                // Get the current offset datetime
                OffsetDateTime odt1 = OffsetDateTime.now();
                System.out.println("Current offset datetime: " + odt1);
```

439

```
                    // Create an offset datetime
                    OffsetDateTime odt2 = OffsetDateTime.of(2012, 5, 11,
                                                    18, 10, 30, 0,
                                                    offset);
                    System.out.println("An offset datetime: " + odt2);

                    // Get the local date and time from the offset datetime
                    LocalDate ld1 = odt1.toLocalDate();
                    LocalTime lt1 = odt1.toLocalTime();
                    System.out.println("Current Local Date: " + ld1);
                    System.out.println("Current Local Time: " + lt1);

                    // Get the instant from the offset datetime
                    Instant i1 = odt1.toInstant();
                    System.out.println("Current Instant: " + i1);

                    // Create an offset datetime from the instant
                    ZoneId usChicago = ZoneId.of("America/Chicago");
                    OffsetDateTime odt3 = OffsetDateTime.ofInstant(i1, usChicago);
                    System.out.println("Offset datetime from instant: " + odt3);
            }
    }
```

```
Current offset time: 08:43:35.074-06:00
An offset time: 16:40:28+05:30
Current offset datetime: 2014-01-06T08:43:35.121-06:00
An offset datetime: 2012-05-11T18:10:30+05:30
Current Local Date: 2014-01-06
Current Local Time: 08:43:35.121
Current Instant: 2014-01-06T14:43:35.121Z
Offset datetime from instant: 2014-01-06T08:43:35.121-06:00
```

Zoned Datetime

An instance of the ZonedDateTime class represents a datetime with time zone rules. The time zone rules include a zone offset and rules for its variation because of Daylight Saving Time. There are no ZonedDate and ZonedTime; they do not make sense.

The relationships between a ZonedDateTime and a LocalDateTime can be represented as

ZonedDateTime = LocalDateTime + ZoneId

The following is an example of creating a ZonedDateTime from a LocalDateTime:

```
ZoneId usCentral = ZoneId.of("America/Chicago");
LocalDateTime ldt = LocalDateTime.of(2012, Month.MAY, 11, 7, 30);
ZonedDateTime zdt = ZonedDateTime.of(ldt, usCentral);
System.out.println(zdt);
```

```
2012-05-11T07:30-05:00[America/Chicago]
```

Not all combinations of a `LocalDateTime` and a `ZoneId` result in a valid `ZonedDateTime`. There may be a gap or overlap on the local timeline in a time zone because of the Daylight Saving Time change. For example, in the America/Chicago time zone on March 10, 2013 at 02:00, the clock was moved an hour forward, thus leaving a gap of one hour on the local timeline; the time between 02:00 and 02:59 did not exist. In the same America/Chicago time zone on November 3, 2013 at 02:00, the clock was moved an hour backward, thus creating an overlap of one hour on the local timeline; the time between 01:00 and 01:59 existed twice. The Date-Time API has well-defined rules to handle such gaps and overlaps.

- If the local datetime falls in the middle of the gap, the time is moved forward by the same amount as the gap. For example, if you want to construct a zoned datetime for the time zone America/Chicago for March 10, 2013 at 02:30:00, you will get March 10, 2013 at 3:30:00. The time is moved forward by an hour, which is equal to the gap of an hour.

- If the local datetime falls in the middle of the overlap, the time is valid. In the gap, two zone offsets exist: one the earlier offset that existed before moving the clock backward and one the later offset that exists after moving the clock backward. By default, for the time in the gap, the zone offset that existed earlier is used. The `ZonedDateTime` class contains `withEarlierOffsetAtOverlap()` and `withLaterOffsetAtOverlap()`, which let you select the desired zone offset if the time falls in the overlap.

The following snippet of code demonstrates the results of `ZonedDateTime` with the time falling in the gap and overlap:

```
ZoneId usChicago = ZoneId.of("America/Chicago");

// 2013-03-10T02:30 did not exist in America/Chicago time zone
LocalDateTime ldt = LocalDateTime.of(2013, Month.MARCH, 10, 2, 30);
ZonedDateTime zdt = ZonedDateTime.of(ldt, usChicago);
System.out.println(zdt);

// 2013-10-03T01:30 existed twice in America/Chicago time zone
LocalDateTime ldt2 = LocalDateTime.of(2013, Month.NOVEMBER, 3, 1, 30);
ZonedDateTime zdt2 = ZonedDateTime.of(ldt2, usChicago);
System.out.println(zdt2);

// Try using the two rules for overlaps: one will use the earlier
// offset -05:00 (the default) and another the later offset -06:00
System.out.println(zdt2.withEarlierOffsetAtOverlap());
System.out.println(zdt2.withLaterOffsetAtOverlap());
```

```
2013-03-10T03:30-05:00[America/Chicago]
2013-11-03T01:30-05:00[America/Chicago]
2013-11-03T01:30-05:00[America/Chicago]
2013-11-03T01:30-06:00[America/Chicago]
```

The ZonedDateTime class contains a static factory method ofLocal(LocalDateTime localDateTime, ZoneId zone, ZoneOffset preferredOffset). You can use this method to create a ZonedDateTime by specifying the preferred zone offset in case there are two zone offsets available for the local time in the specified zone. If the specified referred zone offset is invalid, the earlier zone offset for the overlap is used. The following snippet of code demonstrates the use of this method. When I provide an invalid preferred offset -07:00, the earlier offset -05:00 is used.

```
ZoneId usChicago = ZoneId.of("America/Chicago");
ZoneOffset offset5 = ZoneOffset.of("-05:00");
ZoneOffset offset6 = ZoneOffset.of("-06:00");
ZoneOffset offset7 = ZoneOffset.of("-07:00");

// At 2013-10-03T01:30, -05:00 and -06:00 offsets were valid for
// the time zone America/Chicago
LocalDateTime ldt = LocalDateTime.of(2013, Month.NOVEMBER, 3, 1, 30);
ZonedDateTime zdt5 = ZonedDateTime.ofLocal(ldt, usChicago, offset5);
ZonedDateTime zdt6 = ZonedDateTime.ofLocal(ldt, usChicago, offset6);
ZonedDateTime zdt7 = ZonedDateTime.ofLocal(ldt, usChicago, offset7);
System.out.println("With offset " + offset5 + ": " + zdt5);
System.out.println("With offset " + offset6 + ": " + zdt6);
System.out.println("With offset " + offset7 + ": " + zdt7);
```

```
With offset -05:00: 2013-11-03T01:30-05:00[America/Chicago]
With offset -06:00: 2013-11-03T01:30-06:00[America/Chicago]
With offset -07:00: 2013-11-03T01:30-05:00[America/Chicago]
```

The ZonedDateTime class contains several methods to convert it to local and offset date, time and datetime representations, compare its instances, and obtain its new instances by changes some of its fields. Listing 12-9 shows how to work with zoned datetimes. You will get a different output for the current date and time.

Listing 12-9. Using the ZonedDateTime Class

```
// ZonedDateTimeTest.java
package com.jdojo.datetime;

import java.time.Instant;
import java.time.LocalDateTime;
import java.time.Month;
import java.time.OffsetDateTime;
import java.time.ZoneId;
import java.time.ZoneOffset;
import java.time.ZonedDateTime;

public class ZonedDateTimeTest {
        public static void main(String[] args) {
                // Get the current zoned datetime for the system default time zone
                ZonedDateTime zdt1 = ZonedDateTime.now();
                System.out.println("Current zoned datetime:" + zdt1);

                // Create a local datetime
                LocalDateTime ldt = LocalDateTime.of(2012, Month.MARCH, 11, 7, 30);
```

```
            // Create some zoned datetimes
            ZoneId usCentralZone = ZoneId.of("America/Chicago");
            ZonedDateTime zdt2 = ZonedDateTime.of(ldt, usCentralZone);
            System.out.println(zdt2);

            // Get zone offset and zone id
            ZoneOffset offset = zdt2.getOffset();
            ZoneId zone = zdt2.getZone();
            System.out.println("Offset:" + offset + ", Zone:" + zone);

            // Subtract 10 hours. Zone-offset changes from -05:00 to -06:00
            ZonedDateTime zdt3 = zdt2.minusHours(10);
            System.out.println(zdt3);

            // Create a datetime in Asia/Kolkata time zone
            ZoneId indiaKolkataZone = ZoneId.of("Asia/Kolkata");
            ZonedDateTime zdt4 = ZonedDateTime.of(ldt, indiaKolkataZone);
            System.out.println(zdt4);

            // Perform some conversions on zoned date time
            LocalDateTime ldt2 = zdt4.toLocalDateTime();
            OffsetDateTime odt = zdt4.toOffsetDateTime();
            Instant i1 = zdt4.toInstant();
            System.out.println("To local datetime: " + ldt2);
            System.out.println("To offset datetime: " + odt);
            System.out.println("To instant: " + i1);
        }
}
```

```
Current zoned datetime:2014-01-07T21:20:58.200-06:00[America/Chicago]
2012-03-11T07:30-05:00[America/Chicago]
Offset:-05:00, Zone:America/Chicago
2012-03-10T20:30-06:00[America/Chicago]
2012-03-11T07:30+05:30[Asia/Kolkata]
To local datetime: 2012-03-11T07:30
To offset datetime: 2012-03-11T07:30+05:30
To instant: 2012-03-11T02:00:00Z
```

Same Instant, Different Times

Sometimes you want to convert a datetime in a time zone to a datetime in another time zone. It is similar to asking the date and time in India when it is May 14, 2012 16:30 in Chicago. You can get this in several ways. You can use the toInstant() method of the ZonedDateTime class to get the instant from the first zoned datetime and use the ofInstant() method to create the second zoned datetime. You can also use the withZoneSameInstant(ZoneId newZoneId) method of the ZonedDateTime class, as shown in Listing 12-10, to achieve the same result.

Listing 12-10. Converting a Datetime in a Time Zone to Another Time Zone

```java
// DateTimeZoneConversion.java
package com.jdojo.datetime;

import java.time.LocalDateTime;
import java.time.Month;
import java.time.ZoneId;
import java.time.ZonedDateTime;

public class DateTimeZoneConversion {
        public static void main(String[] args) {
                LocalDateTime ldt = LocalDateTime.of(2012, Month.MAY, 14, 16, 30);

                ZoneId usCentral = ZoneId.of("America/Chicago");
                ZonedDateTime zdt = ZonedDateTime.of(ldt, usCentral);
                System.out.println("In US Central Time Zone:" + zdt);

                ZoneId asiaKolkata = ZoneId.of("Asia/Kolkata");
                ZonedDateTime zdt2 = zdt.withZoneSameInstant(asiaKolkata);
                System.out.println("In Asia/Kolkata Time Zone:" + zdt2);

                ZonedDateTime zdt3 = zdt.withZoneSameInstant(ZoneId.of("Z"));
                System.out.println("In UTC Time Zone:" + zdt3);
        }
}
```

```
In US Central Time Zone:2012-05-14T16:30-05:00[America/Chicago]
In Asia/Kolkata Time Zone:2012-05-15T03:00+05:30[Asia/Kolkata]
In UTC Time Zone:2012-05-14T21:30Z
```

Clocks

The Clock class is an abstraction for the real-world clock. It provides access to the current instant, date, and time in a time zone. You can obtain a clock for the system default time zone.

```java
Clock clock = Clock.systemDefaultZone();
```

You can also get a clock for a specified time zone.

```java
// Get a clock for Asia/Kolkata time zone
ZoneId asiaKolkata = ZoneId.of("Asia/Kolkata");
Clock clock2 = Clock.system(asiaKolkata);
```

To get the current instant, date, and time from a clock, you can use the now(Clock c) method of the datetime related classes.

```java
// Get the system default clock
Clock clock = Clock.systemDefaultZone();
```

```
// Get the current instant of the clock
Instant instant1 = clock.instant();

// Get the current instant using the clock and the Instant class
Instant instant2 = Instant.now(clock);

// Get the local date using the clock
LocalDate ld = LocalDate.now(clock);

// Get the zoned datetime using the clock
ZonedDateTime zdt = ZonedDateTime.now(clock);
```

The now() method without arguments in all date, time, and datetime classes uses the system default clock for the default time zone. The following two statements use the same clock:

```
LocalTime lt1 = LocalTime.now();
LocalTime lt2 = LocalTime.now(Clock.systemDefaultZone());
```

The systemUTC() method of the Clock class returns a clock for the UTC time zone. You can also obtain a fixed clock that always returns the same time. A fixed clock is useful in testing when you want your test cases to use the same current time and not depend on the current time of the system clock. You can use the fixed(Instant fixedInstant, ZoneId zone) static method of the Clock class to get a clock with a fixed instant in a specified time zone. The Clock class also lets you obtain a clock that gives time at a fixed offset from another clock.

A clock is always aware of its time zone. You can obtain the system default time zone using the Clock class as follows:

```
ZoneId defaultZone = Clock.systemDefaultZone().getZone();
```

■ **Tip**   The default implementation of the Clock class ignores the leap seconds. You can also extend the Clock class to implement your own clock.

Periods

A period is an amount of time defined in terms of calendar fields years, months, and days. A duration is also an amount of time measured in terms of seconds and nanoseconds. Negative periods are supported.

What is the difference between a period and a duration? A duration represents an exact number of nanoseconds, whereas a period represents an inexact amount of time. A period is for humans what a duration is for machines.

Some examples of periods are 1 day, 2 months, 5 days, 3 months and 2 days, etc. When someone mentions a 2 month period, you do not know the exact amount of nanoseconds in that 2 months. A 2 month period may mean different number of days (and hence different nanoseconds) depending on when that period starts. For example, a 2 month period from midnight January 1 may represent 59 or 60 days depending on whether the year is a leap year or not. Similarly, a period of 1 day may represent 23, 24, or 25 hours depending on the day whether that day observes the start/end of the Daylight Saving Time or not.

An instance of the Period class represents a period. Use one of the following static factory methods to create a Period:

- static Period of(int years, int months, int days)

- static Period ofDays(int days)

- static Period ofMonths(int months)

- static Period ofWeeks(int weeks)

- static Period ofYears(int years)

The following snippet of code creates some instances of the Period class:

```
Period p1 = Period.of(2, 3, 5);    // 2 years, 3 months, and 5 days
Period p2 = Period.ofDays(25);     // 25 days
Period p3 = Period.ofMonths(-3);   // -3 months
Period p4 = Period.ofWeeks(3);     // 3 weeks (21 days)
System.out.println(p1);
System.out.println(p2);
System.out.println(p3);
System.out.println(p4);
```

```
P2Y3M5D
P25D
P-3M
P21D
```

You can perform additions, subtractions, multiplications, and negation on a period. The division operation performs an integer division, for example, 7 divided by 3 is 2. The following snippet of code shows some of the operations and their results on periods:

```
Period p1 = Period.ofDays(15);     // P15D
Period p2 = p1.plusDays(12);       // P27D
Period p3 = p1.minusDays(12);      // P3D
Period p4 = p1.negated();          // P-15D
Period p5 = p1.multipliedBy(3);    // P45D
```

Use the plus() and minus() methods of the Period class to add one period to another and to subtract one period from another. Use the normalized() method of the Period class to normalize the years and months. The method ensures that the month value stays within 0 to 11. For example, a period of "2 years and 15 months" will be normalized to "3 years and 3 months."

```
Period p1 = Period.of(2, 3, 5);
Period p2 = Period.of(1, 15, 28);

System.out.println("p1: " + p1);
System.out.println("p2: " + p2);
System.out.println("p1.plus(p2): " + p1.plus(p2));
System.out.println("p1.plus(p2).normalized(): " + p1.plus(p2).normalized());
System.out.println("p1.minus(p2): " + p1.minus(p2));
```

```
p1: P2Y3M5D
p2: P1Y15M28D
p1.plus(p2): P3Y18M33D
p1.plus(p2).normalized(): P4Y6M33D
p1.minus(p2): P1Y-12M-23D
```

There is a big difference in the way the Date-Time API treats computations based on periods and durations. Computations including periods behave the way humans would expect. For example, when you add a period of one day to a ZonedDateTime, the date component changes to the next day, keeping the time the same, irrespective of how many hours the day had (23, 24, or 25 hours). However, when you add a duration of a day, it will always add 24 hours. Let's walk through an example to clarify this.

On 2012-03-11T02:00, the clocks in the US Central time zone were moved forward by one hour, making 2012-03-11 a 23-hour day. Suppose you give a person a datetime of 2012-03-10T07:30 in the US Central time zone. If you ask him what would be the datetime after a day, his answer would be 2012-03-11T07:30. His answer is natural because, for humans, adding one day to the current datetime gives the next day with the same time. Let's ask the same question of a machine. Ask the machine to add 24 hours, which is considered the same as 1 day, to 2012-03-10T07:30. The machine's response would be 2012-03-11T08:30 because it will add exactly 24 hours to the initial datetime, knowing that the hour between 02:00 and 03:00 did not exist. Listing 12-11 demonstrates this discussion using a Java program.

Listing 12-11. Difference in Adding a Period and Duration to a Datetime

```java
// PeriodTest.java
package com.jdojo.datetime;

import java.time.Duration;
import java.time.LocalDateTime;
import java.time.Month;
import java.time.Period;
import java.time.ZoneId;
import java.time.ZonedDateTime;

public class PeriodTest {
        public static void main(String[] args) {
                ZoneId usCentral = ZoneId.of("America/Chicago");
                LocalDateTime ldt = LocalDateTime.of(2012, Month.MARCH, 10, 7, 30);
                ZonedDateTime zdt1 = ZonedDateTime.of(ldt, usCentral);
                Period p1 = Period.ofDays(1);
                Duration d1 = Duration.ofHours(24);

                // Add a period of 1 day and a duration of 24 hours
                ZonedDateTime zdt2 = zdt1.plus(p1);
                ZonedDateTime zdt3 = zdt1.plus(d1);

                System.out.println("Start Datetime: " + zdt1);
                System.out.println("After 1 Day period: " + zdt2);
                System.out.println("After 24 Hours duration: " + zdt3);
        }
}
```

```
Start Datetime: 2012-03-10T07:30-06:00[America/Chicago]
After 1 Day period: 2012-03-11T07:30-05:00[America/Chicago]
After 24 Hours duration: 2012-03-11T08:30-05:00[America/Chicago]
```

Period Between Two Dates and Times

It is a common requirement to compute the amount of time elapsed between two dates, times, and datetimes. For example, you may need to compute the number of days between two local dates or the number of hours between two local datetimes. The Date-Time API provides methods to compute the elapsed period between two dates and times. There are two ways to get the amount of time between two dates and times.

- Use the between() method on one of the constants in the ChronoUnit enum.

- Use the until() method on one of the datetime-related classes, for example, LocalDate, LocalTime, LocalDateTime, ZonedDateTime, etc.

The ChronoUnit enum has a between() method, which takes two datetime objects and returns a long. The method returns the amount of time elapsed from the first argument to the second argument. If the second argument occurs before the first one, it returns a negative amount. The returned amount is the complete number of units between two dates and times. For example, if you call HOURS.between(lt1, lt2), where lt1 and lt2 are 07:00 and 09:30 respectively, it will return 2, not 2.5. However, if you call MINUTES.between(lt1, lt2), it will return 150.

The until() method takes two parameters. The first parameter is the end date or time. The second parameter is the time unit in which to compute the elapsed time. The program in Listing 12-12 shows how to use both methods to compute the amount of time between two dates and times.

Listing 12-12. Computing the Amount of Time Elapsed Between Two Dates and Times

```java
// TimeBetween.java
package com.jdojo.datetime;

import java.time.LocalDate;
import java.time.LocalTime;
import java.time.Month;
import static java.time.temporal.ChronoUnit.DAYS;
import static java.time.temporal.ChronoUnit.HOURS;
import static java.time.temporal.ChronoUnit.MINUTES;

public class TimeBetween {
        public static void main(String[] args) {
                LocalDate ld1 = LocalDate.of(2014, Month.JANUARY, 7);
                LocalDate ld2 = LocalDate.of(2014, Month.MAY, 18);
                long days = DAYS.between(ld1, ld2);

                LocalTime lt1 = LocalTime.of(7, 0);
                LocalTime lt2 = LocalTime.of(9, 30);
                long hours = HOURS.between(lt1, lt2);
                long minutes = MINUTES.between(lt1, lt2);

                System.out.println("Using between (days): " + days);
                System.out.println("Using between (hours): " + hours);
                System.out.println("Using between (minutes): " + minutes);
```

```
         // Using the until() method
         long days2 = ld1.until(ld2, DAYS);
         long hours2 = lt1.until(lt2, HOURS);
         long minutes2 = lt1.until(lt2, MINUTES);

         System.out.println("Using until (days): " + days2);
         System.out.println("Using until (hours): " + hours2);
         System.out.println("Using until (minutes): " + minutes2);
      }
}
```

```
Using between (days): 131
Using between (hours): 2
Using between (minutes): 150
Using until (days): 131
Using until (hours): 2
Using until (minutes): 150
```

It is not always possible to compute the amount of time elapsed between two dates and times. For example, you cannot tell the number of hours between a LocalDate and a LocalDateTime as the LocalDate does not store a time component. If such parameters are passed to the methods, a runtime exception is thrown. The rule is that the specified end date/time should be convertible to the start date/time.

Partials

A partial is a date, time, or datetime that does not fully specify an instant on a timeline, but still makes sense to humans. With some more information, a partial may match multiple instants on the timeline. For example, December 25 is not a complete date that can be determined uniquely on a timeline; however, it makes sense when we talk about Christmas. Similarly, January 1 makes sense as New Year's Day.

You must have a date, time, and time zone to identify an instant uniquely on the timeline. If you have some, but not all, of the three pieces of information, you have a partial. You cannot obtain an Instant from a partial without supplying some more pieces of information. I already discussed some partials in previous sections.

A LocalDate, LocalTime, LocalDateTime, and OffsetTime are examples of partials. An OffsetDateTime and ZonedDateTime are not partials; they have information to identify an instant on the timeline uniquely.

I will discuss three more partials in this section:

- Year

- YearMonth

- MonthDay

The names of these partials easily describe them. A Year represents a year, for example, 2012, 2013, etc. A YearMonth represents a valid combination of a year and a month, for example, 2012–05, 2013–09, etc. A MonthDay represents a valid combination of a month and a day of month, for example, - -12-15. Listing 12-13 shows some of the operations you can perform on these partials.

Listing 12-13. Using Year, YearMonth, and MonthDay Partials

```java
// Partials.java
package com.jdojo.datetime;

import java.time.Month;
import java.time.MonthDay;
import java.time.Year;
import java.time.YearMonth;

public class Partials {
    public static void main(String[] args) {
        // Use Year
        Year y1 = Year.of(2012);    // 2012
        Year y2 = y1.minusYears(1); // 2011
        Year y3 = y1.plusYears(1);  // 2013
        Year y4 = Year.now();       // current year
        if (y1.isLeap()) {
            System.out.println(y1 + " is a leap year.");
        }
        else {
            System.out.println(y1 + " is not a leap year.");
        }

        // Use YearMonth
        YearMonth ym1 = YearMonth.of(2012, Month.MAY); // 2012-05

        // Get the number of days in the month
        int monthLen = ym1.lengthOfMonth(); // 31
        System.out.println("Days in month in " + ym1 + ": " + monthLen);

        // Get the number of days in the year
        int yearLen = ym1.lengthOfYear(); // 366
        System.out.println("Days in year in " + ym1 + ": " + yearLen);

        // Use MonthDay
        MonthDay md1 = MonthDay.of(Month.DECEMBER, 25);
        MonthDay md2 = MonthDay.of(Month.FEBRUARY, 29);
        if (md2.isValidYear(2009)) {
            System.out.println(md2 + " occurred in 2009");
        }
        else {
            System.out.println(md2 + " did not occur in 2009");
        }
    }
}
```

```
2012 is a leap year.
Days in month in 2012-05: 31
Days in year in 2012-05: 366
--02-29 did not occur in 2009.
```

Finally, Listing 12-14 contains an example of combining two partials to get another partial. It's the complete program to compute Christmas days for the next five years.

Listing 12-14. Combining a Year and MonthDay to get a LocalDate

```
// ChristmasDay.java
package com.jdojo.datetime;

import java.time.LocalDate;
import java.time.Month;
import java.time.MonthDay;
import java.time.Year;
import java.time.format.TextStyle;
import java.util.Locale;

public class ChristmasDay {
    public static void main(String[] args) {
        MonthDay dec25 = MonthDay.of(Month.DECEMBER, 25);
        Year year = Year.now();

        // Construct and print Christmas days in next five years
        for (int i = 1; i <= 5; i++) {
            LocalDate ld = year.plusYears(i).atMonthDay(dec25);
            int yr = ld.getYear();
            String weekDay = ld.getDayOfWeek()
                            .getDisplayName(TextStyle.FULL, Locale.getDefault());
            System.out.format("Christmas in %d is on %s.%n", yr, weekDay);
        }
    }
}
```

```
Christmas in 2015 is on Friday.
Christmas in 2016 is on Sunday.
Christmas in 2017 is on Monday.
Christmas in 2018 is on Tuesday.
Christmas in 2019 is on Wednesday.
```

The program creates a MonthDay partial for December 25 and keeps combining a year to it to get a LocalDate. You can rewrite the program in Listing 12-14 using the LocalDate class as shown below. It shows the versatility of the Date-Time API, which allows you do achieve the same result in different ways.

```
LocalDate ld = LocalDate.of(Year.now().getValue(), Month.DECEMBER, 25);
for (int i = 1; i <= 5; i++) {
    ld = ld.withYear(ld.getYear() + 1);
    // format and print ld here
}
```

Adjusting Dates

Sometimes you want to adjust a date and time to have a particular characteristic, for example, the first Monday of the month, the next Tuesday, etc. You can perform adjustments to a date and time using an instance of the TemporalAdjuster interface. The interface has one method, adjustInto(), that takes a Temporal and returns a Temporal. The Date-Time API provides several commonly used datetime adjusters. If they do not suit your needs, you can roll out your own adjusters. I will discuss examples of both.

A TemporalAdjusters class is provided. It consists of all static methods that return different types of predefined date adjusters. The datetime-related classes contain a with(TemporalAdjuster adjuster) method. You need to pass the returned object from one of the methods of the TemporalAdjusters class to the with() method. The with() method will return a copy of the original datetime object by adjusting its components using the logic in the adjuster. The following snippet of code computes the first Monday after January 1, 2014:

```
import java.time.DayOfWeek;
import java.time.LocalDate;
import java.time.Month;
import java.time.temporal.TemporalAdjusters;
...
LocalDate ld1 = LocalDate.of(2014, Month.JANUARY, 1);
LocalDate ld2 = ld1.with(TemporalAdjusters.next(DayOfWeek.MONDAY));
System.out.println(ld1);
System.out.println(ld2);
```

```
2014-01-01
2014-01-06
```

The method names are self-explanatory, as you can see in Table 12-3.

Table 12-3. *List of Some Useful Methods in the TemporalAdjusters Class*

Method	Description
next(DayOfWeek dayOfWeek)	Returns an adjuster that adjusts the date to be the first specified day of week after the date being adjusted.
nextOrSame(DayOfWeek dayOfWeek)	Returns an adjuster that adjusts the date to be the first specified day of week after the date being adjusted. If the date being adjusted is already on the specified day of week, it returns the same date.
previous(DayOfWeek dayOfWeek)	Returns an adjuster that adjusts the date to be the first specified day of week before the date being adjusted.
previousOrSame(DayOfWeek dayOfWeek)	Returns an adjuster that adjusts the date to be the first specified day of week before the date being adjusted. If the date being adjusted is already on the specified day of week, it returns the same date.
firstInMonth(DayOfWeek dayOfWeek), lastInMonth(DayOfWeek dayOfWeek)	Each returns an adjuster that adjusts the date to be the first/last (respectively) specified day of week in the month represented by the date being adjusted.

(continued)

Table 12-3. (*continued*)

Method	Description
dayOfWeekInMonth(int ordinal, DayOfWeek dayOfWeek)	Returns an adjuster that adjusts the date to be the specified ordinal day of week in the month represented by the date being adjusted. It is suitable for computing dates like the third Monday in January 2014.
firstDayOfMonth() lastDayOfMonth()	Each returns an adjuster that adjusts the date to be the first/last day of the month represented by the date being adjusted.
firstDayOfYear() lastDayOfYear()	Each returns an adjuster that adjusts the date to be the first/last day of the year represented by the date being adjusted.
firstDayOfNextMonth()	Returns an adjuster that adjusts the date to be the first day of the next month represented by the date being adjusted.
firstDayOfNextYear()	Returns an adjuster that adjusts the date to be the first day of the next year represented by the date being adjusted.
ofDateAdjuster(UnaryOperator<LocalDate> dateBasedAdjuster)	A convenience method for developers to write their own LocalDate-based adjusters.

The TemporalAdjuster class provides a dayOfWeekInMonth() method. This method returns a date adjuster that adjusts a date to the specified ordinal day of week, for example, the first Sunday of month, the third Friday of month, etc. The specified ordinal value may be between 1 and 5. If the ordinal is 5 and the month does not have a fifth specified dayOfWeek, it returns the first specified dayOfWeek from the next month. The following snippet of code requests the date adjuster the fifth Sunday in May 2012. The date adjuster returns the first Sunday in June 2012 because May 2012 does not have a fifth Sunday.

```
LocalDate ld1 = LocalDate.of(2012, Month.MAY, 22);
LocalDate ld2 = ld1.with(TemporalAdjusters.dayOfWeekInMonth(5, DayOfWeek.SUNDAY));
System.out.println(ld1);
System.out.println(ld2);
```

```
2012-05-22
2012-06-03
```

You can use a date adjuster with other methods to perform a complex adjustment. You can obtain the date for the second Friday of month after 3 months and 14 days from today as follows:

```
LocalDate date = LocalDate.now()
                    .plusMonths(3)
                    .plusDays(14)
                    .with(DateAdjusters.dayOfWeekInMonth(2, DayOfWeek.FRIDAY));
```

You can use the ofDateAdjuster() method to create your own date adjuster for a LocalDate. The following snippet of code creates a date adjuster and uses it. The adjuster adds 3 months and 2 days to the date being adjusted. Note that I have used a lambda expression to create the adjuster, which I have not discussed yet.

```java
// Create an adjuster that retruns a date after 3 months and 2 days
TemporalAdjuster adjuster =
        TemporalAdjusters.ofDateAdjuster((LocalDate date) -> date.plusMonths(3).plusDays(2));

// Use the adjuster
LocalDate today = LocalDate.now();
LocalDate dayAfter3Mon2Day = today.with(adjuster);
System.out.println("Today: " + today);
System.out.println("After 3 months and 2 days: " + dayAfter3Mon2Day);
```

```
Today: 2014-03-01
After 3 months and 2 days: 2014-06-03
```

Listing 12-15 demonstrates how to how adjust dates.

Listing 12-15. Adjusting Dates and Times

```java
// AdjustDates.java
package com.jdojo.datetime;

import java.time.DayOfWeek;
import java.time.LocalDate;
import java.time.temporal.TemporalAdjuster;
import java.time.temporal.TemporalAdjusters;

public class AdjustDates {
        public static void main(String[] args) {
                LocalDate today = LocalDate.now();
                System.out.println("Today: " + today);

                // Use a DateAdjuster to adjust today's date to the next Monday
                LocalDate nextMonday = today.with(TemporalAdjusters.next(DayOfWeek.MONDAY));
                System.out.println("Next Monday: " + nextMonday);

                // Use a DateAdjuster to adjust today's date to the last day of month
                LocalDate lastDayOfMonth = today.with(TemporalAdjusters.lastDayOfMonth());
                System.out.println("Last day of month: " + lastDayOfMonth);

                // Create an adjuster that retruns a date after 3 months and 2 days
                TemporalAdjuster adjuster = TemporalAdjusters.ofDateAdjuster(
                                (LocalDate date) -> date.plusMonths(3).plusDays(2));
                LocalDate dayAfter3Mon2Day = today.with(adjuster);
                System.out.println("Date after adding 3 months and 2 days: " + dayAfter3Mon2Day);
        }
}
```

```
Today: 2014-01-08
Next Monday: 2014-01-13
Last day of month: 2014-01-31
Date after adding 3 months and 2 days: 2014-04-10
```

Let's create a custom date adjuster. If the date being adjusted is on weekends or Friday 13, it returns the next Monday. Otherwise, it returns the original date. That is, the adjuster will return only weekdays, except Friday 13. Listing 12-16 contains the complete code for the adjuster. The adjuster has been defined as a constant in the class. Using the adjuster is as easy as passing the CustomAdjusters.WEEKDAYS_WITH_NO_FRIDAY_13 constant to the with() method of the datetime classes that can supply a LocalDate.

```
LocalDate ld = LocalDate.of(2013, Month.DECEMBER, 13); // Friday
LocalDate ldAdjusted = ld.with(CustomAdjusters.WEEKDAYS_WITH_NO_FRIDAY_13); // Next Monday
```

Listing 12-16. Creating a Custom Date Adjuster

```java
// CustomAdjusters.java
package com.jdojo.datetime;

import java.time.DayOfWeek;
import static java.time.DayOfWeek.FRIDAY;
import static java.time.DayOfWeek.MONDAY;
import static java.time.DayOfWeek.SATURDAY;
import static java.time.DayOfWeek.SUNDAY;
import java.time.LocalDate;
import java.time.temporal.TemporalAdjuster;
import java.time.temporal.TemporalAdjusters;

public class CustomAdjusters {
        public final static TemporalAdjuster WEEKDAYS_WITH_NO_FRIDAY_13 =
                        TemporalAdjusters.ofDateAdjuster(CustomAdjusters::getWeekDayNoFriday13);

        // No public constructor as it is a utility class
        private CustomAdjusters() { }

        private static LocalDate getWeekDayNoFriday13(LocalDate date) {
                // Initialize the new date with the original one
                LocalDate newDate = date;

                DayOfWeek day = date.getDayOfWeek();
                if (day == SATURDAY || day == SUNDAY || (day == FRIDAY && date.getDayOfMonth() == 13)) {
                        // Return next Monday
                        newDate = date.with(TemporalAdjusters.next(MONDAY));
                }
                return newDate;
        }
}
```

Listing 12-17 demonstrates how to use the custom date adjuster. December 12, 2013 was on Thursday. You use the adjuster to adjust December 12, 13, and 14 in 2013. December 12, 2013 is returned without any adjustments. The other two dates are adjusted to next Monday, which is December 16, 2013. Note that the adjuster can be used on any datetime object that can supply a LocalDate. The program uses it to adjust a ZonedDateTime.

Listing 12-17. Using the Custom Date Adjuster

```java
// CustomAdjusterTest.java
package com.jdojo.datetime;

import java.time.LocalDate;
import java.time.LocalTime;
import java.time.Month;
import java.time.ZoneId;
import java.time.ZonedDateTime;

public class CustomAdjusterTest {
        public static void main(String[] args) {
                LocalDate ld1 = LocalDate.of(2013, Month.DECEMBER, 12); // Thursday
                LocalDate ld2 = LocalDate.of(2013, Month.DECEMBER, 13); // Friday
                LocalDate ld3 = LocalDate.of(2013, Month.DECEMBER, 14); // Saturday

                LocalDate ld1Adjusted = ld1.with(CustomAdjusters.WEEKDAYS_WITH_NO_FRIDAY_13);
                System.out.println(ld1 + " adjusted to " + ld1Adjusted);

                LocalDate ld2Adjusted = ld2.with(CustomAdjusters.WEEKDAYS_WITH_NO_FRIDAY_13);
                System.out.println(ld2 + " adjusted to " + ld2Adjusted);

                LocalDate ld3Adjusted = ld3.with(CustomAdjusters.WEEKDAYS_WITH_NO_FRIDAY_13);
                System.out.println(ld3 + " adjusted to " + ld3Adjusted);

                // Use it to adjust a ZonedDateTime
                ZonedDateTime zdt =
                        ZonedDateTime.of(ld2, LocalTime.of(8, 45), ZoneId.of("America/Chicago"));
                ZonedDateTime zdtAdjusted = zdt.with(CustomAdjusters.WEEKDAYS_WITH_NO_FRIDAY_13);
                System.out.println(zdt + " adjusted to " + zdtAdjusted);
        }
}
```

```
2013-12-12 adjusted to 2013-12-12
2013-12-13 adjusted to 2013-12-16
2013-12-14 adjusted to 2013-12-16
2013-12-13T08:45-06:00[America/Chicago] adjusted to 2013-12-16T08:45-06:00[America/Chicago]
```

Querying Datetime Objects

All datetime classes support queries. A query is a request for information. Note that you can obtain the components of a datetime object, for example, the year from a LocalDate, using the get(TemporalField field) method of the datetime object. Use a query to request information that is not available as components. For example, you can query a LocalDate whether it is a Friday 13. The result of a query can be of any type.

An instance of the TemporalQuery<R> interface represents a query. All datetime classes contain a query() method, which takes a TemporalQuery as a parameter and returns a result.

TemporalQueries is a utility class that contains several predefined queries as its static methods, as shown in Table 12-4. If a datetime object does not have the information sought in the query, the query returns null. For example, the query for a LocalDate from a LocalTime object returns null. Chronology is an interface that is used to identify and manipulate dates in a calendar system.

Table 12-4. *List of Utility Methods in the TemporalQueries Class*

Method	Return Type	Description
chronology()	TemporalQuery<Chronology>	A query to get the chronology.
localDate()	TemporalQuery<LocalDate>	A query to get the LocalDate.
localTime()	TemporalQuery<LocalTime>	A query to get the LocalTime.
offset()	TemporalQuery<ZoneOffset>	A query to get the ZoneOffset.
precision()	TemporalQuery<TemporalUnit>	A query to get the smallest supported unit.
zone()	TemporalQuery<ZoneId>	A query to get the ZoneId. If the ZoneId is not available it queries for ZoneOffset. It returns null if both are not available, for example, a LocalDate has neither.
zoneId()	TemporalQuery<ZoneId>	A query to get the ZoneId. If ZoneId is not available, it returns null.

The program in Listing 12-18 shows how to use predefined queries. It uses queries to get the precision and LocalDate from a LocalDate, a LocalTime, and a ZonedDateTime.

Listing 12-18. Querying Datetime Objects

```java
// QueryTest.java
package com.jdojo.datetime;

import java.time.LocalDate;
import java.time.LocalTime;
import java.time.ZonedDateTime;
import java.time.temporal.TemporalQueries;
import java.time.temporal.TemporalQuery;
import java.time.temporal.TemporalUnit;

public class QueryTest {
    public static void main(String[] args) {
        // Get references of the precision and local date queries
        TemporalQuery<TemporalUnit> precisionQuery = TemporalQueries.precision();
        TemporalQuery<LocalDate> localDateQuery = TemporalQueries.localDate();
```

```
                    // Query a LocalDate
                    LocalDate ld = LocalDate.now();
                    TemporalUnit precision = ld.query(precisionQuery);
                    LocalDate queryDate = ld.query(localDateQuery);
                    System.out.println("Precision of LocalDate: " + precision);
                    System.out.println("LocalDate of LocalDate: " + queryDate);

                    // Query a LocalTime
                    LocalTime lt = LocalTime.now();
                    precision = lt.query(precisionQuery);
                    queryDate = lt.query(localDateQuery);
                    System.out.println("Precision of LocalTime: " + precision);
                    System.out.println("LocalDate of LocalTime: " + queryDate);

                    // Query a ZonedDateTime
                    ZonedDateTime zdt = ZonedDateTime.now();
                    precision = zdt.query(precisionQuery);
                    queryDate = zdt.query(localDateQuery);
                    System.out.println("Precision of ZonedDateTime: " + precision);
                    System.out.println("LocalDate of ZonedDateTime: " + queryDate);
        }
}
```

```
Precision of LocalDate: Days
LocalDate of LocalDate: 2014-01-11
Precision of LocalTime: Nanos
LocalDate of LocalTime: null
Precision of ZonedDateTime: Nanos
LocalDate of ZonedDateTime: 2014-01-11
```

Creating and using a custom query is easy. You can create a custom query in two ways.

- Create a class that implements the TemporalQuery interface and use instances of the class as a query.

- Use any method reference as a query. The method should take a TemporalAccessor and return an object. The return type of the method defines the result type for the query.

Listing 12-19 contains the code for a Friday13Query class. The class implements the TemporalQuery interface. The queryFrom() method is part of the interface implementation. The method returns true if the datetime object contains a date that falls on Friday 13. Otherwise, it returns false. The query returns false if the datetime object does not contain a day of month and day of week information, for example a LocalTime object. The class defines a constant IS_FRIDAY_13 that can be used as a query.

Listing 12-19. A Class Implementing the TemporalQuery Interface

```
// Friday13Query.java
package com.jdojo.datetime;

import java.time.DayOfWeek;
import java.time.temporal.TemporalAccessor;
import java.time.temporal.TemporalQuery;
```

```
import static java.time.temporal.ChronoField.DAY_OF_MONTH;
import static java.time.temporal.ChronoField.DAY_OF_WEEK;
import static java.time.DayOfWeek.FRIDAY;

public class Friday13Query implements TemporalQuery<Boolean> {
        public final static Friday13Query IS_FRIDAY_13 = new Friday13Query();

        // Prevent outside code from creating objects of this class
        private Friday13Query() {}

        @Override
        public Boolean queryFrom(TemporalAccessor temporal) {
                if (temporal.isSupported(DAY_OF_MONTH) && temporal.isSupported(DAY_OF_WEEK)) {
                        int dayOfMonth = temporal.get(DAY_OF_MONTH);
                        int weekDay = temporal.get(DAY_OF_WEEK);
                        DayOfWeek dayOfWeek = DayOfWeek.of(weekDay);
                        if (dayOfMonth == 13 && dayOfWeek == FRIDAY) {
                                return Boolean.TRUE;
                        }
                }
                return Boolean.FALSE;
        }
}
```

The following snippet of code uses the Friday13Query with three datetime objects. The first LocalDate falls on Friday 13, as you can see in the output that the query returns true.

```
LocalDate ld1 = LocalDate.of(2013, 12, 13);
Boolean isFriday13 = ld1.query(Friday13Query.IS_FRIDAY_13);
System.out.println("Date: " + ld1 + ", isFriday13: " + isFriday13);

LocalDate ld2 = LocalDate.of(2014, 1, 10);
isFriday13 = ld2.query(Friday13Query.IS_FRIDAY_13);
System.out.println("Date: " + ld2 + ", isFriday13: " + isFriday13);

LocalTime lt = LocalTime.of(7, 30, 45);
isFriday13 = lt.query(Friday13Query.IS_FRIDAY_13);
System.out.println("Time: " + lt + ", isFriday13: " + isFriday13);
```

```
Date: 2013-12-13, isFriday13: true
Date: 2014-01-10, isFriday13: false
Time: 07:30:45, isFriday13: false
```

Listing 12-20 contains the code for a CustomQueries class. The class contains a static method isFriday13(). The method reference for isFriday13() method can be used as a query.

Listing 12-20. A CustomQueries Class with a IsFriday13 Method That Can Be Used a Query

```java
// CustomQueries.java
package com.jdojo.datetime;

import java.time.DayOfWeek;
import static java.time.DayOfWeek.FRIDAY;
import static java.time.temporal.ChronoField.DAY_OF_MONTH;
import static java.time.temporal.ChronoField.DAY_OF_WEEK;
import java.time.temporal.TemporalAccessor;

public class CustomQueries {
        public static Boolean isFriday13(TemporalAccessor temporal) {
                if (temporal.isSupported(DAY_OF_MONTH) && temporal.isSupported(DAY_OF_WEEK)) {
                        int dayOfMonth = temporal.get(DAY_OF_MONTH);
                        int weekDay = temporal.get(DAY_OF_WEEK);
                        DayOfWeek dayOfWeek = DayOfWeek.of(weekDay);
                        if (dayOfMonth == 13 && dayOfWeek == FRIDAY) {
                                return Boolean.TRUE;
                        }
                }
                return Boolean.FALSE;
        }
}
```

The following snippet of code uses the method reference of the isFriday13() method in the Custom query class as a query. The code uses the same datetime objects as in the above example and you get the result.

```java
LocalDate ld1 = LocalDate.of(2013, 12, 13);
Boolean isFriday13 = ld1.query(CustomQueries::isFriday13);
System.out.println("Date: " + ld1 + ", isFriday13: " + isFriday13);

LocalDate ld2 = LocalDate.of(2014, 1, 10);
isFriday13 = ld2.query(CustomQueries::isFriday13);
System.out.println("Date: " + ld2 + ", isFriday13: " + isFriday13);

LocalTime lt = LocalTime.of(7, 30, 45);
isFriday13 = lt.query(CustomQueries::isFriday13);
System.out.println("Time: " + lt + ", isFriday13: " + isFriday13);
```

```
Date: 2013-12-13, isFriday13: true
Date: 2014-01-10, isFriday13: false
Time: 07:30:45, isFriday13: false
```

It is typical of the Date-Time API to provide multiple choices to perform the same task. Let's consider a task of getting the LocalTime from a ZonedDateTime. The program in Listing 12-21 shows five ways of achieving this.

Listing 12-21. Multiple Ways of Getting the LocalTime from a ZonedDateTime

```java
// LocalTimeFromZonedDateTime.java
package com.jdojo.datetime;

import java.time.LocalTime;
import java.time.ZonedDateTime;
import java.time.temporal.TemporalQueries;

public class LocalTimeFromZonedDateTime {
        public static void main(String[] args) {
                ZonedDateTime zdt = ZonedDateTime.now();

                // Use the toLocalTime() method of the ZonedDateTime class (preferred)
                LocalTime lt1 = zdt.toLocalTime();

                // Use the from() methdo of the LocalTime class
                LocalTime lt2 = LocalTime.from(zdt);

                // Use the localTime() query
                LocalTime lt3 = zdt.query(TemporalQueries.localTime());

                // Use the LocalTime::from method as a query
                LocalTime lt4 = zdt.query(LocalTime::from);

                // Get all time components and construct a LocalTime
                int hours = zdt.getHour();
                int minutes = zdt.getMinute();
                int seconds = zdt.getSecond();
                int nanos = zdt.getNano();
                LocalTime lt5 = LocalTime.of(hours, minutes, seconds, nanos);

                // Print all LocalTimes
                System.out.println("lt1: " + lt1);
                System.out.println("lt2: " + lt2);
                System.out.println("lt3: " + lt3);
                System.out.println("lt4: " + lt4);
                System.out.println("lt5: " + lt5);
        }
}
```

```
lt1: 22:51:01.925
lt2: 22:51:01.925
lt3: 22:51:01.925
lt4: 22:51:01.925
lt5: 22:51:01.925
```

Which method is the correct way? Most of the time, all methods will execute the same logic. However, some methods are more readable than others. In this case, the code calling the toLocalTime() method of the ZonedDateTime class should be used as it is straightforward and most readable. At least, you should not extract the time components from the ZonedDateTime to construct the LocalTime, as shown in the fifth method in the example.

Non-ISO Calendar Systems

The date classes such as LocalDate use the ISO calendar system, which is the Gregorian calendar. The Date-Time API also lets you use other calendars such as Thai Buddhist calendar, Hijrah calendar, Minguo calendar, and Japanese calendar. The non-ISO calendar-related classes are in the java.time.chrono package.

There is an XxxChronology and XxxDate class for each of the available non-ISO calendar system. The XxxChronology class represents the Xxx calendar system whereas XxxDate class represents a date in the Xxx calendar system. Each XxxChronology class contains an INSTANCE constant that represents a singleton instance of that class. For example, HijrahChronology and HijrahDate are classes that you will be using to work with the Hijrah calendar system. The following snippet of code shows two ways to get the current date in the Thai Buddhist calendar:

```
import java.time.chrono.ThaiBuddhistChronology;
import java.time.chrono.ThaiBuddhistDate;
...
ThaiBuddhistChronology thaiBuddhistChrono = ThaiBuddhistChronology.INSTANCE;
ThaiBuddhistDate now = thaiBuddhistChrono.dateNow();
ThaiBuddhistDate now2 = ThaiBuddhistDate.now();
System.out.println("Current Date in Thai Buddhist: " + now);
System.out.println("Current Date in Thai Buddhist: " + now2);
```

```
Current Date in Thai Buddhist: ThaiBuddhist BE 2557-01-09
Current Date in Thai Buddhist: ThaiBuddhist BE 2557-01-09
```

You can also convert dates in one calendar system to another. ISO dates to non-ISO dates conversion is also allowed. Converting dates from one calendar system to another is just a matter of calling the from() static method of the target date class and passing the source date object as its parameter. Listing 12-22 shows how to convert ISO date to Thai Buddhist date and vice versa.

Listing 12-22. Using the Thai Buddhist and ISO Calendars

```
// InterCalendarDates.java
package com.jdojo.datetime;

import java.time.LocalDate;
import java.time.chrono.ThaiBuddhistDate;

public class InterCalendarDates {
        public static void main(String[] args) {
                ThaiBuddhistDate thaiBuddhistNow = ThaiBuddhistDate.now();
                LocalDate isoNow = LocalDate.now();
                System.out.println("Thai Buddhist Current Date: " + thaiBuddhistNow);
                System.out.println("ISO Current Date: " + isoNow);
```

```
                // Convert Thai Buddhist date to ISO date and vice versa
                ThaiBuddhistDate thaiBuddhistNow2 = ThaiBuddhistDate.from(isoNow);
                LocalDate isoNow2 = LocalDate.from(thaiBuddhistNow);
                System.out.println("Thai Buddhist Current Date from ISO: " + thaiBuddhistNow2);
                System.out.println("ISO Current Date from Thai Buddhist: " + isoNow2);
        }
}
```

```
Thai Buddhist Current Date: ThaiBuddhist BE 2557-01-09
ISO Current Date: 2014-01-09
Thai Buddhist Current Date from ISO: ThaiBuddhist BE 2557-01-09
ISO Current Date from Thai Buddhist: 2014-01-09
```

Formatting Dates and Times

An object of the DateTimeFormatter class lets you format and parse a datetime object. By formatting, I mean representing a datetime object in a user-defined textual form, for example, representing a LocalDate May 24, 2012 as "05/24/2012." Sometimes formatting is also referred as printing, because formatting features also let you print (or output) a textual representation of a datetime object to an Appendable object such as a StringBuilder.

Parsing is the reverse of formatting. It lets you construct a datetime object from a textual representation of a datetime. Creating a LocalDate object from the text "05/24/2012" to represent May 24, 2012 is an example of parsing.

Different ways of formatting and parsing datetimes exist. Learning how to format datetimes may be difficult, if you do not learn it the right way. The most important point to keep in mind is that formatting and parsing are always performed by an object of the DateTimeFormatter class. The difference lies in how you create that object. The DateTimeFormatter class does not provide any public constructors. You must obtain its object indirectly. In the beginning, the confusion lies in how to get its object. Use one of the following two methods of the DateTimeFormatter class to format a date, time, or datetime:

- String format(TemporalAccessor temporal)

- void formatTo(TemporalAccessor temporal, Appendable appendable)

The format() method takes a date, time, or datetime object and returns a textual representation of the object based on the rules of the formatter. The formatTo() method lets you write the textual representation of the object to an Appendable, for example, a file, a StringBuilder, etc.

To format a datetime object, a formatter needs two pieces of information: a format pattern and a locale. Sometimes one or both pieces of information are defaulted for you; sometimes, you provide them.

You can perform formatting in several ways. They all use, directly or indirectly, a DateTimeFormatter object.

- Using pre-defined standard datetime formatters

- Using the format() method of the datetime classes

- Using user-defined patterns

- Using the DateTimeFormatterBuilder class

Using Predefined Formatters

Predefined formatters are defined as constants in the DateTimeFormatter class. They are listed in in Table 12-5. Most of the formatters use ISO datetime formats; some formatters use a slightly modified version of ISO formats.

Table 12-5. *List of Predefined Datetime Formatters*

Formatter	Description	Example
BASIC_ISO_DATE	An ISO date formatter to format and parse a date without using a separator between two date components.	20140109, 20140109-0600
ISO_DATE, ISO_TIME, ISO_DATE_TIME	Date, time, and datetime formatters to format and parse dates, times, and datetimes using the ISO separators.	2014-01-09, 2014-01-09-06:00, 15:38:32.927, 15:38:32.943-06:00, 2014-01-09T15:20:07.747-06:00, 2014-01-09T15:20:07.825-06:00[America/Chicago]
ISO_INSTANT	An instant formatter to format and parse an instant (or a datetime object representing an instant such as a ZonedDateTime) in UTC format.	2014-01-09T21:23:56.870Z
ISO_LOCAL_DATE, ISO_LOCAL_TIME, ISO_LOCAL_DATE_TIME	Date, time, and datetime formatters to format or parse dates, times, and datetimes without an offset.	2014-01-09, 15:30:14.352, 2014-01-09T15:29:11.384
ISO_OFFSET_DATE, ISO_OFFSET_TIME, ISO_OFFSET_DATE_TIME	Date, time, and datetime formatters to format and parse dates, times, and datetimes with an offset using ISO format.	2014-01-09-06:00, 15:34:29.851-06:00, 2014-01-09T15:33:07.07-06:0
ISO_ZONED_DATE_TIME	A datetime formatter to format and parse a datetime with a zone id, if available.	2014-01-09T15:45:49.112-06:00, 2014-01-09T15:45:49.128-06:00[America/Chicago]
ISO_ORDINAL_DATE	A date formatter to format and parse a date with year and day-of-year.	2014-009
ISO_WEEK_DATE	A date formatter to format and parse week-based dates. The format is year-Wweek_of_year-day_of_week. For example, '2014-W02-4' means the fourth day of the second week in 2014.	2014-W02-4, 2014-W02-4-06:00
RFC_1123_DATE_TIME	A datetime formatter to format and parse datetimes for e-mails using the RFC1123 specification.	Thu, 9 Jan 2014 15:50:44 -060

Using the predefined formatters is easy: just pass the date/time object to the format(). The following snippet of code uses ISO_DATE formatter to format a LocalDate, an OffsetDateTime, and ZonedDateTime. You may get a different output as it formats and prints the current date.

```
import java.time.LocalDate;
import java.time.OffsetDateTime;
import java.time.ZonedDateTime;
import static java.time.format.DateTimeFormatter.ISO_DATE;
...
```

```
// Format dates using the ISO_DATE formatter
String ldStr = ISO_DATE.format(LocalDate.now());
String odtStr = ISO_DATE.format(OffsetDateTime.now());
String zdtStr = ISO_DATE.format(ZonedDateTime.now());

System.out.println("Local Date; " + ldStr);
System.out.println("Offset Datetime: " + odtStr);
System.out.println("Zoned Datetime: " + zdtStr);
```

```
Local Date; 2014-01-09
Offset Datetime: 2014-01-09-06:00
Zoned Datetime: 2014-01-09-06:00
```

Pay attention to the names of the predefined formatters. The datetime object being formatted must contain the components as suggested by their names. For example, the ISO_DATE formatter expects the presence of the date components, and hence, it should be not used to format time-only objects such as a LocalTime. Similarly, the SIO_TIME formatter should be used to format a LocalDate.

```
// A runtime error as a LocalTime does not contain date components
String ltStr = ISO_DATE.format(LocalTime.now());
```

Using the format( ) Method of Datetime Classes

You can format a datetime object using its format() method. The format() method takes an object of the DateTimeFormatter class. The following snippet of code uses this approach. The ISO_DATE formatter is used.

```
import java.time.LocalDate;
import java.time.OffsetDateTime;
import java.time.ZonedDateTime;
import static java.time.format.DateTimeFormatter.ISO_DATE;
...
LocalDate ld = LocalDate.now();
String ldStr = ld.format(ISO_DATE);
System.out.println("Local Date: " + ldStr);

OffsetDateTime odt = OffsetDateTime.now();
String odtStr = odt.format(ISO_DATE);
System.out.println("Offset Datetime: " + odtStr);

ZonedDateTime zdt = ZonedDateTime.now();
String zdtStr = zdt.format(ISO_DATE);
System.out.println("Zoned Datetime: " + zdtStr);
```

```
local Date: 2014-01-09
Offset Datetime: 2014-01-09-06:00
Zoned Datetime: 2014-01-09-06:00
```

Using User-Defined Patterns

One of the most commonly used methods in the DateTimeFormatter class is the ofPattern() method, which returns a DateTimeFormatter object with the specified format pattern and locale.

- static DateTimeFormatter ofPattern(String pattern)

- static DateTimeFormatter ofPattern(String pattern, Locale locale)

The following snippet obtains two formatters to format a date in "Month day, Year" format. The first formatter formats the datetime in the default locale and the second one in the German locale.

```
// Get a formatter for the default locale
DateTimeFormatter fmt1 = DateTimeFormatter.ofPattern("MMMM dd, yyyy");

// Get a formatter for the German locale
DateTimeFormatter fmt2 = DateTimeFormatter.ofPattern("MMMM dd, yyyy", Locale.GERMAN);
```

Sometimes you have a DateTimeFormatter object for a pattern and a locale. You want to use the same pattern to format a datetime in another locale. The DateTimeFormatter class has a withLocale() method that returns a DateTimeFormatter object for the specified locale that uses the same pattern. In the above snippet of code, you could have replaced the second statement with the following one:

```
// Get a formatter for the German locale using the same pattern as fmt1
DateTimeFormatter fmt2 = fmt1.withLocale(Locale.GERMAN);
```

■ **Tip** Use the getLocale() method of the DateTimeFormatter class to know the locale that it will use to format datetimes.

Datetime formatting is performed based on a pattern. A formatting pattern is a sequence of characters that have special meanings. For example, MMMM in a pattern uses the fully spelled name of a month, such as January, February, etc.; MMM uses the short form of a month name, such as Jan, Feb, etc.; MM uses two digits month number, such as 01, 02, etc.; M uses one or two digits month number, such as 1, 2, 10, 11, etc.

In a format pattern, some characters have special meanings and some are used literally. Characters with special meanings will be interpreted by the formatter and they will be replaced with datetime components. A formatter outputs the literal characters as they appear in the pattern. All letters 'A' to 'Z' and 'a' to 'z' are reserved as pattern letters, although not all are used. If you want to include a literal string in a pattern, you need to enclose it in single quotes. To output a single quote, you need to use two consecutive single quotes.

A datetime formatter outputs any non-letter characters, other than [,] and a single quote, directly. However, it is recommended that you enclose them in single quotes. Suppose you have a local date of May 29, 2012. Both patterns of "1997 MMMM dd, yyyy" and "'1997' MMMM dd, yyyy" will output 1997 May 29, 2012; however, the latter, which uses single quotes around the literal 1997, is recommended.

Table 12-6 lists the symbols used in patterns and their meanings. All examples in the table use "2012-07-29T07:30:12.789-05:00[America/Chicago]" as the input datetime.

Table 12-6. *Datetime Formatting Symbols, Their Descriptions with Examples*

Symbol	Description	Examples	
		Pattern	**Output**
G	Era	G	AD
		GGGG	Anno Domini
		GGGGG	A
u	Year It can be a positive or negative number. After an era start date, it is a positive number. Before an era start date, it is a negative number. For example, the year value for 2014 AD is 2014 and the year value for 2014 BC is -2014.	u/uuu/uuuu	2012
		uu	12
		uuuuu	02012
y	Year of era It counts the year forward or backward from the era start date. It is always a positive number. For example, the year value for 2014 AD is 2014 and the year value for 2014 BC is 2015. In Common Era, year 0 is 1 BC.	y/yyy/yyyy	2012
		yy	12
		yyyyy	02012
D	Day of year (1 -366)	D	150
M/L	Month of year	M	5
		MM	05
		MMM	Jul
		MMMM	July
d	Day of month The pattern d will output values like 1, 2, 10, 29, etc. The pattern dd will zero-pad the values as 01, 02, 10, 29, etc. to make them always two digits. The pattern ddd will output values like 001, 010, 029, etc.	d	29
Q/q	Quarter of year	Q	3
		QQ	03
		QQQ	Q3
		QQQQ	3rd quarter
Y	Week-based year	Y	2012
		YY	12
		YYY/YYYY	2012
w	Week of week-based year	w	31
W	Week of month	W	5
E	Day of week	E	7
		EE	07
		EEE	Sun
		EEEEE	Sunday

(continued)

Table 12-6. (*continued*)

Symbol	Description	Examples	
F	Day of week in month	F	1
a	AM/PM of day	a	AM
h	Clock hour of AM/PM (1-12)	h	7
K	Hour of AM/PM (0-11)	K	7
k	Clock hour of AM/PM (1-24)	k	7
H	Hour of day (0-23)	H	7
		HH	07
m	Minute of hour	mm	30
s	Second of minute	ss	12
S	Fraction of second	SSSSSSSSS	000000789
A	Millisecond of day	A	27012000
n	Nanosecond of second	n	789
N	Nanosecond of day	N	27012000000789
V	Time zone ID	VV	America/Chicago
z	Time zone name	z	CDT
Z	Zone offset When the zone offset is zero, it outputs '+0000' or '+00:00' depending on whether you use Z, ZZ, or ZZZ.	Z	-0500
		ZZ	-0500
		ZZZ	-05:00
		ZZZZ	GMT-05:00
O	Localized zone offset	O	GMT-5
X	Zone offset Unlike the symbol 'Z', it prints Z for the zone offset Zero. X outputs only the hour such as '+09'; XX outputs the hour and minute, without a colon such as '+0830'; XXX outputs the hour and minute with a colon such as '+08:30'; XXXX outputs the hour, minute, and optional second, without a colon such as '+083045'; and, XXXXX outputs the hour, minute, and option second, with a colon such as '+08:30:45'.	XXX	-05:00
x	Same as X, except that it prints '+00' for the zone offset zero, not 'Z'.	xx	-0500
p	Pad next It pads the output of the pattern following it with spaces. For example, if mm outputs 30, pppmm will output ' 30' and ppppmm will output ' 30'. The number of p determines the width of the output.	pppmm	' 30' (Single quotes have been shown to display the padding with a space.)

(continued)

Table 12-6. (*continued*)

Symbol	Description	Examples	

'	Escape for text
	Text within single quotes is output directly. To output a single quote, use two consecutive single quotes.
		`'Hello'`
		
		`'Hello' MMMM`
			`Hello`
			
			`Hello July`

' '	A single quote	`'''Hello''' MMMM`	`'Hello' July`
[ ]	An optional section Please refer to the discussion for an example.		
#, {, }	They are reserved for future use.		

You can have optional sections in a pattern string. The symbols [and] denote the start and the end of an optional section, respectively. A pattern enclosed within an optional section is output only if information is available for all its elements. Otherwise, an optional section is skipped. An optional section may be nested inside another optional section. Listing 12-23 shows how to use an optional section in a pattern. The optional section contains time information. When you format a date, the optional section is skipped.

Listing 12-23. Using an Optional Section in a Datetime Formatting Pattern

```java
// OptionalSectionTest.java
package com.jdojo.datetime;

import java.time.LocalDate;
import java.time.LocalDateTime;
import java.time.LocalTime;
import java.time.Month;
import java.time.format.DateTimeFormatter;

public class OptionalSectionTest {
        public static void main(String[] args) {
                // A pattern with an optional section
                String pattern = "MM/dd/yyyy[ 'at' HH:mm:ss]";
                DateTimeFormatter fmt = DateTimeFormatter.ofPattern(pattern);

                LocalDate ld = LocalDate.of(2012, Month.MAY, 30);
                LocalTime lt = LocalTime.of(17, 30, 12);
                LocalDateTime ldt = LocalDateTime.of(ld,lt);

                // Format a date. Optional section will be skipped because a
                // date does not have time (HH, mm, and ss) information.
                String str1 = fmt.format(ld);
                System.out.println(str1);

                // Format a datetime. Optional section will be output.
                String str2 = fmt.format(ldt);
                System.out.println(str2);
        }
}
```

```
05/30/2012
05/30/2012 at 17:30:12
```

Listing 12-24 shows how to use different patterns to format dates and times.

Listing 12-24. Using Patterns to Format Dates and Times

```java
// FormattingDateTime.java
package com.jdojo.datetime;

import java.time.LocalDate;
import java.time.LocalTime;
import java.time.Month;
import java.time.ZoneId;
import java.time.ZonedDateTime;
import java.time.format.DateTimeFormatter;
import java.time.temporal.Temporal;
import java.util.Locale;

public class FormattingDateTime {
        public static void main(String[] args) {
                LocalDate ld = LocalDate.of(2012, Month.APRIL, 30);
                System.out.println("Formatting date: " + ld);
                format(ld, "M/d/yyyy");
                format(ld, "MM/dd/yyyy");
                format(ld, "MMM dd, yyyy");
                format(ld, "MMMM dd, yyyy");
                format(ld, "EEEE, MMMM dd, yyyy");
                format(ld, "'Month' q 'in' QQQ");
                format(ld, "[MM-dd-yyyy][' at' HH:mm:ss]");

                LocalTime lt = LocalTime.of(16, 30, 5, 78899);
                System.out.println("\nFormatting time:" + lt);
                format(lt, "HH:mm:ss");
                format(lt, "KK:mm:ss a");
                format(lt, "[MM-dd-yyyy][' at' HH:mm:ss]");

                ZoneId usCentral = ZoneId.of("America/Chicago");
                ZonedDateTime zdt = ZonedDateTime.of(ld, lt, usCentral);
                System.out.println("\nFormatting zoned datetime:" + zdt);
                format(zdt, "MM/dd/yyyy HH:mm:ssXXX");
                format(zdt, "MM/dd/yyyy VV");
                format(zdt, "[MM-dd-yyyy][' at' HH:mm:ss]");
        }

        public static void format(Temporal co, String pattern) {
                DateTimeFormatter fmt = DateTimeFormatter.ofPattern(pattern, Locale.US);
                String str = fmt.format(co);
                System.out.println(pattern + ": " + str);
        }
}
```

```
Formatting date: 2012-04-30
M/d/yyyy: 4/30/2012
MM/dd/yyyy: 04/30/2012
MMM dd, yyyy: Apr 30, 2012
MMMM dd, yyyy: April 30, 2012
EEEE, MMMM dd, yyyy: Monday, April 30, 2012
'Month' q 'in' QQQ: Month 2 in Q2
[MM-dd-yyyy][' at' HH:mm:ss]: 04-30-2012

Formatting time:16:30:05.000078899
HH:mm:ss: 16:30:05
KK:mm:ss a: 04:30:05 PM
[MM-dd-yyyy][' at' HH:mm:ss]:  at 16:30:05

Formatting zoned datetime:2012-04-30T16:30:05.000078899-05:00[America/Chicago]
MM/dd/yyyy HH:mm:ssXXX: 04/30/2012 16:30:05-05:00
MM/dd/yyyy VV: 04/30/2012 America/Chicago
[MM-dd-yyyy][' at' HH:mm:ss]: 04-30-2012 at 16:30:05
```

Using Locale Specific Formats

The DateTimeFormatter class has several methods that return a DateTimeFormatter with a predefined formatting pattern suitable for humans to read. Use the following methods to obtain a reference to such formatters:

- DateTimeFormatter ofLocalizedDate(FormatStyle dateStyle)

- DateTimeFormatter ofLocalizedDateTime(FormatStyle dateTimeStyle)

- DateTimeFormatter ofLocalizedDateTime(FormatStyle dateStyle, FormatStyle timeStyle)

- DateTimeFormatter ofLocalizedTime(FormatStyle timeStyle)

These methods accept an argument of FormatStyle enum type, which has four constants: SHORT, MEDIUM, LONG, and FULL. These constants are used to output formatted date and time with a varying degree of detail. The details in the output are locale-specific. The methods use the system default locale. For a different locale, use the withLocal() method to obtain a new DateTimeFormatter with the specified locale.

Listing 12-25 shows how to use some predefined locale-specific formats. It formats dates and times in US (default), German, and Indian locales.

Listing 12-25. Using Predefined Format Patterns

```
// LocalizedFormats.java
package com.jdojo.datetime;

import java.time.LocalDate;
import java.time.LocalDateTime;
import java.time.LocalTime;
import java.time.Month;
import java.time.format.DateTimeFormatter;
import static java.time.format.FormatStyle.FULL;
```

```java
import static java.time.format.FormatStyle.LONG;
import static java.time.format.FormatStyle.MEDIUM;
import static java.time.format.FormatStyle.SHORT;

import java.util.Locale;

public class LocalizedFormats {
        public static void main(String[] args) {
                LocalDate ld = LocalDate.of(2012, Month.APRIL, 19);
                LocalTime lt = LocalTime.of(16, 30, 20);
                LocalDateTime ldt = LocalDateTime.of(ld, lt);

                DateTimeFormatter fmt = DateTimeFormatter.ofLocalizedDate(SHORT);
                System.out.println("Formatter Default Locale: " + fmt.getLocale());
                System.out.println("Short Date: " + fmt.format(ld));

                fmt = DateTimeFormatter.ofLocalizedDate(MEDIUM);
                System.out.println("Medium Date: " + fmt.format(ld));

                fmt = DateTimeFormatter.ofLocalizedDate(LONG);
                System.out.println("Long Date: " + fmt.format(ld));

                fmt = DateTimeFormatter.ofLocalizedDate(FULL);
                System.out.println("Full Date: " + fmt.format(ld));

                fmt = DateTimeFormatter.ofLocalizedTime(SHORT);
                System.out.println("Short Time: " + fmt.format(lt));

                fmt = DateTimeFormatter.ofLocalizedDateTime(SHORT);
                System.out.println("Short Datetime: " + fmt.format(ldt));

                fmt = DateTimeFormatter.ofLocalizedDateTime(MEDIUM);
                System.out.println("Medium Datetime: " + fmt.format(ldt));

                // Use German locale to format the datetime in medius style
                fmt = DateTimeFormatter.ofLocalizedDateTime(MEDIUM)
                                        .withLocale(Locale.GERMAN);
                System.out.println("German Medium Datetime: " + fmt.format(ldt));

                // Use Indian(English) locale to format datetime in short style
                fmt = DateTimeFormatter.ofLocalizedDateTime(SHORT)
                                        .withLocale(new Locale("en", "IN"));
                System.out.println("Indian(en) Short Datetime: " + fmt.format(ldt));

                // Use Indian(English) locale to format datetime in medium style
                fmt = DateTimeFormatter.ofLocalizedDateTime(MEDIUM)
                                        .withLocale(new Locale("en","IN"));
                System.out.println("Indian(en) Medium Datetime: " + fmt.format(ldt));

        }
}
```

```
Formatter Default Locale: en_US
Short Date: 4/19/12
Medium Date: Apr 19, 2012
Long Date: April 19, 2012
Full Date: Thursday, April 19, 2012
Short Time: 4:30 PM
Short Datetime: 4/19/12 4:30 PM
Medium Datetime: Apr 19, 2012 4:30:20 PM
German Medium Datetime: 19.04.2012 16:30:20
Indian(en) Short Datetime: 19/4/12 4:30 PM
Indian(en) Medium Datetime: 19 Apr, 2012 4:30:20 PM
```

Using the DateTimeFormatterBuilder Class

Internally, all datetime formatters are obtained using `DateTimeFormatterBuilder`. Typically, you will not need to use this class. The previously discussed methods are sufficient in almost all use cases. The class has a no-args constructor and many appendXxx() methods. You create an instance of the class and call those appendXxx() methods to build the desired formatter. Finally, call the `toFomatter()` method to get a `DateTimeFormatter` object. The following snippet of code builds a `DateTimeFormatter` object to format a date in the format like "Christmas in YEAR is on WEEK_DAY":

```java
import java.time.LocalDate;
import java.time.format.DateTimeFormatter;
import java.time.format.DateTimeFormatterBuilder;
import static java.time.format.TextStyle.FULL_STANDALONE;
import static java.time.temporal.ChronoField.DAY_OF_WEEK;
import static java.time.temporal.ChronoField.YEAR;
...
DateTimeFormatter formatter = new DateTimeFormatterBuilder()
                                .appendLiteral("Christmas in ")
                                .appendValue(YEAR)
                                .appendLiteral(" is on ")
                                .appendText(DAY_OF_WEEK, FULL_STANDALONE)
                                .toFormatter();
LocalDate ld = LocalDate.of(2014, 12, 25);
String str = ld.format(formatter);
System.out.println(str);
```

```
Christmas in 2014 is on Thursday
```

You can create the same formatter using a pattern, which is a lot easier to write and read than the above code using the `DateTimeFormatterBuilder`.

```
LocalDate ld = LocalDate.of(2014, 12, 25);
String pattern = "'Christmas in' yyyy 'is on' EEEE";
DateTimeFormatter formatter = DateTimeFormatter.ofPattern(pattern);
String str = ld.format(formatter);
System.out.println(str);
```

```
Christmas in 2014 is on Thursday
```

Parsing Dates and Times

Parsing is the process of creating a date, time, or datetime object from a string. Like formatting, parsing is also handled by a DateTimeFormatter. Please refer to the previous section, "Formatting Dates and Times," for details on how to get an instance of the DateTimeFormatter class. The same symbols used for formatting are also used as parsing symbols.

There are two ways to parse a string into a datetime object:

- Using the parse() method of the datetime class

- Using the parse() method of the DateTimeFormatter class

■ **Tip** A DateTimeParseException is thrown if the text cannot be parsed. It is a runtime exception. The class contains two methods to provide the error details. The getErrorIndex() method returns the index in the text where the error occurred. The getParsedString() method returns the text being parsed. It is good practice to handle this exception while parsing a datetime.

Each datetime class has two overloaded versions of the parse() static method. The return type of the parse() method is the same as the defining datetime class. The following are the two version of the parse() method in LocalDate class:

- static LocalDate parse(CharSequence text)

- static LocalDate parse(CharSequence text, DateTimeFormatter formatter)

The first version of the parse() method takes the textual representation of the datetime object in ISO format. For example, for a LocalDate, the text should be in the yyyy-mm-dd format. The second version lets you specify a DateTimeFormatter. The following snippet of code parses two strings into two LocalDate objects:

```
// Parse a LocalDate in ISO format
LocalDate ld1 = LocalDate.parse("2014-01-10");

// Parse a LocalDate in MM/dd/yyyy format
DateTimeFormatter formatter = DateTimeFormatter.ofPattern("MM/dd/yyyy");
LocalDate ld2 = LocalDate.parse("01/10/2014", formatter);

System.out.println("ld1: " + ld1);
System.out.println("ld2: " + ld2);
```

```
ld1: 2014-01-10
ld2: 2014-01-10
```

The DateTimeFormatter class contains several parse() methods to facilitate parsing of strings into datetime objects. The DateTimeFormatter class does not know the type of datetime object that can be formed from the strings. Therefore, most of them return a TemporalAccessor object that you can query to get the datetime components. You can pass the TemporalAccessor object to the from() method of the datetime class to get the specific datetime object. The following snippet of code shows how to parse a string in MM/dd/yyyy format using a DateTimeFormatter object to construct a LocalDate:

```
import java.time.LocalDate;
import java.time.format.DateTimeFormatter;
import java.time.temporal.TemporalAccessor;
...
DateTimeFormatter formatter = DateTimeFormatter.ofPattern("MM/dd/yyyy");
TemporalAccessor ta = formatter.parse("01/10/2014");
LocalDate ld = LocalDate.from(ta);
System.out.println(ld);
```

2014-01-10

Another version of the parse() method takes a TemporalQuery that can be used to parse the string directly into a specific datetime object. The following snippet of code uses this version of the parse() method. The second parameter is the method reference of the from() method of the LocalDate class. You can think of the following snippet of code as shorthand for the above code:

```
DateTimeFormatter formatter = DateTimeFormatter.ofPattern("MM/dd/yyyy");
LocalDate ld = formatter.parse("01/10/2014", LocalDate::from);
System.out.println(ld);
```

2014-01-10

The DateTimeFormatter class contains a parseBest() method. Using this method needs little explanation. Suppose you receive a string as an argument to a method. The argument may contain varying pieces of information for date and time. In such a case, you want to parse the string using the most pieces of information. Consider the following pattern:

```
yyyy-MM-dd['T'HH:mm:ss[Z]]
```

The above pattern has two optional sections. A text with this pattern may be fully parsed to an OffsetDateTime, and partially parsed to a LocalDateTime and a LocalDate. You can create a parser for this pattern as

```
DateTimeFormatter formatter = DateTimeFormatter.ofPattern("yyyy-MM-dd['T'HH:mm:ss[Z]]");
```

The following snippet of code specifies OffsetDateTime, LocalDateTime, and LocalDate as the preferred parsed result types:

```
String text = ...
TemporalAccessor ta = formatter.parseBest(text,
                                          OffsetDateTime::from,
                                          LocalDateTime::from,
                                          LocalDate::from);
```

The method will try to parse the text as the specified types in order and return the first successful result. Typically, a call to the parseBest() method is followed by a series of if-else statement with an instanceof operator to check what type of object was returned. Listing 12-26 shows how to use the parseBest() method. Notice that the fourth text is in invalid format and parsing it throws an exception.

Listing 12-26. Using the parseBest( ) Method of the DateTimeFormatter Class

```java
// ParseBestTest.java
package com.jdojo.datetime;

import java.time.LocalDate;
import java.time.LocalDateTime;
import java.time.OffsetDateTime;
import java.time.format.DateTimeFormatter;
import java.time.format.DateTimeParseException;
import java.time.temporal.TemporalAccessor;

public class ParseBestTest {
        public static void main(String[] args) {
                DateTimeFormatter parser = DateTimeFormatter.ofPattern("yyyy-MM-
dd['T'HH:mm:ss[Z]]");
                parseStr(parser, "2012-05-31");
                parseStr(parser, "2012-05-31T16:30:12");
                parseStr(parser, "2012-05-31T16:30:12-0500");
                parseStr(parser, "2012-05-31Hello");
        }

        public static void parseStr(DateTimeFormatter formatter, String text) {
                try {
                        TemporalAccessor ta = formatter.parseBest(text,
                                                        OffsetDateTime::from,
                                                        LocalDateTime::from,
                                                        LocalDate::from);
                        if (ta instanceof OffsetDateTime) {
                                OffsetDateTime odt = OffsetDateTime.from(ta);
                                System.out.println("OffsetDateTime: " + odt);
                        } else if (ta instanceof LocalDateTime) {
                                LocalDateTime ldt = LocalDateTime.from(ta);
                                System.out.println("LocalDateTime: " + ldt);
                        } else if (ta instanceof LocalDate) {
                                LocalDate ld = LocalDate.from(ta);
                                System.out.println("LocalDate: " + ld);
                        } else {
                                System.out.println("Parsing returned: " + ta);
                        }
                }
                catch (DateTimeParseException e) {
                        System.out.println(e.getMessage());
                }
        }
}
```

```
LocalDate: 2012-05-31
LocalDateTime: 2012-05-31T16:30:12
OffsetDateTime: 2012-05-31T16:30:12-05:00
Text '2012-05-31Hello' could not be parsed, unparsed text found at index 10
```

Legacy Datetime Classes

I'll refer to the datetime-related classes that were available before Java 8 as legacy datetime classes. The main legacy classes are Date, Calendar, and GregorianCalendar. They are in the java.util package. Please refer to the section "Interoperability with Legacy Datetime Classes" for how to convert Date and Calendar objects to datetime objects of the new Date-Time API and vice versa.

The Date Class

An object of the Date class represents an instant in time. A Date object stores the number of milliseconds elapsed since the epoch, midnight January 1, 1970 UTC.

■ **Tip** The Date class in the legacy Date-Time API is similar to the Instant class in the new Date-Time API. They have the precision of millisecond and nanosecond, respectively.

Most of the constructors and methods of the Date class have been deprecated since JDK1.1. The default constructor of the Date class is used to create a Date object with the current system datetime. Listing 12-27 illustrates the use of the Date class. You may get a different output because it prints the current date and time.

Listing 12-27. Using the Date Class

```java
// CurrentLegacyDate.java
package com.jdojo.datetime;

import java.util.Date;

public class CurrentLegacyDate {
    public static void main (String[] args) {
        // Create a new Date object
        Date currentDate = new Date();
        System.out.println("Current date: " + currentDate);

        // Get the milliseconds value of the current date
        long millis = currentDate.getTime();
        System.out.println("Current datetime in millis: " + millis);
    }
}
```

```
Current date: Sat Jan 11 11:19:55 CST 2014
Current datetime in millis: 1389460795979
```

A Date object works with a 1900-based year. When you call the setYear() method of this object to set the year as 2012, you will need to pass 112 (2012 - 1900 = 112). Its getYear() method returns 112 for the year 2012. Months in this class range from 0 to 11 where January is 0, February is 2 . . . and December is 11.

The Calendar Class

Calendar is an abstract class. An abstract class cannot be instantiated. I will discuss abstract classes in detail in the chapter on inheritance. The GregorianCalendar class is a concrete class, which inherits the Calendar class.

The Calendar class declares some final static fields to represent date fields. For example, Calendar.JANUARY can be used to specify the January month in a date. The GregorianCalendar class has a default constructor, which create an object to represent the current datetime. You can also create a GregorianCalendar object to represent a specific date using its other constructors. It also lets you obtain the current date in a particular time zone.

```
// Get the current date in the system default time zone
GregorianCalendar currentDate = new GregorianCalendar();

// Get GregorianCalendar object representing March 26, 2003 06:30:45 AM
GregorianCalendar someDate = new GregorianCalendar(2003, Calendar.MARCH, 26, 6, 30, 45);

// Get Indian time zone, which is GMT+05:30
TimeZone indianTZ = TimeZone.getTimeZone("GMT+05:30");

// Get current date in India
GregorianCalendar indianDate = new GregorianCalendar(indianTZ);

// Get Moscow time zone, which is GMT+03:00
TimeZone moscowTZ = TimeZone.getTimeZone("GMT+03:00");

// Get current date in Moscow
GregorianCalendar moscowDate = new GregorianCalendar(moscowTZ);
```

■ **Tip** A Date contains a datetime. A GregorianCalendar contains a datetime with a time zone.

The month part of a date ranges from 0 to 11. That is, January is 0, February is 1, and so on. It is easier to use the constants declared for months and the other date fields in the Calendar class rather than using their integer values. For example, you should use Calendar.JANUARY constant to represent the January month in your program instead of a 0. You can get the value of a field in a datetime using the get() method by passing the requested field as an argument.

```
// Create a GregorianCalendar object
GregorianCalendar gc = new GregorianCalendar();

// year will contain the current year value
int year = gc.get(Calendar.YEAR);

// month will contain the current month value
int month = gc.get(Calendar.MONTH);
```

```
// day will contain day of month of the current date
int day = gc.get(Calendar.DAY_OF_MONTH);

// hour will contain hour value
int hour = gc.get(Calendar.HOUR);

// minute will contain minute value
int minute = gc.get(Calendar.MINUTE);

// second will contain second values
int second = gc.get(Calendar.SECOND);
```

You can set the date interpretation to be lenient or not lenient by using the setLenient() method of the GregorianCalendar class. By default, it is lenient. If the date interpretation is lenient, a date such as March 35, 2003 is interpreted as April 5, 2003. If date interpretation is not lenient, such a date will result in an error. You can also compare two dates, whether one date occurs before or after another, by using before() and after() methods. There are two methods, add() and roll(), which need explanation. They are described below.

The add( ) Method

The add() method is used to add an amount to a particular field in a date. The amount being added may be negative or positive. Suppose you have the date of December 1, 2003 stored in a GregorianCalendar object. You want to add 5 to the month field. The value for the month field will be 16, which is out of range (0 – 11). In such a case, the larger date field (here, year is larger than month) will be adjusted to accommodate the overflow. The date, after adding 5 to the month field, will be May 1, 2004. The following snippet of code illustrates this concept:

```
GregorianCalendar gc = new GregorianCalendar(2003, Calendar.DECEMBER, 1);
gc.add(Calendar.MONTH, 5); // Now gc represents May 1, 2004
```

This method may result in adjusting smaller fields, too. Suppose you have the date of January 30, 2003 stored in a GregorianCalendar object. You add 1 to the month field. The new month field does not overflow. However, the resulting date, February 30, 2003, is not a valid date. The day of month must be between 1 and 28 in the month of February 2003. In this case, the day of month field is automatically adjusted. It is set to the nearest possible valid value, which is 28. The resulting date will be February 28, 2003.

The roll( ) Method

The roll() method works the same as the add() method, except it does not change the larger field when the field being changed overflows. It may adjust the smaller fields to make the date a valid date. It is an overloaded method.

- void roll(int field, int amount)
- void roll(int field, boolean up)

The second version rolls up/down the specified field by a single unit of time, whereas the first version rolls the specified field by the specified amount. Therefore, gc.roll(Calendar.MONTH, 1) is the same as gc.roll(Calendar. MONTH, true) and gc.roll(Calendar.MONTH, -1) is the same as gc.roll(Calendar.MONTH, false). Listing 12-28 illustrates the use of some of the methods of the GregorianCalendar class. You may get a different output.

Listing 12-28. Using the GregorianCalendar Class

```java
// GregorianDate .java
package com.jdojo.datetime;

import java.util.Calendar;
import java.util.Date;
import java.util.GregorianCalendar;

public class GregorianDate {
        public static void main(String[] args) {
                GregorianCalendar gc = new GregorianCalendar();
                System.out.println("Current Date: " + getStr(gc));

                // Add 1 year
                gc.add(Calendar.YEAR, 1);
                System.out.println("After adding a year: " + getStr(gc));

                // Add 15 days
                gc.add(Calendar.DATE, 15);
                System.out.println("After adding 15 days: " + getStr(gc));

                long millis = gc.getTimeInMillis();
                Date dt = gc.getTime();
                System.out.println("Time in millis: " + millis);
                System.out.println("Time as Date: " + dt);
        }

        public static String getStr(GregorianCalendar gc) {
                int day = gc.get(Calendar.DAY_OF_MONTH);
                int month = gc.get(Calendar.MONTH);
                int year = gc.get(Calendar.YEAR);
                int hour = gc.get(Calendar.HOUR);
                int minute = gc.get(Calendar.MINUTE);
                int second = gc.get(Calendar.SECOND);

                String str = day + "/" + (month + 1) + "/" + year + " " +
                                hour + ":" + minute + ":" + second;
                return str;
        }
}
```

```
Current Date: 11/1/2014 11:35:22
After adding a year: 11/1/2015 11:35:22
After adding 15 days: 26/1/2015 11:35:22
Time in millis: 1422293722726
Time as Date: Mon Jan 26 11:35:22 CST 2015
```

Interoperability with Legacy Datetime Classes

The legacy datetime classes have been around for over 18 years. The new Date-Time API is not going to replace them overnight. As a Java developer, you will be tasked to maintain applications that use the legacy classes. Java 8 provides interoperability between the legacy classes and the new Date-Time API. New methods have been added to the legacy classes to convert their objects to the new Date-Time classes and vice versa. Interoperability of the following legacy classes will be discussed in this section:

- java.util.Date
- java.util.Calendar
- java.util.GregorianCalendar
- java.util.TimeZone
- java.sql.Date
- java.sql.Time
- java.sql.Timestamp
- java.nio.file.attribute.FileTime

Table 12-7 contains the list of legacy datetime classes and their new Date-Time counterparts. All legacy classes, except the Calendar class, provides two-way conversion. The toXxx() methods are instance methods. They return an object of the new datetime class. The other methods are static methods, which accept an object of the new datetime class and return an object of the legacy class. For example, the from() method in the java.util.Date class is a static method, which takes an Instant argument and returns a java.util.Date. The toInstant() method is an instance method and converts a java.util.Date into an Instant.

Table 12-7. *Conversion Between New Datetime and Legacy Datetime Classes*

Legacy Class	New Methods in Legacy Class	Equivalent New Datetime Class
java.util.Date	from(), toInstant()	Instant
Calendar	toInstant()	None
GregorianCalendar	from(), toZonedDateTime()	ZonedDateTime
TimeZone	getTimeZone(), toZoneId()	ZoneId
java.sql.Date	valueOf(), toLocalDate()	LocalDate
Time	valueOf(), toLocalTime()	LocalTime
Timestamp	from(), toInstant()	Instant
	valueOf(), toLocalDateTime()	LocalDateTime
FileTime	from(), toInstant()	Instant

Listing 12-29 shows how to convert a Date to an Instant and vice versa.

Listing 12-29. Converting a Date to an Instant and Vice Versa

```java
// DateAndInstant.java
package com.jdojo.datetime;

import java.util.Date;
import java.time.Instant;

public class DateAndInstant {
        public static void main(String[] args) {
                // Get the current date
                Date dt = new Date();
                System.out.println("Date: " + dt);

                // Convert the Date to an Insatnt
                Instant in = dt.toInstant();
                System.out.println("Instant: " + in);

                // Convert the Instant back to a Date
                Date dt2 = Date.from(in);
                System.out.println("Date: " + dt2);
        }
}
```

```
Date: Sat Jan 11 14:45:02 CST 2014
Instant: 2014-01-11T20:45:02.265Z
Date: Sat Jan 11 14:45:02 CST 2014
```

Typically, the legacy code uses GregorianCalendar to store date, time, and datetime. You can convert it to a ZonedDateTime, which can be converted to any other classes in the new Date-Time API. The Calendar class provides a toInstant() method to convert its instance to an Instant. The Calendar class is abstract. Typically, you would have an instance of its concrete subclass class, for example, GregorianCalendar. Therefore, converting an Instant to a GregorianCalendar would be a two-step process:

- Convert the Instant to a ZonedDateTime,

- Use the from() static method of the GregorianCalendar class to get a GregorianCalendar.

The program in Listing 12-30 shows how to convert a GregorianCalendar to a ZonedDateTime and vice versa. The program also shows how to get a LocalDate, LocalTime, etc. from a GregorianCalendar. You may get a little different output because the output depends on the system's default time zone.

Listing 12-30. Converting a GregorianCalendar to New Datetime Types and Vice Versa

```java
// GregorianCalendarAndNewDateTime.java
package com.jdojo.datetime;

import java.time.LocalDate;
import java.time.LocalDateTime;
import java.time.LocalTime;
import java.time.OffsetDateTime;
```

```java
import java.time.OffsetTime;
import java.time.ZoneId;
import java.time.ZonedDateTime;

import java.util.GregorianCalendar;
import java.util.TimeZone;

public class GregorianCalendarAndNewDateTime {
        public static void main(String[] args) {
                // Create a GC for the default time zone
                GregorianCalendar gc = new GregorianCalendar(2014, 1, 11, 15, 45, 50);
                System.out.println("Gregorian Calendar: " + gc.getTime());

                // Convert the GC to a LocalDate
                LocalDate ld = gc.toZonedDateTime().toLocalDate();
                System.out.println("Local Date: " + ld);

                // Convert the GC to a LocalTime
                LocalTime lt = gc.toZonedDateTime().toLocalTime();
                System.out.println("Local Time: " + lt);

                // Convert the GC to a LocalDateTime
                LocalDateTime ldt = gc.toZonedDateTime().toLocalDateTime();
                System.out.println("Local DateTime: " + ldt);

                // Convert the GC to an OffsetDate
                OffsetDateTime od = gc.toZonedDateTime().toOffsetDateTime();
                System.out.println("Offset Date: " + od);

                // Convert the GC to an OffsetTime
                OffsetTime ot = gc.toZonedDateTime().toOffsetDateTime().toOffsetTime();
                System.out.println("Offset Time: " + ot);

                // Convert the GC to an ZonedDateTime
                ZonedDateTime zdt = gc.toZonedDateTime();
                System.out.println("Zoned DateTime: " + zdt);

                // Convert the ZonedDateTime to a GC. In GC month starts at 0
                // and in new API at 1
                ZoneId zoneId = zdt.getZone();
                TimeZone timeZone = TimeZone.getTimeZone(zoneId);
                System.out.println("Zone ID: " + zoneId);
                System.out.println("Time Zone ID: " + timeZone.getID());

                GregorianCalendar gc2 = GregorianCalendar.from(zdt);
                System.out.println("Gregorian Calendar: " + gc2.getTime());
        }
}
```

```
Gregorian Calendar: Tue Feb 11 15:45:50 CST 2014
Local Date: 2014-02-11
Local Time: 15:45:50
Local DateTime: 2014-02-11T15:45:50
Offset Date: 2014-02-11T15:45:50-06:00
Offset Time: 15:45:50-06:00
Zoned DateTime: 2014-02-11T15:45:50-06:00[America/Chicago]
Zone ID: America/Chicago
Time Zone ID: America/Chicago
Gregorian Calendar: Tue Feb 11 15:45:50 CST 2014
```

Summary

Through the java.time packages, Java 8 provides a comprehensive Date-Time API to work with date, time, and datetime. By default, most of the classes are based on the ISO-8601 standards. The main classes are

- Instant

- LocalDate

- LocalTime

- LocalDateTime

- OffsetTime

- OffsetDateTime

- ZonedDateTime

The Instant class represents an instant on the timeline and it is suitable for machines, for example, as timestamps for event. The LocalDate, LocalTime, and LocalDateTime classes represents human readable date, time, and datetime without a time zone. The OffsetTime and OffsetDateTime represent a time and datetime with a zone offset from UTC. The ZoneDateTime class represents a datetime for a time zone with zone rules, which will adjust the time according to the daylight saving time changes in the time zone.

The Date-Time API provides classes for representing an amount of time used with machines and humans. The Duration class represents an amount of time for machines whereas the Period class represents an amount of time as perceived by humans. The Date-Time API provides extensive support for formatting and parsing date and times through the java.time.format.DateTimeFormatter class. The Date-Time API supports non-ISO calendar systems through the java.time.chrono package. Built-in supports for Hijrah, Japanese, Minguo, and Thai Buddhist calendars are provided. The API is extensible and supports building your calendar systems.

■ ■ ■

CHAPTER 13

Formatting Data

Java provides a rich set of APIs for formatting data. The data may include simple values such as a numbers or objects such as strings, dates, and other types of objects. In this chapter, you will learn

- How to format and parse dates and numbers
- How to use the printf-style formatting
- How to create a class that uses a custom formatter

Formatting Dates

Java 8 provides a Date-Time API to work with dates and times, and to format and parse them. The Date-Time API was discussed in Chapter 12. If you are writing new code that is related to dates and times, you are advised to use the new Date-Time API. This section is provided in case you need to work with legacy code that uses old ways of formatting dates and time that existed before Java 8.

In this section, I will discuss how to format dates. I will also discuss how to parse a string to create a date object. You can format dates in predefined formats or formats of your choice. The Java library provides two classes to format dates:

- java.text.DateFormat
- java.text.SimpleDateFormat

Use the DateFormat class to format dates using a predefined format. It is an abstract class. The class is abstract, so you cannot create an instance of this class using the new operator. You can call one of its getXxxInstance() methods, where Xxx can be Date, DateTime, or Time, to get the formatter object, or just getInstance(). The formatted text depends on two things: style and locale. Use the format() method of the DateFormat class to format a date and time. The style of formatting determines how much datetime information is included in the formatted text, whereas the locale determines how all pieces of information are assembled. The DateFormat class defines five styles as constants:

- DateFormat.DEFAULT
- DateFormat.SHORT
- DateFormat.MEDIUM
- DateFormat.LONG
- DateFormat.FULL

The DEFAULT format is the same as MEDIUM, unless you use getInstance() where the default is SHORT. Table 13-1 shows the same date formatted in different styles for a US locale.

Table 13-1. *Predefined Date Format Styles and Formatted Text for Locale as United States*

Style	Formatted Date
DEFAULT	Mar 27, 2003
SHORT	3/27/03
MEDIUM	Mar 27, 2003
LONG	March 27, 2003
FULL	Thursday, March 27, 2003

The program listed in Listing 13-1 displays dates in short and medium formats for locales as default (which is US for the JVM running this example), France, and Germany. The program prints the current date. It will print different formats of the same date when you run this program. Your results will be different than those displayed since it displays different formats for today's date.

Listing 13-1. Using the Predefined Date Formats

```java
// PredefinedDateFormats.java
package com.jdojo.format;

import java.text.DateFormat;
import java.util.Date;
import java.util.Locale;

public class PredefinedDateFormats {
    public static void main(String[] args) {
        // Get the current date
        Date today = new Date();

        // Print date in the default locale format
        Locale defaultLocale = Locale.getDefault();
        printLocaleDetails(defaultLocale);
        printDate(defaultLocale, today);

        // Print date in French format
        printLocaleDetails(Locale.FRANCE);
        printDate(Locale.FRANCE, today);

        // Print date in German format. We could also use Locale.GERMANY
        // instead of new Locale ("de", "DE").
        Locale germanLocale = new Locale ("de", "DE");
        printLocaleDetails(germanLocale);
        printDate(germanLocale, today);
    }

    public static void printLocaleDetails (Locale locale){
        String languageCode = locale.getLanguage();
        String languageName = locale.getDisplayLanguage();
        String countryCode = locale.getCountry();
        String countryName = locale.getDisplayCountry();
```

```
                    // Print the locale info
                    System.out.println("Language: " + languageName + "(" +
                                        languageCode + "); " +
                                        "Country: " + countryName +
                                        "(" + countryCode + ")");
        }

        public static void printDate (Locale locale, Date date){
                    DateFormat formatter;
                    String formattedDate;

                    // Format and print the date in SHORT style
                    formatter = DateFormat.getDateInstance(DateFormat.SHORT, locale);
                    formattedDate = formatter.format(date);
                    System.out.println("SHORT: " + formattedDate);

                    // Format and print the date in MEDIUM style
                    formatter = DateFormat.getDateInstance(DateFormat.MEDIUM, locale);
                    formattedDate = formatter.format(date);
                    System.out.println("MEDIUM: " + formattedDate);

                    // Print a blank line at the end
                    System.out.println();
        }
}
```

```
Language: English(en); Country: United States(US)
SHORT: 1/24/14
MEDIUM: Jan 24, 2014

Language: French(fr); Country: France(FR)
SHORT: 24/01/14
MEDIUM: 24 janv. 2014

Language: German(de); Country: Germany(DE)
SHORT: 24.01.14
MEDIUM: 24.01.2014
```

The java.util.Locale class contains constants for some common locales For example, you can use Locale.FRANCE for a locale with language "fr" and country code "FR". Alternatively, you can create a locale object for France like so:

```
Locale frenchLocale = new Locale("fr", "FR") ;
```

To create a Locale, you need to use a two-letter lowercase language code and a two-letter uppercase country code if the Locale class does not declare a constant for that country. Language codes and country codes have been listed in ISO-639 code and ISO-3166 code. Some more examples of creating locales are as follows:

```
Locale hindiIndiaLocale = new Locale("hi", "IN");
Locale bengaliIndiaLocale = new Locale("bn", "IN");
Locale thaiThailandLocale = new Locale("th", "TH");
```

■ **Tip**   Use the `Locale.getDefault()` method to get the default `Locale` for your system.

If you want to use custom date formats, use the `SimpleDateFormat` class. Formatting using the `SimpleDateFormat` class is locale-sensitive. Its default constructor creates a formatter with the default locale and default date format for that locale. You can create a formatter using other constructors where you can specify your own date format and locale. Once you have an object of the `SimpleDateFormat` class, you can call its `format()` method to format the date. If you want to change the date format for subsequent formatting, you can use the `applyPattern()` method by passing the new date format (or pattern) as an argument. For example,

```
// Create a formatter with a pattern dd/MM/yyyy. Note that uppercase M is used
// for month-of-year. Lowercase d denotes day in month, whereas uppercase D //denotes day in year
// Note that / in the date format will appears as /.
SimpleDateFormat simpleFormatter = new SimpleDateFormat("dd/MM/yyyy");

// Get current date
Date today = new Date();

// Format the current date
String formattedDate = simpleFormatter.format(today);

// Print the date
System.out.println("Today is (dd/MM/yyyy): " + formattedDate);

// Change the date format. Now month will be spelled fully.
// Note a comma will appear as a comma. It has no special interpretation.
simpleFormatter.applyPattern("MMMM dd, yyyy");

// Format the current date
formattedDate = simpleFormatter.format(today);

// Print the date
System.out.println("Today is (MMMM dd, yyyy): " + formattedDate);
```

```
Today is (dd/MM/yyyy): 24/01/2014
Today is (MMMM dd, yyyy): January 24, 2014
```

Note that the output will be different when you run this code on your computer. It will print the current date in this format using the default locale. The above output is in the US locale.

Letters that are used to create patterns to format a date and time are listed with their meanings in Table 13-2. The examples are shown as if the date to display is July 10, 1996 at 12:30:55 in the afternoon.

Table 13-2. List of Formatting Symbols for Formatting Date and Time

Letter	Date or Time Component	Presentation	Examples
G	Era designator	Text	AD
y	Year	Year	2003; 03
Y	Week-based year	Year	2003; 03
M	Month in year	Month	March; Mar; 03
w	Week in year	Number	27
W	Week in month	Number	2
D	Day in year	Number	189
d	Day in month	Number	10
F	Day of week in month	Number	2
E	Day in week	Text	Tuesday; Tue
a	AM/PM marker	Text	PM
H	Hour in day (0-23)	Number	0
k	Hour in day (1-24)	Number	24
K	Hour in AM/PM (0-11)	Number	0
h	Hour in AM/PM (1-12)	Number	12
m	Minute in hour	Number	30
s	Second in minute	Number	55
S	Millisecond	Number	978
z	Time zone	General time zone	Pacific Standard Time; PST; GMT-08:00
Z	Time zone	RFC 822 time zone	-0800

You can embed literals inside formatted dates. Suppose you have your birth date (September 19, 1969) stored in a date object and now you want to print it as "I was born on the Day 19 of the month September in 1969". Some parts in the message come from the birth date and others are literals, which are intended to appear in the message as they are. You cannot use any alphabet's a-z and A-Z as literals inside a date pattern. You need to place them inside single quotes to treat them as literals, not part of the formatting pattern. First, you need a Date object to represent September 19, 1969. The Date class' constructor, which takes year, month, and day, has been deprecated. Let's start with the GregorianCalendar class and use its getTime() method to get a Date object. The following snippet of code prints this message:

```
// Create a GregorianCalendar object with September 19, 1969 as date
GregorianCalendar gc = new GregorianCalendar(1969,
Calendar.SEPTEMBER,19);

// Get date object
Date birthDate = gc.getTime();

// Create the pattern. You must place literals inside single quotes
String pattern = "'I was born on the day' dd 'of the month' MMMM 'in' yyyy";
```

489

```
// Create simple date format
SimpleDateFormat simpleFormatter = new SimpleDateFormat(pattern);

// Print the date
System.out.println(simpleFormatter.format(birthDate));
```

```
I was born on the Day 19 of the month September in 1969
```

So far, you have converted date objects into formatted text. Let's look at converting text into Date objects. This is accomplished by using the parse() method of the SimpleDateFormat class. The signature of the parse() method is as follows:

```
public Date parse(String text, ParsePosition startPos)
```

The parse() method takes two arguments. The first argument is the text from which you want to extract the date. The second one is the starting position of the character in the text from where you want to start parsing. The text can have date part embedded in it. For example, you can extract two dates from text such as "First date is 01/01/1995 and second one is 12/12/2001". Because the parser does not know where the date begins in the string, you need to tell it using the ParsePosition object. It simply keeps track of the parsing position. There is only one constructor for the ParsePosition class and it takes an integer, which is the position where parsing starts. After the parse() method is successful, the index for the ParsePosition object is set to the index of the last character of the date text used plus one. Note that the method does not use all the text passed as its first argument. It uses only the text as necessary to create a date object. Let's start with a simple example. Suppose you have a string of "09/19/1969", which represents the date September 19, 1969. You want to get a date object out of this string. The following snippet of code illustrates the steps:

```
// Our text to be parsed
String text = "09/19/1969";

// Create a pattern for the date text "09/19/1969"
String pattern = "MM/dd/yyyy";

// Create a simple date format object to represent this pattern
SimpleDateFormat simpleFormatter = new SimpleDateFormat(pattern);

// Since the date part in text "09/19/1969" start at index zero
// we create a ParsePosition object with value zero
ParsePosition startPos = new ParsePosition(0);

// Parse the text
Date parsedDate = simpleFormatter.parse(text, startPos);

// Here, parsedDate will have September 19, 1969 as date and startPos current index will be set to
// 10, which you can get calling startPos.getIndex() method.
```

Let's parse more complex text. If the text in the previous example were "09/19/1969 Junk", you would have gotten the same result, because after reading 1969, the parser will not look at any more characters in the text. Suppose you have text "XX01/01/1999XX12/31/2000XX". There are two dates embedded in the text. How would you parse these two dates? Note that the text for the first date starts at index 2 (the first two Xs have indices 0 and 1). Once parsing is done for the first date text, the ParsePosition object will point to the third X in the text. You just need to increment its index by two to point to the first character of the second date text. The following snippet of code illustrates the steps:

```
// Our text to be parsed
String text = "XX01/01/1999XX12/31/2000XX";

// Create a pattern for our date text "09/19/1969"
String pattern = "MM/dd/yyyy";

// Create a simple date format object to represent this pattern
SimpleDateFormat simpleFormatter = new SimpleDateFormat(pattern);

// Set the start index at 2
ParsePosition startPos = new ParsePosition(2);

// Parse the text to get the first date (January 1, 1999)
Date firstDate = simpleFormatter.parse(text, startPos);

// Now, startPos has its index set after the last character of the first date parsed.
// To set its index to the next date increment its index by 2.
int currentIndex = startPos.getIndex();
int nextIndex = currentIndex + 2;
startPos.setIndex (nextIndex);

// Parse the text to get the second date (December 31, 2000)
Date secondDate = simpleFormatter.parse(text, startPos);
```

It is left to the readers, as an exercise, to write a program that will extract the date in a date object from the text "I was born on the day 19 of the month September in 1969". The date extracted should be September 19, 1969. (Hint: You already have the pattern for this text in one of the previous examples, when you worked on formatting date objects.)

Here's one more example of parsing text that contains date and time. Suppose you have the text "2003-04-03 09:10:40.325", which represents a timestamp in the format year-month-day hour:minute:second.millisecond. You want to get the time parts of the timestamp. Listing 13-2 shows how to get time parts from this text.

Listing 13-2. Parsing a Timestamp to Get Its Time Parts

```
// ParseTimeStamp.java
package com.jdojo.format;

import java.util.Date;
import java.util.Calendar;
import java.text.ParsePosition;
import java.text.SimpleDateFormat;

public class ParseTimeStamp {
        public static void main(String[] args){
                String input = "2003-04-03 09:10:40.325";

                // Prepare the pattern
                String pattern = "yyyy-MM-dd HH:mm:ss.SSS" ;
```

```
            SimpleDateFormat sdf = new SimpleDateFormat(pattern);

            // Parse the text into a Date object
            Date dt = sdf.parse(input, new ParsePosition(0));
            System.out.println(dt);

            // Get the Calendar instance
            Calendar cal = Calendar.getInstance();

            // Set the time
            cal.setTime(dt);

            // Print time parts
            System.out.println("Hour:" + cal.get(Calendar.HOUR));
            System.out.println("Minute:" + cal.get(Calendar.MINUTE));
            System.out.println("Second:" + cal.get(Calendar.SECOND));
            System.out.println("Millisecond:" +
                            cal.get(Calendar.MILLISECOND));

    }
}
```

```
Thu Apr 03 09:10:40 CST 2003
Hour:9
Minute:10
Second:40
Millisecond:325
```

Formatting Numbers

In this section, I will discuss how to format numbers. I will also discuss how to parse a string to create a Number object. The following two classes can be used to format and parse numbers:

- `java.text.NumberFormat`

- `java.text.DecimalFormat`

The NumberFormat class is used to format a number in a particular locale's predefined format. The DecimalFormat class is used to format a number in a format of your choice in a particular locale. You can use a getXXXInstance() method of the NumberFormat class to get the instance of a formatter object, where Xxx can be replaced by Number, Currency, Integer, or Percent, or just getInstance(). These methods are overloaded. If you call them without any argument, they return a formatter object for the default locale. Call the format() method, passing the number as an argument to get the formatted number as a string.

```
NumberFormat formatter;

// Get number formatter for default locale
formatter = NumberFormatter.getNumberInstance();
```

```
// Get number formatter for French locale
formatter = NumberFormatter.getNumberInstance(Locale.FRENCH);

// Get currency formatter for German
formatter = NumberFormatter.getCurrencyInstance(Locale.GERMAN);
```

Listing 13-3 illustrates how to format numbers in default format for the current locale (the United States is the default locale for this example), French locale, and German locale.

Listing 13-3. Formatting Numbers Using Default Formats

```java
// DefaultNumberFormatters.java
package com.jdojo.format;

import java.util.Locale;
import java.text.NumberFormat;

public class DefaultNumberFormatters {
    public static void main(String[] args){
        double value = 1566789.785 ;

        // Default locale
        printFormatted(Locale.getDefault(), value);

        // Indian locale
        // (Rupee is the Indian currency. Short form is Rs.)
        Locale indianLocale = new Locale("en", "IN");
        printFormatted(indianLocale, value);
    }

    public static void printFormatted(Locale locale, double value) {
        // Get number and currency formatter
        NumberFormat nf = NumberFormat.getInstance(locale);
        NumberFormat cf = NumberFormat.getCurrencyInstance(locale);

        System.out.println("Formatting value: " + value +
                           " for locale: " + locale);
        System.out.println("Number: "   + nf.format(value));
        System.out.println("Currency: " + cf.format(value));
    }
}
```

```
Formatting value: 1566789.785 for locale: en_US
Number: 1,566,789.785
Currency: $1,566,789.78
Formatting value: 1566789.785 for locale: en_IN
Number: 1,566,789.785
Currency: Rs.1,566,789.78
```

To perform more advanced formatting, you can use the DecimalFormat class. It allows you to supply your own format pattern. Once you create an object of the DecimalFormat class, you can change the format pattern using its applyPattern() method. You can specify different patterns for positive and negative numbers. The two patterns are separated by a semicolon. The DecimalFormat class uses round-to-even rounding mode while formatting numbers. For example, if you have specified only two digits after the decimal point in your number format, 12.745 will be rounded to 12.74, because 4 is even; 12.735 will also be rounded to 12,74; and 12.746 will be rounded to 12.75. You can also parse a string to a number using the parse() method. Note that the parse() method returns an object of the java.lang.Number class. You can use xxxValue() methods to get the primitive value, where xxx can be byte, double, float, int, long, and short.

Listing 13-4 illustrates the use of the DecimalFormat class. Note that you can also use the parseDouble() method of the java.lang.Double class to parse a string into a double value. However, the string has to be in the default number format. The advantage of using the parse() method of the DecimalFormat class is that the string can be in any format.

Listing 13-4. Formatting and Parsing Numbers

```java
// DecimalFormatter.java
package com.jdojo.format;

import java.text.ParsePosition;
import java.text.DecimalFormat;

public class DecimalFormatter {
        private static DecimalFormat formatter = new DecimalFormat();
        public static void main (String[] args){
                formatNumber("##.##", 12.745);
                formatNumber("##.##", 12.746);
                formatNumber("0000.0000", 12.735);
                formatNumber("#.##", -12.735);

                // Positive and negative number format
                formatNumber("#.##;(#.##)", -12.735);

                // Parse a string to decimal number
                String str = "XY4,123.983";
                String pattern = "#,###.###";
                formatter.applyPattern(pattern);

                // Create a ParsePosition object to specify the first digit of
                // number in the string. It is 4 in "XY4,123.983"
                // with the index 2.
                ParsePosition pp = new ParsePosition(2);

                Number numberObject = formatter.parse(str, pp);

                double value = numberObject.doubleValue();
                System.out.println("Parsed Value is " + value);
        }

        public static void formatNumber(String pattern, double value) {
                        // Apply the pattern
                        formatter.applyPattern ( pattern );
```

```
                        // Format the number
                        String formattedNumber = formatter.format(value) ;

                        System.out.println("Number:" + value + ", Pattern:" +
                                          pattern + ", Formatted Number:" +
                                          formattedNumber);
        }
}
```

```
Number:12.745, Pattern:##.##, Formatted Number:12.74
Number:12.746, Pattern:##.##, Formatted Number:12.75
Number:12.735, Pattern:0000.0000, Formatted Number:0012.7350
Number:-12.735, Pattern:#.##, Formatted Number:-12.73
Number:-12.735, Pattern:#.##;(#.##), Formatted Number:(12.73)
Parsed Value is 4123.983
```

Printf-style Formatting

In this section, I will discuss how to format objects and values using printf-style formatting similar to that supported by the printf() function in C. First I will cover the general ideas of the printf-style formatting support in Java and then the details of formatting all types of values.

The Big Picture

The java.util.Formatter class supports printf-style formatting, which is similar to the formatting supported by the printf() function in C programming language. If you are familiar with C, C++, and C#, it should be easier for you to understand the discussion in this section. In this section, you will use formatting strings such as "%1$s", "%1$4d", etc. in your code without explaining their meanings. You may not be able to understand them fully; you should ignore them for now. Just focus on the output and try to get the bigger picture of what the Formatter class is intended to accomplish, rather than trying to understand the details. I will discuss the details in the next section. Let's start with a simple example shown in Listing 13-5. You may get a slightly different output.

Listing 13-5. Using C's Printf-style Formatting in Java

```java
// PrintfTest.java
package com.jdojo.format;

import java.util.Date;

public class PrintfTest {
        public static void main(String[] args) {
                // Formatting strings
                System.out.printf("%1$s, %2$s, and %3$s %n", "Fu", "Hu", "Lo");
                System.out.printf("%3$s, %2$s, and %1$s %n", "Fu", "Hu", "Lo");

                // Formatting numbers
                System.out.printf("%1$4d, %2$4d, %3$4d %n", 1, 10, 100);
                System.out.printf("%1$4d, %2$4d, %3$4d %n", 10, 100, 1000);
```

```
            System.out.printf("%1$-4d, %2$-4d, %3$-4d %n", 1, 10, 100);
            System.out.printf("%1$-4d, %2$-4d, %3$-4d %n", 10, 100, 1000);

            // Formatting date and time
            Date dt = new Date();
            System.out.printf("Today is %tD %n", dt);
            System.out.printf("Today is %tF %n", dt);
            System.out.printf("Today is %tc %n", dt);
        }
}
```

```
Fu, Hu, and Lo
Lo, Hu, and Fu
   1,   10,  100
  10,  100, 1000
1, 10, 100
10, 100, 1000
Today is 01/24/14
Today is 2014-01-24
Today is Fri Jan 24 21:41:20 CST 2014
```

You have been using the System.out.println() and System.out.print() methods to print text on the standard output. In fact, System.out is an instance of the java.io.PrintStream class, which has println() and print() instance methods. Java 5 added two more methods, format() and printf(), to the PrintStream class, which can be used to write a formatted output to a PrintStream instance. Both methods work the same. Listing 13-5 uses System.out.printf() method to print the formatted text to the standard output.

Java 5 also added a format() static method to the String class, which returns a formatted string. The formatting behavior of the format()/printf() method of the PrintStream class and the format() static method of the String class is the same. The only difference between them is that the format()/printf() method in the PrintStream class writes the formatted output to an output stream, whereas the format() method of the String class returns the formatted output.

The format()/printf() method of the PrintStream class and the format() static method of the String class are convenience methods. These convenience methods exist to make the job of text formatting easier. However, the Formatter class does the real work. Let's discuss the Formatter class in detail. You will use these convenience methods in the examples.

A Formatter is used to format text. The formatted text can be written to the following destinations:

- An Appendable (e.g. StringBuffer, StringBuilder, Writer, etc.)

- A File

- An OutputStream

- A PrintStream

The following snippet of code accomplishes the same thing as the code in Listing 13-5. This time, you use a Formatter object to format the data. When you call the format() method of the Formatter object, the formatted text is stored in the StringBuilder object, which you pass to the constructor of the Formatter object. When you are done with formatting all text, you call the toString() method of the StringBuilder to get the entire formatted text.

```
// Create an Appendable data storage for our formatted output
StringBuilder sb = new StringBuilder();

// Create a Formatter that will ??? its output to the StringBuffer
Formatter fm = new Formatter(sb);

// Formatting strings
fm.format("%1$s, %2$s, and %3$s %n", "Fu", "Hu", "Lo");
fm.format("%3$s, %2$s, and %1$s %n", "Fu", "Hu", "Lo");

// Formatting numbers
fm.format("%1$4d, %2$4d, %3$4d %n", 1, 10, 100);
fm.format("%1$4d, %2$4d, %3$4d %n", 10, 100, 1000);
fm.format("%1$-4d, %2$-4d, %3$-4d %n", 1, 10, 100);
fm.format("%1$-4d, %2$-4d, %3$-4d %n", 10, 100, 1000);

// Formatting date and time
Date dt = new Date();
fm.format("Today is %tD %n", dt);
fm.format("Today is %tF %n", dt);
fm.format("Today is %tc %n", dt);

// Display the entire formatted string
System.out.println(sb.toString());
```

If you want to write all formatted text to a file, you can do so using the following snippet of code. You will need to handle the FileNotFoundException, which may be thrown from the constructor of the Formatter class if the specified file does not exist. When you are done with the Formatter object, you will need to call its close() method to close the output file.

```
import java.io.File;
import java.io.FileNotFoundException;
import java.util.Formatter;
...
// Let's write the formatted output to C:\xyz.text file
File file = new File("C:\\xyz.txt");
Formatter fm = null;
try {
        // Create a Formatter that will write the output the file
        fm = new Formatter(file);

        // Formatting strings
        fm.format("%1$s, %2$s, and %3$s %n", "Fu", "Hu", "Lo");
        fm.format("%3$s, %2$s, and %1$s %n", "Fu", "Hu", "Lo");

        // Format more text here...
}
catch(FileNotFoundException e) {
        e.printStackTrace();
}
```

```
finally {
        if (fm != null) {
                fm.close();
        }
}
```

The format() method of the Formatter class is overloaded. Its declarations are as follows.

- Formatter format(String format, Object... args)

- Formatter format(Locale l, String format, Object... args)

The first version of the format() method uses the default locale for formatting. The second version allows you to specify a locale. The format()/printf() method of the PrintStream class and the format() method of the String class provide the same two versions of the format() method, which accept the same types of arguments. This discussion of the format() method of the Formatter class equally applies to these convenience methods in the PrintStream and String classes.

The Formatter class uses the locale-specific formatting whenever it is applicable. For example, if you want to format a decimal number, say 12.89, the number is formatted as 12,89 (notice a comma between 12 and 89) in France whereas it is formatted as 12.89 (notice a dot between 12 and 89) in the United States. The locale argument of the format() method is used to format text in a locale-specific format. The following snippet of code demonstrates the effects of locale-specific formatting. Note the difference in the formatted output for US and France for the same input values.

```
System.out.printf(Locale.US, "In US: %1$.2f %n", 12.89);
System.out.printf(Locale.FRANCE, "In France: %1$.2f %n", 12.89);

Date dt = new Date();
System.out.printf(Locale.US, "In US: %tA %n", dt);
System.out.printf(Locale.FRANCE, "In France: %tA %n", dt);
```

```
In US: 12.89
In France: 12,89
In US: Friday
In France: vendredi
```

The Details

Formatting data using a Formatter requires two types of inputs:

- A format string

- A list of values

The format string is the template that defines how the output will look. It contains zero or more occurrences of fixed texts and zero or more embedded format specifiers. No formatting is applied to the fixed text.

A format specifier serves two purposes. It acts as a placeholder for the formatted data inside the format string and it specifies how the data should be formatted.

Let's consider the following example. Suppose you want to print a text with the birth date of a person. The following is an example of such a text:

```
January 16, 1970 is John's birth day.
```

■ **Note**   All outputs in this section are in the US locale unless specified otherwise.

The above text contains fixed text and formatted text. The fixed text should appear in the output literally. The formatted text will depend on the inputs. You can convert the above text into a template as shown:

```
<month> <day>, <year> is <name>'s birth day.
```

You have replaced the text that may vary with placeholders that are enclosed in angle brackets, for example, <month>, <day>, etc. You will need four input values (month, day, year, and name) to use the above template to get a formatted text. For example, if you supply the values for <month>, <day>, <year>, and <name> as "January", "16", "1970", and "John", respectively, the template will produce

```
January 16, 1970 is John's birth day.
```

In this example, you have just replaced the placeholders in your template with their actual values. You did not perform any formatting for the actual values. The formatting that is provided by the Formatter class works in a similar fashion. What we called a placeholder in this example is called a format specifier. What we called a template in this example is called a format string.

A format specifier always starts with a percent sign (%). You can convert your template into a format string, which can be used with the Formatter class as follows:

```
%1$tB %1$td, %1$tY is %2$s's birth day.
```

In this format string, "%1$tB", "%1$td", "%1$tY", and %2$s" are four format specifiers, whereas " ", ", ", "is ", and "'s birth day." are fixed texts.

The following snippet of code uses the above format string to print formatted text. Note that calendar and "John" are the input values for the format string. In this case, the input value calendar is an instance of the Calendar class that encapsulates a date.

```
LocalDate dob = LocalDate.of(1970, Month.JANUARY, 16);
System.out.printf("%1$tB %1$td, %1$tY is %2$s's birth day.", dob, "John");
```

```
January 16, 1970 is John's birth day.
```

The general syntax for a format specifier is as follows:

```
%<argument-index$><flags><width><.precision><conversion>
```

Except the % and <conversion> parts, all other parts are optional. Note that there is no space between any two parts of a format specifier. The % (percent sign) denotes the start of a format specifier inside a format string. If you want to specify % as the part of a fixed text inside a format string, you need to use two consecutive % as %%.

The <argument-index$> denotes the index of the argument that the format specifier refers to. It consists of an integer in base-10 format followed by a $ (dollar sign). The first argument is referred to as 1$, the second as 2$, and so on. You can refer to the same argument multiple times in different format specifiers inside the same format string.

The <flags> denotes the format of the output. It is a set of characters. The valid values for <flags> depend on the data type of the argument that the format specifier refers to.

The <width> denotes the minimum number of characters that need to be written to the output.

Typically, the <.precision> denotes the maximum number of characters to be written to the output. However, its exact meaning varies depending on the value for <conversion>. It is a decimal number. It starts with a dot (.).

The <conversion> denotes how the output should be formatted. Its value depends on the data type of the argument, which the format specifier refers to. It is mandatory.

There are two special format specifiers: "%%" and "%n". The "%%" format specifier outputs "%" (a percent sign) and "%n" outputs a platform-specific newline character. The following snippet of code demonstrates the use of these two special format specifiers:

```
System.out.printf("Interest rate is 10%%.%nJohn%nDonna");
```

```
Interest rate is 10%.
John
Donna
```

You have not supplied any arguments to the printf() method in the code because these two special format specifiers do not work on any arguments. Note the two newlines in the output that are generated by the two "%n" format specifiers in the format string.

Referencing an Argument inside a Format Specifier

I have not covered the conversion part of the format specifier yet. For the discussion in this section, I will use 's' as the conversion character for the format specifiers. The 's' conversion formats its argument as string. In its simplest form, you can use "%s" as a format specifier. Let's consider the following snippet of code and its output:

```
System.out.printf("%s, %s, and %s", "Ken", "Lola", "Matt");
```

```
Ken, Lola, and Matt
```

A format specifier in a format string can refer to an argument in three ways:

- Ordinary indexing
- Explicit indexing
- Relative indexing

Ordinary Indexing

When a format specifier does not specify an argument-index value (as in "%s"), it is called ordinary indexing. In ordinary indexing, the argument-index is determined by the index of the format specifier in the format string. The first format specifier without argument-index has the index of 1, the second has the index of 2, and so on. The format specifier with the index 1 refers to the first argument; the format specifier with the index 2 refers to the second argument; and so on. Figure 13-1 shows the indices of the format specifiers and the arguments.

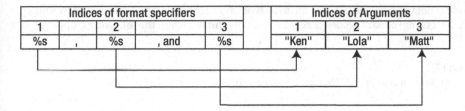

Figure 13-1. *Indexes of format specifiers in a format string and indexes of the arguments*

Figure 13-1 shows how indices are mapped in the above example. The first "%s" format specified refers to the first argument, "Ken". The second "%s" format specified refers to the second argument, "Lola". And, the third "%s" format specified refers to the third argument, "Matt".

If the number of arguments is more than the number of format specifiers in the format string, the extra arguments are ignored. Consider the following snippet of code and its output. It has three format specifiers (three "%s") and four arguments. The fourth argument, "Lo", is an extra argument, which is ignored.

```
System.out.printf("%s, %s, and %s", "Ken", "Lola", "Matt", "Lo");
```

```
Ken, Lola, and Matt
```

A java.util.MissingFormatArgumentException is thrown if a format specifier references a non-existent argument. The following snippet of code will throw the exception because the number of arguments is one less than the number of format specifiers. There are three format specifiers, but only two arguments.

```
// Compiles fine, but throws a runtime exception
System.out.printf("%s, %s, and %s", "Ken", "Lola");
```

Note that the last argument to the format() method of the Formatter class is a varargs argument. You can also pass an array to a varargs argument. The following snippet of code is valid even though it uses three format specifiers and only one argument of array type. The array type argument contains three values for the three format specifiers.

```
String[] names = {"Ken", "Matt", "Lola"};
System.out.printf("%s, %s, and %s", names);
```

```
Ken, Matt, and Lola
```

The following snippet of code is also valid because it passes four values in the array type argument but has only three format specifiers:

```
String[] names = {"Ken", "Matt", "Lola", "Lo"};
System.out.printf("%s, %s, and %s", names);
```

```
Ken, Matt, and Lola
```

The following snippet of code is not valid because it uses an array type argument that has only two elements and there are three format specifiers. A `MissingFormatArgumentException` will be thrown when the following snippet of code is run.

```
String[] names = {"Ken", "Matt"};
System.out.printf("%s, %s, and %s", names); // Throws an exception
```

Explicit Indexing

When a format specifier specifies an argument index explicitly, it is called explicit indexing. Note that an argument index is specified just after the % sign in a format specifier. It is an integer in the decimal format and it ends with $ (a dollar sign). Consider the following snippet of code and its output. It uses three format specifiers: "%1$s", "%2$s", and "%3$s", which use explicit indexing.

```
System.out.printf("%1$s, %2$s, and %3$s", "Ken", "Lola", "Matt");
```

```
Ken, Lola, and Matt
```

When a format specifier uses explicit indexing, it can refer to an argument at any index in the argument list using the index of the argument. Consider the following snippet of code:

```
System.out.printf("%3$s, %1$s, and %2$s", "Lola", "Matt", "Ken");
```

```
Ken, Lola, and Matt
```

This snippet of code has the same output as the snippet of code before it. However, in this case, the values in the argument list are not in the same order. The first format specifier, "%3$s", refers to the third argument, "Ken"; the second format specifier, "%1$s", refers to the first argument, "Lola"; and the third format specifier, "%2$s", refers to the second argument, "Matt".

It is allowed to reference the same argument multiple times using explicit indexing. It is also allowed not to reference some arguments inside the format string. In the following snippet of code, the first argument of "Lola" is not referenced and the third argument of "Ken" is referenced twice:

```
System.out.printf("%3$s, %2$s, and %3$s", "Lola", "Matt", "Ken");
```

```
Ken, Matt, and Ken
```

Relative Indexing

There is a third way to refer to an argument inside a format specifier, which is called relative indexing. In relative indexing, a format specifier uses the same argument that was used by the previous format specifier. Relative indexing does not use an argument-index value. Rather, it uses '<' character as a flag in the format specifier. Since in relative indexing, a format specifier uses the same argument that is used by the previous format specifier, it cannot be used with the first format specifier. Remember that to use a relative indexing, there must be a previous format specifier, which implies that you cannot use the relative indexing for the first format specifier.

Consider the following snippet of code and its output, which uses relative indexing:

```
System.out.printf("%1$s, %<s, %<s, %2$s, and %<s", "Ken", "Matt");
```

```
Ken, Ken, Ken, Matt, and Matt
```

This snippet of code uses five format specifiers: "%1$s", "%<s", "%<s", "%2$s", and "%<s". It uses two arguments: "Ken" and "Matt". Note that it is possible to have less number of arguments than the number of format specifiers if some format specifiers use relative indexing. The first format specifier of "%1$s" uses explicit indexing to reference the first argument of "Ken". The second format specifier of "%<s" uses relative indexing (notice '<' flag) and, therefore, it will use the same argument, which was used by the previous format specifier, "1$s". This way, both the first and the second format specifiers use the first argument of "Ken". This is confirmed by the output that displays "Ken" as the first two names. The third format specifier of "%<s" also uses relative indexing. It will use the same argument as used by the previous format specifier (the second format specifier). Since the second format specifier used the first argument of "Ken", the third one will also use the same argument. This is confirmed in the output that shows "Ken" as the third name. The fourth "%2$s" format specifier uses explicit indexing to use the second argument of "Matt". The fifth and the last format specifier of "%<s" uses relative indexing and it will use the same argument that is used by its previous format specifier (the fourth format specifier). Since the fourth format specifier uses the second argument of "Matt", the fifth format specifier will also use the second argument of "Matt". This is confirmed in the output that displays "Matt" as the fifth name.

The following statement will throw a `java.util.MissingFormatArgumentException` because it uses relative indexing for the first format specifier:

```
System.out.printf("%<s, %<s, %<s, %2$s, and %<s", "Ken", "Matt");
```

It is possible to mix all three types of indexing to reference arguments inside different format specifiers in the same format string. Consider the following statement and its output:

```
System.out.printf("%1$s, %s, %<s, %s, and %<s", "Ken", "Matt");
```

```
Ken, Ken, Ken, Matt, and Matt
```

The first format specifier uses the explicit indexing to use the first argument of "Ken". The second and the fourth format specifiers (both "%s") use ordinary indexing. The third and the fifth format specifiers (both "%<s") use relative indexing. It is clear from the rule of relative indexing that the third and fifth format specifiers will use the same arguments as used by the second and the fourth format specifiers, respectively. Which arguments will be used by the second and the fourth format specifiers? The answer is simple. When you have some format specifiers that use ordinary indexing and some explicit indexing, just for the purpose of understanding this rule, ignore the format specifiers that use explicit indexing and number the format specifiers that use ordinary indexing as 1, 2, and so on. Using this rule, you can think of the above statement the same as the following one:

```
System.out.printf("%1$s, %1$s, %<s, %2$s, and %<s", "Ken", "Matt");
```

Notice that you have replaced the first occurrence of "%s" with %1$s" and the second occurrence with "%2$s" as if they are using explicit indexing. This explains the output generated by the above statement.

Using Flags in a Format Specifier

Flags act as modifiers. They modify the formatted output. Table 13-3 lists all flags that can be used in a format specifier.

Table 13-3. *List of Valid Flags, Their Descriptions, and Examples of Their Usage*

Flag	Description	Examples		
		Format String	**Argument**	**Formatted Text**
'-'	The result is left justified. Note that the result is right justified when you do not use the '-' flag in a format specifier.	'"%6s"'	"Ken"	' Ken'
		'"%-6s"'	"Ken"	'Ken '
'#'	The argument is formatted in alternate form depending on the conversion part of the format specifier. The example shows the same decimal number, 6270185, being formatted to a hexadecimal format. When '#' flag is used, the hexadecimal number is prefixed with "0x".	"%x"	6270185	5face9
		"%#x"	6270185	0x5face9
'+'	The result contains a + sign for positive values. It applies only to numeric values.	"%d"	105	105
		"%+d"	105	+105
' '	The result contains a leading space for positive values. It applies only to numeric values.	'"%d"'	105	'105'
		'"% d"'	105	' 105'
'0'	The result is zero padded. It applies only to numeric values.	'"%6d"'	105	' 105'
		'"%06d"'	105	'000105'
','	The result contains a locale-specific grouping separator. It applied only to numeric values. For example, a comma is used as a thousand-separator in US locale, whereas a space is used in France locale.	"%,d"	89105	89,105 (US Locale)
		"%,d"	89105	89 105 (France locale)
'('	The result is enclosed in parentheses for a negative number. It applies only to numeric values.	"%d"	-1969	-1969
		"%(d"	-1969	(1969)
'<'	It causes the argument for the previous format specifier to be reused. It is mostly used in formatting dates and times.	"%s and %<s"	"Ken"	Ken and Ken

The valid use of a flag depends on the context of its use. Depending on the value being formatted, it is allowed to use multiple flags in a format specifier. For example, the format specifier "%1$,0(12d" uses three flags: ',', '0', and '('. If -122899 is used as the argument by this format specifier, it will output (000122,899). The effects of using each flag will be discussed in detail when I discuss formatting for different data types in the sections to follow.

Conversion Characters

Different conversion characters are used to format values of different data types. For example, 's' is used to format a value as a string. The valid values for other parts in a format specifier are also determined by the conversion character in the format specifier and the data type of the argument that the format specifier references. We can broadly classify the formatting types based on data types in four categories:

- General formatting
- Character formatting
- Numeric formatting
- Date/Time formatting

Many of the conversion characters have uppercase variants. For example, 'S' is the uppercase variant of 's'. The uppercase variant converts the formatted output to uppercase as if output.toUpperCase() method was called, where output is the reference to the formatted output string. The following statement and its output demonstrate the effect of using the uppercase variant 'S'. Note that 's' produces "Ken" and 'S' produces "KEN" for the same input value "Ken".

```
System.out.printf("%s and %<S", "Ken");
```

```
Ken and KEN
```

General Formatting

The general formatting can be used to format values of any data types. Table 13-4 has the list of conversions that are available under the general formatting category.

Table 13-4. *List of Conversion Characters for General Formatting*

Conversion	Uppercase Variant	Description
'b'	'B'	It produces "true" or "false" based on the value of the argument. It produces "false" for a null argument and for a Boolean argument whose value is false. Otherwise, it produces "true."
'h'	'H'	It produces a string that is the hash code value in hexadecimal format of the argument. If the argument is null, it produces "null."
's'	'S'	It produces a string representation of the argument. If the argument is null, it produces a "null" string. If the argument implements the Formattable interface, it invokes the formatTo() method on the argument and the returned value is the result. If the argument does not implement the Formattable interface, toString() method is invoked on the argument to get the result.

The general syntax for a format specifier for general formatting is

```
%<argument_index$><flags><width><.precision><conversion>
```

The width denotes the minimum number of characters to be written to the output. If the length of the string representation of the argument is less than the width value, the result will be padded with spaces. The space padding is performed to the left of the argument value. If '-' flag is used, space padding is performed to the right. The value of width alone does not decide the content of the result. The values of width and precision together decide the final content of the result.

The precision denotes the maximum number of characters to be written to the output. The precision is applied to the argument before the width is applied. You need to understand the consequences of applying the precision before the width. If the precision is less than the length of the argument, the argument is truncated to the length that is equal to the precision, and space padding is performed to match the length of the output to the value of the width. Consider the following snippet of code:

```
System.out.printf("'%4.1s'", "Ken");
```

```
'   K'
```

The argument is "Ken" and the format specifier is "%4.1s", where 4 is the width and 1 is the precision. First, the precision is applied that will truncate the value "Ken" to "K". Now, the width is applied, which states that a minimum of four characters should be written to the output. However, after the precision is applied, you have only one character left. Therefore, "K" will be left padded with three spaces to match the width value of four.

Consider the following snippet of code:

```
System.out.printf("'%1.4s'", "Ken");
```

```
'Ken'
```

The argument value is "Ken" and the format specifier is "%1.4s" where 1 is the width and 4 is the precision. Because the precision value of 4 is greater than the length of the argument, which is 3, there is no effect of the precision. Because the width value of 1 is less than the width of the result after precision is applied, there is no effect of the width value on the output.

The following are some examples of using Boolean, string and hash code formatting conversions. Note that the hash code formatting conversion ('h' and 'H') outputs the hash code value of the argument in a hexadecimal format. These examples also demonstrate the effect of using the uppercase variants of the conversions.

```
// Boolean conversion
System.out.printf("'%b', '%5b', '%.3b'%n", true, false, true);
System.out.printf("'%b', '%5b', '%.3b'%n", "Ken", "Matt", "Lola");
System.out.printf("'%B', '%5B', '%.3B'%n", "Ken", "Matt", "Lola");
System.out.printf("%b %n", 1969);
System.out.printf("%b %n", new Object());
```

```
'true', 'false', 'tru'
'true', ' true', 'tru'
'TRUE', ' TRUE', 'TRU'
true
true
```

```
// String conversion
System.out.printf("'%s', '%5s', '%.3s'%n", "Ken", "Matt", "Lola");
System.out.printf("'%S', '%5S', '%.3S'%n", "Ken", "Matt", "Lola");

// Use '-' flag to left-justify the result. You must use width when you specify the '-' flag
System.out.printf("'%S', '%-5S', '%.3S'%n", "Ken", "Matt", "Lola");
System.out.printf("%s %n", 1969);
System.out.printf("%s %n", true);
System.out.printf("%s %n", new Object());
```

```
'Ken', ' Matt', 'Lol'
'KEN', ' MATT', 'LOL'
'KEN', 'MATT ', 'LOL'
1969
true
java.lang.Object@de6f34
```

```
// Hash Code conversion
System.out.printf("'%h', '%5h', '%.3h'%n", "Ken", "Matt", "Lola");
System.out.printf("'%H', '%5H', '%.3H'%n", "Ken", "Matt", "Lola");
System.out.printf("%h %n", 1969);
System.out.printf("%h %n", true);
System.out.printf("%h %n", new Object());
```

```
'12634', '247b34', '243'
'12634', '247B34', '243'
7b1
4cf
156ee8e
```

If you pass a value of a primitive type as an argument to the format() method of the Formatter class (or the printf() method of the PrintStream class), the primitive type value is converted to a reference type using an appropriate type of wrapper class using the autoboxing rules. For example, the statement

```
System.out.println("%s", 1969);
```

will be converted to

```
System.out.println("%s", new Integer(1969));
```

Writing a Custom Formatter

The Formatter class supports custom formatting through 's' and 'S' conversions. If the argument implements java.util.Formattable interface, the 's' conversion calls the formatTo() method on the argument to get the formatted result. The formatTo() method is passed the reference of a Formatter object, flags, width, and precision values that are used in the format specifier. You can apply any custom logic inside the formatTo() method of the class to format the objects of your class. Listing 13-6 contains the code for a FormattablePerson class, which implements the Formattable interface.

Listing 13-6. Implementing a Custom Formatter Using the Formattable Interface

```java
// FormattablePerson.java
package com.jdojo.format;

import java.util.Formattable;
import java.util.Formatter;
import java.util.FormattableFlags;

public class FormattablePerson implements Formattable {
        private String firstName = "Unknown";
        private String lastName = "Unknown";

        public FormattablePerson(String firstName, String lastName ) {
                this.firstName = firstName;
                this.lastName = lastName;
        }

        // Other code goes here...

        public void formatTo(Formatter formatter, int flags, int width, int precision) {
                String str = this.firstName + " " + this.lastName;

                int alternateFlagValue = FormattableFlags.ALTERNATE & flags;
                if (alternateFlagValue == FormattableFlags.ALTERNATE) {
                        str = this.lastName + ", " + this.firstName;
                }

                // Check if uppercase variant of the conversio is being used
                int upperFlagValue = FormattableFlags.UPPERCASE & flags;
                if (upperFlagValue == FormattableFlags.UPPERCASE) {
                        str = str.toUpperCase();
                }

                // Call the format() method of formatter argument,
                // so our result is stored in it and the caller will get it
                formatter.format(str);
        }
}
```

Your Formattable person has a first name and a last name. You have kept the logic inside the formatTo() method simple. You check for alternate flag '#'. If this flag is used in the format specifier, you format the person name in the "LastName, FirstName" format. If the alternate flag is not used, you format the person name in the "FirstName LastName" format. You also support uppercase variant 'S' of 's' conversion. If 'S' conversion is used, you format the person name in uppercase. Your logic does not use other values of the flags, width, and precision. The flags are passed in as an int value as bitmask. To check if a flag was passed, you will need to use the bitwise & operator. The operand to be used in the bitwise & operator are defined by constants in the java.util.FormattableFlags class. For example, to check if the format specifier uses a left-justify '-' flag, you will need to use the following logic:

```java
int leftJustifiedFlagValue = FormattableFlags.LEFT_JUSTIFY & flags;
if (leftJustifiedFlagValue == FormattableFlags.LEFT_JUSTIFY) {
        // Left-justified flag '-' is used
}
```

```
else {
        // Left-justified flag '-' is not used
}
```

You can use your `FormattablePerson` objects with format specifiers using string conversion `'s'` and `'S'` as shown below:

```
FormattablePerson fp = new FormattablePerson("Ken", "Smith");
System.out.printf("%s %n", fp );
System.out.printf("%#s %n", fp );
System.out.printf("%S %n", fp );
System.out.printf("%#S %n", fp );
```

```
Ken Smith
Smith, Ken
KEN SMITH
SMITH, KEN
```

Character Formatting

Character formatting may be applied to the values of char primitive data type or `Character` objects. It can also be applied to the values of byte, `Byte`, short, `Short`, int, or `Integer` types if their values are valid Unicode code points. You can test if an integer value represents a valid Unicode code point by using the `isValidCodePoint(int value)` static method of the `Character` class.

The conversion character for character formatting is `'c'`. Its uppercase variant is `'C'`. The flag `'#'` and the precision are not supported for character formatting. The flag `'-'` and width have the same meaning as in the context of the general formatting. The following snippet of code demonstrates the use of character formatting:

```
System.out.printf("%c %n", 'a');
System.out.printf("%C %n", 'a');
System.out.printf("%C %n", 98);
System.out.printf("'%5C' %n", 100);
System.out.printf("'%-5C' %n", 100);
```

```
a
A
B
'    D'
'D    '
```

Numeric Formatting

Numeric formatting can be broadly classified into two categories:

- Integral number formatting
- Floating-point number formatting

Many locale-specific formatting are automatically applied when a numeric value is formatted. For example, the numeric digits that are used for number formatting are always locale-specific. If the formatted number contains a decimal separator or group separators, they are always replaced with locale-specific decimal separator or group separators, respectively. The following snippet of code shows the same number 1234567890 formatted differently for three different locales US, Indian, and Thailand:

```
Locale englishUS = new Locale ("en", "US");
Locale hindiIndia = new Locale ("hi", "IN");
Locale thaiThailand = new Locale ("th", "TH", "TH");
System.out.printf(englishUS, "%d %n", 1234567890);
System.out.printf(hindiIndia, "%d %n", 1234567890);
System.out.printf(thaiThailand, "%d %n", 1234567890);
```

1234567890

१२३४५६७८९०

๑๒๓๔๕๖๗๘๙๐

Integral Number Formatting

The integral number formatting deals with formatting whole numbers. It can be applied to format values of byte, Byte, short, Short, int, Integer, long, Long and BigInteger. Table 13-5 has the list of conversions that are available under integral number formatting category.

Table 13-5. *List of Conversions Applicable to byte, Byte, short, Short, int, Integer, long, Long, and BigInteger Data Types*

Conversion	Uppercase variant	Description
'd'		It formats the argument in locale-specific decimal integer (base-10). The '#' flag cannot be used with this conversion.
'o'		It formats the argument as a base-8 integer without any localization. If '#' flag is used with this conversion, the output always begins with a '0' (a zero). The '(', '+', ' ', and ',' flags cannot be used with this conversion.
'x'	'X'	It formats the argument as a base-16 integer without any localization. If '#' flag is used with this conversion, the output always begins with a "0x". When the uppercase variant 'X' is used with '#' flag, the output always begins with "0X". The '(', '+', ' ', and ',' flags cannot be used with this conversion with an argument of byte, Byte, short, Short, int, Integer, long, and Long data types. The ',' flag cannot be used with this conversion with an argument of BigInteger data type.

The general syntax for a format specifier for integral number formatting is as follows:

```
%<argument_index$><flags><width><conversion>
```

Note that precision part in a format specifier is not applicable to integral number formatting. The following snippet of code demonstrates the use of the 'd' conversion with various flags to format integers:

```
System.out.printf("'%d' %n", 1969);
System.out.printf("'%6d' %n", 1969);
System.out.printf("'%-6d' %n", 1969);
System.out.printf("'%06d' %n", 1969);
System.out.printf("'%(d' %n", 1969);
System.out.printf("'%(d' %n", -1969);
System.out.printf("'% d' %n", 1969);
System.out.printf("'% d' %n", -1969);
System.out.printf("'%+d' %n", 1969);
System.out.printf("'%+d' %n", -1969);
```

```
'1969'
'  1969'
'1969  '
'001969'
'1969'
'(1969)'
' 1969'
'-1969'
'+1969'
'-1969'
```

When conversions 'o' and 'x' are used with a negative argument of byte, Byte, short, Short, int, Integer, long, and Long data types, the argument value is first converted to an unsigned number by adding a number 2^N to it, where N is the number of bits used to represent the value of the data type of the argument. For example, if the argument data type is byte, which takes 8 bits to store the value, the argument value of -X will be converted to a positive value of -X + 256 by adding 256 to it and the result contain the base-8 or base-16 equivalent of the value -X + 256. The conversions 'o' and 'x' do not transform the negative argument value to an unsigned value for a BigInteger argument type. Consider the following snippet of code and the output:

```
byte b1 = 9;
byte b2 = -9;
System.out.printf("%o %n", b1);
System.out.printf("%o %n", b2);
```

```
11
367
```

The conversion 'o' outputs the base-8 integer 11 for a positive decimal integer 9. However, when a negative decimal integer -9 is used with the 'o' conversion, -9 is converted to a positive number -9 + 256 (=247). The final output contains 367, which is the base-8 equivalent of the decimal 247.

The following snippet of code shows some more examples of 'o' and 'x' conversions for int and BigInteger argument types:

```
System.out.printf("%o %n", 1969);
System.out.printf("%o %n", -1969);
System.out.printf("%o %n", new BigInteger("1969"));
System.out.printf("%o %n", new BigInteger("-1969"));

System.out.printf("%x %n", 1969);
System.out.printf("%x %n", -1969);
System.out.printf("%x %n", new BigInteger("1969"));
System.out.printf("%x %n", new BigInteger("-1969"));

System.out.printf("%#o %n", 1969);
System.out.printf("%#x %n", 1969);
System.out.printf("%#o %n", new BigInteger("1969"));
System.out.printf("%#x %n", new BigInteger("1969"));
```

```
3661
37777774117
3661
-3661
7b1
fffff84f
7b1
-7b1
03661
0x7b1
03661
0x7b1
```

Floating-Point Number Formatting

Floating-point number formatting deals with formatting numbers, which have a whole part and a fraction part. It can be applied to format values of float, Float, double, Double, and BigDecimal data types. Table 13-6 contains the list of conversions used for formatting floating-point number formatting.

Table 13-6. *List of Conversions Applicable to float, Float, double, Double, and BigDecimal Data Types*

Conversion	Uppercase Variant	Description
'e'	'E'	It formats the argument in a locale-specific computerized scientific notation, for example, 1.969919e+03. The output contains one digit followed by a decimal separator, which is followed by exponent part. For example, 1969.919 will be formatted as 1.969919e+03 if the precision is 6. Precision is the number of digits after the decimal separator. The group separator flag ',' cannot be used with this conversion.
'g'	'G'	It formats the argument in a locale-specific general scientific notation. Depending on the value of the argument, it acts as 'e' conversion or 'f' conversion. It applies rounding to the value of the argument depending on the value of the precision.
		If the value after rounding is greater than or equal to 10^{-4} but less than $10^{precision}$, it formats the value as if 'f' conversion is used.
		If the value after rounding is less than 10^{-4} or greater than or equal to $10^{precision}$, it formats the value as if 'e' conversion is used.
		Note that the total number of significant digits in the result is equal to the value of the precision. By default, precision of 6 is used.
'f'		It formats the argument in a locale-specific decimal format. Precision is the number of digits after the decimal separator. The value is rounded depending on the specified value of the precision.
'a'	'A'	It formats the argument in hexadecimal exponential form. It is not applicable to the argument of BigDecimal type.

The general syntax for a format specifier for floating-point number formatting is

```
%<argument_index$><flags><width><.precision><conversion>
```

The precision has different meanings. The meanings depend on the conversion character. By default, the value of precision is 6. For 'e' and 'f' conversions, the precision is the number of digits after the decimal separator. For the 'g' conversion, the precision is the total number of digits in the resulting magnitude after rounding. Precision is not applicable to the 'a' conversion.

The following snippet of code shows how to format floating-point numbers with the default precision, which is 6:

```
System.out.printf("%e %n", 10.2);
System.out.printf("%f %n", 10.2);
System.out.printf("%g %n", 10.2);

System.out.printf("%e %n", 0.000002079);
System.out.printf("%f %n", 0.000002079);
System.out.printf("%g %n", 0.000002079);

System.out.printf("%a %n", 0.000002079);
```

```
1.020000e+01
10.200000
10.2000
2.079000e-06
0.000002
2.07900e-06
'1.97e+03'
0x1.1709e564a6d14p-19
```

The following snippet of code shows the effects of using width and precision in floating-point number formatting:

```
System.out.printf("%.2e %n", 1969.27);
System.out.printf("%.2f %n", 1969.27);
System.out.printf("%.2g %n", 1969.27);

System.out.printf("'%8.2e' %n", 1969.27);
System.out.printf("'%8.2f' %n", 1969.27);
System.out.printf("'%8.2g' %n", 1969.27);

System.out.printf("'%10.2e' %n", 1969.27);
System.out.printf("'%10.2f' %n", 1969.27);
System.out.printf("'%10.2g' %n", 1969.27);

System.out.printf("'%-10.2e' %n", 1969.27);
System.out.printf("'%-10.2f' %n", 1969.27);
System.out.printf("'%-10.2g' %n", 1969.27);

System.out.printf("'%010.2e' %n", 1969.27);
System.out.printf("'%010.2f' %n", 1969.27);
System.out.printf("'%010.2g' %n", 1969.27);
```

```
1.97e+03
1969.27
2.0e+03
'1.97e+03'
' 1969.27'
' 2.0e+03'
'  1.97e+03'
'   1969.27'
'   2.0e+03'
'1.97e+03  '
'1969.27   '
'2.0e+03   '
'001.97e+03'
'0001969.27'
'0002.0e+03'
```

If the argument value for a floating-point conversion is NaN or Infinity, the output contains the strings "NaN" and "Infinity", respectively. The following snippet of code shows the formatting of floating-point numbers when their values are NaN or infinities:

```
System.out.printf("%.2e %n", Double.NaN);
System.out.printf("%.2f %n", Double.POSITIVE_INFINITY);
System.out.printf("%.2g %n", Double.NEGATIVE_INFINITY);
System.out.printf("%(f %n", Double.POSITIVE_INFINITY);
System.out.printf("%(f %n", Double.NEGATIVE_INFINITY);
```

```
NaN
Infinity
-Infinity
Infinity
(Infinity)
```

Formatting Dates and Times

Date/time formatting deals with formatting date, time, and datetime. It can be applied to format values of long, Long, java.util.Calandar, java.util.Date, and java.time.temporal.TemporalAccessor types. The value in a long/Long type argument is interpreted as the milliseconds passed since January 1, 1970 midnight UTC.

■ **Note** TemporalAccessor is an interface added in Java 8. It is part of the new Date-Time API. All classes in the API that specify some kind of date, time, or both are TemporalAccessor. LocalDate, LocalTime, LocalDateTime, and ZonedDateTime are some examples of TemporalAccessor. Please refer to Chapter 12 for more details on using the new Date-Time API.

The 't' conversion character is used to format date/time values. It has an uppercase variant 'T'. The general syntax for a format specifier for date/time formatting is as follows:

```
%<argument_index$><flags><width><conversion>
```

Note that precision part in a format specifier is not applicable to date/time formatting. For date/time formatting, the conversion is a two-character sequence. The first character in the conversion is always 't' or 'T'. The second character is called the conversion suffix, which determines the format of the date/time argument. Table 13-7,13-8 and Table 13-9 list all the conversion suffixes that can be used with 't'/'T' data/time conversion character.

Table 13-7. *List of Suffix Characters for Time Formatting*

Conversion Suffix	Description
'H'	A two-digit hour of the day for the 24-hour clock. The valid values are 00 to 23. 00 is used for midnight.
'I'	A two-digit hour of the day for the 12-hour clock. The valid values are 01 to 12. The 01 value corresponds to one o'clock in the morning or afternoon.
'k'	It behaves the same as the 'H' suffix except that it does not add a leading zero to the output. Valid values are 0 to 23.
'l'	It behaves the same as 'I' suffix except that it does not add a leading zero. Valid values are 1 to 12.
'M'	A two-digit minute within an hour. Valid values are 00 to 59.
'S'	A two-digit second within a minute. Valid values are 00 to 60. The value 60 is a special value that is required to support leap seconds.
'L'	A three-digit millisecond within a second. Valid values are 000 to 999.
'N'	A nine-digit nanosecond within a second. The valid values are 000000000 to 999999999. The precision of the nanosecond value is dependent on the precision that is supported by the operating system.
'p'	It outputs a locale-specific morning or afternoon marker in lowercase. For example, for US locale, it will output "am" or "pm". If you want the output in uppercase (e.g., "AM" and "PM" for US locale), you need to use the uppercase variant 'T' as the conversion character..
'z'	It outputs the numeric time zone offset from GMT (e.g., +0530).
'Z'	It is a string abbreviation of the time zone (e.g., CST, EST, IST, etc).
's'	It outputs seconds since the beginning of the epoch starting at January 1, 1970 midnight UTC.
'Q'	It outputs milliseconds since the beginning of the epoch starting at January 1, 1970 midnight UTC.

Table 13-8. *List of Suffix Characters for Date Formatting*

Conversion Suffix	Description
'B'	Locale-specific full name of the month, such as "January", "February", etc. for US locale.
'b'	Locale-specific abbreviated month name, such as "Jan", "Feb", etc. for US locale.
'h'	Same as 'b'
'A'	Locale-specific full name of the day of the week, such as "Sunday", "Monday", etc. for US locale.
'a'	Locale-specific short name of the day of the week, such as "Sun", "Mon", etc. for US locale.
'C'	It divides the four-digit year by 100 and formats the result as two digits. It adds a leading zero if the resulting number is one digit. It ignores the fraction part from the result of the division by 100. Valid values are 00 to 99. For example, if the four-digit year is 2011, it will output 20; if the four-digit year is 12, it will output 00.

(continued)

Table 13-8. (*continued*)

Conversion Suffix	Description
'Y'	At least a four-digit year. It adds leading zeros if the year contains less than four digits. For example, if the year is 789, it will output 0789; if the year is 2011, it will output 2011; if the year is 20189, it will output 20189.
'y'	The last two digits of the year. It adds leading zero if necessary. For example, if the year is 9, it will output 09; if the year is 123, it will output 23; if the year is 2011, it will output 11.
'j'	A three-digit day of the year. Valid values are 000 to 366.
'm'	A two-digit month. Valid values are 01 to 13. The special value of 13 is required to support lunar calendar.
'd'	A two-digit day of the month. Valid values are 01 to 31.
'e'	Day of the month. Valid values are 1 to 31. It behaves the same as 'd' except that it does not add a leading zero to the output.

Table 13-9. *List of Suffix Characters for Date/Time Formatting*

Conversion Suffix	Description
'R'	It formats time in 24-hour clock format as "hour:minute". Its effects is the same as using "%tH:%tM" as a format specifier. Examples are "11:23", "01:35", "21:30", etc.
'T'	It formats time in 24-hour clock format as "hour:minute:second". Its effects is the same as using "%tH:%tM:%tS" as a format specifier. Examples are"11:23:10", "01:35:01", "21:30:34", etc.
'r'	It formats time in 12-hour clock format as "hour:minute:second morning/afternoon marker". Its effects is the same as using "%tI:%tM:%tS %Tp" as a format specifier. The morning/afternoon marker may be locale-specific. "09:23:45 AM", "09:30:00 PM", etc. are example for US locale.
'D'	It formats the date as "%tm/%td/%ty", such as "01/19/11".
'F'	It formats the date as "%tY-%tm-%td", such as "2011-01-19".
'c'	It formats the date and time as "%ta %tb %td %tT %tZ %tY", such as "Wed Jan 19 11:52:06 CST 2011".

The data/time conversion applies localization wherever it is applicable. The following snippet of code formats the same date and time, January 25, 2014 11:48:16 AM, in US, Indian, and Thai locales. Note the use of the '<' flag in the format specifier. It lets you use the argument that holds the date and time value in multiple format specifiers.

```
Locale englishUS = Locale.US;
Locale hindiIndia = new Locale ("hi", "IN");
Locale thaiThailand = new Locale ("th", "TH", "TH");

// Construct a LocalDateTime
LocalDateTime ldt = LocalDateTime.of(2014, Month.JANUARY, 25, 11, 48, 16);

System.out.printf(englishUS, "In US: %tB %<te, %<tY %<tT %<Tp%n", ldt);
System.out.printf(hindiIndia, "In India: %tB %<te, %<tY %<tT %<Tp%n", ldt);
System.out.printf(thaiThailand, "In Thailand: %tB %<te, %<tY %<tT %<Tp%n", ldt);
```

```
In US: January 25, 2014 11:48:16 AM

In India: जनवरी २५, २०१४ ११:४८:१६ पूर्वाह्न

In Thailand: มกราคม ๒๕, ๒๐๑๔ ๑๑:๔๘:๑๖ ก่อนเที่ยง
```

The following snippet of code formats the current date and time in the default locale (US in this case). You will get different output when you run the code. It uses a `ZonedDateTime` argument that holds the current date/time with time zone.

```
ZonedDateTime currentTime = ZonedDateTime.now();

System.out.printf("%tA %<tB %<te, %<tY %n", currentTime);
System.out.printf("%TA %<TB %<te, %<tY %n", currentTime);
System.out.printf("%tD %n", currentTime);
System.out.printf("%tF %n", currentTime);
System.out.printf("%tc %n", currentTime);
System.out.printf("%Tc %n", currentTime);
```

```
Saturday January 25, 2014
SATURDAY JANUARY 25, 2014
01/25/14
2014-01-25
Sat Jan 25 00:47:26 CST 2014
SAT JAN 25 00:47:26 CST 2014
```

Note the effect of using the uppercase variant `'T'` as the conversion character. It formats the argument in uppercase letters. The definition of uppercase depends on the locale that is used. If the locale does not have different uppercase and lowercase letters, the output will be the same when you use `'T'` or `'t'` as the conversion character.

Summary

In this chapter, you learned how to format dates and times using the `DateFormat` and `SimpleDateFormat` classes in the `java.text` package. The `DateFormat` class formats dates and times using predefined formats whereas the `SimpleDateFormat` class lets you specify custom formats.

The `NumberFormat` class is used to format a number in a particular locale's predefined format. The `DecimalFormat` class is used to format a number in a format of your choice in a particular locale.

You can use `printf`-style formatting using the `java.util.Formatter` class to format strings, numbers, and date/time. It lets you send the formatted output to a `StringBuilder`, a `StringBuffer`, a `File`, an `OutputStream`, a `PrintStream`, etc. You have been using the `System.out.format()` and `System.out.printf()` methods to send the formatted output to the standard output. Use the `static String.format()`method to get a formatted string. Use a `Formatter` to send the formatted output to the destination of your choice. You can implement the `Formattable` interface to apply a custom formatting to the objects of the class.

■ ■ ■

CHAPTER 14

Regular Expressions

In this chapter, you will learn

- How to create regular expressions
- How to use convenience methods in the `String` class to perform regular expression-based find-and-replace
- How to use the `Pattern` class to compile regular expressions
- How to use the `Matcher` class to match a regular expression against an input string
- How to use groups in regular expressions
- How to perform advanced find-and-replace using the `Matcher` class

What Is a Regular Expression?

A regular expression is a way to describe a pattern in a sequence of characters. The pattern may be used to validate the sequence of characters, to search through the sequence of characters, to replace the sequence of characters matching the pattern with other sequence of characters, etc.

Let's start with an example. Suppose you have a string, which may be an e-mail address. How would you make sure that the string is in a valid e-mail address format? At this point, you are not interested in the existence of the e-mail address. You just want to validate its format.

You would like to validate the string against some rules. For example, it must contain an @ sign, which is preceded by at least one character and followed by a domain name. Optionally, you may specify that the text preceding the @ sign must contain only letters, digits, underscores, and hyphens. The domain name must contain a dot. You may want to add some more validations. If you just want to check for a @ character in a string, you can do it by calling `email.indexOf('@')`, where `email` is the reference of the string holding the e-mail address. If you want to make sure that there is only one @ character in the e-mail string, you need add more logic to the code. In such cases, you may end up with 20 to 50, or even more, lines of code depending on the number of validations you want to perform. This is where regular expressions come in handy. It will make your e-mail address validation easy. You can accomplish it in just one line of code. Doesn't that sound too good to be true? Just a little while ago, you were told that you might end up with 50 lines of code. Now you are told that you could accomplish the same in just one line of code. This is true. It can be done in one line of code. Before I go into the details of how to do this, let's list the steps needed to accomplish this task.

- To validate these kinds of strings, you need to recognize the pattern you are looking for. For example, in the simplest form of e-mail address validation, the string should consist of some text (at least one character) plus an @ sign followed by some text for domain name. Let's ignore any other details for now.

- You need a way to express the recognized pattern. A regular expression is used to describe such a pattern.

- You need a program that can match the pattern against the input string. Such a program is also known as a regular expression engine.

Suppose you want to test whether a string is of the form X@X, where X is any character. Strings "a@a", "b@f", "3@h" are in this form. You can observe a pattern here. The pattern is "A character followed by @, which is followed by a character." How do you express this pattern in Java?

The string ".@." will represent your regular expression in this case. In ".@.", the dots have a special meaning. They represent any character. All characters that have special meanings inside a regular expression are called metacharacters. I will discuss metacharacters in the next section. The String class contains a matches() method. It takes a regular expression as an argument and returns true if the whole string matches the regular expression. Otherwise, it returns false. The signature of this method is

```
boolean matches(String regex)
```

The program listed in Listing 14-1 illustrates the use of the matches() method of the String class.

Listing 14-1. Matching a String Against a Pattern

```java
// RegexMatch.java
package com.jdojo.regex;

public class RegexMatch {
    public static void main(String[] args) {
        // Prepare a regular expression to represent a pattern
        String regex = ".@.";

        // Try matching many strings against the regular expression
        RegexMatch.matchIt("a@k", regex);
        RegexMatch.matchIt("webmaster@jdojo.com", regex);
        RegexMatch.matchIt("r@j", regex);
        RegexMatch.matchIt("a%N", regex);
        RegexMatch.matchIt(".@.", regex);
    }

    public static void matchIt(String str, String regex) {
        // Test for pattern match
        if (str.matches(regex)) {
            System.out.println(str + " matches the regex " + regex);
        }
        else {
            System.out.println(str + " does not match the regex " + regex);
        }
    }
}
```

```
a@k matches the regex .@.
webmaster@jdojo.com does not match the regex .@.
r@j matches the regex .@.
a%N does not match the regex .@.
.@. matches the regex .@.
```

Some important points to note are the following:

- The regular expression ".@." did not match "webmaster@jdojo.com", because a dot means only one character and the String.matches() method matches the pattern in the regular expression against the entire string. Note that the string "webmaster@jdojo.com" has the pattern represented by .@.; that is, a character followed by @ and another character. However, the pattern matches part of the string, not the entire string. The "r@j" part of "webmaster@jdojo.com" matches that pattern. I will present some examples where you will match the pattern anywhere in the string rather than match the entire string.

- If you want to match a dot character in a string, you need to escape the dot in the regular expression. The regular expression ".\\.." will match any string of three characters in which the middle character is a dot character. For example, The method call "a.b".matches(".\\..") will return true; the method call "...".matches(".\\..") will return true; the method calls "abc".matches(".\\..") and "aa.ca".matches(".\\..") will return false.

You can also replace the matching string with another string. The String class has two methods to do the match replacement:

- String replaceAll(String regex, String replacementString):
- String replaceFirst(String regex, String replacementString):

The replaceAll() method replaces strings, which match the pattern represented by the specified regex, with the specified replacementString. It returns the new string after replacement. Some examples of using the replaceAll() method are as follows:

```
String regex = ".@.";

// newStr will contain "webmaste***dojo.com"
String newStr = "webmaster@jdojo.com".replaceAll(regex,"***");

// newStr will contain "***"
newStr = "A@B".replaceAll(regex,"***");

// newStr will contain "***and***"
newStr = "A@BandH@G".replaceAll(regex,"***");

// newStr will contain "B%T" (same as the original string)
newStr = "B%T".replaceAll(regex,"***");
```

The replaceFirst() method replaces the first occurrence of the match with the replacementString. It returns the new string after replacement. Some examples of using the replaceFirst() method are as follows:

```
String regex = ".@.";

// newStr will contain "webmaste***dojo.com"
String newStr = "webmaster@jdojo.com".replaceFirst(regex, "***");

// newStr will contain "***"
newStr = "A@B".replaceFirst(regex, "***");

// newStr will contain "***andH@G"
newStr = "A@BandH@G".replaceFirst(regex, "***");

// newStr will contain "B%T" (same as the original string)
newStr = "B%T".replaceFirst(regex, "***");
```

Metacharacters

Metacharacters are characters with special meanings. They are used in regular expressions. Sometimes metacharacters do not have any special meanings and they are treated as ordinary characters. They are treated as ordinary characters or metacharacters depending on the context in which they are used. The metacharacters supported by the regular expressions in Java are as follows:

- ((a left parenthesis)
-) (a right parenthesis)
- [(a left bracket)
-] (a right bracket)
- { (a left brace)
- { (a right brace)
- \ (a backslash)
- ^ (a caret)
- $ (a dollar sign)
- | (a vertical bar)
- ? (a question mark)
- * (an asterisk)
- + (an addition sign)
- . (a dot or period)
- < (a less-than sign)
- > (a greater-than sign)
- - (a hyphen)
- = (an equal to sign)
- ! (an exclamation mark)

Character Classes

The metacharacters [and] (left and right brackets) are used to specify a character class inside a regular expression. A character class is a set of characters. The regular expression engine will attempt to match one character from the set. Note that a character class has no relation with a class construct or class files in Java. The character class "[ABC]" will match characters A, B, or C. For example, the strings "A@V", "B@V", and "C@V" will match the regular expression "[ABC]@.". However, the string "H@V" will not match the regular expression "[ABC]@." because @ is not preceded by A, B, or C. As another example, the strings "man" or "men" will match the regular expression "m[ae]n".

When I use the word "match", I mean that the pattern exists in a string. I do not mean that the whole string matches the pattern. For example, "WEB@JDOJO.COM" matches the pattern "[ABC]@.", because @ is preceded by B. The string "A@BAND@YEA@U" matches the pattern "[ABC]@." twice even though the string contains three @ signs. The second @ is not a part of any match, because it is preceded by D and not A, B, or C.

You can also specify a range of characters using a character class. The range is expressed using a hyphen (-) character. For example, "[A-Z]" in a regular expression represents any uppercase English letters; "[0-9]" represents any digit between 0 and 9. If you use ^ in the beginning of a character class, it means complement (meaning not). For example, "[^ABC]" means any character except A, B, and C. The character class "[^A-Z]" represents any character except uppercase English letters. If you use ^ anywhere in a character class except in the beginning, it loses its special meaning (i.e. the special meaning of complement) and it matches just a ^ character. For example, "[ABC^]" will match A, B, C, or ^.

You can also include two or more ranges in one character class. For example, "[a-zA-Z]" matches any character a through z and A through Z. "[a-zA-Z0-9]" matches any character a through z (uppercase and lowercase), and any digit 0 through 9. Some examples of character classes are listed in Table 14-1.

Table 14-1. *Examples of Character Classes*

Character Classes	Meaning	Category
[abc]	Character a, b, or c	Simple character class
[^xyz]	A character except x, y, and z	Complement or negation
[a-p]	Characters a through p	Range
[a-cx-z]	Characters a through c, or x through z, which would include a, b, c, x, y, or z.	Union
[0-9&&[4-8]]	Intersection of two ranges (4, 5, 6, 7, or 8)	Intersection
[a-z&&[^aeiou]]	All lowercase letters minus vowels. In other words, a lowercase letter, which is not a vowel. That is, all lowercase consonants.	Subtraction

Predefined Character Classes

Some frequently used predefined character classes are listed in Table 14-2.

Table 14-2. *List of the Predefined Regular Expression Character Classes*

Predefined Character Classes	Meaning
. (a dot)	Any character (may or may not match line terminators). Please refer to the section "Line terminators" in the API documentation of the java.util.regex.Pattern class for more details.
\d	A digit. Same as [0-9]
\D	A non-digit. Same as [^0-9]
\s	A whitespace character. Same as [\t\n\x0B\f\r]. The list includes a space, a tab, a new line, a vertical tab, a form feed, and a carriage return characters.
\S	A non-whitespace character. Same as [^\s]
\w	A word character. Same as [a-zA-Z_0-9]. The list includes lowercase letters, uppercase letter, underscore, and decimal digits.
\W	A non-word character. Same as [^\w]

If you allow all uppercase and lowercase letters, underscore and digits in your e-mail address validations, the regular expression to validate e-mail addresses of only three characters would be "\w@\w". Now you are one step ahead in your e-mail address validation process. Instead of allowing only A, B, or C in the first part of e-mail (as expressed by regular expression [ABC]@.), now you are allowing any word character as the first part as well as second part.

More Powers to Regular Expressions

Until now, you have seen only three methods of the String class using the regular expressions. The package java.util.regex contains three classes to support the full version of regular expressions. The classes are

- Pattern
- Matcher
- PatternSyntaxException

A Pattern holds the compiled form of a regular expression. The compiled form of a regular expression is its specialized in-memory representation to facilitate faster string matching. A Matcher associates the string to be matched with a Pattern and it performs the actual match. A PatternSyntaxException represents an error in a malformed regular expression.

Compiling Regular Expressions

A Pattern holds the compiled form of a regular expression. It is immutable. It can be shared. It has no public constructor. The class contains a static compile() method, which returns a Pattern object. The compile() method is overloaded.

- static Pattern compile(String regex)
- static Pattern compile(String regex, int flags)

The following snippet of code compiles a regular expression into a Pattern object:

```
// Prepare a regular expression
String regex = "[a-z]@.";

// Compile the regular expression into a Pattern object
Pattern p = Pattern.compile(regex);
```

The second version of the compile() method lets you specify flags that modify the way the pattern is matched. The flags parameter is a bit mask. The flags are defines as int constants in the Pattern class, as listed in Table 14-3.

Table 14-3. *List of Flags Defined in the Pattern Class*

Flag	Description
Pattern.CANON_EQ	Enables canonical equivalence. If this flag is set, two characters match only if their full canonical decompositions match.
Pattern.CASE_INSENSITIVE	Enables case-insensitive matching. This flag sets the case-insensitive matching only for US-ASCII charset. For case-insensitive matching of Unicode charset, the UNICODE_CASE flag should also be set in conjunction with this flag.
Pattern.COMMENTS	Permits whitespace and comments in pattern. When this flag is set, whitespace is ignored and embedded comments starting with # are ignored until the end of a line.
Pattern.DOTALL	Enables dotall mode. By default, the expression . does not match line terminators. When this flag is set, the expression matches any character, including a line terminator.
Pattern.LITERAL	Enables literal parsing of the pattern. When this flag is set, the characters in the regular expression are treated literally. That is, metacharacters and escape sequences have no special meanings. CASE_INSENSTIVE and UNICODE_CASE flags retain their effects when used with this flag.
Pattern.MULTILINE	Enables multiline mode. By default, the expressions ^ and $ match the beginning and the end of the entire input sequence. When this flag is set, they match just after and just before a line terminator or the end of the input sequence, respectively.
Pattern.UNICODE_CASE	Enables Unicode-aware case folding. When this flag is set in conjunction with the CASE_INSENSITIVE flag, the case-insensitive matching is performed according to the Unicode Standard.
Pattern.UNICODE_CHARACTER_CLASS	Enables the Unicode version of predefined character classes and POSIX character classes. Setting this flag also has the effect of setting the UNICODE_CASE flag. When this flag is set, the (US-ASCII only) Predefined character classes and POSIX character classes are in conformance with Unicode Technical Standard #18: Unicode Regular Expression Annex C: Compatibility Properties.
Pattern.UNIX_LINES	Enables Unix lines mode. When this flag is set, only the \n character is recognized as a line terminator.

The following snippet of code compiles a regular expression setting the CASE_INSENSTIVE and DOTALL flags, so the matching will be case-insensitive for US-ASCII charset and the expression. will match a line terminator. For example, "A@\n" will be matched by the following pattern:

```
// Prepare a regular expression
String regex = "[a-z]@.";

// Compile the regular expression into a Pattern object setting the
// CASE_INSENSITIVE and DOTALL flags
Pattern p = Pattern.compile(regex, Pattern.CASE_INSENSITIVE|Pattern.DOTALL);
```

Creating a Matcher

An instance of the Matcher class is used to perform a match on a sequence of characters by interpreting the compiled pattern held in a Pattern object. It has no public constructor. The matcher() method of the Pattern class is used to get an instance of the Matcher class. The method takes the string to be matched by the pattern as an argument.

```
// Create a Pattern object
String regex = "[a-z]@.";

Pattern p = Pattern.compile(regex);

// String to perform the match
String str = "abc@yahoo.com,123@cnn.com,ksharan@jdojo.com";

// Get a matcher object using Pattern object p for str
Matcher m = p.matcher(str);
```

At this point, the Matcher object m has associated the pattern represented in the Pattern object p with the sequence of characters in str. It is ready to start the match operation. Typically, a matcher object is used to find a match in the sequence of characters. The match may succeed or fail. If the match succeeds, you may be interested in knowing the start and end positions of the match and the matched text. You can query a Matcher object to get all these pieces of information.

Matching the Pattern

You need to use the following methods of the Matcher to perform the match on the input:

- The find() method
- The start() method
- The end() method
- The group() method

The find() method is used to find a match for the pattern in the input. If the find succeeds, it returns true. Otherwise, it returns false. The first call to this method starts the search for the pattern at the beginning of the input. If the previous call to this method was successful, the next call to this method starts the search after the previous match. Typically, a call to the find() method is used in a while-loop to find all the matches. It is an overloaded method. Another version of the find() method takes an integer argument, which is the offset to start the find for a match.

The start() method returns the start index of the previous match. Typically, it is used after a successful find() method call.

The end() method returns the index of the last character in the matched string plus one. Therefore, after a successful invocation of the find() method, the difference between the values returned by the end() and start() methods will give you the length of the matched string. Using the substring() method of the String class, you can get the matched string as follows:

```
// Continued from previous fragment of code
if (m.find()) {
        // str is the string we are looking into
        String foundStr = str.substring(m.start(), m.end());

        System.out.println("Found string is:" + foundStr);
}
```

The group() method returns the found string by the previous successful find() method call. Recall that you can also get the previous matched string using the substring() method of the String class by using the start and end of the match. Therefore, the above snippet of code can be replaced by the following code:

```
if (m.find()) {
        String foundStr = m.group();
        System.out.println("Found text is:" + foundStr);
}
```

Listing 14-2 illustrates the use of these methods. The validations for the method's arguments have been omitted for clarity. The program attempts to find the "[abc]@." pattern in different strings.

Listing 14-2. Using Pattern and Matcher Classes

```
// PatternMatcher.java
package com.jdojo.regex;

import java.util.regex.Pattern;
import java.util.regex.Matcher;

public class PatternMatcher {
        public static void main(String[] args) {
                String regex = "[abc]@.";

                String source = "cric@jdojo.com is a valid email address";
                PatternMatcher.findPattern(regex, source);

                source = "kelly@jdojo.com is invalid";
                PatternMatcher.findPattern(regex, source);

                source = "a@band@yea@u";
                PatternMatcher.findPattern(regex, source);

                source = "There is an @ sign here";
                PatternMatcher.findPattern(regex, source);
        }
```

```java
    public static void findPattern(String regex, String source) {
        // Compile regex into a Pattern object
        Pattern p = Pattern.compile(regex);

        // Get a Matcher object
        Matcher m = p.matcher(source);

        // Print regex and source text
        System.out.println("\nRegex:" + regex);
        System.out.println("Text:" + source);

        // Perform find
        boolean found = false;
        while (m.find()) {
                                          System.out.println("Matched Text:" + m.group() +
                        ", Start:" + m.start() +
                        ", " + "End:" + m.end());

                // We found at least one match. Set the found flag to true
                found = true;
        }

        if (!found) {
                // We did not find any match
                System.out.println("No match found");
        }
    }
}
```

```
Regex:[abc]@.
Text:cric@jdojo.com is a valid email address
Matched Text:c@j, Start:3, End:6

Regex:[abc]@.
Text:kelly@jdojo.com is invalid
No match found

Regex:[abc]@.
Text:a@band@yea@u
Matched Text:a@b, Start:0, End:3
Matched Text:a@u, Start:9, End:12

Regex:[abc]@.
Text:There is an @ sign here
No match found
```

Beware of Backslashes

Beware of using backslashes in regular expressions. The character class \w (that is, a backslash followed by a "w") represents a word character. Recall that a backslash character is also used as a part of an escape character. Therefore, \w must be written as \\w as a string literal. You can also use a backslash to nullify the special meaning of metacharacters. For example, [marks the beginning of a character class. What would be the regular expression that will match a digit enclosed in brackets, for example, [1], [5], etc.? Note that the regular expression [0-9] will match any digit. The digit may or may not be enclosed in a bracket. You may think about using [[0-9]]. It will not give you any error message; however, it will not do the job either. You can also embed a character class within another. For example, you can write [a-z[0-9]], which is the same as [a-z0-9]. In this case, the first [in [[0-9]] should be treated as an ordinary character, not as a metacharacter. You must use a backslash as \[[0-9]\]. To write this regular expression as a string literal, you need to use two backslashes as \\[[0-9]\\]].

Quantifiers in Regular Expressions

You can also specify the number of times a character in a regular expression may match the sequence of characters. If you want to match all two digit integers, your regular expression would be \d\d, which is the same as [0-9][0-9]. What would be the regular expression to match any integer? You cannot write the regular expression to match any integer with the knowledge you have gained so far. You need to be able to express a pattern "one digit or more" using a regular expression. Here comes the concept of quantifiers. Quantifiers and their meanings are listed in Table 14-4.

Table 14-4. Quantifiers and Their Meaning

Quantifiers	Meaning
*	Zero or more times
+	One or more times
?	Once or not at all
{m}	Exactly m times
{m, }	At least m times
{m, n}	At least m, but not more than n times

It is important to note that quantifiers must follow a character or character class for which it specifies the quantity. The regular expression to match any integer would be \d+, which says that match one or more number of digits. Is this solution for matching integer correct? No, it is not. Suppose your text is "This is text123 which contains 10 and 120". If you run your pattern \d+ against this string, it will match against 123, 10, and 120. Note that 123 is not used as an integer; rather it is a part of word text123. If you are looking for integers inside text, certainly 123 in text123 does not qualify as an integer. You want to match all integers that form a word in the text.

Necessity is the mother of invention. Now you need to specify that the match should be performed only on word boundaries, not inside text having embedded integers. This is necessary to exclude integer 123 from your previous result. The next section discusses the use of metacharacters to match boundaries.

With the knowledge you have gained in this section, let's improve your e-mail address validation. Inside an e-mail address, there must be one and only one @ sign. To specify one and only one character, you use that character one time in the regular expression although you can use {1} as the quantifier. For example, X{1} and X means the same inside a regular expression. You are fine on this account. However, your solution until now supports only one character before and after the @ sign. In reality, there can be more than one character before and after the @ sign in an e-mail address. You can specify the pattern to validate an e-mail address as \w+@\w+, which means: one or more word characters, an @ sign, and one or more word characters.

Matching Boundaries

Until now, you did not care about the location of the pattern match in the text. Sometimes, you may be interested in knowing if the match occurred in the beginning of a line. You may be interested in finding and replacing a particular match only if the match was found in a word, not as part of any word. For example, you may want to replace the word "apple" inside a string with the word "orange." Suppose your string is "I have an apple and five pineapples". Certainly, you do not want to replace all occurrences of "apple" with "orange" in this string. If you do, your new string would be "I have an orange and five pineoranges". In fact, you want the new string to be "I have an orange and five pineapples". You want to match the word "apple" as a standalone word, not the part of any other word.

Table 14-5 lists all boundary matchers that can be used in a regular expression.

Table 14-5. *List of Boundary Matchers Inside Regular Expressions*

Boundary Matchers	Meaning
^	The beginning of a line
$	The end of a line
\b	A word boundary
\B	A non-word boundary
\A	The beginning of the input
\G	The end of previous match
\Z	The end of the input but for the final terminator, if any
\z	The end of the input

In Java, a word character is defined by [a-zA-Z_0-9]. A word boundary is a zero-width match that can match the following:

- Between a word character and a non-word character

- Start of the string and a word character

- A word character and the end of the string

A non-word boundary is also a zero-width match and it is the opposite of the word boundary. It matches the following:

- The empty string

- Between two word characters

- Between two non-word characters

- Between a non-word character and the start or end of the string

The regular expression to match the word apple would be \bapple\b, which means the following: a word boundary, the word apple, and a word boundary. Listing 14-3 demonstrates how to match a word boundary using a regular expression.

Listing 14-3. Matching a Word Boundary

```java
// MatchBoundary.java
package com.jdojo.regex;

public class MatchBoundary {
        public static void main(String[] args) {
                // Prepare regular expression. Use \\b to get \b inside the string literal.
                String regex = "\\bapple\\b";
                String replacementStr = "orange";
                String inputStr = "I have an apple and five pineapples";
                String newStr = inputStr.replaceAll(regex, replacementStr);

                System.out.println("Regular Expression: " + regex);
                System.out.println("Input String: " + inputStr);
                System.out.println("Replacement String: " + replacementStr);
                System.out.println("New String: " + newStr);
        }
}
```

```
Regular Expression: \bapple\b
Input String: I have an apple and five pineapples
Replacement String: orange
New String: I have an orange and five pineapples
```

There are two boundary matchers: ^ (beginning of a line) and \A (beginning of the input). Input string may consist of multiple lines. In that case, \A will match the beginning of the entire input string, whereas ^ will match the beginning of each line in the input. For example, regular expression "^The" will match the input string, which is in the beginning of any line.

Groups and Back Referencing

You can treat multiple characters as a unit by using them as a group. A group is created inside a regular expression by enclosing one or more characters inside parentheses. (ab), ab(z), ab(ab)(xyz), (the((is)(is))) are examples of groups. Each group in a regular expression has a group number. The group number starts at 1. The Matcher class has a method groupCount() that returns the number of groups in the pattern associated with the Matcher instance. There is a special group called group 0 (zero). It refers to the entire regular expression. The group 0 is not reported by the groupCount() method.

How is each group numbered? Each left parenthesis inside a regular expression marks the start of a new group. Table 14-6 lists some examples of group numbering in a regular expression. Note that I have also listed group 0 for all regular expressions although it is not reported by the groupCount() method of the Matcher class. The last example in the list shows that the group 0 is present, even if there are no explicit groups present in the regular expression.

Table 14-6. *Examples of Groups in Regular Expressions*

Regular Expression: AB(XY)

Number of groups reported by Matcher class's groupCount() method: 1

Group Number	Group Text
0	AB(XY)
1	(XY)

Regular Expression: (AB)(XY)

Number of groups reported by Matcher class's groupCount() method: 2

Group Number	Group Text
0	(AB)(XY)
1	(AB)
2	(XY)

Regular Expression: ((A)((X)(Y)))

Number of groups reported by Matcher class's groupCount() method: 5

Group Number	Group Text
0	((A)((X)(Y)))
1	((A)((X)(Y)))
2	(A)
3	((X)(Y))
4	(X)
5	(Y)

Regular Expression: ABXY

Number of groups reported by Matcher class's groupCount() method: 0

Group Number	Group Text
0	ABXY

You can also back reference group numbers in a regular expression. Suppose you want to match text that starts with "ab" followed by "xy", which is followed by "ab". You can write a regular expression as "abxyab". You can also achieve the same result by forming a group that contains "ab" and back referencing it as "(ab)xy\1". Here, "\1" refers to group 1, which is "(ab)" in this case. You can use "\2" to refer to group 2, "\3" to refer to group 3, and so on. How will regular expression "(ab)xy\12" be interpreted? You have used "\12" as the group back reference. The regular expression engine is smart enough to detect that it contains only one group in "(ab)xy\12". It uses "\1" as back reference to group 1, which is "(ab)" and 2 as an ordinary character. Therefore, the regular expression "(ab)xy\12" is the same as "abxyab2". If a regular expression has 12 or more groups, \12 in the regular expression will refer to the twelfth group.

You can also fetch part of a matched text by using a group number in the regular expression. The group() method in the Matcher class is overloaded. You have already seen the group() method, which takes no arguments. Another version of the method takes a group number as an argument and returns the matched text by that group. Suppose you have phone numbers embedded in the input text. All phone numbers occurs as a word and are ten digits long. The first three digits are the area code. The regular expression \b\d{10}\b will match all phone numbers in the input text.

However, to get the first three digits (the area code), you will have to write extra code. If you form a regular expression using groups, you can get the area code using the group number. The regular expression placing the first three digits of a phone number in a group would be \b(\d{3})\d{7}\b. If m is the reference to a Matcher object associated with this pattern, m.group(1) will return the first three digits of the phone number after a successful match. You can also use m.group(0) to get the entire matched text. Listing 14-4 illustrates the use of groups in regular expressions to get the area code part of phone numbers. Note that 2339829 does not match the pattern because it has only 7 digits.

Listing 14-4. Using Groups in Regular Expressions

```java
// PhoneMatcher.java
package com.jdojo.regex;

import java.util.regex.Pattern;
import java.util.regex.Matcher;

public class PhoneMatcher {
    public static void main(String[] args) {
        // Prepare a regular expression: A group of 3 digits followed by 7 digits.
        String regex = "\\b(\\d{3})\\d{7}\\b";

        // Compile the regular expression
        Pattern p = Pattern.compile(regex);

        String source = "3342449027, 2339829, and 6152534734";

        // Get the Matcher object
        Matcher m = p.matcher(source);

        // Start matching and display the found area codes
        while(m.find()) {
            String phone = m.group();
            String areaCode = m.group(1);
            System.out.println("Phone: " + phone + ", Area Code: " + areaCode);
        }
    }
}
```

```
Phone: 3342449027, Area Code: 334
Phone: 6152534734, Area Code: 615
```

Groups are also used to format or replace the matched string with another string. Suppose you want to format all 10-digit phone numbers as (XXX) XXX-XXXX, where X denotes a digit. As you can see, the phone number is in three groups: the first three digits, the next three digits, and the last four digits. You need to form a regular expression using three groups so you can refer to the three matched groups by their group numbers. The regular expression would be \b(\d{3})(\d{3})(\d{4})\b. The \b in the beginning and in the end denotes that you are interested in matching ten digits only at word boundaries. The following snippet of code illustrates how you can display formatted phone numbers:

```java
// Prepare the regular expression
String regex = "\\b(\\d{3})(\\d{3})(\\d{4})\\b";

// Compile the regular expression
Pattern p = Pattern.compile(regex);
```

```
String source = "3342449027, 2339829, and 6152534734";

// Get Matcher object
Matcher m = p.matcher(source);

// Start match and display formatted phone numbers
while(m.find()) {
        System.out.println("Phone: " + m.group() + ", Formatted Phone: (" + m.group(1) + ") " +
                           m.group(2) + "-"  + m.group(3));
}
```

```
Phone: 3342449027, Formatted Phone: (334) 244-9027
Phone: 6152534734, Formatted Phone: (615) 253-4734
```

You can also replace all 10-digit phone numbers in the input text by formatted phone numbers. You have already learned how to replace the matched text with another text using the replaceAll() method of the String class. The Matcher class also has a replaceAll() method, which accomplishes the same. The problem you are facing in replacing the phone numbers by the formatted phone numbers is getting the matched parts of the matched phone numbers. In this case, the replacement text also contains the matched text. You do not know what text matches the pattern in advance. Groups come to your rescue. $n, where n is a group number, inside a replacement text refers to the matched text for group n. For example, $1 refers to the first matched group. The replacement text to replace the phone numbers with the formatted phone numbers will be ($1) $2-$3. Listing 14-5 illustrates the technique of referencing groups in a replacement text.

Listing 14-5. Back Referencing a Group in a Replacement Text

```
// MatchAndReplace.java
package com.jdojo.regex;

import java.util.regex.Matcher;
import java.util.regex.Pattern;

public class MatchAndReplace {
        public static void main(String[] args) {
                // Prepare the regular expression
                String regex = "\\b(\\d{3})(\\d{3})(\\d{4})\\b";
                String replacementText = "($1) $2-$3";
                String source = "3342449027, 2339829, and 6152534734";

                // Compile the regular expression
                Pattern p = Pattern.compile(regex);

                // Get Matcher object
                Matcher m = p.matcher(source);

                // Replace the phone numbers by formatted phone numbers
                String formattedSource = m.replaceAll(replacementText);

                System.out.println("Text: " + source );
                System.out.println("Formatted Text: " + formattedSource );
        }
}
```

```
Text: 3342449027, 2339829, and 6152534734
Formatted Text: (334) 244-9027, 2339829, and (615) 253-4734
```

You can also achieve the same result by using the String class. You do not need to use the Pattern and Matcher classes at all. The following snippet of code illustrates the same concept as above, using the String class instead. The String class uses Pattern and Matcher class internally to get the result.

```
// Prepare the regular expression
String regex = "\\b(\\d{3})(\\d{3})(\\d{4})\\b";
String replacementText = "($1) $2-$3";
String source = "3342449027, 2339829, and 6152534734";

// Use replaceAll() method of the String class
String formattedSource = source.replaceAll(regex, replacementText);
```

Using Named Groups

Using group numbers in a big regular expression is cumbersome. Java 7 added support for named groups in regular expressions. You can do everything with the group name as you were able to do using the group numbers in the previous section.

- You can name a group.

- You can back reference groups using their names.

- You can reference group names in replacement text.

- You can get the matched text using the group names.

As before, you need to use a pair of parentheses to create a group. The start parenthesis is followed by a ? and a group name placed in angle brackets. The format to define a named group is

```
(?<groupName>pattern)
```

The group name must consist of only letters and digits: a through z, A through Z, and 0 through 9. The group name must start with a letter. The following is an example of a regular expression that uses three named groups. The group names are areaCode, prefix, and lineNumber. The regular expression is to match a 10-digit phone number.

```
\b(?<areaCode>\d{3})(?<prefix>\d{3})(?<lineNumber>\d{4})\b
```

You can use \k<groupName> to back reference the group named groupName. The area code and prefix parts in a phone number use the same pattern. You can rewrite the above regular expression that back reference the areaCode group as the following:

```
\b(?<areaCode>\d{3})\k<areaCode>(?<lineNumber>\d{4})\b
```

You can reference a named group in a replacement text as ${groupName}. The following snippet of code shows a regular expression with three named groups and a replacement text referencing those three groups using their names:

```
String regex = "\\b(?<areaCode>\\d{3})(?<prefix>\\d{3})(?<lineNumber>\\d{4})\\b";
String replacementText = "(${areaCode}) ${prefix}-${lineNumber}";
```

When you name a group, the group still gets a group number, as discussed in the previous section. You can still refer to a group by its group number even though it has a name. The above snippet code is rewritten as follows in which the third group, which has been named lineNumber, is referenced using its group number in as $3 in the replacement text:

```
String regex = "\\b(?<areaCode>\\d{3})(?<prefix>\\d{3})(?<lineNumber>\\d{4})\\b";
String replacementText = "(${areaCode}) ${prefix}-$3";
```

After a successful match, you can use the group(String groupName) method of the Matcher class to get the matched text for the group.

Listing 14-6 shows how to use group names in a regular expression and how to use the names in a replacement text.

Listing 14-6. Using Named Groups in Regular Expressions

```java
// NamedGroups.java
package com.jdojo.regex;

import java.util.regex.Matcher;
import java.util.regex.Pattern;

public class NamedGroups {
        public static void main(String[] args) {
                // Prepare the regular expression
                String regex =
                        "\\b(?<areaCode>\\d{3})(?<prefix>\\d{3})(?<lineNumber>\\d{4})\\b";

                // Reference first two groups by names and the thrd oen as its number
                String replacementText = "(${areaCode}) ${prefix}-$3";

                String source = "3342449027, 2339829, and 6152534734";

                // Compile the regular expression
                Pattern p = Pattern.compile(regex);

                // Get Matcher object
                Matcher m = p.matcher(source);

                // Replace the phone numbers by formatted phone numbers
                String formattedSource = m.replaceAll(replacementText);

                System.out.println("Text: " + source);
                System.out.println("Formatted Text: " + formattedSource);
        }
}
```

```
Text: 3342449027, 2339829, and 6152534734
Formatted Text: (334) 244-9027, 2339829, and (615) 253-4734
```

After a successful match using the find() method of the Matcher class, you can use its start() and end() methods to know the match boundary for groups. These methods are overloaded:

- int start()

- int start(int groupNumber)

- int start(String groupName)

- int end()

- int end(int groupNumber)

- int end(String groupName)

The methods that take no arguments return the start and end of the previous match. Other two sets of methods return the start and end of a group in the previous match. Java 8 added the two methods start(String groupName) and end(String groupName). The following snippet of code uses the previous example of matching 10-digit phone number in a string. It prints the start of each group for each successful match.

```
// Prepare the regular expression
String regex = "\\b(?<areaCode>\\d{3})(?<prefix>\\d{3})(?<lineNumber>\\d{4})\\b";

String source = "3342449027, 2339829, and 6152534734";
System.out.println("Source Text: " + source);

// Compile the regular expression
Pattern p = Pattern.compile(regex);

// Get Matcher object
Matcher m = p.matcher(source);

while(m.find()) {
        String matchedText = m.group();
        int start1 = m.start("areaCode");
        int start2 = m.start("prefix");
        int start3 = m.start("lineNumber");
        System.out.print("Matched Text:" + matchedText);
        System.out.print(". Area code start:" + start1);
        System.out.print(", Prefix start:" + start2);
        System.out.println(", Line Number start:" + start3);
}
```

```
Source Text: 3342449027, 2339829, and 6152534734
Matched Text:3342449027. Area code start:0, Prefix start:3, Line Number start:6
Matched Text:6152534734. Area code start:25, Prefix start:28, Line Number start:31
```

Resetting the Matcher

If you have finished matching a pattern against input text and you want to restart matching from the beginning of the input text again, you need to use the reset() method of the Matcher class. After a call to the reset() method, the next call to match a pattern will start from the beginning of the input text. The reset() method is overloaded. Another version allows you to associate a different input text with the pattern. These two versions of reset() methods allow you to reuse any existing instance of the Matcher class if your pattern remains the same. This enhances the performance of your program by avoiding the need to recreate a new Matcher object to perform matches against the same pattern.

Final Words on E-mail Validations

You now have learned the major parts of regular expressions. You are ready to complete your e-mail address validation example. Your e-mail addresses will be validated against the following rules:

- All e-mail addresses will be of the form name@domain.

- The name part must start with an alphanumeric character (a-z, A-Z, 0-9).

- The name part must have at least one character.

- The name part may have any alphanumeric character (a-z, A-Z, 0-9), underscore, hyphen, or dot.

- The dot in the domain part must contain at least one dot.

- The dot in domain name must be preceded and followed by at least one alphanumeric character.

- You should also be able to refer to the name and the domain parts using group numbers. This validation states that you place name and domain part as groups inside the regular expression.

The following regular expression will match an e-mail address according to the above rules. Group 1 is the name part whereas group 2 is the domain part.

```
([a-zA-Z0-9]+[\\w\\-.]*)@([a-zA-Z0-9]+\\.[a-zA-Z0-9\\-.]+)
```

The more validations you add, the more complex the regular expression. Readers are encouraged to add some more validations for e-mail addresses and modify the above regular expression accordingly. This regular expression allows two consecutive dots in the domain part. How would you prevent that?

Find-and-Replace Using Regular Expressions

Find-and-replace is a very powerful technique supported by regular expressions in Java. Sometimes you may be required to find a pattern and replace it depending upon the text it matches; that is, the replacement text is decided based on some conditions. The Java regular expression designers visualized this need and they have included two methods in the Matcher class that let you accomplish this task:

- Matcher appendReplacement(StringBuffer sb, String replacement)

- StringBuffer appendTail(StringBuffer sb)

Let's consider the following text:

"A train carrying 125 men and women was traveling at the speed of 100 miles per hour. The train fare was 75 dollars per person."

You want to find all numbers in the text (e.g., 125, 100, and 75) and replace them as follows:

- "100" by "a hundred"

- "> 100" by "more than a hundred"

- "< 100" by "less than a hundred"

After replacement, the above text should read as follows:

"A train carrying more than a hundred men and women was traveling at the speed of a hundred miles per hour. The train fare was less than a hundred dollars per person."

To accomplish this task, you need to find all numbers embedded in the text, compare the found number with 100, and decide on the replacement text. Such a situation also arises when you find and replace text using a text editor. The text editor highlights the word you were searching for, you enter a new word, and text editor does the replacement for you. You can also create a find/replace program as found in text editors using these two methods. Typically, these methods are used in conjunction with the find() method of the Matcher class. The steps that are performed to accomplish find and replace texts using these two methods are outlined below.

- Create a Pattern object.

- Create a Matcher object.

- Create a StringBuffer object to hold the result.

- Use the find() method in a loop to match the pattern.

- Call the appendReplacement() and appendTail() methods depending on the position of the found match.

Let's create a Pattern by compiling the regular expression. Since you want to find all numbers, your regular expression would be \b\d+\b. Note the first and last \b. They specify that you are interested in numbers only on word boundaries.

```
String regex = "\\b\\d+\\b";
Pattern p = Pattern.compile(regex);
```

Create a Matcher by associating the pattern with the text.

```
String text = "A train carrying 125 men and women was traveling" +
              " at the speed of 100 miles per hour. The train" +
              " fare was 75 dollars per person.";
Matcher m = p.matcher(text);
```

Create a StringBuffer to hold the new text

```
StringBuffer sb = new StringBuffer();
```

Start using the find() method on the Matcher object to find a match. When you invoke the find() method for the first time, the number 125 will match the pattern. At this point, you would like to prepare the replacement text depending on the matched text as:

```
String replacementText = "";

// Get the matched text. Recall that group() method returns the whole matched text
String matchedText = m.group();

// Convert the text into integer for comparison
int num = Integer.parseInt(matchedText);

// Prepare the replacement text
if (num == 100) {
        replacementText = "a hundred";
}
else if (num < 100) {
        replacementText = "less than a hundred";
}
else {
        replacementText = "more than a hundred";
}
```

Now, you will call the appendReplacement() method on the Matcher object, passing an empty StringBuffer and replacementText as arguments. In this case, replacementText has a string "more than hundred" because the find() method call matched the number 125.

```
m.appendReplacement(sb, replacementText);
```

It is interesting to know what the appendReplacement() method call does. It checks if there was a previous match. Because this is the first call to the find() method, there is no previous match. For the first match, it appends the text starting from the beginning of the input text until the character before the matching text. In your case, the following text is appended to the StringBuffer. At this point, the text in the StringBuffer is

```
"A train carrying "
```

Now the appendReplacement() method appends the text in the replacementText argument to the StringBuffer. This will change the StringBuffer contents to

```
"A train carrying more than a hundred"
```

The appendReplacement() method does one more thing. It sets the append position (an internal state of the Matcher object) to the character position just after the first matching text. In your case, the append position will be set to the character following 125, which is the position of the space character that follows 125. This finishes the first find and replace step.

You will call the find() method of the Matcher object again. It will find the pattern, that is, another number, which is 100. You will compute the value of the replacement text using the same procedure as you did after the first match. This time, the replacementText will contain the string "a hundred". You call appendReplacement() method as follows:

```
m.appendReplacement(sb, replacementText);
```

Again, it checks if there was a previous match. Since this was the second call to the find() method, it will find a previous match and it will use the append position saved by the last appendReplacement() call as the starting position. The last character to be appended will be the character just before the second match. It will also set the append position to the character position following the number 100. At this point, the StringBuffer contains the following text:

"A train carrying more than a hundred men and women was traveling at the speed of a hundred"

When you call the find() method for the third time, it will find the number 75 and the StringBuffer buffer content will be as follows after the replacement. The append position will be set to the character position following the number 75.

"A train carrying more than a hundred men and women was traveling at the speed of a hundred miles per hour. The train fare was less than a hundred"

If you call the find() method again, it will not find any match. However, the StringBuffer does not contain the text following the last match, which is "dollars per person." To append the text following the last match, you need to call the appendTail() method. It appends the text to the StringBuffer starting at append position until the end of the input string. The call to this method

```
m.appendTail(sb);
```

will modify the StringBuffer to

"A train carrying more than a hundred men and women was traveling
at the speed of a hundred miles per hour. The train fare was less than
a hundred dollars per person."

What will the content of the StringBuffer be if you would have called the appendTail() method just after the second call to the appendReplacement() method? The complete program is shown in Listing 14-7.

Listing 14-7. Find-and-Replace Using Regular Expressions and appendReplacement() and appendTail() Methods

```java
// AdvancedFindReplace.java
package com.jdojo.regex;

import java.util.regex.Pattern;
import java.util.regex.Matcher;

public class AdvancedFindReplace {
    public static void main (String[] args) {
        String regex = "\\b\\d+\\b";
        StringBuffer sb = new StringBuffer();
        String replacementText = "";
        String matchedText = "";

        String text = "A train carrying 125 men and women was traveling at" +
                " the speed of 100 miles per hour. " +
                "The train fare was 75 dollars per person." ;

        Pattern p = Pattern.compile(regex);
        Matcher m = p.matcher(text);

        while (m.find()) {
            matchedText = m.group();
```

```
                    // Convert the text into an integer for comparing
                    int num = Integer.parseInt(matchedText);

                    // Prepare the replacement text
                    if (num == 100) {
                            replacementText = "a hundred";
                    }
                    else if (num < 100) {
                            replacementText = "less than a hundred";
                    }
                    else {
                            replacementText = "more than a hundred";
                    }

                    m.appendReplacement(sb, replacementText);
            }

            // Append the tail
            m.appendTail(sb);

            // Display the old and new text
            System.out.println("Old Text: " + text);
            System.out.println("New Text: " + sb.toString());
    }
}
```

Old Text: A train carrying 125 men and women was traveling at the speed of 100 miles per hour. The train fare was 75 dollars per person.

New Text: A train carrying more than a hundred men and women was traveling at the speed of a hundred miles per hour. The train fare was less than a hundred dollars per person.

Summary

A regular expression is a sequence of characters used as a pattern to match some text. Java provides comprehensive support for using regular expressions through the Pattern and Matcher classes. Several convenience methods for using regular expression exist in the String class.

A Pattern object represents a compiled regular expression. A Matcher object is used to associate a Pattern with an input text to be searched for the pattern. The find() method of the Matcher class is used to find a match for the pattern in the input text. Regular expressions allow you to use groups. Groups are automatically numbered from 1 and N. The first group from left is number 1. A special group 0 exists that is the entire regular expression. Starting with Java 7, you can also name groups. You can refer to the groups by numbers and their names.

CHAPTER 15

■ ■ ■

Arrays

In this chapter, you will learn:

- How to declare array variables
- How to create arrays
- How to access elements of an array
- How to use a `for` loop and a `for`-each loop to iterate through elements an array
- How to copy elements of one array to another array
- How to copy primitive and reference types arrays
- How to use multi-dimensional arrays
- How to use an `ArrayList` when a variable-length array is needed
- How to convert elements of an `ArrayList` to an array and vice versa

What Is an Array?

An array is a fixed-length data structure that is used to hold more than one value of the same data type. Let's consider an example, which will explain why we need arrays. Suppose you have been asked to declare variables to hold employee ids of three employees. The employee ids will be integers. The variable declarations to hold three integer values will look like

```
int empId1, empId2, empId3;
```

What do you do if the number of employees increases to five? You may modify your variable declarations to look like

```
int empId1, empId2, empId3, empId4, empId5;
```

What do you do if the number of employees increases to 1,000? You definitely would not want to declare 1,000 `int` variables like `empId1`, `empId2`...`empId1000`. Even if you do that, the resulting code would be unmanageable and clumsy. Arrays come to your rescue in such situations. Using an array, you can declare a variable of a type, which can hold as many values of that type as you want. In fact, Java has a restriction on the number of values an array can hold. An array can hold a maximum of 2,147,483,647 values, which is the maximum value of the `int` data type.

What makes a variable an array? Placing [ ] (empty brackets) after the data type or after the variable name in a variable declaration makes the variable an array. For example,

```
int empId;
```

is a simple variable declaration. Here, `int` is the data type and `empId` is the variable name. This declaration means that the `empId` variable can hold one integer value. Placing [ ] after the data type in the above declaration as in

```
int[] empId;
```

makes `empId` an array variable. The above declaration is read as "empId is an array of int." You can also make the `empId` variable an array by placing the [ ] after the variable name, like so:

```
int empId[];
```

Both of the above declarations are valid. This book uses the first convention to declare an array. I started our discussion with an example of variable declaration to hold three employee ids. Until now, you have prepared the ground to hold more than one value in one variable. That is, your `empId` variable declared as an array of `int` is capable of holding more than one `int` value. How many values can your `empId` array variable hold? The answer is you do not know yet. You cannot specify the number of values an array can hold at the time you declare the array. The subsequent sections explain how to specify the number of values an array can hold. You can declare an array to hold multiple values of a data type (primitive or reference). The following are more examples of array declarations:

```
// salary can hold multiple float values
float[] salary;

// name can hold multiple references to String objects
String[] name;

// emp can hold multiple references to Employee objects
Employee[] emp;
```

■ **Tip** An array is a fixed-length data structure to store data items of the same type. All elements of an array are stored contiguously in memory.

Arrays Are Objects

All arrays in Java are objects. Every object in Java belongs to a class; so does every array object. You can create an array object using the new operator. You have used the new operator with a constructor to create an object of a class. The name of a constructor is the same as the name of the class. What is the name of the class of an array object? The answer to this question is not so obvious. I will answer this question later in this chapter.

For now, let's concentrate on how to create an array object of a particular type. The array object creation expression starts with the new operator, followed by the data type of the values you want to store in the array, followed by an integer enclosed in [ ] (brackets), which is the number of values you want to store in the array. The general syntax for array creation expression is as follows:

```
// Creates an array object of type ArrayDataType of ArrayLength length
new ArrayDataType[ArrayLength];
```

Continuing with our discussion, you can now create an array to store five `int` employee ids as follows:

```
new int[5];
```

In this expression, 5 is the length of the array (also called the dimension of the array). The word "dimension" is also used in another context. You can have an array of dimension one, two, three, or more. An array with more than one dimension is called a multi-dimensional array. I will cover the multi-dimensional array later in this chapter. In this book, I will refer to 5 in the above expression as the length of the array, not as the dimension of the array.

Note that the above expression creates an array object in memory, which allocates memory to store five integers. The new operator returns the reference of the new object in memory. If you want to use this object later in your code, you must store that reference in an object reference variable. The reference variable type must match the type of object reference returned by the new operator. In the above case, the new operator will return an object reference of int array type. You have already seen how to declare a reference variable of int array type. It is declared as

```
int[] empId;
```

To store the array object reference in `empId`, you can write

```
empId = new int[5];
```

You can also combine the declaration of an array and its creation in one statement as

```
int[] empId = new int[5];
```

How would you create an array to store 252 employee ids? You can do this as

```
int[] empId = new int[252];
```

You can also use an expression to specify the length of an array while creating the array.

```
int total = 23;
int[] array1 = new int[total];      // array1 has 23 elements
int[] array2 = new int[total * 3]; // array2 has 69 elements
```

Because all arrays are objects, their references can be assigned to a reference variable of the `Object` type. For example,

```
int[] empId = new int[5]; // Create an array object
Object obj = empId;        // A valid assignment
```

However, if you have the reference of an array in a reference variable of the `Object` type, you need to cast it to the appropriate array type before you can assign it to an array reference variable or access elements by index. Remember that every array is an object. However, not every object is necessarily an array.

```
// Assume that obj is a reference of the Object type that holds a reference of int[]
int[] tempIds = (int[])obj;
```

Accessing Array Elements

Once you create an array object using the new operator, you can refer to each individual element of the array using an element's index enclosed in brackets. The index for the first element is 0, the second element 1, the third element 2, and so on. This is called zero-based indexing. The index for the last element of an array is the length of the array minus 1. If you have an array of length 5, the indexes of the array elements would be 0, 1, 2, 3, and 4. Consider the following statement:

```
int[] empId = new int[5];
```

The length of the empId array is 5; its elements can be referred to as empId[0], empId[1], empId[2], empId[3], and empId[4].

It is a runtime error to refer to a non-existing element of an array. For example, using empId[5] in your code will throw an exception, because empId has a length of 5 and empId[5] refers to the sixth element, which is non-existent. You can assign values to elements of an array as follows:

```
empId[0] = 10;  // Assign 10 to the first element of empId
empId[1] = 20;  // Assign 20 to the second element of empId
empId[2] = 30;  // Assign 30 to the third element of empId
empId[3] = 40;  // Assign 40 to the fourth element of empId
empId[4] = 50;  // Assign 50 to the fifth element of empId
```

Table 15-1 shows the details of an array. It shows the indexes, values, and references of the elements of the array after the above statements are executed.

Table 15-1. *Array Elements in Memory for the empId Array*

Element's Index	0	1	2	3	4
Element's Value	10	20	30	40	50
Element's Reference	empId[0]	empId[1]	empId[2]	empId[3]	empId[4]

The following statement assigns the value of the third element of the empId array to an int variable temp:

```
int temp = empId[2]; // Assigns 30 to temp
```

Length of an Array

An array object has a public final instance variable named length, which contains the number of elements in the array.

```
int[] empId = new int[5];  // Create an array of length 5
int len = empId.length;    // 5 will be assigned to len
```

Note that length is the property of the array object you create. Until you create the array object, you cannot use its length property. The following code fragment illustrates this:

```
// salary is a reference variable, which can refer to an array of int.
// At this point, it is not referring to any array object.
int[] salary;
```

```
// A runtime error. salary is not referring to any array object yet.
int len = salary.length;

// Create an int array of length 1000 and assign its reference to salary
salary = new int[1000];

// Correct. len2 has a value 1000
int len2 = salary.length;
```

Typically, elements of arrays are accessed using loops. If you want to do any processing with all of the elements of an array, you execute a loop starting from index 0 (zero) to length minus 1. For example, to assign the values 10, 20, 30, 40, and 50 to the elements of the empId array of length 5, you would execute a for loop as shown:

```
for (int i = 0 ; i < empId.length; i++) {
        empId[i] = (i + 1) * 10;
}
```

It is important to note that while executing the loop, the loop condition must check for array index/subscript for being less than the length of array as in "i < empId.length" because the array index starts with 0, not 1. Another common mistake made by programmers while processing an array using a for loop is to start the loop counter at 1 as opposed to 0. What will happen if you change the initialization part of the for loop in the above code from int i = 0 to int i = 1? It would not give you any errors. However, the first element, empId[0], would not be processed and would not be assigned the value of 10.

You cannot change the length of an array after it is created. You may be tempted to modify the length property.

```
int[] roll = new int[5]; // Create an array of 5 elements

// A compile-time error. The length property of an array is final. You cannot modify it.
roll.length = 10;
```

You can have a zero-length array. Such an array is called an empty array.

```
// Create an array of length zero
int[] emptyArray = new int[0];

// Will assign zero to len
int len = emptyArray.length;
```

■ **Tip**   Arrays use zero-based indexing. That is, the first element of an array has an index of zero. Arrays are created dynamically at runtime. The length of an array cannot be modified after it has been created. If you need to modify the length of an array, you must create a new array and copy the elements from the old array to the new array. It is valid to create an array of length zero.

Initializing Array Elements

Recall from Chapter 6 that, unlike class member variables (instance and static variables), local variables are not initialized by default. You cannot access a local variable in your code unless it has been assigned a value. The same rule applies to the blank final variables. The compiler uses Rules of Definite Assignment to make sure that all variables have been initialized before their values are used in a program.

Array elements are always initialized irrespective of the scope in which the array is created. Array elements of primitive data type are initialized to the default value for their data types. For example, the numeric array elements are initialized to zero, boolean elements to false, and the reference type elements to null. The following snippet of code illustrates the array initialization:

```
// intArray[0], intArray[1] and intArray[2] are initialized to zero by default.
int[] intArray = new int[3];

// bArray[0] and bArray[1] are initialized to false.
boolean[] bArray = new boolean[2];

// An example of a reference type array.
// strArray[0] and strArray[1] are initialized to null.
String[] strArray = new String[2]

// Another example of a reference type array.
// All 100 elements of the person array are initialized to null.
Person[] person = new Person[100];
```

Listing 15-1 illustrates the array initialization for an instance variable and some local variables.

Listing 15-1. Default Initialization of Array Elements

```
// ArrayInit.java
package com.jdojo.array;

public class ArrayInit {
        private boolean[] bArray = new boolean[3];  // An instance variable

        public ArrayInit() {
                // Display the initial value for elements of the instance
                // variable bArray
                for (int i = 0; i < bArray.length; i++) {
                        System.out.println("bArray[" + i + "]:" + bArray[i]);
                }
        }

        public static void main(String[] args) {
                System.out.println("int array initialization:");

                int[] empId = new int[3];  // A local array variable
                for (int i = 0; i < empId.length; i++) {
                        System.out.println("empId[" + i + "]:" + empId[i]);
                }

                System.out.println("boolean array initialization:");

                // Initial value for bArray elements are displayed
                // inside the constructor
                new ArrayInit();

                System.out.println("Reference type array initialization:");
```

```
        String[] name = new String[3];   // A local array variable
        for (int i = 0; i < name.length; i++) {
                System.out.println("name[" + i + "]:" + name[i]);
        }
    }
}
```

```
int array initialization:
empId[0]:0
empId[1]:0
empId[2]:0
boolean array initialization:
bArray[0]:false
bArray[1]:false
bArray[2]:false
Reference type array initialization:
name[0]:null
name[1]:null
name[2]:null
```

Beware of Reference Type Arrays

Array elements of a primitive type contain values of that primitive type, whereas array elements of a reference type contain the reference of objects. Suppose you have an int array of

```
int[] empId = new int[5];
```

Here, empId[0],empId[1]...empId[4] contain an int value.
Suppose you have an array of String, like so:

```
String[] name = new String[5];
```

Here, name[0], name[1]...name[4] may contain a reference of a String object. Note that the String objects, the elements of the name array, have not been created yet. As discussed in the previous section, all elements of the name array contain null at this point. You need to create the String objects and assign their references to the elements of the array one by one as shown:

```
name[0] = new String("name1");
name[1] = new String("name2");
name[2] = new String("name3");
name[3] = new String("name4");
name[4] = new String("name5");
```

It is a common mistake to refer to the elements of an array of reference type just after creating the array and before assigning a valid object reference to each element. The following code illustrates this common mistake:

```
// Create an array of String
String[] name = new String[5];

// A runtime error as name[0] is null
int len = name[0].length();

// Assign a valid string object to all elements of the array
for (int i = 0; i < name.length; i++){
        name[i] = "name" + ( i + 1 );
}

// Now you can get the length of the first element
int len2 = name[0].length(); // Correct. len2 has value 5
```

The concept of initialization of the String reference type array is depicted in Figure 15-1. This concept applies to all reference types.

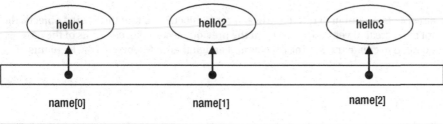

Figure 15-1. *Reference type array initialization*

All elements of an array are stored contiguously in memory. In case of a reference type array, the array elements store the references of the objects. Those references in the elements are stored contiguously, not the objects they are referring to. The objects are stored on heap and their locations are, typically, not contiguous.

Explicit Array Initialization

You can initialize elements of an array explicitly when you declare the array or when you create the array object using the new operator. The initial values for elements are separated by a comma and enclosed in braces ({}).

```
// Initialize the array at the time of declaration
int[] empId = {1, 2, 3, 4, 5};
```

This code creates an array of int of length 5, and initializes its elements to 1, 2, 3, 4, and 5. Note that you do not specify the length of an array when you specify the array initialization list at the time of the array declaration. The length of the array is the same as the number of values specified in the array initialization list. Here, the length of the empId array will be 5, because you passed 5 values in the initialization list {1, 2, 3, 4, 5}.

A comma may follow the last value in initialization list.

```
int[] empId = {1, 2, 3, 4, 5, }; // A comma after the last value 5 is valid.
```

Alternatively, you can initialize the elements of an array as shown:

```
int[] empId = new int[]{1, 2, 3, 4, 5};
```

Note that you cannot specify the length of an array if you specify the array initialization list. The length of the array is the same as the number of values specified in the initialization list.

It is valid to create an empty array by using an empty initialization list.

```
int[] emptyNumList = { };
```

For a reference type array, you can specify the list of objects in the initialization list. The following snippet of code illustrates array initialization for String and Account types. Assume that the Account class exists and it has a constructor, which takes an account number as an argument.

```
// Create a String array with two Strings "Sara" and "Truman"
String[] name = {new String("Sara"), new String("Truman")};

// You can also use String literals
String[] names = {"Sara", "Truman"};

// Create an Account array with two Account objects
Account[] ac = new Account[]{new Account(1), new Account(2)};
```

■ **Tip** When you use an initialization list to initialize the elements of an array, you cannot specify the length of the array. The length of the array is set to the number of values in the initialization list.

Limitations of Using Arrays

An array in Java cannot be expanded or shrunk after it is created. Suppose you have an array of 100 elements, and later, you need to keep only 15 elements. You cannot get rid of the remaining 85 elements. If you need 135 elements, you cannot append 35 more elements to it. You can deal with the first limitation (memory cannot be freed for unused array elements) if you have enough memory available to your application. However, there is no way out if you need to add more elements to an existing array. The only solution is to create another array of the desired length, and copy the array elements from the original array to the new array. You can copy array elements from one array to another in two ways:

- Using a loop
- Using the static `arraycopy()` method of the `java.lang.System` class

Suppose you have an `int` array of the length `originalLength` and you want to modify its length to `newLength`. You can apply the first method of copying arrays as shown in the following snippet of code:

```
int originalLength = 100;
int newLength = 15;
int[] ids = new int[originalLength];

// Do some processing here...

// Create a temporary array of new length
int[] tempIds = new int[newLength];

// While copying array elements we have to check if the new length
// is less than or greater than original length
int elementsToCopy = 0;

if (originalLength > newLength) {
        elementsToCopy = newLength;
}
else {
        elementsToCopy = originalLength;
}

// Copy the elements from the original array to the new array
for (int i = 0; i < elementsToCopy; i++){
        tempIds[i] = ids[i];
}

// Finally assign the reference of new array to ids
ids = tempIds;
```

Another way to copy elements of an array to another array is by using the `arraycopy()` method of the `System` class. The signature of the `arraycopy()` method is as follows:

```
public static void arraycopy(Object sourceArray, int sourceStartPosition,
                          Object destinationArray,
                          int destinationStartPosition,
                          int lengthToBeCopied)
```

Here,

- sourceArray is the reference to the source array.

- sourceStartPosition is the starting index in the source array from where the copying of elements will start.

- destinationArray is the reference to the destination array.

- destinationStartPosition is the start index in the destination array from where new elements from source array will be copied.

- lengthToBeCopied is the number of elements to be copied from the source array to the destination array.

You can replace the previous for loop with the following code:

```
// Now copy array elements using the arraycopy() method
System.arraycopy (ids, 0, tempIds, 0, elementsToCopy);
```

The objects of the two classes, java.util.ArrayList and java.util.Vector, can be used in place of an array, where the length of the array needs to be modified. You can think of the objects of these two classes as variable length arrays. The next section discusses these two classes in detail.

Listing 15-2 demonstrates how to copy an array using a for loop and the System.arraycopy() method.

Listing 15-2. Copying an Array Using a for Loop and the System.arraycopy() Method

```
// ArrayCopyTest.java
package com.jdojo.array;

import java.util.Arrays;

public class ArrayCopyTest {
        public static void main(String[] args) {
                // Have an array with 5 elements
                int[] data = {1, 2, 3, 4, 5 };

                // Expand the data array to 7 elements
                int[] eData = expandArray(data, 7);

                // Truncate the data array to 3 elements
                int[] tData = expandArray(data, 3);

                System.out.println("Using for-loop...");
                System.out.println("Original Array: " + Arrays.toString(data));
                System.out.println("Expanded Array: " + Arrays.toString(eData));
                System.out.println("Truncated Array: " + Arrays.toString(tData));

                // Copy data array to new arrays
                eData = new int[9];
                tData = new int[2];
                System.arraycopy(data, 0, eData, 0, 5);
                System.arraycopy(data, 0, tData, 0, 2);
```

```
                System.out.println("Using System.arraycopy() method...");
                System.out.println("Original Array: " + Arrays.toString(data));
                System.out.println("Expanded Array: " + Arrays.toString(eData));
                System.out.println("Truncated Array: " + Arrays.toString(tData));
        }

        // Uses a for-loop to copy an array
        public static int[] expandArray(int[] oldArray, int newLength) {
                int originalLength = oldArray.length;
                int[] newArray = new int[newLength];
                int elementsToCopy = 0;

                if (originalLength > newLength) {
                        elementsToCopy = newLength;
                }
                else {
                        elementsToCopy = originalLength;
                }

                for (int i = 0; i < elementsToCopy; i++) {
                        newArray[i] = oldArray[i];
                }
                return newArray;
        }
}
```

```
Using for-loop...
Original Array: [1, 2, 3, 4, 5]
Expanded Array: [1, 2, 3, 4, 5, 0, 0]
Truncated Array: [1, 2, 3]
Using System.arraycopy() method...
Original Array: [1, 2, 3, 4, 5]
Expanded Array: [1, 2, 3, 4, 5, 0, 0, 0, 0]
Truncated Array: [1, 2]
```

The Arrays class is in the java.util package. It contains many convenience methods to deal with arrays. For example, it contains methods for converting an array to a string format, sorting an array, etc. You used the Arrays.toString() static method to get the contents of an array in the string format. The method is overloaded; you can use it to get the content of any type of array in string format. In this example, you used a for loop and the System.arraycopy() method to copy arrays. Notice that using the arraycopy() method is much more powerful than that of a for loop. For example, the arraycopy() method is designed to handle copying of the elements of an array from one region to another region in the same array. It takes care of any overlap in the source and the destination regions within the array.

Variable-Length Arrays

You know that Java does not provide variable-length arrays. However, Java libraries provide some classes whose objects can be used as variable-length arrays. These classes provide methods to obtain an array representation of their elements. ArrayList and Vector are two classes in the java.util package that can be used whenever variable-length arrays are needed.

ArrayList and Vector classes work the same way, except that the methods in the Vector class are synchronized, whereas methods in ArrayList are not. If your object list is accessed and modified by multiple threads simultaneously, use the Vector class, which will be slower but thread safe. Otherwise, you should use the ArrayList class. For the rest of the discussion, I will refer to ArrayList only. However, the discussion applies to Vector as well.

The big difference between arrays and the ArrayList class is that the later works with only objects, not with primitive data types. The ArrayList class is a generic class and it takes the type of its elements as the type parameter. If you want to work with primitive values, you need to declare an ArrayList of one of the wrapper classes. For example, use ArrayList<Integer> to work with int elements.

The following code fragment illustrates the use of the ArrayList class:

```
import java.util.ArrayList;
// Create an ArrayList of Integer
ArrayList<Integer> ids = new ArrayList<>();

// Get the size of array list
int total = ids.size(); // total will be zero at this point

// Print the details of array list
System.out.println("ArrayList size is " + total);
System.out.println("ArrayList elements are " + ids);

// Add three ids 10, 20, 30 to the  array list.
ids.add(new Integer(10)); // Adding an Integer object.
ids.add(20);              // Adding an int. Autoboxing is at play.
ids.add(30);              // Adding an int. Autoboxing is at play.

// Get the size of the array list
total = ids.size(); // total will be 3

// Print the details of array list
System.out.println("ArrayList size is " + total);
System.out.println("ArrayList elements are " + ids);

// Clear all elements from array list
ids.clear();

// Get the size of the array list
total = ids.size(); // total will be 0
// Print the details of array list
System.out.println("ArrayList size is " + total);
System.out.println("ArrayList elements are " + ids);
```

```
ArrayList size is 0
ArrayList elements are []
ArrayList size is 3
ArrayList elements are [10, 20, 30]
ArrayList size is 0
ArrayList elements are []
```

You can make one important observation from the above output. You can print the list of all elements in an ArrayList just by passing its reference to the System.out.println() method. The toString() method of the ArrayList class returns a string that is a comma-separated string representation of its elements enclosed in brackets ([]).

Like arrays, ArrayList uses zero-based indexing. That is, the first element of ArrayList has an index of zero. You can get the element stored at any index by using the get() method.

```
// Get the element at the index 0 (the first element)
Integer firstId = ids.get(0);

// Get the element at the index 1 (the second element)
int secondId = ids.get(1); // Autounboxing is at play
```

You can check if the ArrayList contains an object using its contains() method.

```
Integer id20 = 20;
Integer id50 = 50;

// Add three objects to the arraylist
ids.add(10);
ids.add(20);
ids.add(30);

// Check if the array list contains id20 and id50
boolean found20 = ids.contains(id20); // found20 will be true
boolean found50 = ids.contains(id50); // found50 will be false
```

You can iterate through the elements of an ArrayList in one of the two ways: using a loop or using an iterator. In this chapter, I will discuss how to iterate through elements of an ArrayList using a for loop. Please refer to the chapter on *Collections* in the book *Beginning Java Language Features* (ISBN 978-1-4302-6658-7) to learn how to iterate through elements of an ArrayList (or any type of collection or set) using an iterator. The following snippet of code shows how to use a for loop to iterate through the elements of an ArrayList:

```
// Get the size of the ArrayList
int total = ids.size();

// Iterate through all elements
for (int i = 0; i < total; i++) {
        int temp = ids.get(i);
        // Do some processing...
}
```

If you want to iterate through all elements of the ArrayList without caring for their indexes, you can use the for-each loop as shown:

```
// Iterate through all elements
for (int temp : ids) {
        // Do some processing with temp...
}
```

Listing 15-3 illustrates the use of a for loop to iterate through elements of an ArrayList. It also shows you how to remove an element from an ArrayList using the remove() method.

Listing 15-3. Iterating Through Elements of an ArrayList

```java
// NameIterator.java
package com.jdojo.array;

import java.util.ArrayList;

public class NameIterator {
        public static void main(String[] args) {
                // Create an ArrayList of String
                ArrayList<String> nameList = new ArrayList<String>();

                //Add some names
                nameList.add("Christopher");
                nameList.add("Kathleen");
                nameList.add("Ann");

                // Get the count of names in the list
                int count = nameList.size();

                // Let us print the name list
                System.out.println("List of names...");
                for(int i = 0; i < count; i++) {
                        String name = nameList.get(i);
                        System.out.println(name);
                }

                // Let us remove Kathleen from the list
                nameList.remove("Kathleen");

                // Get the count of names in the list again
                count = nameList.size();

                // Let us print the name list again
                System.out.println("After removing Kathleen...");
                for(int i = 0; i < count; i++) {
                        String name = nameList.get(i);
                        System.out.println(name);
                }
        }
}
```

```
List of names...
Christopher
Kathleen
Ann
After removing Kathleen...
Christopher
Ann
```

Passing an Array as a Parameter

You can pass an array as a parameter to a method or a constructor. The type of array you pass to the method must be assignment compatible to the formal parameter type. The syntax for an array type parameter declaration for a method is the same as for the other data types. That is, parameter declaration should start with the array type, followed by one or more whitespaces and the argument name, as shown:

```
modifiers returnType methodName(ArrayType argumentName, ...)
```

The following are some examples of method declarations with array arguments:

```
// The processSalary() method has two parameters:
// 1. id is an array of int
// 2. salary is an array of double
public static void processSalary(int[] id, double[] salary) {
        // Code goes here...
}

// The setAKA() method has two parameters:
// 1. id is int (It is simply int type, not array of int)
// 2. aka is an array of String
public static void setAKA(int id, String[] aka) {
        // Code goes here...
}

// The printStates() metohd has one parameter:
// 1. stateNames is an array of String
public static void printStates(String[] stateNames) {
        // Code goes here...
}
```

The following code fragment for a method mimics the toString() method of ArrayList. It accepts an int array and returns the comma-separated values enclosed in brackets ([ ]).

```
public static String arrayToString(int[] source) {
        if (source == null) {
                return null;
        }

        // Use StringBuilder to improve performance
        StringBuilder result = new StringBuilder("[");

        for (int i = 0; i < source.length; i++) {
                if (i == source.length - 1) {
                        result.append(source[i]);
                }
                else {
                        result.append(source[i] + ",");
                }
        }

        result.append("]");
        return result.toString();
}
```

The above method may be called as follows:

```
int[] ids = {10, 15, 19};
String str = arrayToString(ids);   // Pass ids int array to arrayToString() method
```

Because an array is an object, the array reference is passed to the method. The method, which receives an array parameter, can modify the elements of the array. Listing 15-4 illustrates how a method can change the elements of its array parameter; this example also shows how to implement the swap() method to swap two integers using an array.

Listing 15-4. Passing an Array as a Method Parameter

```
// Swap.java
package com.jdojo.array;

public class Swap {
        public static void main(String[] args) {
                int[] num = {17, 80};

                System.out.println("Before swap");
                System.out.println("#1: " + num[0]);
                System.out.println("#2: " + num[1]);

                // Call the swpa() method passing teh num array
                swap(num);

                System.out.println("After swap");
                System.out.println("#1: " + num[0]);
                System.out.println("#2: " + num[1]);
        }

        // The swap() method accepts an int array as argument and swaps the values
        // if array contains two values.
        public static void swap (int[] source) {
                if (source != null && source.length == 2) {
                        // Swap the first and the second elements
                        int temp = source[0];
                        source[0] = source[1];
                        source[1] = temp;
                }
        }
}
```

```
Before swap
#1: 17
#2: 80
After swap
#1: 80
#2: 17
```

Recall, in Chapter 6, that we were not able to implement a method for swapping two integers using method's parameters of primitive types. It was so, because, for primitive types, the actual parameters are copied to the formal parameter. Here, we were able to swap two integers inside the swap() method, because we used an array as the parameter. The array's reference is passed to the method, not the copy of the elements of the array.

There is a risk when an array is passed to a method. The method may modify the array elements, which, sometimes, may not be desired or intended. In such a case, you should pass a copy of the array to the method, not the original array. If the method modifies the array, your original array is not affected.

You can make a quick copy of your array using array's clone() method. The phrase "quick copy" warrants special attention. For primitive types, the cloned array will have a true copy of the original array. A new array of the same length is created and the value of each element in the original array is copied to the corresponding element of the cloned array. However, for reference types, the reference of the object stored in each element of the original array is copied to the corresponding element of the cloned array. This is known as a shallow copy, whereas the former type, where the object (or the value) is copied, is known as a deep copy. In case of a shallow copy, elements of both arrays, the original and the cloned, refer to the same object in memory. You can modify the objects using their references stored in the original array as well as the cloned array. In this case, even if you pass a copy of the original array to a method, your original array can be modified inside the method. The solution to this problem is to make a deep copy of your original array to pass it to the method. The following snippet of code illustrates the cloning of an int array and a String array. Note that the return type of the clone() method is Object and you need to cast the returned value to an appropriate array type.

```
// Create an array of 3 integers 1,2,3
int[] ids = {1, 2, 3};

// Declare an array of int named clonedIds.
int[] clonedIds;

// The clonedIds array has the same values as the ids array.
clonedIds = (int[])ids.clone()

// Create an array of 3 strings.
String[] names  = {"Lisa", "Pat", "Kathy"};

// Declare an array of String named clonedNames.
String[] clonedNames;

// The clonedNames array has the reference of the same three strings as the names array.
clonedNames = (String[])names.clone();
```

The cloning process for primitive array ids and reference array names in the above snippet of code is depicted in Figure 15-2 through Figure 15-5.

Memory state after the following statements are executed.
int[ ] ids = {1,2,3};
int[ ] clonedIds;

Figure 15-2. *The ids array is populated and the clonedIds array is declared*

Memory state after the following statement is executed.
clonedIds = (int [ ]) ids.clone ( );

Figure 15-3. *The ids array is cloned in the clonedIds array*

Memory state after the following statements are executed.
String names = {"Lisa", "Pat", "Kathy"};
String[ ] clonedNames;

Figure 15-4. *The names array is populated and the clonedNmaes array is declared*

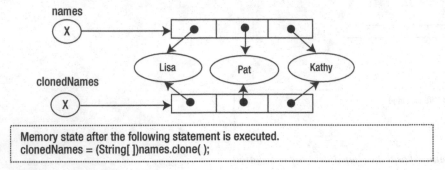

Memory state after the following statement is executed.
clonedNames = (String[ ])names.clone( );

Figure 15-5. *The names array is cloned in the clonedNames array*

Notice that when the names array is cloned, the clonedNames array elements refer to the same String objects in memory. When you mention a method of modifying an array parameter passed to it, you may mean one or all of the following three things:

- Array parameter reference
- Elements of the array parameter
- The object referred by the array parameter elements

Array Parameter Reference

Because an array is an object, a copy of its reference is passed to a method. If the method changes the array parameter, the actual parameter is not affected. Listing 15-5 illustrates this. The main( ) method passes array to the tryArrayChange( ) method, which in turn assigns a different array reference to the parameter. The output shows that the array in the main( ) method remains unaffected.

Listing 15-5. Modifying an Array Parameter Inside a Method

```java
// ModifyArrayParam.java
package com.jdojo.array;

import java.util.Arrays;

public class ModifyArrayParam {
    public static void main(String[] args) {
        int[] origNum = {101, 307, 78};
        System.out.println("Before method call:" + Arrays.toString(origNum));

        // Pass the array to the method
        tryArrayChange(origNum);

        System.out.println("After method call:" + Arrays.toString(origNum));
    }

    public static void tryArrayChange(int[] num) {
        System.out.println("Inside method-1:" + Arrays.toString(num));
```

```
        // Create and store a new int array in num
        num = new int[]{10, 20};

        System.out.println("Inside method-2:" + Arrays.toString(num));
    }
}
```

```
Before method call:[101, 307, 78]
Inside method-1:[101, 307, 78]
Inside method-2:[10, 20]
After method call:[101, 307, 78]
```

If you do not want your method to change the array reference inside the method body, you must declare the method parameter as final, like so:

```
public static void tryArrayChange(final int[] num) {
        // An error. num is final and cannot be changed
        num = new int[]{10, 20};
}
```

Elements of the Array Parameter

The values stored in the elements of an array parameter can always be changed inside a method. Listing 15-6 illustrates this.

Listing 15-6. Modifying Elements of an Array Parameter Inside a Method

```
// ModifyArrayElements.java
package com.jdojo.array;

import java.util.Arrays;

public class ModifyArrayElements {
        public static void main(String[] args) {
                int[] origNum = {10, 89, 7};
                String[] origNames = {"Mike", "John"};
                System.out.println("Before method call, origNum:" + Arrays.toString(origNum));
                System.out.println("Before method call, origNames:" +
                                Arrays.toString(origNames));

                // Call methods passing the arrays
                tryElementChange(origNum);
                tryElementChange(origNames);

                System.out.println("After method call, origNum:" + Arrays.toString(origNum));
                System.out.println("After method call, origNames:" +
                                Arrays.toString(origNames));
        }
```

```java
        public static void tryElementChange(int[] num) {
                // If array has at least one element, store 1116 in
                // its first element
                if (num != null && num.length > 0) {
                        num[0] = 1116;
                }
        }

        public static void tryElementChange(String[] names) {
                // If array has at least one element, store "Twinkle" in
                // its first element
                if (names != null && names.length > 0) {
                        names[0] = "Twinkle";
                }
        }
}
```

```
Before method call, origNum:[10, 89, 7]
Before method call, origNames:[Mike, John]
After method call, origNum:[1116, 89, 7]
After method call, origNames:[Twinkle, John]
```

Notice that first element of the arrays changed after the method calls. You can change the elements of an array parameter inside a method, even if the array parameter is declared final.

The Object Referred by the Array Parameter Elements

This section applies to array parameters of only the reference type. If the array's reference type is mutable, you can change the state of the object stored in the array elements. In the previous section, I discussed replacing the reference stored in an array element by a new object reference. This section discusses changing the state of the object referred to by the elements of the array. Consider an Item, as shown in Listing 15-7.

Listing 15-7. An Item Class

```java
// Item.java
package com.jdojo.array;

public class Item {
        private double price;
        private String name;

        public Item (String name, double initialPrice) {
                this.name = name;
                this.price = initialPrice;
        }

        public double getPrice() {
                return this.price;
        }
```

```
        public void setPrice(double newPrice ) {
                this.price = newPrice;
        }

        public String toString() {
                return "[" + this.name + ", " + this.price + "]";
        }
}
```

Listing 15-8 illustrates this. The main() method creates an array of Item. The array is passed to the tryStateChange() method, which changes the price of the first element in the array to 10.38. The output shows that the price is changed for the original element in the array created in the main() method.

Listing 15-8. Modifying the States of Array Elements of an Array Parameter Inside a Method

```
// ModifyArrayElementState.java
package com.jdojo.array;

public class ModifyArrayElementState {
        public static void main(String[] args) {
                Item[] myItems = {new Item("Pen", 25.11), new Item("Pencil", 0.10)};
                System.out.println("Before method call #1:" + myItems[0]);
                System.out.println("Before method call #2:" + myItems[1]);

                // Call the method passing the array of Item
                tryStateChange(myItems);

                System.out.println("After method call #1:" + myItems[0]);
                System.out.println("After method call #2:" + myItems[1]);
        }

        public static void tryStateChange(Item[] allItems) {
                if (allItems != null && allItems.length > 0) {
                        // Change the price of first item to 10.38
                        allItems[0].setPrice(10.38);
                }
        }
}
```

```
Before method call #1:[Pen, 25.11]
Before method call #2:[Pencil, 0.1]
After method call #1:[Pen, 10.38]
After method call #2:[Pencil, 0.1]
```

■ **Tip** The clone() method can be used to make a clone of an array. For a reference array, the clone() method performs a shallow copy. An array should be passed to a method and returned from a method with caution. If a method may modify its array parameter and you do not want your actual array parameter to get affected by that method call, you must pass a deep copy of your array to that method.

If you store the state of an object in an array instance variable, you should think carefully before returning the reference of that array from any methods of your class. The caller of that method will get the handle of the array instance variable and will be able to change the state of the objects of that class outside the class. This situation is illustrated in following example:

```java
public class MagicNumber {
        // Magic numbers are not supposed to be changed It can be look up though
        private int[] magicNumbers = {5, 11, 21, 51, 101};

        // Other codes go here...

        public int[] getMagicNumbers () {
                /* Never do the following. If you do this, caller of this
                   method will be able to change the magic numbers.
                */
                // return this.magicNumbers;

                /* Do the following instead. In case of reference array, make a deep copy, and
                   return that copy. For primitive array you can use the clone() method */
                return (int[])magicNumbers.clone();
        }
}
```

You can also create an array and pass it to a method without storing the array reference in a variable. Suppose there is a method named setNumbers(int[] nums), which takes an int array as a parameter. You can call this method as shown:

```java
setNumbers(new int[]{10, 20, 30});
```

Command-Line Arguments

A Java application can be launched from a command prompt (a command prompt in Windows and a shell prompt in UNIX). It can also be launched from within a Java development environment tool, such as NetBeans, JDeveloper, etc. A Java application is run at the command line like so:

```
java <<options-list>> <<classname>>
```

<<options-list>> is optional. You can also pass command-line arguments to a Java application by specifying arguments after the class name.

```
java <<classname>> <<List of Command-line Arguments>>
```

Each argument in the argument list is separated by a space. For example, the following command runs the com.jdojo.array.Test class and passes three names as the command-line arguments:

```
java com.jdojo.array.Test Cat Dog Rat
```

What happens to these three command-line arguments when the Test class is run? The operating system passes the list of the arguments to the JVM. Sometimes the operating system may expand the list of arguments by interpreting their meanings and may pass a modified arguments list to the JVM. The JVM parses the argument lists using a space as a separator. It creates an array of String whose length is the same as the number of arguments in the list. It populates the String array with the items in the arguments list sequentially. Finally, the JVM passes this String array to the main() method of the Test class that you are running. This is the time when you use the String array argument passed to the main() method. If there is no command-line argument, the JVM creates a String array of length zero and passes it to the main() method. If you want to pass space-separated words as one argument, you can enclose them in double quotes. You can also avoid the operating system interpretation of special characters by enclosing them in double quotes. Let's create a class called CommandLine as shown in Listing 15-9.

Listing 15-9. Processing Command-line Arguments Inside the main() Method

```java
// CommandLine.java
package com.jdojo.array;

public class CommandLine {
        public static void main(String[] args) {
                // args contains all command-line arguments
                System.out.println("Total Arguments:" + args.length);

                // Display all arguments
                for(int i = 0 ; i < args.length; i++) {
                        System.out.println("Argument #" + (i+1) + ":" + args[i]);
                }
        }
}
```

Table 15-2 shows the command to run the com.jdojo.array.CommandLine class and the corresponding output.

Table 15-2. *Output of Command-line Argument Program Using Different Arguments*

Command	Output
java com.jdojo.array.CommandLine	Total Arguments:0
java com.jdojo.array.CommandLine Cat Dog Rat	Total Arguments:3 Argument #1:Cat Argument #2:Dog Argument #3:Rat
java com.jdojo.array.CommandLine "Cat Dog Rat"	Total Arguments:1 Argument #1:Cat Dog Rat
java com.jdojo.array.CommandLine 29 Dogs	Total Arguments:2 Argument #1:29 Argument #2:Dogs

What is the use of command-line arguments? They let you change the behavior of your program without re-compiling it. For example, you may want to sort the contents of a file in ascending or descending order. You may pass command-line arguments, which will specify the sorting order. If there is no sorting order specified on the command line, you may assume ascending order by default. If you call the sorting class com.jdojo.array.SortFile, you may run it in the following ways.

To sort employee.txt file in ascending order:

```
java com.jdojo.array.SortFile employee.txt asc
```

To sort department.txt file in descending order:

```
java com.jdojo.array.SortFile department.txt desc
```

To sort salary.txt in ascending order:

```
java com.jdojo.array.SortFile salary.txt
```

Depending on the second element, if any, of the String array passed to the main() method of the SortFile class, you may sort the file differently.

Note that all command-line arguments are passed to the main() method as a String. If you pass a numeric argument, you need to convert the string argument to a number. To illustrate this numeric argument conversion, let's develop a mini calculator class, which takes an expression as command-line argument and prints the result. The mini calculator supports only four basic operations: add, subtract, multiply and divide; see Listing 15-10.

Listing 15-10. A Mini Command-line Calculator

```java
// Calc.java
package com.jdojo.array;

import java.util.Arrays;

public class Calc {
        public static void main(String[] args) {
                // Print the list of commandline argument
                System.out.println(Arrays.toString(args));

                // Make sure we received three arguments and the
                // the second argument has only one character to indicate operation.
                if (!(args.length == 3 && args[1].length() == 1)) {
                        printUsage();
                        return;  // Stop the program here
                }

                // Parse the two number operands. Place the parsing code inside a try-catch,
                // so we will handle the error in case both operands are not numbers.
                double n1 = 0.0;
                double n2 = 0.0;
                try {
                        n1 = Double.parseDouble(args[0]);
                        n2 = Double.parseDouble(args[2]);
                }
                catch (NumberFormatException e) {
                        System.out.println("Both operands must be a number");
                        printUsage();
                        return; // Stop the program here
                }
```

```
                String operation = args[1];
                double result = compute(n1, n2, operation);

                // Print the result
                System.out.println(args[0] + args[1] + args[2] + "=" + result);
        }

    public static double compute(double n1, double n2, String operation)
        {
                // Initialize the result with not-a-number
                double result = Double.NaN;

                switch (operation) {
                    case "+":
                            result = n1 + n2;
                            break;
                    case "-":
                            result = n1 - n2;
                            break;
                    case "*":
                            result = n1 * n2;
                            break;
                    case "/":
                            result = n1 / n2;
                            break;
                    default:
                            System.out.println("Invalid operation:" + operation);
                }

                return result;
        }

    public static void printUsage() {
            System.out.println("Usage: java com.jdojo.array.Calc expr");
            System.out.println("Where expr could be:");
            System.out.println("n1 + n1");
            System.out.println("n1 - n2");
            System.out.println("n1 * n2");
            System.out.println("n1 / n2");
            System.out.println("n1 and n2 are two numbers");
        }
}
```

You may use the Calc class as follows.

```
java com.jdojo.array.Calc 3 + 7
java com.jdojo.array.Calc 78.9 * 98.5
```

You may get an error when you try to use * (asterisk) to multiply two numbers. The operating system may interpret it as all files names in the current directory. To avoid such errors, you can enclose the operator in double quotes or the escape character provided by the operating system.

```
java com.jdojo.array.Calc 7 "*" 8
```

■ **Tip**   If your program uses command-line arguments, it is not a 100% Java program. This is because the program does not fit in the category of "write once, run everywhere." Some operating systems do not have a command prompt, and therefore, you may not be able to use the command-line argument feature. Additionally, an operating system may interpret the metacharacters in the command-line arguments differently.

Multi-Dimensional Arrays

If a data element in a list is identified using more than one dimension, you can use a multi-dimensional array to represent the list in your program. For example, a data element in a table is identified by two dimensions, row and column. You can store a tabular data in your Java program in a two dimensional array. You can declare a multi-dimensional array by using a pair of brackets ([]) for each dimension in the array declaration. For example, you can declare a two dimensional array of int as shown:

```
int[][] table;
```

Here, table is a reference variable that can hold a reference to a two-dimensional array of int. At the time of declaration, memory is allocated only for the reference variable table, not for any array elements. The memory state after the above code is executed is depicted in Figure 15-6.

table

Figure 15-6.   *Memory state after the declaration of a two-dimensional array*

A two-dimensional array of int with three rows and two columns can be created as shown:

```
table = new int[3][2];
```

The memory state after execution of this code is depicted in Figure 15-7. All elements have been shown to have a value of zero, because all elements of a numeric array are initialized to zero by default. The rules for default initialization of array elements of a multi-dimensional array are the same as that of a single dimensional array as discussed previously in this chapter.

table

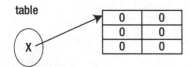

Figure 15-7.   *Memory state after the creation of a two-dimensional array*

The indexes of each dimension in a multi-dimensional array are zero-based. Each element of the `table` array can be accessed as `table[rownumber][columnNumber]`. The row number and the column number always starts at zero. For example, you can assign a value to the first row and the second column in the `table` array as shown:

```
table[0][1] = 32;
```

You can assign a value 71 to the third row and the first column like so:

```
table[2][0] = 71;
```

The memory state after the above two assignments is depicted in Figure 15-8.

Figure 15-8. *Memory state after two assignments to the two-dimensional array elements*

Java does not support a multi-dimensional array in a true sense. Rather, it supports an array of arrays. Using an array of arrays, you can implement the same functionality as provided by multi-dimensional arrays. When you create a two-dimensional array, the elements of the first array are of an array type, which can refer to a single dimensional array. The size of each single-dimensional array need not be the same. Considering the array of arrays concept for the `table` two-dimensional array, you can depict the memory state after array creation and assignments of two values as shown in Figure 15-9.

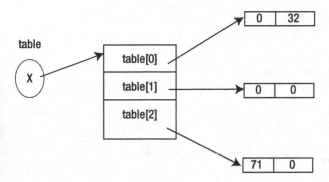

Figure 15-9. *An array of arrays*

The name of the two-dimensional array, `table`, refers to an array of three elements. Each element of the array is a one-dimensional array of `int`. The data type of `table[0]`, `table[1]` and `table[2]` is an `int` array. The length of `table[0]`, `table[1]` and `table[2]` is each 2.

You must specify the dimension of at least the first level array at the time you create a multi-dimensional array. For example, when you create a two-dimensional array, you must specify at least the first dimension, which is the number of rows. You can achieve the same results as the above code fragment as follows:

```
table = new int[3][];
```

This statement creates only first level of array. Only table[0], table[1] and table[2] exist at this time. They are referring to null. At this time, table.length has a value of 3. Since table[0], table[1] and table[2] are referring to null, you cannot use length attribute on them. That is, you have created three rows in a table, but you do not know how many columns each row will contain. Since table[0], table[1] and table[2] are arrays of int, you can assign them values as

```
table[0] = new int[2]; // Create two columns for row 1
table[1] = new int[2]; // Create two columns for row 2
table[2] = new int[2]; // Create two columns for row 3
```

You have completed the creation of the two-dimensional array, which has the three rows and each row has two columns. You can assign the values to some cells as

```
table[0][1] = 32;
table[2][0] = 71;
```

It is also possible to create a two-dimensional array with different number of columns for each row. Such an array is called a ragged array. Listing 15-11 illustrates working with a ragged array.

Listing 15-11. An Example of a Ragged Array

```
// RaggedArray.java
package com.jdojo.array;

public class RaggedArray {
        public static void main(String[] args) {
                // Create a two-dimensional array of 3 rows
                int[][] raggedArr = new int[3][];

                // Add 2 columns to the first row
                raggedArr[0] = new int[2];

                // Add 1 column to the second row
                raggedArr[1] = new int[1];

                // Add 3 columns to the third row
                raggedArr[2] = new int[3];

                // Assign values to all elements of raggedArr
                raggedArr[0][0] = 1;
                raggedArr[0][1] = 2;
                raggedArr[1][0] = 3;
                raggedArr[2][0] = 4;
                raggedArr[2][1] = 5;
                raggedArr[2][2] = 6;
```

```
            // Print all elements. One row at one line
            System.out.println(raggedArr[0][0] + "\t" + raggedArr[0][1]);
            System.out.println(raggedArr[1][0]);
            System.out.println(raggedArr[2][0] + "\t" + raggedArr[2][1] + "\t" + raggedArr[2][2]);
        }
}
```

```
1    2
3
4    5    6
```

■ **Tip**   Java supports an array of arrays, which can be used to achieve functionalities provided by a multi-dimensional array. Multi-dimensional arrays are widely used in scientific and engineering applications. If you are using arrays in your business application program that have more than two dimensions, you may need to reconsider the choice of multi-dimensional arrays as the choice for your data structure.

Accessing Elements of a Multi-Dimensional Array

Typically, a multi-dimensional array is populated using nested for loops. The number of for loops used to populate a multi-dimensional array equals the number of dimensions in the array. For example, two for loops are used to populate a two-dimensional array. Typically, a loop is used to access the elements of a multi-dimensional array. Listing 15-12 illustrates how to populate and access elements of a two-dimensional array.

Listing 15-12. Accessing Elements of a Multi-dimensional Array

```java
// MDAccess.java
package com.jdojo.array;

public class MDAccess {
        public static void main(String[] args){
                int[][] ra = new int[3][];
                ra[0] = new int[2];
                ra[1] = new int[1];
                ra[2] = new int[3];

                // Populate the ragged array using for loops
                for(int i = 0; i < ra.length; i++) {
                        for(int j = 0; j < ra[i].length; j++){
                                ra[i][j] = i + j;
                        }
                }

                // Print the array using for loops
                for(int i = 0; i < ra.length; i++) {
                        for (int j = 0; j < ra[i].length; j++){
                                System.out.print(ra[i][j] + "\t");
                        }
```

```
                    // Add a new line after each row is printed
                    System.out.println();
            }
        }
}
```

```
0    1
1
2    3    4
```

Initializing Multi-Dimensional Arrays

You may initialize the elements of a multi-dimensional array by supplying the list of values at the time of its declaration or at the time of creation. You cannot specify the length of any dimension if you initialize the array with a list of values. The number of initial values for each dimension will determine the length of each dimension in the array. Since many dimensions are involved in a multi-dimensional array, the list of values for a level is enclosed in braces. For a two-dimensional array, the list of values for each row is enclosed in a pair of braces, like so:

```
int[][] arr = {{10, 20, 30}, {11, 22}, {222, 333, 444, 555}};
```

This statement creates a two-dimensional array with three rows. The first row contains three columns with values 10, 20, and 30. The second row contains two columns with values 11 and 22. The third row contains four columns with values 222, 333, 444, and 555. A zero-row and zero-column two-dimensional array can be created as shown:

```
int[][] empty2D = { };
```

Initialization of a multi-dimensional array of reference type follows the same rule. You can initialize a two-dimensional String array like so:

```
String[][] acronymList = {{"JMF", "Java Media Framework"},
                          {"JSP", "Java Server Pages"},
                          {"JMS", "Java Message Service"}};
```

You can initialize the elements of a multi-dimensional array at the time you create it.

```
int[][] arr = new int[][]{{1, 2}, {3,4,5}};
```

Enhanced for Loop for Arrays

Java 5 introduced an enhanced for loop that lets you loop through elements of an array in a cleaner way. The enhanced for loop is also known as for-each loop. The syntax is as follows:

```
for(DataType e : array) {
        // Loop body goes here...

        // e contains one element of the array at a time
}
```

The for-each loop uses the same for keyword used by the basic for loop. Its body is executed as many times as the number of elements in the array. DataType e is a variable declaration, where e is the variable name and DataType is its data type. The data type of the variable e should be assignment-compatible with the type of the array. The variable declaration is followed by a colon (:), which is followed by the reference of the array that you want to loop through. The for-each loop assigns the value of an element of the array to the variable e, which you can use inside the body of the loop. The following snippet of code uses a for-each loop to print all elements of an int array:

```
int[] numList = {1, 2, 3};
for(int num : numList) {
        System.out.println(num);
}
```

```
1
2
3
```

You can accomplish the same thing using the basic for loop, as follows:

```
int[] numList = {1, 2, 3};
for(int i = 0; i < numList.length; i++) {
        int num = numList[i];
        System.out.println(num);
}
```

```
1
2
3
```

Note that the for-each loop provides a way to loop through elements of an array, which is cleaner than the basic for loop. However, it is not a replacement for the basic for loop because you cannot use it in all circumstances. For example, you cannot access the index of the array element and you cannot modify the value of the element inside the loop as you do not have the index of the element.

Array Declaration Syntax

You can declare an array by placing brackets ([]) after the data type of the array or after the name of the array reference variable. For example, the following declaration

```
int[] empIds;
int[][] points2D;
int[][][] points3D;
Person[] persons;
```

is equivalent to

```
int empIds[];
int points2D[][];
int points3D[][][];
Person persons[];
```

Java also allows you to mix two syntaxes. In the same array declaration, you can place some brackets after the data type and some after the variable name. For example, you can declare a two-dimensional array of int as follows:

```
int[] points2D[];
```

You can declare a two-dimensional and a three-dimensional array of int in one declaration statement as

```
int[] points2D[], points3D[][];
```

or

```
int[][] points2D, points3D[];
```

Runtime Array Bounds Checks

At runtime, Java checks array bounds for every access to an array element. If the array bounds are exceeded, an java.lang.ArrayIndexOutOfBoundsException is thrown. The only requirement for array index values at compile time is that they must be integers. The Java compiler does not check if the value of an array index is less than zero or beyond its length. This check must be performed at runtime, before every access to an array element is allowed. Runtime array bounds checks slow down the program execution for two reasons:

- The first reason is the cost of bound checks itself. To check the array bounds, the length of array must be loaded in memory and two comparisons (one for less than zero and one for greater than or equal to its length) must be performed.

- The second reason is that an exception must be thrown when the array bounds are exceeded. Java must do some housekeeping and get ready to throw an exception if the array bounds are exceeded.

Listing 15-13 illustrates the exception thrown if the array bounds are exceeded. The program creates an array of int named test, which has a length of 3. The program cannot access the fourth element (test[3] as it does not exist. An ArrayIndexOutOfBoundsException is thrown when such an attempt is made.

Listing 15-13. Array Bounds Checks

```java
// ArrayBounds.java
package com.jdojo.array;

public class ArrayBounds {
    public static void main(String[] args) {
        int[] test = new int[3];

        System.out.println("Assigning 12 to the first element");
        test[0] = 12;  // index 0 is between 0 and 2. Ok

        System.out.println("Assigning 79 to the fourth element");

        // index 3 is not between 0 and 2. At runtime, an exception is thrown.
        test[3] = 79;

        System.out.println("We will not get here");
    }
}
```

```
Assigning 12 to the first element
Assigning 79 to the fourth element
Exception in thread "main" java.lang.ArrayIndexOutOfBoundsException: 3
        at com.jdojo.array.ArrayBounds.main(ArrayBounds.java:14)
```

It is good practice to check for array length before accessing its elements. The fact that array bounds violation throws an exception may be misused as shown in the following snippet of code, which prints values stored in an array:

```java
/* Do not use this code, even if it works.*/
// Create an array
int[] arr = new int[10];

// Populate the array here...

// Print the array. Wrong way
try {
        // Start an infinite loop. When we are done with all elements an
        // exception is thrown and we will be in catch block and hence out of the loop.
        int counter = 0;
        while (true) {
                System.out.println(arr[counter++]);
        }
}
catch (ArrayIndexOutOfBoundsException e) {
        // We are done with printing array elements
}
// Do some processing here...
```

The above snippet of code uses an infinite while loop to print values of the elements of an array and relies on the exception throwing mechanism to check for array bounds. The right way is to use a for loop and check for array index value using the length property of the array.

What Is the Class of an Array Object

Arrays are objects. Because every object has a class, you must have a class for every array. All methods of the Object class can be used on arrays. Because the getClass() method of the Object class gives the reference of the class for any object in Java, you will use this method to get the class name for all arrays. Listing 15-14 illustrates how to get the class name of an array.

Listing 15-14. Knowing the Class of an Array

```java
// ArrayClass.java
package com.jdojo.array;

public class ArrayClass {
        public static void main (String[] args){
                int[] iArr = new int[2];
                int[][] iiArr = new int[2][2];
                int[][][] iiiArr = new int[2][2][2];
```

```
        String[] sArr   = {"A", "B"} ;
        String[][] ssArr = {{"AA"}, {"BB"}} ;
        String[][][] sssArr = {} ; // A 3D empty array of string

        // Print the class name for all arrays
        System.out.println("int[]:" + getClassName(iArr));
        System.out.println("int[][]:" + getClassName(iiArr));
        System.out.println("int[][][]:" + getClassName(iiiArr));
        System.out.println("String[]:" + getClassName(sArr));
        System.out.println("String[][]:" + getClassName(ssArr));
        System.out.println("String[][][]:" + getClassName(sssArr));
    }

    // Any java object can be passed to getClassName() method.
    // Since every array is an object, we can also pass an array to this method.
    public static String getClassName(Object obj) {
        // Get the reference of its class
        Class c = obj.getClass();

        // Get the name of the class
        String className = c.getName();
        return className;
    }
}
```

```
int[]:[I
int[][]:[[I
int[][][]:[[[I
String[]:[Ljava.lang.String;
String[][]:[[Ljava.lang.String;
String[][][]:[[[Ljava.lang.String;
```

The class name of an array starts with left bracket(s) ([ ). The number of left brackets is equal to the dimension of the array. For an int array, the left bracket(s) is followed by a character I. For a reference type array, the left bracket(s) is followed by a character L, followed by the name of the class name, which is followed by a semicolon. The class names for one-dimensional primitive arrays and a reference type are shown in Table 15-3.

Table 15-3. *Class Name of Arrays*

Array Type	Class Name
byte[]	[B
short[]	[S
int[]	[I
long[]	[J
char[]	[C
float[]	[F
double[]	[D
boolean[]	[Z
com.jdojo.Person[]	[Lcom.jdojo.Person;

The class names of arrays are not available at compile time for declaring or creating them. You must use the syntax described in this chapter to create an array. That is, you cannot write the following to create an int array:

```
[I myIntArray;
```

Rather, you must write the following to create an int array:

```
int[] myIntArray;
```

Array Assignment Compatibility

The data type of each element of an array is the same as the data type of the array. For example, each element of an int[] array is an int; each element of a String[] array is a String. The value assigned to an element of an array must be assignment-compatible to its data type. For example, it is allowed to assign a byte value to an element of an int array, because byte is assignment compatible to int. However, it is not allowed to assign a float value to an element of an int array, because float is not assignment compatible to int.

```
byte bValue = 10;
float fValue = 10.5f;
int[] sequence = new int[10];

sequence[0] = bValue; // Ok
sequence[1] = fValue; // A compile-time error
```

The same rule must be followed when dealing with a reference type array. If there is a reference type array of type T, its elements can be assigned an object reference of type S, if and only if, S is assignment compatible to T. The subclass object reference is always assignment compatible to the superclass reference variable. Because the Object class is the superclass of all classes in Java, you can use an array of Object class to store objects of any class. For example,

```
Object[] genericArray = new Object[4];

genericArray[0] = new String("Hello");   // Ok
genericArray[1] = new Person("Daniel");  // Ok. Assuming Person class exists
genericArray[2] = new Account(189);      // Ok. Assuming Account class exist
genericArray[3] = null;                  // Ok. null can be assigned to any reference type
```

You need to perform a cast at the time you read back the object from the array, as shown:

```
/* Compiler will flag an error for the following statement. genericArray is of Object type and an
Object reference cannot be assigned to a String reference variable. Even though genericArray[0]
contains a String object reference, we need to cast it to String as we do in next statement.
*/
String s = genericArray[0]; // A compile-time error

String str = (String)genericArray[0]; // Ok
Person p = (Person)genericArray[1];    // Ok
Account a = (Account)genericArray[2]; // Ok
```

If you try to cast the array element to a type, whose actual type is not assignment compatible to the new type, a java.lang.ClassCastException is thrown. For example, the following statement will throw a ClassCastException at runtime:

```
String str = (String)genericArray[1]; // Person cannot be cast to String
```

You cannot store an object reference of the superclass in an array of the subclass. The following snippet of code illustrates this:

```
String[] names = new String[3];
names[0] = new Object(); // An error. Object is superclass of String
names[1] = new Person(); // An error. Person is not subclass of String
names[2] = null;         // Ok.
```

Finally, an array reference can be assigned to another array reference of another type if the former type is assignment compatible to the latter type.

```
Object[] obj = new Object[3];
String[] str = new String[2];
Account[] a = new Account[5];

obj = str;               // Ok
str = (String[]) obj; // Ok. Because obj has String array reference

obj = a;

// ClassCastException error. obj has the reference of an Account array and
// an Account cannot be converted to a String
str = (String[]) obj;

a = (Account[]) obj; // Ok
```

Converting an ArrayList/Vector to an Array

An ArrayList can be used when the number of elements in the list is not precisely known. Once the number of elements in the list is fixed, you may want to convert an ArrayList to an array. You may do this for one of the following reasons:

- The program semantics may require you to use an array, not an ArrayList. For example, you may need to pass an array to a method, but you have data stored in an ArrayList.

- You may want to store user inputs in an array. However, you do not know the number of values the user will input. In such a case, you can store values in an ArrayList while accepting input from the user. At the end, you can convert the ArrayList to an array.

- Accessing array elements is faster than accessing ArrayList elements. If you have an ArrayList and you want to access the elements multiple times, you may want to convert the ArrayList to an array for better performance.

The ArrayList class has an overloaded method named toArray():

- Object[ ]   toArray( )

- <T> T[ ]   toArray(T[ ] a)

The first method returns the elements of ArrayList as an array of Object. The second method takes an array of any type as argument. All ArrayList elements are copied to the passed array if there is enough space and the same array is returned. If there is not enough space in the passed array, a new array is created. The type of new array is the same as the passed array. The length of the new array is equal to the size of ArrayList. Listing 15-15 shows how to convert an ArrayList to an array.

Listing 15-15. An ArrayList to an Array Conversion

```java
// ArrayListToArray.java
package com.jdojo.array;

import java.util.ArrayList;
import java.util.Arrays;

public class ArrayListToArray {
        public static void main(String[] args){
                ArrayList<String> al = new ArrayList<String>();
                al.add("cat");
                al.add("dog");
                al.add("rat");

                // Print the content of arrayList
                System.out.println("ArrayList:" + al);

                // Create an array of teh same length as teh ArrayList
                String[] s1 = new String[al.size()];

                // Copy the ArrayList elements to teh array
                String[] s2 = al.toArray(s1);
```

```
            // s1 has enough space to copy all ArrayList elements.
            // al.toArray(s1) returns s1 itself
            System.out.println("s1 == s2:" + (s1 == s2));
            System.out.println("s1:" + Arrays.toString(s1));
            System.out.println("s2:" + Arrays.toString(s2));

            // Create an array of string with 1 element.
            s1 = new String[1];
            s1[0] = "hello" ; // Store hello in first element

            // Copy ArrayList to the array s1
            s2 = al.toArray(s1);

            /* Since s1 doesn't have sufficient space to copy all ArrayList elements,
            al.toArray(s1) creates a new String array with 3 elements in it. All elements of
            arraylist are copied to new array. Finally, new array is returned. Here, s1 ==
            s2 is false. s1 will be untouched by the method call.
            */
            System.out.println("s1 == s2:" + (s1 == s2));
            System.out.println("s1:" + Arrays.toString(s1));
            System.out.println("s2:" + Arrays.toString(s2));
        }
}
```

```
ArrayList:[cat, dog, rat]
s1 == s2:true
s1:[cat, dog, rat]
s2:[cat, dog, rat]
s1 == s2:false
s1:[hello]
s2:[cat, dog, rat]
```

Summary

An array is a data structure to store multiple data values of the same type in memory. All array elements are allocated contiguous space in memory. Array elements are accessed using their indexes. Arrays use zero-based indexing. The first element has an index of zero.

Arrays in Java are objects. Java supports fixed-length arrays. That is, once an array is created, its length cannot be changed. Use an ArrayList if you need a variable-length array. The ArrayList class provides a toArray() method to convert its elements to an array. Java supports multi-dimensional arrays in the form of ragged arrays that are arrays of arrays. You can clone an array using the clone() method. A shallow-cloning is done for reference arrays.

CHAPTER 16

■ ■ ■

Inheritance

In this chapter, you will learn

- What inheritance is

- How to inherit a class from another class

- The difference between early binding and late binding

- What method overriding is and how to override methods

- What field hiding and method hiding are and how to use them in your code

- What abstract classes are and where to use them

- How to declare final classes and methods

- The difference between "is-a," "has-a," and "part-of" relationships

What is Inheritance?

Sometimes you may need the same functionality at multiple places in your application. There are different ways to write code to achieve this. One way is to copy the same code in all places where you need the same functionality. If you follow this logic, you need to make changes at all places when the functionality changes. Let's consider an example where you need the same functionality at three different places. Suppose you have an application that deals with three kinds of objects: planets, employees, and managers. Further, suppose that all three kinds of objects have a name. You create three classes: Planet, Employee, and Manager to represent the three kinds of objects. Each class has an instance variable called name and two methods called getName() and setName(). If you think about the code in three classes to maintain the name of their objects, you would find that they are the same. You might have written code for one class and copied it to other two classes. You may realize the problem in maintaining this kind of code when the same code is copied multiple places. If you need to handle the name differently later, you will need to make changes in three places. Inheritance is the feature of object-oriented programming that helps in such circumstances to avoid copying the same code at multiple places, thus facilitating code reuse. Inheritance also lets you customize the code without changing the existing code. Inheritance offers much more than just the code reuse and customization.

Inheritance is one of the cornerstones of object-oriented programming languages. It lets you create a new class by reusing code from an existing class. The new class is called a subclass and the existing class is called the superclass. A superclass contains the code that is reused and customized by the subclass. It is said that the subclass inherits from the superclass. A superclass is also known as a base class or a parent class. A subclass is also known as a derived class or a child class. Technically, it may be possible to inherit a class from any existing class. However, practically it is not always a good idea to inherit a new class from any existing class. Inheritance in software development works much the same way as inheritance in normal human life. You inherit something from your parents; your parents inherit something from their parents, and so on. If you look at inheritance in human lives, there exists a relationship between humans for inheritance to occur. Similarly, there exists a relationship between objects of the superclass and the subclass. The relationship that must exist between the superclass and the subclass in order for inheritance to be effective is called an "is-a" relationship. You need to ask yourself a simple question before you should inherit a class Q from a class P: "Is an object of class P also an object of class Q?" If the answer is yes, class Q may inherit from class P. Let's consider three classes Planet, Employee, and Manager. Let's ask the same question using these three classes one-by-one.

- Is a planet an employee? That is, does an "is-a" relationship exist between a planet and an employee? The answer is no. Is an employee a planet? The answer is no.

- Is a planet a manager? The answer is no. Is a manager a planet? The answer is no.

- Is an employee a manager? The answer is maybe. An employee may be a manager, a clerk, a programmer, or any other type of employee. However, an employee is not necessarily always a manager. Is a manager an employee? The answer is yes.

You asked six questions using the three classes. You got "yes" as the answer in only one case. This is the only case that is fit for using inheritance. The Manager class should inherit from the Employee class.

How does a class inherit another class? It is very simple to inherit a class from another class. You need to use the keyword extends followed by the superclass name in the class declaration of your subclass. The general syntax is

```
<<class modifiers>>class <<SubclassName>> extends <<SuperclassName>> {
        // Code for the Subclass goes here
}
```

For example, the following code declares a class Q, which inherits from class P:

```
public class Q extends P {
        // Code for class Q goes here
}
```

You can use either the simple name or the fully qualified name of the superclass in a class declaration. If the subclass and the superclass do not reside in the same package, you may need to import the superclass name to use its simple name in the extends clause. Suppose the fully qualified names of class P and Q are pkg1.P and pkg2.Q, respectively. The above declaration may be rewritten in one of the following two ways: using simple name of the superclass or using the fully qualified name of the superclass.

```
// #1 - Use the simple name of P in the extends clause and use an import statement.
package pkg2;

import pkg1.P;

public class Q extends P {
        // Code for class Q goes here
}

// #2 - Use the fully qualified name of P. No need to use an import statement.
package pkg2;

public class Q extends pkg1.P {
        // Code for class Q goes here
}
```

Let's look at the simplest example of inheritance in Java. Let's start with an Employee class as listed in Listing 16-1.

Listing 16-1. An Employee Class

```java
// Employee.java
package com.jdojo.inheritance;

public class Employee {
        private String name = "Unknown";

        public void setName(String name) {
                this.name = name;
        }

        public String getName() {
                return name;
        }
}
```

It is a simple class with a `private` instance variable name and two `public` methods, `setName()` and `getName()`. The instance variable is used to store the name for an employee and the two methods are used to get and set the name instance variable. Note that there is no special code in the Employee class. It is one of the simplest classes you can write in Java. It is easy to write and understand the following snippet of code that uses the Employee class:

```java
Employee emp = new Employee();
emp.setName("John Jacobs");
String empName = emp.getName();
System.out.println("Employee Name: " + empName);
```

Employee Name: John Jacobs

Listing 16-2 contains the code for the Manager class, which inherits from the Employee class. Note the use of the keyword extends to indicate that the Employee class is the superclass and the Manager class is the subclass. The Manager class does not contain any code, except the declaration. That is all you need in the Manager class for now.

Listing 16-2. A Manager Class

```java
// Manager.java
package com.jdojo.inheritance;

public class Manager extends Employee {
        // No code is needed for now
}
```

Let's test the Manager class. Listing 16-3 contains the code.

Listing 16-3. Testing the Manager Class

```java
// SimplestInheritanceTest.java
package com.jdojo.inheritance;

public class SimplestInheritanceTest {
        public static void main(String[] args) {
                // Create an object of the Manager class
                Manager mgr = new Manager();

                // Set the name of the manager
                mgr.setName("Leslie Zanders");

                // Get the name of the manager
                String mgrName = mgr.getName();

                // Display the manager name
                System.out.println("Manager Name: " + mgrName);
        }
}
```

```
Manager Name: Leslie Zanders
```

Even if you did not write any code for the Manager class, it works the same as the Employee class, because it inherits from the Employee class. You create a manager object by using the Manager class's constructor.

```java
Manager mgr = new Manager();
```

After the manager object is created, the code looks similar to the one you used for dealing with an Employee object. You used the setName() and getName() methods with the manager object.

```java
mgr.setName("Leslie Zanders");
String mgrName = mgr.getName();
```

Note that the Manager class does not declare the setName() and getName() methods. Neither does it declare the name instance variable. However, it appears that all of them have been declared inside the Manager class, because it uses the "extends Employee" clause in its declaration. When a class inherits from another class, it inherits its superclass members (instance variables, methods, etc.). There are many rules that govern inheritance. I will discuss those rules in details one-by-one later in this chapter.

Object Class is the Default Superclass

If a class does not specify a superclass using the keyword extends in its class declaration, it inherits from the java.lang.Object class. For example, the following two class declarations for class P are the same:

```java
// #1 - "extends Object" is implicitly added for class P
public class P {
        // Code for class P goes here
}
```

```
// #2 - "extends Object" is explicitly added for class P
public class P extends Object {
        // Code for class P goes here
}
```

In the previous chapters, you did not use the extends clause to declare your classes. They were implicitly inherited from the Object class. This is the reason that objects of those classes were able to use the methods of the Object class. Consider the following snippet of code:

```
Employee emp = new Employee();
int hc = emp.hashCode();
String str = emp.toString();
```

Note that the Employee class does not specify its superclass using an extends clause. This means that it inherits from the Object class. The Object class declares the hashCode() and toString() methods. Because the Employee class is implicitly a subclass of the Object class, it can use these methods as if they have been included in its own declaration. You have been using inheritance from the very first Java program you wrote, although you were not aware of it. This section has demonstrated the power of inheritance that comes as code reuse. You will see other benefits of inheritance later in this chapter.

Inheritance and Hierarchical Relationship

I touched upon this point in the previous section that inheritance should be used only if an "is-a" relationship exists between the subclass and the superclass. A subclass can have its own subclasses, which in turn can have their own subclasses, and so on. All classes in an inheritance chain form a tree-like structure, which is known as an inheritance hierarchy or a class hierarchy. All classes above a class in the inheritance hierarchy are called ancestors for that class. All classes below a class in the inheritance hierarchy are called descendants of that class.

Java allows single inheritance for a class. That is, a class can have only one superclass (or parent). However, a class can be the superclass for multiple classes. All classes in Java have a superclass except the Object class. The Object class sits at the top of the inheritance hierarchies for all classes in Java. Figure 16-1 shows a sample inheritance hierarchy for the Employee class and its descendants using a UML (Unified Modeling Language) diagram. In a UML diagram, a superclass and a subclass are connected using an arrow pointing from the subclass to the superclass.

Figure 16-1. A sample Inheritance class hierarchy

Sometimes, the term "immediate superclass" is used to mean the ancestor class, which is one level up in the inheritance hierarchy whereas the term "superclass" is used to mean an ancestor class at any level. This book uses the term "superclass" to mean ancestor of a class, which is one level up in the inheritance hierarchy. For example, `Programmer` is the superclass of `SystemProgrammer`, whereas `Employee` and `Object` are ancestors of `SystemProgrammer`. Sometimes, the term "immediate subclass" is used to mean a descendant class, which is one level down in the inheritance hierarchy, whereas the term "subclass" is used to mean a descendant class at any level. This book uses the term "subclass" to mean a descendant of a class, which is one level down in the inheritance hierarchy. For example, `Employee` is a subclass of `Object`, whereas `Clerk`, `Programmer`, and `Manager` are subclasses of `Employee`. `Clerk`, `Programmer`, `ApplicationProgrammer`, `SystemProgrammer`, `DatabaseProgrammer`, `Manager`, `FullTimeManager`, and `PartTimeManager` are all descendants of `Employee`. If a class is a descendant of another class, it is also a descendant of the ancestor of that class. For example, all descendants of the `Employee` class are also descendants of the `Object` class. All descendants of the `Manager` class are also descendants of the `Employee` class and the `Object` class.

What Is Inherited by a Subclass?

A subclass does not inherit everything from its superclass. However, a subclass may use, directly or indirectly, everything from its superclass. Let's discuss the distinction between "a subclass *inheriting* something from its superclass" and "a subclass *using* something from its superclass."

Let's take a real world example. Suppose your parent (a superclass) has money in a bank account. The money belongs to your parent. You (a subclass) need some money. If you *inherit* the money, you would just use the money at will as if the money is yours. If you can just *use* the money, you cannot get to the parent's money directly. Rather, you need to ask your parents for money and they will give it to you. In both cases, you used your parent's money. In the case of inheritance, the money appears to be owned by you. That is, you have direct access to it. In the second case, your parent's money was available to you for use without you having direct access to it. In the latter case, you had to go through your parents to use their money.

A subclass inherits non-private members of its superclass. I will discuss this rule in detail shortly. Note that constructors and initializers (static and instance) are not members of a class, and therefore, they are not inherited. Members of a class are all members that are declared inside the body of the class and members that it inherits from the superclass. This definition of members of a class has a trickle-down effect. Suppose there are three classes: A, B, and C. The class A inherits from the `Object` class. The class B inherits from the class A, and the class C inherits from the class B. Suppose class A declares a private member m1 and a non-private member m2. The members of class A are m1, m2, and all inherited members from the `Object` class. Note that m1 and m2 members of class A are *declared members*, whereas others are *inherited members*. Members of class B will be any members that are declared in class B and all non-private members of class A. The member m1 is declared `private` in class A, so it is not inherited by class B. The same logic applies to the members of class C. Note that non-private members of the `Object` class trickle down to class A, B, and C through the inheritance hierarchy. The non-private members of class A trickle down to class B, which in turn trickle down to class C, through the inheritance hierarchy.

There are four access modifiers: `private`, `public`, `protected`, and package-level. The absence of the `private`, `public`, and `protected` access modifier is considered as the default or package-level access. The access level modifier of a class member determines two things:

- Who can access (or use) that class member directly

- Whether a subclass inherits that class member or not

Access modifiers are also used with non-members (e.g. constructors) of a class. In such cases, an access modifier role is only one: "who can access that non-member?"

If a class member is declared `private`, it is accessible only inside the class that declares it. A `private` class member is not inherited by subclasses of that class.

A `public` class member is accessible from everywhere in the application. A subclass inherits all `public` members of its superclass.

If a class member is declared protected, it is accessible in the package in which it is declared. A protected class member is always accessible inside the body of a subclass whether the subclass is in the same package as the class or in a different package. A protected class member is inherited by a subclass. The protected access modifier is used with a class member when you want subclasses to access and inherit the class member. Note that a protected class member can be accessed through the package in which it is declared and inside subclasses. If you want to provide access to a class member only from inside its package, you should use a package-level access modifier, not a protected access modifier.

If a class member is declared package-level, it is accessible only inside the package in which the class is declared. A package-level class member is inherited only if the superclass and subclass are in the same package. If the superclass and the subclass are in different packages, the subclass does not inherit package-level members from its superclass.

■ **Tip**   The access modifiers build on each other where you start with no access to the outside world (private), and add to it, first package (default), then subclasses (protected), and then the world (public).

Let's look at your example of inheritance in Listing 16-1 and Listing 16-2. The Employee class has three members: a name field, a getName() method, and a setName() method. The name field has been declared private and hence it is not accessible inside the Manager class because it is not inherited. The getName() and setName() methods have been declared public and they are accessible from anywhere including the Manager class. They are inherited from the Employee class by the Manager class, though since they are public, the fact they are inherited doesn't matter.

Upcasting and Downcasting

An "is-a" relationship in the real world translates into inheritance class hierarchy in software. A class is a type in Java. When you express the "is-a" relationship using inheritance, you create a subclass, which is a more specific type of the superclass. For example, a Manager is a specific type of Employee. An Employee is a specific type of Object. As you move up in the inheritance hierarchy, you move from a specific type to a more general type. How does inheritance affect the client code? In this context, the client code is any code that uses the classes in a class hierarchy. Inheritance guarantees that whatever behavior is present in a class will also be present in its subclass. A method in a class represents a behavior of the objects of that class. This means that whatever behavior a client code expects to be present in a class will also be present in the class's subclass. This leads to the conclusion that if client code works with a class, it will also work with the class's subclass, because a subclass guarantees at least the same behaviors as its superclass. For example, the Manager class provides at least the same behaviors as provided by its superclass Employee.

Consider the following snippet of code:

```
Employee emp;
emp = new Employee();
emp.setName("Richard Castillo");
String name = emp.getName();
```

This snippet of code compiles without any errors. When the compiler comes across emp.setName("Richard Castillo") and emp.getName() calls, it checks the declared type of the emp variable. It finds that the declared type of the emp variable is Employee. It makes sure that the Employee class has setName() and getName() methods that conform to the call being made. It finds that the Employee class does have a setName() method that takes a String as a parameter. It finds that the Employee class does have a getName() method that takes no parameters and returns a String. After verifying these two facts, the compiler is fine with the emp.setName() and emp.getName() method calls.

With the point in mind that a subclass guarantees at least the same behavior (methods) as its superclass, let's consider the following snippet of code:

```
Employee emp;
emp = new Manager(); // A Manager object assigned to an Employee variable
emp.setName("Richard Castillo");
String name = emp.getName();
```

The compiler will compile the above snippet of code too, even though you have changed the code this time to assign the emp variable an object of the Manager class. It will pass the setName() and getName() method calls on the same basis as described in the previous case. It also passes the assignment statement

```
emp = new Manager();
```

The compile-time type of "new Manager()" expression is the Manager type. The compile-time type (or declared type) of the emp variable is Employee type. Since the Manager class inherits from the Employee class, an object of the Manager class "is-a" object of the Employee class. Simply, you say that a manager is always an employee. Such an assignment (from subclass to superclass) is called upcasting and it is always allowed in Java. It is also called a widening conversion because an object of the Manager class (more specific type) is assigned to a reference variable of the Employee type (a more generic type). All of the following assignments are allowed and they are all examples of upcasting:

```
Object obj;
Employee emp;
Manager mgr;
PartTimeManager ptm;

// An employee is always an object
obj = emp;

// A manager is always an employee
emp = mgr;

// A part-time manager is always a manager
mgr = ptm;

// A part-time manager is always an employee
emp = ptm;

// A part-time manager is always an object
obj = ptm;
```

Use a simple rule to check if an assignment is a case of upcasting. Look at the compile-time type (declared type) of the expression on the right side of the assignment operator (e.g. b in a = b). If the compile-time type of the right hand operand is a subclass of the compile-time type of the left-hand operand, it is a case of upcasting, and the assignment is safe and allowed. Upcasting is a direct technical translation of the fact that an object of a subclass "is-a" object of the superclass, too.

Upcasting is a very powerful feature of inheritance. It lets you write polymorphic code that works with classes that exists and classes that will be added in future. It lets you code your application logic in terms of a superclass that will always work with all subclasses (existing subclasses or subclasses to be added). It lets you write generic code without worrying about a specific type (class) with which the code will be used at runtime. Listing 16-4 is a simple utility class to test your upcasting rule. It has a printName() static method that accepts an argument of the Employee type. The printName() method uses the getName() method of the Employee class to get the name of the employee object and prints the name on the standard output.

Listing 16-4. *A Utility Class That Uses Employee Type Parameter in Its printName() Method*

```java
// EmpUtil.java
package com.jdojo.inheritance;

public class EmpUtil {
        public static void printName(Employee emp){
                // Get the name of employee
                String name = emp.getName();

                // Print employee name
                System.out.println(name);
        }
}
```

Listing 16-5 contains code to test the upcasting rule using the EmpUtil class.

Listing 16-5. *A Test Class to Test the Upcasting Rule*

```java
// UpcastTest.java
package com.jdojo.inheritance;

public class UpcastTest {
        public static void main(String[] args) {
                Employee emp = new Employee();
                emp.setName("Ken Wood");

                Manager mgr = new Manager();
                mgr.setName("Ken Furr"); // Inheritance of setName() at work

                // Print names
                EmpUtil.printName(emp);
                EmpUtil.printName(mgr); // Upcasting at work
        }
}
```

```
Ken Wood
Ken Furr
```

The main() method creates two objects (emp and mgr): one of the Employee class and one of the Manager class. It sets names for both objects. Finally, it calls the printName() method of the EmpUtil class to print the names of both objects. The first call to EmpUtil.printName(emp) is fine, because the printName() method accepts an Employee object and you have passed an Employee object (emp). The second call, EmpUtil.printName(mgr), is fine because of the upcasting rule. The printName(Employee emp) accepts an Employee object and you were able to pass a Manager object (mgr) instead, because a manager is always an employee and upcasting rules allows the assignment of a subclass object to a variable of superclass type.

591

Assigning a superclass reference to a subclass variable is called downcasting (or narrowing conversion). Downcasting is the opposite of upcasting. In upcasting, the assignment moves up the class hierarchy whereas in downcasting the assignment moves down the class hierarchy. The Java compiler cannot make sure at compile time that downcasting is legal or not. Let's consider the following snippet of code:

```
Employee emp;
Manager mgr = new Manager();
emp = mgr; // Ok. Upcasting
mgr = emp; // A compiler error. Downcasting
```

The assignment emp = mgr is allowed because of upcasting. However, the assignment mgr = emp is not allowed because it is a case of downcasting where a variable of superclass (Employee) is being assigned to a variable of subclass (Manager). The compiler is right in assuming that every manager is an employee (upcasting). However, not every employee is a manager (downcasting). In the above snippet of code, you would like the downcasting to work because you know for sure that the emp variable holds a reference to a Manager. Java imposes an additional rule in order for your downcast to succeed at compile-time. You need to give additional assurance to the compiler that you have considered the assignment of a superclass reference to a subclass reference variable and you would like the compiler to pass it. You give this assurance by adding a typecast to the assignment, as shown:

```
mgr = (Manager)emp; // OK. Downcast at work
```

The above downcasting with a typecast succeeds at compile-time. However, the Java runtime will perform an additional verification. The job of the compiler is just to make sure that the declared type of mgr variable, which is Manager, is assignment compatible with the typecast being used, which is Manager. The compiler cannot check what type of object emp variable will actually refer to at runtime. The Java runtime verifies the correctness of the typecast (Manager)emp in the above statement.

The type of the object to which the emp variable refers at runtime is also called its runtime type. The runtime compares the runtime type of the emp variable and the Manager type (Manager type is used in the typecast). If the runtime type of emp variable is assignment compatible with the type used in typecast, the typecast succeeds at runtime. Otherwise, runtime throws a java.lang.ClassCastException.

Let's consider the following snippet of code assuming that you have a subclass of the Manager class, which is called PartTimeManager.

```
Employee emp;
Manager mgr = new Manager();
PartTimeManager ptm = new PartTimeManager();
emp = mgr; // Upcasting. OK
ptm = (PartTimeManager)emp; // Downcasting. OK at compile-time. A runtime error.
```

The last assignment, which uses downcasting, succeeds at compile-time because the declared type of the ptm variable and the typecast type are the same. The runtime type of emp is Manager, because the emp = mgr statement assigns a Manager object's reference to it. When the runtime attempts to execute the "(PartTimeManager emp)" part of the downcasting, it finds that the runtime type of emp, which is Manager, is not assignment compatible with the typecast type, which is PartTimeManager. This is the reason that the runtime will throw a ClassCastException.

You can think of a statement that involves a downcasting as having two parts for the verification purpose. Suppose the statement is a2 = (K)b2. The compiler's job is to verify that the declared type of a2 is assignment compatible with type K. The runtime's job is to verify that the runtime type of b2 is assignment compatible with type K. If any of the two checks fails, you get an error at compile-time or runtime depending of which check fails. Figure 16-2 depicts this scenario.

Figure 16-2. *Runtime and compile-time checks made for downcasting*

■ **Tip** The Object class is at the top of every class hierarchy in Java. This allows you to assign a reference of any class type to a variable of the Object type. The following type of assignment is always allowed:

```
Object obj = new AnyJavaClass(); // Upcasting
```

Whether downcasting from an Object type to another class type will succeed depends on the downcasting rule as discussed above.

The instanceof Operator

How can you be sure that a downcasting will always succeed at runtime? Java has an instanceof operator, which helps you determine that whether a reference variable has a reference to an object of a class or a subclass of the class at runtime. It takes two operands and evaluates to a boolean value true or false. Its syntax is

```
<<Class Reference Variable>>instanceof <<Class Name or Interface>>
```

If <<Class Reference Variable>>refers to an object of class <<Class Name>>or any of its descendants, instanceof returns true. Otherwise, it returns false. Note that if <<Class Reference Variable>>is null, instanceof always returns false.

You should use the instanceof operator before downcasting to check if the reference variable you are trying to downcast is of the type you expected it to be. For example, if you want to check if a variable of Employee type refers to a Manager object at runtime, you would write

```
Manager mgr = new Manager();
Employee emp = mgr;
if (emp instanceof Manager) {
        // The following downcast will always succeed
        mgr = (Manager)emp;
}
else {
        // emp is not a Manager type
}
```

The instanceof operator goes through two types of checks: compile-time check and runtime check. The compiler checks if it is ever possible for the left-hand operand to refer to an object of the right-hand operand. This check may not be obvious to you at this point. The purpose of using the instanceof operator is to compare the runtime type of a reference variable to a type. In short, it compares two types. Does it ever make sense to compare a mango with an employee? You would say no. The compiler adds checks for this kind of illogical comparison using the `instanceof` operator. It makes sure that it is possible for the left-hand operand of the `instanceof` operator to hold a reference of an object of the right-hand operand type. If it is not possible, the compiler generates an error. It is easy to find out whether the compiler will generate an error for using the `instanceof` operator or not. Consider the following snippet of code:

```
Manager mgr = null;
if (mgr instanceof Clerk) { //  A compile-time error
}
```

The variable `mgr` can hold a reference of `Manager` type or its descendant type. However, it can never hold a reference of the `Clerk` type. The `Clerk` type is not in the same inheritance-chain as the `Manager` class, although it is in the same inheritance tree. For the same reason, the following use of the `instanceof` operator will generate a compiler error because the `String` class is not in the inheritance-chain of the `Employee` class.

```
String str = "test";
if (str instanceof Employee) { // A compile-time error
}
```

■ **Tip** An object is considered an instance of a class if that object is of that class type, or its direct or indirect descendant type. You can use the `instanceof` operator to check if an object is an instance of a class or not.

Sometimes you may end up writing code that uses the `instanceof` operator to test for multiple conditions at one place, as follows:

```
Employee emp;

// Some logic goes here...

if (emp instanceof Employee) {
        // Code to deal with a employee
}
else if (emp instanceof Manager) {
        // Code to deal with a manager
}
else if (emp instanceof Clerk) {
        // Code to deal with a clerk
}
```

You should avoid writing this kind of code. If you add a new subclass of `Employee`, you will need to add the logic for the new subclass to the above code. Usually, this kind of code indicates a design flaw. Always ask yourself the question, "Will this code keep working when I add a new class to the existing class hierarchy?" If the answer is yes, you are fine. Otherwise, reconsider the design.

The `equals()` method is the one place in which you will often end up using the `instanceof` operator. It is defined in the `Object` class and the method is inherited by all classes. It takes an `Object` argument. It returns `true` if the argument and the object on which this method is called are considered equal. Otherwise, it returns `false`. Objects of each class may be compared for equality differently. For example, two employees may be considered equal if they work for the same company and in the same department and have same employee id. What happens if a `Manager` object is passed to the equals() method of the Employee class? Since a manager is also an employee, it should compare the two for equality. The following snippet of code shows you a possible implementation of the equals() method for the Employee class:

```java
// Employee.java
package com.jdojo.inheritance;

public class Employee {
        private String name = "Unknown";

        public void setName(String name) {
                this.name = name;
        }

        public String getName() {
                return name;
        }

        public boolean equals(Object obj) {
                boolean isEqual = false;

                // We compare objects of the Employee class with the objects of
                // Employee class or its descendants
                if (obj instanceof Employee) {
                        // If two have the same name, consider them equal.
                        Employee e = (Employee)obj;
                        String n = e.getName();
                        isEqual = n.equals(this.name);
                }

                return isEqual;
        }
}
```

After you have added the equals() method to the Employee class, you can write code like the following, which compares two objects of the Employee type for equality based on their names:

```java
Employee emp = new Employee();
emp.setName("John Jacobs");

Manager mgr = new Manager();
mgr.setName("John Jacobs");

System.out.println(mgr.equals(emp)); // prints true
System.out.println(emp.equals(mgr)); // prints true
System.out.println(emp.equals("John Jacobs")); // prints false
```

In the third comparison, you compare an Employee object with a String object, which returns false. Comparing an Employee and a Manager object returns true because they have the same names.

Binding

Classes have methods and fields; we write code to access them as follows. Assume that myMethod() and xyz are members of the MyClass class, which is the declared type of the myObject reference variable.

```
MyClass myobject = get an object reference;
myObject.myMethod();    // Which myMethod() to call?
int a = myObject.xyz;   // Which xyz to access?
```

Binding is the process of identifying the accessed method's code (myMethod() in this case) or the field (xyz in this case), which will be used when the code executes. In other words, binding is a process of making a decision, which method's code or field will be accessed, when the code executes. There are two stages where the binding can happen: compile time and runtime. When the binding occurs at compile time, it is known as early binding. Early binding is also known as static binding or compile-time binding. When the binding occurs at runtime, it is known as late binding. Late binding is also known as dynamic binding or runtime binding.

Early Binding

Early binding is simple to understand compared to late binding. In early binding, the decision about which method code and field will be accessed is made by the compiler at compile time. For a method call, the compiler decides which method from which class will be executed when the code having the method call is executed. For a field access, the compiler decides which field from which class will be accessed when the code having the field access is executed. Early binding is used for the following types of methods and fields of a class in Java:

- All types of fields: static and non-static

- Static methods

- Non-static final methods

In early binding, a method or a field is accessed based on the declared type (or compile-time type) of the variable (or expression) accessing the method or the field. For example, if early binding is used for an a2.m1() method call, if a2 has been declared of type A, the m1() method in class A will be called when a2.m1() is executed.

Let's look at a detailed example that demonstrates the early binding rules. Let's consider two classes listed in Listing 16-6 and Listing 16-7.

Listing 16-6. An EarlyBindingSuper Class That Has a Static Field, an Instance Field, and a Static Method

```java
// EarlyBindingSuper.java
package com.jdojo.inheritance;

public class EarlyBindingSuper {
        // An instance variable
        public String str = "EarlyBindingSuper";

        // A static variable
        public static int count = 100;

        public static void print() {
                System.out.println("Inside EarlyBindingSuper.print()");
        }
}
```

Listing 16-7. An EarlyBindingSub Class, Which Inherits from EarlyBindingSuper Class and Has a Static Field, an Instance Field, and a Static Method, Which Are of the Same Type as in Its Superclass

```java
// EarlyBindingSub.java
package com.jdojo.inheritance;

public class EarlyBindingSub extends EarlyBindingSuper{
        // An instance variable
        public String str = "EarlyBindingSub";

        // A static variable
        public static int count = 200;

        public static void print() {
                System.out.println("Inside EarlyBindingSub.print()");
        }
}
```

The EarlyBindingSuper class declares two fields: str and count. The str field is declared non-static and count is declared static. The print() method is declared static.

The EarlyBindingSub class inherits from the EarlyBindingSuper class and it declares the same types of fields and methods, which have the same names. Fields are set to different values and the method prints a different message in the EarlyBindingSub class, so you can know which one is accessed when you execute your code. The EarlyBindingTest class in Listing 16-8 demonstrates the result of the early binding.

Listing 16-8. A Test Class to Demonstrate Early Binding for Fields and Methods

```java
// EarlyBindingTest.java
package com.jdojo.inheritance;

public class EarlyBindingTest {
        public static void main(String[] args) {
                EarlyBindingSuper ebSuper = new EarlyBindingSuper();
                EarlyBindingSub ebSub = new EarlyBindingSub();

                // Will access EarlyBindingSuper.str
                System.out.println(ebSuper.str);

                // Will access EarlyBindingSuper.count
                System.out.println(ebSuper.count);

                // Will access EarlyBindingSuper.print()
                ebSuper.print();

                System.out.println("-----------------------------");

                // Will access EarlyBindingSub.str
                System.out.println(ebSub.str);

                // Will access EarlyBindingSub.count
                System.out.println(ebSub.count);
```

```
            // Will access EarlyBindingSub.print()
            ebSub.print();

            System.out.println("-----------------------------");

            // Will access EarlyBindingSuper.str
            System.out.println(((EarlyBindingSuper)ebSub).str);

            // Will access EarlyBindingSuper.count
            System.out.println(((EarlyBindingSuper)ebSub).count);

            // Will access EarlyBindingSuper.print()
            ((EarlyBindingSuper)ebSub).print();

            System.out.println("-----------------------------");

            // Assign the ebSub to ebSuper
            ebSuper = ebSub; // Upcasting

            /* Now access methods and fields using ebSuper variable, which is
             referring to a EarlyBindingSub object
            */

            // Will access EarlyBindingSuper.str
            System.out.println(ebSuper.str);

            // Will access EarlyBindingSuper.count
            System.out.println(ebSuper.count);

            // Will access EarlyBindingSuper.print()
            ebSuper.print();
            System.out.println("-----------------------------");
        }
}
```

```
EarlyBindingSuper
100
Inside EarlyBindingSuper.print()
-----------------------------
EarlyBindingSub
200
Inside EarlyBindingSub.print()
-----------------------------
EarlyBindingSuper
100
Inside EarlyBindingSuper.print()
-----------------------------
EarlyBindingSuper
100
Inside EarlyBindingSuper.print()
-----------------------------
```

The main() method creates an object of each type EarlyBindingSuper and EarlyBindingSub.

```
EarlyBindingSuper ebSuper = new EarlyBindingSuper();
EarlyBindingSub ebSub = new EarlyBindingSub();
```

According to early binding rules, the statements ebSuper.str, ebSuper.count, and ebSuper.print() will always access the str and count fields, and the print() method of the EarlyBindingSuper class because you have declared ebSuper of the EarlyBindingSuper type. This decision is made by the compiler because str and count are fields and for fields, Java always uses early binding. The print() method is a static method and Java always uses early binding for static methods. The same rule applies when you access these members using ebSub variable.

The output of the following statements may not be obvious.

```
// Will access EarlyBindingSuper.str
System.out.println(((EarlyBindingSuper)ebSub).str);

// Will access EarlyBindingSuper.count
System.out.println(((EarlyBindingSuper)ebSub).count);

// Will access EarlyBindingSuper.print()
((EarlyBindingSuper)ebSub).print();
```

The above three statements use an expression to access fields and methods. When you write ebSub.str, you access str field using ebSub variable directly. It is clear that ebSub variable is of type EarlyBindingSub and therefore, ebSub.str will access str field of the EarlyBindingSub class. When you use typecast, the compile-time type of the expression changes. For example, the compile-time type of ebSub is EarlyBindingSub. However, the compile-time type of the expression, (EarlyBindingSuper)ebSub, is EarlyBindingSuper. This is the reason that all of the above three statements will access fields and methods from the EarlyBindingSuper class, not from the EarlyBindingSub class even though they all use the ebSub variable, which is of the EarlyBindingSub type. The output of Listing 16-8 validates our discussion about the early binding rules.

■ **Tip**　You can also access static fields and methods of a class using the name of the class, for example, EarlyBindingSub.str. The early binding rules still apply and the compiler will bind the access to those fields and methods to the class whose name is used to access them. Using the class name to access static members of the class should be preferred for readability.

Late Binding

Binding for all non-static, non-final methods follows the rules of late binding. That is, if your code accesses a non-static method, which is not declared as final, the decision as to which version of the method is called is made at runtime. The version of the method that will be called depends on the runtime type of the object on which the method call is made, not on its compile-time type. Let's consider the following snippet of code, which creates an object of the Manager class and assigns the reference to a variable emp of the Employee class. The emp variable accesses the setName() method.

```
Employee emp = new Manager();
emp.setName("John Jacobs");
```

The compiler performs only one check for the emp.setName() method call in the above code. It makes sure that the declared type of the emp variable, which is Employee, has a method called setName(String s). The compiler detects that the setName(String s) method in the Employee class is an instance method, which is not final. For an instance method call, the compiler does not perform binding. It will leave this work for runtime. The method call, emp.setName("John Jacobs"), is the case of late binding. At runtime, the JVM decides which setName(String s) method should be called. The JVM gets the runtime type of the emp variable. The runtime type of the emp variable is Manager when the emp.setName("John Jacobs") statement is looked at in the above code snippet. The JVM traverses up the class hierarchy starting from the runtime type (that is, Manager) of the emp variable looking for the definition of a setName(String s) method. First, it looks at the Manager class and it finds that the Manager class does not declare a setName(String s) method. The JVM now moves one level up the class hierarchy, which is the Employee class. It finds that the Employee class declares a setName(String s) method. Once the JVM finds a matching method definition, it binds the call to that method and stops the search. Recall that the Object class is always at the top of all class hierarchies in Java. The JVM continues its search for a method definition up to the Object class. If it does not find a matching method in the Object class, it throws a runtime exception.

Let's look at an example that will demonstrate the late binding process. Listing 16-9 and Listing 16-10 have code for LateBindingSuper and LateBindingSub classes, respectively. The LateBindingSub class inherits from the LateBindingSuper class. It defines the same instance method print() as defined in the LateBindingSuper class. The print() method in both classes prints different messages so that you can see which method is being called.

Listing 16-9. A LateBindingSuper Class, Which Has an Instance Method Named print()

```java
// LateBindingSuper.java
package com.jdojo.inheritance;

public class LateBindingSuper {
    public void print() {
        System.out.println("Inside LateBindingSuper.print()");
    }
}
```

Listing 16-10. A LateBindingSub Class, Which Has an Instance Method Named print()

```java
// LateBindingSub.java
package com.jdojo.inheritance;

public class LateBindingSub extends LateBindingSuper{
    public void print() {
        System.out.println("Inside LateBindingSub.print()");
    }
}
```

Listing 16-11 demonstrates the result of late binding.

Listing 16-11. A Test Class to Demonstrate Early Binding for Fields and Methods

```java
// LateBindingTest.java
package com.jdojo.inheritance;

public class LateBindingTest {
    public static void main(String[] args) {
        LateBindingSuper lbSuper = new LateBindingSuper();
        LateBindingSub lbSub = new LateBindingSub();
```

```
                // Will access LateBindingSuper.print()
                lbSuper.print(); // #1

                // Will access LateBindingSub.print()
                lbSub.print();    // #2

                // Will access LateBindingSub.print()
                ((LateBindingSuper)lbSub).print(); // #3

                // Assign the lbSub to lbSuper
                lbSuper = lbSub; // Upcasting

                // Will access LateBindingSub.print() because lbSuper
                // is referring to a LateBindingSub object
                lbSuper.print(); // #4
        }
}
```

```
Inside LateBindingSuper.print()
Inside LateBindingSub.print()
Inside LateBindingSub.print()
Inside LateBindingSub.print()
```

The main() method creates an object of each type LateBindingSuper and LateBindingSub.

```
LateBindingSuper lbSuper = new LateBindingSuper();
LateBindingSub lbSub = new LateBindingSub();
```

The calls to the print() method are labeled #1, #2, #3 and #4, so we may refer to them in our discussion.

Both variables, lbSuper and lbSub, are used to access the print() instance method. The runtime decides which version of the print() method is called. When you use lbSuper.print(), which print() method is called depends on the object to which lbSuper variable is referring to at that point in time. Recall that a reference variable of a class type may also refer to an object of any of its descendant. The lbSuper variable may refer to an object of LateBindingSuper or LateBindingSub.

When the statement #1, lbSuper.print(), is ready to execute, the runtime will need to find the code for the print() method. The runtime looks for the runtime type of the lbSuper variable and it finds that the lbSuper variable is referring to an object of LateBindingSuper type. It looks for a print() method in the LateBindingSuper class and finds it. Therefore, the runtime binds the print() method call in the statement labeled #1 to the print() method of the LateBindingSuper class. This is confirmed by the first line in the output.

The logic for binding the print() method in statement #2 is the same as for the statement labeled #1, but the class this time is LateBindingSub.

Statement #3 is tricky. When you use a typecast such as (LateBindingSuper)lbSub, the object to which lbSub refers to at runtime does not change. Using a typecast, all you say is that you want to use the object to which lbSub variable refers as an object of LateBindingSuper type. However, the object itself never changes. You can verify this by using the following code, which gets the class name of an object:

```
// Both s1 and s2 have "com.jdojo.inheritance.LateBindingSub" class name
LateBindingSub lbSub = new LateBindingSub();
String s1 = lbSub.getClass().getName();
String s2 = ((LateBindingSuper)lbSub).getClass().getName();
```

When statement #3 is ready to execute, at that time the expression with the typecast still refers to an object of LateBindingSub type, and therefore, the print() method of the LateBindingSub class will be called. This is confirmed by the third line in the output.

Let's consider two lines of code to discuss statement #4:

```
lbSuper = lbSub; // Upcasting
lbSuper.print(); // #4
```

The first source line assigns lbSub to lbSuper. The effect of this line is that lbSuper variable starts referring to an object of LateBindingSub object. When statement #4 is ready to execute, the runtime needs to find the code for the print() method. The runtime finds that the runtime type of the lbSuper variable is the LateBindingSub class. It looks for the print() method in the LateBindingSub class and finds it right there. Therefore, statement #4 executes the print() method in the LateBindingSub class. This is confirmed by the fourth line in the output.

■ **Tip**   Late binding incurs a small performance overhead compared to early binding because the method calls are resolved at runtime. However, many techniques (e.g. virtual method table) can be used to implement late binding, so the performance hit is minimal or negligible. The benefit of late binding overshadows the little performance hit. It lets you implement inclusion polymorphism. When you write code like a2.print(), the a2 variable exhibits polymorphic behavior with respect to the print() method. The same code, a2.print(), may call the print() method of the class of the a2 variable or any of its descendant classes depending on what type of object a2 is referring to at runtime. Inheritance and late binding lets you write polymorphic code, which is written in terms of superclass type and works for all subclass types as well.

Method Overriding

Redefining an instance method in a class, which is inherited from the superclass, is called method overriding. Let's consider the following declarations of class A and class B:

```
public class A {
        public void print() {
                System.out.println("A");
        }
}

public class B extends A {
        public void print() {
                System.out.println("B");
        }
}
```

Class B is a subclass of class A. Class B inherits the print() method from its superclass and redefines it. It is said that the print() method in class B overrides the print() method of class A. It is like class B telling class A, "Thanks for being my superclass and letting me inherit your print() method. However, I need to work differently. I am going to

redefine it my way, without affecting your print() method in any way. You can keep using your print() method."
If a class overrides a method, it affects the overriding class and its subclasses. Consider the following declaration
of class C:

```
public class C extends B {
        // Inherits B.print()
}
```

Class C does not declare any methods. What method does class C inherit: A.print() or B.print(), or both? It
inherits the print() method from class B. A class always inherits what is available from its immediate superclass
(declared in superclass or inherited by its super superclass). If a class D inherits from class C, it will inherit print()
method of class B through class C.

```
public class D extends C {
        // Inherits B.print() through C
}
```

Let's consider two more classes E and F, which inherit from D and E, respectively. Class E overrides the print()
method of class B, which it inherited from class D.

```
public class E extends D {
        public void print() {
                System.out.println("E");
        }
}
```

```
public class F extends E {
        // Inherits E.print() through E
}
```

What will be the output of the following snippet of code?

```
A a = new A();
a.print();      // will print A
a = new B();
a.print();      // will print B
a = new C();
a.print();      // will print B
a = new D();
a.print();      // will print B
a = new E();
a.print();      // will print E
a = new F();
a.print();      // will print E
```

The comments in the code tell you what will be printed. Can you figure out why you get this output? There are
three things at work. First, you can assign an object of a descendant of class A to a variable of class A type. This is the
reason that you have called a.print() in all statements. Second, the print() method has been overridden by some
of the descendants of class A in the class hierarchy. Third, late binding performs the magic of calling the appropriate
print() method depending on the class of the object to which the variable is referring to at runtime.

Let's consider the following definitions of two classes S and T:

```java
public class S {
        public void print() {
                System.out.println("S");
        }
}

public class T extends S {
        public void print(String msg) {
                System.out.println(msg);
        }
}
```

Does the print() method in class T override the print() method in its superclass S? The answer is no. The print() method in class T does not override the print() method in class S. This is called method overloading. Class T will now have two print() methods: one inherited from its superclass S, which takes no arguments and one declared in it, which takes a String argument. However, both methods of class T have the same name print. This is the reason that it is called method overloading because the same method name is used more than once in the same class.

Here are the rules when a class is said to override a method, which it inherits from its superclass.

Method Overriding Rule #1

The method must be an instance method. Overriding does not apply to static methods.

Method Overriding Rule #2

The overriding method must have the same name as the overridden method.

Method Overriding Rule #3

The overriding method must have the same number of parameters of the same type in the same order as the overridden method. Java 5 has changed this rule slightly when the methods use generic types as their parameters. When the method's parameters use generic type, you need to consider the erasure of the generic type parameter, not the generic type itself when comparing with other methods to check if one overrides another. I will revisit this rule in later to discuss it in detail with examples. For now, let's consider a method as overriding another method if they have the same number of parameters of the same type in the same order. Note that the name of the parameter does not matter. For example, void print(String str) and void print(String msg) are considered the same method. The different names of the parameters, str and msg, do not make them different methods.

Method Overriding Rule #4

Before Java 5, the return type of the overriding and the overridden methods must be the same. In Java 5, this rule remains the same for return types of primitive data types. However, it has changed for return types of reference data types. If the return type of the overridden method is a reference type, the return type of the overriding method must be assignment compatible to the return type of the overridden method. Suppose a class has a method definition of R1 m1(), which is overridden by a method definition R2 m1();. This method overriding is allowed only if an instance of R2 can be assigned to a variable of R1 type without any typecast. Let's consider the following snippet of code that defines three classes P, Q, and R:

```java
public class P {
        public Employee getEmp() {
                // Code goes here
        }
}
```

```
public class Q extends P {
        public Employee getEmp() {
                // code goes here
        }
}

public class R extends P {
        public Manager getEmp() {
                // code goes here
        }
}
```

Class P defines a getEmp() method that returns an object of Employee type. The getEmp() method of Class Q overrides the getEmp() method of its superclass P because it has the same name, number of parameters (zero in this case) of the same type in the same order, and the same return type, Employee. The getEmp() method of class R also overrides the getEmp() method of class P even though its return type Manager is different from the return type of the overridden method, which is Employee. The getEmp() method of class R overrides its superclass getEmp() method because an instance of Manager type can always be assigned to a variable of Employee type without any typecast.

Method Overriding Rule #5

The access level of the overriding method must be at least the same or more relaxed than that of the overridden method. The three access levels are public, protected and package-level that allow for inheritance. Recall that private members are not inherited and hence cannot be overridden. The order of access level from the most relaxed to the strictest is public, protected, and package-level. If the overridden method has public access level, the overriding method must have the public access level because public is the most relaxed access level. If the overridden method has protected access level, the overriding method may have public or protected access level. If the overridden method has package-level access, the overriding method may have public, protected, or package-level access. Table 16-1 summarizes this rule. I will discuss why this rule exists shortly.

Table 16-1. *List of Allowed Access Levels for an Overriding Method*

Overridden Method Access Level	Allowed Overriding Method Access Level
public	public
protected	public, protected
package-level	public, protected, package-level

Method Overriding Rule #6

A method may include a list of checked exceptions in its throws clause. Although it is allowed to include an unchecked exception in the throws clause of a method, it is not required. In this section, I am discussing only checked exceptions. The overriding method cannot add a new exception to the list of exceptions in the overridden method. It may remove one or all exceptions or it may replace an exception with another exception, which is one of the descendants of the exception listed in the overridden method. Let's consider the following class definitions:

```
public class G {
        public void m1() throws CheckedException1, CheckedException2 {
                // Code goes here
        }
}
```

If a class overrides m1() method of class G, it must not add any new checked exception to it. The following code will not compile, because it has added a new checked exception CheckException3 in the overridden method m1():

```
public class H extends G {
        public void m1() throws CheckedException1, CheckedException2, CheckedException3 {
                // Code goes here
        }
}
```

The following class declarations override the m1() method in class G and they are all valid. In class I, the method m1() removes both exceptions. In class J, it removes one exception and keeps one. In class K, it keeps one and replaces the other one with a descendant type assuming that the CheckedException22 is a descendant class of CheckedException2.

```
public class I extends G {
        // m1() removes all exceptions
        public void m1() throws {
                // Code goes here
        }
}
```

```
public class J extends G {
        // m1() removes one exception and keeps one
        public void m1() throws CheckedException1 {
                // Code goes here
        }
}
```

```
public class J extends G {
        // m1() removes keep one and replaces one with a subclass
        public void m1() throws CheckedException1, CheckedException22 {
                // Code goes here
        }
}
```

The rules about the return type and the list of exceptions of an overriding method may not be obvious. I will discuss the reasons behind these rules. There is a reason behind these rules, which is "A variable of a class type can hold the reference of an object of any of its descendants." When you write code using the superclass type, that code must also work without any modification with objects of subclass types. Let's consider the following definition of class P assuming the EmpNotFoundException is a checked exception class:

```
public class P {
        public Employee getEmp(int empId) throws EmpNotFoundException {
                // code goes here
        }
}
```

You can write the following snippet of code:

```
P p = // get an object reference of P or its descendant;
try {
        Employee emp = p.getEmp(10);
}
catch (EmpNotFoundException e) {
        // Handle the exception here
}
```

There are two points that need to be considered in the above snippet of code. First, the variable p, which is of type P, can point to an object of type P or to an object of any descendant of class P. Second, when p.getEmp(10) method is called, the compiler verifies that the declared type of variable p (P class) has a getEmp() method, which accepts one parameter of type int, returns an Employee type object and throws EmpNotFoundException. These pieces of information are verified by the compiler with class P. The assumption made (and verified, too) by the compiler about the getEmp() method should never be invalidated at runtime. Otherwise, it will result in a chaos; code compiles, but might not run.

Let's consider one of the possible cases of overriding the getEmp() method as shown:

```
public class Q extends P {
        public Manager getEmp(int empId) {
                // code goes here
        }
}
```

If the variable p is assigned an object of class Q, the code

```
Employee emp = p.getEmp(10);
```

inside the try-catch block is still valid. In this case, the variable p will refer to an object of class Q whose getEmp() method returns a Manager object and does not throw any exception. Returning a Manager object from the getEmp() method is fine because you can assign a Manager object to the emp variable, which is a case of upcasting. Not throwing an exception from the getEmp() method is also fine because the code was ready to handle the exception (by using a try-catch block) in case the exception was thrown.

What is the reason behind the access level rules for overriding methods? Note that when a variable p accesses the getEmp() method, the compiler verifies that the code, where p.getEmp() is used, has access to the getEmp() method of class P. If the subclasses of P reduces the access level, the same code, p.getEmp(), may not work at runtime, because the code executing the statement may not have access to the getEmp() method in the descendant of class P.

Let's consider the following definition of class Q2, which inherits from class P. It overrides the getEmp() method and replaces the EmpNoFoundException with another checked exception named BadEmpIdException.

```
// Won't compile
public class Q2 extends P {
        public Manager getEmp(int empId) throws BadEmpIdException {
                // code goes here
        }
}
```

Suppose the code, which was written in terms of P type, gets a reference of a Q2 object as follows:

```
P p = new Q2();
try {
        Employee emp = p.getEmp(10);
}
catch(EmpNotFoundException e) {
        // Handle exception here
}
```

Note that the `try-catch` block is not prepared to handle the `BadEmpIdException`, which the method `getEmp()` of the Q2 class may throw. This is the reason why declaration of class Q2 would not compile.

To summarize the rules of overriding, let's break down the parts of a method declaration as follows:

- Name of the method

- Number of parameters

- Type of parameters

- Order of parameters

- Return type of parameters

- Access level

- List of checked exceptions in the throws clause

The first four parts must always be the same in the overriding and the overridden methods. Before Java 5, the return type must be the same in the overriding and the overridden methods. From Java 5, if the return type is a reference type, overriding a method's return type could also be a subtype (any descendant) of the return type of the overridden method. Access level and list of exceptions in the overridden method may be thought of as its constraints. An overriding method may relax (or even remove) the constraints of the overridden method. However, an overriding method can never have more restrictive constraints than that of the overridden method.

■ **Tip** The rules of overriding a method are complex. It may take you a long time to master them. All rules are directly supported by the compiler. If you make a mistake in the source code while overriding a method, the compiler will generate a nice (not always) error message that will give you a clue about your mistake. There is a golden rule about method overriding that helps you avoid mistakes: "Whatever code is written using the superclass type must also work with the subclass type."

Accessing Overridden Method

Sometimes you may need to access the overridden method from a subclass. A subclass can use the keyword super as a qualifier to call the overridden method of the superclass. Note that the Object class has no superclass. It is illegal to use the keyword super in the Object class. As a programmer, you will never need to write code for the Object class anyway as it is part of the Java class library.

Let's consider the code for the AOSuper class in Listing 16-12. It has a print() method, which prints a message on the standard output.

Listing 16-12. An AOSuper Class

```java
// AOSuper.java
package com.jdojo.inheritance;

public class AOSuper {
        public void print() {
                System.out.println("Inside AOSuper.print()");
        }
}
```

The code in Listing 16-13 contains the declaration for an AOSub class, which inherits from the AOSuper class.

Listing 16-13. An AOSub Class, Which Inherits from the AOSuper Class

```java
// AOSub.java
package com.jdojo.inheritance;

public class AOSub extends AOSuper {
        public void print() {
                // Call print() method of AOSuper class
                super.print();

                // Print a message
                System.out.println("Inside AOSub.print()");
        }

        public void callOverridenPrint() {
                // Call print() method of AOSuper class
                super.print();
        }
}
```

The AOSub class overrides the print() method of the AOSuper class. Note the super.print() method call inside the print() and the callOverridenPrint() methods of the AOSub class. It will call the print() method of AOSuper class. The output of Listing 16-14 shows that a method call with a super qualifier calls the overridden method in the superclass.

Listing 16-14. A Test Class to Test a Method Call with the super Qualifier

```java
// AOTest.java
package com.jdojo.inheritance;

public class AOTest {
        public static void main(String[] args) {
                AOSub aoSub = new AOSub();
                aoSub.print();
                aoSub.callOverridenPrint();
        }
}
```

```
Inside AOSuper.print()
Inside AOSub.print()
Inside AOSuper.print()
```

There is no way to directly call a method of the superclass of the superclass. You can call the overridden method of the superclass (only the immediate ancestor) using the keyword super. Suppose there are three classes: A, B, and C, where class B inherits from class A, and class C inherits from class B. There is no way to call methods of class A from inside class C. If class C needs to call a method of class A, you need to provide a method in class B that will call method of class A. Class C will call the method of class B, which in turn will call the method of class A.

■ **Tip** When a method call is made using the keyword super, Java uses early binding, even though the method is an instance method. Another instance when Java uses early biding for an instance method call is a private method call because a private method cannot be invoked from outside its defining class. A private method cannot be overridden either. The keyword super refers to the instance fields and methods or constructors of the immediate ancestor of the class in which it appears.

Method Overloading

Having more than one method with the same name in the same class is called method overloading. Methods with the same name in a class could be declared methods, inherited methods, or a combination of both. Overloaded methods must have different number of parameters, different types of parameters, or both. The return type, access level and throws clause of a method play no role in making it an overloaded method. The m1() method of the OME1 class is an example of an overloaded method.

```
public class OME1 {
        public void m1(int a) {
                // Code goes here
        }

        public void m1(int a, int b) {
                // Code goes here
        }

        public int m1(String a) {
                // Code goes here
        }

        public int m1(String a, int b) throws CheckedException1 {
                // Code goes here
        }
}
```

The following is an example of an incorrect attempt to overload the m2() method in class OME2:

```
// Won't compile
public class OME2 {
        public void m2(int p1) {
                // Code goes here
        }

        public void m2(int p2) {
                // Code goes here
        }
}
```

Using different names for parameters (p1 and p2) does not make the m2() method overloaded. The code for the OME2 class would not compile because it has a duplicate declaration for the m2() method. Both methods have the same number and type of parameters, which makes it not overloaded.

The order of the parameters may play a role in making a method overloaded. The m3() method of the OME3 class is overloaded because parameter types are different. Both methods have one parameter of type int and another of type double. However, they are in a different order.

```
public class OME3 {
        public void m3(int p1, double p2) {
                // Code goes here
        }

        public void m3(double p1, int p2) {
                // Code goes here
        }
}
```

Use a simple rule to check if two methods can be termed as an overloaded method. List the name of the methods and the type of their parameters from left to right separated by a comma. You can use any other separator. If the two methods of a class having the same name give you different lists, they are overloaded. Otherwise, they are not overloaded. If you make such lists for m1(), m2(), and m3() methods in class OME1, OME2, and OME3 classes, you will come up with the following results:

```
// Method list for m1 in class OME1 - Overloaded
m1,int
m1,int,int
m1,String
m1,String,int

// Method list for m2 in class OME2 - Not Overloaded
m2,int
m2,int

// Method list for m3 in class OME3 - Overloaded
m3,int,double
m3,double,int
```

You should realize that the results for the m2() method in class OME2 are the same for both versions and hence OME2.m2() is not overloaded.

Table 16-2 lists some important differences between method overriding and method overloading.

Table 16-2. *Some Important Differences Between Method Overriding and Method Overloading*

Method Overriding	Method Overloading
Overriding involves inheritance and at least two classes.	Overloading has nothing to do with inheritance. Overloading involves only one class.
It occurs when a class defines a method with the same name, the same number of parameters of the same type in the same order as defined by its superclass.	It occurs when a class defines more than one method with the same name. All methods with the same name must differ at least in one respect from others - the number of parameters, their types or orders.
The return type of the overriding method must be assignment substitutable with the return type of the overridden method.	Return types of overloaded methods do not play any roles in overloading.
The overriding method cannot have additional throws clause than the overridden method. It can have the same or less restrictive list of exceptions as the overridden method.	Throws clauses of overloaded methods do not play any roles in overloading.
Overriding applies only to instance (non-static) methods.	Any method (static or non-static) can be overloaded.

Method overloading is another kind of polymorphism where the same method name has different meanings. Method overloading is bound at compile time as opposed to method overriding that is bound at runtime. Note that the compiler only resolves the version of the overloaded methods that will be called. It determines which version of the overloaded method will be called matching the actual parameters with the formal parameters of the overloaded methods. If the overloaded method is an instance method, which code will be executed is still determined at runtime using late binding.

For an overloaded method call, the compiler chooses the most specific method. If it does not find an exact match, it will try to look for a more generic version by converting the actual parameter type to a more generic type using the rules of automatic type widening. Listing 16-15 demonstrates how the compiler chooses an overloaded method.

Listing 16-15. A Test Program That Demonstrates How the Compiler Chooses the Most Specific Method from Several Versions of an Overloaded Method

```
// OverloadingTest.java
package com.jdojo.inheritance;

public class OverloadingTest {
        public double add(int a, int b) {
                System.out.println("Inside add(int a, int b)");
                double s = a + b;
                return s;
        }

        public double add(double a, double b) {
                System.out.println("Inside add(double a, double b)");
                double s = a + b;
                return s;
        }
```

```java
        public void test(Employee e) {
                System.out.println("Inside test(Employee e)");
        }

        public void test(Manager e) {
                System.out.println("Inside test(Manager m)");
        }

        public static void main(String[] args) {
                OverloadingTest ot = new OverloadingTest();

                int i = 10;
                int j = 15;
                double d1 = 10.4;
                double d2 = 2.5;
                float f1 = 2.3F;
                float f2 = 4.5F;
                short s1 = 2;
                short s2 = 6;

                ot.add(i, j);
                ot.add(d1, j);
                ot.add(i, s1);
                ot.add(s1, s2);
                ot.add(f1, f2);
                ot.add(f1, s2);

                Employee emp = new Employee();
                Manager mgr = new Manager();
                ot.test(emp);
                ot.test(mgr);

                emp = mgr;
                ot.test(emp);
        }
}
```

```
Inside add(int a, int b)
Inside add(double a, double b)
Inside add(int a, int b)
Inside add(int a, int b)
Inside add(double a, double b)
Inside add(double a, double b)
Inside test(Employee e)
Inside test(Manager m)
Inside test(Employee e)
```

Note that the compiler knows only the compile-time type (the declared type) of the actual and the formal parameters. Let's look at the ot.add(f1, s2) method call. The types of actual parameters are float and short. There is no add(float, short) method in the OverloadingTest class. The compiler tries to widen the type of the first argument to a double data type and it finds a match based on the first parameter add(double, double).

Still, the second parameter type does not match; the actual type is short and the formal type is double. Java allows automatic widening from short to double. The compiler converts the short type to the double type and binds add(f1, s2) call to add(double, double) method. When ot.test(mgr) is called, the compiler looks for an exact match and, in this case, it finds one, test(Manager m), and binds the call to this version of the test() method. Suppose the test(Manager m) method is not present in the OverloadingTest class. The compiler will bind ot.test(mgr) call to test(Employee e) method because a Manager type can be widened (using upcasting) to Employee type automatically.

Sometimes, overloaded methods and automatic type widening may confuse the compiler resulting in a compiler error. Consider Listings 16-16 and 16-17 for an Adder class with an overloaded add() method and how to test it.

Listing 16-16. The Adder Class, Which Has Overloaded add().method

```java
// Adder.java
package com.jdojo.inheritance;

public class Adder {
    public double add(int a, double b) {
        return a + b;
    }

    public double add(double a, int b) {
        return a + b;
    }
}
```

Listing 16-17. Testing add() Method of the Adder Class

```java
// AdderTest.java
package com.jdojo.inheritance;

public class AdderTest {
    public static void main(String[] args) {
        Adder a = new Adder();
        double d = a.add(2, 3); // A compile-time error
    }
}
```

An attempt to compile the AdderTest class generates the following error:

```
"AdderTest.java": reference to add is ambiguous, both method add(int,double) in
com.jdojo.inheritance.Adder and method add(double,int) in com.jdojo.inheritance.Adder match at
line 7, column 18
```

The error message states that compiler is not able to decide which one of the two add() methods in the Adder class to call for a.add(3, 7) method invocation. The compiler is confused in deciding if it should widen the int type of 3 to make it double type 3.0 and call the add(double, int) or if it should widen the int type of 7 to make it double type 7.0 and call the add(int, double). In situations like this, you need to help the compiler by using a typecast as follows:

```java
double d1 = a.add((double)2, 3); // OK. Will use add(double, int)
double d2 = a.add(2, (double)3); // OK. Will use add(int, double)
```

Inheritance and Constructors

An object has two things: state and behavior. Instance variables in a class represent the state of its objects. Instance methods represent the behavior of its objects. Each object of a class maintains its own state. When you create an object of a class, memory is allocated for all instance variables declared in the class and all instance variables declared in its ancestors at all levels. Your Employee class declares a name instance variable. When you create an object of the Employee class, the memory is allocated for its name instance variable. When an object of the Manager class is created, memory is allocated for the name field that is present in its superclass Employee. After all, a manager has a similar state as that of an employee. A manager behaves similar to an employee.

Let's look at an example. Consider two classes, U and V, as shown:

```java
public class U {
        private int id;
        protected String name;
}

public class V extends U {
        protected double salary;
        protected String address;
}
```

Figure 16-3 depicts the memory allocation when objects of class U and V are created. When an object of class U is created, memory is allocated only for the instance variables that are declared in class U. When an object of class V is created, memory is allocated for all instance variables in class U and class V.

Figure 16-3. *Memory allocation for an object includes all instance variable of the class and all its ancestors*

Let's get to the main topic of discussion for this section, which is constructors. Constructors are not members of a class and they are not inherited by subclasses. They are used to initialize instance variables. When you create an object of a class, the object contains instance variables from the class and all of its ancestors. To initialize the instance variables of ancestor classes, the constructors of ancestor classes must be called. Let's consider the following two classes, CSuper and CSub, as shown in Listing 16-18 and Listing 16-19. The CTest class in Listing 16-20 is used to create an object of the CSub class.

Listing 16-18. A CSuper Class with a no-args Constructor

```java
// CSuper.java
package com.jdojo.inheritance;

public class CSuper {
        public CSuper() {
                System.out.println("Inside CSuper() constructor.");
        }
}
```

Listing 16-19. A CSub Class, Which Inherits from the CSuper Class and Has a no-args Constructor

```java
//CSub.java
package com.jdojo.inheritance;

public class CSub extends CSuper {
        public CSub() {
                System.out.println("Inside CSub() constructor.");
        }
}
```

Listing 16-20. A Test Class, Which Demonstrates That Constructors for all Ancestors Are Called When an Object of a Class Is Created Starting at the Top of the Class Hierarchy and Going Down

```java
// CTest.java
package com.jdojo.inheritance;

public class CTest {
        public static void main(String[] args) {
                CSub cs = new CSub();
        }
}
```

```
Inside CSuper() constructor.
Inside CSub() constructor.
```

The output of the CTest class shows that the constructor of the CSuper class is called first, and then the constructor of the CSub class. In fact, the constructor of the Object class is called before the constructor of the CSuper class. You cannot print the fact the constructor of the Object class is called because the Object class is not your class, and therefore you cannot modify it. The question is, "How does the constructor of the CSuper class get called?" The answer to this question is based on the rule that when an object of a class is created, memory is allocated for all instance variables including instance variables in all its ancestor classes. Instance variables for all classes must be initialized by calling their constructors. The compiler helps you to enforce this rule to the most extent. The compiler injects the call to the immediate ancestor's no-args constructor as the first statement in every constructor you add to your class. The keyword super is used in many contexts. It also refers to the immediate ancestor of a class. If it is followed by parentheses, it refers to the constructor of the superclass. If superclass constructor accepts parameters, you can pass a list of parameters within parentheses similar to a method call. The following are examples of calling constructor of a superclass:

```
// Call no-args constructor of superclass
super();

// Call superclass constructor with a String argument
super("Hello");

// Call superclass constructor with two double arguments
super(10.5, 89.2);
```

You can call constructor of the superclass explicitly or let the compiler inject the call to the no-args constructor for you. When you compile the CSuper and CSub class, the compiler modifies their constructors' code, which looks as shown in Listing 16-21 and Listing 16-22.

Listing 16-21. Compiler Injection of a super() Call to Call the Immediate Ancestor's no-args Constructor

```
// CSuper.java
package com.jdojo.inheritance;

public class CSuper {
        public CSuper() {
                super();  // Injected by the compiler
                System.out.println("Inside CSuper() constructor.");
        }
}
```

Listing 16-22. Compiler Injection of a super() Call to Call the Immediate Ancestor's no-args Constructor

```
// CSub.java
package com.jdojo.inheritance;

public class CSub extends CSuper {
        public CSub() {
                super();  // Injected by the compiler
                System.out.println("Inside CSub() constructor.");
        }
}
```

■ **Tip** The keyword super refers to the immediate ancestor of a class. You can call superclass constructors using the super keyword only as the first statement inside a constructor.

You can also call the no-args constructor or any other constructors of the superclass explicitly as the first statement inside constructors of your class. The compiler injects the no-args constructor call only if you have not added one explicitly. Let's try to improve your Employee and Manager classes. Let's add a constructor to the Employee class that accepts the name of the employee as a parameter. You will call the new class Employee2, as shown in Listing 16-23.

Listing 16-23. Employee2 Class, Which Is a Modified Version of the Original Employee Class. It Has Added a Constructor That Accepts a String Argument

```java
// Employee2.java
package com.jdojo.inheritance;

public class Employee2 {
        private String name = "Unknown";

        public Employee2(String name) {
                this.name = name;
        }

        public void setName(String name) {
                this.name = name;
        }

        public String getName() {
                return name;
        }
}
```

Let's call your new Manager class Manager2, which inherits from the Employee2 class.

```java
// Manager2.java
package com.jdojo.inheritance;

// Won't compile
public class Manager2 extends Employee2 {
        // No code for now
}
```

The above code for the Manager2 class does not compile. It generates the following compiler error:

```
Error(4,23): constructor Employee2() not found in class com.jdojo.inheritance.Employee2
```

You have not added any constructor for the Manager2 class. Therefore, the compiler will add a no-args constructor for it. It will also try to inject a super()call as the first statement inside the no-args constructor, which will call the no-args constructor of the Employee2 class. However, the Employee2 class does not have a no-args constructor. This is the reason that you get the above error. The code for the Manager2 class looks as follows, after it is modified by the compiler. You may notice that that the super() call is invalid, because the Employee2 class does not have a no-args constructor.

```java
// Code for Manager2 class after compiler injects a no-args constructor with a call to super()
package com.jdojo.inheritance;

// Won't compile
public class Manager2 extends Employee2 {
        // Injected by the compiler
        public Manager2() {
                super();  // Calls the nonexistent no-args constructor of Employee2 class
        }
}
```

So, how do you fix the Manager2 class? There are many ways to fix it. Some of the ways you can fix the Manager2 class are as follows.

You can add a no-args constructor to the Employee2 class, like so:

```
public class Employee2 {
        // A no-args constructor
        public Employee2() {
        }
        /* All other code for class remains the same */
}
```

After adding a no-args constructor to the Employee2 class, the code for the Manager2 class will compile fine.

You can add a no-args constructor to the Manager2 class and explicitly call the constructor of the Employee2 class with a String argument as

```
public class Manager2 extends Employee2 {
        public Manager2() {
                // Call constructor of Employee2 class explicitly
                super("Unknown");
        }
}
```

You can add a constructor to the Manager2 class, which takes a String argument and pass the argument value to the Employee2 class constructor. This way, you can create a Manager by passing the name of the Manager as a parameter to its constructor.

```
public class Manager2 extends Employee2 {
        public Manager2(String name) {
                // Call constructor of Employee2 class explicitly
                super(name);
        }
}
```

Normally, the third option is used where you would provide a way to create an object of the Manager2 class with manager's name. Note that Manager2 class does not have access to the name instance variable of the Employee2 class. Still, you can initialize the name instance variable in the Employee2 class from the Manager2 class using the super keyword and invoking the constructor of the Employee2 class. Listing 16-24 has the complete code for the Manager2 class that will compile. Listing 16-25 has code to test the Manager2 class and its output shows that it works as expected.

Listing 16-24. A Manager2 Class That Has a Constructor That Accepts a String Argument. It Calls the Constructor of the Employee2 Class Explicitly

```
// Manager2.java
package com.jdojo.inheritance;

public class Manager2 extends Employee2 {
        public Manager2(String name) {
                super(name);
        }
}
```

Listing 16-25. A Test Class to Test the Manager2 Class

```java
// Manager2Test.java
package com.jdojo.inheritance;

public class Manager2Test {
        public static void main(String[] args) {
                Manager2 mgr = new Manager2("John Jacobs");
                String name = mgr.getName();
                System.out.println("Manager name: " + name);
        }
}
```

Manager name: John Jacobs

■ **Tip** Every class must call the constructor of its superclass from its constructors directly or indirectly. If the superclass does not have a no-args constructor, you must call any other constructors of the superclass explicitly as we have done in Listing 16-24.

I need to discuss a few more rules about using the constructors of the superclass from the subclass. Let's consider the following definition of classes X and Y, which are in two different packages:

```java
// X.java
package com.jdojo.inheritance.pkg1;

public class X {
        // X() has package-level access
        X() {
        }
}
```

```java
// Y.java
package com.jdojo.inheritance.pkg2;

import com.jdojo.inheritance.pkg1.X;

public class Y extends X {
        public Y() {
        }
}
```

The code for class Y would not compile. It generates a compiler error as follows:

```
Error(7):  X() is not public in com.jdojo.inheritance.pkg1.X; cannot be accessed from outside
package
```

The error states that the no-args constructor in class X has a package-level access. Therefore, it cannot be accessed from class Y, which is in a different package. You received this error because the compiler will modify class Y definition as follows:

```java
// Compiler modified version of class Y
// Y.java
package com.jdojo.inheritance.pkg2;

import com.jdojo.inheritance.pkg1.X;

public class Y extends X {
        public Y() {
                super(); // Injected by the compiler to call X() constructor
        }
}
```

The no-args constructor of class X has a package-level access. Therefore, it can only be accessed from com.jdojo.inheritance.pkg1 package. How do you fix class Y? It is tricky to suggest a solution in such a case. The solution depends on the design that is used behind the creation of class X and class Y. However, for the class Y to compile, you must create a constructor for the class X, which has a public or protected access, so it can be accessed from class Y.

Here is another rule for using constructors along with inheritance. The superclass constructor must be called explicitly or implicitly from inside the constructor of a class using the super keyword. However, the access to a superclass constructor from a class is controlled by the access level of the constructor of the superclass. Sometimes, consequences of the access level of the constructors of a class could be that it cannot be accessed at all. Consider the following definition of the class called NoSubclassingAllowed:

```java
public class NoSubclassingAllowed {
        private NoSubclassingAllowed() {
        }
        // Other code goes here
}
```

NoSubclassingAllowed has explicitly declared a private constructor. A private constructor cannot be accessed from anywhere including subclasses. For a subclass to exist, it must be able to call at least one of the constructors of its superclass. This concludes that the NoSubclassingAllowed class cannot be inherited by any other classes. This is one of the ways to disable inheritance for a class. The following code will not compile, which tries to subclass the NoSubclassingAllowed class, which has no accessible constructors:

```java
// Won't compile.
public class LetUsTryInVain extends NoSubclassingAllowed {
}
```

One thing you may notice is that no one can create an object of the NoSubclassingAllowed class because its constructor is not accessible from outside. Classes like this one provide methods that create its object and return it to the caller. This is also a way to control and encapsulate object creation of a class.

Recall from Chapter 6 that you can call a constructor of a class from another constructor of the same class using the this keyword and this call must be the first statement in the constructor's body. When you look at the rule to call another constructor of the same class and constructor of the superclass, you would find that both state that the call must be the first statement inside the body of the constructor. The result of these two rules is that from one constructor either you can use this() to call another constructor of the same class or super() to call a constructor of the superclass, but not both. This rule also ensures that the constructor of the superclass is always called once and only once.

Method Hiding

A class also inherits all non-private static methods from its superclass. Redefining an inherited static method in a class is known as method hiding. The redefined static method in a subclass is said to hide the static method of its superclass. Recall that redefining a non-static method in a class is called method overriding. Listing 16-26 contains code for a MHidingSuper class, which has a `static print()` method. Listing 16-27 has the code for a MHidingSub class that inherits from the MHidingSuper class. It redefines the `print()` method, which hides the `print()` method in the MHidingSuper class. The `print()` method in MHidingSub is an example of method hiding.

Listing 16-26. A MHidingSuper Class That Has a Static Method

```java
// MHidingSuper.java
package com.jdojo.inheritance;

public class MHidingSuper {
        public static void print() {
                System.out.println("Inside MHidingSuper.print()");
        }
}
```

Listing 16-27. A MHidingSub Class That Hides the print() of its Superclass

```java
// MHidingSub.java
package com.jdojo.inheritance;

public class MHidingSub extends MHidingSuper {
        public static void print() {
                System.out.println("Inside MHidingSub.print()");
        }
}
```

All rules about the redefined method (name, access level, return types, and exception) for method hiding are the same as for method overriding. Please refer to the "Method Overriding" section for more detailed discussion on these rules. One rule that is different for method hiding is the binding rule. Early binding is used for `static` methods. Based on the compile-time type of the expression, the compiler determines what code will be executed at runtime for a `static` method call. Note that you can use the class name as well as a reference variable to invoke a `static` method. There is no ambiguity about method binding, when you use a class name to invoke a `static` method. The compiler binds the `static` method that is defined (or redefined) in the class. If a class does not define (or redefine) the `static` method, the compiler binds the method that the class inherits from its superclass. If the compiler does not find a defined/redefined/inherited method in the class, it generates an error. Listing 16-28 contains the code that demonstrates the early binding rules for method hiding for `static` methods of a class.

Listing 16-28. A Test Class to Demonstrate Method Hiding

```java
// MHidingTest.java
package com.jdojo.inheritance;

public class MHidingTest {
        public static void main(String[] args) {
                MHidingSuper mhSuper = new MHidingSub();
                MHidingSub mhSub = new MHidingSub();
```

```
                    System.out.println("#1");

                    // #1
                    MHidingSuper.print();
                    mhSuper.print();

                    System.out.println("#2");

                    // #2
                    MHidingSub.print();
                    mhSub.print();
                    ((MHidingSuper) mhSub).print();

                    System.out.println("#3");

                    // #3
                    mhSuper = mhSub;
                    mhSuper.print();
                    ((MHidingSub) mhSuper).print();
          }
}
```

```
#1
Inside MHidingSuper.print()
Inside MHidingSuper.print()
#2
Inside MHidingSub.print()
Inside MHidingSub.print()
Inside MHidingSuper.print()
#3
Inside MHidingSuper.print()
Inside MHidingSub.print()
```

The test code has three sections labeled #1, #2, and #3. Let's discuss how early binding is performed by the compiler in each section.

```
// #1
MHidingSuper.print();
mhSuper.print();
```

The first call, MHidingSuper.print(), is made using a class name. The compiler binds this call to execute the print() method of the MHidingSuper class. The second call, mhSuper.print(), is made using the reference variable mhSuper. The compile-time type (or declared type) of the mhSuper variable is MHidingSuper. Therefore, the compiler binds this call to execute the print() method of the MHidingSuper class.

```
// #2
MHidingSub.print();
mhSub.print();
((MHidingSuper)mhSub).print();
```

The first two calls in section #2 are similar to the two calls in section #1. They are bound to the print() method of the MHidingSub class. The third call, ((MHidingSuper)mhSub).print(), needs a little explanation. The compile-time type of the mhSub variable is MHidingSub. When you use a typecast (MHidingSuper) on the mhSub variable, the compile-time type of the expression (MHidingSuper)mhSub becomes MHidingSuper. When you call the print() method on this expression, the compiler binds it to its compile-time type, which is MHidingSuper. Therefore, the third method call in section #2 is bound to the print() method of the MHidingSuper class.

```
// #3
mhSuper = mhSub;
mhSuper.print();
((MHidingSub)mhSuper).print();
```

The first statement in section #3 assigns a reference of MHidingSub object to the mhSuper reference variable. After the first statement is executed, the mhSuper variable is referring to an object of the MHidingSub class. When the first call to the print() method is made, the compiler looks at the compile-time type (or declared type) of mhSuper variable, which is MHidingSuper. Therefore, the compiler binds the call mhSuper.print() to the print() method of the MHidingSuper class. The second call to the print() method is bound to the print() method of the MHidingSub class because the typecast (MHidingSub) makes the type of the entire expression as MHidingSub.

■ **Tip** A static method of a class cannot hide an instance method of its superclass. If you want to invoke a hidden method of the superclass from inside a class, you need to qualify the hidden method call with the superclass name. For example, if you want to call the print() method of the MHidingSuper class from inside the MHidingSub class, you need to use MHidingSuper.print(). Inside the MHidingSub class, the call to the print() method, without using the class name or a variable, refers to the hiding method print() of the MHidingSub class.

Field Hiding

A field declaration (static or non-static) in a class hides the inherited field with the same name in its superclass. The type of the field and its access level are not considered in the case of field hiding. Field hiding occurs solely based on the field name. Early binding is used for field access. That is, the compiler-time type of the class is used to bind the field access. Consider the following declaration of two classes G and H:

```
public class G {
        protected int x = 200;
        protected String y = "Hello";
        protected double z = 10.5;
}

public class H extends G {
        protected int x = 400;        // Hides x in class G
        protected String y = "Bye";   // Hides y in class G
        protected String z = "OK";    // Hides z in class G
}
```

The field declarations x, y, and z in class H hide the inherited fields x, y, and z in class G. It is to be emphasized that the same field name in a class alone hides a field of its superclass. Data types of the hidden and the hiding fields are immaterial. For example, the data type of z in class G is double, whereas data type of z in class H is String. Still, the field z in class H hides the field z in class G. The simple names of fields x, y, and z in class H refer to the hiding fields, not inherited fields. Therefore, if you use the simple name x in class H, it refers to the field x declared in class H, not in class G. If you want to refer to the field x in class G from inside class H, you need to use the keyword super, for example, super.x.

In Listing 16-29, the FHidingSuper class declares fields num and name. In Listing 16-30, the FHidingSub class inherits from the FHidingSuper class and it inherits the num and name fields from it. The print() method of the FHidingSub class prints the values of the num and name fields. The print() method uses simple names of num and name fields and they refer to the inherited fields from the FHidingSuper class. When you run the FHidingTest class in Listing 16-31, the output shows that the FHidingSub class really inherits num and name fields from its superclass.

Listing 16-29. FHidingSuper Class with Two Protected Instance Fields

```java
// FHidingSuper.java
package com.jdojo.inheritance;

public class FHidingSuper {
        protected int num = 100;
        protected String name = "John Jacobs";
}
```

Listing 16-30. FHidingSub Class, Which Inherits from the FHidingSuper Class and Inherits Fields num and name

```java
// FHidingSub.java
package com.jdojo.inheritance;

public class FHidingSub extends FHidingSuper {
        public void print() {
                System.out.println("num: " + num);
                System.out.println("name: " + name);
        }
}
```

Listing 16-31. A Test Class to Demonstrate field's Inheritances

```java
// FHidingTest.java
package com.jdojo.inheritance;

public class FHidingTest {
        public static void main(String[] args) {
                FHidingSub fhSub = new FHidingSub();
                fhSub.print();
        }
}
```

```
num: 100
name: John Jacobs
```

Let's consider the definition of class FHidingSub2 listed in Listing 16-32.

Listing 16-32. A FHidingSub2 Class That Inherits from FHidingSuper and Declares Two Variables with the Same Name as Declared in Its Superclass

```java
// FHidingSub2.java
package com.jdojo.inheritance;

public class FHidingSub2 extends FHidingSuper {
        // Hides num field in FHidingSuper class
        private int num = 200;

        // Hides name field in FHidingSuper class
        private String name = "Wally Inman";

        public void print() {
                System.out.println("num: " + num);
                System.out.println("name: " + name);
        }
}
```

The FHidingSub2 class inherits from the FHidingSuper class. It declares two fields num and name, which have the same names as the two fields declared in its superclass. This is a case of field hiding. The num and name fields in FHidingSub2 hide the num and name fields that are inherited from the FHidingSuper class. When the num and name fields are used by their simple names inside the FHidingSub2 class, they refer to the fields declared in the FHidingSub2 class, not to the inherited fields from the FHidingSuper class. This is verified by running the FHidingTest2 class as listed in Listing 16-33.

Listing 16-33. A Test Class to Demonstrate Field Hiding

```java
// FHidingTest2.java
package com.jdojo.inheritance;

public class FHidingTest2 {
        public static void main(String[] args) {
                FHidingSub2 fhSub2 = new FHidingSub2();
                fhSub2.print();
        }
}
```

```
num: 200
name: Wally Inman
```

The FHidingSub2 class has four fields, two inherited (num and name) and two declared (num and name). If you want to refer to the inherited fields from the superclass, you need to qualify the field names with the keyword super. For example, super.num and super.name inside FHidingSub2 refers to the num and name fields in FHidingSuper class.

The print() method of the FHidingSub3 class in Listing 16-34 uses the keyword super to access hidden fields of the superclass and uses the simple names of the fields to access fields from its own class. The output of Listing 16-35 verifies this.

Listing 16-34. A FHidingSub3 Class That Demonstrates How to Access Hidden Fields of Superclass Using the super Keyword

```java
// FHidingSub3.java
package com.jdojo.inheritance;

public class FHidingSub3 extends FHidingSuper {
        // Hides the num field in FHidingSuper class
        private int num = 200;

        // Hides the name field in FHidingSuper class
        private String name = "Wally Inman";

        public void print() {
                // FHidingSub3.num
                System.out.println("num: " + num);

                // FHidingSuper.num
                System.out.println("super.num: " + super.num);

                // FHidingSub3.name
                System.out.println("name: " + name);

                // FHidingSuper.name
                System.out.println("super.name: " + super.name);
        }
}
```

Listing 16-35. A Test Class That Accesses Hidden Fields

```java
// FHidingTest3.java
package com.jdojo.inheritance;

public class FHidingTest3 {
        public static void main(String[] args) {
                FHidingSub3 fhSub3 = new FHidingSub3();
                fhSub3.print();
        }
}
```

```
num: 200
super.num: 100
name: Wally Inman
super.name: John Jacobs
```

Recall that when an object is created, the Java runtime allocates memory for all instance variables in the class of the object and all of its ancestors. When you create an object of the FHidingSub2 or FHidingSub3.class, memory will be allocated for the four instance variables as shown in Figure 16-4.

627

Figure 16-4. *Memory layout for objects of FHidingSuper and FHidingSub2 classes*

Let's summarize the field hiding rules:

- Field hiding occurs when a class declares a variable with the same name as an inherited variable from its superclass.

- Field hiding occurs only based on the name of the field. Access level, data type, and the type of field (static or non-static) are not considered for field hiding. For example, a static field can hide an instance field. A field of int type can hide a field of String type, etc. A private field in a class can hide a protected field in its superclass. A public field in a class can hide a protected field in its superclass.

- A class should use the keyword super to access the hidden fields of the superclass. The class can use the simple names to access the redefined fields in its body.

Disabling Inheritance

You can disable subclassing for a class by declaring the class final. You have seen the use of the final keyword before for declaring constants. The same final keyword is used in a class declaration. A final class cannot be subclassed. The following snippet of code declares a final class named Security:

```
public final class Security {
        // Code goes here
}
```

The following declaration of class CrackedSecurity will not compile:

```
// Won't compile. Cannot inherit from Security
public final class CrackedSecurity extends Security {
        // Code goes here
}
```

You can also declare a method as final. A final method cannot be overridden or hidden by a subclass. Since a final method cannot be overridden or hidden, a call to a final method may be inlined by a code optimizer for better performance.

```
public class A {
        public final void m1() {
                // Code goes here
        }

        public void m2() {
                // Code goes here
        }
}

public class B extends A {
        // Cannot override A.m1() here because it is final in class A

        // OK to override m2() because it is not final in class A
        public void m2() {
                // Code goes here
        }
}
```

You will find many classes and methods in the Java class libraries that are declared final. Most notably, the String class is final. Why would you declare a class or a method as final? In other words, why would you want to prevent subclassing of a class or overriding/hiding of a method? The main reasons for doing this are security, correctness, and performance. If your class is important for security reasons, you do not want someone to inherit from your class and mess with the security that your class is supposed to implement. Sometimes, you declare a class/method final to preserve the correctness of the program. A final method may result in better performance at runtime because a code optimizer is free to inline the final method calls.

Abstract Classes and Methods

Sometimes you may create a class just to represent a concept rather than to represent objects. Suppose you want to develop classes to represent different shapes. A shape is just an idea or a concept. It does not exist in reality. Suppose someone asks you to draw a shape. Your immediate response would be, "What shape do you want me to draw?" If someone asks you to draw a circle or a rectangle, it makes sense to you. Java lets you create a class whose objects cannot be created. Its purpose is just to represent an idea, which is common to objects of other classes. Such a class is called an abstract class. The term "concrete class" is used to denote a class that is not abstract and whose objects can be created. So far, all your classes have been concrete classes.

You need to use the abstract keyword in the class declaration to declare an abstract class. For example, the following code declares a Shape class abstract:

```
public abstract class Shape {
        // No code for now
}
```

Because the Shape class has been declared abstract, you cannot create its object even though it has a public constructor (the default one added by the compiler). You can declare a variable of an abstract class as you do for a concrete class. The following code snippet shows some valid and invalid uses of Shape class:

```
Shape s;     // OK
new Shape(); // An error. Cannot create a Shape object
```

If you look at the definition of the Shape class, it looks the same as any other concrete classes, except the use of the abstract keyword in the declaration. A class has instance variables and instance methods to define the state and behavior of its objects. By declaring a class abstract, you indicate that the class has some incomplete method definitions (behaviors) for its objects and it must be considered incomplete for object creation purposes.

What is an incomplete method in a class? A method which has a declaration, but no body, is an incomplete method. Missing body of a method does not mean an empty body. It means no body. The braces that follow the method's declaration indicate the body of the method. In the case of an incomplete method, the braces are replaced with a semicolon. If a method is incomplete, you must indicate it by using the abstract keyword in the method's declaration. Your Shape class does not know how to draw a shape until you mention a specific shape. However, one thing is sure that you should be able to draw a shape no matter what kind of shape it is. In this case, you know the behavior name (draw), but you do not know how to implement it. Therefore, draw is a good candidate to be declared as an abstract method (or incomplete method) in the Shape class. The Shape class looks as follows with an abstract draw() method:

```java
public abstract class Shape {
        public Shape() {
        }

        public abstract void draw();
}
```

When you declare a class abstract, it does not necessarily mean that it has at least one abstract method. An abstract class may have all concrete methods. It may have all abstract methods. It may have some concrete and some abstract methods. If you have an abstract class, it means that an object of that class cannot exist. However, if a class has an abstract method (either declared or inherited), it must be declared abstract. Declaring a class as abstract is like placing an "under construction" sign in front of a building. If an "under construction" sign is placed in front of a building, it is not supposed to be used (not supposed to be created in case of a class). It does not matter whether the building is complete or not. An "under construction" sign is enough to indicate that it cannot be used. However, if some parts of the building are incomplete (like a class having abstract methods), you must place an "under construction" sign in front of it (must declare the class abstract) to avoid any mishap, in case someone attempts to use it.

■ **Tip** You cannot create objects of an abstract class. If a class has an abstract method, declared or inherited, the class must be declared abstract. If a class does not have any abstract methods, you can still declare the class abstract. An abstract method is declared the same way as any other methods, except that its body is indicated by a semicolon.

Listing 16-36 has the complete code for your Shape class.

Listing 16-36. An Abstract Shape Class with One Instance Variable, Two Constructors, and One Abstract Method

```java
// Shape.java
package com.jdojo.inheritance;

public abstract class Shape {
        private String name;

        public Shape() {
                this.name = "Unknown shape";
        }
```

```java
    public Shape(String name) {
            this.name = name;
    }

    public String getName() {
            return this.name;
    }

    public void setName(String name) {
            this.name = name;
    }

    // Abstract methods
    public abstract void draw();
    public abstract double getArea();
    public abstract double getPerimeter();
}
```

Each shape will have a name. The name instance variable stores the name of the shape. The getName() and setName() methods let you read and change the name of the shape, respectively. Two constructors let you set the name of the shape or leave the name as the default name "Unknown shape". A shape does not know how to draw, so it has declared its draw() method abstract. A shape also does not know how to compute its area and perimeter, so it has declared getArea() and getPerimeter() methods abstract.

An abstract class guarantees the use of inheritance, at least theoretically. Otherwise, an abstract class by itself is useless. For example, until someone supplies the implementations for the abstract methods of the Shape class, its other parts (instance variables, concrete methods, and constructors) are of no use. You create subclasses of an abstract class, which override the abstract methods providing implementations for them.

Listing 16-37 has code for a Rectangle class, which inherits from the Shape class.

Listing 16-37. A Rectangle Class, Which Inherits from the Shape Class

```java
// Rectangle.java
package com.jdojo.inheritance;

public class Rectangle extends Shape {
        private double width;
        private double height;

        public Rectangle(double width, double height) {
                // Set the shape name as "Rectangle"
                super("Rectangle");
                this.width = width;
                this.height = height;
        }

        // Provide an implementation for inherited abstract draw() method
        public void draw() {
                System.out.println("Drawing a rectangle...");
        }
```

```
        // Provide an implementation for inherited abstract getArea() method
        public double getArea() {
                return width * height;
        }


        // Provide an implementation for inherited abstract getPerimeter() method
        public double getPerimeter() {
                return 2.0 * (width + height);
        }
}
```

Note that you have not declared the Rectangle class abstract, which means that it is a concrete class and its objects can be created. An abstract method is also inherited by a subclass like any other methods. Since the Rectangle class is not declared abstract, it must override all three abstract methods of its superclass and provide implementations for them. If the Rectangle class does not override all abstract methods of its superclass and provides implementation for them, it is considered incomplete and must be declared abstract. Your Rectangle class overrides the draw(), getArea(), and getPerimeter() methods of the Shape class and provides implementation (body within braces) for them. The instance variables width and height are used to keep track of width and height of the rectangle. Inside the constructor, you call the constructor of the Shape class using super keyword, super("Rectangle"), to set its name. Listing 16-38 has code for a Circle class, which inherits from the Shape class. It also overrides three abstract methods of the Shape class and provides implementations for them.

Listing 16-38. A Circle Class, Which Inherits from Shape Class

```
// Circle.java
package com.jdojo.inheritance;

public class Circle extends Shape {
        private double radius;

        public Circle(double radius) {
                super("Circle");
                this.radius = radius;
        }

        // Provide an implementation for inherited abstract draw() method
        public void draw() {
                System.out.println("Drawing a circle...");
        }

        // Provide an implementation for inherited abstract getArea() method
        public double getArea() {
                return Math.PI * radius * radius;
        }

        // Provide an implementation for inherited abstract getPerimeter() method
        public double getPerimeter() {
                return 2.0 * Math.PI * radius;
        }
}
```

It is time to use your abstract Shape class along with its concrete subclasses Rectangle and Circle. Note that the only restriction that is applied to an abstract class, when it is used in code, is that you cannot create its objects. Apart from this restriction, you can use it the same way you can use a concrete class. For example, you can declare a variable of an abstract class type; you can call methods of the abstract class using that variable, etc. How do you call a method on a Shape variable, if you cannot create an object of the Shape class? This is a good point. Let's consider the following snippet of code:

```
// Upcasting at work
Shape s = new Rectangle(2.0, 5.0);

// Late binding at work. s.getArea() will call the getArea() method of
// the Rectangle class.
double area = s.getArea();
```

If you look at the above code, it makes sense. The first statement creates a Rectangle and assigns its reference to a variable of the Shape class, which is a simple case of upcasting. In the second statement, you are calling the getArea() method using the s variable. The compiler only verifies the existence of the getArea() method in the Shape class, which is the declared type of the s variables. The compiler does not care whether the getArea() method in the Shape class is incomplete (abstract) or not. It does not care if the getArea() method is abstract in the Shape class because it is an instance method and it knows that late binding at runtime will decide which code for the getArea() method will be executed. All it cares about is the existence of a method declaration of the getArea() method. At runtime, the late binding process finds that the variable s is referring to a Rectangle and it calls the getArea() method of the Rectangle class. Is it not like having one's cake and eating it too. Have an abstract class (incomplete class) and use it too? If you look at the above two lines of code, you would find that these magical two statements involve so many concepts of object-oriented programming: abstract class, abstract method, upcasting, method overriding, late binding, and runtime polymorphism. All of these features are involved in the above two statements to giving you the ability to write generic and polymorphic code.

Consider a ShapeUtil class as shown in Listing 16-39.

Listing 16-39. A ShapeUtil Class That Has Utility Methods to Draw Any Shapes and Print Details About Them

```
// ShapeUtil.java
package com.jdojo.inheritance;

public class ShapeUtil {
        public static void drawShapes(Shape[] list) {
                for (int i = 0; i < list.length; i++) {
                        // Draw a shape, no matter what it is
                        list[i].draw(); // Late binding
                }
        }

        public static void printShapeDetails(Shape[] list) {
                for (int i = 0; i < list.length; i++) {
                        // Gather details about the shape
                        String name = list[i].getName(); // Late Binding
                        double area = list[i].getArea(); // Late binding
                        double perimeter = list[i].getPerimeter(); // Late binding
```

```
                        // Print details
                        System.out.println("Name: " + name);
                        System.out.println("Area: " + area);
                        System.out.println("Perimeter: " + perimeter);
                }
        }
}
```

The ShapeUtil class contains two static methods: drawShapes() and printShapeDetails(). Both accept an array of Shape objects as a parameter. The drawShapes() method draws all the shapes by calling the draw() method of each element in the array passed to it. The printShapeDetails() method prints details, name, area, and perimeter of the shapes passed to it. The beauty of the code in the ShapeUtil class is that it never refers to any subclasses of the Shape class. It has no knowledge about the Rectangle or Circle class at all. It does not even care if a Rectangle class or a Circle class exists, although the code will work with Rectangles, Circles, and objects of any descendants of the Shape class. You may argue that you could have written the same code even if you did not declare the Shape class as abstract. So, what is the big deal about declaring the Shape class as abstract? You are getting two advantages by declaring the Shape class as abstract:

- If you did not declare the Shape class abstract, you were forced to provide implementations for the three abstract methods in the class. Since the Shape class does not know what shape object it will take the form of, it is not appropriate for it to provide implementations for these methods. For now, let's assume that you can handle this issue by providing an empty body for the draw() method and returning zero (or maybe a negative number) from the getArea() and getPerimeter() methods in the Shape class. Let's move to the next advantage, which is more compelling.

- You are forced to declare the Shape class as abstract because you had declared three abstract methods in it. The greatest advantage of declaring an abstract method in a class is to force its subclasses to override and provide implementation for it. The abstract methods in the Shape class forced the Rectangle and Circle subclasses to override them and provide implementations for them. Was it not what you wanted?

Listing 16-40 has code that tests the ShapeUtil class along with the Shape, Rectangle, and Circle classes. It creates an array of Shape objects. It populates one element of the array with a Rectangle and another with a Circle. It passes the array to the drawShapes() and printShapeDetails() methods of the ShapeUtil class, which draws the shapes and prints their details according to the type of objects placed in the array.

Listing 16-40. A Test Class to Test Shape, Rectangle, Circle, and the ShapeUtil Class

```
// ShapeUtilTest
package com.jdojo.inheritance;

public class ShapeUtilTest {
        public static void main(String[] args) {
                // Create some shapes, draw, and print their details
                Shape[] shapeList = new Shape[2];
                shapeList[0] = new Rectangle(2.0, 4.0);  // Upcasting
                shapeList[1] = new Circle(5.0);          // Upcasting

                // Draw all shapes
                ShapeUtil.drawShapes(shapeList);

                // Print details of all shapes
                ShapeUtil.printShapeDetails(shapeList);
        }
}
```

```
Drawing a rectangle...
Drawing a circle...
Name: Rectangle
Area: 8.0
Perimeter: 12.0
Name: Circle
Area: 78.53981633974483
Perimeter: 31.41592653589793
```

You have finished discussing the main rules of declaring classes and methods abstract. However, there are many other rules that govern the use of abstract classes and methods in a Java program. Most of those rules (if not all) are listed below. All rules point to only one basic rule: "Abstract class should be subclassed to be useful and the subclass should override and provide implementation for the abstract methods."

- A class may be declared abstract even if it does not have an abstract method.

- A class must be declared abstract if it declares or inherits an abstract method. If the class overrides and provides implementations for all inherited abstract methods and does not declare any abstract methods, it does not have to be declared abstract. Although it could be declared abstract.

- You cannot create an object of an abstract class. However, you can declare a variable of the abstract class type and call methods using it.

- An abstract class cannot be declared final. Recall that a final class cannot be subclassed, which conflicts with the requirement of an abstract class that it must be subclassed to be useful in a true sense.

- An abstract class should not declare all constructors private. Otherwise, the abstract class cannot be subclassed. Note that constructors of all ancestor classes (including an abstract class) are always invoked when an object of a class is created. When you create an object of a Rectangle class, constructors for the Object class and the Shape class are also invoked. If you declare all constructors of an abstract class private, you cannot create a subclass for your abstract class, which makes it the same as declaring an abstract final class.

- An abstract method cannot be declared static. Note that an abstract method must be overridden and implemented by a subclass. A static method cannot be overridden. However, it can be hidden.

- An abstract method cannot be declared private. Recall that a private method is not inherited and hence it cannot be overridden. The requirement for an abstract method is that a subclass must be able to override and provide implementation for it.

An abstract method cannot be declared native, strictfp, or synchronized. These keywords refer to implementation details of a method. The native keyword denotes that a method is implemented in native code as opposed to Java code. The strictfp keyword denotes that the code inside a method uses FP-strict rules for floating-point computations. Please refer to http://en.wikipedia.org/wiki/Strictfp for more details on the strictfp keyword and its usage. The synchronized keyword denotes that the object on which the method is invoked must be locked by the thread before it can execute method's code. Since an abstract method does not have an implementation, the keywords that imply an implementation cannot be used for an abstract method.

- An abstract method in a class can override an `abstract` method in its superclass without providing an implementation. The subclass `abstract` method may refine the return type or exception list of the overridden `abstract` method. Let's consider the following code. Class B overrides the `abstract` `m1()` method of class A and it does not provide its implementation. It only removes one exception from the throws clause. Class C overrides the `m1()` method of class B and provides implementation for it. Note that the change in return type or exception list as shown in `m1()` method for class B and class C must follow the rules of method overriding.

```
public abstract class A {
        public abstract void m1() throws CE1, CE2;
}

public abstract class B extends A {
        public abstract void m1() throws CE1;
}

public class C extends B {
        public void m1() {
                // Code goes here
        }
}
```

- A concrete instance method may be overridden by an `abstract` instance method. This can be done to force the subclasses to provide implementation for that method. All classes in Java inherit `equals()`, `hashCode()`, and `toString()` methods of the `Object` class. Suppose you have a class CA and you want all its subclasses to override and provide implementation for the `equals()`, `hashCode()`, and `toString()` methods of the `Object` class. You need to override these three methods in class CA and declare them `abstract`, like so:

```
public abstract class CA {
        public abstract int hashCode();
        public abstract boolean equals(Object obj);
        public abstract String toString();
            // Other code goes here
}
```

- In this case, concrete methods of the `Object` class have been overridden by `abstract` methods in the CA class. All concrete subclasses of CA are forced to override and provide implementations for the `equals()`, `hashCode()`, and `toString()` methods.

Method Overriding and Generic Method Signatures

Java 5 introduced the concept of generic types. If you are using a version of Java prior to Java 5, this section does not apply. Java 5 lets you declare generic methods. When Java code with generics types is compiled, the generic types are transformed into raw types. The process that is used to transform the generic type parameters information is known as type erasure. Let's consider the GenericSuper class in Listing 16-41. It has a generic type parameter T. It has two methods, `m1()` and `m2()`. Its `m1()` method uses the generic type T as its parameter type. Its `m2()` method defines a new generic type to use it as its parameter type.

Listing 16-41. A Sample Class That Uses Generic Type Parameters

```java
// GenericSuper.java
package com.jdojo.inheritance;

public class GenericSuper<T> {
        public void m1(T a) {
                // Code goes here
        }

        public <P extends Employee> void m2(P a) {
                // Code goes here
        }
}
```

When the GenericSuper class is compiled, the erasure transforms the code during compilation and the resulting code looks as shown in Listing 16-42.

Listing 16-42. The GenericSuper Class Transformed Code During Compilation After Erasure Is Used

```java
// GenericSuper.java
package com.jdojo.inheritance;

public class GenericSuper {
        public void m1(Object a) {
                // Code goes here
        }

        public void m2(Employee a) {
                // Code goes here
        }
}
```

The GenericSub class in Listing 16-43 inherits the GenericSuper class.

Listing 16-43. A GenericSub Class Inherits from the GenericSuper Class and Overrides m1() and m2() Methods

```java
// GenericSub.java
package com.jdojo.inheritance;

public class GenericSub extends GenericSuper {
        public void m1(Object a) {
                // Code goes here
        }

        public void m2(Employee a) {
                // Code goes here
        }
}
```

637

In the GenericSub class, the m1() and m2() methods override the corresponding methods in the GenericSuper class. If you compare the methods m1() and m2() between Listing 16-41 and Listing 16-43 for overriding rules, you would think that they do not have the same signature because the code in Listing 16-41 uses generics. The rules for checking for override equivalent method signature is that if a method uses generic parameters, you need to compare its erasure, not the generic version of its declaration. When you compare erasure of m1() and m2() method's declaration in the GenericSuper class (in Listing 16-42) with m1() and m2() methods declarations in Listing 16-43, you would find that m1() and m2() methods are overridden in the GenericSub class.

Typo Danger in Method Overriding

Sometimes it is easy to get it wrong when you try to override a method in a class. It may seem that you have overridden a method when it is not overridden. Let's consider the following two classes, C1 and C2:

```java
// C1.java
package com.jdojo.inheritance;

public class C1 {
        public void m1(double num) {
                System.out.println("Inside C1.m1(): " + num);
        }
}

// C2.java
package com.jdojo.inheritance;

public class C2 extends C1 {
        public void m1(int num) {
                System.out.println("Inside C2.m1(): " + num);
        }
}
```

The intent was that the m1() method in class C2 overrides the m1() method of class C1. However, this is not true. It is a case of method overloading, not method overriding. The m1() method in C2 is overloaded; m1(double num) is inherited from class C1 and m1(int num) is declared in C2. Things becomes more difficult when you start running your program and you do not get the desired results. Consider the following code snippet;

```java
C1 c = new C2();
c.m1(10);  // Which method is called - C1.m() or C2.m2()?
```

What should be printed when you execute the above code? It prints the following:

```
Inside C1.m1(): 10.0
```

Are you surprised to see the output of the above snippet of code? Let's discuss in detail what happens when the above snippet of code is compiled and executed. When the compiler comes across the second statement, c.m1(10), it does the following thing: it finds out the compile-time type of the reference variable c, which is C1.

It looks for a method named m1 in C1. The argument value 10 passed to the method m1() is an int. The compiler looks for a method named m1 (inherited or declared) in C1, which takes an int parameter. It finds that class C1 has a method m1(double num), which accepts a double parameter. It tries type-widening conversion and finds that m1(double num) method in class C1 can be used for c.m1(10) method call. At this time, the compiler binds the method signature for the call. Note that the compiler binds the method signature, not the method code. The method code is bound at runtime because m1() is an instance method. The compiler does not decide which m1() method's code will be executed for c.m1(10). Keep in mind that the compiler's decision is solely based on its knowledge about class C1. When c.m1(10) is compiled, the compiler does not know (or care) about the existence of any other class, for example, C2. You can see what code is generated for c.m1(10) method call by the Java compiler. You need to use the javap command line utility with a -c option to disassemble the compiled code as follows. You need to pass the fully qualified name of the class to the javap command.

```
javap -c your-fully-qualified-class-name
```

For the above code snippet that contains the c.m1(10) call, the javap will print instructions that are generated by the compiler. I have shown only one instruction:

```
12:  invokevirtual  #14; // Method com/jdojo/inheritance /C1.m1:(D)V
```

The invokevirtual instruction is used to denote a call to an instance method that will use late binding. The #14 (it may be different for you) indicates the method table entry number, which is the entry for the C1.m1(D)V method. The syntax is a little cryptic for you. The character D denotes double, which is the parameter type and V denotes void, which is the return type of the method m1().

At runtime, when the JVM attempts to run c.m1(10), it uses the late binding mechanism to find the method code that it will execute. Note that the JVM will search for m(D)V method signature, which is the compiler syntax for void m1(double). It starts the search by looking at the runtime type of c, which is class C2. Class C2 does not have a method named m1, which accepts a parameter of type double. The search moves up in the class hierarchy to class C1. The JVM finds the method in class C1 and it executed it. This is the reason that you got the output that indicates that m1(double num) in the class C1 is called for c.m1(10).

Such mistakes are very difficult to hunt down. Java 5 lets you avoid such mistakes by using the @Override annotation. Please refer to Chapter 1 on annotations in the book *Beginning Java Language Features* (ISBN 978-1-4302-6658-7) for more details. The annotation has compiler support. The compiler will make sure a method that is annotated with the @Override annotation really overrides a method in its superclass. Otherwise, it will generate an error. Using the @Override annotation is easy. Just add it to the method declaration anywhere before the method's return type. The following code for class C2 uses @Override annotation for the m1() method:

```
public class C2 extends C1 {
    @Override
    public void m1(int num) {
        System.out.println("Inside C2.m1(): " + num);
    }
}
```

When you compile the above code for class C2, the compiler will generate an error stating that the method m1() in class C2 does not override any method in its superclass. Using the @Override annotation with a method that is supposed to override a superclass method saves you a lot of debugging time. Note that the @Override annotation does not change the way method overriding works. It is used as an indicator to the compiler that it needs to make sure the method really overrides the method of its superclass.

Is-a, has-a, and part-of Relationships

A software application, which is designed based on object-oriented paradigm, consists of interacting objects. Objects of one class may be related to objects of another class in some ways. Is-a, has-a, and part-of are the three most commonly used relationships that exist between objects of two classes. I have already discussed that an is-a relationship is modeled using inheritance between two classes. For example, the relationship "A part-time manager *is-a* manager" is modeled by inheriting PartTimeManager class from the Manager class.

Sometimes an object of a class contains an object of another class, which indicates a whole-part relationship. This relationship is called aggregation. It is also known as has-a relationship. The example of has-a relationship is "A person has an address." As a whole-part relationship, the person represents the whole and the address represents the part. Java does not have any special feature that lets you indicate a has-a relationship in your code. In Java code, aggregation is implemented by using an instance variable in the whole, which is of the type part. In this example, the Person class will have an instance variable of type Address, as shown below. Note that an object of the Address class is created outside of a Person class and passed in to the Person class constructor.

```java
public class Address {
        // Code goes here
}

public class Person {
        // Person has-a Address
        private Address addr;

        public Person(Address addr) {
                this.addr = addr;
        }

        // Other code goes here
}
```

Composition is a special case of aggregation in which the whole controls the life cycle of the part. It is also known as part-of relationship. Sometimes, has-a and part-of relationships are used interchangeably. The main difference between aggregation and composition is that in composition the whole controls the creation/destruction of the part. In composition, the part cannot exist by itself. Rather, the part is created and destroyed as a part of the whole. Consider the relationship "A CPU is part-of a computer." You can also rephrase the relationship as "A computer has a CPU." Does the existence of a CPU outside a computer make sense? The answer is no. It is true that a computer and a CPU represent a whole-part relationship. However, there are some more constraints to this whole-part relationship and that is, "The existence of a CPU makes sense only inside a computer." You can implement composition in Java code by declaring an instance variable of a type part and creating the part object as part of creation of the whole as shown below. A CPU is created when a Computer is created. The CPU is destroyed when the computer is destroyed.

```java
public class CPU {
        // Code goes here
}

public class Computer {
        // CPU part-of Computer
        private CPU cpu = new CPU();

        // Other code goes here
}
```

Java has a special class type called inner class, which can also be used to represent composition. An object of an inner class can exist only within an object of its enclosing class. The enclosing class would be the whole and the inner class would be the part. You can represent the part-of relationship between CPU and computer using an inner class, as follows:

```
public class Computer {
        private CPU cpu = new CPU();

        // CPU is an inner class of Computer
        private class CPU {
                // Code goes here
        }

        // Other code goes here for Computer class
}
```

Compare this implementation of composition between a computer and a CPU with the previous one. When you use an inner class, an object of the CPU class cannot exist without an object of the Computer class. This restriction may be problematic when the object of the same class, say CPU, is part of another object in a composition relationship.

Composition also denotes owner-owned relationship. A computer is an owner and a CPU is owned by the computer. The owned object cannot exist without the owner object. Typically, but not necessarily, the owned object is destroyed when the owner object is destroyed. Sometimes, when the owner object is being destroyed, it passes the reference of the owned object to another owner. In such cases, the owned object survives the death of its current owner. The point to note is that the owned object always has an owner.

Sometimes programmers get confused between the choice of using inheritance and composition and they use inheritance instead of composition. You can find this kind of mistake in the Java class library where the java.util.Stack class is inherited from java.util.Vector class. A Vector is a list of objects. A Stack is also a list of objects, but is not simply a list of object as Vector is. A Stack is supposed to allow you to add an object to its top and remove an object from its top. However, a Vector allows you to add/remove an object at any position. Since the Stack class inherits from the Vector class, it also inherits methods that will let you add/remove an object at any position, which are simply wrong operations for a stack. The Stack class should have used composition to use a Vector object as its internal representation rather than inheriting from it. The following code snippet shows the correct use of a "has-a" relationship between the Stack and Vector classes:

```
public class Stack {
        // Stack has-a Vector
        private Vector items = new Vector();

        // Other code goes here
}
```

■ **Tip**   Whenever you are in doubt in choosing between composition and inheritance, give preference to composition. Both let you share the code. However, inheritance forces your class to be in a specific class hierarchy. Inheritance also creates a subtype, whereas composition is used to create a new type.

No Multiple Inheritance of Classes

Typically, a class signifies implementation. Java does not support multiple inheritance of implementation. That is, a class in Java cannot have more than one superclass. Inheritance lets a class inherit implementation and/or interface from its superclass. In the case of implementation inheritance, the superclass provides implementation for functionality that its subclass inherits and reuses. For example, the Employee class has implemented the getName() and setName() methods, which are inherited by the Manager class. In the case of interface inheritance, the superclass provides specification for functionality that its subclass inherits and implements. Note that declaring abstract methods in Java defines a specification whereas declaring a concrete (non-abstract) method defines an implementation. For example, the Shape class has specification for a draw() method, which is inherited by its subclasses (e.g. Rectangle and Circle). It does not provide any implementation for the draw() method. All concrete subclasses of the Shape class must provide implementation for its draw() method.

Multiple inheritance is defined as having a class inherit from more than one superclass. It poses some problems when a class inherits an implementation from multiple superclasses. Suppose there are two classes, Singer and Employee, and both provide implementation for processing salary (say pay() method). Further, suppose you inherit a class SingerEmployee, which inherits from the Singer and Employee classes. The new class, SingerEmployee, inherits the pay() method from two different superclasses, which have different implementations. When the pay() method is invoked on a SingerEmployee, which pay() method should be used—from the Employee class or from the Singer class? Multiple inheritance makes programmer's job as well as language designer's job complex. Java supports multiple inheritance of interfaces (or types), not implementations. It has a construct, called interface, which is different from a class. An interface can inherit from multiple interfaces. A class can implement multiple interfaces. Java's approach to support only multiple inheritance of types avoids problems for programmers as well as its designers. Multiple types inheritance is easier to understand and design than the multiple implementations inheritance.

Summary

Inheritance lets you define a class based on the definition on another class. Inheritance is one of the techniques to implement inclusion polymorphism. It promotes code reuse. It lets you write code in terms of a class that works for the class and all its subclasses. The subclass inherits members on its superclass based on some rules. Constructors are not members of a class and they are not inherited by subclasses.

The keyword extends is used to inherit a class from another class. If a class declaration does not contain the keyword extends, the class implicitly inherits from the Object class. Inheritance creates a tree-like class hierarchy—the Object class being at the top of all class hierarchy. The Object class itself does not have a superclass.

Java supports two types of binding: early binding and late binding. In early binding, the compiler determines the fields and methods that will be accessed, based on the compile-time type of the references accessing the fields and methods. Java uses early binding for accessing all types of fields and static methods. In late binding, the runtime type of the reference variable determines the method that is executed. Inheritance along with late binding makes it possible to use runtime polymorphism in Java. Java uses late binding for accessing instance methods.

A variable of a superclass can always be assigned a reference of its subclasses. This is called upcasting. When a variable of a subclass is type cast and assigned to a variable of the superclass, it is called downcasting. For a downcasting to succeed at runtime, the variable of the superclass must contain a reference of the subclass or the subclasses of the subclass. The instanceof operator is used to test whether a reference variable is an instance of a specific class.

You can declare abstract classes and methods. The keyword abstract is used to declare abstract classes and methods. Abstract classes cannot be instantiated. If a class contains an abstract method, the class must be declared abstract. A class can be declared abstract even if it contains no abstract methods. Abstract methods are supposed to be overridden and provided an implementation by subclasses.

A subclass may access the constructors, methods, and fields of its superclass using the keyword super. The call to access the constructor of the superclass must be the first statement in the constructor of the subclass.

Redefining the static methods of a superclass inside a subclass is called method hiding. A field with the same name as a field in the superclass hides the field in the superclass and it is called field hiding. The hidden methods may be accessed from the subclass using the superclass class name as the qualifier for the method. You can use the keyword super to access the hidden fields from the subclass.

Classes and methods may be declared final. A final class cannot be subclasses. A final method cannot be overridden. Declaring all constructors of a class private also stops subclassing for that class.

■■■■

CHAPTER 17

Interfaces

In this chapter, you will learn

- What interfaces are
- How to declare interfaces
- How to declare abstract, default, and static methods in interfaces
- How to fully and partially implement interfaces in a class
- How to evolve interfaces after they are published
- How to inherit an interface from other interfaces
- Using the instanceof operator with interfaces
- What marker interfaces are
- How interfaces can be used to implement polymorphism
- How dynamic binding applies to method calls on interface type variables

What Is an Interface?

The interface is a very important concept in Java programming. The knowledge of a Java developer is incomplete unless he understands the role of interfaces in Java programming. It is better understood by examples than by a formal definition. Let's discuss a simple example that will set the stage for the detailed discussion about the need for interfaces, before I provide its formal definition.

A Java application consists of interacting objects. An object interacts with other objects by sending messages. The ability of an object to receive messages is implemented by providing methods in the object's class. Suppose there is a class called Person, which provides a walk() method. The walk() method gives the ability to receive a "walk" message to every object of the Person class. Let's define the Person class as follows:

```
public class Person {
      private String name;

      public Person(String name) {
            this.name = name;
      }

      public void walk() {
            System.out.println(name + " (a person) is walking.");
      }
}
```

An object of the Person class will have a name that will be set in its constructor. When it receives a "walk" message, that is, when its walk() method is called, it prints a message in the standard output.

Let's create a utility class named Walkables, which is used to send a specific message to a collection of objects. Let's assume that you want to add a letThemWalk() static method to the Walkables class, which accepts an array of Person objects. It sends a "walk" message to all the elements in the array. You can define your Walkables class as follows. The method does what its name suggests; that is, it lets everyone walk!

```java
public class Walkables {
        public static void letThemWalk(Person[] list){
                for(Person person : list) {
                        person.walk();
                }
        }
}
```

The following snippet of code can be used to test the Person and Walkables classes:

```java
public class WalkablesTest {
        public static void main(String[] args) {
                Person[] persons = new Person[3];
                persons[0] = new Person("Jack");
                persons[1] = new Person("Jeff");
                persons[2] = new Person("John");

                // Let everyone walk
                Walkables.letThemWalk(persons);
        }
}
```

```
Jack (a person) is walking.
Jeff (a person) is walking.
John (a person) is walking.
```

So far, you don't see any problem with the design of the Person and Walkables classes, right? They perform the actions they were designed to perform. The design of the Person class guarantees that its objects will respond to a "walk" message. By declaring the Person array as the parameter type for the letThemWalk() method in the Walkables class, the compiler makes sure that the call to persons[i].walk() is valid, because a Person object is guaranteed to respond to the "walk" message.

Let's expand this project by adding a new class called Duck, which represents a duck in the real world. We all know that a duck can also walk. A duck can do many other things that a person can or cannot do. However, for the purpose of our discussion, we'll focus on only the walking ability of ducks. You can define your Duck class as follows:

```java
public class Duck {
        private String name;

        public Duck(String name) {
                this.name = name;
        }

        public void walk() {
                System.out.println(name + " (a duck) is walking.");
        }
}
```

You may notice that there is a similarity between the Person and Duck classes. An object of both classes can respond to a "walk" message as both of them provide a walk() method. However, the similarity between the two classes ends right there. They are not linked in any other ways at all, except for the fact that both of them have the Object class as their common ancestor. The introduction of the Duck class has expanded the walking ability of objects in your application. Before there were ducks, only people could walk. After you add the Duck class, ducks can walk as well.

Now, you want to let ducks walk using your Walkables class. Can your Walkables class let the ducks walk? No. It cannot let the ducks walk unless you make some changes. The ability of a Duck to walk does not pose any problem for the existing Walkables class. The problem at this point is that the letThemWalk() method has declared its parameter type as an array of Person. A Duck is not a Person. You cannot write code as shown below. A Duck object cannot be assigned to a reference variable of the type Person. The following snippet of code will not compile:

```
Person[] list = new Person[3];
persons[0] = new Person("Jack");
persons[1] = new Duck("Jeff"); // A compile-time error
persons[2] = new Person("John");
Walkables.letThemWalk(list);
```

How do you solve this problem so your Walkables class will let a person and a duck walk together? There are three ways to solve this problem with your existing knowledge of the Java programming language. Note that we are not talking about interfaces at this point. You will solve this problem efficiently and correctly using interfaces at the end of this section. Let's just forget about the title of this chapter for now, so you can appreciate the important role that an interface plays in the Java programming. The three ways to solve this problem can be listed as follows:

- Change the parameter type of the letThemWalk() method of the Walkables class from an array of Person to an array of Object. Use reflection to invoke the walk() method on all elements of the passed-in array. Do not worry about the term "reflection" at this point. This is covered in Chapter 3 book of *Beginning Java Language Features* (Apress, 2014).

- Define a new static method called letDucksWalk(Duck[] ducks) in the Walkables class. Call this method when you want ducks to walk.

- Inherit the Person and Duck classes from a common ancestor class, say Animal class, and add a walk() method in the Animal class. Change the parameter type of the letThemWalk() method of the Walkables class from an array of Person to an array of Animal.

Let's look at each of the three solutions in detail.

Proposed Solution #1

You can implement the first solution by adding the two methods to the Walkables class, as shown:

```
// Walkables.java
import java.lang.reflect.Method;

public class Walkables {
        public static void letThemWalk(Object[] list) {
                for (int i = 0; i < list.length; i++) {
                        // Get the walk method reference
                        Method walkMethod = getWalkMethod(list[i]);
```

```
                    if (walkMethod != null) {
                        try {
                                // Invoke the walk() method
                                walkMethod.invoke(list[i]);
                        }
                        catch (Exception e) {
                                e.printStackTrace();
                        }
                    }
                }
            }
        }

        public static Method getWalkMethod(Object obj) {
            Class c = obj.getClass();
            Method walkMethod = null;
            try {
                    walkMethod = c.getMethod("walk");
                    return walkMethod;
            }
            catch (NoSuchMethodException e) {
                    // walk() method does not exist
            }
            return null;
        }
}
```

The getWalkMethod() method looks for a walk() method in the specified object's class. If it finds a walk() method, it returns the reference of the found method. Otherwise, it returns null. You have changed the parameter type of the letThemWalk() method from an array of Person to an array of Object. You can use the following snippet of code to test the modified Walkables class:

```
Object[] objects = new Object[4];
objects[0] = new Person("Jack");
objects[1] = new Duck("Jeff");
objects[2] = new Person("John");
objects[3] = new Object(); // Does not have a walk() method

// Let everyone walk
Walkables.letThemWalk(objects);
```

```
Jack (a person) is walking.
Jeff (a duck) is walking.
John (a person) is walking.
```

The output shows that your solution works. It lets persons and ducks walk together. At the same time, it does not force an object to walk if that object does not know how to walk. You passed four objects to the letThemWalk() method and no attempt was made to invoke the walk() method on the fourth element of the array because the Object class does not have a walk() method.

Let's reject this solution for the very simple reason that you used reflection to invoke the walk() method on all objects passed in and you relied on the fact that all objects that know how to walk will have a method named "walk." This solution is easily and silently broken if you change the method name, say in the Person class, from walk() to walkMe(). Your program will keep working without any errors, but when you call the letThemWalk() method with a Person object, its changed walkMe() method will not be invoked.

Proposed Solution #2

Let's look at the second proposed solution. You propose to add a new method letDucksWalk() to your Walkables class, as shown:

```
public class Walkables {
        public static void letThemWalk(Person[] list) {
                for (Person person : list) {
                        person.walk();
                }
        }

        public static void letDucksWalk(Duck[] list) {
                for (Duck duck : list) {
                        duck.walk();
                }
        }
}
```

This solves the problem in the sense that it will let all ducks walk. However, it is not an ideal solution either. It still will not let persons and ducks walk together. Another problem with this solution is extensibility. It is not an extensible solution. If you look at the two methods, letThemWalk() and letDucksWalk(), you will find that except for the parameter types, Person and Duck, they have the same logic. What happens if you add a new class called Cat whose objects can walk too? This solution would force you to add another method, letCatsWalk(Cat[] cats), to the Walkables class. Therefore, you should reject this solution because it is not extensible.

Proposed Solution #3

Let's look at the third proposed solution. It proposes to inherit the Person class and the Duck class from a common ancestor class, say, Animal, which has a walk() method. It will also make you change the parameter of the letThemWalk() method in the Walkables class from a Person array to an Animal array. This solution is very close to the one you are looking for, and it may be considered a good solution in some situations. However, you reject this solution for the following two reasons:

- This solution forces you to have a common ancestor in your class hierarchy. For example, all classes whose objects know how to walk must have the same ancestor (direct or indirect). Suppose you create a new class called Dog whose object can walk. Under this proposed solution the Dog class must be inherited from the Animal class, so you can use the letThemWalk() method to let a Dog walk. Sometimes you want to add the walking ability to objects of a class, which is already inherited from another class. In such cases, it is not possible to change the superclass of the existing classes to the Animal class.

- Suppose you go forward with this solution. You add a new class called Fish, which inherits the Animal class. An object of the Fish class does not know how to walk. Because the Fish class is inherited from the Animal class, it will also inherit the walk() method, which is the ability to walk. Definitely, you will need to override the walk() method inside the Fish class. Now the question arises, how should the Fish class implement the walk() method? Should it respond by stating "I am a fish and I do not know how to walk."? Should it throw an exception stating "It is illegal to ask a fish to walk."?

You can see that the third solution seems to be a very close solution. However, it is not an ideal one. It also proves a point that inheritance is a good thing to use in Java programs, but it does not always provide an ideal solution.

An Ideal Solution

You are looking for a solution that should provide two things:

- A single method, letThemWalk(), in the Walkables class, should be able to send a "walk" message (that is, invoke the walk() method) on all objects that are passed to it as its parameter. This method should work with all types of objects that can walk (which you have now or you will have in future).

- If you want to add the ability to walk to objects of an existing class, you should not be forced to change the superclass of the class.

Interfaces in Java provide a perfect solution in this scenario. Before you start discussing interfaces in detail, let's complete the solution to the problem presented in this section. First, you need to define an interface. For now, just think of an interface as a programming contract.

An interface is declared using the keyword interface, which can have abstract method declarations. Note that an abstract method does not have a body. Each interface should be given a name. Your interface is named Walkable. It contains one method called walk(). The complete code for your Walkable interface is shown in Listing 17-1.

Listing 17-1. The Declaration for a Walkable Interface

```java
// Walkable.java
package com.jdojo.interfaces;

public interface Walkable {
        void walk();
}
```

All classes whose objects can walk should implement the Walkable interface. A class can implement one or more interfaces using the keyword implements in its declaration. By implementing an interface, a class guarantees that it will provide an implementation for all methods declared in the interface or the class will declare itself abstract. For now, let's ignore the second part and assume that the class implements all methods of the interfaces it implements. If a class implements the Walkable interface, it must provide implementation for the walk() method.

Objects of the Person and Duck classes need the ability to walk. You need to implement the Walkable interface to these classes. Listing 17-2 and Listing 17-3 have the complete revised code for these classes.

Listing 17-2. The Revised Person Class, Which Implements the Walkable Interface

```java
// Person.java
package com.jdojo.interfaces;

public class Person implements Walkable {
        private String name;
```

```
        public Person(String name) {
                this.name = name;
        }

        public void walk() {
                System.out.println(name + " (a person) is walking.");
        }
}
```

Listing 17-3. The Revised Duck Class, Which Implements the Walkable Interface

```
// Duck.java
package com.jdojo.interfaces;

public class Duck implements Walkable {
        private String name;

        public Duck(String name) {
                this.name = name;
        }

        public void walk() {
                System.out.println(name + " (a duck) is walking.");
        }
}
```

Note that the declarations of the revised classes have a minor difference from their original declarations. Both of them have a new implements Walkable clause added to their declarations. Since both of them implement the Walkable interface, they must provide the implementation for the walk() method as declared in the Walkable interface. You did not have to define a fresh walk() method as you had it implemented from the very beginning. If these classes did not have a walk() method, you had to add it to them at this stage.

Before you revise the code for your Walkables class, let's look at other things that you can do with the Walkable interface. Like a class, an interface defines a new reference type. When you define a class, it defines a new reference type and it lets you declare variable of that type. Similarly, when you define a new interface (e.g. Walkable), you can define a reference variable of the new interface type. The variable scope could be local, instance, static, or a method parameter. The following declaration is valid:

```
Walkable w; // w is a reference variable of type Walkable
```

You cannot create an object of an interface type. The following code is invalid:

```
new Walkable(); // A compile-time error
```

You can create an object of only a class type. However, an interface type variable can refer to any object whose class implements that interface. Because the Person and Duck classes implement the Walkable interface, a reference variable of the Walkable type can refer to an object of these classes.

```
Walkable w1 = new Person("Jack"); // OK
Walkable w2 = new Duck("Jeff");   // OK

// A compile-time error as the Object class does not implement the Walkable interface
Walkable w3 = new Object();
```

649

What can you do with the reference variable of an interface type? You can access any members of the interface using its reference type variable. Since your Walkable interface has only one member, which is the walk() method, you can write code as shown:

```
// Let the person walk
w1.walk();

// Let the duck walk
w2.walk();
```

When you invoke the walk() method on w1, it invokes the walk() method of the Person object because w1 is referring to a Person object. When you invoke the walk() method on w2, it invokes the walk() method of the Duck object because w2 is referring to a Duck object. When you call a method using a reference variable of an interface type, it calls the method on the object to which it is referring. With this knowledge about an interface, let's revise the code for your Walkables class. Listing 17-4 contains the revised code. Note that in the revised code for the letThemWalk() method, all you had to do is to change the parameter type from Person to Walkable. Everything else remains the same.

Listing 17-4. The Revised Walkables Class

```java
// Walkables.java
package com.jdojo.interfaces;

public class Walkables {
        public static void letThemWalk(Walkable[] list) {
                for (Walkable w : list) {
                        w.walk();
                }
        }
}
```

Listing 17-5 shows how to test your revised classes with the Walkable interface. It creates an array of the Walkable type. Declaring an array of an interface type is allowed because an array provides a shortcut to create many variables of the same type. This time, you can pass objects of the Person class as well as the Duck class in one array of the Walkable type to the letThemWalk() method of the Walkables class, which lets everyone walk together, as shown in the output.

Listing 17-5. A Test Class to Test the Revised Person, Duck, and Walkables Classes

```java
// WalkablesTest.java
package com.jdojo.interfaces;

public class WalkablesTest {
        public static void main(String[] args) {
                Walkable[] w = new Walkable[3];
                w[0] = new Person("Jack");
                w[1] = new Duck("Jeff");
                w[2] = new Person("John");

                // Let everyone walk
                Walkables.letThemWalk(w);
        }
}
```

Jack (a person) is walking.
Jeff (a duck) is walking.
John (a person) is walking.

How will your existing code change if you want to create a new class called Cat whose objects should have the ability to walk? You will be surprised to see that you do not need to change anything in your existing code at all. The Cat class should implement the Walkable interface and that is all. Listing 17-6 contains the code for the Cat class.

Listing 17-6. A Cat Class

```java
// Cat.java
package com.jdojo.interfaces;

public class Cat implements Walkable {
        private String name;

        public Cat(String name) {
                this.name = name;
        }

        public void walk() {
                System.out.println(name + " (a cat) is walking.");
        }
}
```

You can use the following snippet of code to test the new Cat class with the existing code. Looking at the output, you have made persons, ducks, and cats walk together by using the Walkable interface! This is one of the uses of an interface in Java: it lets you put unrelated classes under one umbrella.

```java
Walkable[] w = new Walkable[4];
w[0] = new Person("Jack");
w[1] = new Duck("Jeff");
w[2] = new Person("John");
w[3] = new Cat("Jace");

// Let everyone walk
Walkables.letThemWalk(w);
```

Jack (a person) is walking.
Jeff (a duck) is walking.
John (a person) is walking.
Jace (a cat) is walking.

You have achieved the objective of making different kinds of objects walk together using the interface construct. So, what is an interface anyway?

An interface in Java defines a reference type to specify an abstract concept. It is implemented by classes that provide an implementation of the concept. Prior to Java 8, an interface could contain only abstract methods, so it represented a pure abstract concept. Java 8 allows an interface to have static and default methods that can also contain implementation. Interfaces let you define a relationship between unrelated classes through the abstract concept. In your example, the Walkable interface represented a concept that enabled you to treat the two unrelated classes of Person and Duck the same way because both implemented the same concept.

It is time to go over details of how to create and use interfaces in a Java program. As I discuss the technical details of interfaces, I will also go over proper uses and common misuses of interfaces.

Declaring an Interface

An interface can be declared as a top-level interface, a nested interface, or an annotation type. I will discuss nested interfaces later in this chapter. Annotation type interfaces are discussed in a separate chapter in a different book. I will use the term *interface* to mean a top-level interface. The general (incomplete) syntax for declaring an interface is

```
<modifiers> interface <interface-name> {
        Constant-Declaration
        Method-Declaration
        Nested-Type-Declaration
}
```

An interface declaration starts with list of modifiers, which may be empty. Like a class, an interface can have a public or package-level scope. The keyword public is used to indicate that the interface has a public scope. A public interface can be referred to from anywhere in the application. Absence of a scope-modifier indicates that the interface has a package-level scope. An interface with a package-level scope can be referred to only within the members of its package.

The keyword interface is used to declare an interface. The keyword is followed by the name of the interface. The name of an interface is a valid Java identifier. An interface body follows its name, which is placed inside braces. Members of an interface are declared inside the body. In a special case, the body of an interface can be empty. The following is the simplest interface declaration:

```
package com.jdojo.interfaces;

interface Updatable {
        // The interface body is empty
}
```

This code declares an interface named Updatable, which has a package-level scope. It can be used only inside the com.jdojo.interfaces package because it has a package-level scope. It does not contain any member declarations.

Like a class, an interface has a simple name and a fully qualified name. The identifier that follows the keyword interface is its simple name. The fully qualified name of an interface is formed by using its package name and the simple name separated by a dot. In the above example, Updatable is the simple name and com.jdojo.interfaces. Updatable is the fully qualified name. The rules of using simple and fully qualified name of an interface are the same as that of a class.

The following code declares an interface named ReadOnly. It has a public scope. That is, the definition of the ReadOnly interface is available anywhere in the application, not only inside the com.jdojo.interfaces package.

```
package com.jdojo.interfaces;

public interface ReadOnly {
        // The interface body is empty
}
```

An interface declaration is implicitly abstract. You can declare Updatable and ReadOnly interfaces as follows without changing their meanings. In other words, an interface declaration is always abstract whether you declare it abstract explicitly or not.

```
abstract interface Updatable {
}

public abstract interface ReadOnly {
}
```

■ **Note**   Interfaces in Java are implicitly abstract. Using the keyword `abstract` in their declarations is obsolete and it should not be used in new programs. The above examples are only for illustration purpose.

Declaring Interface Members

An interface can have three types of members:

- Constant fields
- Abstract, static, and default methods
- Static types (nested interfaces and classes)

Note that an interface declaration is much like a class declaration, except that an interface cannot have mutable instance and class variables. Unlike a class, an interface cannot be instantiated. All members of an interface are implicitly public.

Constant Fields Declarations

You can declare constant fields in an interface as shown in Listing 17-7. It declares an interface named Choices, which has declarations of two fields: YES and NO. Both are of int data type.

Listing 17-7. Declaring Fields in an Interface

```
// Choices.java
package com.jdojo.interfaces;

public interface Choices {
        public static final int YES = 1;
        public static final int NO = 2;
}
```

All fields in an interface are implicitly `public`, `static`, and `final`. Although the interface declaration syntax permits the use of these keywords in a field declaration, their use is redundant. It is recommended not to use these keywords when declaring fields in an interface. The Choices interface can be declared as follows without changing its meaning:

```
public interface Choices {
        int YES = 1;
        int NO = 2;
}
```

You can access the fields in an interface using the dot notation in the form of

```
<interface-name>.<field-name>
```

You can use Choices.YES and Choices.NO to access the values of YES and NO fields in the Choices interface. Listing 17-8 demonstrates how to use the dot notation to access fields of an interface.

Listing 17-8. Accessing Fields of an Interface

```
// ChoicesTest.java
package com.jdojo.interfaces;

public class ChoicesTest {
        public static void main(String[] args) {
                System.out.println("Choices.YES = " + Choices.YES);
                System.out.println("Choices.NO = " + Choices.NO);
        }
}
```

```
Choices.YES = 1
Choices.NO = 2
```

Fields in an interface are always final whether the keyword final is used in its declaration or not. This implies that you must initialize a field at the time of declaration. You can initialize a field with a compile-time or runtime constant expression. Since a final field (constant field) is assigned a value only once, you cannot set the value of the field of an interface, except in its declaration. The following snippet of code generates a compile-time error:

```
Choices.YES = 5; // A compile-time error
```

The following snippet of code shows some valid and invalid field declarations for an interface:

```
/* All fields declarations are valid in the ValidFields interface */
public interface ValidFields {
        int X = 10;

        // You can use one field to initialize another if the referenced
        // field is declared before the one that references it.
        int Y = X;
        double N = X + 10.5;

        boolean YES = true;
         boolean NO = false;

        // Assuming Test is a class that exists
        Test TEST = new Test();
}

/* Examples of invalid field declarations. */
public interface InvalidFields {
        int X;       // Invalid. X is not initialized
        int Y = Z;   // Invalid. Forward referencing of Z is not allowed.
        int Z = 10;  // Valid by itself.
        Test TEST;   // Invalid. TEST is not initialized, assuming a Test class exists
}
```

■ Tip It is a convention to use all uppercase letters in the name of a field in an interface to indicate that they are constants. However, Java does not impose any restrictions on naming the fields of an interface as long as they follow the naming rules for identifiers. Fields of an interface are always `public`. However, the accessibility of `public` fields from outside the declaring package depends on the scope of the interface. For example, if an interface is declared to have a package-level scope, its fields are not accessible outside the package because the interface itself is not accessible outside the package, even though its fields are always `public`.

You are advised not to declare an interface to only have constant fields in it. The proper (and most commonly used) use of an interface is to declare a set of methods to define APIs. If you want to group constants in one construct, use a class, not an interface. If you are using Java 5 or a higher version, consider using enum to declare your constants. Using enum provides type safety and compile-time checks for your constants.

Methods Declarations

You can declare three types of methods in an interface:

- Abstract methods
- Static methods
- Default methods

Prior to Java 8, you could declare only abstract methods in interfaces. The modifiers `static` and `default` are used to declare static and default methods, respectively. The lack of `static` and `default` modifiers makes a method abstract. The following is an example of an interface with all three types of methods:

```
interface AnInterface {
        // An abstract method
        int m1();

        // A static method
        static int m2() {
                // The method implementation goes here
        }

        // A default method
        default int m3() {
                // The method implementation goes here
        }
}
```

The following sections discuss each method type declaration in detail.

Abstract Methods Declarations

The main purpose of declaring an interface is to create an abstract specification (or concept) by declaring zero or more abstract methods. All method declarations in an interface are implicitly `abstract` and `public` unless they are declared `static` or `default`. Like in a class, an abstract method in an interface does not have an implementation.

The body of the abstract method is always represented by a semicolon, not by a pair of braces. The following snippet of code declares an interface named Player:

```
public interface Player {
        public abstract void play();
        public abstract void stop();
        public abstract void forward();
        public abstract void rewind();
}
```

The Player interface has four methods: play(), stop(), forward(), and rewind(). The Player interface is a specification for an audio/video player. A real player, for example, a DVD player, will provide the concrete implementation of the specification by implementing all four methods of the Player interface.

Use of the abstract and public keywords in a method declaration in an interface is redundant, even though allowed by the compiler, because a method in an interface is implicitly abstract and public. The above declaration of the Player interface can be rewritten as follows without changing its meaning:

```
public interface Player {
        void play();
        void stop();
        void forward();
        void rewind();
}
```

Abstract method declarations in an interface may include parameters, a return type, and a throws clause. The following snippet of code declares an ATM interface. It declares four methods. If the account information is wrong, the login() method throws an AccountNotFoundException. The withdraw() method throws an InsufficientBalanceException when the user attempts to withdraw an amount, which will reduce the balance to an amount lower than the required minimum balance amount.

```
public interface ATM {
        boolean login(int account) throws AccountNotFoundException;
        boolean deposit(double amount);
        boolean withdraw(double amount) throws InsufficientBalanceException;
        double getBalance();
}
```

Abstract methods of an interface are inherited by classes that implement the interface, and classes override them to provide an implementation. This implies that an abstract method in an interface cannot be declared final as the final keyword in a method declaration indicates that the method is final and it cannot be overridden. However, a class may declare the overridden method of an interface final indicating that the subclasses cannot override the method.

Static Methods Declarations

Let's refer to the code for the Walkables class shown in Listing 17-4. It is a utility class that contains a static method called letThemWalk(). Creating such a utility class for providing static methods for working with an interface was common prior to Java 8. You will find a number of interface/utility-class pairs in the Java library, for example, Collection/Collections, Path/Paths, Channel/Channels, Executor/Executors, etc. Following this convention, you named your interface/utility-class pair as Walkable/Walkables. Java designers realized the necessity of the extra utility classes along with interfaces. From Java 8, you can have static methods in interfaces. A static method contains the static modifier. They are implicitly public. You can redefine the Walkable interface as shown in Listing 17-9 to include the letThemWalk() method and get rid of the Walkables class altogether.

Listing 17-9. The Revised Walkable Interface with an Additional Static Convenience Method

```java
// Walkable.java
package com.jdojo.interfaces;

public interface Walkable {
        // An abstract method
        void walk();

        // A static convenience method
        public static void letThemWalk(Walkable[] list) {
                for (int i = 0; i < list.length; i++) {
                        list[i].walk();
                }
        }
}
```

You can use the static methods of an interface using the dot notation.

```
<interface-name>.<static-method>
```

The following snippet of code calls the Walkable.letThemWalk() method:

```java
Walkable[] w = new Walkable[4];
w[0] = new Person("Jack");
w[1] = new Duck("Jeff");
w[2] = new Person("John");
w[3] = new Cat("Jace");

// Let everyone walk
Walkable.letThemWalk(w);
```

```
Jack (a person) is walking.
Jeff (a duck) is walking.
John (a person) is walking.
Jace (a cat) is walking.
```

Unlike static methods in a class, static methods in an interface are not inherited by implementing classes or subinterfaces. An interface that inherits from another interface is called a subinterface. There is only one way to call the static methods of an interface: by using the interface name. A static method m() of an interface I must be called using I.m(). You can use the unqualified name m() of the method to call it only within the body of the interface or when you import the method using a static import statement.

Default Methods Declarations

A default method in an interface is declared with the modifier default. A default method provides a default implementation for the classes that implements the interface, but does not override the default method.

The default methods are a new, exciting feature in Java 8. Prior to Java 8, interfaces could have only abstract methods. Why were default methods added in Java 8? The short answer is that they were added so the existing interfaces may evolve. At this point, the answer may be hard to understand. Let's look at an example to clear it.

Suppose, prior to Java 8, you want create a specification for movable objects to describe their locations in a 2D plane. Let's create the specification by creating an interface named Movable, as shown in Listing 17-10.

Listing 17-10. A Movable Interface

```java
// Movable.java
package com.jdojo.interfaces;

public interface Movable {
        void setX(double x);
        void setY(double y);
        double getX();
        double getY();
}
```

The interface declares four abstract methods. The setX() and setY() methods let the a Movable change the location using the absolute positioning. The getX() and getY() methods return the current location in terms of the x and y coordinates.

Consider the Pen class in Listing 17-11. It implements the Movable interface, and as part of the specification, it provides implementation for the four methods of the interface. The class contains two instance variables called x and y to track the location of the pen.

Listing 17-11. A Pen Class That Implements the Movable Interface

```java
// Pen.java
package com.jdojo.interfaces;

public class Pen implements Movable {
        private double x;
        private double y;

        public Pen() {
                // By default, the pen is at (0.0, 0.0)
        }

        public Pen(double x, double y) {
                this.x = x;
                this.y = y;
        }

        public void setX(double x) {
                this.x = x;
        }

        public void setY(double y) {
                this.y = y;
        }
```

```
        public double getX() {
                return x;
        }

        public double getY() {
                return y;
        }

        public String toString() {
                return "Pen(" + x + ", " + y + ")";
        }
}
```

The following snippet of code uses the Movable interface and the Pen class:

```
// Create a Pen and assign its reference to a Movable variable
Movable p1 = new Pen();
System.out.println(p1);

// Move the Pen
p1.setX(10.0);
p1.setY(5.0);
System.out.println(p1);
```

```
Pen(0.0, 0.0)
Pen(10.0, 5.0)
```

So far, there is nothing extraordinary going on with the Movable interface and the Pen class. Suppose the Movable interface is part of a library that you have developed. You have distributed the library to your customers. Customers have implemented the Movable interface in their classes.

Now comes a twist in the story. Some customers have requested that the Movable interface include specifications for changing the location using relative coordinates. They want you to add a move() method to the Movable interface as follows. The requested part is shown in boldface.

```
public interface Movable {
        void setX(double x);
        void setY(double y);
        double getX();
        double getY();
        void move(double deltaX, double deltaY);
}
```

You are a nice business person; you always want a happy customer. You obliged the customer. You made the changes and redistributed the new version of your library. After a few hours, you get calls from several angry customers. They are angry because the new version of the library broke their existing code. Let's analyze what went wrong.

Prior to Java 8, all methods in an interface were implicitly abstract. Therefore, the new method move() is an abstract method. All classes that are implementing the Movable interface must provide the implementation for the new method. Note that customers already have several classes, for example, the Pen class, implementing the Movable interface. All those classes will not compile anymore unless the new method is added to those classes. The moral of the story is that, prior to Java 8, it was not possible to add methods to an interface after it has been distributed to the public, without breaking the existing code.

Java libraries have published hundreds of interfaces, which were used thousands of times by customers worldwide. Java designers were in a dire need of a way to evolve the existing interfaces without breaking the existing code. They explored several solutions. Default methods were the accepted solution to evolve interfaces. A default method can be added to an existing interface. It provides a default implementation for the method. All classes implementing the interface will inherit the default implementation, thus not breaking them. Classes may choose to override the default implementation.

A default method is declared using the keyword default. A default method cannot be declared abstract or static. It must provide an implementation. Otherwise, a compile-time error occurs. Listing 17-12 shows the revised code for the Movable interface. It contains a default method move() that is defined in terms of the existing four methods.

Listing 17-12. The Movable Interface with a Default Method

```java
// Movable.java
package com.jdojo.interfaces;

public interface Movable {
        void setX(double x);
        void setY(double y);
        double getX();
        double getY();

        // A default method
        default void move(double deltaX, double deltaY) {
                double newX = getX() + deltaX;
                double newY = getY() + deltaY;
                setX(newX);
                setY(newY);
        }
}
```

Any existing classes, including the Pen class, that implement the Movable interface will continue to compile and work as before. The new move() method with its default implementation is available for all those classes. Listing 17-13 shows the usage of the old and new methods of the Movable interface with the Pen class.

Listing 17-13. Testing the New Movable Interface with the Existing Pen Class

```java
// MovableTest.java
package com.jdojo.interfaces;

public class MovableTest {
        public static void main(String[] args) {
                // Create a Pen and assign its reference to a Movable variable
                Movable p1 = new Pen();
                System.out.println(p1);

                // Move the Pen using absolute cocoordinates
                p1.setX(10.0);
                p1.setY(5.0);
                System.out.println(p1);
```

```java
                // Move the Pen using relative cocordinates
                p1.move(5.0, 2.0);
                System.out.println(p1);
        }
}
```

Another common use of default methods is to declare optional methods in an interface. Consider a Named interface as shown in Listing 17-14.

Listing 17-14. A Named Interface Using Default Methods to Provide Optional Methods

```java
// Named.java
package com.jdojo.interfaces;

public interface Named {
    void setName(String name);

    default String getName() {
        return "John Doe";
    }

    default void setNickname(String nickname) {
        throw new UnsupportedOperationException("setNickname");
    }

    default String getNickname() {
        throw new UnsupportedOperationException("getNickname");
    }
}
```

The interface provides specification for getting and setting the official name and nickname. Not everything has a nickname. The interface provides methods to get and set the nickname as default methods making them optional. If a class implements the Named interface, it can override the setNickname() and getNickname() methods to provide implementation, if the class supports a nickname. Otherwise, the class does not have to do anything for these methods. They simply throw a runtime exception to indicate that they are not supported. The interface declares the getName() method as default and provides a sensible default implementation for it by return "John Doe" as the default name. The classes implementing the Named interface are expected to override the getName() method to return the real name.

You have just touched the tip of the iceberg in terms of the benefits and power that default methods have brought to the Java language. It has given a new life to the existing Java APIs. In Java 8, default methods have been added to several interfaces in the Java library to provide more expressiveness and functionality for the existing APIs.

What are the similarities and differences between a concrete method in a class and a default method in an interface?

- Both provide an implementation.

- Both have access to the keyword this in the same way. That is, the keyword this is the reference of the object on which the method is called.

- The major difference lies in the access to the state of the object. A concrete method in a class can access the instance variables of the class. However, a default method does not have access to the instance of variables of the class implementing the interface. The default method has access to the other members of the interface, for example other methods, constants, and type members. For example, the default method in the Movable interface is written using the other member methods getX(), getY(), setX(), and setY().

- Needless to say that both types of methods can use their parameters.

- Both methods can have a throws clause.

You are not done with default methods yet. I will discuss their roles in inheritance shortly.

Nested Type Declarations

A nested type declaration in an interface defines a new reference type. You can declare a class, interface, enum, and annotation as nested types. I have not discussed enum and annotation yet, so I will restrict the discussion to nested interfaces and classes in this section. An interface/class declared inside an interface is called a nested interface/class.

An interface and a class define new reference types, so do a nested interface and a nested class. Sometimes a type makes more sense as a nested type. Suppose you have an ATM interface and you want to define another interface called ATMCard. The ATMCard interface can be defined as a top-level interface or a nested interface of ATM. Since an ATM card is used with an ATM, it might make more sense to define ATMCard as a nested interface of the ATM interface. Since you are defining ATMCard as a nested interface of ATM, you can also drop the "ATM" from its name and you can name it just Card, as shown:

```
public interface ATM {
        boolean login(int account) throws AccountNotFoundException;
        boolean deposit(double amount);
        boolean withdraw(double amount) throws InsufficientFundException;
        double getBalance();

        // Card is a nested interface. You can omit the keywors public and static.
        public static interface Card {
                String getNumber();
                String getSecurityCode();
                LocalDate getExpirationDate();
                String getCardHolderName();
        }
}
```

A nested interface is always accessed through its enclosing interface. In the above snippet of code, ATM is a top-level interface (or simply an interface) and Card is a nested interface. The ATM interface is also called an enclosing interface for the Card interface. The fully qualified name of the ATM interface is com.jdojo.interfaces.ATM; the fully qualified name of the nested Card interface is com.jdojo.interfaces.ATM.Card. All nested types are implicitly public and static. The above code snippet used the keywords public and static to declare the ATMCard interface, which are redundant.

You can also declare a nested class inside an interface. You may not understand the use of a nested class described in this section until you know how to implement an interface, which is described in the next section. The following discussion is included here to complete the discussion about the nested types of an interface. You may revisit this section after reading about how to implement an interface in the next few sections.

It is not common to declare a nested class inside an interface. However, you should not be surprised if you find an interface that declares a nested class as its member. What advantage does it offer to have a nested class inside an interface? There is only one advantage of doing this and it is a better organization of related entities: interfaces and classes. Suppose you want to develop a Job interface that will let the user submit a job to a job scheduler. The following is the code for the Job interface:

```
public interface Job {
        public void runJob();
}
```

Suppose each department must submit a job every day, even if they do not have something to run. It suggests that sometimes you need an empty job or a job with nothing real to do. The developer of the Job interface may provide a constant, which represents a trivial implementation of the Job interface as listed in Listing 17-15. It has a nested class called EmptyJob, which implements the enclosing Job interface.

Listing 17-15. The Job Interface with a Nested Class and a Constant Field

```java
// Job.java
package com.jdojo.interfaces;

public interface Job {
        // A nested class
        class EmptyJob implements Job {
                private EmptyJob() {
                        // Do not allow outside to create its object
                }

                public void runJob() {
                        System.out.println("Nothing serious to run...");
                }
        }

        // A constant field
        Job EMPTY_JOB = new EmptyJob();

        // An abstract method
        void runJob();
}
```

If a department does not have a meaningful job to submit, it can use Job.EMPTY_JOB constant as a job. The fully qualified name of the EmptyJob class is com.jdojo.interfaces.Job.EmptyJob. Note that the enclosing interface Job provides an additional namespace for the EmptyJob class. Inside the Job interface, the EmptyJob class can be referred to by its simple name of EmptyJob. However, outside the Job interface, it must be referred to as Job.EmptyJob. You may notice that a trivial job object is represented by the Job.EMPTY_JOB constant. You have made the constructor for the EmptyJob nested class private, so no one outside the interface can create its object. Listing 17-16 shows how to use the class. Typically, in such cases, you would make the constructor of the Job.EmptyJob class private so its object cannot be created outside the Job interface because the EMPTY_JOB constant already provides an object of this class.

Listing 17-16. A Test Program to Test the Job Interface and Its Nested EmptyJob Class

```java
// JobTest.java
package com.jdojo.interfaces;

public class JobTest {
        public static void main(String[] args) {
                submitJob(Job.EMPTY_JOB);
        }

        public static void submitJob(Job job) {
                job.runJob();
        }
}
```

Nothing serious to run...

An Interface Defines a New Type

An interface defines a new reference type. You can use an interface type anywhere you can use a reference type. For example, you can use an interface type to declare a variable (instance, static, or local), to declare a parameter type in a method, as a return type of a method, etc.

Consider the following interface declaration named Swimmable, which declares a method swim() as shown in Listing 17-17. The SwimmableTest class in Listing 17-18 shows how to use the Swimmable interface as a reference data type.

Listing 17-17. The Declaration for a Swimmable Interface

```
// Swimmable.java
package com.jdojo.interfaces;

public interface Swimmable {
    void swim();
}
```

Listing 17-18. A Test Class That Demonstrates the Use of an Interface Type as a Variable Type

```
// SwimmableTest.java
package com.jdojo.interfaces;

public class SwimmableTest {
    // Interface type to define instance variable
    private Swimmable iSwimmable;

    // Interface type to define parameter type for a constructor
    public SwimmableTest(Swimmable aSwimmable) {
        this.iSwimmable = aSwimmable;
    }

    // Interface type to define return type of a method
    public Swimmable getSwimmable() {
        return this.iSwimmable;
    }

    // Interface type to define parameter type for a method
    public void setSwimmable(Swimmable newSwimmable) {
        this.iSwimmable = newSwimmable;
    }

    public void letItSwim(){
        // Interface type to declare a local variable
        Swimmable localSwimmable = null;

        localSwimmable = this.iSwimmable;

        // An interface variable can be used to invoke any method
        // declared in the interface and the Object class
        localSwimmable.swim();
    }
}
```

The SwimmableTest class uses the new type defined by the Swimmable interface in a number of ways. The purpose of the class is just to demonstrate the use of an interface as a new type. It uses the Swimmable interface as a type to declare

- An instance variable named iSwimmable.

- A parameter named aSwimmable for its constructor.

- The return type of its getSwimmable() method.

- A parameter named newSwimmable for its setSwimmable() method.

- A local variable named localSwimmable inside its letItSwim() method. Inside the method, you could have invoked swim() method directly on the instance variable, iSwimmable. You used a local variable just to demonstrate that an interface type can be used anywhere a type can be used.

At this point, two questions about interfaces need to be answered.

- What object in memory does a variable of an interface type refer to?

- What can you do with a variable of an interface type?

Since an interface defines a reference type, what object in memory does a variable of an interface type refer to? Let's expand on this question with an example. You have a Swimmable interface and you can declare a reference variable of type Swimmable as follows:

```
Swimmable sw;
```

What is the value of the variable sw at this point? A variable of a reference data type refers to an object in memory. To be precise, let's rephrase the question as "What object in memory does sw refer to?" You cannot answer this question completely at this point. The partial and unexplained answer is that a variable of an interface type refers to an object in memory whose class implements that interface. The answer will be clearer when I discuss implementing an interface in the next section. You cannot create an object of an interface type. An interface is implicitly abstract and it does not have a constructor. That is, you cannot use an interface type with the new operator to create an object. The following code would not compile:

```
Swimmable sw2 = new Swimmable(); // A compile-time error
```

In this statement, the use of the new operator causes the compile-time error, not the Swimmable sw2 part. The Swimmable sw2 part is a variable declaration, which is valid.

However, one thing is certain: a variable of an interface type can refer to an object in memory. This scenario is depicted in Figure 17-1.

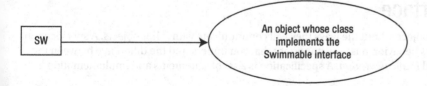

Figure 17-1. A Swimmable type variable (sw) referring to an object in memory

Let's answer the second question. What can you do with the variable of an interface type? All rules for a reference type variable equally apply to a variable of an interface type. A few important things that you can do with a variable of a reference type are as follows:

- You can assign a reference of an object in memory including a null reference value.

```
Swimmable sw2 = null;
```

- You can access any constant fields declared in an interface using a variable of the interface type or directly using the interface name. It is preferred to access the constants of an interface using the interface name. Consider the Choices interface with two constants called YES and NO. You can access the value of the two constants using the simple name of the interface as Choices.YES, Choices.NO, and using the interface reference variable sw2.YES, and sw2.NO.

- You can use a variable of an interface type to invoke any methods declared in the interface. For example, a variable of the Swimmable type can invoke the swim() method as

```
Swimmable sw3 = get an object instance of the Swimmable type...
sw3.swim();
```

- A variable of an interface type can invoke any method of the java.lang.Object class. This rule is not very obvious. However, if you think carefully, it is a very simple and important rule. A variable of an interface type can refer to an object in memory. No matter what object in memory it refers to, the object will always be of a class type. All classes in Java must have the Object class as their direct/indirect superclass. As a result, all objects in Java have access to all methods of the Object class. Therefore, it is logical to allow an interface type variable to access all methods of the Object class. The following snippet of code calls the hashCode(), getClass(), and toString() methods of the Object class using a Swimmable type variable:

```
Swimmable sw4 = get a Swimmable type object...
int hc = sw4.hashCode();
Class c = sw4.getClass();
String str = sw4.toString();
```

- Another important rule to remember is that an instance or static variable of an interface type is initialized to null by default. As is the case with all types of local variables, a local variable of an interface type is not initialized by default. You must explicitly assign it a value before you can use it.

Implementing an Interface

An interface defines a specification for objects about the ways they will communicate with other objects. A specification is a contract or agreement for an object's behavior. It is very important that you understand the difference between the two terms *specification* (or *contract*) and *implementation*. A specification is a set of statements and implementation is the realization of those statements.

Let's take a real-world example. The statement "Jack will give ten dollars to John on June 8, 2014." is a specification. When Jack gives ten dollars to John on June 8, 2014, the specification is executed. You can restate it as when Jack gives ten dollars to John on June 8, 2014, the specification is implemented. Sometimes, while discussing interface, a specification is also referred to as a contract, a protocol, an agreement, a plan, or a draft. No matter which term you use to refer to a specification, it is always abstract. The implementation of a specification could be partial or complete. Jack may give seven dollars to John on June 8, 2014, and, in that case, the specification has not been implemented completely.

An interface specifies a protocol that an object guarantees to offer when it interacts with other objects. It specifies the protocol in terms of abstract and default methods. A specification is implemented at some time by someone, and so is the case with an interface. An interface is implemented by a class. When a class implements an interface, the class provides implementations for all abstract methods of the interface. A class may provide a partial implementation of the abstract methods of the interface, and in that case, the class must declare itself `abstract`.

A class that implements an interface uses an "implements" clause to specify the name of the interface. An "implements" clause consists of the keyword `implements`, followed by a comma-separated list of interface types. A class can implement multiple interfaces. Let's focus on a class implementing only one interface for now. The general syntax for a class declaration that implements an interface looks as follows:

```
<modifiers> class <class-Name> implements <comma-separated-list-of-interfaces> {
        // Class body goes here
}
```

Suppose there is a Fish class.

```
public class Fish {
        // Code for Fish class goes here
}
```

Now, you want to implement the Swimmable interface in the Fish class. The following code shows the Fish class that declares that it implements the Swimmable interface:

```
public class Fish implements Swimmable {
        // Code for the Fish class goes here
}
```

The text in boldface font shows the changed code. The above code for the Fish class will not compile. A class inherits all abstract and default methods from the interfaces it implements. Therefore, the Fish class inherits the abstract swim() method from the Swimmable interface. A class must be declared abstract if it contains (inherited or declared) abstract methods. You have not declared the Fish class abstract. This is the reason the above declaration will not compile. In the following code, the Fish class overrides the swim() method to provide an implementation:

```
public class Fish implements Swimmable {
        // Override and implement the swim() method
        public void swim() {
                // Code for swim method goes here
        }

        // More code for the Fish class goes here
}
```

The class that implements an interface must override to implement all abstract methods declared in the interface. Otherwise, the class must be declared abstract. Note that default methods of an interface are also inherited by the implementing classes. The implanting classes may choose (but is not required) to override the default methods. The static methods in an interface are not inherited by the implementing classes.

A class implementing interfaces can have other methods that are not inherited from the implemented interfaces. Other methods can have the same name and different number and/or types of parameters than the one declared in the implemented interfaces.

In your case, the only requirement for the Fish class is that it must have a swim() method, which accepts no parameters and returns void as declared in the Swimmable interface. The following code defines two swim() methods in the Fish class. The first one with no parameters implements the swim() method of the Swimmable interface. The second one, swim(double distanceInYards), has nothing to do with the Swimmable interface implementation by the Fish class.

```java
public class Fish implements Swimmable {
        // Override the swim() method in the Swimmable interface
        public void swim() {
                // More code goes here
        }

        // A valid method for the class Fish. This method declaration has nothing to do
        // with the Swimmable interface's swim()
        public void swim(double distanceInYards) {
                // More code goes here
        }
}
```

Listing 17-19 has the complete code for the Fish class. A Fish object will have a name, which is supplied in its constructor. It implements the swim() method of Swimmable interface to print a message on the standard output.

Listing 17-19. Code for the Fish Class That Implements the Swimmable Interface

```java
// Fish.java
package com.jdojo.interfaces;

public class Fish implements Swimmable {
        private String name;

        public Fish(String name) {
                this.name = name;
        }

        public void swim() {
                System.out.println(name + " (a fish) is swimming.");
        }
}
```

How do you create an object of a class that implements an interface? You create an object of a class the same way (by using the new operator with its constructor) whether it implements an interface or not. You can create an object of the Fish class as

```java
// Create an object of the Fish class
Fish fifi = new Fish("Fifi");
```

When you execute the statement new Fish("Fifi"), it creates an object in memory and that object's type is Fish (the type defined by its class). When a class implements an interface, its object has one more type, which is the type defined by the implemented interface. In your case, the object created by executing has two types: Fish and Swimmable. In fact it has a third type, too, which is the Object type by virtue of the Fish class inheriting the Object class, which happened by default. Since an object of the Fish class has two types, Fish and Swimmable, you can assign the reference of a Fish object to a variable of the Fish type as well as to a variable of the Swimmable type. The following code summarizes this:

```
Fish guppi = new Fish("Guppi");
Swimmable hilda = new Fish("Hilda");
```

The variable guppi is of the Fish type. It is referring to the Guppi fish object. There is no surprise in the first assignment; a Fish object being assigned to a variable of the Fish type. The second assignment is also valid because the Fish class implements the Swimmable interface and every object of the Fish class is also of the Swimmable type. At this point hilda is a variable of the Swimmable type. It is referring to the Hilda fish object. The following assignment is always valid:

```
// A Fish is always Swimmable
hilda = guppi;
```

However, the other way is not valid. Assigning a variable of the Swimmable type to a variable of the Fish type generates a compile-time error.

```
// A Swimmable is not always a Fish
guppi = hilda; // A compile-time error
```

Why does the above assignment generate a compile-time error? The reason is very simple. An object of the Fish class is always Swimmable because the Fish class implements the Swimmable interface. Since a variable of the Fish type can only refer to a Fish object, which is always Swimmable, the assignment hilda = guppi is always valid. However, a variable of the Swimmable type can refer to any object whose class implements the Swimmable interface, not necessarily only to a Fish object. For example, consider a class Turtle, which implements the Swimmable interface.

```
public class Turtle implements Swimmable {
        public void swim() {
                System.out.println("Turtle can swim too!");
        }
}
```

You can assign an object of the Turtle class to hilda variable.

```
hilda = new Turtle(); // OK. A Turtle is always Swimmable
```

If the assignment guppi = hilda is allowed at this point, a Fish variable guppi will be referring to a Turtle object! This would be a disaster. The Java runtime would throw an exception, even if the compiler had allowed this assignment. This kind of assignment is not allowed for the following reason:

A Fish is always Swimmable. However, not every Swimmable is a Fish.

Suppose you know (programmatically) for sure that a variable of the Swimmable type contains reference to a Fish object. If you want to assign the Swimmable type variable to a variable of the Fish type, you can do so by using a type cast, as shown:

```
// The compiler will pass it. The runtime may throw a ClassCastException.
guppi = (Fish)hilda;
```

The compiler will not complain about the above statement. It assumes that you have made sure that the hilda variable is referring to a Fish object and the cast (Fish)hilda will succeed at runtime. If, by any chance, the hilda variable is not referring to a Fish object, the Java runtime will throw a ClassCastException. For example, the following snippet of code will pass the compiler check, but will throw a ClassCastException:

```
Fish fred = new Fish("Fred");
Swimmable turti = new Turtle();

// OK for the compiler, but not ok for the runtime. turti is a Turtle, not a Fish at runtime.
// fred can refer to only a Fish, not a Turtle
fred = (Fish)turti;
```

Listing 17-20 has a short but complete code that lets you test the Fish class and the Swimmable interface.

Listing 17-20. Demonstrating That a Variable of an Interface Can Store the Reference of the Object of the Class Implementing the Interface

```
// FishTest.java
package com.jdojo.interfaces;

public class FishTest {
        public static void main(String[] args) {
                Swimmable finny = new Fish("Finny");
                finny.swim();
        }
}
```

```
Finny (a fish) is swimming.
```

Implementing Interface Methods

When a class fully implements an interface, it provides an implementation for all abstract methods of the implemented interfaces by overriding the methods. A method declaration in an interface includes constraints (or rules) for the methods. For example, a method may declare a throws clause in its declaration. The throws clause in the method declaration is a constraint for the method. If the throws clause declares some checked exceptions, the caller of that method must be ready to handle them. Methods in an interface are implicitly public. This defines another constraint on the methods, which states that all methods of an interface are accessible publicly, with an assumption that the interface itself is accessible publicly.

Let's consider a Banker interface, defined as follows:

```
public interface Banker {
        double withdraw(double amount) throws InsufficientFundException;
        void deposit(double amount) throws FundLimitExceededException;
}
```

The Banker interface declares two methods called withdraw() and deposit(). Let's consider the following implementation of the Banker interface in the MinimumBalanceBank class. The overridden methods in this class have exactly the same constraints as defined in the Banker interface. Both methods are declared public and both of them throw the same exception as declared in their declarations in the Banker interface.

```
public class MinimumBalanceBank implements Banker {
        public double withdraw(double amount) throws InsufficientFundException {
                // Code for this method goes here
        }

        public void deposit(double amount) throws FundLimitExceededException {
                // Code for this method goes here
        }
}
```

Let's consider the following implementation of the Banker interface in the NoLimitBank class. The NoLimitBank has rules that a customer can have unlimited overdraft (wish it happened in reality) and there is no upper limit on the balance. NoLimitBank has dropped the throws clause when it overrode the withdraw() and deposit() methods of the Banker interface.

```
public class NoLimitBank implements Banker {
        public double withdraw(double amount) {
                // Code for this method goes here
        }

        public void deposit(double amount) {
                // Code for this method goes here
        }
}
```

The code for NoLimitBank is valid, even though its two methods that overrode the Banker interface methods have dropped the throws clause. Dropping constraints (exceptions in this case) is allowed when a class overrides an interface method. An exception in the throws clause imposes a restriction that the caller must handle the exception. If you use the Banker type to write the code, here is how you will call the withdraw() method:

```
Banker b = get a Banker type object;
try {
        double amount = b.withdraw(1000.90);
        // More code goes here
}
catch (InsufficientFundException e) {
        // Handle the exception here
}
```

At compile-time, when the b.withdraw() method is called, the compiler forces you to handle the exception thrown from the withdraw() method because it knows the type of the variable b is Banker and the Banker type's withdraw() method throws an InsufficientFundException. If you assign an object of NoLimitBank to the variable b in the above code, no exception will be thrown from the withdraw() method of the NoLimitBank class when b.withdraw() is called, even though the call to withdraw() method is inside a try-catch block. The compiler cannot check the runtime type of variable b. Its safety check is based on the compile-time types of the variable b. It would never be a problem if the runtime throws a fewer number of exceptions or no exceptions than expected in the code, Consider the following implementation of the Banker interface by the UnstablePredictableBank class:

```
// The following code will not compile
public class UnstablePredictableBank implements Banker {
        public double withdraw(double amount)
                throws InsufficientFundException, ArbitraryException {
                // Code for this method goes here
        }

        public void deposit(double amount) throws FundLimitExceededException {
                // Code for this method goes here
        }
}
```

This time, the withdraw() method adds a new exception, ArbitraryException, which adds a new constraint to the overridden method. Adding constraints to an overridden method is never allowed.

Consider the following snippet of code:

```
Banker b = new UnstablePredictableBank();
try {
        double amount = b.withdraw(1000.90);
        // More code goes here
}
catch (InsufficientFundException e) {
        // Handle exception here
}
```

The compiler does not know that at runtime the variable b, which is of type Banker, will refer to an object of the UnstablePredictableBank type. Therefore, the compiler will force you to handle only the InsufficientFundException when you call b.withdraw(). What happens when ArbitraryException is thrown from the withdraw() method at runtime? Your code is not ready to handle it. This is the reason that you cannot add new exceptions to a method declaration in a class, which overrides a method in its implementing interface.

If a class overrides a method of the implemented interface, that method must be declared public. Recall that all methods in an interface are implicitly public, and public is the least restricting scope modifier for a method. Declaring a method in the class that overrides an interface method as private, protected, or package-level is like restricting the scope of the overridden method (like placing more constraints). The following snippet of code will not compile because the withdraw() and deposit() methods are not declared public:

```
// Code would not compile
public class UnstablePredictableBank implements Banker{
        // withdraw() method must be public
        private double withdraw(double amount) throws InsufficientFundException {
                // Code for this method goes here
        }

        // deposit() method must be public
        protected void deposit(double amount) throws FundLimitExceededException {
                // Code for this method goes here
        }
}
```

■ **Tip** Use a general rule of thumb to check if adding or dropping a constraint is allowed in a class method, which overrides an interface's method. Write code using an interface type variable that is assigned an object of the class that implements the interface. If the code makes sense to you (of course, it has to make sense to the compiler too), it is allowed. Otherwise, it is not allowed. Suppose J is an interface, which declares a method m1(), Suppose the class C implements the interface J and it modifies the declaration of the method m1(). If the following code makes sense and compiles, the modification in the m1() declaration inside the class C is fine.

```
J obj = new C(); // Or any object of any subclass of C
obj.m1();
```

Another rule of thumb is to see if the overriding method in the class is relaxing the restrictions declared in the interface for the same method. If an overriding method relaxes the constraints of the overridden method, it is fine. Otherwise, the compiler will generate an error.

Implementing Multiple Interfaces

A class can implement multiple interfaces. All interfaces that a class implements are listed after the keyword implements in the class declaration. Interface names in the list are separated by a comma. By implementing multiple interfaces, the class agrees to provide the implementation for all abstract methods in all interfaces. Suppose there are two interfaces called Adder and Subtractor, declared as follows:

```
public interface Adder {
        int add(int n1, int n2);
}

public interface Subtractor {
        int subtract(int n1, int n2);
}
```

If an ArithOps class implements the two interfaces, its declaration would look as shown:

```
public class ArithOps implements Adder, Subtractor {
        // Override the add() method of the Adder interface
        public int add(int n1, n2) {
                return n1 + n2;
        }

        // Override the subtract() method of the Subtractor interface
        public int subtract(int n1, n2) {
                return n1 - n2;
        }

        // Other code for the class goes here
}
```

There is no limit on the maximum number of interfaces implemented by a class. When a class implements an interface, its objects get an additional type. If a class implements multiple interfaces, its objects get as many new types as the number of implemented interfaces. Consider the object of the ArithOps class, which can be created by executing new ArithOps(). The object of the ArithOps class gets two additional types, which are Adder and Subtractor. The following snippet of code shows the result of the object of the ArithOps class getting two new types. You can treat an object of ArithOps as ArithOps type, Adder type, or Subtractor type. Of course, every object in Java can always be treated as an Object type.

```
ArithOps a = new ArithOps();
Adder b = new ArithOps();
Subtractor c = new ArithOps();
b = a;
c = a;
```

Let's look at a more concrete and complete example. You already have two interfaces, Walkable and Swimmable. If a class implements the Walkable interface, it must provide the implementation for the walk() method. If you want an object of a class to be treated as the Walkable type, the class would implement the Walkable interface. The same argument goes for the Swimmable interface. If a class implements both interfaces, Walkable and Swimmable, its objects can be treated as a Walkable type as well as a Swimmable type. The only thing that the class must do is to provide implementation for both the walk() and swim() methods. Let's create a Turtle class, which implements both of these interfaces. A Turtle object will have ability to walk as well as swim.

Listing 17-21 has the code for the Turtle class. A turtle can bite too. You have added this behavior to the Turtle objects by adding a bite() method to the Turtle class. Note that adding the bite() method to the Turtle class has nothing to do with implementations of two interfaces. A class, which implements interfaces, can have any number of additional methods of its own.

Listing 17-21. A Turtle Class, Which Implements the Walkable and Swimmable Interfaces

```java
// Turtle.java
package com.jdojo.interfaces;

public class Turtle implements Walkable, Swimmable{
        private String name;

        public Turtle(String name) {
                this.name = name;
        }

        // Adding a bite() method to the Turtle class
        public void bite() {
                System.out.println(name + " (a turtle) is biting.");
        }

        // Implementation for the walk() method of the Walkable interface
        public void walk() {
                System.out.println(name + " (a turtle) is walking.");
        }

        // Implementation for the swim() method of the Swimmable interface
        public void swim() {
                System.out.println(name + " (a turtle) is swimming.");
        }
}
```

Listing 17-22 shows using a Turtle object as a Turtle type, Walkable type, and Swimmable type.

Listing 17-22. Using the Turtle Class

```java
// TurtleTest.java
package com.jdojo.interfaces;

public class TurtleTest {
    public static void main(String[] args) {
        Turtle turti = new Turtle("Turti");

        // Using Turtle type as Turtle, Walkable and Swimmable
        letItBite(turti);
        letItWalk(turti);
        letItSwim(turti);
    }

    public static void letItBite(Turtle t) {
        t.bite();
    }

    public static void letItWalk(Walkable w) {
        w.walk();
    }

    public static void letItSwim(Swimmable s) {
        s.swim();;
    }
}
```

```
Turti (a turtle) is biting.
Turti (a turtle) is walking.
Turti (a turtle) is swimming.
```

Note that a Turtle type variable can access all three methods, bite(), walk(), and swim() like so:

```java
Turtle t = new Turtle("Turti");
t.bite();
t.walk();
t.swim();
```

When you use a Turtle object as the Walkable type, you can access only the walk() method. When you use a Turtle object as the Swimmable type, you can access only the swim() method. The following snippet of code demonstrates this rule:

```java
Turtle t = new Turtle("Trach");
Walkable w = t;
w.walk(); // OK. Using w, you can access only the walk() method of Turtle object

Swimmable s = t;
s.swim(); // OK. Using s you can access only the swim() method
```

Partially Implementing an Interface

A class agrees to provide an implementation for all abstract methods of the interfaces it implements. However, a class does not have to provide implementations for all methods. In other words, a class can provide partial implementations of the implemented interfaces. Recall that an interface is implicitly abstract (means incomplete). If a class does not provide the full implementation of interfaces, it must be declared abstract (means incomplete). Otherwise, the compiler will refuse to compile the class. Consider an interface named IABC, which has three methods m1(), m2(), and m3().

```
package com.jdojo.interfaces;

public interface IABC {
        void m1();
        void m2();
        void m3();
}
```

Suppose a class named ABCImpl implements the IABC interface and it does not provide implementations for all three methods.

```
package com.jdojo.interfaces;

// A compile-time error
public class ABCImpl implements IABC {
        // Provides implementation for only one method of the IABC interface
        public void m1() {
                // Code for the method goes here
        }
}
```

The above code for the ABCImpl class would not compile. It agrees to provide implementations for all three methods of the IABC interface. However, the body of the class does not keep the promise. It provides an implementation for only for one method, m1(). Because the class ABCImpl did not provide implementations for the other two methods of the IABC interface, the ABCImpl class is incomplete, which must be declared abstract to indicate its incompleteness. If you attempt to compile the ABCImpl class, the compiler will generate the following errors:

```
Error(3,14): class com.jdojo.interfaces.ABCImpl should be declared abstract; it does not define
method m2() of interface com.jdojo.interfaces.IABC
Error(3,14): class com.jdojo.interfaces.ABCImpl should be declared abstract; it does not define
method m3() of interface com.jdojo.interfaces.IABC
```

The compiler error is loud and clear. It states that the ABCImpl class must be declared abstract because it did not implement the m2() and m3() methods of the IABC interface.

The following snippet of code fixes the compiler error by declaring the class abstract:

```
package com.jdojo.interfaces;

public abstract class ABCImpl implements IABC {
        public void m1() {
                // Code for the method goes here
        }
}
```

The implication of declaring a class as abstract is that it cannot be instantiated. The following code will generate a compile-time error:

```
new ABCImpl(); // A compile-time error. ABCImpl is abstract
```

The only way to use the ABCImpl class is to inherit another class from it and provide the missing implementations for the m2() and m3() methods of the IABC interface. The following is the declaration for a new class DEFImpl, which inherits from the ABCImpl class:

```
package com.jdojo.interfaces;

public class DEFImpl extends ABCImpl {
        // Other code goes here

        public void m2() {
                // Code for the method goes here
        }

        public void m3() {
                // Code for the method goes here
        }
}
```

The DEFImpl class provides implementations for the m2() and m3() methods of the ABCImpl class. Note that the DEFImpl class inherits the m1(), m2(), and m3() methods from its superclass ABCImpl and m3(). The compiler does not force you to declare the DEFImpl class as an abstract class anymore. You can still declare the DEFImpl class abstract, if you want to.

You can create an object of the DEFImpl class because it is not abstract. What are the types of an object of the DEFImpl class? It has four types: DEFImpl, ABCImpl, Object, and IABC. An object of the DEFImpl class is also of the ABCImpl type because DEFImpl inherits from ABCImpl. An object of the ABCImpl class is also of type IABC because ABCImpl implements IABC interface. Since a DEFImpl is an ABCImpl, and an ABCImpl is an IABC, it is logical that a DEFImpl is also an IABC. This rule has been demonstrated by the following snippet of code. An object of the DEFImpl class has been assigned to variables of DEFImpl, Object, ABCImpl, and IABC types.

```
DEFImpl d = new DEFImpl();
Object obj = d;
ABCImpl a = d;
IABC ia = d;
```

The Supertype-Subtype Relationship

Implementing an interface to a class establishes a supertype-subtype relationship. The class becomes a subtype of all the interfaces it implements and all interfaces become a supertype of the class. The rule of substitution applies in this supertype-subtype relationship. The rule of substitution is that a subtype can replace its supertype everywhere. Let's consider the following class declaration for a class C, which implements three interfaces J, K, and L:

```
public class C implements J, K, L {
        // Code for class C goes here
}
```

The above code establishes supertype-subtype relationship between three the interfaces J, K, and L, and the class C. Recall that an interface declaration defines a new type. Suppose that you have already declared three interfaces: J, K, and L. The three interface declarations define three types: type J, type K, and type L. The declaration of the class C defines a fourth type: type C. What is the relationship between the four types, J, K, L, and C? Class C is a subtype of types J, K and L; type J is a supertype of type C; type K is a supertype of type C; and, type L is a supertype of type C. The implication of this supertype-subtype relationship is that wherever a value of type J, K, or L is required, you can safely substitute a value of type C. The following snippet code demonstrates this rule:

```
C cObject = new C();

// cObject is of type C. It can always be used where J, K or L type is expected.
J jobject = cObject; // OK
K kobject = cObject; // OK
L lobject = cObject; // OK
```

Interface Inheritance

An interface can inherit from another interface. Unlike a class, an interface can inherit from multiple interfaces. Consider the Singer, Writer, and Player interfaces shown in Listing 17-23, Listing 17-24, and Listing 17-25.

Listing 17-23. A Singer Interface

```
// Singer.java
package com.jdojo.interfaces;

public interface Singer {
        void sing();
        void setRate(double rate);
        double getRate();
}
```

Listing 17-24. A Writer Interface

```
// Writer.java
package com.jdojo.interfaces;

public interface Writer {
        void write();
        void setRate(double rate);
        double getRate();
}
```

Listing 17-25. A Player Interface

```
// Player.java
package com.jdojo.interfaces;

public interface Player {
    void play();
    void setRate(double rate);
```

```
    default double getRate() {
        return 300.0;
    }
}
```

All three types of professionals (singers, writers, and players) perform their jobs and they are paid. The three interfaces contain two types of methods. One type of method signifies the job they do, for example, sing(), write(), and play(). Another type of method signifies their minimum hourly rates. The Singer and Write interfaces have declared the setRate() and getRate() methods abstract, letting the implementing classes to specify their implementation. The Player interface declares the setRate() method abstract and provides a default implementation for the getRate() method.

Like a class inheriting from another class, an interface uses the keyword extends to inherit from other interfaces. The keyword extends is followed by a comma-separated list of inherited interface names. The inherited interfaces are known as superinterfaces and the interface inheriting them is known as subinterface. An interface inherits the following members of its superinterfaces:

- Abstract and default methods

- Constant fields

- Nested types

■ **Tip** An interface does not inherit static methods from its superinterfaces.

An interface may override the inherited abstract and default methods that it inherits from its superinterfaces. If the interface contains constant fields and nested types with the same names as the inherited constant fields and nested types from the superinterfaces, the constant fields and nested types in the interface are said to hide the respective names of their inherited counterparts.

Suppose you want to create an interface to represent charity singers who do not charge for singing. A charity singer is also a singer. You will create an interface named CharitySinger that inherits from the Singer interface, as shown:

```
public interface CharitySinger extends Singer {
}
```

At this point, the CharitySinger interface inherits the three abstract methods from the Singer interface. Any class implementing the CharitySinger interface will need to implement those three methods. Because charity singers do not charge for singing, the CharitySinger interface may override the setRate() and getRate() methods and provide a default implementation using default methods shown in Listing 17-26.

Listing 17-26. A CharitySinger Interface

```
// CharitySinger.java
package com.jdojo.interfaces;

public interface CharitySinger extends Singer {
        @Override
        default void setRate(double rate) {
                // A no-op
        }
```

```
        @Override
        default double getRate() {
                return 0.0;
        }
}
```

The setRate() method is a no-op. The getRate() method returns zero. The class that implements the CharitySinger interface will need to implement the sing() method and provide an implementation for it. The class will inherit the default methods setRate() and getRate().

It is possible that the same person is a singer as well as a writer. You can create an interface named SingerWriter, which inherits from the two interfaces Singer and Writer, as shown in Listing 17-27.

Listing 17-27. A SingerWriter Interface That Inherits from Singer and Writer Interfaces

```
// SingerWriter.java
package com.jdojo.interfaces;

public interface SingerWriter extends Singer, Writer {
        // No code
}
```

How many methods does the SingerWriter interface have? It inherits three abstract methods from the Singer interface and three abstract methods from the Writer interface. It inherits methods setRate() and getRate() twice – once from the Singer interface and once from the Writer interface. These methods have the same declarations in both superinterfaces and they are abstract. This does not cause a problem as both methods are abstract. The class that implements the SingerWriter interface will need to provide implementation for both methods only once.

Listing 17-28 shows the code for a Melodist class that implements the SingerWriter interface. Note that it overrides the setRate() and getRate() methods only once.

Listing 17-28. A Melodist Class That Implements the SingerWriter Interface

```
// Melodist.java
package com.jdojo.interfaces;

public class Melodist implements SingerWriter {
        private String name;
        private double rate = 500.00;

        public Melodist(String name) {
                this.name = name;
        }

        @Override
        public void sing() {
                System.out.println(name + " is singing.");
        }

        @Override
        public void setRate(double rate) {
                this.rate = rate;
        }
```

```
        @Override
        public double getRate() {
                return rate;
        }

        @Override
        public void write() {
                System.out.println(name + " is writing");
        }
}
```

The following snippet of code shows how to use the Melodist class:

```
SingerWriter purcell = new Melodist("Henry Purcell");
purcell.setRate(700.00);
purcell.write();
purcell.sing();
```

```
Henry Purcell is writing
Henry Purcell is singing.
```

A person may sing as well as play games. Let's create a SingerPlayer interface to represent this kind of persons. Let's inherit the interface from the Singer and Player interfaces as shown:

```
public interface SingerPlayer extends Singer, Player {
        // No code for now
}
```

Trying to compile the SingerPlayer interface results in the following error:

```
SingerPlayer.java:4: error: interface SingerPlayer inherits abstract and default for getRate() from
types Player and Singer
```

The error resulted from the conflict in the two inherited versions of the getRate() method. The Singer interface declares the getRate() method abstract and the Player interface declares it default. This causes a conflict. The compiler cannot decide which method to inherit. This kind of conflict may arise when multiple versions of the same default method are inherited from different superinterfaces. Consider the following declaration of the CharitySingerPlayer interface:

```
public interface CharitySingerPlayer extends CharitySinger, Player {
}
```

Trying to compile the CharitySingerPlayer interface results in the following error:

```
CharitySingerPlayer.java:4: error: interface CharitySingerPlayer inherits unrelated defaults for
getRate() from types CharitySinger and Player
CharitySingerPlayer.java:4: error: interface CharitySingerPlayer inherits abstract and default for
setRate(double) from types CharitySinger and Player
```

This time, the error is because of two reasons:

- The interface inherits two default getRate() methods, one from the CharitySinger interface and one from the Player interface.

- The interface inherits a default setRate() method from the CharitySinger interface and an abstract setRate() method from the Player interface.

This type of conflict was not possible before Java 8 as the default methods were not available. The compiler does not know which method to inherit when it encounters a combination of abstract-default or default-default method. To resolve such conflicts, the interface needs to override the method in the interface.

There are several ways to resolve the conflict. All involve overriding the conflicting method in the interface.

- You can override the conflicting method with an abstract method.

- You can override the conflicting method with a default method and provide a new implementation.

- You can override the conflicting method with a default method and call one of the methods of the superinterfaces.

Let's resolve the conflict in the SingerPlayer interface. Listing 17-29 contains a declaration for the interface that overrides the getRate() method with an abstract getRate() method. Any class implementing the SingerPlayer interface will have to provide an implementation for the getRate() method.

Listing 17-29. Overriding the Conflicting Method with an Abstract Method

```
// SingerPlayer.java
package com.jdojo.interfaces;

public interface SingerPlayer extends Singer, Player {
        // Override the getRate() method with an abstract method
        @Override
        double getRate();
}
```

The declaration in Listing 17-30 for the SingerPlayer resolves the conflict by overriding the getRate() method with a default getRate() method, which simply returns a value 700.00. Any class implementing the SingerPlayer interface will inherit the default implementation of the getRate() method.

Listing 17-30. Overriding the Conflicting Method with a Default Method

```
// SingerPlayer.java
package com.jdojo.interfaces;

public interface SingerPlayer extends Singer, Player {
        // Override the getRate() method with a default method
        @Override
        default double getRate() {
                return 700.00;
        }
}
```

Sometimes an interface may want to access the override default methods of its superinterfaces. Java 8 introduced a new syntax for calling the overridden default methods of direct superinterfaces from an interface. The new syntax uses the keyword super as shown:

```
SuperInterfaceName.super.superInterfaceDefaultMethod(arg1, arg2...)
```

■ **Tip** Using the keyword super, only the default methods of the direct superinterfaces can be accessed. Accessing default methods of the superinterfaces of superinterfaces are not supported by the syntax. You cannot access the abstract methods of the superinterfaces using this syntax.

Listing 17-31 contains the declaration for the SingerPlayer that resolves the conflict by overriding the getRate() method with a default getRate() method. The method calls the getRate() method of the Player interface using the Player.super.getRate() call, multiplies the value by 3.5, and returns it. It simply implements a rule that a SingerPlayer is paid minimum 3.5 times a Player is paid. Any class implementing the SingerPlayer interface will inherit the default implementation of the getRate() method.

Listing 17-31. Overriding the Conflicting Method with a Default Method That Calls the Method in the Superinterface

```java
// SingerPlayer.java
package com.jdojo.interfaces;

public interface SingerPlayer extends Singer, Player{
        // Override the getRate() method with a default method that calls the
        // Player superinterface getRate() method
        @Override
        default double getRate() {
                double playerRate = Player.super.getRate();
                double singerPlayerRate = playerRate * 3.5;
                return singerPlayerRate;
        }
}
```

Listing 17-32 contains the code for the CharitySingerPlayer interface. It overrides the setRate() method with an abstract method and the getRate() method with a default method. The getRate() method calls the default getRate() method of the Player interface.

Listing 17-32. Overriding the Conflicting Methods in the CharitySinger Interface

```java
// CharitySingerPlayer.java
package com.jdojo.interfaces;

public interface CharitySingerPlayer extends CharitySinger, Player {
        // Override the setRate() method with an abstract method
        @Override
        void setRate(double rate);

        // Override the getRate() method with a default method that calls the
        // Player superinterface getRate() method
        @Override
```

```
        default double getRate() {
                return Player.super.getRate();
        }
}
```

The Superinterface-Subinterface Relationship

Interface inheritance establishes a *superinterface-subinterface* (also called *supertype-subtype)* relationship. When the interface CharitySinger inherits from the Singer interface, the Singer interface is known as the superinterface of the CharitySinger interface, and the CharitySinger interface is known as the subinterface of the Singer interface. An interface can have multiple superinterfaces and an interface can be a subinterface for multiple interfaces. A reference of a subinterface can be assigned to a variable of the superinterface. Consider the following snippet of code to demonstrate the use of superinterface-subinterface relationship. Comments in the code explain why an assignment will succeed or fail.

```
public interface Shape {
        // Code goes here
}

public interface Line extends Shape {
        // Code goes here
}

public interface Circle extends Shape {
        // Code goes here
}
```

The following is sample code that you can write using these interfaces with comments explaining what the code is supposed to do:

```
Shape shape = get an object reference of a Shape;
Line line = get an object reference of a Line;
Circle circle = get an object reference of a Circle;

/* More code goes here... */

shape = line;   // Always fine. A Line is always a Shape.
shape = circle; // Always fine. A Circle is always a Shape.

// A compile-time error. A Shape is not always a Line. A Shape may be a Circle.
// Must use a cast to compile.
line = shape;

// Ok with the compiler. The shape variable must refer to a Line at runtime.
// Otherwise, the runtime will throw a ClassCastException.
line =(Line)shape;
```

Inheriting Conflicting Implementations

Before Java 8, it was not possible for a class to inherit multiple implementations (non-abstract methods) from multiple supertypes. Introduction of default methods made it possible for a class to inherit conflicting implementations from its superclass and superinterfaces.

When a class inherits a method with the same signature from multiple paths (superclass and superinterfaces), Java uses the three simple rules in order to resolve the conflict.

1. **The superclass always wins:** If a class inherits a method (abstract or concrete) from its superclass and a method with the same signature from one of its superinterfaces, the superclass wins. That is, the class inherits the method of the superclass and the methods in the superinterfaces are ignored. This rule treats a default method in an interface as a fallback if the same method is not available in the class through the class hierarchy.

2. **The most specific superinterface wins:** This rule is used if the first rule did not resolve the conflict. If the inherited default method comes from multiple superinterfaces, the method from the most specific superinterface is inherited by the class.

3. **The class must override the conflicting method:** This rule is used if the above two rules did not resolve the conflict. In this case, the developer must override the conflicting method in the class.

Let's discuss different scenarios where the above three rules will apply.

The Superclass Always Wins

This rule is simple to apply. If a class inherits or declares a method, the methods with the same signature in the superinterfaces will be ignored.

Example #1

Consider the following two classes, `Employee` and `Manager`.

```java
public abstract class Employee {
    private double rate;

    public abstract void setRate(double rate);

    public double getRate() {
        return rate;
    }
}

public abstract class Manager extends Employee implements CharitySinger {
        // Code goes here
}
```

The Manager class inherits from the Employee class. The following five methods are available to the Manager class for inheritance:

- The abstract `CharitySinger.sing()` method

- The default `CharitySinger.setRate()` method

- The default CharitySinger.getRate() method

- The abstract Employee.setRate() method

- The concrete Employee.getRate() method

There is no conflict for the sing() method. Therefore, the Manager class inherits the sing() method from the CharitySinger interface. There are two choices for the setRate() and getRate() methods. The two methods are available in the superclass. Therefore, the Manager class inherits the setRate() and getRate() methods from the Employee class.

Example #2

The "superclass always wins" rule implies that the methods declared in the Object class cannot be overridden with a default method in an interface. The following declaration for the Runner interface will not compile:

```
// Won't compile
public interface Runner {
        void run();

        // Not allowed
        default String toString() {
                return "WhoCares";
        }
}
```

Before I give the reasons behind this rule, let's assume that the Runner interface compiles. Suppose a Thinker class implements the Runner interface as shown:

```
public class Thinker implements Runner {
        public void run() {
                System.out.println();
        }

        // Which method is inherited - Object.toString() or Runner.toString()?
}
```

The Thinker class has two choices for inheriting the toString() method: one from the superclass Object and one from the superinterface Runner. Remember that the superclass always wins, and therefore, the Thinker class inherits the toString() method from the Object class, not the Runner interface. This argument is true for all methods in the Object class and all classes. Because such default methods in an interface will never be used by any class, it is not allowed for interfaces to override the methods of the Object class with a default method.

Example #3

Default methods in interfaces cannot be declared final for two reasons:

- Default methods are intended to be overridden in classes.

- If a default method is added in an existing interface, all implementing classes should continue to work if they contained a method with the same signature.

Let's consider a Sizeable interface and a Bag class that implement the interface.

```java
public interface Sizeable {
      int size();
}

public class Bag implements Sizeable {
      private int size;

      @Override
      public int size() {
            return size;
      }

      public boolean isEmpty() {
            return (size == 0);
      }

      // More code goes here
}
```

The Bag class overrides the size() method of the Sizeable interface. The class contains an additional concrete method isEmpty(). There is no problem at this point. Now, the designer of the Sizeable interface decides to add a default isEmpty() method to the interface that will look as follows:

```java
public interface Sizeable {
      int size();

      // A new default method. Cannot declare it final
      default boolean isEmpty() {
            return (size() == 0);
      }
}
```

After the new default isEmpty() method is added to the Sizeable interface, the Bag class will continue to work. The class simply overrides the default isEmpty() method of the Sizeable interface. If it were allowed to declare the default isEmpty() method final, it would have resulted in an error as a final method is not allowed to be overridden. The rule not to allow a final default method ensures backward-compatibility. The existing classes will continue to work if the class contains a method and a default method with the same signature is added in the interfaces the class implements.

The Most Specific Superinterface Wins

This rule tries to resolve the inheritance of a complicating method with the same signature from multiple interfaces. If the same method (abstract or default) is inherited from multiple superinterfaces through different paths, the most specific path is used. Suppose I1 is an interface with a method m(). I2 is a subinterface of I1 and I2 overrides the method m(). If a class Test implements both interfaces I1 and I2, it has two choices of inheriting the m() method

I1.m() and I2.m(). In this case, I2.m() is considered most specific as it overrides I1.m(). I will summarize this rule as follows:

- Make a list of all choices of the method with the same signature that are available from different superinterfaces.

- Remove all methods from the list that have been overridden by others in the list.

- If you are left with only one choice, that is the method the class will inherit.

Consider the following Employee class. It implements Singer and SingerPlayer interfaces.

```java
public class Employee implements Singer, SingerPlayer {
        // Code goes here
}
```

There are no conflicts in inheriting the play() methods, which is inherited from the SingerPlayer interface. There is no conflict in inheriting the sing() method as both superinterfaces leads to the same sing() method that is in the Singer interface.

Which setRate() method is inherited by the Employee class? You have the following choices:

- Singer.setRate()

- SingerPlayer.setRate()

Both choices lead to an abstract setRate() method. Therefore, there is no conflict. However, the SingerPlayer.setRate() method is most specific in this case as it overrides the Singer.setRate() method.

Which getRate() method is inherited by the Employee class? You have the following choices:

- Singer.getRate()

- SingerPlayer.getRate()

The Singer.getRate() method has been overridden by the SingerPlayer.getRate() method. Therefore, Singer.getRate() is removed as a choice, which leaves you only one choice, SingerPlayer.getRate(). Therefore, the Employee class inherits the default getRate() method from the SingerPlayer interface.

The Class Must Override the Conflicting Method

If the above two rules were not able to resolve the conflicting method's inheritance, the class must override the method and choose what it wants to do inside the method. It may implement the method in a completely new way or it may choose to call one of the methods in the superinterfaces. You can call the default method of one of the superinterfaces of a class using the following syntax:

```java
SuperInterfaceName.super.superInterfaceDefaultMethod(arg1, arg2...)
```

If you want to call one of the methods in the superclass of a class, you can use the following syntax:

```java
ClassName.super.superClassMethod(arg1, arg2...)
```

Consider the following declaration for a MultiTalented class, which inherits from the Singer and Player interfaces:

```java
// Won't compile
public abstract class MultiTalented implements Singer, Player {
}
```

The above class declaration will not compile. The class inherits the sing(), play(), and setRate() methods without any conflicts. There are two choices to inherit the getRate() method:

- The abstract Singer.getRate() method

- The default Player.getRate() method

None of the two versions of the getRate() method are more specific than others. In this case, the MultiTalented class must override the getRate() method to resolve the conflict.

The following code for the MultiTalented class will compile. It overrides the getRate() method to resolve the conflict. The method calls the default getRate() method of the Player interface and performs other logic. The class is still declared abstract as it does not implemented abstract methods from the Singer and Player interfaces.

```
public abstract class MultiTalented implements Singer, Player {
        // A MultiTalented is paid the rate of a Player plus 200.00
        @Override
        public double getRate() {
                // Get the default rate for a Player from the Player interafce
                double playerRate = Player.super.getRate();
                double rate = playerRate + 200.00;
                return rate;
        }
}
```

The instanceof Operator

You can use the instanceof operator to evaluate if a reference type variable refers to an object of a specific class or its class implements a specific interface. It is a two-operand operator and it evaluates to a boolean value. The general syntax of the instanceof operator is

<<referenceVariable>> instanceof <<referenceType>>

Let's consider the following snippet of code that defines interfaces Generous and Munificent, and classes Giver, GenerousGiver, MunificentGiver, and StingyGiver. Figure 17-2 shows a class diagram for these interfaces and classes.

Figure 17-2. *A class diagram showing the relationship between interfaces and classes: Generous, Munificent, Object, Giver, GenerousGiver, MunificentGiver, and StingyGiver*

```java
public interface Generous {
      void give();
}

public interface Munificent extends Generous {
      void giveALot();
}

public class Giver {
}

public class GenerousGiver extends Giver implements Generous {
      public void give() {
      }
}

public class MunificentGiver extends Giver implements Munificent {
      public void give() {
      }

      public void giveALot() {
      }
}

public final class StingyGiver extends Giver {
      public void giveALittle() {
      }
}
```

Every expression in Java has two types, a compile-time type and a runtime type. The compile-time type is also known as the static type or the declared type. The runtime type is also known as the dynamic type or the actual type. The compile-time type of an expression is known at compile time. The runtime type of an expression is known when the expression is actually executed. Consider the following statement:

```java
Munificent john = new MunificentGiver();
```

The above code involves one variable declaration, Munificent john, and one expression, new MunificentGiver(). The compile time type of the variable john is Munificent. The compile-time type of the expression new MunificentGiver() is MunificentGiver. At runtime, the variable john will have a reference to an object of the MunificentGiver class and its runtime type will be MunificentGiver. The runtime type for the expression new MunificentGiver() will be the same as its compile-time type, which is MunificentGiver.

The instanceof operator performs compile-time check as well as runtime check. At compile-time, it checks if it is possible for its left-hand operand to point to an instance of its right-hand operand type. It is allowed for the left-hand operand to point to the null reference. If it is possible for the left-hand operand to have a reference of its right-hand operand type, the code passes the compiler check. For example, the following code would compile and it will print true at runtime:

```java
Munificent john = new MunificentGiver();
if (john instanceof Munificent) {
      System.out.println("true");
}
```

```
else {
        System.out.println("false");
}
```

Looking at the compile-time type of john, which is Munificent, the compiler is assured that john will refer to either null or an object whose class implements the Munificent interface. Therefore, the compiler will not complain about "john instanceof Munificent" expression.

Let's consider the following snippet of code, which compiles and prints false:

```
Giver donna = new Giver();
if (donna instanceof Munificent) {
        System.out.println("true");
}
else {
        System.out.println("false");
}
```

The compile-time type of the variable donna is Giver. At runtime, it also points to an object of the Giver type. That is, its runtime type is Giver. When the compiler attempts to compile the "donna instanceof Munificent" expression, it asks a question: "Is it possible that the variable donna whose compile-time type is Giver may point to an object of a class that implements the Munificent interface?" The answer is yes. Are you getting confused by the answer? The compiler does not look at the whole statement Giver donna = new Giver(); in the above snippet of code when it evaluates the instanceof operator. It just looks at the compile-time type of variable donna, which is Giver. The Giver class itself does not implement the Munificent interface. However, any subclass of the Giver class might implement the Munificent interface and the variable donna may refer to the object of any such classes. For example, it is possible to write code as shown:

```
Giver donna = new MunificentGiver();
```

In this case, the compile-time type of the variable donna remains the Giver type. However, at runtime, it will refer to an object whose class implements the Munificent interface. The job of the compiler is just to make sure about a "possibility" that may be true or false at runtime. When the variable donna refers to an object of the Giver class, donna instanceof Munificent will return false at runtime, because the Giver class does not implement the Munificent interface. When the variable donna refers to an object of the MunificentGiver class, donna instanceof Munificent will return true at runtime because the MunificentGiver class implements the Munificent interface.

The following snippet of code will compile and print false:

```
Giver kim = new StingyGiver();
if (kim instanceof Munificent) {
        System.out.println("true");
}
else {
        System.out.println("false");
}
```

Let's consider a variation of the above code as follows:

```
StingyGiver jim = new StingyGiver();
if (jim instanceof Munificent) { // A compile-time error
        System.out.println("true");
}
```

```
else {
        System.out.println("false");
}
```

This time, the compiler will refuse to compile the above code. Let's apply the logic and try to figure out what is wrong with the code. The compiler will generate an error about the jim instanceof Munificent expression. It is saying that it knows for sure that there is no possibility at runtime that the variable jim can refer to an object whose class implements the Munificent interface. How can the compiler be so sure about this possibility? It is easy. You have declared the StingyGiver class as final, which means it cannot be subclassed. This implies that the variable jim whose compile-time type is StingyGiver can only refer to an object whose class is StingyGiver. The compiler also knows that the StingyGiver class and none of its ancestor classes implement the Munificent interface. With all these reasoning, the compiler determines that you have a logical error in your program and you need to fix it.

If the instanceof operator returns true at runtime, it means that its left-hand operand can be safely cast to the type represented by its right-hand operand. Typically, your logic will be as follows when you need to use the instanceof operator:

```
ABC a = null;
DEF d = null;
if (x instanceof ABC) {
        // Safe to cast x to ABC type
        a = (ABC)x;
}
else if (x instanceof DEF) {
        // Safe to cast x to DEF type
        d = (DEF)x;
}
```

If the left-hand operand of the instanceof operator is null or a reference variable, which points to null at runtime, it returns false. The following snippet of code will also print false:

```
Giver ken = null;
if (ken instanceof Munificent) {
        System.out.println("true");
}
else {
        System.out.println("false");
}
```

You can conclude that if v instanceof XYZ returns true, you can assume the following two things safely:

- v is not null. That is, v is pointing to a valid object in memory.

- The cast (XYZ)v will always succeed. That is, the following code is guaranteed to work at runtime without a ClassCastException:

    ```
    XYZ x = (XYZ)v;
    ```

Marker Interfaces

You can declare an interface with no members. Note that an interface can have members in two ways: by declaring its own members or by inheriting members from its superinterfaces. When an interface has no members (declared or inherited), it is known as a *marker* interface. A marker interface is also called a *tag* interface. What is the use of a marker interface? Why would any class implement a marker interface? As the name suggests, a marker interface is used to mark the class with a special meaning that can be used in a particular context. The meaning added to a class by a marker interface depends on the context. The developer of the marker interface has to document the meaning of the interface and the consumer of the interface will make use of its intended meaning. For example, let's declare a marker interface called Funny, as shown below. The meaning of this Funny interface is up to the developer who uses it.

```
public interface Funny {
        // No code goes here
}
```

Every interface defines a new type, so does a marker interface. Therefore, you can declare a variable of type Funny.

```
Funny simon = an object of a class that implements the Funny interface;
```

What can you access using the variable simon, which is of type Funny? You cannot access anything using the simon variable, except the all methods of the Object class. You could do that without implementing the Funny interface to your class, too. Typically, a marker interface is used with the instanceof operator to check if a reference type variable refers to an object, whose class implements the marker interface. For example, you may write code like

```
Object obj = any java object;
...
if (obj instanceof Funny) {
        // obj is an object whose class implements the Funny interface. Display a message on the
        // standard output that we are using a Funny object. Or, do something that is intended
        // by the developer of the Funny interface
        System.out.println("Using a Funny object");
}
```

Java API has many marker interfaces. The java.lang.Cloneable, java.io.Serializable, and java.rmi.Remote are a few of the marker interfaces in the Java class library. If a class implements the Cloneable interface, it means that the developer of that class intended to allow the cloning of the objects of that class. You need to take additional steps of overriding the clone() method of the Object class in your class, so the clone() method can be called on objects of your class because the clone() method has been declared protected in the Object class. Even though your class overrides the clone() method, the object of your class cannot be cloned until your class implements the Cloneable marker interface. You can see that implementing Cloneable interface associates a meaning to the class that its object can be cloned. When the clone() method of the Object class is invoked, Java performs a check if the object's class implements the Cloneable interface. If the object's class does not implement the Cloneable interface, it throws an exception at runtime.

Java 5 introduced a specialized form of interface known as annotations. It can be used to associate a meaning to any element, for example, a class, a method, a variable, a package, etc., of a Java program. I will discuss annotations in the next chapter.

Functional Interfaces

An interface with just one abstract method is known as a *functional* interface. The static and default methods are not counted to designate an interface a functional interface. No additional steps, other than what I have already discussed, are needed to declare an interface as functional. I will discuss more about functional interfaces in the chapter on lambda expressions. The Walkable and Swimmable interfaces are examples of functional interfaces as they contain only one abstract method. The Singer interface is an example of a non-function interface as it contains more than one abstract method.

Comparing Objects

When you have a group of objects, sometimes you may want to order them based on some criteria. The java.lang.Comparable and java.util.Comparator are two commonly used interfaces for the purpose of ordering objects. I will discuss both interfaces in this section.

Using the Comparable Interface

A class implements the Comparable interface if objects of the class need to be compared for sorting purposes. For example, you may want to compare two objects of a Person class when sorting a collection of persons in an array or a list. The criteria you use to compare the two objects depend on the context. For example, when you need to display many persons, you may want to display them sorted by their last names, person ids, addresses, or telephone numbers.

The ordering on the objects of a class that is imposed by the Comparable interface is also called the class's *natural ordering*. The Comparable interface contains an abstract compareTo() method that takes one parameter. The method returns zero if the two objects being compared are considered equal; it returns a negative integer if the object is less than the specified parameter; it returns a positive integer if the object is greater than the specified parameter.

The Comparable interface is a generic interface declared as follows:

```
public interface Comparable<T> {
        public int compareTo(T o);
}
```

The String class and wrapper classes (Integer, Double, Float, etc.) implement the Comparable interface. The String class's compareTo() method sorts strings lexicographically. All wrapper classes for the numeric primitive types compare the two objects numerically.

Before Java 5, the compareTo() method must accept only the Object type argument. However, from Java 5, you need to use a parameter type for the Comparable interface, which indicates the type of parameter to its compareTo() method. It is typical to compare objects of the same type. Before Java 5, you needed to perform a check inside the compareTo() method to determine if the object being passed to the argument is of the same type or not. When you use the generic version of the Comparable interface, the compareTo() method's parameter type can be specified as shown below. The following class declaration for the class A implements the Comparable<A> interface using A as its generic type, which states that the class A supports only comparing objects of its own type:

```
public class A implement Comparable<A> {
        public int compareTo(A a) {
                /* Code goes here */
        }
}
```

Listing 17-33 contains the code for a ComparablePerson class that implements the Comparable<ComparablePerson> interface. In the compareTo() method, first you compare the two objects based on their last names. If the last names are the same, you compare their first names. You have used the compareTo() method of the String class to compare the last and first names of two comparable persons. Note that the compareTo() method does not handle null values.

Listing 17-33. A ComparablePerson Class That Implements the Comparable Interface

```java
// ComparablePerson.java
package com.jdojo.interfaces;

public class ComparablePerson implements Comparable<ComparablePerson> {
        private String firstName;
        private String lastName;

        public ComparablePerson(String firstName, String lastName) {
                this.firstName = firstName;
                this.lastName = lastName;
        }

        public String getFirstName() {
                return firstName;
        }

        public void setFirstName(String firstName) {
                this.firstName = firstName;
        }

        public String getLastName() {
                return lastName;
        }

        public void setLastName(String lastName) {
                this.lastName = lastName;
        }

        // Compares two persons based on their last names. If last names are
        // the same, use first names
        public int compareTo(ComparablePerson anotherPerson) {
                int diff = getLastName().compareTo(anotherPerson.getLastName());
                if (diff == 0) {
                        diff = getFirstName().compareTo(anotherPerson.getFirstName());
                }
                return diff;
        }

        public String toString() {
                return getLastName() + ", " + getFirstName();
        }
}
```

Listing 17-34 contains the code that tests the ComparablePerson class by sorting their objects in an array. The output shows that objects of the ComparablePerson class are sorted by last name and first name.

Listing 17-34. A Test Class to Test the ComparablePerson Class and the Comparable Interface

```java
// ComparablePersonTest.java
package com.jdojo.interfaces;

import java.util.Arrays;

public class ComparablePersonTest {
        public static void main(String[] args) {
                ComparablePerson[] persons = new ComparablePerson[] {
                                new ComparablePerson("John", "Jacobs"),
                                new ComparablePerson("Jeff", "Jacobs"),
                                new ComparablePerson("Wally", "Inman")};

                System.out.println("Before sorting...");
                print(persons);

                // Sort the persons list
                Arrays.sort(persons);

                System.out.println("\nAfter sorting...");
                print(persons);
        }

        public static void print(ComparablePerson[] persons) {
                for(ComparablePerson person: persons){
                        System.out.println(person);
                }
        }
}
```

```
Before sorting...
Jacobs, John
Jacobs, Jeff
Inman, Wally

After sorting...
Inman, Wally
Jacobs, Jeff
Jacobs, John
```

Using the Comparator Interface

The Comparable interface imposes a specified ordering on objects of a class. Sometimes you may want to specify a different ordering for objects of the class from the ordering specified in the class by the Comparable interface. Sometimes you may want to specify a particular ordering for the objects of a class that does not implement the Comparable interface. For example, you may want to specify ordering on objects of the ComparablePerson class based on the first name and the last name, as opposed to the ordering specified by its compareTo() method of the Comparable interface, which is the last name and the first name. The Comparator interface lets you specify a custom ordering on objects of any class. Typically, the Java API dealing with a collection of objects requires a Comparator object to specify a custom ordering. The Comparator interface is a generic interface.

```
public interface Comparator<T> {
        int compare(T o1, T o2);
        boolean equals(Object obj);

        // Default and static methods are not shown here
}
```

The Comparator interface has been overhauled in Java 8. Several static and default methods have been added to the interface. I will discuss some of the new methods in this chapter and some later in the chapter on lambda expressions.

Typically, you do not need to implement the equals() method of the Comparator interface. Every class in Java inherits the equals() method from the Object class and that is fine in most cases. The compare() method takes two parameters and it returns an integer. It returns a negative integer, zero, or a positive integer if the first argument is less than, equal to, or greater than the second argument, respectively.

Listing 17-35 and Listing 17-36 contain two implementations of the Comparator interface: one compares two ComparablePerson objects based on their first name and another based on their last names.

Listing 17-35. A Comparator Comparing ComparablePersons Based on Their First Names

```
// FirstNameComparator.java
package com.jdojo.interfaces;

import java.util.Comparator;

public class FirstNameComparator implements Comparator<ComparablePerson> {
        public int compare(ComparablePerson p1, ComparablePerson p2) {
                String firstName1 = p1.getFirstName();
                String firstName2 = p2.getFirstName();
                int diff = firstName1.compareTo(firstName2);
                return diff;
        }
}
```

Listing 17-36. A Comparator Comparing ComparablePersons Based on Their Last Names

```
// LastNameComparator.java
package com.jdojo.interfaces;

import java.util.Comparator;

public class LastNameComparator implements Comparator<ComparablePerson> {
        public int compare(ComparablePerson p1, ComparablePerson p2) {
                String lastName1 = p1.getLastName();
                String lastName2 = p2.getFirstName();
                int diff = lastName1.compareTo(lastName2);
                return diff;
        }
}
```

Using a `Comparator` is easy. Create its object and pass it to the methods that take a collection of objects and a comparator to compare them. For example, to sort an array of `ComparablePerson` objects, pass the array and a `FirstNameComparator` to the static `sort()` method of the `Arrays` class.

```
ComparablePerson[] persons = create and populate the array...

// Sort the persons array based on first name
Comparator fnComparator = new FirstNameComparator();
Arrays.sort(persons, fnComparator);
```

You can use a similar logic to sort the array based on the last name.

```
// Sort the persons array based on last name
Comparator lnComparator = new LastNameComparator();
Arrays.sort(persons, lnComparator);
```

Prior to Java 8, if you wanted to the array based on the first name followed by the last name, you needed to create another implementation of the `Comparator` interface. Thanks to Java 8's adding of default methods to interfaces, you do not need to create a new implementation of the `Comparator` interface. The `Comparator` class contains a `thenComparing()` default method declared as follows:

```
default Comparator<T> thenComparing(Comparator<? super T> other)
```

The `thenComparing()` method takes a `Comparator` as an argument and returns a new `Comparator`. The new `Comparator` is used for ordering if the two objects being compared are equal using the original `Comparator`. The following snippet of code combines the first name and last `Comparators` to create a new `Comparator`:

```
// Sort using first name, then last name
Comparator firstLastComparator = fnComparator.thenComparing(lnComparator);
Arrays.sort(persons, firstLastComparator);
```

■ **Tip** You can chain the call to the `thenComparing()` method to create a `Comparator` that imposes the ordering on several nested levels.

There is another useful addition to the `Comparator` interface in Java 8: a default method named `reversed()`. The method returns a new `Comparator` that imposes the reverse ordering of the original `Comparator`. If you want to sort the array of persons based on first name, then last name in descending order, you can do so as follows:

```
// Sort using first name, then last name in reversed order
Comparator firstLastReverseComparator = firstLastComparator.reversed();
Arrays.sort(persons, firstLastReverseComparator);
```

Comparators do not handle null values well. Typically, they throw a `NullPointerException`. Java 8 added two useful, null-friendly, convenience static methods to the `Comparator` interface.

- `static <T> Comparator<T> nullsFirst(Comparator<? super T> comparator)`
- `static <T> Comparator<T> nullsLast(Comparator<? super T> comparator)`

These methods take a Comparator and return a null-friendly Comparator place the null values first or last.

```
// Sort using first name, then last name, placing null values first
Comparator nullFirstComparator = Comparator.nullsFirst(firstLastComparator);
Arrays.sort(persons, nullFirstComparator);
```

Listing 17-37 uses an object of this class to sort objects of the ComparablePerson class. As the output indicates, this time you are able to sort a list of comparable persons based on their first names and last names. If you want to sort a list of objects of the ComparablePerson in any other order, you will need to use an object of the Comparator interface that imposes the desired order.

Listing 17-37. A Test Class That Uses a Comparator Object to Sort ComparablePerson Objects

```
// ComparablePersonTest2.java
package com.jdojo.interfaces;

import java.util.Arrays;
import java.util.Comparator;

public class ComparablePersonTest2 {
        public static void main(String[] args) {
                ComparablePerson[] persons = new ComparablePerson[]{
                        new ComparablePerson("John", "Jacobs"),
                        new ComparablePerson("Jeff", "Jacobs"),
                        new ComparablePerson("Wally", "Inman")};

                System.out.println("Original array...");
                print(persons);

                // Sort using first name
                Comparator<ComparablePerson> fnComparator = new FirstNameComparator();
                Arrays.sort(persons, fnComparator);
                System.out.println("\nAfter sorting on first name...");
                print(persons);

                // Sort using last name
                Comparator<ComparablePerson> lnComparator = new LastNameComparator();
                Arrays.sort(persons, lnComparator);
                System.out.println("\nAfter sorting on last name...");
                print(persons);

                // Sort using first name, then last name
                Comparator<ComparablePerson> firstLastComparator =
                        fnComparator.thenComparing(lnComparator);
                Arrays.sort(persons, firstLastComparator);
                System.out.println("\nAfter sorting on first, then last name...");
                print(persons);

                // Sort using first name, then last name in reversed order
                Comparator<ComparablePerson> firstLastReverseComparator =
                        firstLastComparator.reversed();
```

```
            Arrays.sort(persons, firstLastReverseComparator);
            System.out.println("\nAfter sorting on first, then last name in reversed...");
            print(persons);

            // Sort using first name, then last name using null first
            Comparator<ComparablePerson> nullFirstComparator =
                    Comparator.nullsFirst(firstLastComparator);
            ComparablePerson[] personsWithNulls = new ComparablePerson[]{
                    new ComparablePerson("John", "Jacobs"),
                    null,
                    new ComparablePerson("Jeff", "Jacobs"),
                    new ComparablePerson("Wally", "Inman"),
                    null};

            Arrays.sort(personsWithNulls, nullFirstComparator);
            System.out.println("\nAfter sorting on first, then last name " +
                            "using null first...");
            print(personsWithNulls);
    }

    public static void print(ComparablePerson[] persons) {
            for (ComparablePerson person : persons) {
                    System.out.println(person);
            }
    }
}
```

```
Original array...
Jacobs, John
Jacobs, Jeff
Inman, Wally

After sorting on first name...
Jacobs, Jeff
Jacobs, John
Inman, Wally

After sorting on last name...
Inman, Wally
Jacobs, John
Jacobs, Jeff

After sorting on first, then last name...
Jacobs, Jeff
Jacobs, John
Inman, Wally

After sorting on first, then last name in reversed...
Inman, Wally
Jacobs, John
Jacobs, Jeff
```

```
After sorting on first, then last name using null first...
null
null
Jacobs, Jeff
Jacobs, John
Inman, Wally
```

Polymorphism—One Object, Many Views

Polymorphism refers to the ability of an object to take on many forms. I will use the term "view" instead of the term "form." The term "view" gives better understanding of polymorphism in the context of interfaces. Let's rephrase the definition of polymorphism: It is an ability of an object to provide its different views. Interfaces let you create a polymorphic object. Consider the Turtle class declaration shown in Listing 17-21. It implements Swimmable and Walkable interfaces. You create a Turtle object as shown:

```
Turtle turti = new Turtle("Turti");
```

Because the Turtle class implements the Walkable and Swimmable interfaces, you can treat the turti object as a Walkable or a Swimmable.

```
Walkable turtiWalkable = turti;
Swimmable turtiSwimmable = turti;
```

Since every class in Java is inherited from the Object class, you can also treat the turti object as an Object.

```
Object turiObject = turti;
```

Figure 17-3 shows four different views of the same Turtle object. Note that there is only one object, which is of the Turtle class. When you look at a house from different directions (top, front, back, left, right, etc.), you get different views of the same house. Nevertheless, there is only one house. Note that when you are looking at a house from its front, you do not get to see its other views, from example, the back view or the left view. Like a house, a Java object can exhibit different views of itself, which is called polymorphism.

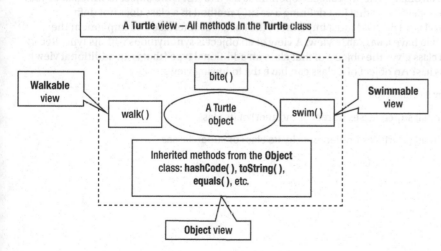

Figure 17-3. Polymorphism— one object, many views. Four different views of a Turtle object

What defines a particular view of a Java object and how do you get that view of the object? A view is something that is available for an outsider (in technical terms, for clients or users of the class). The set of methods (accessible to clients) defined in a type (a class or an interface) defines a view of an object of that type. For example, the Walkable type defines one method: walk(). If you get a Walkable view of an object, it means that you have access to only the walk() method of that object. Similarly, if you have a Swimmable view of an object, you can access only the swim() method of that object. How about having a Turtle view of a Turtle object? The Turtle class defines three methods: bite(), walk(), and swim(). It also inherits methods from the Object class. Therefore, if you have a Turtle view of an object, you can access all methods that are available in the Turtle class (directly declared or inherited from its superclass and superinterfaces). Every class in Java is inherited, directly or indirectly, from the Object class. By virtue of this, every object in Java has at least two views: one view defined by the set of methods that are available (declared or inherited) in the object's class and another view defined by the set of methods defined in the Object class. When you are using the Object view of an object, you can access methods of only the Object class.

You get different views of an object by accessing it using reference variables of different types. For example, to get the Walkable view of a Turtle object you do any of the following things:

```
Turtle t = new Turtle("Turti");
Walkable w2 = t; // w2 gives Walkable view of Turtle object
Walkable w3 = new Turtle(); // w3 gives Walkable view of Turtle object
```

With this knowledge of a Java object that can support different views, Let's look at the use of the instanceof operator. It is used to test if an object supports a specific view or not. Consider the following snippet of code:

```
Object anObject = get any object reference;
if(anObject instanceof Walkable) {
        // anObject has a Walkable view
        Walkable w = (Walkable)anObject;

        // Now access the Walkable view of the object using w
}
else {
        // anObject does not have a Walkable view
}
```

The anObject variable refers to an object. The instanceof operator is used to test if the object to which anObject variable refers to supports a Walkable view. Note that just defining a walk() method in a class does not define a Walkable view for the objects of that class. The class must implement the Walkable interface and implement the walk() method in order for its object to have a Walkable view. A view of an object is synonymous with its type. Recall that implementing an interface to a class gives the objects of that class an additional type (that is an additional view). How many views an object of a class has? An object of a class can have the following views:

- A view that is defined by its class type

- Views that are defined by all superclasses (direct or indirect) of its class

- Views that are defined by all interfaces implements by its class or superclasses (direct or indirect)

Dynamic Binding and Interfaces

Java uses dynamic binding (also known as runtime binding or late binding) when a method is invoked using a variable of an interface type. Consider the following code:

```
Walkable john = a Walkable object reference...
john.walk();
```

The variable john has two types: a compile-time type and a runtime type. Its compile-time type is its declared type, which is Walkable. The compiler knows about the compile-time type of a variable. When the code john.walk() is compiled, the compiler has to verify that this call is valid according to all pieces of information that are available at compile time. The compiler adds instruction similar to the following for the john.walk() method invocation:

```
invokeinterface #5,  1; //InterfaceMethod com/jdojo/interfaces/Walkable.walk:()V
```

The above instruction states that the john.walk() method invocation is being made on a variable of an interface type, which is Walkable. The object to which the variable john refers at runtime is its runtime type. The compiler does not know about the runtime type of the variable john. The variable john may refer to an object of a Person class, a Turtle class, a Duck class, or any other class that implements the Walkable interface. The compiler does not state which implementation of the walk() method should be used, when john.walk() is executed. The runtime decides the implementation of the walk() method to invoke as follows:

- It gets the information about the class of the object to which the variable john refers to. For example, consider the following snippet of code:

  ```
  Walkable john = new Person("John"); // john refers to a Person object
  john.walk();
  ```

  Here, the class type of the object to which the variable john refers to at runtime is Person.

- It looks for the walk() method implementation in the class that is determined in the previous step. If the walk() method implementation is not found in that class, the runtime looks for the walk() method's implementation in the ancestor class recursively.

- If the walk() method's implementation is found in the previous step, it is executed as soon as it is found. That is, if the walk() method's implementation is found in the class of the object to which the variable john refers to, the runtime executes that method implementation and it does not look for the method any further in its ancestor class.

If the walk() method's implementation is not found in the class hierarchy, the inheritance hierarchy of the superinterfaces implemented by the class is searched. If a walk() method is found using the most specific rules of finding methods in interfaces described previously, that method is invoked if it is a default method. If multiple default walk() methods are found, an IncompatibleClassChangeError is thrown. If an abstract walk() method is found, an AbstractMethodError is thrown.

- If the walk() method's implementation is still not found, a NoSuchMethodError is thrown. If all classes are consistently compiled, you should not get this error.

Summary

An interface is a specification that is meant to be implemented by classes. An interface may contain members that are static constants, abstract methods, default methods, static methods, and nested types. An interface cannot have instance variables. An interface cannot be instantiated.

An interface with no members is known as a market interface. An interface with only one abstract method is known as a functional interface.

A class implements interfaces. The keyword implements is used in a class declaration to implement interfaces. The class implementing an interface inherits all members from the interface, except the static methods. If the class inherits abstract methods from the implemented interfaces, it needs to override them and provide an implementation or it should declare itself abstract. The class-implementing interfaces are subtypes of the implemented interfaces and the implemented interfaces are supertypes of the class. A class inherits the same methods from multiple supertypes (superclasses or superinterfaces) with the same signature; in such a case, the method from the superclass takes precedence; if all methods are inherited from superinterfaces, the most specific method is used; if there are still multiple candidates, the class must override the method to resolve the conflict.

An interface may inherit from other interfaces. The keyword extends is used in the interface declaration to specify all inherited interfaces. The interfaces from which the interface is inherited are known as superinterfaces and the interface itself is known as a subinterface. A subinterface inherits all members of its superinterfaces, except their static methods. A conflict may arise if an interface inherits a method combination default-default or default-abstract with the same signature from multiple superinterfaces. The conflict is resolved in two steps: the most specific candidate is used; if there are multiple most specific candidates, the interface must override the conflicting method.

Before Java 8, it was not possible, without breaking the code, to evolve interfaces after they are published. From Java 8, you can add default and static methods to existing interfaces.

Dynamic binding is used when an abstract or default method is called using a variable of an interface type. Static binding is used when the static methods of an interface is called. Note that the static methods of an interface can be called using only one syntax.

```
InterfaceName.staticMethodName(arg1, arg2...)
```

■■■

CHAPTER 18

Enum Types

In this chapter, you will learn

- What enum types are

- How to declare enum types and enum constants

- How to use enums in switch statements

- How to associate data and methods to enum constants

- How to declare nested enums

- How to implement interfaces to an enum type

- How to perform a reverse lookup for enum constants

- How to use EnumSet to work with ranges of enum constants

What Is an Enum Type?

An enum (also known as enumeration and enumerated data type) lets you create an ordered list of constants as a type. Before we discuss what an enum is and why we need it, let's consider a problem and solve it using Java features that were available before Java 5. Suppose you are working on a defect tracking application in which you need to represent the severity of a defect. The application lets you specify the severity of a defect as low, medium, high, and urgent. A typical way to represent the four types of severity before Java 5 was to declare four int constants in a class, say Severity, as shown:

```
public class Severity {
        public static final int LOW = 0;
        public static final int MEDIUM = 1;
        public static final int HIGH = 2;
        public static final int URGENT = 3;
}
```

Suppose you want to write a utility class named DefectUtil that has a method to compute the projected turnaround days for a defect based on its severity. The code for the DefectUtil class may look like the following:

```
public class DefectUtil {
        public static int getProjectedTurnaroundDays(int severity) {
                int days = 0;
```

```
        switch (severity) {
                case Severity.LOW:
                        days = 30;
                        break;
                case Severity.MEDIUM:
                        days = 15;
                        break;
                case Severity.HIGH:
                        days = 7;
                        break;
                case Severity.URGENT:
                        days = 1;
                        break;
        }

        return days;
    }

    // Other code for the DefectUtil class goes here
}
```

The following are a few problems with the above approach in handling the severity of a defect:

- Since a severity is represented as an integer constant, you can pass any integer value to the getProjectedTurnaroundDays() method, not just 0, 1, 2, and 3, which are the valid values for the severity type. You may want to add a check inside this method so only valid severity values can be passed to it. Otherwise, the method may throw an exception. However, that does not solve the problem forever. You will need to update the code that checks for valid severity values whenever you add new severity types.

- If you change the value for a severity constant, you must recompile the code that uses it to reflect the changes. When you compile the DefectUtil class, Severity.LOW is replaced with 0, Severity.MEDIUM is replaced with 1, and so on. If you change the value for the constant LOW in the Severity class to 10, you must recompile the DefectUtil class to reflect this change. Otherwise, the DefectUtil class will still keep using the value 1.

- When you save the value of the severity on disk, its corresponding integer value will be saved, for example, 0, 1, 2, etc., not the string values LOW, MEDIUM, HIGH, etc. You must maintain a separate map to convert from an integer value to its corresponding string representation for all severity types.

- When you print the severity value of a defect, it will print an integer, for example, 0, 1, 2, etc. An integer value for a severity does not mean anything to the users.

- Note that the severity types of the defects have a specific order. For example, a LOW severity defect is given less priority than a MEDIUM severity defect. Since severity is being represented by an arbitrary number, you must write code using hard-coded values to maintain the order of the constants defined in the Severity class. Suppose you add another severity type of VERY_HIGH, which has less priority than URGENT and more priority than HIGH. Now you must change the code that handles ordering of severity type because you have added one in the middle of the existing severity types.

- There is no automatic way (except by hard coding) that will let you list all severity types.

You would agree that representing the severity types using integer constants is difficult to maintain. That was the only easily implemented solution available before Java 5 to define enumerated constants. You could have solved this problem effectively before Java 5. However, the amount of code you had to write was disproportionate to the problem. The enum type in Java 5 solves this problem in a simple and effective way.

According to the Merriam-Webster online dictionary, the term "enumerate" means "to specify one after another." This is exactly what the enum type lets you do. It lets you specify constants in a specific order. The constants defined in an enum type are instances of that enum type. You define an enum type using the keyword enum. Its simplest general syntax is

```
<access-modifier> enum <enum-type-name> {
        // List of comma separated names of enum constants
}
```

The value for `<access-modifiers>` is the same as the access modifier for a class: public, private, protected, or package-level. The `<enum-type-name>` is a valid Java identifier. The body of the enum type is placed within braces following its name. The body of the enum type can have a list of comma-separated constants and other elements that are similar to the elements you have in a class, for example, instance variables, methods, etc. Most of the time, the enum body includes only constants. The following code declares an enum type called Gender, which declares two constants, MALE and FEMALE:

```
public enum Gender {
        MALE, FEMALE; // The semi-colon is optional in this case
}
```

■ **Tip** It is a convention to name the enum constants in uppercase. The semicolon after the last enum constant is optional if there is no code that follows the list of constants.

Listing 18-1 declares a public enum type called Severity with four enum constants: LOW, MEDIUM, HIGH, and URGENT.

Listing 18-1. Declaration of a Severity Enum

```
// Severity.java
package com.jdojo.enums;

public enum Severity {
        LOW, MEDIUM, HIGH, URGENT;
}
```

A public enum type can be accessed from anywhere in the application. Just like a public class, you need to save the code in Listing 18-1 in a file named Severity.java. When you compile the code, the compiler will create a Severity.class file. Note that except for the use of the enum keyword and the body part, everything for the Severity enum type looks the same as if it is a class declaration. In fact, Java implements an enum type as a class. The compiler does a lot of work for an enum type and generates code for it that is essentially a class. You need to place an enum type in a package as you have been placing all classes in a package. You can use an import statement to import an enum type, as you import a class type, into a compilation unit.

You declare a variable of an enum type the same way you declare a variable of a class type.

```
// Declare defectSeverity variable of the Severity enum type
Severity defectSeverity;
```

You can assign null to an enum type variable, like so:

```
Severity defectSeverity = null;
```

What other values can you assign to an enum type variable? An enum type defines two things:

- The enum constants, which are the only valid values for its type

- The order for those constants

The Severity enum type defines four enum constants. Therefore, a variable of the Severity enum type can have only one of the four values—LOW, MEDIUM, HIGH, and URGENT—or null. You can use dot notation to refer to the enum constants by using the enum type name as the qualifier. The following snippet of code assigns values to a variable of Severity enum type:

```
Severity low = Severity.LOW;
Severity medium = Severity.MEDIUM;
Severity high = Severity.HIGH;
Severity urgent = Severity.URGENT;
```

You cannot instantiate an enum type. The following code that attempts to instantiate the Severity enum type results in a compile-time error:

```
Severity badAttempt = new Severity(); // A compile-time error
```

■ **Tip** An enum type acts as a type as well as a factory. It declares a new type and a list of valid instances of that type as its constants.

An enum type also assigns an order number (or position number), called ordinal, to all of its constants. The ordinal starts with zero and it is incremented by one as you move from first to last in the list of constants. The first enum constant is assigned the ordinal value of zero, the second of 1, the third of 2, and so on. The ordinal values assigned to constants declared in Severity enum type are 0 to LOW, 1 to MEDIUM, 2 to HIGH, and 3 to URGENT. If you change the order of the constants in the enum type body, or add new ones, their ordinal values will change accordingly.

Each enum constant has a name. The name of an enum constant is the same as the identifier specified for the constant in its declaration. For example, the name for the LOW constant in the Severity enum type is "LOW."

You can read the name and the ordinal of an enum constant using the name() and ordinal() methods, respectively. Each enum type has a static method named values() that returns an array of constants in the order they are declared in its body. The program in Listing 18-2 prints the name and ordinal of all enum constants declared in the Severity enum type.

Listing 18-2. Listing Name and Ordinal of Enum Type Constants

```java
// ListEnumConstants.java
package com.jdojo.enums;

public class ListEnumConstants {
        public static void main(String[] args) {
                for(Severity s : Severity.values()) {
                        String name = s.name();
                        int ordinal = s.ordinal();
                        System.out.println(name + "(" + ordinal + ")");
                }
        }
}
```

```
LOW(0)
MEDIUM(1)
HIGH(2)
URGENT(3)
```

Superclass of an Enum Type

An enum type is similar to a Java class type. In fact, the compiler creates a class when an enum type is compiled. You can treat an enum type as a class type for all practical purposes. However, there are some rules that apply only to the enum type. An enum type can also have constructors, fields, and methods. Did I not say that an enum type cannot be instantiated? (In other words, new Severity() is invalid.) Why do you need constructors for an enum type if it cannot be instantiated?

Here is the reason why you need constructors for an enum type. An enum type is instantiated only in the code generated by the compiler. All enum constants are objects of the same enum type. These instances are created and named the same as the enum constants in the code generated by the compiler. The compiler is playing the tricks. The compiler generates code for an enum type similar to the one shown below. The following sample code is just to give you an idea what goes on behind the scenes. The actual code generated by the compiler may be different from the one shown below. For example, the code for the valueOf() method gives you a sense that it compares the name with enum constant names and returns the matching constant instance. In reality, the compiler generates code for a valueOf() method that makes a call to the valueOf() method in the Enum superclass.

```java
// Transformed code for Severity enum type declaration
package com.jdojo.enums;

public final class Severity extends Enum {
        public static final Severity LOW;
        public static final Severity MEDIUM;
        public static final Severity HIGH;
        public static final Severity URGENT;
```

```
        // Create constants when class is loaded
        static {
                LOW    = new Severity("LOW", 0);
                MEDIUM = new Severity("MEDIUM", 1);
                HIGH   = new Severity("HIGH", 2);
                URGENT = new Severity("URGENT", 3);
        }

        // The private constructor to prevent direct instantiation
        private Severity(String name, int ordinal) {
                super(name, ordinal);
        }

        public static Severity[] values() {
                return new Severity[] { LOW, MEDIUM, HIGH, URGENT };
        }

        public static Severity valueOf(String name) {
                if (LOW.name().equals(name)) {
                        return LOW;
                }

                if (MEDIUM.name().equals(name)) {
                        return MEDIUM;
                }

                if (HIGH.name().equals(name)) {
                        return HIGH;
                }

                if (URGENT.name().equals(name)) {
                        return URGENT;
                }

                throw new IllegalArgumentException(
                                "Invalid enum constant" + name);
        }
}
```

By looking at the transformed code for the Severity enum declaration, the following points can be made:

- Every enum type implicitly extends java.lang.Enum class. This means that all methods
  defined in the Enum class can be used with all enum types. Table 18-1 lists the methods that are
  defined in the Enum class.

Table 18-1. *List of Methods in the Enum Class That Are Available in All Enum Types*

Method Name	Description
`public final String name()`	Returns the name of the enum constant exactly as declared in the enum type declaration.
`public final int ordinal()`	Returns the order (or position) of the enum constant as declared in the enum type declaration.
`public final boolean equals(Object other)`	Returns true if the specified object is equal to the enum constant. Otherwise, it returns false. Note that an enum type cannot be instantiated directly and it has a fixed number of instances, which are equal to the number of enum constants it declares. It implies that the == operator and the equals() method return the same result, when they are used on two enum constants.
`public final int hashCode()`	Returns the hash code value for an enum constant.
`public final int compareTo(E o)`	Compares the order of this enum constant with the order of the specified enum constant. It returns the difference in ordinal value of this enum constant and the specified enum constant. Note that to compare two enum constants they must be of the same enum type. Otherwise, a runtime exception is thrown.
`public final Class<E> getDeclaringClass()`	Returns the class object for the class that declares the enum constant. Two enum constants are considered to be of the same enum type if this method returns the same class object for both. Note that the class object returned by the getClass() method, which every enum type inherits from the Object class, might not be the same as the class object returned by this method. When an enum constant has a body, the actual class of the object for that enum constant is not the same as the declaring class; actually, it is one of the subclasses of the declaring class.
`public String toString()`	By default, it returns the name of the enum constant, which is the same as the return value of the name() method. Note that this method is not declared final and hence you can override it to return a more meaningful string representation for each enum constant.
`public static <T extends Enum<T>>T valueOf(Class<T> enumType, String name)`	Returns an enum constant of the specified enum type and name. For example, you can use the following code to get the LOW enum constant value of the Severity enum type in your code: `Severity lowSeverity = Enum.valueOf(Severity.class, "LOW")`
`protected final Object clone() throws CloneNotSupportedException`	The Enum class redefines the clone() method. It declares the method final, so it cannot be overridden by any enum type. The method always throws an exception. This is done intentionally to prevent cloning of enum constants. This makes sure that only one set of enum constants exists for each enum type.
`protected final void finalize()`	The Enum class declares it final so that it cannot be overridden by any enum type. It provides an empty body. Since you cannot create an instance of an enum type, except its constants, it makes no sense to have a finalize() method for your enum type.

- An enum type is implicitly `final`. In some situations (discussed later), the compiler cannot declare it as `final` as it has done in the sample code for the `Severity` class.

- The compiler adds two static methods, `values()` and `valueOf()`, to every enum type. The `values()` method returns the array of enum constants in the same order they are declared in the enum type. You have seen the use of the `values()` method in Listing 18-2. The `valueOf()` method is used to get the instance of an enum type using the constant name as a string. For example, `Severity.valueOf("LOW")` will return the `Severity.LOW` constant. The `valueOf()` method facilitates reverse lookup—from a string value to an enum type value.

- The `Enum` class implements the `java.lang.Comparable` and `java.io.Serializable` interfaces. This means instances of every enum type can be compared and serialized. The `Enum` class makes sure that during the deserialization process no other instances of an enum type are created than the ones declared as the enum constants. You can use the `compareTo()` method to determine if one enum constant is declared before or after another enum constant. Note that you can also determine the order of two enum constants by comparing their ordinals. The `compareTo()` method does the same, with one more check, that the enum constants being compared must be of the same enum type. The following code snippet shows how to compare two enum constants:

```
Severity s1 = Severity.LOW;
Severity s2 = Severity.HIGH;

// s1.compareTo(s2) returns s1.ordinal() - s2.ordinal()
int diff = s1.compareTo(s2);
if (diff > 0) {
        System.out.println(s1 + " occurs after " + s2);
}
else {
        System.out.println(s1 + " occurs before " + s2);
}
```

Using Enum Types in switch Statements

You can use enum types in switch statements. When the switch expression is of an enum type, all case labels must be unqualified enum constants of the same enum type. The switch statement deduces the enum type name from the type of its expression. You may include a default label.

The following is a revised version of the `DefectUtil` class using a switch statement. Now you do not need to handle the exceptional case of receiving a null value in the `severity` parameter inside `getProjectedTurnaroundDays()` method. If the enum expression of the switch statement evaluates to null, it throws a `NullPointerException`.

```
// DefectUtil.java
package com.jdojo.enums;

public class DefectUtil {
        public static int getProjectedTurnaroundDays(Severity severity) {
                int days = 0;
                switch (severity) {
                        // Must use the unqualified name LOW, not Severity.LOW
                        case LOW:
                                days = 30;
                                break;
```

```
                    case MEDIUM:
                            days = 15;
                            break;
                    case HIGH:
                            days = 7;
                            break;
                    case URGENT:
                            days = 1;
                            break;
            }

            return days;
        }
}
```

Associating Data and Methods to Enum Constants

Generally, you declare an enum type just to have some enum constants, as you have done in the Severity enum type. Since an enum type is actually a class type, you can declare pretty much everything inside an enum type body that you can declare inside a class body. Let's associate one data element, projected turnaround days, with each of your Severity enum constants. You will name your enhanced Severity enum type as SmartSeverity. Listing 18-3 has code for the SmartSeverity enum type, which is very different from the code for the Severity enum type.

Listing 18-3. A SmartSeverity enum Type Declaration, Which Uses Fields, Constructors, and Methods

```
// SmartSeverity.java
package com.jdojo.enums;

public enum SmartSeverity {
        LOW(30), MEDIUM(15), HIGH(7), URGENT(1);

        // Declare an instance variable
        private int projectedTurnaroundDays;

        // Declare a private constructor
        private SmartSeverity(int projectedTurnaroundDays) {
                this.projectedTurnaroundDays = projectedTurnaroundDays;
        }

        // Declare a public method to get the turnaround days
        public int getProjectedTurnaroundDays() {
                return projectedTurnaroundDays;
        }
}
```

Let's discuss the new things that are in the SmartSeverity enum type.

- It declares an instance variable projectedTurnaroundDays, which will store the value of the projected turnaround days for each enum constant.

```
// Declare an instance variable
private int projectedTurnaroundDays;
```

713

- It defines a private constructor, which accepts an int parameter. It stores the value of its parameter in the instance variable. You can add multiple constructors to an enum type. If you do not add a constructor, a no-args constructor is added. You cannot add a public or protected constructor to an enum type. All constructors in an enum type declaration go through parameter and code transformation by the compiler and their access levels are changed to private. Many things are added or changed in the constructor of an enum type by the compiler. As a programmer, you do not need to know the details of the changes made by the compiler.

```
// Declare a private constructor
private SmartSeverity(int projectedTurnaroundDays){
    this.projectedTurnaroundDays = projectedTurnaroundDays;
}
```

- It declares a public method getProjectedTurnaroundDays(), which returns the value of the projected turnaround days for an enum constant (or the instance of the enum type).

- The enum constant declarations have changed to

```
LOW(30), MEDIUM(15), HIGH(7), URGENT(1);
```

This change is not obvious. Now every enum constant name is followed by an integer value in parentheses, for example, LOW(30). This syntax is shorthand for calling the constructor with an int parameter type. When an enum constant is created, the value inside the parentheses will be passed to the constructor that you have added. By simply using the name of the enum constant (for example, LOW in the constant declaration), you invoke a default no-args constructor.

The program in Listing 18-4 tests the SmartSeverity enum type. It prints the names of the constants, their ordinals, and their projected turnaround days. Note that the logic to compute the projected turnaround days is encapsulated inside the declaration of the enum type itself. The SmartSeverity enum type combines the code for the Severity enum type and the getProjectedTurnaroundDays() method in the DefectUtil class. You do not have to write a switch statement anymore to get the projected turnaround days. Each enum constant knows about its projected turnaround days.

Listing 18-4. A Test Class to Test the SmartSeverity Enum Type

```
// SmartSeverityTest.java
package com.jdojo.enums;

public class SmartSeverityTest {
    public static void main(String[] args) {
        for(SmartSeverity s : SmartSeverity.values()) {
            String name = s.name();
            int ordinal = s.ordinal();
            int days = s.getProjectedTurnaroundDays();
            System.out.println("name=" + name +
                                ", ordinal=" + ordinal +
                                ", days=" + days);
        }
    }
}
```

```
name=LOW, ordinal=0, days=30
name=MEDIUM, ordinal=1, days=15
name=HIGH, ordinal=2, days=7
name=URGENT, ordinal=3, days=1
```

Associating a Body to an Enum Constant

SmartSeverity is an example of adding data and methods to an enum type. The code in the getProjectedTurnaroundDays() method is the same for all enum constants. You can also associate a different body to each enum constant. The body can have fields and methods. The body for an enum constant is placed inside braces following its name. If the enum constant accepts arguments, its body follows its argument list. The syntax for associating a body to an enum constant is as follows:

```
<access-modifier> enum <enum-type-name> {
      CONST1 {
              // Body for CONST1 goes here
      },
      CONST2 {
              // Body for CONST2 goes here
      },
      CONST3(arguments-list) {
              // Body of CONST3 goes here
      };

      // Other code goes here
}
```

It is a little different game when you add a body to an enum constant. The compiler creates an anonymous class, which inherits from the enum type. It moves the body of the enum constant to the body of that anonymous class. Anonymous classes are covered in Chapter 2 of the book *Beginning Java Language Features* (ISBN:978-1-4302-6658-7). I will use it briefly to complete the discussion of the enum type. For now, you can think of it just as a different way of declaring and creating a new class at the same time.

Consider an ETemp enum type, as shown:

```
public enum ETemp {
      C1 {
              // Body of constant C1
              public int getValue() {
                      return 100;
              }
      },
      C2,
      C3;
}
```

The body of the ETemp enum type declares three constants: C1, C2, and C3. You have added a body to the C1 constant. The compiler will transform the code for ETemp into something like the following code:

```
public enum ETemp {
        public static final ETemp C1 = new ETemp() {
                // Body of constant C1
                public int getValue() {
                        return 100;
                }
        };
        public static final ETemp C2 = new ETemp();
        public static final ETemp C3 = new ETemp();

        // Other code goes here
}
```

Note that the constant C1 is declared of type ETemp and assigned an object using an anonymous class. The ETemp enum type has no knowledge of the getValue() method defined in the anonymous class. Therefore, it is useless for all practical purposes because you cannot call the method as ETemp.C1.getValue().

To let the client code use the getValue() method, you must declare a getValue() method for the ETemp enum type. If you want all constants of ETemp to override and provide implementation for this method, you need to declare it as abstract. If you want it to be overridden by some, but not all constants, you need to declare it non-abstract and provide a default implementation for it. The following code declares a getValue() method for the ETemp enum type, which returns 0. The C1 constant has its body, which overrides the getValue() method and returns 100. Note that the constants C2 and C3 do not have to have a body; they do not need to override the getValue() method. Now, you can use the getValue() method on the ETemp enum type.

```
public enum ETemp {
        C1 {
                // Body of constant C1
                public int getValue() {
                        return 100;
                }
        },
        C2,
        C3;

        // Provide the default implementation for the getValue() method
        public int getValue() {
                return 0;
        }
}
```

The following code rewrites the above version of ETemp and declares the getValue() method abstract. An abstract method for an enum type forces you to provide a body for all constants and override that method. Now all constants have a body. The body of each constant overrides and provides implementation for the getValue() method.

```java
public enum ETemp {
    C1 {
        // Body of constant C1
        public int getValue() {
            return 100;
        }
    },
    C2 {
        // Body of constant C2
        public int getValue() {
            return 0;
        }
    },
    C3 {
        // Body of constant C3
        public int getValue() {
            return 0;
        }
    };

    // Provide default implementation for getValue() method
    public abstract int getValue();
}
```

Let's enhance your SmartSeverity enum type. You are running out of good names for your enum type. You will name the new one SuperSmartSeverity. Listing 18-5 has the code.

Listing 18-5. Using a Body for Enum Constants

```java
// SuperSmartSeverity.java
package com.jdojo.enums;

public enum SuperSmartSeverity {
    LOW("Low Priority", 30) {
        public double getProjectedCost() {
            return 1000.0;
        }
    },
    MEDIUM("Medium Priority", 15) {
        public double getProjectedCost() {
            return 2000.0;
        }
    },
    HIGH("High Priority", 7) {
        public double getProjectedCost() {
            return 3000.0;
        }
    },
    URGENT("Urgent Priority", 1) {
        public double getProjectedCost() {
            return 5000.0;
        }
    };
```

```java
        // Declare instance variables
        private String description;
        private int projectedTurnaroundDays;

        // Declare a private constructor
        private SuperSmartSeverity(String description,
                                    int projectedTurnaroundDays){
                this.description = description;
                this.projectedTurnaroundDays = projectedTurnaroundDays;
        }

        // Declare a public method to get the turn around days
        public int getProjectedTurnaroundDays() {
                return projectedTurnaroundDays;
        }

        // Override the toString() method in the Enum class to return description
        @Override
        public String toString() {
                return this.description;
        }

        // Provide getProjectedCost() abstract method, so all constants
        // override and provide implementation for it in their body
        public abstract double getProjectedCost();
}
```

The following are new features in the SuperSmartSeverity enum type:

- It has added an abstract method getProjectedCost() to return the projected cost of each type of severity.

- It has a body for each constant that provides implementation for the getProjectedCost() method. Note that declaring an abstract method in an enum type forces you to provide a body for all its constants.

- It has added another parameter to the constructor, which is a nicer name for the severity type.

- It has overridden the toString() method in the Enum class. The toString() method in the Enum class returns the name of the constant. Your toString() method returns a brief and more intuitive name for each constant.

■ **Tip** Typically, you do not need to write this kind of complex code for an enum type. Java enum is very powerful. It has features for you to utilize, if you need them.

The code in Listing 18-6 demonstrates the use of the new features added to the SuperSmartSeverity enum type.

Listing 18-6. A Test Class to Test the SuperSmartSeverity Enum Type

```java
// SuperSmartSeverityTest.java
package com.jdojo.enums;

public class SuperSmartSeverityTest {
        public static void main(String[] args) {
                for(SuperSmartSeverity s : SuperSmartSeverity.values()) {
                        String name = s.name();
                        String desc = s.toString();
                        int ordinal = s.ordinal();
                        int projectedTurnaroundDays =
                                s.getProjectedTurnaroundDays();
                        double projectedCost = s.getProjectedCost();
                        System.out.println("name=" + name +
                                ", description=" + desc +
                                ", ordinal=" + ordinal +
                                ", turnaround days=" +
                                projectedTurnaroundDays +
                                ", projected cost=" + projectedCost);
                }
        }
}
```

```
name=LOW, description=Low Priority, ordinal=0, turnaround days=30, projected cost=1000.0
name=MEDIUM, description=Medium Priority, ordinal=1, turnaround days=15, projected cost=2000.0
name=HIGH, description=High Priority, ordinal=2, turnaround days=7, projected cost=3000.0
name=URGENT, description=Urgent Priority, ordinal=3, turnaround days=1, projected cost=5000.0
```

Comparing Two Enum Constants

You can compare two enum constants in three ways:

- Using the compareTo() method of the Enum class

- Using the equals() method of the Enum class

- Using the == operator

The compareTo() method of the Enum class lets you compare two enum constants of the same enum type. It returns the difference in ordinal for the two enum constants. If both enum constants are the same, it returns zero. The following snippet of code will print -3 because the difference of the ordinals for LOW(ordinal=0) and URGENT(ordinal=3) is -3. A negative value means the constant being compared occurs before the one being compared against.

```java
Severity s1 = Severity.LOW;
Severity s2 = Severity.URGENT;
int diff = s1.compareTo(s2);
System.out.println(diff);
```

-3

Suppose you have another enum called BasicColor.

```
public enum BasicColor {
        RED, GREEN, BLUE;
}
```

The following snippet of code will not compile because it tries to compare the two enum constants, belonging to different enum types:

```
int diff = BasicColor.RED.compareTo(Severity.URGENT); // A compile-time error
```

You can use the equals() method of the Enum class to compare two enum constants for equality. An enum constant is equal only to itself. Note that the equals() method can be invoked on two enum constants of different types. If the two enum constants are from different enum types, the method returns false.

```
Severity s1 = Severity.LOW;
Severity s2 = Severity.URGENT;
BasicColor c = BasicColor.BLUE;
System.out.println(s1.equals(s1));
System.out.println(s1.equals(s2));
System.out.println(s1.equals(c));
```

```
true
false
false
```

You can also use the equality operator (==) to compare two enum constants for equality. Both operands to the == operator must be of the same enum type. Otherwise, you get a compile-time error.

```
Severity s1 = Severity.LOW;
Severity s2 = Severity.URGENT;
BasicColor c = BasicColor.BLUE;
System.out.println(s1 == s1);
System.out.println(s1 == s2);

// A compile-time error. Cannot compare Severity and BasicColor enum types
//System.out.println(s1 == c);
```

```
true
false
```

Nested Enum Types

You can have a nested enum type declaration. You can declare a nested enum type inside a class, an interface, or another enum type. Nested enum types are implicitly static. You can also declare a nested enum type static explicitly in its declaration. Since an enum type is always static, whether you declare it or not, you cannot declare a local enum type (e.g. inside a method's body). You can use any of the access modifiers (public, private, protected, or package) level for a nested enum type. Listing 18-7 shows the code that declares a nested public enum type named Gender inside a Person class.

Listing 18-7. A Gender Enum Type as a Nested Enum Type Inside a Person Class

```
// Person.java
package com.jdojo.enums;

public class Person {
        public enum Gender {MALE, FEMALE}
}
```

The Person.Gender enum type can be accessed from anywhere in the application because it has been declared public. You need to import the enum type to use its simple name in other packages, as shown in the following code:

```
// Test.java
package com.jdojo.enums.pkg1;

import com.jdojo.enums.Person.Gender;

public class Test {
        public static void main(String[] args) {
                Gender m = Gender.MALE;
                Gender f = Gender.FEMALE;
                System.out.println(m);
                System.out.println(f);
        }
}
```

You can also use the simple name of an enum constant by importing the enum constants using static imports. The following code snippet uses MALE and FEMALE simple names of constants of Person.Gender enum type. Note that the first import statement is needed to import the Gender type itself to use its simple name in the code.

```
// Test.java
package com.jdojo.enums.pkg1;

import com.jdojo.enums.Person.Gender;
import static com.jdojo.enums.Person.Gender.*;

public class Test {
        public static void main(String[] args) {
                Gender m = MALE;
                Gender f = FEMALE;
                System.out.println(m);
                System.out.println(f);
        }
}
```

You can also nest an enum type inside another enum type or an interface. The following are valid enum type declarations:

```
public enum OuterEnum {
      C1, C2, C3;

      public enum NestedEnum {
            C4, C5, C6;
      }
}

public interface MyInterface {
      int operation1();
      int operation2();

      public enum AnotherNestedEnum {
            CC1, CC2, CC3;
      }
}
```

Implementing an Interface to an Enum Type

An enum type may implement interfaces. The rules for an enum type implementing an interface are the same as the rules for a class implementing an interface. An enum type is never inherited by another enum type. Therefore, you cannot declare an enum type as abstract. This also implies that if an enum type implements an interface, it must also provide implementation for all abstract methods in that interface.

The program in Listing 18-8 declares a Command interface. The program in Listing 18-9 declares an enum type called CommandList that implements the Command interface. Each enum constant implements the execute() method of the Command interface. Alternatively, you can implement the execute() method in the enum type body and omit the implementations from some or all enum constants. Listing 18-10 demonstrates using the enum constants in the CommandList enum type as Command type.

Listing 18-8. A Command Interface

```
// Command.java
package com.jdojo.enums;

public interface Command {
      void execute();
}
```

Listing 18-9. A CommandList Enum Type Implementing the Command Interface

```
// CommandList.java
package com.jdojo.enums;

public enum CommandList implements Command {
      RUN {
```

```
                public void execute() {
                        System.out.println("Running...");
                }
        },
        JUMP {
                public void execute() {
                        System.out.println("Jumping...");
                }
        };

        // Force all constants to implement the execute() method.
        public abstract void execute();
}
```

Listing 18-10. Using the CommandList Enum Constants as Command Types

```
// CommandTest.java
package com.jdojo.enums;

public class CommandTest {
        public static void main(String... args) {
                // Execute all commands in the command list
                for(Command cmd : CommandList.values()) {
                        cmd.execute();
                }
        }
}
```

```
Running...
Jumping...
```

Reverse Lookup for Enum Constants

You can get the reference of an enum constant if you know its name or position in the list. This is known as reverse lookup based on the name or ordinal of an enum constant. You can use the valueOf() method, which is added by the compiler to an enum type, to perform reverse lookup based on a name. You can use the array returned by the values() method, which is added by the compiler to an enum type, to perform reverse lookup by ordinal. Note that the order of the values in the array that is returned by values() method is the same as the order in which the enum constants are declared. The ordinal of enum constants starts at zero. This implies that the ordinal value of an enum constant can be used as an index in the array that is returned by the values() method. The following snippet of code demonstrates how to reverse look up enum constants:

```
Severity low1 = Severity.valueOf("LOW"); // A reverse lookup using a name
Severity low2 = Severity.values()[0];    // A reverse lookup using an ordinal
System.out.println(low1);
System.out.println(low2);
System.out.println(low1 == low2);
```

```
LOW
LOW
true
```

The reverse lookup for enum constants is case-sensitive. If you use an invalid constant name with the valueOf() method, an IllegalArgumentException is thrown. For example, Severity.valueOf("low") will throw an IllegalArgumentException stating that no enum constant "low" exists in the Severity enum.

Range of Enum Constants

The Java API provides a java.util.EnumSet collection class to work with ranges of enum constants of an enum type. The implementation of the EnumSet class is very efficient. Suppose you have an enum type called Day as shown in Listing 18-11.

Listing 18-11. A Day Enum Type

```java
// Day.java
package com.jdojo.enums;

public enum Day {
        MONDAY, TUESDAY, WEDNESDAY, THURSDAY, FRIDAY, SATURDAY, SUNDAY;
}
```

You can work with a range of days using the EnumSet class, for example, you can get all days between MONDAY and FRIDAY. An EnumSet can contain enum constants only from one enum type. Listing 18-12 demonstrates how to use the EnumSet class to work with the range for enum constants.

Listing 18-12. A Test Class to Demonstrate How to Use the EnumSet Class

```java
// EnumSetTest.java
package com.jdojo.enums;

import java.util.EnumSet;

public class EnumSetTest {
        public static void main(String[] args) {
                // Get all constants of the Day enum
                EnumSet<Day> allDays = EnumSet.allOf(Day.class);
                print(allDays, "All days: " );

                // Get all constants from MONDAY to FRIDAY of the Day enum
                EnumSet<Day> weekDays = EnumSet.range(Day.MONDAY, Day.FRIDAY);
                print(weekDays, "Weekdays: ");

                // Get all constants that are not from MONDAY to FRIDAY of the
                // Day enum Essentially, we will get days representing weekends
                EnumSet<Day> weekends = EnumSet.complementOf(weekDays);
                print(weekends, "Weekends: ");
        }
```

```
    public static void print(EnumSet<Day> days, String msg) {
            System.out.print(msg);
            for(Day d : days) {
                    System.out.print(d + " ");
            }
            System.out.println();
    }
}
```

```
All days: MONDAY TUESDAY WEDNESDAY THURSDAY FRIDAY SATURDAY SUNDAY
Weekdays: MONDAY TUESDAY WEDNESDAY THURSDAY FRIDAY
Weekends: SATURDAY SUNDAY
```

Summary

Like a class and an interface, an enum defines a new reference type in Java. An enum type consists of a pre-defined, ordered set of values, which are known as the elements or constants of the enum type. Constants of the enum type have a name and an ordinal. You can obtain the reference of an enum constant using its name and ordinal, and vice versa. Typically, an enum type is used to define type-safe constants.

An enum type has several things that a class has. It has constructors, instance variables, and methods. However, the constructors of an enum type are implicitly private. An enum type can also implement interfaces just as a class can.

You can declare a variable of the enum type. The variable can be assigned null or one of the constants of the enum type. Every enum type is implicitly inherited from the java.lang.Enum class. An enum type can be used in the switch statements. Java provides an efficient implementation of an EnumSet class to work with a range of enum constants of a specific enum type.

APPENDIX A

■ ■ ■

Character Encodings

A character is the basic unit of a writing system, for example, a letter of the English alphabet, and an ideograph of an ideographic writing system such as Chinese and Japanese ideographs. In the written form, a character is identified by its shape, also known as glyph. The identification of a character with its shape is not precise. It depends on many factors, for example, a hyphen is identified as a minus sign in a mathematical expression; some Greek and Latin letters have the same shapes, but they are considered different characters in two written scripts. Computers understand only numbers, more precisely, only bits 0 and 1. Therefore, it was necessary to convert, with the advent of computers, the characters into codes (or bit combinations) inside the computer's memory, so that the text (sequence of characters) could be stored and reproduced. However, different computers may represent different characters with the same bit combinations, which may lead to misinterpretation of text stored by one computer system and reproduced by another. Therefore, for correct exchange of information between two computer systems, it is necessary that one computer system understand unambiguously the coded form of the characters represented in bit combination produced by another computer system and vice versa. Before we begin our discussion of some widely used character encodings, it is necessary to understand some commonly used terms.

- An abstract character is a unit of textual information, for example, Latin capital letter A ('A').

- A character repertoire is defined as the set of characters to be encoded. A character repertoire can be fixed or open. In a fixed character repertoire, once the set of characters to be encoded is decided, it is never changed. ASCII and POSIX portable character repertoire are examples of a fixed character repertoire. In an open character repertoire, a new character may be added any time. Unicode and Windows Western European repertoires are examples of an open character repertoire. The EURO currency sign and Indian RUPEE sign were added to Unicode because it is an open repertoire.

- A coded character set is defined as a mapping from a set of non-negative integers (also known as code positions, code points, code values, character numbers, and code space) to a set of abstract characters. The integer that maps to a character is called the code point for that character and the character is called an encoded character. A coded character set is also called a character encoding, coded character repertoire, character set definition, or code page. Figure A-1 depicts two different coded character sets; both of them have the same character repertoire, which is the set of three characters (A, B, and C) and the same code points, which is the set of three non-negative integers (1, 2, and 3).

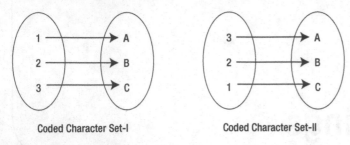

Figure A-1. *Two coded character sets having the same character repertoire and code points*

To define a coded character set, you need to specify three things:

- A set of code points

- A set of characters

- The mapping between the set of code points and the set of characters

The number of bits used to represent a character determines how many distinct characters can be represented in a coded character set. Some widely used coded character sets are as follows.

ASCII

ASCII, the American Standard Code for Information Interchange, is a 7-bit coded character set. ASCII has 2^7 (=128) code points and so it represents 128 distinct characters whose numeric values range from 0 (binary 0000000) to 127 (binary 1111111). The characters NUL and DELETE are represented by code points 0000000 and 1111111, respectively. There are historical reasons to assign these code points to NUL and DELETE characters. It was common to use punched paper tapes to store data for processing by the time ASCII was developed. A 1 bit was used to represent a hole on the paper tape whereas a 0 bit represented the absence of a hole. Since a row of seven 0 bits would be indistinguishable from blank tape, the coding 0000000 would have to represent a NUL character, that is, the absence of any effect. Since holes, once punched, could not be erased but an erroneous character could always be converted into 111111, this bit pattern was adopted as DELETE character.

ASCII uses the first 32 bit combinations (or code points) to represent control characters. This range includes the NUL character, but not the DELETE character. Therefore, it leaves 95 bit combinations for printing characters.

$$128 - 32(Control\ Characters) - 1(DELETE) = 95$$

All printing characters are arranged in the order that could be used for sorting purposes. The SPACE character is normally sorted before any other printing character. Therefore, the SPACE character is allocated the first position among the printing characters. The code point for SPACE character in ASCII is 32, or 1100000. The code point range of 48 to 57 represents 0 to 9 digits, 65 to 90 represents 26 uppercase letters A to Z, and 97 to122 represents 26 lowercase letters a to z. Modern computers use an 8-bit combination, also known as a byte, as the smallest unit for storage. Therefore, on modern computers, a 7-bit ASCII character uses 8 bits (or 1 byte) of memory of which the most significant bit is always set to 0; for example, SPACE is stored as 01100000, DELETE is stored as 0111111. Table A-1 contains the list of characters in the ASCII character set.

Table A-1. *ASCII Character Set*

Decimal	Hexadecimal	Binary	Character	Official Name
0	0	0	NUL	NULL
1	1	1	SOH	Start of heading
2	2	10	STX	Start of text
3	3	11	ETX	End of text
4	4	100	EOT	End of transmission
5	5	101	ENQ	Enquiry
6	6	110	ACK	Acknowledge
7	7	111	BEL	Bell
8	8	1000	BS	Backspace
9	9	1001	TAB	Horizontal tab
10	0A	1010	LF	Line feed (new line)
11	0B	1011	VT	Vertical tab
12	0C	1100	FF	Form feed (new page)
13	0D	1101	CR	Carriage return
14	0E	1110	SO	Shift out
15	0F	1111	SI	Shift in
16	10	10000	DLE	Data link escape
17	11	10001	DC1	Device control 1
18	12	10010	DC2	Device control 2
19	13	10011	DC3	Device control 3
20	14	10100	DC4	Device control 4
21	15	10101	NAK	Negative acknowledge
22	16	10110	SYN	Synchronous idle
23	17	10111	ETB	End of transmission block
24	18	11000	CAN	Cancel
25	19	11001	EM	End of medium
26	1A	11010	SUB	Substitute
27	1B	11011	ESC	Escape
28	1C	11100	FS	File separator
29	1D	11101	GS	Group separator
30	1E	11110	RS	Record separator
31	1F	11111	US	Unit separator

(continued)

Table A-1. (*continued*)

Decimal	Hexadecimal	Binary	Character	Official Name
32	20	100000	SP	Space
33	21	100001	!	Exclamation mark
34	22	100010	"	Quotation mark
35	23	100011	#	Number sign
36	24	100100	$	Dollar sign
37	25	100101	%	Percent sign
38	26	100110	&	Ampersand
39	27	100111	'	Apostrophe
40	28	101000	(	Left parenthesis
41	29	101001	)	Right parenthesis
42	2A	101010	*	Asterisk
43	2B	101011	+	Plus sign
44	2C	101100	,	Comma
45	2D	101101	-	Hyphen/minus
46	2E	101110	.	Full stop/period
47	2F	101111	/	Solidus /slash
48	30	110000	0	Digit zero
49	31	110001	1	Digit one
50	32	110010	2	Digit two
51	33	110011	3	Digit three
52	34	110100	4	Digit four
53	35	110101	5	Digit five
54	36	110110	6	Digit six
55	37	110111	7	Digit seven
56	38	111000	8	Digit eight
57	39	111001	9	Digit nine
58	3A	111010	:	Colon
59	3B	111011	;	Semicolon
60	3C	111100	<	Less-than sign
61	3D	111101	=	Equals sign
62	3E	111110	>	Greater-than sign
63	3F	111111	?	Question mark

(*continued*)

Table A-1. (*continued*)

Decimal	Hexadecimal	Binary	Character	Official Name
64	40	1000000	@	Commercial at
65	41	1000001	A	Latin capital letter A
66	42	1000010	B	Latin capital letter B
67	43	1000011	C	Latin capital letter C
68	44	1000100	D	Latin capital letter D
69	45	1000101	E	Latin capital letter E
70	46	1000110	F	Latin capital letter F
71	47	1000111	G	Latin capital letter G
72	48	1001000	H	Latin capital letter H
73	49	1001001	I	Latin capital letter I
74	4A	1001010	J	Latin capital letter J
75	4B	1001011	K	Latin capital letter K
76	4C	1001100	L	Latin capital letter L
77	4D	1001101	M	Latin capital letter M
78	4E	1001110	N	Latin capital letter N
79	4F	1001111	O	Latin capital letter O
80	50	1010000	P	Latin capital letter P
81	51	1010001	Q	Latin capital letter Q
82	52	1010010	R	Latin capital letter R
83	53	1010011	S	Latin capital letter S
84	54	1010100	T	Latin capital letter T
85	55	1010101	U	Latin capital letter U
86	56	1010110	V	Latin capital letter V
87	57	1010111	W	Latin capital letter W
88	58	1011000	X	Latin capital letter X
89	59	1011001	Y	Latin capital letter Y
90	5A	1011010	Z	Latin capital letter Z
91	5B	1011011	[	Left square bracket /Opening square bracket
92	5C	1011100	\	Reverse solidus/Backslash
93	5D	1011101	]	Right square bracket/Closing square bracket
94	5E	1011110	^	Circumflex accent
95	5F	1011111	_	Low line/Spacing underscore

(*continued*)

Table A-1. (*continued*)

Decimal	Hexadecimal	Binary	Character	Official Name
96	60	1100000	`	Grave accent
97	61	1100001	a	Latin small letter A
98	62	1100010	b	Latin small letter B
99	63	1100011	c	Latin small letter C
100	64	1100100	d	Latin small letter D
101	65	1100101	e	Latin small letter E
102	66	1100110	f	Latin small letter F
103	67	1100111	g	Latin small letter G
104	68	1101000	h	Latin small letter H
105	69	1101001	i	Latin small letter I
106	6A	1101010	j	Latin small letter J
107	6B	1101011	k	Latin small letter K
108	6C	1101100	l	Latin small letter L
109	6D	1101101	m	Latin small letter M
110	6E	1101110	n	Latin small letter N
111	6F	1101111	o	Latin small letter O
112	70	1110000	p	Latin small letter P
113	71	1110001	q	Latin small letter Q
114	72	1110010	r	Latin small letter R
115	73	1110011	s	Latin small letter S
116	74	1110100	t	Latin small letter T
117	75	1110101	u	Latin small letter U
118	76	1110110	v	Latin small letter V
119	77	1110111	w	Latin small letter W
120	78	1111000	x	Latin small letter X
121	79	1111001	y	Latin small letter Y
122	7A	1111010	z	Latin small letter Z
123	7B	1111011	{	Left curly bracket/Opening curly bracket
124	7C	1111100	|	Vertical line/Vertical bar
125	7D	1111101	}	Right curly bracket/Closing curly bracket
126	7E	1111110	~	Tilde
127	7F	1111111	DEL	DELETE

8-bit Character Sets

The ASCII character set worked fine for the English language. Representing the alphabets from other languages, for example, French and German, led to the development of an 8-bit character set. An 8-bit character set defines 2^8 (or 256) character positions whose numeric values range from 0 to 255. The bit combination for an 8-bit character set ranges from 00000000 to 11111111. The 8-bit character set is divided into two parts. The first part represents characters, which are the same as in ASCII character set. The second part introduces 128 new characters. The first 32 positions in the second part are reserved for control characters. Therefore, there are two control character areas in an 8-bit character set: 0-31 and 128-159. Since SPACE and DELETE characters are already defined in the first part, an 8-bit character set can accommodate 192 printing characters (95 + 97) including SPACE. ISO Latin-1 is one of the examples of an 8-bit character set.

Even an 8-bit character set is not large enough to accommodate most of the alphabets of all languages in the world. This lead to the development of a bigger (may be the biggest) character set, which is known as the Universal Character Set (UCS).

Universal Multiple-Octet Coded Character Set (UCS)

The Universal Multiple-Octet Coded Character Set, simply known as UCS, is intended to provide a single coded character set for the encoding of written forms of all the languages of the world and of a wide range of additional symbols that may be used in conjunction with such languages. It is intended not only to cover languages in current use, but also languages of the past and such additions as may be required in the future. The UCS uses a 4-octet (1 octet is 8 bits) structure to represent a character. However, the most significant bit of the most significant octet is constrained to be 0, which permits its use for private internal purposes in a data processing system. The remaining 31 bits allow us to represent more than two thousand million characters. The four octets are named as

- The Group-Octet, or G

- The Plane-Octet, or P

- The Row-Octet, or R

- The Cell-Octet, or C

G is the most significant octet and C is the least significant octet. So, the whole code range for UCS is viewed as a four-dimensional structure composed of

- 128 groups

- 256 planes in each group

- 256 rows in each plane

- 256 cells in each row

Two hexadecimal digits (0-9, A-F) specify the values of any octet. The values of G are restricted to the range 00-7F. The plane with G=00 and P=00 is known as Basic Multilingual Plane (BMP). The row of BMP with R=00 represents the same set of characters as 8-bit ISO Latin-I. Therefore, the first 128 characters of ASCII, ISO Latin-1 and BMP with R=00 match. Characters 129th to 256th of ISO Latin-I and that of BMP with R=00 match. This makes UCS compatible with the existing 7-bit ASCII and 8-bit ISO Latin-I. Further, BMP has been divided into five zones.

- A-zone: It is used for alphabetic and symbolic scripts together with various symbols. The code position available for A-zone ranges from 0000-4DFF. The code positions 0000-001F and 0080-009F are reserved for control characters. The code position 007F is reserved for the DELETE character. Thus, it has 19903 code positions available for graphics characters.

- I-zone: It is used for Chinese/Japanese/Korean (CJK) unified ideographs. Its range is 4E00-9FFF, so 20992 code positions are available in this zone.

- O-zone: It is used for Korean Hangul syllabic scripts and for other scripts, like ?. Its range is A000-D7FF, so 14336 code positions are available in this zone.

- S-zone: It is reserved for use with transformation format UTF-16. The transformation format UTF-16 will be described shortly. Its range is D800-DFFF, so 2048 code positions are available in this zone.

- R-zone: It is known as the restricted zone. It can be used only in special circumstances. One of the uses of this zone is for specific user-defined characters. However, in this case an agreement is necessary between the sender and the recipient to communicate successfully. Its range is E000-FFFD, so 8190 code positions are available in this zone.

UCS is closely related to another popular character set called Unicode, which has been prepared by the Unicode Consortium. Unicode uses a 2-octet (16 bits) coding structure and hence it can accommodate 2^{16} (= 65536) distinct characters. The Unicode can be considered as the 16-bit coding of the BMP of UCS. These two character sets, Unicode and UCS, were developed and are maintained by two different organizations. However, they cooperate to keep Unicode and UCS compatible. If a computer system uses the Unicode character set to store some text, each character in the text has to be allocated 16 bits even if all characters in the text are from ASCII character set. Note that the first 128 characters of Unicode match with that of ASCII, and a character in ASCII can be represented only in 8-bits. So, to use 16 bits to represent all characters in Unicode is wasteful of computer memory. An alternative would be to use 8 bits for all characters from ASCII and 16 bits for characters outside the range of ASCII. However, this method of using different bits to represent different characters from Unicode has to be consistent and uniform, resulting in no ambiguity when data is stored or interchanged between different computer systems. This issue led to the development of character encoding method. Currently, there are four character-encoding methods specified in ISO/IEC 10646-1.

- UCS-2

- UCS-4

- UTF-16

- UTF-8

UCS-2

This is a 2-octet BMP form of encoding, which allows the use of two octets to represent a character from the BMP. This is a fixed-length encoding method. That is, each character from BMP is represented exactly by two octets.

UCS-4

This encoding method is also called the 4-octet canonical form of encoding, which uses four octets for every character in UCS. This is also a fixed-length encoding method.

UTF-16 (UCS Transformation Format 16)

Once characters outside the BMP are used, the UCS-2 encoding method cannot be applied to represent them. In this case, the encoding must switch over to use UCS-4, which will just double the use of resources, such as memory, network bandwidth, etc. The transformation format UTF-16 has been designed to avoid such a waste of memory and other resources, which would have resulted in using the UCS-4 encoding method. The UTF-16 is a variable-length encoding method. In the UTF-16 encoding method, UCS-2 is used for all characters within BMP and UCS-4 is used for encoding the characters outside BMP.

UTF-8 (UCS Transformation Format 8)

This is a variable-length encoding method, which may use 1 to 6 octets to represent a character from UCS. All ASCII characters are encoded using one octet. In the UTF-8 format of character encoding, characters are represented using one or more octets as shown in Table A-2.

Table A-2. *List of Legal UTF-8 Sequences*

Number of Octets	Bit Patterns Used	UCS Code
1	Octet 1: 0xxxxxxx	00000000-0000007F
2	Octet 1: 110xxxxx Octet 2: 10xxxxxx	00000080-000007FF
3	Octet 1: 1110xxxx Octet 2: 10xxxxxx Octet 3: 10xxxxxx	00000800-0000FFFF
4	Octet 1: 11110xxx Octet 2: 10xxxxxx Octet 3: 10xxxxxx Octet 4: 10xxxxxx	00010000-001FFFFF
5	Octet 1: 111110xx Octet 2: 10xxxxxx Octet 3: 10xxxxxx Octet 4: 10xxxxxx Octet 5: 10xxxxxx	00200000-03FFFFFF
6	Octet 1: 1111110x Octet 2: 10xxxxxx Octet 3: 10xxxxxx Octet 4: 10xxxxxx Octet 5: 10xxxxxx Octet 6: 10xxxxxx	04000000-7FFFFFFF

The "x" in the table indicates either a 0 or a 1. Note that, in UTF-8 format, an octet that starts with a 0 bit indicates that it is representing an ASCII character. An octet starting with 110 bits combinations indicates that it is the first octet of the 2-octet representation of a character, and so on. Also note that, in the case an octet is a part of a multi-octet character representation, the octet other than the first one starts with a 10 bits pattern. Security checks can be easily implemented for UTF-8 encoded data. UTF-8 octet sequences, which do not conform to the octet-sequences shown in the table, are considered invalid.

Java and Character Encodings

Java stores and manipulates all characters and strings as Unicode characters. In serialization and byte codes, Java uses the UTF-8 encoding of the Unicode character set. All implementations of Java virtual machine are required to support the character encoding methods, as shown in Table A-3.

Table A-3. *List of the Supported Character Encodings by a JVM*

Character Encoding	Description
ASCII	7-bit ASCII (also known as ISO646-US, the Basic Latin block of the Unicode character set)
ISO-8859-1	ISO Latin Alphabet No. 1 (also known as ISO-LATIN-1)
UTF-8	8-bit Unicode Transformation Format
UTF-16BE	16-bit Unicode Transformation Format, big-endian byte order. Big-endian was discussed in Chapter 3
UTF-16LE	16-bit Unicode Transformation Format, little-endian byte order. Little-endian was discussed in Chapter 3
UTF-16	16-bit Unicode Transformation Format, byte order specified by a mandatory initial byte-order mark (either order accepted on input, big-endian used on output)

Java supports UTF-8 format with the following two significant modifications:

- Java uses 16 bits to represent a NUL character in a class file whereas standard UTF-8 uses only 8 bits. This compromise has been made to make it easier for other languages to parse a Java class file where a NUL character is not allowed within a string. However, in some cases Java uses standard UTF-8 format to represent NUL character.

- Java recognizes only 1-octet, 2-octet, and 3-octet UTF-8 formats whereas standard UTF-8 format may use 1-octet, 2-octet, 3-octet, 4-octet, 5-octet, and 6-octet sequences. This is because Java supports Unicode character set and all characters from Unicode can be represented in 1-, 2- or 3-octet formats of UTF-8.

When you compile the Java source code, by default, the Java compiler assumes that the source code file has been written using the platform's default encoding (also known as local codepage or native encoding). The platform's default character encoding is Latin-1 on Windows and Solaris and MacRoman on Mac. Note that Windows does not use true Latin-1 character encoding. It uses a variation of Latin-1 that includes fewer control characters and more printing characters .You can specify a file-encoding name (or codepage name) to control how the compiler interprets characters beyond the ASCII character set. At the time of compiling your Java source code, you can pass the character-encoding name used in your source code file to Java compiler. The following command tells Java compiler (javac) that the Java source code Test.java has been written using a traditional Chinese encoding named Big5. Now, the Java compiler will convert all characters encoded in Big5 to Unicode.

```
javac -encoding Big5 Test.java
```

The JDK includes the native2ascii tool, which can be used to convert files, which contain other character encoding into files containing Latin-1 and/or Unicode-encoded characters. The general syntax of using native2ascii tool is

```
native2ascii option inputfile outputfile
```

For example, the following command converts all characters in Source.java file into Unicode-encoded character and places the output in Destination.java file assuming that the Source.java file has been written using the platform's default encoding:

```
native2ascii Source.java Destination.java
```

The following command converts all characters in the Source.java file into Unicode-encoded characters and places the output in the Destination.java file. It is assumed that the Source.java file has been written using Chinese Big5 encoding.

```
native2ascii -encoding Big5 Source.java Destination.java
```

The following command performs the reverse operation, that is, converts a file Source.java with Latin-1 and/or Unicode-encoded characters to a file Destination.java with native-encoded characters:

```
native2ascii -reverse Source.java Destination.java
```

The native2ascii tool uses the standard output for the output if the outputfile name is omitted. It uses standard input for the input if the inputfile name is omitted too.

■ ■ ■

Documentation Comments

The Java programming language lets you include comments in the source code that can be used to prepare documentation for the application. Such comments are known as documentation comments or Javadoc comments. JDK provides a javadoc command-line tool to extract the documentation comments from the source codes and generate documentation in HTML format. The javadoc tool is located in the bin directory of the JDK_HOME directory. For example, if you have installed the JDK in C:\java8 directory, the javadoc tool will be located in the C:\java8\bin directory.

Although a documentation comment can appear anywhere in Java source code, the javadoc tool uses only those documentation comments to generate the HTML pages that appear just before the declaration of classes, nested classes, interfaces, enums, annotations, constructors, methods, and fields. Note that the tool does not generate documentation for the documentation comments that are written for anonymous classes, package declarations, and import declarations. You need to write the documentation comments in a separate special file for a package, which will be used by the tool to generate documentation for that package.

A documentation comment starts with /** characters and ends with */ characters. The leading asterisks (*) on each line of the documentation comment are ignored. The following is an example of a documentation comment that is written for the Calc class declaration:

```
// Calc.java
package com.jdojo.utility;

/**
 * A utility class to perform basic calculations on numbers. All
 * methods in this class are <code>static</code>. It provides methods
 * to perform addition, subtraction, multiplication, and division.
 *
 * @author Kishori Sharan
 */
public final class Calc {
        // Code for Calc class goes here
}
```

It is important to note that the documentation comment must appear just before the declaration of the program element for which it is intended. Otherwise, it will be ignored by the javadoc tool, or shown for the wrong element. The following two documentation comments are not the same:

```
/* Example #1 */
/**
 * This documentation comment is intended for the class declaration
 * Xyz. However, it will be ignored by the javadoc tool, because there
 * is a package declaration between this documentation comment and the
```

```
 * Xyz class declaration. Note that a documentation comment for a package
 * declaration is written differently and it is not written in the
 * source code.
 */
package com.jdojo.utility;

public class Xyz {
        /* Code for Xyz class goes here */
}


/* Example #2 */
package com.jdojo.utility;

/**
 * This documentation comment is intended for the class declaration
 * Xyz. It will be used by the javadoc tool, because it appears just
 * before the Xyz class declaration.
 */
public class Xyz {
        /* Code for Xyz class goes here */
}
```

Writing Documentation Comments

You can write three types of comments in Java source code:

- Single-line comments

- Multi-line comments

- Documentation comments

The first two types of comments are free-form comments and they are meant for the developers to read. The third type of the comment is meant to be processed by the javadoc tool to generate HTML documents for the source code.

The textual part of the documentation comment may include HTML tags, and those tags will be interpreted as HTML in the generated HTML document. For example, to display the text "Hello" in boldface font as part of the documentation comment, you can write <b>Hello<b> as shown:

```
/**
 * You can include HTML tags in documentation comments. This will
 * display <b>Hello</b> in boldface font.
 */
```

Apart from HTML tags, you can also use some special tags. A tag in a documentation comment is a special type of keywords that is interpreted and processed by the javadoc tool. Two types of tags can be used:

- Block tags

- In-line tags

A block tag is of the following form:

```
@tagName tagText
```

A block tag starts with an @ character, which is followed by the tag name. The tag text follows the tag name. The following is an example of a block tag, which uses @author block tag and "Kishori Sharan" as the tag text:

```
@author Kishori Sharan
```

A block tag must appear in the beginning of a line in a documentation comment. Note that the asterisks, white spaces, and the /** characters are ignored by the javadoc tool if they appear in the beginning of a line. When I state that a block tag must appear in the beginning of a line, I mean the beginning of a line after ignoring these characters. The following is an example of using @author and @since block tags. The @author tag lets you specify an author name and the @since tag allows you to specify the version since the API was introduced.

```
/**
 * A utility class to perform basic calculations on numbers.
 * All methods in this class are <code>static</code>. It
 * provides methods to perform addition, subtraction, multiplication, and division.
 *
 * @author Kishori Sharan
 * @since Version 1.0
 */
public final class Calc {
        // code
}
```

If a line in a documentation comment starts with an @ character, it will be interpreted as the start of a block tag. If you want to start a line with an @ character without getting it interpreted as the start of a block tag, you need to use the HTML entity &#064 instead of the @ character. However, an @ character may appear as part of the text inside a line, provided the prior character isn't a {, which is explained more below.

The associated text with a block tag may appear in multiple lines, which includes all text that follows the tag name until another block tag or the end of the documentation comment is encountered.

An inline tag can appear anywhere in the documentation comment where text can appear. It is of the form

```
{@tagName tagText}
```

An inline tag is enclosed inside braces ({ and }). The following is an example of a documentation comment that uses a {@code text} inline tag to display the text "n1 + n2" in code font:

```
/**
 * An example of inline tag. It computes {@code n1 + n2}.
 */
```

■ **Tip** When you are writing documentation comment, make sure that the first sentence of the description selection of the comment is a summary sentence. The comment for a package, a class, and a member is split into two sections: a summary section and a detail section. The first sentence of the comment is displayed in the summary section and the entire comment is displayed in the detail section in the documentation.

List of Block and Inline Tags

Not all tags can be used for the documentation comment in all contexts. Table B-1 has the list of all block tags and inline tags, and the contexts in which they can be used.

Table B-1. *List of Block and Inline Tags, and the Contexts in Which They Can Be Used*

Tag	Overview	Package	Class, Interface, Enum, and Annotation	Field	Constructor and Method
@author	Yes	Yes	Yes	No	No
@deprecated	No	No	Yes	Yes	Yes
@exception	No	No	No	No	Yes
@param	No	No	No	No	Yes
@return	No	No	No	No	Yes (Methods only)
@see	Yes	Yes	Yes	Yes	Yes
@serial	No	Yes	Yes	Yes	No
@serialData	No	No	No	No	Yes (Methods only)
@serialField	No	No	No	Yes	No
@since	Yes	Yes	Yes	Yes	Yes
@throws	No	No	No	No	Yes
@version	Yes	Yes	Yes	No	No
{@code}	Yes	Yes	Yes	Yes	Yes
{@docRoot}	Yes	Yes	Yes	Yes	Yes
{@inheritDoc}	No	No	No	No	Yes (Methods only)
{@link}	Yes	Yes	Yes	Yes	Yes
{@linkplain}	Yes	Yes	Yes	Yes	Yes
{@literal}	Yes	Yes	Yes	Yes	Yes
{@value}	No	No	No	Yes	No

The Overview column in the table may not be obvious, because there is no such construct as "overview" in the Java programming language. The javadoc tool lets you add documentation comments for the entire application in one place, which is called an overview comment. The overview comment is displayed on the overview page that is generated by the tool. I will discuss an example of how to include an overview comment in the generated documentation later. The following sections will describe the tags in brief.

@author <author-name(s)>

The @author tag adds the author name or names under the Author section in the documentation. A documentation comment may contain multiple @author tags. If you have multiple author names, you can use only one @author tag to specify all author names or you can use a separate @author tag to specify each author name. If you use multiple @author tags, all author names will be concatenated using a locale-specific separator and placed under one Author entry. Table B-2 shows the effects of using one and multiple @author tags. Note that the table shows only the Author entry from the generated text.

Table B-2. *The Effects of Using One and Multiple @author Tags in Documentation Comments*

Documentation Comment	Generated Author Entry

```/**```
 ```* A dummy class.```
 ```*```
 ```* @author Kishori Sharan```
 ```*/```
	Author:
	 Kishori Sharan

```/**```
 ```* A dummy class.```
 ```*```
 ```* @author Kishori Sharan```
 ```* @author Greg Langham```
 ```* @author John Jacobs```
 ```*/```
	Author:
	 Kishori Sharan, Greg Langham, John Jacobs

@deprecated <explanation-text>

The @deprecated tag is used to generate documentation for program elements that should no longer be used, although they may function correctly. The explanation text for this tag should explain why the program element should not be used. If there is a replacement for the deprecated program element, the explanation text should contain a link to or explanation about the replacement. The following documentation comment uses the @deprecated tag for the Dummy class. It provides a link to Dummy2 class, which is the replacement class.

```
/**
 * A dummy class.
 *
 * @deprecated As of version 1.1. Use {@link com.jdojo.utility.Dummy2 Dummy2} instead.
 */
public class Dummy {
}
```

@exception <class-name> <description>

The @exception tag is a synonym for @throws tag. Please refer to the description of the @throws tag for details.

@param <parameter-name> <description>

The @param is applicable only to classes, methods, and constructors. It generates a Parameters section with the specified parameter-name and the description. If the parameter is a type parameter, the specified parameter-name should be enclosed in angle brackets (<>). The following is an example of using the @param tags to document the parameters of a method:

```
/**
 * Returns the result of multiplication of <code>n1</code> and
 * <code>n2</code>. It may return incorrect result if the value of
 * the multiplication of <code>n1</code> and <code>n2</code> exceeds
 * the range of the <code>int</code> data type.
 *
```

```
 * @param n1 The multiplicand
 * @param n2 The multiplier
 * @return Returns the result of multiplication of <code>n1</code> and <code>n2</code>
 */
public static int multiply(int n1, int n2) {
        return n1 * n2;
}
```

The following is an example of using the @param tags to document the type parameters of a class:

```
/**
 * Wraps an object of any type.
 *
 * @param <T> Type of the object wrapped in the Wrapper
 */
public class Wrapper<T> {
        // Code for the Wrapper class goes here
}
```

@return <description>

It is valid only for methods. It adds a Returns section with the specified `description`. The specified `description` should contain the return type and the description of value that is returned from the method. Please refer to the example of the @param tag to see how to use @return tag in a documentation comment.

@see <reference>

It adds a See Also section with a link or text that points to the specified `reference`. A documentation comment can have multiple @see tags. All @see tags will be displayed under one See Also section for a documentation comment. You can specify the `reference` in one of the three following forms:

```
@see "text"
@see <a href="URL">label</a>
@see package.Classname#member label
```

In the first form, the reference is specified as a text that is enclosed in double quotes. The javadoc tool adds the specified text in the See Also section, without any link.

In the second form, the reference is specified using an HTML anchor tag (<a> tag). The javadoc tool generates a hyperlink that points to the specified URL. If specified, the specified `label` is displayed as the link text.

In the third form, the reference is specified to a class, an interface, a field, a constructor, or a method. Note that if you are referencing a field, a constructor, or a method, its name is preceded by a hash sign (#), not a dot. The javadoc tool generates a link to the reference that has the specified `label` as the visible text. The label is optional. If label is omitted, the tool uses a suitable text for the link that is derived from the first argument to the @see tag. The reference to the program element could use the fully qualified name or a partial name. The tool uses the same rules as the Java compiler to resolve the partial name of a program element.

The following is an example of how to use different forms of the @see tag. It assumes that Calc class is in the same package as the Dummy class and the Calc class contains add() and multiply() methods.

```
package com.jdojo.utility;

/**
 * A dummy class.
 *
 * @see "Online Java Tutorial"
 * @see <a href="http://www.oracle.com">Oracle Website</a>
 * @see com.jdojo.utility.Calc Calculator
 * @see com.jdojo.utility.Calc#add(int, int) Add Method
 * @see com.jdojo.utility.Calc#multiply(int, int)
 */
public class Dummy {
}
```

The generated See Also section for the Dummy class would look as shown:

See Also:

```
"Online Java Tutorial" Oracle Website, Calculator, Add Method,
    Calc.multiply(int, int)
```

@serial <field-description or include/exclude>

The javadoc tool generates a Serialized Form page that contains all pieces of information about serialized forms of all serialized classes. The tool creates a See Also section for serialized classes that contains a link to the Serialized Form page. A class needs to implement java.io.Serializable or java.io.Externalizable interface to be added to the Serialized Form page.

The @serial tag is used to add a description for default serializable fields of a class. The specified description will be added to the Serialized Form page for the field. The following is an example of using the @serial tag for a field:

```
/**
 * A dummy class.
 */
public class Dummy implements java.io.Serializable {
    /**
     * @serial The description for value field goes here
     */
    private int value;
}
```

You may include or exclude a package or a class from appearing on the Serialized Form page by using the `include` or exclude argument with the `@serial` tag. If the `@serial` tag is used at both package and class levels, the class level tag takes precedence. By default, a serializable class that is `public` or `protected` is included in the Serialized Form page. The following documentation comment excludes the Dummy class from the Serialized Form page:

```
/**
 * A dummy class. It will not appear on the serialized Form page.
 *
 * @serial exclude
 */
public class Dummy implements java.io.Serializable {
        /**
         * @serial The description for value field goes here
         */
        private int value;
}
```

@serialData <data-description>

A class that implement `java.io.Externalizable` interface needs to implement `readExternal()` and `writeExternal()` methods. A serializable class may also implement `writeObject()`, `readObject()`, `writeReplace()`, and `readResolve()` methods to customize the serialization of the objects of the class. The `@serialData` tag may be used with the documentation comments of any of these six methods. The data description text should describe the types and the order of the data in the serialized form.

@serialField <field-name> <field-type> <field-description>

A serializable class can include a `serialPersistentFields` field that is an array of `ObjectStreamField`. The `@serialField` tag describes each component of that array. The description of the elements will appear in the Serialized Form page. The following documentation comment uses `@serialField` tags to document the `name` and the `height` components of the `ObjectStreamField`:

```
package com.jdojo.utility;

import java.io.ObjectStreamField;
import java.io.Serializable;

/**
 * A class to represent a person
 */
public class Person implements Serializable {
        private String name;
        private String gender;
        private double height;

        /**
         * @serialField name String The name of the person
         * @serialField height double The height of the person in feet
         */
```

```
        private static final ObjectStreamField[] serialPersistentFields
                        = {new ObjectStreamField("name", String.class),
                           new ObjectStreamField("height", double.class)
                          };
}
```

@since <description>

The @since tag adds a Since section to the documentation. The specified `description` indicates the release of the software that added the program element being documented. The following documentation comment shows how to use @since tag:

```
/**
 * A dummy class.
 *
 * @since 1.0
 */
public class Dummy {
}
```

@throws <class-name> <description>

The @throws tag is a synonym for @exception tag. It adds a Throws section to the documentation. It is used to describe an exception that may be thrown from a constructor or a method. Multiple @throws tag can be used in a documentation comment. If a method throws a checked exception and there is no @throws tag, the javadoc tool will add one without a description to make sure that all checked exceptions are documented. The following documentation comment for the divide() method shows how to use the @throws tag. If you do not provide the fully qualified name of the class, the javadoc tool will use the same search order as used by the Java compiler to resolve the partial class name.

```
/**
 * Returns the result of integer division of <code>n1</code> by
 * <code>n2</code>.
 *
 * @param n1 The dividend
 * @param n2 The divisor
 * @return Returns the result of <code>n1 / n2</code>
 * @throws ArithmeticException If <code>n2</code> is zero.
 */
public static int divide(int n1, int n2) throws ArithmeticException {
        return n1 / n2;
}
```

@version <version-text>

The @version tag adds a Version section to the generated documentation. The version text should contain the current version of the program element. The @since tag is used to specify the version of the software when a program element was added whereas the @version tag is used to specify the current version. The following documentation comment shows how to use @version tag:

```
/**
 * A dummy class.
 *
 * @since 1.0
 * @version 1.6
 */
public class Dummy {
}
```

{@code <text>}

It displays the specified text in code font without interpreting the text as HTML markup or nested documentation comments tag. It is equivalent to

```
<code>{@literal <text>}</code>
```

{@docRoot}

It resolves to the relative path of the root directory of the generated documents. It is used in the URL part of links. Suppose you have a file called myfiles/copyright.html that is located under the root directory of the generated documents. If you want to include a link to the copyright.html file in your documentation comment, you can do the following:

```
/**
 * A dummy class.  Please read
 * the <a href="{@docRoot}/myfiles/copyright.html">Copyright</a> page.
 */
public class Dummy {
}
```

{@inheritDoc}

It copies the documentation of a method from the nearest inheritable class or the implementable interface. Note that for this tag to copy the documentation, the method in which this tag appears must override a method in its parent class or implement a method of the implemented interfaces.

This tag may be used only inside the main description in the documentation comment for a method or inside the text argument of @return, @param, and @throws tags for a method. If it appears inside the main description, it copies the main description of the overridden method. If it appears in other tag's text, it copies the tag's text from the overridden method.

If a method overrides a method in the parent class or implements a method of an interface, the javadoc tool automatically copies the documentation for the main description, @return , @param and @throws if the main description of these tags is missing in the overriding method.

The following documentation comment demonstrates the use of {@ inheritDoc} tag. It is used inside the documentation comment for the getId() method of the SmartPerson class. It is used inside the main description as well as the text section of the @return tag. Note that the @param tag is missing from the getId() method of SmartPerson class. The javadoc tool will automatically copy the documentation for the @param tag from the getId() method of the Person class.

```
/**
 * A class to represent a person
 */
public class Person {
        /**
         * Returns the person id.
         * @param x The value to add to the id
         * @return The person id.
         */
        public int getId(int x) {
                return x + 10;
        }
}

/**
 * A class to represent a smart person
 */
public class SmartPerson extends Person {
        /**
         * {@inheritDoc}
         * @return {@inheritDoc}
         */
        public int getId(int x) {
                return 20 + x;
        }
}
```

The generated documentation for the getId() method of the SmartPerson class is as follows:

getId
public int **getId**(int x)
        Returns the person id.

Overrides:
getId in class Person

Parameters:
x - The value to add to the id

Returns:
The person id.

{@link <package.class#member> <label>}

It inserts an inline link with the specified label as the text for the link. This tag generates a link that is similar to the link generated by one of the forms of the @see tag. The main difference between the two are that this tag is an inline tag, whereas the @see tag is a block tag. The following documentation comment shows how to use this tag. The use of this tag below will create a link with the text "add", which will point to the documentation of the add() method of the Calc class.

```
/**
 * A dummy class.  Please see
 * {@link com.jdojo.utility.Calc#add(int, int) add} method of the
 * Calc class to learn how to add two integers.
 *
 */
public class Dummy {
}
```

{@linkplain <package.class#member> <label>}

It works similarly to the {@link} tag, except that it displays the label for the link in plain text, whereas the {@link} displays the label for the link in code font. Please refer to the description of {@link} tag for more details.

{@literal <text>}

It displays the specified text without interpreting it as HTML markup or a nested documentation comment tag. Note that HTML tags are enclosed in angle brackets (<>). If you want to use angle brackets in documentation comments, you will need to use HTML entities < and >. If you do not want to use HTML entities, you can use this tag with your raw text. For example, it is valid to write {@literal x < y} anywhere in the documentation comment rather than writing x < y.

{@value <package.class#field>}

It is used to copy the value of a static and final field (a constant field). If it is used without the argument, it copies the value of the constant field at its location. The following documentation comments show how to use {@value} tag. In the documentation comment for MULTIPLIER field, it uses {@value} tag without an argument, which will insert the value of the MULTIPLIER field. In the documentation comment for the DIVISOR field, it uses both forms of the {@value} tag, one with an argument and one without an argument. The argument, #MULTIPLIER, refers to the MULTIPLIER field of the same class.

```
/**
 * A dummy class.
 */
public class Dummy {
        /**
         * The MULTIPLIER is {@value}
         */
        public static final int MULTIPLIER = 2000;

        /**
         * The value of MULTIPLIER is {@value #MULTIPLIER}.
```

```
      * The value of DIVISOR is {@value}.
      */
     public final static int DIVISOR = 1000;
}
```

The following is the generated documentation comment that shows the effects of using {@value} tag:

MULTIPLIER
```
public static final int MULTIPLIER
```

The MULTIPLIER is 2000

DIVISOR
```
public static final int DIVISOR
```
The value of MULTIPLIER is <u>2000</u>. The value of DIVISOR is 1000.

Documenting Packages

A package declaration appears multiple times in an application. There needs to be a simpler and separate way to document a package. You can document a package by placing either of the following two files, but not both, in the package directory along with the source files (.java files):

- package-info.java
- package.html

■ **Tip**   If both package-info.java and package.html files are available, the package-info.java file is used.

When you run the javadoc tool, it automatically uses the documentation in one of these two files as the documentation for your package. The package-info.java file was introduced in JDK5.0. The first sentence of the package documentation should be a summary statement about the package. The first sentence of the package documentation is displayed in the package summary description.

com/jdojo/utility/package-info.java file

It contains the package declaration with documentation comments for a package. In package-info.java file, a package is documented the same way any other program elements are documented. The content of the package-info.java file for com.jdojo.utility package is as follows:

```
/**
 * Contains utility classes. More description for
 * com.jdojo.utility package goes here.
 * @since 1.1
 * @version 1.9
 */
package com.jdojo.utility;
```

com/jdojo/utility/package.html file

It is a regular HTML file with HTML tags. The HTML contents within the <body> and </body> tags is used as the package documentation. It does not contain a package declaration. It does not use /** and */ characters as start and end of the documentation comment. However, you can use documentation tags that are valid for the package. The content of the package.html file for com.jdojo.utility package is as shown:

```
<html>
        <body>
                Contains utility classes. More description for
                com.jdojo.utility package goes here.
                @since 1.1
                @version 1.9
        </body>
</html>
```

Overview Documentation

The overview documentation is used to write documentation for the entire application in a separate HTML file. There is no rule for naming the overview documentation file. Generally, the overview documentation file is named as overview.html. The comment is placed inside the <body> and </body> tags in the HTML file. You need to pass the path of the overview documentation comment file to the javadoc tool using the –overview command-line option. The following is a sample overview comment contained in an HTML file:

```
<html>
<body>
API documentation for the dummy application. More overview text goes here.
@author Who Knows
@version 1.2
</body>
</html>
```

Including Unprocessed Files in Documentation

Sometimes you may want to include some files with your Java documentation, which you reference inside the documentation comments. For example, you may want to display graphics or source code. The javadoc tool lets you include files, which it copies to the generated documentation directory without processing them. You need to create a directory called doc-files under any package directory that contains .java source files, and copy your extra files in that directory. The javadoc tool will copy all your files to the destination directory without processing them.

Skipping Source Files Processing

Sometimes you may have some Java source files that you do not want the javadoc tool to process. For example, you may have some test files for which you do not want to generate documentation. The javadoc tool looks at the file name before it decides to process the content of the file. If the file name is not a valid Java identifier, it skips that file. If you have a .java source file, which javadoc tool should skip, you need to name that file such that the name is not a valid Java identifier. For example, you may include a hyphen (-) in the file name to skip it. Note that this strategy of skipping source file processing is needed when you are using javadoc tool to generate documentation by passing it wildcards (*) or package name. If you supply the javadoc tool the list of source files to process, you do not need to use this strategy.

An Example of Documentation Comments

Listing B-1 has the source code for a Calc class. It is a trivial class. Its purpose is only to demonstrate how to write documentation comments. It uses many of the tags, which we discussed earlier. Figure B-1 shows the generated HTML page (partially shown) for the Calc class documentation.

Listing B-1. Calc Class Source Code with Documentation Comment

```java
// Calc.java
package com.jdojo.utility;

/**
 * A utility class to perform basic calculations on numbers.
 * All methods in this class are <code>static</code>. It
 * provides methods to perform addition, subtraction,
 * multiplication and division.
 *
 * @author Kishori Sharan
 * @since Version 1.0
 */
public final class Calc {
        /**
         * Stop someone from instantiating this class. This class is not
         * meant for instantiation as all its methods are
         * <code>static</code>.
         */
        private Calc() {
        }

        /**
         * Performs addition on two numbers. It returns the result of
         * <code> n1 + n2 </code>as an <code>int</code>. If the result
         * of <code>n1 + n2</code> exceeds the range of the
         * <code>int</code> data type, it will not return the correct
         * result. For bigger numbers, use {@link #add(long, long)}.
         *
         * @param n1 The first number
         * @param n2 The second number
         * @return Returns the value of <code>n1 + n2</code>
         */
        public static int add(int n1, int n2) {
                return n1 + n2;
        }

        /**
         * Performs addition on two numbers. It returns the result of
         * <code>n1 + n2</code> as a <code>long</code>.
         *
         * @param n1 The first number
         * @param n2 The second number
         * @return Returns the value of <code>n1 + n2</code>
         */
```

```java
        public static long add(long n1, long n2) {
                return n1 + n2;
        }

        /**
         * Returns the result of <code>n1 - n2</code>.
         *
         * @param n1 The first number
         * @param n2 The second number
         * @return Returns the result of <code>n1 - n2</code>
         */
        public static int subtract(int n1, int n2) {
                return n1 - n2;
        }

        /**
         * Returns the result of multiplication of <code>n1</code> and
         * <code>n2</code>. It may return incorrect result if the value of
         * the multiplication of <code>n1</code> and <code>n2</code>
         * exceeds the range of the <code>int</code> data type.
         *
         * @param n1 The multiplicand
         * @param n2 The multiplier
         * @return Returns the result of multiplication of
         *         <code>n1</code> and <code>n2</code>
         */
        public static int multiply(int n1, int n2) {
                return n1 * n2;
        }

        /**
         * Returns the result of integer division of <code>n1</code> by
         * <code>n2</code>.
         *
         * @param n1 The dividend
         * @param n2 The divisor
         * @return Returns the result of <code>n1 / n2</code>
         * @throws ArithmeticException If <code>n2</code> is zero.
         */
        public static int divide(int n1, int n2) throws ArithmeticException {
                return n1 / n2;
        }
}
```

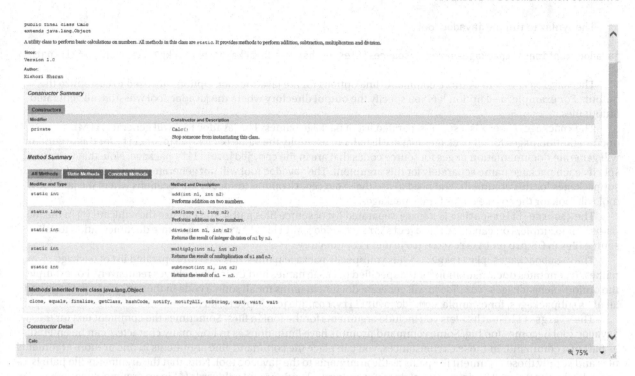

```
public final class Calc
extends java.lang.Object
```

A utility class to perform basic calculations on numbers. All methods in this class are static. It provides methods to perform addition, subtraction, multiplication and division.

Since:
Version 1.0
Author:
Kishori Sharan

Constructor Summary

Constructors

Modifier	Constructor and Description
private	Calc() Stop someone from instantiating this class.

Method Summary

All Methods   Static Methods   Concrete Methods

Modifier and Type	Method and Description
static int	add(int n1, int n2) Performs addition on two numbers.
static long	add(long n1, long n2) Performs addition on two numbers.
static int	divide(int n1, int n2) Returns the result of integer division of n1 by n2.
static int	multiply(int n1, int n2) Returns the result of multiplication of n1 and n2.
static int	subtract(int n1, int n2) Returns the result of n1 - n2.

Methods inherited from class java.lang.Object

clone, equals, finalize, getClass, hashCode, notify, notifyAll, toString, wait, wait, wait

Constructor Detail

Calc

🔍 75%   ▼

Figure B-1. *The generated HTML page for the Calc class documentation comment*

Running the javadoc Tool

You need to run the javadoc command-line tool to generate HTML pages for your documentation comments in the source files (.java files). For these examples of running the javadoc tool, I assume that the following files contain documentation comments:

```
C:\projects\src\overview.html
C:\projects\src\com\jdojo\chapter2\package-info.java
C:\projects\src\com\jdojo\chapter2\Welcome.java
C:\projects\src\com\jdojo\utility\Calc.java
C:\projects\src\com\jdojo\utility\Dummy.java
C:\projects\src\com\jdojo\utility\package-info.java
```

The overview.html file is the overview documentation file for the documentation. There are two package-info. java files, one for com.jdojo.chapter2 package and one for com.jdojo.utility package. Welcome.java, Calc.java and Dummy.java are Java source files.

You will need to open the command prompt, for example a DOS prompt in Windows, to run the javadoc tool. All of the following examples of running the javadoc tool assume that the current directory is C:\projects. I will use relative paths to the files and directories in the examples that will be relative to C:\projects directory. If you do not get the desired results with the relative paths, you can absolute paths. For example, if you use src in your commands, it means C:\projects\src and you can always replace src with C:\projects\src in the examples. You will use C:\projects\docs directory to store the documentation comments files that are generated by the javadoc tool.

The syntax to run the javadoc tool is

```
javadoc <options> <package-names> <source-files-paths> <-subpackages pkg1:pkg2...> <@args-file-paths>
```

The `<options>` is zero or more command-line options for the javadoc tool. Options are used to customize the output. For example, a -d option lets you specify the output directory where the javadoc tool will store all generated output files.

The `<package-names>` is a space-separated list of package names. The javadoc tool will generate HTML documentation pages for all packages that are listed. For example, the value of `com.jdojo.utility` for this argument will generate documentation pages for source codes that are in the `com.jdojo.utility` package. Note that you must specify each package name separately for this argument. The javadoc tool will not generate documentation for any subpackages for this argument. You need to use the -sourcepath option to specify the locations where the javadoc tool will look for the source codes for the packages.

The `<source-files-paths>` is a space-separated list of source files paths. You can use the wildcard (*) in the file paths. For example, you can use `C:\projects\src\com.jdojo\utility\*.java` to generate documentation for all source files in `C:\projects\src\com.jdojo\utility` directory.

The `<-subpackages pkg1:pkg2...>` lets you specify package names. It is a colon-separated list of package names. It generates documentation for the specified package names and their subpackages recursively. For example, the option -subpackages `com.jdojo` will generate documentations for all source code in the `com.jdojo` package and all of its subpackages, for example, `com.jdojo.utility`, `com.jdojo.chapter2`, etc.

The `<@args-file-paths>` lets you include arguments for the tool in files. Sometimes the comment text for the javadoc tool becomes too big. Some command prompts have limitations as to how many characters can be entered as part of a command. In those circumstances, you can place the command-line arguments in one or more arguments files and supply those argument file paths as the arguments to the javadoc tool. Note that the arguments file path is preceded by the @ sign. The javadoc tool does not support -J options and wildcards (*) in an argument file.

■ **Tip** The javadoc tool provides many options to customize the generated output files. To list all options, you can run it using the -help option, as in javadoc -help. You can use a -J-version option to print the version of the javadoc tool, as in javadoc -J-version.

I need to discuss the -sourcepath option for the javadoc tool before you look at some examples of running it. Sometimes the javadoc tool has to find the source files (.java files). For example, when you pass the package names or subpackage names to generate documentation to the javadoc tool, it needs to find all files that have the source code for those packages. By default, the javadoc tool uses the CLASSPATH to search for the source files. If the CLASSPATH is not set, it uses the current directory to search for the source files. The -sourcepath option is used to specify the locations where the javadoc tool can search for source files. The package name is concatenated to each entry in the -sourcepath value to locate the source files. In Windows, the -sourcepath option is a semicolon-separated list of directories, whereas in UNIX-like operating systems, it is a colon-separated list of directories.

The following command will generate documentation for all source code in the `com.jdojo.utility` package. It will place the output files in `C:\projects\docs` directory. The argument to the -sourcepath option is `src`, which indicates that the javadoc tool will look for the source files (.java files) under `C:\projects\src` directory.

```
C:\projects>javadoc -d docs -sourcepath src com.jdojo.utility
```

The following command will generate documentation for all source code under `com.jdojo` package and its subpackages. It will place the output in `C:\projects\docs` directory.

```
C:\projects>javadoc -d docs -sourcepath src -subpackages com.jdojo
```

The following command will generate documentation for only Dummy.java source file:

```
C:\projects>javadoc -d docs src/com/jdojo/utility/Dummay.java
```

The following command is entered on one line even though it is shown on two lines. It will generate documentation for all source code under the com.jdojo package and its subpackages. It will include the overview comments from C:\projects\src\overview.html file. It will place the output in the C:\projects\docs directory.

```
C:\projects>javadoc -d docs -overview src\overview.html -sourcepath src -subpackages com.jdojo
```

By default, the javadoc tool does not generate documentation for the @author and @version tags. You need to use the -author and -version options to include the text for @author and @version tags in the generated documentation, respectively.

The following command will generate documentation for com.jdojo.utility package. The documentation will include text for @author and @version tags.

```
C:\projects>javadoc -d docs –author –version -sourcepath src com.jdojo.utility
```

You can use one or more argument files to store all the arguments to the javadoc tool. Note that -J options and wildcards (*) are not supported in argument files. You must use the command line to enter these two types of arguments. Suppose the following is the contents of a file named args.txt, which is placed in C:\projects directory:

```
-d docs
-author
-sourcepath src
-subpackages com.jdojo
```

You can run the javadoc tool that will use arguments from the args.txt file, as shown below. All relative paths in the argument file are resolved with respect to the current directory.

```
C:\projects>javadoc @args.txt
```

You can split the arguments for the javadoc in multiple files. You can pass multiple argument files to the javadoc tool by separating them by a space, as shown below. Options can be distributed among multiple argument files in any order. You can use a relative path (e.g., args.txt) or its absolute path (e.g., C:\projects\args.txt) of the argument file to the javadoc tool.

```
C:\projects>javadoc @args1.txt @args2.txt @args3.txt
```

Generated Documentation Files

The javadoc tool generates many HTML files. All generated files can be classified into three categories:

- Files for classes, interfaces, enums, annotations, packages, and overviews
- Files to cross-reference some pieces of information from one HTML page to another, such as an index page, a class hierarchy page for each package, a Use page for each package, etc.
- Support files

The tool generates one HTML file per class/interface/enum/annotation. The files are placed in directories that mimic the package hierarchies of classes, interfaces, enums, and annotations. The file names are the same as the program elements for which they contain the documentation. A `package-summary.html` file is included in every package directory that contains package documentation. An `overview-summary.html` file is generated for all packages to serve as overview documentation.

The generated HTML pages include the class hierarchy pages, a deprecated API page, constants values pages, serialized forms pages, etc. These files have self-explanatory names and they contain a hyphen in their names. Support files include any image files, a `help-doc.html` file to describe the generated documentation files, etc.

Viewing Generated HTML Documentation

You can view the documentation generated by the `javadoc` tool in an HTML page using HTML frames or with no frames. The `javadoc` tool generates two files, `index.html` and `overview-summary.html`, which are placed at the root in the output directory. You need to open the `index.html` file in a browser, for example, Microsoft Internet Explorer, Google Chrome, Mozilla Firefox, Safari, etc., to view the documentation using HTML frames. You can open the `overview-summary.html` file in a browser to view the documentation without HTML frames. The HTML frames are organized as shown in Figure B-2 .

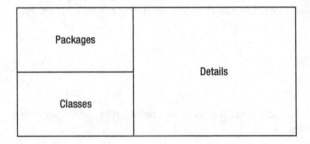

Figure B-2. *Arrangement of the HTML frames that are generated by the javadoc tool*

The `index.html` page has three frames. The upper-left frame contains the list of packages. If the documentation that you generate belongs to only one package, this frame is not generated. That is, you must generate documentation for at least two packages in order for the `javadoc` tool to generate the Packages frame. The lower-left frame contains the list of classes, interfaces, enums, exceptions, and annotations in a package that is selected from the Packages frame. The frame on the right side displays the details of the selection from the left frames.

Summary

Java allows writing comments in source code that can be used to generate documentation. The documentation comment starts with /** and ends with */. The `javadoc` tool, which is included in the JDK is used to extract and generate the documentation comments from source code. The tool generates documentation in HTML format. The tool contains support for many custom tags with special meaning. It also lets you use HTML tags inside the documentation.

APPENDIX C

■ ■ ■

Compact Profiles

The Java Development Kit (JDK) consists of the Java Language, development tools such as Java compiler, debugger, etc., and the Java Runtime Environment (JRE). The JRE is a subset of JDK and it consists of libraries, the Java virtual machine, and deployment toolkits. Libraries in the JRE can be subdivided into the following four categories:

- Lang and util base libraries
- Other base libraries
- Integration libraries
- User interface toolkits

Before Java SE 8, the JRE distribution was based on the all-or-nothing strategy. There was only one bundle of the JRE for a platform that contained libraries in all the four categories. This was a problem for resource-constrained devices. Suppose you had developed an application for Raspberry PI that uses only the lang and util base libraries. However, you had to deploy the full JRE that contained libraries in all the four categories. This simply used more space on the device than needed.

Java SE 8 introduced the concept of compact profiles that is a way to define subsets of the JRE libraries. A JRE bundle may contain one of those subsets of libraries or all libraries. The JRE containing a subset of the libraries is called a compact profile; the JRE containing all libraries is called the full JRE as it used to be before Java SE 8. Now, you can develop applications using JDK 8 and deploy them using one of the compact profiles to memory-constrained small devices. You can have a compact profile that may take as little as 11MB of space on a device running on Linux. Java SE 8 defines three compact profiles that are named as follows:

- compact1
- compact2
- compact3

Each profile specifies a set of Java API packages. Any packages not contained in the three compact profiles are part of the full JRE. Table C-1 lists the high-level library names in each compact profile and the full JRE.

Table C-1. *List of the Library Names for Compact Profiles and the Full JRE*

Full JRE	Accessibility	AWT	Beans
	CORBA	Drag and Drop	IDL
	Image I/O	Input Methods	Java 2D
	JAX-WS	JNI	Preferences
	Print Service	RMI-IIOP	Sound
	Swing		
compact3	Instrumentation	JMX	Management
	Security	XML JAXP	
compact2	JDBC	RMI	XML JAXP
compact1	Collections	Concurrency	Core (java.lang.*)
	Date and Time	Extension Mechanism	Input/Output
	Internationalization	JAR	JNDI
	Logging	Networking	Override Mechanism
	Ref Objects	Reflection	Regular Expressions
	Scripting	Security	Serialization
	Versioning	ZIP	

■ **Tip** The full JRE (the complete Java SE platform) is not considered a profile. A profile, even the smallest one, implements the entire JVM and the entire Java language. Sub-setting for a profile happens only for the packages from the Java libraries, not other parts of the JRE.

Table C-2 contains the list of packages added in each profile. Note that the list of packages is additive. That is, the compact2 profile contains all packages from the compact1 profile and the packages listed under the compact2 profile; the compact3 profile contains all the packages in the compact1 and compact2 profiles and the packages listed for the compact3 profile. In other words, compact2 is a superset of compact1; compact3 is a superset of compact2; and, the full JRE is a superset of compact3.

Table C-2. *List of Packages in the compact1, compact2, and compact3 Profiles*

compact3 Additions	java.lang.instrument	javax.management.monitor	javax.security.sasl
	java.lang.management	javax.management.openmbean	javax.sql.rowset
	java.security.acl	javax.management.relation	javax.sql.rowset.serial
	java.util.prefs	javax.management.remote	javax.sql.rowset.spi
	javax.annotation.processing	javax.management.remote.rmi	javax.tools
	javax.lang.model	javax.management.timer	javax.xml.crypto
	javax.lang.model.element	javax.naming	javax.xml.crypto.dom
	javax.lang.model.type	javax.naming.directory	javax.xml.crypto.dsig
	javax.lang.model.util	javax.naming.event	javax.xml.crypto.dsig.dom
	javax.management	javax.naming.ldap	javax.xml.crypto.dsig.keyinfo
	javax.management.loading	javax.naming.spi	javax.xml.crypto.dsig.spec
	javax.management.modelmbean	javax.security.auth.kerberos	org.ietf.jgss
compact2 Additions	java.rmi	javax.xml.datatype	javax.xml.validation
	java.rmi.activation	javax.xml.namespace	javax.xml.xpath
	java.rmi.dgc	javax.xml.parsers	org.w3c.dom
	java.rmi.registry	javax.xml.stream	org.w3c.dom.bootstrap
	java.rmi.server	javax.xml.stream.events	org.w3c.dom.events
	java.sql	javax.xml.stream.util	org.w3c.dom.ls
	javax.rmi.ssl	javax.xml.transform	org.xml.sax
	javax.sql	javax.xml.transform.dom	org.xml.sax.ext
	javax.transaction	javax.xml.transform.sax	org.xml.sax.helpers
	javax.transaction.xa	javax.xml.transform.stax	
	javax.xml	javax.xml.transform.stream	
compact1	java.io	java.security.cert	java.util.regex
	java.lang	java.security.interfaces	java.util.spi
	java.lang.annotation	java.security.spec	java.util.stream
	java.lang.invoke	java.text	java.util.zip
	java.lang.ref	java.text.spi	javax.crypto
	java.lang.reflect	java.time	javax.crypto.interfaces
	java.math	java.time.chrono	javax.crypto.spec

(continued)

Table C-2. (*continued*)

java.net	java.time.format	javax.net
java.nio	java.time.temporal	javax.net.ssl
java.nio.channels	java.time.zone	javax.script
java.nio.channels.spi	java.util	javax.security.auth
java.nio.charset	java.util.concurrent	javax.security.auth. callback
java.nio.charset.spi	java.util.concurrent.atomic	javax.security.auth.login
java.nio.file	java.util.concurrent.locks	javax.security.auth.spi
java.nio.file.attribute	java.util.function	javax.security.auth.x500
java.nio.file.spi	java.util.jar	javax.security.cert
java.security	java.util.logging	

The JDK 8 contains several enhancements to development tools to support developing applications targeting a specific compact profile. It has also added new tools such as jdeps to analyze the Java source code for dependencies on compact profiles. I will discuss those enhancements in subsequent sections.

Before the Java SE Embedded 8, different JRE bundles were made available for downloads targeting different embedded platforms for small devices. Beginning Java SE Embedded 8, Oracle does not provide JRE bundles for downloads; rather, it provides Java development kits for Java SE Embedded 8 (also called EJDK 8) that enable you to create custom JRE bundles containing a specific compact profile on the specific embedded platform. I will discuss EJDK 8 in detail in the "Creating Custom JREs using the EJDK" section.

Enhancement in the javac Command

In JDK 8, you can compile source code targeting one of the compact profiles or the full JRE. The option -profile is used with the javac command to specify one of the compact profiles: compact1, compact2, or compact3. Absence of this option assumes the full JRE. The javac command checks whether the APIs used in the source code are available in the specified profile. The following command compiles Welcome.java targeting the compact1 profile:

```
javac -profile compact1 Welcome.java
```

If you are using the NetBeans IDE to develop your Java application, you can choose the profile option for the Java compiler in the project properties dialog as shown in Figure C-1. To open the project properties dialog, right-click the project and select the Properties option. Select one of the profiles in the Profiles drop-down field.

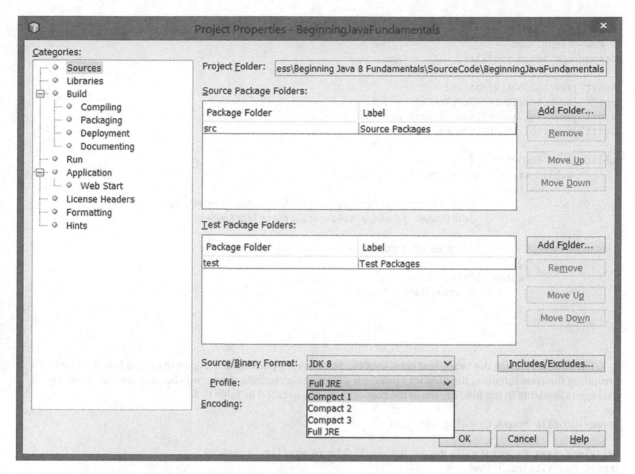

Figure C-1. *Setting the -profile option for the Java compiler in the NetBeans IDE for a Java project*

If the Java source code uses Java SE APIs outside the specified profile, the javac command generates an error. Consider the code for the SwingTest and RowSetTest classes as shown in Listing C-1 and Listing C-2, respectively.

Listing C-1. A SwingTest Class That Uses a Class from the javax.swing Package

```java
// SwingTest.java
package com.jdojo.profiles;

import javax.swing.JFrame;

public class SwingTest {
    public static void main(String[] args) {
        JFrame frame = new JFrame("Compact Profiles");
        frame.setSize(300, 300);
        frame.setVisible(true);
    }
}
```

Listing C-2. A RowSetTest Class That Uses Classes from the javax.sql Package

```
// RowSetTest.java
package com.jdojo.profiles;

import java.sql.SQLException;
import javax.sql.rowset.JdbcRowSet;
import javax.sql.rowset.RowSetFactory;
import javax.sql.rowset.RowSetProvider;

public class RowSetTest {
        public static void main(String[] args) {
                try {
                        RowSetFactory rsFactory = RowSetProvider.newFactory();
                        JdbcRowSet jdbcRs = rsFactory.createJdbcRowSet();

                        // More code goes here
                }
                catch (SQLException e) {
                        e.printStackTrace();
                }
        }
}
```

The source code for the SwingTest class uses the javax.swing package that is part of the full JRE. If you try compiling the class targeting the compact3 profile, it will generate compile-time errors because the javax.swing package is available in the full JRE, not in the compact3 profile, as listed in Table C-2.

```
javac -profile compact3 SwingTest.java

SwingTest.java:4: error: JFrame is not available in profile 'compact3'
import javax.swing.JFrame;
               ^
SwingTest.java:8: error: JFrame is not available in profile 'compact3'
           JFrame frame = new JFrame("Compact Profiles");
               ^
SwingTest.java:8: error: JFrame is not available in profile 'compact3'
           JFrame frame = new JFrame("Compact Profiles");
                              ^

3 errors
```

The following command using the full JRE compiles the SwingTest.java fine:

```
javac SwingTest.java
```

The following command will compile the RowSetTest class file fine as the command uses compact3 as the -profile option that matches the packages used inside the RowSetTest class:

```
javac -profile compact3 RowSetTest.java
```

Enhancement in Java API Documentation

The API documentation for Java SE 8 has some enhancements that let you browse the APIs by profiles and show the profiles in which packages and classes are included. Figure C-2 shows a screenshot of the new look of the Java API documentation page. Now you can browse the Java SE APIs for a specific profile or for the full JRE.

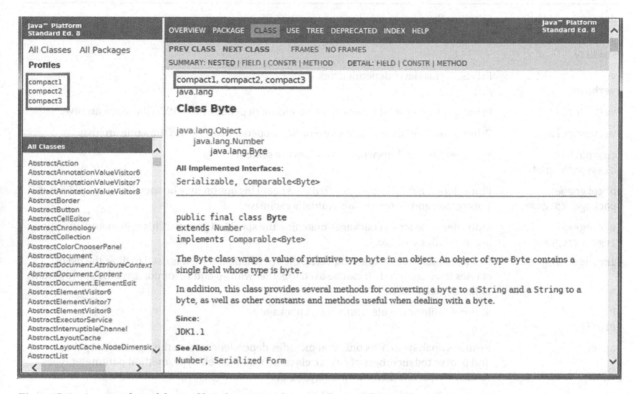

Figure C-2. *A screenshot of the profile information shown in the Java SE API documentation*

When you open the API documentation using frames, three types of links are provided in the top area of the top-left frame: All Classes, All Packages, and All Profiles. Clicking the All Profiles link shows the list of profiles (marked inside a rectangle in the figure). Clicking a profile will show you all packages available in that profile. The right frame displays the list of profiles that includes the class. If a class is included only in the full JRE, the list of profiles will be shown blank.

Checking for Profile Dependencies

JDK 8 added a new class dependency analyzer tool called jdeps. It shows the package-level and class-level dependencies of Java class files. It can also analyze dependencies of classes on compact profiles to help you determine which profile you need for the deployment of your application. By default, it prints the output on the standard output. Using the –dotoutput option, you can send the output to a file in DOT file format. DOT is a plain text graph description language that is readable by humans as well as computer programs. The general syntax for using the tool is

```
jdeps <options> <classes>
```

Here, <classes> can be a pathname to a .class file, a directory, a JAR file, or a fully qualified class name. Table C-3 lists all the options for the jdeps tool.

Table C-3. *List of Options for the jdeps Tool*

Option	Description
-dotoutput <dir>	Specifies the destination directory for DOT file output.
-s -summary	Prints dependency summary only.
-v -verbose	Prints all class level dependencies.
-verbose:package	Prints package-level dependencies excluding dependencies within the same archive.
-verbose:class	Prints class-level dependencies excluding dependencies within the same archive.
-cp <path> -classpath <path>	Specifies the locations where class files are searched.
-p <pkgname> -package <pkgname>	Finds dependences in the specified package. This option may be specified multiple times. This option and –e option are mutually exclusive.
-e <regex> -regex <regex>	Finds dependences in packages matching the specified pattern. This option and –p option are mutually exclusive.
-include <regex>	Restricts analysis to classes matching the specified pattern. It is used to filter the list of classes to be analyzed. It can be used together with -p and -e options, which apply pattern to the dependences.
-P -profile	Shows profile or the file containing a package.
-apionly	Restricts analysis to APIs only that includes dependences from the signature of public and protected members of public classes including field type, method parameter types, returned type, checked exception types, etc.
-R -recursive	Recursively traverses all dependencies.
-jdkinternals	Finds class-level dependences on JDK internal APIs. By default, it analyzes all classes on –cp and input files unless -include option is specified. It cannot be used with -p, -e, and -s options.
-version	Prints the version information.
-h -? -help	Prints a help message for the jdeps tool listing all options with a brief description.

The following command prints the dependencies for the SwingTest class:

```
jdeps SwingTest.class
SwingTest.class -> C:\java8\jre\lib\rt.jar
   com.jdojo.profiles (SwingTest.class)
      -> java.lang
      -> javax.swing
```

The following command prints the dependencies with the profile information for the SwingTest class:

```
jdeps -profile SwingTest.class
SwingTest.class -> C:\java8\jre\lib\rt.jar (Full JRE)
   com.jdojo.profiles (SwingTest.class)
      -> java.lang                         compact1
      -> javax.swing                       Full JRE
```

The following command prints the dependencies with the profile information for both SwingTest and RowSetTest classes:

```
jdeps -profile SwingTest.class RowSetTest.class
SwingTest.class -> C:\java8\jre\lib\rt.jar (Full JRE)
   com.jdojo.profiles (SwingTest.class)
      -> java.lang                         compact1
      -> javax.swing                       Full JRE
RowSetTest.class -> C:\java8\jre\lib\rt.jar (compact3)
   com.jdojo.profiles (RowSetTest.class)
      -> java.lang                         compact1
      -> java.sql                          compact2
      -> javax.sql.rowset                  compact3
```

The following command will create three DOT files in the mydotdir directory: SwingTest.class.dot, RowSetTest.class.dot, and summary.dot:

```
jdeps -profile -dotoutput mydotdir SwingTest.class RowSetTest.class
```

The contents of the SwingTest.class.dot file will be

```
digraph "SwingTest.class" {
   // Path: SwingTest.class
   "com.jdojo.profiles"           -> "java.lang (compact1)";
   "com.jdojo.profiles"           -> "javax.swing (Full JRE)";
}
```

The contents of the RowSetTest.class.dot file will be

```
digraph "RowSetTest.class" {
   // Path: RowSetTest.class
   "com.jdojo.profiles"           -> "java.lang (compact1)";
   "com.jdojo.profiles"           -> "java.sql (compact2)";
   "com.jdojo.profiles"           -> "javax.sql.rowset (compact3)";
}
```

The contents of the summary.dot file will be

```
digraph "summary" {
   "SwingTest.class"       -> "rt.jar"[label="Full JRE\n",fontsize=9];
   "RowSetTest.class"      -> "rt.jar"[label="compact3\n",fontsize=9];
}
```

Creating Custom JREs Using the EJDK

Oracle provides Java development kits for Java SE Embedded 8 (also called EJDK 8), enabling you to create custom JRE bundles containing packages for a specific compact profile. Note that the EJDK is not a development kit used for Java application development; rather, it is a tool to create a compact profile or the full JRE for specific platforms and CPU architectures. EJDK 8 is available for the following Java SE Embedded platforms/CPU architectures:

- Linux/ARMv7 - VFP, HardFP ABI, Little Endian

- Linux /ARMv6/7- VFP, SoftFP ABI, Little Endian

- Linux/ARMv5 - Headless - SoftFP ABI, Little Endian

- Linux/ Power Architecture - Headless - e600 CPU variant with a Classic Floating Point Unit

- Linux /Power Architecture - Headless - e500v2 with double-precision SPE Floating Point Unit

- Linux /x86 Small Footprint - Headless

■ **Note**   At the time of this writing, EJDKs support creating custom JREs only on Linux platform. You cannot create custom JREs for Windows and Mac using EJDKs. However, you can download and use EJDKs on Windows to create custom JREs for the listed platforms (Linux) and the CPU architectures.

Installing EJDK

You need to perform the following steps to install EJDK:

- Make sure you have installed JDK or JRE for Java SE 8 on your machine. One of them (JDK or JRE) is required when you use EJDK 8.

- Download the EJDK installation file from the download page, www.oracle.com/technetwork/java/embedded/downloads/javase/index.html. There is a separate EDJK for all supported platforms. Please download the EJDK installation file for the platform on which you will be deploying your custom created JRE. In the example, I will use EJDK 8 for the Linux/x86 platform. The installation files have the extension .tar.gz.

- Unzip the EJDK installation file into a directory such as /home/ksharan, On Linux, you can use the gunzip or gzip tool to unzip the file; on Windows, you can use any ZIP tool such as 7-zip or WinZip. When you unzip the file on Windows, you need to unzip it twice as a .tar.gz files uses double compression.

- Unzipping the EJDK installation file will create an ejdk1.8.0 directory that contains the EJDK files. At this point, you should have a directory called /home/ksharan/ejdk1.8.0. This completes the installation of the EJDK 8. On Windows, the path may be C:\ksharan\ejdk1.8.0.

Running the jrecreate Command

The ejdk1.8.0 directory contains three subdirectories:

- bin
- lib
- target (e.g. named linux_i586 for EJDK on Linux/x86)

On Linux, you can use the ls command to list the contents of the ejdk1.8.0 directory:

```
[/home/ksharan]$ ls ejdk1.8.0
bin  lib  linux_i586
```

The bin directory contains the following files:

- jrecreate.bat
- jrecreate.sh
- jrecreate.config.properties

There are two files for the jrecreate command: one with extension .bat and one with extension .sh. Both files are the jrecreate tool. You need to use the jrecreate.bat file on Windows and the jrecreate.sh file on Linux. I will use the jrecreate.sh file because I ran all examples on Linux.

The jrecreate.config.properties file is a configuration file for the jrecreate tool. Typically, you do not need to change anything in this file. You can look at the file's contents; it contains comments that explain the purpose of properties and how to change them. I will not cover editing this file. I will focus on only the jrecreate tool.

The lib directory contains the implementation files for the jrecreate command.

The target directory is named differently on different platforms. The name represents the platform and the CPU architecture. For example, the directory is named linux_i586 for Linux/x86; it is named linux_ppc for Linux/Power Architecture – Headless -e600 CPU variant with a Classic Floating Point Unit.

You are just one step away from using the jrecreate command to create custom JREs. The command depends on the JAVA_HOME environment variable to work, which must be set to the installed JDK or JRE directory for Java SE 8. If the JAVA_HOME is not set, running the jrecreate command will print an error message stating that the JAVA_HOME is not set.

On Linux, assuming the JDK or JRE for Java SE 8 is installed in /home/ksharan/java8, you can use the following command to set the JAVA_HOME environment variable:

```
[/home/ksharan]$ export JAVA_HOME=/home/ksharan/java8
```

On Windows, assuming that the JDK or JRE for Java SE 8 is installed in C:\java8, you can set the JAVA_HOME environment variable as follows:

```
C:\>SET JAVA_HOME=C:\java8
```

On Linux, the syntax to run the jrecreate command is

```
jrecreate.sh <options>
```

On Windows, the syntax to run the jrecreate command is

```
jrecreate.bat <options>
```

The jrecreate command takes several options. One of the options is required that specifies the destination directory in which the custom JRE files are generated. The option to specify the destination directory is -d (or --dest) and its value is the path of a directory.

Table C-4 lists all the options for the jrecreate command with their descriptions. Note that most of the options have a short name and a long name. The options with the short names start with one hyphen such as -d and the options with the long names start with two hyphens such as --dest.

Table C-4. *List of Options and Their Descriptions for the jrecreate Command*

Option	Description
-d path --dest path	Specifies the directory in which to write the JRE files. The directory must not exist. An error occurs if the directory already exists.
-p profile --profile profile	Specifies the compact profile name to be created. Valid values are compact1, compact2, and compact3. If it is not specified, the full JRE is created.
--vm jvm	Specifies the JVM type to be included in the created JRE. The valid options are one of the following: minimal, client, server, and all. If this option is not specified, the --profile option is used to select a JVM as follows: For compact1 and compact2, minimal is selected and for compact3, client is selected. If --profile is not specified, the JRE includes all available JVMs.
-x extension --extension extension	Specifies optional components to be included in the generated JRE. It accepts a comma-separated list (with no spaces) as well as a single value. Valid values are fx:graphics, fx:controls, sunec, sunpkcs11, locales, charsets, nashorn. Selecting fx:controls automatically includes fx:graphics.
-g --debug	Includes java level debugging supports. The default is to include no debugging support.
-k --keep-debug-info	Does not strip debugging information from class and unsigned JAR files during JRE creation.
--no-compression	Does not compress unsigned JAR files. This option does not apply to the signed JAR files. The default is to compress the unsigned JAR files.
-n --dry-run	Performs the dry run of the requested operation without creating the JRE.
-v --verbose	Displays verbose output.
--ejdk-home path	Specify the path to the root of EJDK distribution.
-h --help	Summarizes the command-line options.

The following command creates the full JRE in the `fulljre` directory:

```
[/home/ksharan]$ ejdk1.8.0/bin/jrecreate.sh -d fulljre
Building JRE using Options {
    ejdk-home: /home/ksharan/ejdk1.8.0
    dest: /home/ksharan/compact1jre
    target: linux_i586
    vm: all
    runtime: jre
    debug: false
    keep-debug-info: false
    no-compression: false
    dry-run: false
    verbose: false
    extension: []
}

Target JRE Size is 55,209 KB (on disk usage may be greater).
Embedded JRE created successfully
```

■ **Tip** If you get any errors running the `jrecreate` command, you may try setting the `EJDK_HOME` environment variable to the directory containing the EJDK that is the path to the EJDK installation directory.

Notice that size of the full JRE with no debugging options on Linux/x86 is 55MB. If you want to create a JRE with a custom profile such as `compact1`, `compact2` or `compact3`, you will need to specify the profile name using the `-p` (or `--profile`) option. The following command creates a JRE with profile `compact1`; the JRE files will be copied to `compact1jre` directory:

```
[/home/ksharan]$ ejdk1.8.0/bin/jrecreate.sh -p compact1 -d compact1jre
Building JRE using Options {
    ejdk-home: /home/ksharan/ejdk1.8.0
    dest: /home/ksharan/compact1jre
    target: linux_i586
    vm: minimal
    runtime: compact1 profile
    debug: false
    keep-debug-info: false
    no-compression: false
    dry-run: false
    verbose: false
    extension: []
}

Target JRE Size is 10,811 KB (on disk usage may be greater).
Embedded JRE created successfully
```

Notice the size of the JRE with the `compact1` profile on Linux/x86 is approximately 11MB, which is a significant reduction in size from 55MB for the full JRE.

The destination directory for the custom JRE contains several files and sub-directories. You can list them as follows:

```
[/home/ksharan]$ ls compact1jre
bin  COPYRIGHT  README   THIRDPARTYLICENSEREADME.txt
bom  lib        release  Welcome.html
```

The bin directory contains the java command that you will use to run your Java classes. The following command shows the version of the JRE created:

```
[/home/ksharan]$ ./compact1jre/bin/java -version
java version "1.8.0"
Java(TM) SE Embedded Runtime Environment (build 1.8.0-b132, profile compact1, headless)
Java HotSpot(TM) Embedded Minimal VM (build 25.0-b70, mixed mode)
```

Notice that version information for the JRE also contains the profile name, which is compact1 in the output. Listing C-3 contains the code for a HelloCompact1 class that has dependency on the compact1 profile.

Listing C-3. A HelloCompact1 Class That Uses Classes from Only the compact1 Profile

```
// HelloCompact1.java
package com.jdojo.profiles;

public class HelloCompact1 {
        public static void main(String[] args) {
                System.out.println("Hello, compact1 profile!");
        }
}
```

Assuming that the HelloCompact1 class is copied to the /home/ksharan/classes directory with its package structure, the following command uses the compact1 profile to run the class:

```
[/home/ksharan]$ ./compact1jre/bin/java -cp /home/ksharan/classes com.jdojo.profiles.HelloProfile

Hello, compact1 profile!
```

Recall that the RowSetTest class uses the compact3 profile. Running the class using the compact1 profile via the following command generates a runtime exception, as shown in the output:

```
[/home/ksharan]$ ./compact1jre/bin/java -cp /home/ksharan/classes com.jdojo.profiles.RowSetTest

Exception in thread "main" java.lang.NoClassDefFoundError: java/sql/SQLException
        at java.lang.Class.getDeclaredMethods0(Native Method)
        at java.lang.Class.privateGetDeclaredMethods(Unknown Source)
        at java.lang.Class.getMethod0(Unknown Source)
        at java.lang.Class.getMethod(Unknown Source)
        at sun.launcher.LauncherHelper.validateMainClass(Unknown Source)
        at sun.launcher.LauncherHelper.checkAndLoadMain(Unknown Source)
```

```
Caused by: java.lang.ClassNotFoundException: java.sql.SQLException
        at java.net.URLClassLoader$1.run(Unknown Source)
        at java.net.URLClassLoader$1.run(Unknown Source)
        at java.security.AccessController.doPrivileged(Native Method)
        at java.net.URLClassLoader.findClass(Unknown Source)
        at java.lang.ClassLoader.loadClass(Unknown Source)
        at sun.misc.Launcher$AppClassLoader.loadClass(Unknown Source)
        at java.lang.ClassLoader.loadClass(Unknown Source)
        ... 6 more
```

Deploying the Custom JRE

The directory specified as the -d (or --dest) option's value is the directory that contains all the required files for the custom JRE. To deploy the JRE, you will need to copy all the files from the JRE directory to the target device. The actual steps or commands needed to copy the JRE files vary from device to device. Please refer to the documentation for your device on how to deploy the JRE files.

■ **Tip** If you use the jrecreate.bat file on Windows to create the custom JRE, you will need to copy the JRE files from Windows to the Linux platform running on the device. In this case, the java command in the JRE bundle may not be recognized as a command on the Linux platform. After you copy the JRE files, you may have to run the following command on Linux to make the java file executable:

```
$ chmod +x java
```

Running the Custom JRE

Running the custom JRE on a device is the same as running any other JRE: run the java command from the bin directory in the deployed JRE directory. Sometimes you may have to set the PATH environment variable on the device to point it to the bin directory containing the java command. Assuming that you have copied the custom JRE files to the /mydevice/jre8 directory on the device, you can use the following command to set the PATH environment variable:

```
$ export PATH=$PATH:/mydevice/jre8/bin
```

Index

Get the eBook for only $10!

Now you can take the weightless companion with you anywhere, anytime. Your purchase of this book entitles you to 3 electronic versions for only $10.

This Apress title will prove so indispensible that you'll want to carry it with you everywhere, which is why we are offering the eBook in **3 formats** for only $10 if you have already purchased the print book.

Convenient and fully searchable, the PDF version enables you to easily find and copy code—or perform examples by quickly toggling between instructions and applications. The MOBI format is ideal for your Kindle, while the ePUB can be utilized on a variety of mobile devices.

Go to www.apress.com/promo/tendollars to purchase your companion eBook.

Apress®
THE EXPERT'S VOICE™

Printed in the United States
By Bookmasters